Newnham Learning Centre

CRITICAL THINKING

CRITICAL THINKING

A STUDENT'S INTRODUCTION

Greg Bassham

William Irwin

Henry Nardone

James M. Wallace

King's College

McGraw
Graw
Hill

Boston   Burr Ridge, IL   Dubuque, IA   Madison, WI   New York
San Francisco   St. Louis   Bangkok   Bogotá   Caracas   Kuala Lumpur
Lisbon   London   Madrid   Mexico City   Milan   Montreal   New Delhi
Santiago   Seoul   Singapore   Sydney   Taipei   Toronto

McGraw-Hill Higher Education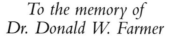
*A Division of The **McGraw-Hill** Companies*

To the memory of
Dr. Donald W. Farmer

1 2 3 4 5 6 7 9 0 DOC/DOC 0 9 8 7 6 5 4 3 2 1

Library of Congress Cataloging-in-Publication Data
Critical thinking: a student's introduction / by Greg Bassham . . . [et al.].
   p. cm.
Includes index.
ISBN 0-7674-1739-9
1. Critical thinking.   I. Bassham, Gregory
B809.2.C745 2001
160 — dc21   2001018044

Sponsoring editor, Kenneth King; production editor, April Wells-Hayes; manuscript editor; Carole Crouse; design manager, Susan Breitbard; text and cover designer, Glenda King; art manager and illustrator, Emma Ghiselli; manufacturing manager, Randy Hurst. Cover: © Jean-Francois Causse/Stone. The text was set in 11/12.5 Bembo by G&S Typesetters and printed on 45# Somerset Matte, PMS 3272, by R. R. Donnelley and Sons.

Text credits appear on a continuation of the copyright page, page 566.

www.mhhe.com

PREFACE

This text is the product of four authors (three philosophy professors and an English professor), but it reflects a single, shared vision of what critical thinking is and how it can best be taught and learned. At the core of that vision is the conviction that critical thinking must begin where students are, not where instructors and textbook writers would like them to be.

Our students are diverse in their backgrounds and abilities, and many lack the relatively sophisticated reading and critical thinking skills presupposed by many other textbooks in the field. For such students, we needed a learner-friendly text that covers all the basics of critical thinking, includes a wealth of challenging, thought-provoking exercises, and is written in a way that our students find clear, comprehensible, and relevant to their daily lives. Because we could find no text that adequately combined these virtues, we decided to write our own.

To help readers not only develop the skills of critical thinking but apply them as well, we have included many traditional exercises and many others that ask students either to collaborate with one another or to work independently and compare their answers. These exercises are designed to encourage students to see that their critical thinking skills, although useful to them as individuals facing an increasingly more commercial and often mercenary world, are best honed in communities, where students can guide and direct one another and test their abilities in practical settings.

Students today live in two worlds—an academic one that demands clarity, rigor, and thoughtful, well-substantiated conclusions, and another world, one in which viewpoints fly like confetti on talk shows, pop psychologists "solve" complicated problems in thirty seconds, and "evidence" for any claim is just an easy mouse click away. Students come to us struggling to find their way in and between these two worlds. This text will help them navigate the journey.

OVERVIEW OF THE TEXT

Critical Thinking: A Student's Introduction is designed to provide a versatile and comprehensive introduction to critical thinking. The book is divided into seven major parts:

1. *The Fundamentals:* Chapters 1–3 introduce students to the basics of critical thinking and logic in clear, reader-friendly language.
2. *Language:* Chapter 4 discusses the uses and pitfalls of language, emphasizing the ways in which language is used to hinder clear, effective thinking.
3. *Fallacies:* Chapters 5 and 6 teach students how to recognize and avoid twenty of the most common logical fallacies.
4. *Argument Analysis and Evaluation:* Chapters 7 and 8 offer a clear, step-by-step introduction to the complex but essential skills of argument analysis and evaluation.
5. *Traditional Topics in Informal Logic:* Chapters 9–11 offer a clear, simplified, introduction to three traditional topics in informal logic: categorical logic, propositional logic, and inductive reasoning.
6. *Researching and Writing Argumentative Essays:* Chapters 12–13 provide students with specific, detailed guidance in producing well-researched, properly documented, and well-written argumentative essays.
7. *Practical Applications:* Chapters 14 and 15 invite students to apply what they have learned by reflecting critically on two areas in which *uncritical* thinking is particularly common: the media (Chapter 14) and pseudoscience and the paranormal (Chapter 15).

Depending on the instructor's preferences and the students' needs, this text can be taught in varying ways. For instructors who stress argument analysis and evaluation, we suggest Chapters 1–8. For instructors who emphasize informal logic, we recommend Chapters 1–6 and 9–11. For instructors who prefer a strong focus on writing, we suggest Chapters 1–6 and 12–13. And for instructors who stress practical applications of critical thinking, we recommend Chapters 1–6 and 14–15.

STRENGTHS AND DISTINCTIVE FEATURES OF THE TEXT

There are many features, we think, that set this text apart from other critical thinking texts:

1. A versatile, student-centered approach that covers all the basics of critical thinking—and more—in clear, reader-friendly language.
2. A text written for today's students, many of whom are seriously underprepared in basic skills and general background knowledge.

3. An abundance of interesting (and often humorous or thought-provoking), classroom-tested exercises of suitable difficulty.

4. An emphasis on active, collaborative learning.

5. A strong focus on writing, with complete chapters on using and evaluating sources (Chapter 12) and writing argumentative essays (Chapter 13).

6. An emphasis on real-world applications of critical thinking, with many examples taken from popular culture and complete chapters on thinking critically about the media (Chapter 14) and science and pseudoscience (Chapter 15).

7. A clear, systematic discussion of critical thinking standards, hindrances, and dispositions.

8. An unusually clear and detailed discussion of the distinction between deductive and inductive reasoning.

9. Thought-provoking marginal quotes, as well as "Critical Thinking Lapses"—outrageous errors in reasoning and thinking.

10. An Internet-based study guide that can be accessed free of charge at www.mhhe.com/bassham. The study guide provides chapter summaries, definitions of key terms, and additional exercises with answers.

11. An Instructor's Manual that includes answer keys, teaching tips, sample tests and quizzes, and an extensive exercise and test bank.

ACKNOWLEDGMENTS

We are grateful to many people for their help and encouragement on this project.

We owe an enormous debt to our reviewers, who provided a wealth of helpful ideas and suggestions. They are David Bowen, University of North Florida; James Brooks, Eastern Kentucky University; Barbara Carlson, Clark University; Rory Conces, University of Nebraska-Omaha; David Detmer, Purdue University-Calumet; Andrew Dzida, Saddleback College; Thomson Faller, University of Portland; Mary Elizabeth Gleason, University of Massachusetts-Lowell; Claude Gratton, University of Nevada-Las Vegas; Jann James, Diablo Valley College; Leemon McHenry, Loyola Marymount University; Tom MacMillan, Mendocino College; and Marty Most, Boise State University. Special thanks are due to Professor Barbara Forrest of Southeastern Louisiana University, whose contributions as a reviewer were truly above and beyond the call of duty.

Thanks are also due to Derrick Boucher, Ken Merrill, Nickolas Pappas, Tod Bassham, Theodore Schick, Jr., and William Drumin, who read and provided helpful feedback on various draft chapters of the book.

We are grateful to the helpful and talented people at Mayfield who guided this book to completion: Julianna Scott Fein and April Wells-Hayes,

Production Editors; Susan Shook Malloy, Developmental Editor; Marty Granahan, Permissions Editor; Linda Toy, Director of Production; and especially Ken King, Senior Philosophy Editor, whose patience, prodding, and wise counsel resulted in innumerable improvements in the text.

Copyeditor Carole Crouse polished and pruned our sprawling and often grammatically challenged manuscript. April Wells-Hayes was courteous and efficient in handling production. Our thanks to both.

For sabbaticals and release time, we gratefully record our thanks to Fr. Thomas O'Hara, CSC, and the Board of Directors of King's College. Without their support, this book could not have been completed.

For their encouragement and the richness of their ideas, we thank our friends on the King's College Critical Thinking Project Team: Jim Dohlon, Bruce Gallup, Tony Grasso, CSC, George Hammerbacher, Peg Hogan, and Charlie Kraszewski.

Over the past four years, we have tried out drafts of this text in our classes. We are tremendously grateful to our students for their enthusiasm and for their many constructive comments and suggestions.

We owe a special debt to our families and significant others for their love and encouragement. Greg thanks his wife, Mia, and son, Dylan, for putting up with many Dadless weekends. Bill thanks Megan Lloyd for the critical thinking lapse that allowed her to marry him. Henry thanks his wife, Beth, and his children, Enrico, Eric, and Nicole, for their love and encouragement. Jim thanks his wife, Debbie, for her patience.

We dedicate this book to the memory of Dr. Donald W. Farmer, friend and mentor, without whose vision and support this book would not have existed.

We would love to hear from you if you have comments, questions, or suggestions for improvement. Write to Greg Bassham at ghbassha@kings.edu, William Irwin at wtirwin@kings.edu, Henry Nardone at hfnardon@kings .edu, and James Wallace at jmwallac@kings.edu. Although all four authors have contributed to every chapter, questions or comments can be most helpfully directed as follows:

Chapters 1–3, 5–9, 15: Greg Bassham or Henry Nardone
Chapters 4, 12–14: James Wallace
Chapters 10–11: William Irwin

CONTENTS

Chapter 5   Logical Fallacies—1   140

Chapter 6   Logical Fallacies—2   162

Chapter 7   Analyzing Arguments   189

Chapter 12   Finding, Evaluating, and Using Sources   351

Chapter 13   Writing Argumentative Essays   407

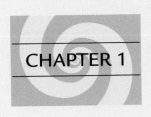

CHAPTER 1

INTRODUCTION TO CRITICAL THINKING

This book is about the power of disciplined thinking. It's about learning to think for yourself and being your own person. It's about the personal empowerment and enrichment that result from learning to use your mind to its fullest potential. In short, it's about becoming a critical thinker.

Critical thinking is what a college education is all about. In many high schools, the emphasis tends to be on "lower-order thinking." Students are simply expected to passively absorb information and then to repeat it back on tests. In college, by contrast, the emphasis is on fostering "higher-order thinking": the active, intelligent evaluation of ideas and information. This doesn't mean that factual information and rote learning are ignored in college. But the main goal of a college education is not to teach students *what to think*. The main goal is to teach students *how to think*—that is, how to become independent, self-directed thinkers and learners.

It needs great boldness to dare to be oneself.
—Albert Camus

WHAT IS CRITICAL THINKING?

Often when we use the word *critical* we mean "negative and fault-finding." This is the sense we have in mind, for example, when we complain about a parent or a friend who we think is unfairly critical of what we do or say. But *critical* also means "involving or exercising skilled judgment or observation." In this sense, critical thinking means thinking clearly and intelligently. More precisely, **critical thinking** is the general term given to a wide range of cognitive skills and intellectual dispositions needed to effectively identify, analyze, and evaluate arguments and truth claims, to discover and overcome personal prejudices and biases, to formulate and present convincing reasons in support of conclusions, and to make reasonable, intelligent decisions about what to believe and what to do.

Put somewhat differently, critical thinking is disciplined thinking governed by clear intellectual standards. Among the most important of these intellectual standards are **clarity, precision, accuracy, relevance, consistency,**

1

logical correctness, completeness, and **fairness.**[1] Let's begin our introduction to critical thinking by looking briefly at each of these important critical thinking standards.

CRITICAL THINKING STANDARDS

Clarity

Before we can effectively evaluate a person's argument or claim, we need to understand clearly what he or she is saying. Unfortunately, that can be difficult, since people often fail to express themselves clearly. Sometimes, this lack of clarity is due to laziness, carelessness, or lack of skill. At other times, it results from a misguided effort to appear clever, learned, or profound. Consider the following passage from philosopher Martin Heidegger's influential but notoriously difficult book *Being and Time:*

> Temporality makes possible the unity of existence, facticity, and falling, and in this way constitutes primordially the totality of the structure of care. The items of care have not been pieced together cumulatively any more than temporality itself has been put together 'in the course of time' ["mit der Zeit"] out of the future, the having been, and the Present. Temporality 'is' not an *entity* at all. It is not, but it *temporalizes* itself. . . . Temporality temporalizes, and indeed it temporalizes possible ways of itself. These make possible the multiplicity of Dasein's modes of Being, and especially the basic possibility of authentic or inauthentic existence.[2]

That may be profound, or it may be nonsense, or it may be both. Whatever exactly it is, it is quite needlessly obscure.

As William Strunk, Jr., and E. B. White remark in their classic *The Elements of Style,* "[m]uddiness is not merely a disturber of prose, it is also a destroyer of life, of hope: death on the highway caused by a badly worded road sign, heartbreak among lovers caused by a misplaced phrase in a well-intentioned letter, anguish of a traveler expecting to be met at a railroad station and not being met because of a slipshod telegram."[3] Only by paying careful attention to language can we avoid such needless miscommunications and disappointments.

Critical thinkers not only strive for clarity of language but also seek maximum clarity of thought. As self-help books constantly remind us, to achieve our personal goals in life we need a clear conception of our goals and priorities, a realistic grasp of our talents and abilities, and a clear understanding of the problems and opportunities we face. Such self-understanding can be achieved only if we value and pursue clarity of thought.

Precision

Detective stories contain some of the best and most interesting examples of critical thinking in fiction. The most famous fictional sleuth is, of course, Sherlock Holmes, the immortal creation of British writer Sir Arthur Conan Doyle.

Everything that can be said can be said clearly.

—Ludwig Wittgenstein

It is wrong to say that good language is important to good thought, merely; for it is the essence of it.

—C. S. Peirce

In Doyle's stories, Holmes is often able to solve complex mysteries when the bungling detectives from Scotland Yard haven't so much as a clue. What is the secret of his success? In a word, an extraordinary commitment to *precision*. First, by careful and highly trained observation, Holmes is able to discover clues that others have overlooked. Then, by a process of precise logical inference, he is able to reason from those clues to discover the solution to the mystery.

> *Really valuable ideas can only be had at the price of close attention.*
> —C. S. Peirce

Everyone recognizes the importance of precision in specialized fields such as medicine, mathematics, architecture, and engineering. Critical thinkers also understand the importance of precise thinking in daily life. They understand that to cut through the confusions and uncertainties that surround many everyday problems and issues, it is often necessary to insist on precise answers to precise questions: What exactly is the problem we're facing? What exactly are the alternatives? What exactly are the advantages and disadvantages of each alternative? Only when we habitually seek such precision are we truly critical thinkers.

Accuracy

There is a well-known saying about computers: "Garbage in, garbage out." Simply put, this means that if you put bad information into a computer, bad information is exactly what you will get out of it. Much the same is true of human thinking and reasoning. No matter how brilliant you may be, you're almost guaranteed to make bad decisions if your decisions are based on false information.

A good example of this is America's long and costly involvement in Vietnam. The policymakers who embroiled us in that conflict were not stupid. On the contrary, they were, in David Halberstam's oft-quoted phrase, "the best and the brightest" of their generation. Of course, the reasons for their repeated failures of judgment are complex and highly controversial; but much of the blame, historians agree, must be placed on false and inadequate information: ignorance of Vietnamese history and culture; an exaggerated estimate of the strategic importance of Vietnam and Southeast Asia; false assumptions about the degree of popular support in South Vietnam, unduly optimistic assessments of the "progress" of the war, and so on. Had American policymakers taken greater pains to learn the truth about such matters, it is likely they would not have made the poor decisions they did.

> *No one can navigate well through life without an accurate map by which to steer. Knowledge is the possession of such a map, and truth is what the map gives us, linking us to reality.*
> —Tom Morris

Critical thinkers don't merely value the truth: they have a *passion* for accurate, timely information. As consumers, citizens, workers, and parents, they strive to make decisions that are as informed as possible. In the spirit of Socrates' famous statement that the unexamined life is not worth living, they never stop learning, growing, and inquiring.

Relevance

Anyone who has ever sat through a boring school assembly or watched a mudslinging political debate can appreciate the importance of staying focused on relevant ideas and information. A favorite debaters' trick is to try to distract an audience's attention by raising an irrelevant issue. Even so great a lawyer as Abraham Lincoln wasn't above such tricks, as the following story told by his law partner illustrates:

> In a case where Judge [Stephen T.] Logan—always earnest and grave—opposed him, Lincoln created no little merriment by his reference to Logan's style of dress. He carried the surprise in store for the latter, till he reached his turn before the jury. Addressing them, he said: "Gentlemen, you must be careful and not permit yourselves to be overcome by the eloquence of counsel for the defense. Judge Logan, I know, is an effective lawyer. I have met him too often to doubt that; but shrewd and careful though he be, still he is sometimes wrong. Since this trial has begun I have discovered that, with all his caution and fastidiousness, he hasn't knowledge enough to put his shirt on right." Logan turned red as crimson, but sure enough, Lincoln was correct, for the former had donned a new shirt, and by mistake had drawn it over his head with the pleated bosom behind. The general laugh which followed destroyed the effect of Logan's eloquence over the jury—the very point at which Lincoln aimed.[4]

Lincoln's ploy was entertaining and succeeded in distracting the attention of the jury. Had the jurors been thinking critically, however, they would have realized that carelessness about one's attire has no logical relevance to the strength of one's arguments.

Consistency

It is easy to see why consistency is essential to critical thinking. Logic tells us that if a person holds inconsistent beliefs, at least one of those beliefs must be false. Critical thinkers love truth and detest falsehood. For that reason, critical thinkers are constantly on the lookout for inconsistencies, both in their own thinking and in the arguments and assertions of others.

There are two kinds of inconsistency critical thinkers are careful to avoid. One is *logical inconsistency,* which involves saying or believing inconsistent things (i.e., things that cannot both or all be true) about a particular matter. The other is *practical inconsistency,* which involves saying one thing and doing another.

Sometimes people are fully aware that their words conflict with their deeds. The politician who cynically breaks her campaign promises once she takes office, the TV evangelist caught in an extramarital affair, the drug counselor arrested for peddling drugs—such people are hypocrites pure and simple. From a critical thinking point of view, such examples are not especially interesting. As a rule, they involve failures of character to a much greater degree than they do failures of critical reasoning.

More interesting from a critical thinking standpoint are cases in which people are not fully aware that their words conflict with their deeds. Such cases highlight an important lesson of critical thinking: that human beings often dis-

Speaking of Inconsistency . . .

Professor Kenneth R. Merrill offers the following tongue-in-cheek advice for writers. What kind of inconsistency does Merrill commit?

1. Watch your spelling. Writters who mis-pele a lott of words are propperly re-guarded as iliterate.
2. Don't forget the apostrophe where its needed, but don't stick it in where theres no need for it. A writers reputation hangs on such trifle's.
3. Don't exaggerate. Overstatement always causes infinite harm.
4. Avoiding foreign phrases is a *conditio sine qua non* for the writer who wants to be *klar und deutlich*. *Le mot juste* is most likely to be found in one's own *lengua madre*.
5. The careful writer must take panes with homophones, which are all to easy too confuse. Though understandable, such confusions great on the reader's nerves. (Some people seem to have a flare for bazaar mistakes of this sort.)
6. Beware of the dangling participle. For-getting this admonition, infelicitous phrases creep into our writing.

7. Clichés should be avoided like the plague. However, hackneyed language is not likely to be a problem for the writer who, since he was knee-high to a grasshopper, has built a better mouse-trap and has kept his shoulder to the wheel.
8. Keep your language simple. Eschew sesquipedalian locutions and fustian rhetoric. Stay clear of the crepuscular—nay, tenebrific and fuliginous—regions of orotund sonorities.
9. Avoid vogue words. Hopefully, the writer will remember that her words basically impact the reader at the dynamic interface of creative thought and action. To be viable, the writer's parameters must enable her to engage the knowledgeable reader in a meaningful dialogue—especially at this point in time, when people tend to prioritize their priorities optimally.
10. Avoid profane or abusive language. It is a damned outrage how many knuckle-dragging slobs vilify people they disagree with.[6]

play a remarkable capacity for self-deception. Author Harold Kushner cites an all-too-typical example:

> Ask the average person which is more important to him, making money or being devoted to his family, and virtually everyone will answer *family* without hesitation. But watch how the average person actually lives out his life. See where he really invests his time and energy, and he will give away the fact that he really does not live by what he says he believes. He has let himself be persuaded that if he leaves for work earlier in the morning and comes home more tired at night, he is proving how devoted he is to his family by expending himself to provide them with all the things they have seen advertised.[5]

Critical thinking helps us become aware of such unconscious practical inconsistencies, enabling us to deal with them on a conscious and rational basis.

It is also common, of course, for people unknowingly to hold inconsistent beliefs about a particular subject. In fact, as Socrates pointed out long ago,

such unconscious logical inconsistency is far more common than most people suspect. Polls show, for instance, that many Americans favor substantial increases in key government programs, large tax cuts, and a balanced budget, without pausing to think that these are probably conflicting goals. Critical thinking helps us to recognize such logical inconsistencies, or, still better, to avoid them altogether.

We have to believe in free will. We've got no choice.

—Isaac Bashevis Singer

Logical Correctness

To think logically is to reason correctly— that is, to draw well-founded conclusions from the beliefs we hold. To think critically, we need accurate and well-supported beliefs. But, just as important, we need to be able to *reason* from those beliefs to conclusions that logically follow from them. Unfortunately, illogical thinking is all too common in human affairs. Bertrand Russell in his classic essay "An Outline of Intellectual Rubbish" provides an amusing example:

> I am sometimes shocked by the blasphemies of those who think themselves pious—for instance, the nuns who never take a bath without wearing a bathrobe all the time. When asked why, since no man can see them, they reply: "Oh, but you forget the good God." Apparently they conceive of the deity as a Peeping Tom, whose omnipotence enables Him to see through bathroom walls, but who is foiled by bathrobes. This view strikes me as curious.[6]

Man is the Reasoning Animal. Such is the claim. I think it is open to dispute. Indeed, my experiments have proven to me that he is the Unreasoning Animal. Note his history. . . . His record is the fantastic record of a maniac.

—Mark Twain

As Russell observes, from the proposition

    1. God sees everything.

the pious nuns correctly drew the conclusion

    2. God sees through bathroom walls.

However, they failed to draw the equally obvious conclusion that

    3. God sees through bathrobes.

Such illogic is, indeed, curious—but not, alas, uncommon.

Completeness

In most contexts, we rightly prefer deep and complete thinking to shallow and superficial thinking. Thus, we justly condemn slipshod criminal investigations, hasty jury deliberations, superficial news stories, and snap medical diagnoses. Of course, there are times when it is impossible or inappropriate to discuss an issue in depth; no one would expect, for example, a thorough and wide-ranging discussion of the ethics of human genetic research in a short newspaper editorial. Generally speaking, however, thinking is better when it is deep rather than shallow, thorough rather than superficial.

It is not much good thinking of a thing unless you think it out.

—H. G. Wells

Fairness

Finally, critical thinking demands that our thinking be fair—that is, open-minded, impartial, and free of distorting biases and preconceptions. That can

> ## Critical Thinking Lapse
>
> The human race are masters of the ridiculous. There was actually a story in our newspaper of a man who was bitten on the tongue while kissing a rattlesnake. He decided to try a nonscientific remedy he heard about to counteract a snakebite. So he wired his mouth to a pickup truck battery and tried to jump-start his tongue. It knocked him out and he ended up in the hospital, where he lost part of his tongue and one lip.[8]

All things excellent are as difficult as they are rare.

—Benedict Spinoza

be very difficult to achieve. Even the most superficial acquaintance with history and the social sciences tells us that people are often strongly disposed to resist unfamiliar ideas, to prejudge issues, to stereotype outsiders, and to identify truth with their own self-interest or the interests of their nation or culture. It is probably unrealistic to suppose that our thinking could ever be completely free of biases and preconceptions; to some extent, we all perceive reality in ways that are powerfully shaped by our individual life experiences and cultural backgrounds. But difficult as it may be to achieve, basic fair-mindedness is an essential attribute of a critical thinker.

EXERCISE 1.1

I. Break into groups of four or five. Choose one member of your group to take notes and be the group reporter. Discuss your education up to this point. To what extent has your education prepared you to think clearly, precisely, accurately, relevantly, consistently, logically, completely, and fairly? Have you ever known a person (e.g., a teacher or a parent) who strongly modeled the critical thinking standards discussed in this section? If so, how did he or she do that?

II. Have you ever been guilty of either practical inconsistency (saying one thing and doing another) or logical inconsistency (believing inconsistent things about a particular topic or issue)? (Hint: Of course you have!) In small groups, think of examples either from your own experience or from that of someone you know. Be prepared to share your examples with the class as a whole.

THE BENEFITS OF CRITICAL THINKING

In the last section we touched briefly on some of the standards governing critical reasoning (clarity, logical correctness, and so forth). Now let's look more specifically at what you can expect to gain from a course in critical thinking.

Critical Thinking in the Classroom

When they first enter college, students are often surprised to discover that their professors seem to care less about *what* they believe than they do about *why* they believe it. In college, as we have seen, the focus is on higher-order thinking: the active, intelligent evaluation of ideas and information. Therefore, critical thinking plays a vital role throughout the college curriculum.

In a critical thinking course, students learn a variety of skills that can greatly improve their classroom performance. These skills include

- understanding the arguments and views of others
- critically evaluating those arguments and views
- developing and defending one's own well-supported arguments and views

Let's look briefly at each of these three skills.

To do well in college you must, of course, be able to *understand* the material you are studying. A course in critical thinking cannot make inherently difficult material easy to comprehend, but critical thinking does teach a variety of skills that, with practice, can significantly improve your ability to understand the arguments and issues discussed in your college textbooks and classes.

In addition, critical thinking can help you to *critically evaluate* what you are learning in class. During your college career, your instructors will often ask you to discuss "critically" some argument or idea introduced in class. Critical thinking teaches a wide range of strategies and skills that can greatly improve your ability to engage in such critical evaluations.

You will also be asked to *develop your own arguments* on particular topics or issues. In an American Government class, for example, you might be asked to write a paper addressing the issue of whether Congress has gone too far in restricting presidential war powers. To write such a paper successfully, you must do more than simply find and assess relevant arguments and information. You must also be able to *marshal arguments and evidence* in a way that convincingly supports your considered view. In our experience, relatively few first-year college students are able to do that very well. The systematic training provided in a course in critical thinking can result in marked improvement in that skill as well.

Critical Thinking in the Workplace

Surveys indicate that fewer than half of today's college graduates can expect to be working in their major field of study within five years of graduation. This statistic speaks volumes about changing workplace realities. Increasingly, employers are looking not for employees with highly specialized career skills, since such skills can usually best be learned on the job, but for workers with good thinking and communication skills—quick learners who can solve problems, think creatively, gather and analyze information, draw appropriate conclusions

We don't want you to axiomatically accept the conventional wisdom on a particular subject. Indeed, your first instinct should be to question it.

—John J. Mearsheimer

There is nothing more practical than sound thinking.

—Foundation for Critical Thinking

Doonesbury © G. B. Trudeau. Reprinted with permission of Universal Press Syndicate. All rights reserved.

from data, and communicate their ideas clearly and effectively. These are exactly the kinds of generalized thinking and problem-solving skills that a course in critical thinking is designed to improve.

Critical Thinking in Life

Critical thinking is valuable in many contexts outside the classroom and the workplace. Let's look briefly at three ways in which this is the case.

First, critical thinking can help us avoid making foolish personal decisions. All of us have at one time or another made decisions about consumer purchases, relationships, personal behavior, and the like that we later realized were seriously mistaken or irrational. Critical thinking can help us to avoid such mistakes by teaching us to think about important life decisions more carefully, clearly, and logically.

Second, critical thinking plays a vital role in promoting democratic processes. Despite what cynics might say, in a democracy it really is "we the people" who have the ultimate say over who governs and for what purposes. It is important, therefore, that citizens' decisions be as informed and as deliberate as possible. Many of today's most serious societal problems—environmental destruction, nuclear proliferation, political gridlock, decaying inner cities, racial prejudice, declining educational standards, to mention just a few—have largely been caused by poor critical thinking. And as Albert Einstein once remarked, "The significant problems we face cannot be solved at the level of thinking we were at when we created them."

Finally, critical thinking is worth studying for its own sake, simply for the personal enrichment and fulfillment it can bring to our lives. One of the most basic truths of the human condition is that most people, most of the time, believe what they are told. Throughout most of recorded history, people accepted without question that the earth was the center of the universe, that demons cause disease, that slavery was just, and that women are inferior to men. Critical thinking, honestly and courageously pursued, can help to free us from the unexamined assumptions, dogmas, and prejudices of our upbringing and our society. It lets us step back from the prevailing customs and ideologies of our culture and ask, "This is what I've been taught, but is it *true*? Does it make *sense*?" In short, critical thinking allows us to lead self-directed, "examined" lives. Such personal liberation is, as the word itself implies, the ultimate goal of a *liberal* arts education. Whatever other benefits it brings, a liberal education can have no greater reward.

> Citizens who think for themselves, rather than uncritically ingesting what their leaders tell them, are the absolutely necessary ingredient of a society that is to remain truly free.
> —Howard Kahane

> Have the courage to use your own intelligence.
> —Immanuel Kant

BARRIERS TO CRITICAL THINKING

The preceding section raises an obvious question: If critical thinking is so important, why is it that *un*critical thinking is so common? Why do so many people—including many highly educated and intelligent people—find critical thinking so difficult?

The reasons, as you might expect, are quite complex. Here is a list of some of the most common barriers to critical thinking:

lack of relevant background information

poor reading skills

bias

prejudice

superstition

egocentrism (self-centered thinking)

sociocentrism (group-centered thinking)

peer pressure

conformism

provincialism

narrowmindedness

closemindedness

distrust in reason

stereotyping

unwarranted assumptions

scapegoating

rationalization

wishful thinking

short-term thinking

selective perception

selective memory

overpowering emotions

self-deception

face-saving

resistance to change

Four of these impediments—egocentrism, sociocentrism, unwarranted assumptions, and wishful thinking—play an especially powerful role in hindering critical thinking.

Egocentrism

Egocentrism is the tendency to see reality as centered on oneself. Egocentrics are selfish, self-absorbed people who view their own interests, ideas, and values as superior to everyone else's. In extreme cases, egocentrism can be a form of a mental illness. Someone who thinks he is God or Napoleon, for instance, is probably certifiably insane. Few of us are that disconnected from reality, but all of us are affected to some degree by egocentric biases.

Egocentrism can occur in a variety of forms. Two common forms are self-interested thinking and self-serving bias.

Self-interested thinking is the tendency to accept and defend beliefs that harmonize with one's own self-interest. Almost no one is immune from self-interested thinking. Most doctors support legislation making it more difficult for them to be sued for medical malpractice; most lawyers do not. Most state university professors strongly support tenure, paid sabbaticals, low teaching loads, and a strong faculty voice in university governance; many state taxpayers and university administrators do not. Most factory workers support laws requiring advance notice of plant closings; most factory owners do not. Most American voters favor campaign finance reform; most elected politicians do not. Of course, some of these beliefs may be supported by good reasons. From a psychological standpoint, however, it is likely that self-interest plays at least some role in shaping the respective attitudes and beliefs.

When a man desires very earnestly to embrace a certain class of doctrines, either in order to join a particular profession, or to please his friends, or to acquire peace of mind, or to rise in the world, or to gratify his passions, . . . he will usually attain his desire.

—W. E. H. Lecky

Self-interested thinking, however understandable it may seem, is a significant obstacle to critical thinking. Everyone finds it tempting at times to reason that "this benefits me; therefore, it must be good;" but from a critical thinking standpoint, such "reasoning" is a sham. Implicit in such thinking is the assumption that "what is most important is what *I* want and need." But why should I, or anyone else, accept such an arbitrary and obviously self-serving assumption? What makes *your* wants and needs so much more important than everyone else's? Critical thinking condemns such special pleading. It demands that we weigh evidence and arguments objectively and impartially. Ultimately, it demands that we revere truth—even when it hurts.

Self-serving bias is the tendency to overrate oneself—to see oneself as being better in some respect than one actually is. We have all known braggarts or know-it-alls who claim to be more talented or knowledgeable than they really are. If you are like most people, you probably think of yourself as being an unusually self-aware person who is largely immune from any such self-deception. If so, then you, too, are probably suffering from self-serving bias.

Studies show that self-serving bias is an extremely common psychological trait. In one survey, one million high school seniors were asked to rate themselves on their "ability to get along with others." *Not a single respondent rated himself below average in such ability.*[9] Other surveys have shown that 90 percent of business managers and over 90 percent of college professors rate their performance as better than average. It is easy, of course, to understand why people tend to overrate themselves. We all like to feel good about ourselves. Nobody likes to think of himself or herself as being "below average" in some important respect. At the same time, however, it is important to be able to look honestly at our personal strengths and weaknesses. We want to set high personal goals, but not goals that are wildly unrealistic. Self-confidence grounded

The one thing that unites all human beings, regardless of age, gender, religion, economic status, or ethnic background, is that, deep down inside, we all believe that we are above-average drivers.

—Dave Barry

in genuine accomplishment is an important element of success. Overconfidence is an obstacle to genuine personal and intellectual growth.

EXERCISE 1.2

Are you overconfident in your beliefs? Here is a simple test to determine if you are. For each of the following ten items, provide a low and a high guess such that you are 90 percent sure the correct answer falls between the two. Your challenge is to be neither too narrow (i.e., overconfident) nor too wide (i.e., underconfident). If you successfully meet the challenge, you should have 10 percent misses—that is, exactly one miss.[10]

	90% Confidence Range	
	LOW	HIGH
1. Martin Luther King's age at death	_____	_____
2. Length of Nile River (in miles)	_____	_____
3. Percentage of African Americans in the U.S.	_____	_____
4. Number of books in the Old Testament	_____	_____
5. Diameter of the moon (in miles)	_____	_____
6. Weight of an empty Boeing 747 (in pounds)	_____	_____
7. Current population of California	_____	_____
8. Year in which Wolfgang Amadeus Mozart was born	_____	_____
9. Air distance from London to Tokyo (in miles)	_____	_____
10. Deepest known point in the ocean (in feet)	_____	_____[11]

Sociocentrism

Sociocentrism is group-centered thinking. Just as egocentrism can hinder rational thinking by focusing excessively on the self, so sociocentrism can hinder rational thinking by focusing excessively on the group.

Sociocentrism can distort critical thinking in many ways. Two of the most important are group bias and the herd instinct.

Group bias is the tendency to see one's own group (nation, tribe, sect, peer group, etc.) as being inherently better than others. Social scientists tell us that such thinking is extremely common throughout human history and across cultures. Just as we seem naturally inclined to hold inflated views of ourselves, so we find it easy to hold inflated views of our family, our community, or our nation. Conversely, we find it easy to look with suspicion or disfavor on those we regard as "outsiders."

Most people absorb group bias unconsciously, usually from early childhood. Most of us grow up thinking that our society's beliefs, institutions, and values are better those of other societies. Consider this exchange between eight-year-old Maurice D. and well-known Swiss scientist and philosopher Jean Piaget:

> **Maurice D.** (8 years, 3 months old): If you didn't have any nationality and you were given a free choice of nationality, which would you choose? *Swiss nationality.* Why? *Because I was born in Switzerland.* Now look, do you think the French and the Swiss are equally nice, or the one nicer or less nice than the other? *The Swiss are nicer.* Why? *The French are always nasty.* Who is more intelligent, the Swiss or the French, or do you think they're just the same? *The Swiss are more intelligent.* Why? *Because they learn French quickly.* If I asked a French boy to choose any nationality he liked, what country do you think he'd choose? *He'd choose France.* Why? *Because he was born in France.* And what would he say about who's nicer? Would he think the Swiss and the French equally nice or one better than the other? *He'd say the French are nicer.* Why? *Because he was born in France.* And who would he think more intelligent? *The French.* Why? *He'd say that the French want to learn quicker than the Swiss.* Now you and the [other] boy don't really give the same answer. Who do you think answered best? *I did.* Why? *Because Switzerland is always better.*[12]

Although most people outgrow such childish nationalistic biases to some extent, few of us manage to outgrow them completely. Clearly, this kind of "mine–is–better" thinking lies at the root of a great deal of human conflict, intolerance, and oppression.

The **herd instinct** (or **conformism**) refers to our tendency to follow the crowd—that is, to conform (often unthinkingly) to authority or to group standards of conduct and belief. The desire to belong, to be part of the in-group, can be among the most powerful of human motivations. As two classic experiments demonstrate, this desire to conform can seriously cripple our powers of critical reasoning and decision making.

In the first experiment, conducted in the 1950s by Solomon Asch, groups of eight college students were asked to match a "standard" line like the following

———————

with three "comparison" lines such as these:

A ———————
B —————————
C ——————

In each group, only one of the eight participants was unaware of the true nature of the experiment; the other seven were confederates working in league with the experimenter. In each case, the single true subject was seated at the end of the table and asked to answer last. In some trials, the seven confederates unanimously gave the correct answer (answer B); in others, they unanimously gave an incorrect answer. The results: When no pressure to conform was present, subjects gave the correct answer more than 99 percent of the time.

> *[T]o those who would investigate the cause of existing opinions, the study of predispositions is much more important than the study of argument.*
> —W. E. H. Lecky

> *When all think alike, then no one is thinking.*
> —Walter Lippmann

However, when faced with the united opposition of their peers, almost a third (32 percent) of the subjects refused to believe their own eyes and gave answers that were obviously incorrect!

Another famous experiment was conducted by Stanley Milgram in the 1960s.[13] In Milgram's experiment, subjects were asked to administer a series of increasingly severe electrical shocks to people whom the subjects could hear but couldn't see. (In fact, no actual shocks were given; the shock "victims" were actually confederates who merely pretended to be in pain.) Subjects were told that they were participating in a study of the effects of punishment on learning. Their task was to act as "teachers" who inflicted progressively more painful shocks on "learners" whenever the latter failed to answer a question correctly. The severity of the shocks was controlled by a series of thirty switches, which ranged in 15-volt intervals from 15 volts ("Slight Shock") to 450 volts ("XXX Danger: Severe Shock"). The purpose of the study was to determine how far ordinary people would go in inflicting pain on total strangers simply because they were asked to do so by someone perceived to be "an authority."

The results were, well, shocking. Over 85 percent of the subjects continued to administer shocks beyond the 300-volt mark, long after the point at which they could hear the victims crying out or pounding on the walls in pain. After the 330-volt mark, the screaming stopped, and for all the subjects knew, the victims were either unconscious or dead. Despite that, nearly two-thirds (65 percent) of the subjects continued to administer shocks, as they were instructed, until they had administered the maximum 450 volts.

The lesson of these studies is clear: "Authority moves us. We are impressed, influenced, and intimidated by authority, so much so that, under the right conditions, we abandon our own values, beliefs, and judgments, even doubt our own immediate sensory experience."[14] As critical thinkers, we need to be aware of the seductive power of peer pressure and reliance on authority, and develop habits of independent thinking and judgment to combat them.

Unwarranted Assumptions and Stereotypes

An **assumption** is something we take for granted, something we believe to be true without any proof or conclusive evidence. Almost everything we think and do is based on assumptions. If the weather report calls for rain, we take an umbrella, because we assume that the meteorologist is not lying, that the report is based on a scientific analysis of weather patterns, that the instruments are accurate, and so forth. There may be no proof that any of this is true, but we realize that it is wiser to take the umbrella than to insist that the weather bureau provide exhaustive evidence to justify its prediction.

Many of our beliefs and opinions are also based on assumptions. One might base support of capital punishment on the assumption that it deters crime. A politician might base opposition to higher taxes on the assumption that most people don't want to pay them. The assumptions may or may not be correct, but without evidence they are really only guesses. Whereas taking an umbrella poses no extra burden, holding a position based on assumptions can be problematic. We all know the frustration and distress of discovering that a belief or an important decision was based on assumptions that turned out to have no basis in fact.

Although we often hear the injunction "Don't assume," it would be impossible to get through a day without making assumptions, and in fact, many of our daily actions are based on assumptions we have drawn from the patterns in our experience. You go to class at the scheduled time because you assume that class is being held at its normal hour and in the same place. You don't call the professor each day to ask if class is being held; you just assume that it is. Such assumptions are *warranted,* which means that there is good reason to hold them. When you see a driver coming toward you with the turn signal on, you have good reason to believe that the driver intends to turn. You may be incorrect, and it might be safer to withhold action until you are certain, but your assumption is not unreasonable.

Unwarranted assumptions, however, are unreasonable. An *unwarranted assumption* is something taken for granted without good reason. Such assumptions often prevent our seeing things clearly. For example, our attraction for someone might cause us to assume that he or she feels the same way and thus to interpret that person's actions incorrectly.

One of the most common types of unwarranted assumptions is a **stereotype.** The word "stereotype" comes from the printing press era, when plates, or stereotypes, were used to produce identical copies of one page. Similarly, when we stereotype, as the word is now used, we assume that individual people have all been stamped from one plate, so that all college sophomores are alike, or all politicians, police officers, African Americans, voters, professors, women, and so forth. When we form an opinion of someone that is based not on his or her individual qualities but, rather, on his or her membership in a particular group, we are assuming that all or virtually all members of that group are alike. Since people are not identical, no matter what race or other similarities they share, stereotypical conceptions will often be false or misleading.

Typically, stereotypes are arrived at through a process known as hasty generalization, in which one draws a conclusion about a large class of things (in this case, people) from a small sample. If we meet one South Bergian who is cruel and rude, we might jump to the conclusion that all South Bergians are cruel and rude. Or we might generalize from what we have heard from a few friends or read in a single news story. Often the media—advertisements, the news, movies, and so forth—encourage stereotyping by the way they portray groups of people.

The practice of thinking critically demands that we become aware of our own thinking, including our assumptions. A *conscious* assumption is one that we are aware of. We know that we are taking something for granted. We might stop and say, "I'm going to assume that this weather report is accurate," or "I'm assuming we have class today." Of course, it would be neither possible nor beneficial to uncover every assumption that informs our thinking. You have made an almost infinite number of assumptions since you awoke this morning. And being conscious of an unwarranted assumption does not justify it; saying "I'm aware of my tendency to stereotype" does not justify stereotyping.

The assumptions we need to become most conscious of are not the ones that lead to our routine behaviors, such as carrying an umbrella or going to class, but the ones upon which we base our more important attitudes, conclusions, actions, and decisions. If we are conscious of our tendency to stereotype, we can take measures to end it. If we are conscious of our assumption that a turn signal means a driver will turn, we might hesitate before pulling out into traffic.

EXERCISE 1.3

I. Read this story and answer the questions that follow.

> When it happened, a disturbing mix of feelings bubbled inside you. It sickened you to watch the boat slip beneath the waves and disappear forever; so much work had gone into maintaining it and keeping it afloat, but at least everyone was safe in the tiny lifeboat you'd had just enough time to launch. You secretly congratulated yourself for having had the foresight to stock the lifeboat with a few emergency items, such as a small amount of food and water, but you knew that a boat built to hold three, maybe four people wasn't going to survive too long with such an overload of passengers.
>
> You looked around at your companions: the brilliant Dr. Brown, whose cleverness and quick wit had impressed you on many occasions; Marie Brown, pregnant and clearly exhausted from the climb into the lifeboat; Lieutenant Ashley Morganstern, a twenty-year veteran who'd seen the most brutal sorts of combat; the lieutenant's secretary and traveling companion, whose shirt you noticed for the first time bore the monogram "LB," but whom everyone called, simply, "Letty"; and Eagle-Eye Sam, the trusted friend who'd been at your side for many years as you sailed the oceans in your precious, now-vanished boat and whose nickname came from his ability to spot the smallest objects seemingly miles away at sea.
>
> Seeing the fear on your passengers' faces, you tried to comfort them: "Don't worry; we'll be fine. They'll be looking for us right away. I'm sure of it." But you weren't so sure. In fact, you knew it wasn't true. It might be days before you were found, since you'd had no time to radio for help. Rescuers probably wouldn't be dispatched until Friday, five days from now, when your failure to show up in port would finally arouse concern.
>
> On the third day, your passengers showed increasing signs of frustration, anger, and fear. "Where are they?" Marie cried. "We can't go on like this!"
>
> You knew she was right. *We can't,* you thought, *not all of us anyway.*
>
> On the fourth day, the food was completely gone and just enough water remained to keep perhaps three people alive for another day, maybe two. Suddenly things got worse. "Is that water?!" Marie screamed, pointing a shaking finger at the bottom of the lifeboat. Horrified, you looked down to see a slight trickle of water seeping in at the very center of the boat. Dr. Brown grabbed a

tee-shirt that was lying in the bottom of the boat and used it like a sponge to absorb the water, wringing it out over the side and plunging it into the invading water again and again. But it was no use; the water began to seep in faster than Brown could work.

"We're too heavy," the lieutenant insisted without emotion. "We've got to lighten the load. Someone has to get out and swim."

"Swim?!" Marie gasped in disbelief. "Are you insane?! There are sharks in these waters!"

"Who's it going to be, Captain?" the lieutenant asked almost coldly, staring you square in the eye. "Which one of us swims?"

"Me. I'll go," you say, swinging your leg out over the side of the boat.

"No," Letty insisted. "You're the only one who knows anything about boats or the ocean. If you go, we'll all die. You must *choose* one of us to sacrifice."

And so you did.

A. Answer the following questions individually.
   1. Which one did you choose? Why? Why didn't you choose the others?
   2. As you read, you probably imagined what the characters looked like. From the image you had of them, describe the following characters in a few sentences:

   The Captain

   Dr. Brown

   Marie Brown

   Lieutenant Ashley Morganstern

   Letty

   Eagle-Eye Sam
   3. What is the relationship between Dr. Brown and Marie Brown?

B. Now form groups of three, and complete the following tasks.
   1. Compare your responses to question 1 in part A. Discuss your reasons for your decisions. Is there any consensus in the group?
   2. Do you all agree on the relationship between Dr. Brown and Marie Brown?
   3. What evidence is there in the story to support your answer to question 3 in part A? Is it possible that they are related in another way or not at all?
   4. Look at your portraits of Dr. Brown. How many assumptions did you and your group members make about the doctor's gender, age, appearance, and profession? What evidence in the story supports your image of the doctor? If your images are similar, what do you think accounts for that similarity? Are your mental images similar to ones we normally see in the media, for example?
   5. Look at your portraits of the other characters. First, what similarities do you find among your group members? Second, what evidence is there in the story to support your assumptions? Are other assumptions possible? Finally, where do you think your mental images came from?

II. In a group of three or four, name and explain a stereotypical conception people may have had about you over the years. Note how that stereotypical conception keeps others from coming to know you more accurately. Turn your page over and exchange papers with other members of your group. See if the other members can determine what stereotype description goes with what member of your group.

Wishful Thinking

> *The easiest thing of all is to deceive one's self; for what a man wishes, he generally believes to be true.*
>
> —Demosthenes

Once, as a little leaguer, one of the authors was thrown out at the plate in a foolish attempt to stretch a triple into a home run, possibly costing the team the game. Angry and disappointed, he refused to believe that he had really been thrown out. "I was safe by a mile," he said plaintively to his disbelieving coaches and teammates. It was only years later, when he was an adult, that he could admit to himself that he really had been out—out, in fact, by a mile.

Have you ever been guilty of wishful thinking—believing something not because you had good evidence for it but simply because you wished it were true? If so, then you're not alone. Throughout human history, reason has done battle with wishful thinking and has usually come out the loser.

> *A man hears what he wants to hear and disregards the rest.*
>
> —Paul Simon

People fear the unknown and invent comforting myths to render the universe less hostile and more predictable. They fear death, and listen credulously to stories of healing crystals, quack cures, and communication with the dead. They fantasize about possessing extraordinary personal powers, and accept uncritically accounts of psychic prediction, levitation, and ESP. They delight in tales of the marvelous and the uncanny, and buy mass-market tabloids that feature headlines such as "Spiritual Sex Channeler: Medium Helps Grieving Widows Make Love to Their Dead Husbands."[15] They kid themselves into thinking, "It can't happen to me," and then find themselves dealing with the consequences of unwanted pregnancies, drunk-driving convictions, drug addiction, or AIDS.

> *The universe is what it is, not what I choose that it should be.*
>
> —Bertrand Russell

EXERCISE 1.4

I. Have you ever been guilty of self-interested thinking, self-serving bias, group bias, the herd instinct, unwarranted assumptions, or wishful thinking? Without embarrassing yourself too much, discuss these critical thinking lapses in groups of three or four. Then share with the class whatever examples you would like to discuss.

II. This textbook gives a number of examples of self-interested thinking, self-serving bias, group bias, the herd instinct, unwarranted assumptions, and wishful thinking. Jot down at least two additional examples of each of these six critical thinking hindrances. Divide into groups of three or four and discuss your examples with the group. Share what you think are the best examples with the class as a whole.

CHARACTERISTICS OF A CRITICAL THINKER

So far in this chapter we have discussed (1) the nature of critical thinking; (2) key critical thinking standards, such as clarity, precision, accuracy, and fairness; (3) the benefits of critical thinking; and (4) some major impediments to critical thinking, including egocentrism, sociocentrism, unwarranted assumptions, and wishful thinking. With this as background, we are now in a position to offer a general profile of a critical thinker. The following list contrasts some of the key intellectual traits of critical thinkers with the relevant traits of uncritical thinkers.[16]

Critical Thinkers	Uncritical Thinkers
Have a passionate drive for clarity, precision, accuracy, relevance, consistency, logicalness, completeness, and fairness.	Often think in ways that are unclear, imprecise, inaccurate, etc.
Are sensitive to ways in which critical thinking can be skewed by egocentrism, sociocentrism, wishful thinking, etc.	Often fall prey to egocentrism, sociocentrism, wishful thinking, etc.
Understand the value of critical thinking, both to individuals and to society as a whole.	See little value in critical thinking.
Are intellectually honest with themselves, acknowledging what they don't know and recognizing their limitations.	Pretend they know more than they do and ignore their limitations.
Listen open-mindedly to opposing points of view and welcome criticisms of beliefs and assumptions.	Are closeminded and resist criticisms of beliefs and assumptions.
Base their beliefs on facts and evidence rather than on personal preference or self-interest.	Often base their beliefs on mere personal preference or self-interest.
Are aware of the biases and preconceptions that shape the way they perceive the world.	Lack awareness of their own biases and preconceptions.
Think independently and are not afraid to disagree with group opinion.	Tend to engage in "group think," uncritically following the beliefs and values of the crowd.

Are able to get to the heart of an issue or problem, without being distracted by details.	Are easily distracted and lack the ability to zero in on the essence of a problem or issue.
Have the intellectual courage to face and assess fairly ideas that challenge even their most basic beliefs.	Fear and resist ideas that challenge their basic beliefs.
Love truth and are curious about a wide range of issues.	Are often relatively indifferent to truth and lack curiosity.
Have the intellectual perseverance to pursue insights or truths, despite obstacles or difficulties.	Tend not to persevere when they encounter intellectual obstacles or difficulties.

A course in critical thinking is like most other things in life: you get out of it what you put into it. If you approach critical thinking as a chore—a pointless general education requirement you need to "get out of the way" before you turn to more "relevant" courses in your major—then a chore it will be. On the other hand, if you approach critical thinking as an opportunity to learn habits of disciplined thinking that are vital to success in school, in your career, and in your life as a liberally educated person, then critical thinking can be a rewarding and even transformative experience. The choice is yours. Good luck, and enjoy!

EXERCISE 1.5

I. Review the list of critical thinking traits on pages 21–22. Then write a 250-word essay in which you address the following questions: Which of the traits listed do you think is your strongest critical thinking trait? Why? Which is your weakest? Why? What could you do to improve in this latter regard? Be specific and realistic.

II. In groups of three or four, define the following critical thinking traits: intellectual honesty, open-mindedness, fair-mindedness, intellectual courage, and intellectual perseverance. (See the list of critical thinking traits on pages 21–22 for some broad hints.) Give an example of each.

III. In groups of three or four, think of examples, either from your own experience or from your knowledge of history or current events, of individuals who possess, or did possess, the quality of intellectual courage to an unusual degree. What about them leads you to think of them as being especially intellectually courageous? Do the same for the qualities of open-mindedness, intellectual honesty, and intellectual perseverance. Be prepared to share your group's best examples with the class.

SUMMARY

1. *Critical thinking* is the general term given to a wide range of cognitive skills and intellectual dispositions needed to effectively identify, analyze, and evaluate arguments and truth claims, to discover and overcome personal prejudices and biases, to formulate and present convincing reasons in support of conclusions, and to make reasonable, intelligent decisions about what to believe and what to do. It is disciplined thinking governed by clear intellectual standards that have proven their value over the course of human history. Among the most important of these intellectual standards are clarity, precision, accuracy, relevance, consistency, logical correctness, completeness, and fairness.

2. Critical thinking is beneficial for many reasons. It can help students do better in school by improving their ability to understand, construct, and criticize arguments. It can help people succeed in their careers by improving their ability to solve problems, think creatively, and communicate their ideas clearly and effectively. It can also reduce the likelihood of making serious mistakes in important personal decisions, promote democratic processes by improving the quality of public decision making, and liberate and empower individuals by freeing them from the unexamined assumptions, dogmas, and prejudices of their upbringing, their society, and their age.

3. Major hindrances to critical thinking include egocentrism, sociocentrism, unwarranted assumptions, and wishful thinking.

   Egocentrism is the tendency to see reality as centered on oneself. Two common forms of egocentrism are self-interested thinking (the tendency to accept and defend beliefs that accord with one's own self-interest) and self-serving bias (the tendency to overrate oneself).

   Sociocentrism is group-centered thinking. Two common varieties of sociocentrism are group bias (the tendency to see one's culture or group as being better than others) and the herd instinct (the tendency to conform, often unthinkingly, to authority or to group standards of conduct and belief).

   Unwarranted assumptions are things we take for granted without good reason. Often, unwarranted assumptions take the form of stereotypes. *Stereotypes* are generalizations about a group of people in which identical characteristics are assigned to all or virtually all members of the group, often without regard to whether such attributions are accurate or not.

   Wishful thinking is believing something because it makes one feel good, not because there is good evidence or rational grounds for thinking it is true.

4. Critical thinkers exhibit a number of traits that distinguish them from uncritical thinkers. Among the most important of these traits are a passionate drive for clarity, precision, accuracy, and other intellectual standards that characterize careful, disciplined thinking; a sensitivity to the ways in which critical thinking can be skewed by egocentrism, wishful thinking, and other psychological obstacles to rational belief; honesty and intellectual humility; open-mindedness; intellectual courage; love of truth; and intellectual perseverance.

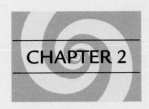

CHAPTER 2

RECOGNIZING ARGUMENTS

As we saw in the previous chapter, critical thinking is centrally concerned with *reasons:* identifying reasons, evaluating reasons, and giving reasons. In critical thinking, passages that present reasons for a claim are called *arguments.* In this chapter we explore the concept of an argument and explain how to distinguish arguments from nonarguments.

WHAT IS AN ARGUMENT?

When people hear the word *argument,* they usually think of some kind of quarrel or dispute. In critical thinking, however, an **argument** is a claim put forward and defended with reasons.

Arguments are composed of one or more premises and a conclusion. **Premises** are statements that are claimed to provide evidence for another statement, the conclusion. The **conclusion** is the statement that the premises are claimed to prove or support.

A **statement** is a sentence that can sensibly be regarded as either true or false.[1] Here are some examples of statements:

Red is a color.

There are nine planets in the solar system.

Canada is in South America.

God does not exist.

Abortion is morally wrong.

I have a headache today.

Stars Wars is a better movie than *Titanic.*

Some of these statements are clearly true, some are clearly false, and some are controversial. However, each of them is a statement, because each can be prefaced with the phrase "It is true that . . ." or "It is false that . . .".

Three things should be noted about statements. First, a sentence may be used to express more than one statement. For example, the grammatical sentence

Roses are red and violets are blue.

expresses two distinct statements ("Roses are red" and "Violets are blue"). Each of these is a statement because each is capable of standing alone as a declarative sentence.

Second, a statement can sometimes be expressed as a phrase or an incomplete clause rather than as a complete declarative sentence. Consider this sentence:

Given the extraordinarily low odds of winning, state lotteries are a kind of tax on the mathematically challenged. (overheard)

Grammatically, this is a single declarative sentence. However, the speaker's intent here is clearly to defend one assertion ("State lotteries are a kind of tax on the mathematically challenged") on the basis of another ("The odds of winning state lotteries are extraordinarily low"). The fact that we have to rephrase the sentence slightly to make this explicit should not obscure the fact that two statements are being offered rather than one.

Third, not all sentences are statements, that is, sentences that either assert or deny that something is the case. Here are some examples of sentences that are not statements:

What time is it? (question)

Hi, Dad! (greeting)

Close the window! (command)

Please send me your current catalog. (request)

Let's go to Mt. Pocono for our anniversary. (proposal)

Insert Tab A into Slot B. (instruction)

Oh, my goodness! (exclamation)

None of these is a statement, because none of them asserts or denies that anything is the case. None says, in effect, "This is a fact. Accept this; it is true." Therefore, sentences like these are not used in arguments.

Not all sentences, however, are as they appear. Some sentences that look like nonstatements are actually statements and can be used in arguments. Here are two examples:

Alyssa, you should quit smoking. Don't you realize how bad that is for your health?

Commencement address: Do not read beauty magazines. They will only make you feel ugly. (Mary Schmich)

The first example contains a *rhetorical question*. Rhetorical questions are sentences that have the grammatical form of questions but are meant to be understood as statements. In our example, the person asking the question isn't really looking for information. She's making an assertion: that smoking is very bad for one's health. This assertion is offered as a reason (premise) to support the conclusion that Alyssa should quit smoking.

The second example includes an *ought imperative,* that is, a sentence that has the form of an imperative or a command but is intended to assert a value or ought judgment about what is good or bad, right or wrong, advisable or inadvisable to do. Grammatically, "Do not read beauty magazines" looks like a command or a suggestion. In this context, however, the speaker is clearly making an assertion: that you *shouldn't* read beauty magazines. Her statement that reading such magazines will only make you feel ugly is offered as a premise to support this value judgment.

How can you tell when a sentence that looks like a command or a suggestion is really an ought imperative? The key question to ask is this: Can I accurately rephrase this sentence so that it refers to what someone should or ought or would be well advised to do? If you can, then the sentence should be treated as a statement.

Consider two further examples. Suppose a drill sergeant says to a new recruit:

> Close that window, soldier! It's freezing in here!

In this context it is clear that the sergeant is issuing an order rather than expressing an ought judgment ("You *ought* to close the window, soldier!"). On the other hand, if one college roommate says to another,

> Don't blow-dry your hair in the tub, Arnold! You could electrocute yourself!

it is likely that the roommate is expressing an ought judgment ("You *shouldn't* blow-dry your hair in the tub!") rather than issuing an order or making a mere suggestion.

As these examples make clear, it is always important to consider the context in which a particular expression is used. A sentence such as "Don't give up the ship!" might be a command in one context and an ought imperative in another. If you are in doubt about whether an argument is being expressed, simply ask yourself: Is this being offered as a reason in defense of some claim? If it is, then an argument is being put forward, regardless of the grammatical form in which the words are expressed.

Critical Thinking Lapse

A 19-year-old man was hospitalized in Salt Lake City after undertaking a personal investigation into the eternal question of whether it is possible to fire a .22-caliber bullet by placing it inside a straw and striking it with a hammer. Answer: sometimes (including this time); it went off and hit him in the stomach.[2]

EXERCISE 2.1

Determine whether, in typical contexts, the following sentences are or are not statements. Exercises marked with the icon (◻) are answered in the back of the book.

◻ 1. Capital punishment is wrong.

2. Can I get you something to drink?

3. Ted Williams is the greatest hitter in baseball history.

◻ 4. What do you say we stop at the next rest stop?

5. Abraham Lincoln was the first president of the United States.

6. Let's party!

◻ 7. I love you.

8. Thou shalt not kill. (said as one of the Ten Commandments)

9. Go, Yankees!

◻ 10. No vehicles are permitted in the park.

11. If Sally calls, tell her I'm at the library.

12. Do not make any marks in this test booklet.

◻ 13. I hope Peter likes his new job.

14. Can't you see that pornography demeans women?

15. Holy cow!

◻ 16. It is a pleasure to meet you.

17. Please print your name legibly.

18. I feel that handguns should be outlawed.

◻ 19. Kill the umpire!

20. I like chocolate ice cream better than vanilla ice cream.

21. Don't drink and drive. (said by your best friend)

◻ 22. Give us this day our daily bread. (said in prayer)

23. Don't you realize how silly that hat looks?

24. What a crock!

◻ 25. Don't forget the rehearsal is Monday night.

IDENTIFYING PREMISES AND CONCLUSIONS

To recap: One of the most fundamental critical thinking skills is that of recognizing arguments. An argument, as used in critical thinking, is a set of claims that consists of one or more premises and a conclusion. The premises are statements offered as reasons why we should accept the conclusion. In deciding whether a sentence is a statement, and hence may be part of an argument, we should look not merely at the grammatical form of the sentence but also at the context in which the sentence is expressed.

In identifying premises and conclusions, we are often helped by indicator words. **Indicator words** are words or phrases that provide clues that premises or conclusions are being put forward. **Premise indicators** indicate that premises are being offered, and **conclusion indicators** indicate that conclusions are being offered. Here are some common premise indicators:

since	because
for	given that
seeing that	being that
inasmuch as	as
in view of the fact that	as indicated by

The following examples illustrate the use of premise indicators.

Having fun can be the spice of life but not its main course, *because* when it is over, nothing of lasting value remains. (Harold Kushner)

Since effective reasoning requires reliable information, it is important to be able to distinguish good sources and trustworthy experts from less useful ones. (Drew E. Hinderer)

I believe that what we do here in the academic world is at least as real and important as what goes on outside our walls. *For* it is here, in our classrooms, that we try to develop the skills in critical thinking and interpretation that are so necessary in the late 20th century when the problems that face us are becoming more complex and the line between truth and illusion is becoming harder to see. (Michael J. Kobre)

Given that suffering depends on brain events (in turn caused by events in the other parts of the body), then *since* the lower animals do not suffer a lot, animals of intermediate complexity (it is reasonable to suppose) suffer only a moderate amount. (Richard Swinburne)

Women are not by any means to blame when they reject the rules of life, which have been introduced into the world, *seeing that* it is men who have made them without their consent. (Montaigne)

To know that God exists in a general and confused way is implanted in us by nature, *inasmuch as* God is man's beatitude. (St. Thomas Aquinas)

I think that, *as* life is action and passion, it is required of a man that he should share the passion and action of his time, at peril of being judged not to have lived. (Oliver Wendell Holmes, Jr.)

Here are some common conclusion indicators:

therefore	thus
hence	consequently
so	accordingly
it follows that	for this reason
that is why	which shows that
wherefore	implies that
as a result	we may infer that
suggests that	proves that

These examples illustrate the use of conclusion indicators:

All human beings possess an inviolable dignity. *Therefore,* abortion is wrong.

You want people to be honest with you. *So* be honest with them.

Sorrow is merely a state of mind and may not be warranted by the circumstance. *Hence* whether or not you feel sad over something is all in the mind. (Lie Zi)

Animals are ordered to man's use in the natural course of things, according to divine providence. *Consequently,* man uses them without any injustice, either by killing them or by employing them in any other way. (St. Thomas Aquinas)

Rapid economic improvements represent a life-or-death imperative throughout the Third World. Its people will not be denied that hope, no matter the environmental costs. *As a result,* that choice must not be forced upon them. (Al Gore)

General scientific laws invariably go beyond the finite amount of observable evidence that is available to support them, and *that is why* they can never be proven in the sense of being logically deduced from that evidence. (A. F. Chalmers)

Our faith comes in moments; our vice is habitual. Yet there is a depth in those brief moments which constrains us to ascribe more reality to them than to all other experiences. *For this reason* the argument which is always forthcoming to silence those who conceive extraordinary hopes of man, namely the appeal to experience, is forever invalid and vain. (Ralph Waldo Emerson)

As our birth brought us the birth of all things, so will our death bring us the death of all things. *Wherefore* it is as foolish to weep because a hundred years from now we shall not be alive, as to weep because we were not living a hundred years ago. (Montaigne)

Understanding arguments would be easier if the expressions just listed were used only to signal premises or conclusions. That isn't the case, however, as the following examples illustrate:

I haven't seen you *since* high school.

You've had that jacket *for* as long as I've known you.

Thus far, everything has been great.

It was *so* cold that even the ski resorts shut down.

I wouldn't mind *seeing that* movie again.

There is water on the floor *because* the sink overflowed.

In none of these examples does the italicized term function as an indicator word. This shows once again why it is so important to consider the context when determining the meaning of an expression.

Many arguments contain no indicator words at all. Here are three examples:

> Protection of wilderness and near-wilderness is imperative. While primal peoples lived in sustainable communities for tens of thousands of years without impairing the viability of ecosystems, modern technocratic-industrial society threatens every ecosystem on Earth and may even be threatening to drastically change the pattern of weather in the biosphere as a whole. (Bill Devall and George Sessions)

> Injustice anywhere is a threat to justice everywhere. We are caught in an inescapable network of mutuality; tied in a single garment of destiny. Whatever affects one directly, affects all indirectly. (Martin Luther King, Jr.)

> I can't be held *completely* responsible for my life. After all, there are many factors outside my control, people and forces that create obstacles and undermine my efforts. And we are free subject to pressure and influences from within ourselves: feelings of greed, fear of death, altruistic impulses, sexual compulsions, need for social acceptance, and so on. (John Chaffee)

The conclusion of the first argument is "Protection of wilderness and near-wilderness is imperative." The conclusion of the second argument is "Injustice anywhere is a threat to justice everywhere." The conclusion of the third argument is "I can't be held completely responsible for my life."

How can we find the conclusion of an argument when the argument contains no indicator words? The following list provides some helpful hints.

Tips on Finding the Conclusion of an Argument

1. Find the main issue and ask yourself what position the writer or speaker is taking on that issue.
2. Look at the beginning or the end of the passage; the conclusion is often (but not always) found in one of those places.
3. Ask yourself, "What is the writer or speaker trying to prove?"
4. Try putting the word "therefore" before one of the statements. If it fits, that statement is probably the conclusion.
5. Try the "because trick." That is, try to find the most appropriate way to fill in the blanks in the following statement: The writer or speaker believes _____ (conclusion) because _____

(premise). The conclusion will naturally come before the word *because*.[3]

Thus far, all the arguments we have examined have been simple arguments. *Simple arguments* have only a single conclusion. But many arguments contain more than one conclusion. Arguments of this sort are called *complex arguments*.

To say that a complex argument can have multiple conclusions is not to say that it can have multiple *independent* (i.e., logically unrelated) conclusions. Consider the following:

> The Weather Service is predicting another cold, snowy winter. Therefore, I should put snow tires on my car. Also, I should invest my life savings in home heating oil stocks.

We might treat this as one argument with two independent conclusions:

1. The Weather Service is predicting another cold, snowy winter. (premise)

Therefore,

2. I should put snow tires on my car. (first conclusion)

and

3. I should invest my life savings in home heating oil stocks. (second conclusion)

To understand the argument in that way, however, is to invite confusion. The two conclusions are completely independent of each other; neither provides any evidence or logical support for the other. There seems to be no good reason, therefore, to regard them as parts of a single argument rather than as conclusions of two separate arguments that share the same premise. Moreover, the premise of the argument ("The Weather Service is predicting another cold, snowy winter") clearly provides much weaker support for the second conclusion ("I should invest my life savings in home heating oil stocks") than it does for the first ("I should put snow tires on my car"). In evaluating the argument, one must treat these two steps independently, and the easiest way to do that is to treat them as two separate arguments.

Does that mean that an argument cannot have more than one conclusion? No, it just means that if an argument does have more than one conclusion, each of the conclusions must be offered in support of a single *main conclusion*. Here is an example of such an argument:

> We know that either Sluggo or Bruiser committed the robbery. But Sluggo couldn't have committed the robbery, because he was in prison when the robbery was committed. Therefore, Bruiser committed the robbery.

In this argument, there are two premises and two conclusions:

1. We know that either Sluggo or Bruiser committed the robbery. (first premise)

2. But Sluggo was in prison when the robbery was committed. (second premise)

Therefore,

3. Sluggo couldn't have committed the robbery. (first conclusion)

Therefore,

4. Bruiser committed the robbery. (second conclusion)

Notice that the first conclusion ("Sluggo couldn't have committed the robbery") is not only a conclusion but also a *premise* offered to support a further conclusion (namely, that "Bruiser committed the robbery"). Conclusions of this sort are called **subconclusions,** because they operate as intermediate or transitional conclusions in a continuing chain of reasoning.

The second conclusion ("Bruiser committed the robbery") is not a step to any further conclusion; it is itself the main point or final conclusion of the argument. Conclusions of this sort are called **main conclusions.**

We are now in a position to define simple and complex arguments more precisely. **Simple arguments** are arguments that contain no subconclusions. They consist of a single conclusion supported by one or more premises. **Complex arguments,** on the other hand, are arguments that contain at least one subconclusion. They consist of a chain of reasoning in which one or more transitional conclusions are offered to support a single main conclusion.

EXERCISE 2.2

I. Identify the premises and conclusions in the following arguments.

1. Since pain is a state of consciousness, a "mental event," it can never be directly observed. (Peter Singer, "Animal Liberation," 1973)
2. The genetic code of DNA and RNA is identical in all species from viruses to mammals. Thus all living things share fundamental biochemical characteristics which indicate that they have all evolved from a single form of life. (Douglas J. Futuyma, *Science on Trial: The Case for Evolution,* 1983)
3. Since everything that begins to exist has a cause of its existence, and since the universe began to exist, we conclude, therefore, the universe has a cause of its existence. (William Lane Craig, *The Kalam Cosmological Argument,* 1979)
4. If a man's thoughts are to have truth and life in them, they must after all be his own fundamental thoughts; for these are the only ones that he can fully and wholly understand. (Arthur Schopenhauer, "On Thinking for One's Self," 1851)
5. He who acts unjustly acts unjustly to himself, because he makes himself bad. (Marcus Aurelius, *Meditations,* c. A.D. 180)
6. I can speak with some authority on the subject of marketing because I once took a marketing class. Moreover, I have purchased many items. (Scott Adams, *The Dilbert Principle,* 1996)

7. The invention or discovery of symbols is doubtless by far the single greatest event in the history of man. Without them, no intellectual advance is possible; with them, there is no limit set to intellectual development except inherent stupidity. (John Dewey, *The Quest for Certainty*, 1929)

8. Science is based on experiment, on a willingness to challenge old dogma, on an openness to see the universe as it really is. Accordingly, science sometimes requires courage—at the very least the courage to question the conventional wisdom. (Carl Sagan, *Broca's Brain: Reflections on the Romance of Science*, 1979)

9. Where our conduct does fall under the commands or prohibitions of law, either the civil or the moral law, the virtuous man is still able to do as he pleases, since he pleases to do what he ought. (Mortimer J. Adler, *Six Great Ideas*, 1981)

10. The extent of a man's, or a people's liberty to live as they desire must be weighed against the claims of many other values, of which equality, or justice, or happiness, or security, or public order are perhaps the most obvious examples. For this reason, it cannot be unlimited. (Isaiah Berlin, *Four Essays on Liberty*, 1969)

11. You know how I know animals have souls? Because on average, the lowest animal is a lot nicer and kinder than most of the human beings that inhabit this Earth. (From a newspaper call-in column, *Wilkes-Barre Times Leader*, August 7, 1999)

12. Devotion signifies a life devoted to God. He therefore is the devout man who lives no longer to his own will, or the way and spirit of the world, but to the sole will of God. (William Law, *A Serious Call to a Devout and Holy Life*, 1728)

13. Democracy has at least one merit, namely, that a member of Parliament cannot be stupider than his constituents, for the more stupid he is, the more stupid they were to elect him. (Bertrand Russell, *Autobiography*, 1967)

14. Don't worry about senility. When it hits you, you won't know it. (Bill Cosby, *Time Flies*, 1987)

15. There is nothing wrong with burning crude [oil] like crazy—oil isn't helping anyone when it sits in the ground—so long as there's a plan for energy alternatives when the cheap oil runs out. (Gregg Easterbrook, "Opportunity Cost," 2000)

16. There is no doubt that certain events recorded at seances are genuine. Who does not recall the famous incident at Sybil Seretsky's when her goldfish sang "I Got Rhythm"—a favorite tune of her recently deceased nephew? (Woody Allen, *Without Feathers*, 1972)

17. So far the states are spending more than 90 percent of the tobacco settlement money on programs unrelated to smoking, such as building highways. This is good, because we need quality highways to handle the sharp increase in the number of Mercedes automobiles purchased by lawyers enriched by the tobacco settlement. (Dave Barry, "War on Smoking Always Has Room for Another Lawyer," 2000)

18. It's part of human nature to be angry at God when bad things happen, but what's the point? If we encourage each other to blame God for injustices,

then aren't we giving the evil or dark side a victory by keeping God's precious children—that's all of us—away from His loving arms? (Letter to the Editor, *Wilkes-Barre Times Leader,* June 11, 1998)

19. In great contests each party claims to act in accordance with the will of God. Both may be, and one must be, wrong. God cannot be for and against the same thing at the same time. (Abraham Lincoln, "Meditation on the Divine Will," 1862)

20. It is a capital mistake to theorize before one has data. Insensibly one begins to twist facts to suit theories, instead of theories to suit facts. (Sherlock Holmes, in Arthur Conan Doyle's *A Scandal in Bohemia,* 1891)

21. Never answer your phone if you have voice mail. People don't call you just because they want to give you something for nothing—they call because they want *you* to work for *them.* (Scott Adams, *The Dilbert Principle,* 1996)

22. Philosophy being nothing else but the study of wisdom and truth, it may with reason be expected that those who have spent most time and pains in it should enjoy a greater calm and serenity of mind, and greater clearness and evidence of knowledge, and be less disturbed with doubts, and difficulties than other men. (George Berkeley, *Principles of Human Knowledge,* 1710)

23. Has it ever occurred to you how lucky you are to be alive? More than 99% of all creatures that have ever lived have died without progeny, but not a single one of your ancestors falls into this group! (Daniel C. Dennett, *Darwin's Dangerous Idea,* 1995)

24. Parenting is all about drawing clear moral boundaries and enforcing acceptable limits to produce conscience and compassion in children. To do otherwise is to create kids who think their rights and interests supersede those of others. (Kathleen Parker, "The Sin of Pride Is Killing Our Children," 1999)

25. When the universe has crushed him man will still be nobler than that which kills him, because he knows that he is dying, and of its victory the universe knows nothing. (Blaise Pascal, *Pensées,* 1670)

II. Identify the premises and the conclusions in the following arguments.

1. Men love the suit so much, we've actually styled our pajamas to look like a tiny suit. Our pajamas have little lapels, little cuffs, simulated breast pockets. Do you need a breast pocket on your pajamas? You put a pen in there, you roll over in the middle of the night, you kill yourself. (Jerry Seinfeld, *Sein-Language,* 1993)

2. Rights are either God-given or evolve out of the democratic process. Most rights are based on the ability of people to agree on a social contract, the ability to make and keep agreements. Animals cannot possibly reach such an agreement with other creatures. They cannot respect anyone else's rights. Therefore they cannot be said to have rights. (Rush Limbaugh, *The Way Things Ought to Be,* 1992)

3. No one need fear to use *he* if common sense supports it. The furor recently raised about *he* would be more impressive if there were a handy substitute for the word. Unfortunately, there isn't—or, at least, no one has come up

with one yet. (William Strunk, Jr., and E. B. White, *The Elements of Style,* 3rd ed., 1979)

4. 'Tis a dangerous thing to engage the authority of scripture in disputes about the natural world, in opposition to reason; lest time, which brings all things to light, should discover that to be evidently false, which we had made scripture assert. (Thomas Burnet, *The Sacred Theory of the Earth,* 1684)

5. All you have shall some day be given; therefore give now, that the season of giving may be yours and not your inheritors'. (Kahlil Gibran, *The Prophet,* 1955)

6. How can anyone in his right mind criticize the state police for the speed traps? If you're not speeding, you don't have to worry about them. It could save your life if some other speeder is stopped. (From a newspaper call-in column, *Wilkes-Barre Times Leader,* July 3, 1998)

7. Philosophy is dangerous whenever it is taken seriously. But so is life. Safety is not an option. Our choices, then, are not between risk and security, but between a life lived consciously, fully, humanly in the most complete sense and a life that just happens. (Douglas J. Soccio, *Archetypes of Wisdom,* 3rd ed., 1998)

8. Our nation protests, encourages, and even intervenes in the affairs of other nations on the basis of its relations to corporations. But if this is the case, how can we dissociate ourselves from the plight of people in these countries? (Louis P. Pojman, *Global Environmental Ethics,* 2000)

9. If a man say, "I love God," and hateth his brother, he is a liar: for he that loveth not his brother whom he hath seen, how can he love God whom he hath not seen? (I John 4:20)

10. If your neighbor presents you with an apparently flawless scientific case that you do not really exist, don't get too rattled even if you cannot find any obvious mistakes in the case. They are there. After all, you have to exist for him to present the case to you at all. (Del Ratzsch, *Philosophy of Science: The Natural Sciences in Christian Perspective,* 1986)

11. Because high school students often rent their books, they have developed the habit of not writing comments in their texts. This is a very bad habit. College-level texts are demanding, and to read them requires interpretation and reflection. The easiest way to get a sense for how a text is proceeding is to jot down the main idea of each paragraph in the margin. (Donald L. Hatcher and L. Ann Spencer, *Reasoning and Writing: An Introduction to Critical Thinking,* 1993)

12. We should be emotionally reconciled to the fact of death, rather than fearing it, once we understand that death is necessary for two important, and very positive, things. First, it is necessary for our appreciation of life. The more vivid our sense of the approach of death, the more we relish the small things in life. And secondly, death is necessary for the continued march of evolutionary improvement, an ongoing progress leading to more valuable states of good, to take place on earth. (Tom Morris, *Philosophy for Dummies,* 1999)

13. Since virtually everyone and every group claim they know what constitutes right versus wrong human action, and since virtually all of these moralities differ from all others to a greater and lesser extent, reason alone tells us

they cannot all be correct. (Michael Shermer, *Why People Believe Weird Things,* 1997)

14. Whether you like it or not, you'd better accept reality the way it occurs: as highly imperfect and filled with most fallible human beings. Your alternative? Continual anxiety and desperate disappointments. (Albert Ellis and Robert A. Harper, *A New Guide to Rational Living,* 1978)

15. Free-will is part of man's dignity. But the angels' dignity surpasses that of men. Therefore, since free-will is in men, with much more reason is it in angels. (St. Thomas Aquinas, *Summa Theologica,* c. 1270)

16. People who believe that they are responsible for what they do will also demand the conditions of responsible choice. They will insist that they not be denied information that is relevant to their choice, and they will want the opportunity to discuss and debate with others. Free speech and free press are thus essential components of a society that regards human beings as responsible moral agents. (Kenneth Strike and Jonas F. Soltis, *The Ethics of Teaching,* 3rd ed., 1998)

17. If having rights requires being able to make moral claims, to grasp and apply moral laws, then many humans—the brain-damaged, the comatose, the senile—who plainly lack those capacities must be without rights. But that is absurd. This proves that rights do not depend on the presence of moral capacities. (Carl Cohen, "The Case for the Use of Animals in Biomedical Research," 1986)

18. It seems not to be true that there is a power in the universe, which watches over the well-being of every individual with parental care and brings all his concerns to a happy ending. . . . Earthquakes, floods, and fires do not differentiate between the good and devout men, and the sinner and unbeliever. And even if we leave inanimate nature out of account and consider the destinies of individual men insofar as they depend on their relations with others of their own kind, it is by no means the rule that virtue is rewarded and wickedness punished, but it happens often enough that the violent, the crafty, and the unprincipled seize the desirable goods of the earth for themselves, while the pious go away empty. (Sigmund Freud, *New Introductory Lectures on Psycho-Analysis,* 1933)

19. It is foolish to argue that we don't need ethics because we have law and religious belief. It is because of ethics (moral reasoning) that we have law in the first place, and we continue to need ethics to refine and perfect our legal system. We also need ethics in order to discuss the practical implications of our religious belief with others who do not share that belief. In addition, in situations when the reasonableness of a particular article of belief is at issue, we need ethics to help us reach a sound decision. (Vincent Ryan Ruggiero, *The Moral Imperative,* 2nd ed., 1984)

20. It is a scientific fact that 1974 was the worst year in world history for rock music. And I am NOT saying this because among the top musical acts to emerge that year were Abba AND Barry Manilow. I am saying it because the hit songs included "Kung Fu Fighting," "Seasons in the Sun," "Billy Don't Be a Hero," "The Night Chicago Died" and "(You're) Having My Baby." (Dave Barry, *Dave Barry Turns Fifty,* 1998)

Critical Thinking Lapse

Larry Walters, a 33-year-old truck driver from North Hollywood, California, had always dreamed about flying. So, on July 2, 1982, Walters tied 42 Army surplus weather balloons to an aluminum lawn chair, strapped himself in, and cut himself loose.

Walters expected to float lazily over the housetops. Instead, he shot up to 16,000 feet.

Soon Walters found himself drifting into the main approach corridor of Los Angeles International Airport. Shivering with cold, he managed to get himself down by shooting out some balloons with a pellet gun.

Eventually, Walters crashed into some power lines, briefly blacking out a small area in Long Beach.

When asked why he had done it, Walters simply replied, "A man can't just sit around."[4]

WHAT IS NOT AN ARGUMENT?

We encounter arguments everywhere in daily life—at school, at work, in magazine ads, in newspaper editorials, in political discussions, in television documentaries, and on radio talk shows. Of course, people don't use language only to offer arguments: they also use it to tell jokes, sing songs, recite poetry, express feelings, report events, ask questions, offer explanations, say prayers, give orders, and exchange wedding vows. How, then, can we distinguish arguments from nonarguments?

The basic test is quite simple. Something counts as an argument only if (1) it is a group of two or more statements and (2) one of those statements (the conclusion) is claimed or intended to be proved or supported by the others (premises). By applying this simple test, we can usually tell whether a given passage is or is not an argument. Now let's look at five types of nonargumentative discourse that are often confused with arguments:

- Reports
- Unsupported statements of belief or opinion
- Conditional statements
- Illustrations
- Explanations

Reports

The purpose of a **report** is simply to convey information about a subject. Here is an example of a report:

Alice Washington was born in 1944 in New York City. She grew up in Harlem and the Bronx and went to segregated public schools, not something of her choosing, nor that of her mother and her father. She finished high school, studied bookkeeping at a secretarial college, and went to work, beginning at 19. When she married, at the age of 25, she had to choose her husband from that segregated "marriage pool," to which our social scientists sometimes quite icily refer, of frequently unemployable black men, some of whom have been involved in drugs or spent some time in prison. From her husband, after many years of what she thought to be monogamous matrimony, she contracted the AIDS virus. She left her husband after he began to beat her. Cancer of her fallopian tubes was detected at this time, then cancer of her uterus. She had three operations. Too frail to keep on with the second of two jobs that she had held, in all, for nearly 20 years, she was forced to turn for mercy to the City of New York.[5]

In this passage, the author is simply reporting a series of generally unfortunate events; his aim is to narrate and inform, not to offer reasons why one statement should be accepted on the basis of others.

Caution is needed, however, with reports *about* arguments. Here is an example of such a passage:

Government is legitimate, according to Hobbes, because living under a government is better than living in a state of nature. The advantages of government are so great that it is worth sacrificing some of our freedom in order to bring about these advantages. For this reason, rational people would consent to sign a social contract and subject themselves to the laws and powers of a government.[6]

This is not an argument, because the author is merely reporting another person's argument, not endorsing it or putting it forward as his own.

Unsupported Statements of Belief or Opinion

Statements of belief or opinion are statements about what a speaker or writer happens to believe. Such statements can be true or false, rational or irrational, but they are parts of arguments only if the speaker or writer claims that they follow from, or support, other claims. Here is an example of a series of **unsupported statements of belief or opinion:**

I believe that it is not dying that people are afraid of. Something else, something more unsettling and more tragic than dying frightens us. We are afraid of never having lived, of coming to the end of our days with the sense that we were never really alive, that we never figured out what life was for.[7]

Because there is no claim that any of these statements follow from, or imply, any other statements, this is not an argument.

Conditional Statements

A **conditional statement** is an "if-then" statement. Here are several examples:

If it rains, then the picnic will be canceled.

If Emilio is a bachelor, then he must be unmarried.

You must speak French if you grew up in Quebec.

If at first you don't succeed, don't try skydiving.[8]

Conditional statements are made up of two basic components. The first part, the statement(s) following the word *if,* is called the **antecedent.** The second part, the statement(s) following the word *then,* is called the **consequent.**

Conditional statements are not arguments, because there is no claim that any statement *follows* from any part of a conditional statement. Thus, if I say, "If you win the homecoming game, then I'll eat my hat," I'm not asserting either that you will win the homecoming game or that I'll eat my hat. I'm only asserting that *if* the first statement is true, then the second statement will also be true. Because there is no claim that any statement follows from, or supports, this conditional statement, no argument has been given.

Although conditional statements are not arguments, it is sometimes easy to confuse them with arguments, because some conditional statements do involve a process of reasoning. Thus, if I say, for example,

If Rhode Island were larger than Ohio, and Ohio were larger than Texas, then Rhode Island would be larger than Texas

it may appear that I have reasoned to a conclusion and, hence, offered an argument. In fact, however, no argument has been given. All I have asserted is that *if* the first two statements are true, then the third statement must also be true. I have not claimed that any of these statements *are* true. Thus, I have not put forward any premises or reasoned to any conclusion. In fact, I have asserted only a single claim: that one statement is true *on the condition* that two other statements are true. True, this claim was arrived at by a process of inference or reasoning, but that does not mean that it is an argument. As we have seen, no single claim by itself is ever an argument.

Conditional statements, accordingly, are not arguments. They can, however, be *parts* of arguments. For example:

If Sturdley fails critical thinking, then he'll be placed on academic probation.
Sturdley will fail critical thinking.
So, Sturdley will be placed on academic probation.

In fact, arguments can be composed entirely of conditional statements:

If Tech scores on this play, then I'll eat my hat.
If I eat my hat, then I'll have a bad case of indigestion.
So, if Tech scores on this play, then I'll have a bad case of indigestion.

Such arguments are sometimes called *chain arguments,* because the antecedent (the *if* part) of the first statement is linked to the consequent (the *then* part) of the last statement by a chain of intervening conditional statements.

Illustrations

Illustrations are intended to provide *examples* of a claim rather than to prove or support the claim.

> Many wildflowers are edible. For example, daisies and day lilies are delicious in salads.

Even though the second statement does provide some evidence for the first, this passage is an illustration rather than an argument. Its purpose is not to provide convincing evidence for a conclusion but merely to provide a few striking or representative examples of a claim.

Distinguishing arguments from illustrations can be difficult for two reasons. First, phrases such as "for example" and "for instance" sometimes occur in arguments rather than illustrations. For example:

> Purists sometimes insist that we should say *between* when two and only two objects are present, *among* if there are more than two. This, however, is an oversimplification. For example, no one would object to *between* in "*The main stumbling block in the present delicate exchanges between Paris, Athens, London and Ankara. . . .*"[9]

Second, there is sometimes a fine line between illustrating a claim and providing convincing evidence for the claim. Consider the following:

> Many of the world's greatest philosophers were bachelors. For instance, Descartes, Locke, Hume, and Kant were all unmarried.

This is a borderline case between an argument and an illustration. Without more information, we cannot tell whether the author's purpose was to provide convincing evidence for a claim or merely to illustrate the claim. Such cases are fairly commonplace and rarely pose any serious difficulty. The general rule here, as with other borderline cases, is simple. Critical thinkers call it the principle of charity (see box).

Applying this simple principle can resolve many otherwise troublesome cases quickly and easily. In the previous example, for instance, it is doubtful whether the four philosophers cited provide sufficient evidence for the claim that "many" of the world's greatest philosophers have been bachelors. It is bet-

> *Read not to contradict and confute, nor to believe and take for granted . . . but to weigh and consider.*
>
> —Francis Bacon

The Principle of Charity

When interpreting an unclear passage, always give the speaker or writer the benefit of the doubt. Never attribute to an arguer a *weaker* argument when the evidence reasonably permits us to attribute to him or her a *stronger* one. And never interpret a passage as a *bad argument* when the evidence reasonably permits us to interpret it as *not an argument at all*.

ter, therefore, to treat these as illustrations of the claim rather than as evidence intended to prove the claim.

Explanations

Consider the following two statements:

> *Titanic* sank because it struck an iceberg.
>
> Capital punishment should be abolished, because innocent people may be mistakenly executed.

On the surface, these two statements look very much alike. Both give reasons, and both use the indicator word "because." However, there is an important difference between the two. The first statement is an explanation and the second is an argument.

An **explanation** tries to show *why* something is the case, not to prove *that* it is the case. In our first example, for instance, it is clear that the speaker isn't trying to argue *that Titanic* sank—everybody already knows that it sank. Instead, he is trying to explain *why* it sank. Of course, you can argue about whether a given explanation is or is not correct. Consider this example:

> Dinosaurs became extinct because of the impact of a large asteroid.

Scientists argue vigorously about whether this is or is not the correct explanation of the apparently sudden extinction of the dinosaurs 65 million years ago. But the fact that this explanation is controversial (i.e., can be argued about) doesn't mean that it is an argument. The intent of the passage is not to argue *that* dinosaurs became extinct but to explain *why* they became extinct.

Explanations have two parts. The statement that is explained is the **explanandum.** The statement that does the explaining is the **explanans.** Thus, in the explanation

> I fell down because I tripped.

the statement "I fell down" is the explanandum and the statement "I tripped" is the explanans.

In everyday speech, we often use "argument" and "explanation" almost interchangeably. Thus, we might say, for example, that the second speaker above is "explaining" why capital punishment should be abolished. This loose way of speaking no doubt contributes greatly to the confusion many students feel in distinguishing arguments from explanations.

Nevertheless, it is important to be able to distinguish arguments from explanations, because the standards for evaluating them are quite different. The fact that Schlomo likes mystery stories may be a more or less satisfactory explanation for *why* he is now reading *The Hound of the Baskervilles,* but plainly it is not a good reason for thinking *that* he is now reading that particular book.

How, then, does one distinguish arguments from explanations? One should always ask two key questions:

First, is the statement that the passage seeks to prove or explain an accepted matter of fact? If it is, then the passage is probably an explanation rather than an argument. (There is usually little point in trying to prove something that is already a matter of common knowledge.)

Second, is it the speaker's or writer's intent to prove or establish *that* something is the case—that is, *to provide reasons or evidence for accepting a claim as true?* Or is it his or her intent to explain *why* something is the case—that is, *to offer an account of why some event has occurred or why something is the way it is?* If the former, then the passage is an argument. If the latter, then the passage is an explanation.

The first test, although often helpful, is far from foolproof. Consider this:

Since all men are mortal, and Socrates is a man, Socrates is mortal.

Here the concluding statement ("Socrates is mortal") is an obvious fact; yet, clearly the passage is an argument.

The first test, therefore, must be used with caution. The second test is both more fundamental and more reliable.

Sometimes neither of the two tests yields a clear answer. In real life, of course, passages don't come neatly labeled as "argument" or "explanation." And the truth is that sometimes we just can't tell whether a passage is meant to be an argument or an explanation.

Suppose, for example, that at a crucial point in the battle of Waterloo Napoleon turned to his generals and exclaimed, "Our right flank is collapsing! The battle is lost!" Was Napoleon explaining *why* the battle was lost, or was he arguing *that* the battle was lost? Without more information, we can't say.

Or consider this quote from ACLU President Nadine Strossen:

Because civil libertarians have learned that free speech is an indispensable instrument for the promotion of other rights and freedoms—including racial equality—we fear that the movement to regulate campus expression will undermine equality, as well as free speech.[10]

What is the author's intent here? Is she trying to *explain* why civil libertarians fear that campus speech codes may undermine both freedom and equality? Or is she offering a *reason* why everyone should be concerned about such possible consequences? Or is she perhaps doing both? Again, it is very difficult to say.

EXERCISE 2.3

Arrange the chairs in the class into a circle. The instructor will give each student a three-by-five-inch index card. On one side of the card, write a very brief example of either an argument or an explanation. On the other side of the card, write "argument" or "explanation," whichever is appropriate to your example. When everyone has finished writing, pass your card to the student sitting to your

---

Critical Thinking Lapse

A 32-year-old Austrian who admitted to making more than 40,000 obscene phone calls was caught when one of his victims managed to obtain his phone number. The woman, who'd been pestered every day for six months, said she was too busy for an obscene call at that moment but would phone back if he left his number.[11]

---

right. Read the card you have received and decide whether it is an argument or an explanation. Then check your answer with the answer indicated on the back. Continue passing the cards until each card has been read. The instructor will then collect the cards and discuss the examples with the class.

Some students find it frustrating that critical thinking doesn't always provide definite, clear-cut answers. In this respect, however, critical thinking simply reflects life. Life is complex and messy, and critical thinking, because it helps us think intelligently about life, naturally reflects that complexity and messiness. Sometimes, despite our best efforts, we can't be sure whether a passage is an argument or an explanation. When that happens, we shouldn't pretend that the passage is clear. Instead, we should look at the various possibilities and say: "Well, it's unclear whether this is an argument or an explanation. However, *if* it is an argument, then it is a good (bad) argument, because _____. And *if* it is an explanation, then it is a good (bad) explanation, because _____." It is often possible to evaluate a passage this way, even if we can't be sure how the passage should be understood.

EXERCISE 2.4

I. Determine which of the following passages contain arguments and which do not.

1. I ate because I was hungry.
2. He must be home. His car is in the driveway.
3. I'm trading in my Ford Explorer for a Toyota Corolla because they're more reliable and get better gas mileage.
4. If Christmas is on a Friday, then the day after Christmas must be a Saturday.
5. Dinosaurs became extinct 65 million years ago, probably as a result of dramatic global cooling that resulted from the impact of a large asteroid.
6. Dogs make better pets than cats because they're more intelligent and obedient.
7. Capital punishment should be abolished because there is no convincing evidence that it deters any more effectively than a sentence of life imprisonment.
8. I'm thirsty. Let's stop for something to drink.
9. I stayed home from school because I was sick.

10. The Cascade Mountain Range contains many majestic peaks. Mt. Rainier and Mt. Hood, for instance, are both over ten thousand feet.

11. The death penalty *costs* too much. Allowing our government to kill citizens compromises the deepest moral values upon which this country was conceived: the inviolable dignity of human persons. (Helen Prejean, CSJ, *Dead Man Walking,* 1994)

12. If there were no maldistribution, if everyone shared equally, and if no grain were fed to animals, all of humanity could be adequately nourished today. (Paul Ehrlich and Anne Ehrlich, *Betrayal of Science and Reason,* 1996)

13. The British statesman William Gladstone thought that we would all be healthier if we chewed each bite of food precisely 32 times. Why else, he argued, did nature endow us with exactly 32 teeth? (Thomas Gilovich, *How We Know What Isn't So,* 1991)

14. [G]uys are extremely reluctant to make commitments, or even to take any steps that might *lead* to commitments. That is why, when a guy goes out on a date with a woman and finds himself really liking her, he often will demonstrate his affection by avoiding her for the rest of his life. (Dave Barry, *Dave Barry's Complete Guide to Guys,* 1995)

15. You can fool all of the people some of the time, and some of the people all the time, but you cannot fool all the people all the time. (Abraham Lincoln, Speech, September 8, 1855)

16. Teaching children the value of money is important. After all, the spending and saving habits they develop in childhood will often shape the way they handle their finances as adults. (Morgan Stanley Dean Witter ad)

17. Productivity and serving the public and taking care of one's own employees are neither mere means nor an afterthought of business but rather its very essence. Then, as every smart entrepreneur knows well enough, the profits will come as a consequence. (Robert C. Solomon, *Ethics and Excellence: Cooperation and Integrity in Business,* 1992)

18. The primary answer to the question "Why study scientific reasoning?" is that it will help you to understand and evaluate scientific information in both your personal life and your work. (Ronald N. Giere, *Understanding Scientific Reasoning,* 4th ed., 1997)

19. Children should be taught not to steal because it is wrong. They should not be taught not to steal because there is a rule against stealing. (J. F. Covaleski, "Discipline and Morality: Beyond Rules and Consequences," 1992)

20. Given that our culture is an increasingly important transmission belt of values to our children and is awash with gratuitous, senseless violence, brutality, and sex; given that the authority of churches and schools is diminished; given that entertainers and sports figures have replaced politicians and moral thinkers as the nation's most admired people yet rarely provide a moral direction to follow, it is a great [benefit] to have political leadership with moral authority. (Mortimer B. Zuckerman, "Voting for Grown-Ups," 2000)

21. The wind blows where it wills, and you hear the sound of it, but you do not know whence it comes or whither it goes; so it is with every one who is born of the Spirit. (John 3:8)

22. Never hit your child. Today health professionals agree that hitting children harms them emotionally as well as physically, fosters rage and self-hate, and often does lasting damage to their self-esteem and sense of worth. (*Dr. Koops's Self-Care Advisor,* 1996)

23. Cynicism is not realistic and tough. It's unrealistic and kind of cowardly because it means you don't have to try. (Peggy Noonan, quoted in *Reader's Digest,* 2000)

24. More than any other time in history, mankind faces a crossroads. One path leads to despair and utter hopelessness, the other, to total extinction. Let us pray that we have the wisdom to choose correctly. (Woody Allen, *Side Effects,* 1981)

25. What's right in the corporation is not what is right in a man's home or in his church. What is right in the corporation is what the guy above you wants from you. That's what morality is in the corporation. (Robert Jackall, *Moral Mazes,* 1988)

26. Man is created to praise, reverence, and serve God our Lord, and by this means to save his soul. All other things on the face of the earth are created for man to help him fulfill the end for which he is created. From this it follows that man is to use these things to the extent that they will help him to attain his end. (St. Ignatius Loyola, S.J., *Spiritual Exercises,* 1541)

27. Above all I delighted in mathematics because of the certainty and evidence of their reasonings. (René Descartes, *Discourse on Method,* 1637)

28. Tradition and folklore contain a large number of fallacious beliefs. For example, many widespread and popular beliefs such as "Don't swim for an hour after eating," "You should rub snow on frost bite," "Reading in the dark will ruin your eyes," "You can catch cold from being chilled," and "The more you cut your hair, the faster it will grow" are not true. (I. W. Kelly et al., "The Moon Was Full and Nothing Happened: A Review of Studies on the Moon and Human Behavior and Human Belief," 1985–86)

29. If you don't listen to radio talk shows, you really should, because it gives you a chance to reassure yourself that a great many people out there are much stupider than you are. (Dave Barry, *Dave Barry's Bad Habits,* 1985)

30. If a bridge collapses, if a dam breaks, if a wing falls off an airplane and people die, I cannot see that as God's doing. I cannot believe that God wanted all those people to die at that moment, or that He wanted some of them to die and had no choice but to condemn the others along with them. I believe that these calamities are all acts of nature, and that there is no moral reason for those particular victims to be singled out for punishment. (Harold Kushner, *When Bad Things Happen to Good People,* 1981)

31. When what is just or unjust is thought to be determined solely by whoever has the power to lay down the law of the land, it unavoidably follows that the law of the land cannot be judged either just or unjust. (Mortimer J. Adler, *Six Great Ideas,* 1981)

32. If you have a variety of spirits or souls, which are eternally alive, and which enter a lump of matter at birth and give it life, and then leave it and allow it

to die, there must be a vast number of spirits, one for each human being who has ever lived or will ever live. (Isaac Asimov, "The Subtlest Difference," 1977)

33. The cause of the Millenium Bug dates back to the 1960s, when computer programmers decided to represent certain types of data in shorthand. Thus 1967 became just "67"; Missouri became just "Mo."; a broiled chicken sandwich with fries and a medium soft drink became just "The No. 4 Combo"; and Charles A. Frecklewanger Jr. became just "Chuck." The programmers did this because, in the 1960s, computer memory was very expensive. Also, back then everybody except Bill Clinton was on drugs. Many of these programmers didn't know what century it was. (Dave Barry, "Come the Millenium, Please Use the Stairs," 1999)

34. So huge and obvious is the body of evidence substantiating our need to cut back on animal products in order to prevent disease that many people have opted to give up their meat-based diets altogether and become vegetarians. (Marilyn Diamond, *The American Vegetarian Cookbook from the Fit for Life Kitchen,* 1990)

35. As the journalist John Taylor pointed out in his 1991 article "Don't Blame Me!" the trend toward universal "victimology" (a new academic discipline!) has snowballed out of control. Thus, lifelong smokers are blaming cigarette companies for their own choice to smoke; vicious criminals blame their actions on oppressive social forces; . . . even participants in "refrigerator races" have sued manufacturers because the warning labels did not specifically warn against the dangers of racing with the mammoth appliances strapped to your back! (John Chaffee, *The Thinker's Way,* 1998)

36. Since human beings have a tripartite soul, says Plato, the highest good for humans cannot be pleasure, since pleasure would be the goal of satisfying only the bodily appetites, which constitutes only one of the three elements of the soul. (T. Z. Lavine, *From Socrates to Sartre: The Philosophic Quest,* 1984)

37. I never throw a key away. I know that as soon as I do, I'll discover a piece of locked luggage which will be useless because the key is gone. (Erma Bombeck, *All I Know about Animal Behavior I Learned in Loehmann's Dressing Room,* 1995)

38. Longevity is perhaps the best single measure of the physical quality of life. (If you're dead, there's little you can do to be happy.) (Carl Sagan, *The Demon-Haunted World: Science as a Candle in the Dark,* 1995)

39. Typically, male desires incline most men towards dominance, while typically female desires incline most women towards nurturance. Consequently, in every society, the overwhelming number of high-status positions in hierarchies are filled by men. (Larry Arnhart, *Darwinian Natural Right,* 1998)

40. Associate as much as you can with people of admirable character and proven sagacity. We become like the people we're around. (Tom Morris, *If Aristotle Ran General Motors,* 1997)

II. Determine whether the following passages are best understood as arguments or as explanations.

1. Neptune is blue because its atmosphere contains methane. (John Fix, *Astronomy: Journey to the Cosmic Frontier,* 2nd ed., 1997)

2. A good schoolmaster is a far more useful citizen than the average bank president, politician, or general, if only because what he transmits is what gives meaning to the life of the banker, the politician, the general. (Clifton Fadiman, *The Lifetime Reading Plan,* 1960)

3. Because Native Americans were not considered to be entitled to equal status with whites, treaties with the "Indians" were ignored. (Bess B. Hess et al., *Sociology,* 4th ed., 1993)

4. We are politically a classless society. Our citizenry as a whole is our ruling class. We should, therefore, be an educationally classless society. (Mortimer Adler, *The Paideia Proposal: An Educational Manifesto,* 1982)

5. Why are there laws of gravity? Because, Einstein revealed, large masses distort space-time, causing objects to move along geodesic paths. (Martin Gardner, "Science and the Unknowable," 1998)

6. The Great Lakes area has a concentration of industry because of the availability of water for manufacturing processes, and because water transportation is an efficient way to move raw materials and products. (Eldon D. Enger and Bradley F. Smith, *Environmental Science,* 6th ed., 1998)

7. True success always starts with an inner vision, however incomplete it might be. That's why most of the books on success by famous coaches, business stars, motivational consultants, and psychologists begin with chapters on goal setting. (Tom Morris, *Philosophy for Dummies,* 1999)

8. It is a fact of life on our beleaguered little planet that widespread torture, famine, and governmental criminal irresponsibility are much more likely to be found in tyrannous than in democratic governments. Why? Because the rulers of the former are much less likely to be thrown out of office for their misdeeds than the rulers of the latter. (Carl Sagan, *The Demon-Haunted World: Science as a Candle in the Dark,* 1995)

9. Men seem to fly around the television more than women. Men get that remote control in their hands, they don't even know what the hell they're not watching. . . . Women don't do this. Women will stop and go, "Well let me see what the show is, before I change the channel. Maybe we can nurture it, work with it, help it grow into something." Men don't do that. Because women nest and men hunt. That's why we watch TV differently. (Jerry Seinfeld, *SeinLanguage,* 1993)

10. Most Americans, I think, are reluctant to make hasty judgments on a public figure's private life, largely because many of us have things in our own private lives we wouldn't like to see up on a billboard in Times Square. (Donald Kaul, "Clinton Lynch Mob Should Save Its Outrage for the Truly Outrageous," 1998)

11. We are bound to run into trouble if we seek rational justifications of every principle we use, for one cannot provide a rational argument for rational argument itself without assuming what we are arguing for. (A. F. Chalmers, *What Is This Thing Called Science?* 3rd ed., 1999)

12. For 26 years television has been free of cigarette ads. Why? Because TV

persuades as nothing else, and we don't want young people—inveterate TV watchers—persuaded. (Charles Krauthammer, "The New Prohibitionism," 1997)

13. Teachers do things in the same way because they all came up through the years of the same type of schooling—they "model" their own teachers. (Diane Ravitch, *The Schools We Deserve*, 1985)

14. I hate books. They only teach us to talk about what we do not know. (Jean-Jacques Rousseau, *Emile*, 1762)

15. Men may live more truly and fully in reading Plato and Shakespeare than at any other time, because then they are participating in essential being and are forgetting their accidental lives. (Allan Bloom, *The Closing of the American Mind*, 1987)

16. Why are firstborns more conservative and influenced by authority? . . . Firstborns, being first, receive considerably more attention from their parents than laterborns, who tend to receive greater freedom and less indoctrination into the ideologies of and obedience to authority. (Michael Shermer, *Why People Believe Weird Things*, 1997)

17. Many people are concerned that the chemical and biological weapons that Saddam Hussein is supposed to be making could be devastating and deadly. I'm not denying they are, but I don't think whatever he manufactures could have much of an effect on the United States, being that we're already tearing ourselves apart and destroying the very fiber that founded this country. (From a newspaper call-in column, *Wilkes-Barre Times Leader*, 1998)

18. Spinoza is the noblest and most lovable of the great philosophers. Intellectually, some others have surpassed him, but ethically he is supreme. As a consequence, he was considered, during his lifetime and for a century after his death, a man of appalling wickedness. (Bertrand Russell, *A History of Western Philosophy*, 1945)

19. I wear glasses primarily so I can look for the things that I keep losing. (Bill Cosby, *Time Flies*, 1987)

20. When someone dies, it is important that those close to him participate in the process; it will help them in their grief, and will help them face their own death more easily. (Elizabeth Kübler-Ross, *Death: The Final Stage of Growth*, 1975)

21. It is unethical to perform laboratory tests on people, so scientists use rats. (Graham R. Thompson and Jonathan Turk, *Earth Science and the Environment*, 1993)

22. All segregation statutes are unjust because segregation distorts the soul and damages the personality. (Martin Luther King, Jr., *Letter from Birmingham Jail*, 1963)

23. The basis for all that the Church believes about the moral dimensions of economic life is its vision of the transcendent worth—the sacredness of human beings. The dignity of the human person, realized in community with others, is the criterion against which all aspects of economic life must be measured. All human beings therefore are ends to be served by the institutions that make up the economy, not means to be exploited for more

narrowly defined goals. (National Conference of Catholic Bishops, *Economic Justice for All: Pastoral Letter on Catholic Social Teaching and the U.S. Economy,* 1986)

24. At certain times in the past, average global temperature was lower than at present. Polar and temperate climates were colder, and possibly wetter, than now. Consequently, vast continental glaciers covered much of North America, Europe, Asia, and parts of the southern continents. (Graham H. Thompson and Jonathan Turk, *Earth Science and the Environment,* 1993)

25. I come from the Lower East Side of New York City and from very rough circumstances. As a matter of fact, I came from a family of fourteen children. Fourteen children. It's true. It happened because my mother was hard of hearing. I'll explain this to you. You see, every night when it was time to retire, my father would turn to my mother and say, "Would you like to go to sleep or what?" My mother, who couldn't hear very well would say, "What?" And that's how it happened. (Jackie Mason, *Jackie Mason's America,* 1983)

SUMMARY

1. Since critical thinking is concerned primarily with understanding, constructing, and critically evaluating arguments, one of the most basic critical thinking skills is that of recognizing arguments.

2. An *argument,* as that term is used in critical thinking, is a claim put forward and defended with reasons. Arguments are composed of one or more premises and a conclusion. *Premises* are statements in an argument offered as evidence or reasons in support of another statement. A *conclusion* is the statement in an argument that the premises are intended to support or prove.

3. *Indicator words* provide clues that premises or conclusions are being offered. Common indicator words include *therefore, consequently, thus, because,* and *since. Premise indicators* provide clues that premises are being offered, and *conclusion indicators* provide clues that conclusions are being offered. Indicator words, however, should be approached with caution, since not all arguments contain indicator words and sometimes indicator words are used in passages that are not arguments.

4. *Simple arguments* are arguments that contain no subconclusions. A *subconclusion* is a statement in an argument that is both a premise and a conclusion. *Complex arguments* are arguments that contain at least one subconclusion.

5. It is important to distinguish arguments from various forms of nonargumentative discourse, such as reports, unsupported statements of belief or opinion, conditional statements, illustrations, and explanations. *Reports*

are statements that are intended simply to convey information about a subject. *Unsupported statements of belief or opinion* are statements that state what a person believes but don't offer evidence or reasons for that belief. *Conditional statements* are "if-then" statements. They claim only that one statement is true *if* another statement is true. *Illustrations* are statements intended to provide examples of a claim, rather than evidence or proof for the claim. *Explanations* are statements intended to explain *why* something is the case rather than to prove *that* it is the case. None of these types of passages is an argument, because none is intended to prove a claim.

BASIC LOGICAL CONCEPTS

Logic is the great
disperser of hazy
and confused
thinking: it clears
up the fogs which
hide from us our
own ignorance,
and make us be-
lieve that we un-
derstand a subject
when we do not.
—John Stuart Mill

In the last chapter we talked about what arguments are and how we can distinguish them from nonarguments. In this chapter we introduce some basic logical concepts necessary to distinguish good arguments from bad.

In evaluating any argument, one should always ask two key questions: Are the premises true? and Do the premises provide good reasons to accept the conclusion?

The first question—how to decide whether an argument's premises are true—will be discussed in Chapter 8. In this chapter we shall focus on the second question. What does it mean to say that an argument's premises provide "good reasons" for its conclusion, and how can we know when such reasons are being offered?

DEDUCTION AND INDUCTION

Before we can effectively evaluate an argument, we need to understand clearly what kind of argument is being offered. Traditionally, arguments have been divided into two types: deductive arguments and inductive arguments. Because the standards for evaluating deductive and inductive arguments are quite different, it is important to understand the difference between these two types of arguments.

All arguments claim to provide support—that is, evidence or reasons—for their conclusions. But arguments differ greatly in the amount of support they claim to provide. Some arguments try to *prove* their conclusions with rigorous, inescapable logic. Others merely try to show that their conclusions are *plausible* or *likely* or *probable* given the premise(s). The first kind of argument is a **deductive argument.** The second kind is an **inductive argument.**

Here are some examples of deductive arguments:

All humans are mortal.
Socrates is human.
Therefore, Socrates is mortal.

All whales are mammals.

All mammals are animals.

Hence, all whales are animals.

If the president lives in the White House, then he lives in Washington, D.C.

The president does live in the White House.

So, the president lives in Washington, D.C.

Public Square is a square.

Therefore, it has four sides.

Notice how the conclusions of these arguments flow from the premises with a kind of inescapable logic. Each conclusion is logically necessary; this means that, given the premises, the conclusion could not possibly be false. Arguments are deductive when their premises are intended to provide this kind of rigorous, airtight logical support for their conclusions.

EXERCISE 3.1

I. Deductive reasoning isn't some technical and specialized form of reasoning engaged in only by logicians or mathematicians. It is something we all do easily and naturally. See if you can solve the following mini-mysteries on your own using your own native reasoning abilities. Then discuss your solutions with a partner.[1]

1. Either Moriarty was the murderer, or Stapleton was the murderer.
   If Stapleton was the murderer, then traces of phosphorus should have been found on the body.
   No traces of phosphorus were found on the body.
   Whodunnit?

2. The murder did not occur in the library.
   If Adler was the murderer, then the weapon was a revolver.
   Either Hope was the murderer, or Adler was the murderer.
   If Hope was the murderer, then the murder took place in the library.
   Whodunnit? With what weapon?

3. The murder was not committed on the moor.
   If Windibank was the murderer, then the weapon was a rope.
   Either Windibank was the murderer, or Calhoun was the murderer.
   If the weapon was a rope, then the murder was committed on the downs.
   If Calhoun was the murderer, then the weapon was a crowbar.
   If the weapon was a crowbar, then the murder was committed on the moor.
   Whodunnit? With what weapon? Where was the murder committed?

The study of logic appeals to no criterion not already present in the learner's mind.

—C. I. Lewis

II. The following logic problems are slightly more difficult than the ones in the previous exercise. See if you can solve the problems on your own. Then discuss your solutions with a partner.

1. At a picnic, Mike went for soft drinks for Amy, Brian, Lisa, and Bill, as well as for himself. He brought back iced tea, grape juice, Diet Coke, Pepsi, and 7–Up.

   Mike doesn't like carbonated drinks.

   Amy would drink either 7–Up or Pepsi.

   Brian likes only sodas.

   Lisa prefers the drink she would put lemon and sugar into.

   Bill likes only clear drinks.

   What drinks did Mike bring for each person?[2]

2. In a certain mythical community, politicians never tell the truth, and nonpoliticians always tell the truth. A stranger meets three natives and asks the first of them, "Are you a politician?" The first native answers the question. The second native then says, "The first native denied being a politician." The third native says that the first native is a politician.

   How many of these three natives are politicians?[3]

III. The following logic problem is moderately challenging. See if you can solve it on your own. Then discuss your solution with a partner.

> Of three prisoners in a certain jail, one had normal vision, the second had only one eye, and the third was totally blind. The jailor told the prisoners that, from three white hats and two red hats, he would select three and put them on the prisoners' heads. None could see what color hat he wore. The jailor offered freedom to the prisoner with normal vision if he could tell what color hat he wore. To prevent a lucky guess, the jailor threatened execution for any incorrect answer. The first prisoner looked at the other prisoners and said that he could not tell what color hat he wore. Next the jailor made the same offer to the one-eyed prisoner. The second prisoner looked at the other prisoners and said he could not tell what hat he wore either. The jailor did not bother making the offer to the blind prisoner, but he agreed to extend the same terms to that prisoner when he made the request. The blind prisoner answered the question correctly.
>
> *What color hat was the blind prisoner wearing, and how did he know?*[4]

> *Much that is taught in college classes grows soon out of date, but the skills of correct reasoning never become obsolete.*
>
> —Irving M. Copi and Carl Cohen

Deductive arguments claim to provide logically conclusive grounds for their conclusions. That is, they attempt to show that their conclusions *must* be true given the premises asserted. Inductive arguments, on the other hand, simply claim that their conclusions are *likely* or *probable* given the premises offered. Here are some examples of inductive arguments:

> Polls show that 75 percent of Republicans favor a school prayer amendment.
>
> Joe is a Republican.
>
> Therefore, Joe probably favors a school prayer amendment.

> Every previous U.S. president has been a man.
>
> Therefore, it is likely that the next U.S. president will be a man.

Every ruby so far discovered has been red.
Probably all rubies are red.

The bank safe was robbed last night.
Whoever robbed the safe knew the safe's combination.
Only two people know the safe's combination: Lefty and Bugsy.
Bugsy needed money to pay his gambling debts.
Bugsy was seen sneaking around outside the bank last night.
It is reasonable to conclude, therefore, that Bugsy robbed the safe.

It is sometimes said that the basic difference between deduction and induction is that deduction moves from general premises to particular conclusions, whereas induction moves from particular premises to general conclusions.[5] That, however, is a misconception.

Here, for example, is a deductive argument that moves not from general premises to a particular conclusion but from particular premises to a general conclusion:

Bush was president from January 20, 1989, to January 20, 1993. (particular premise)
Clinton succeeded Bush and served as president from January 20, 1993, to January 20, 2001. (particular premise)
Bush is a career politician. (particular premise)
Clinton is a career politician. (particular premise)
Therefore, all presidents during the 1990s were career politicians. (general conclusion)

Here is an example of an inductive argument that moves from general premises to a particular conclusion:

All of Stephen King's previous novels have been good. (general premise)
Therefore, Stephen King's next novel will probably be good. (particular conclusion)

In fact, it is possible to find examples of *any* possible combination of general or particular premises or conclusions in deductive or inductive arguments. Thus, it is a mistake to regard any particular pattern of general or particular statements as a defining characteristic of deductive or inductive reasoning.

What makes an argument deductive or inductive is not the pattern of particularity or generality in the premises and conclusion. Rather, it is the *type of support* the premises are claimed to provide for the conclusion. The following list summarizes the key differences between deductive and inductive reasoning.

Key Differences between Deductive and Inductive Arguments

Deductive arguments claim that	Inductive arguments claim that
If the premises are true, then the conclusion *must* be true.	If the premises are true, then the conclusion is *probably* true.

The conclusion follows *necessarily* from the premises.

The premises provide *conclusive* evidence for the truth of the conclusion.

It is *impossible* for all the premises to be true and the conclusion false.

The truth of the premises *guarantees* the truth of the conclusion.

It is *logically inconsistent* to assert the premises and deny the conclusion, meaning that if you accept the premises, you *must* accept the conclusion.

The conclusion follows *probably* from the premises.

The premises provide *good (but not conclusive)* evidence for the truth of the conclusion.

It is *unlikely* that the premises are true and the conclusion false.

The truth of the premises makes the truth of the conclusion *likely*.

Although it is logically consistent to assert the premises and deny the conclusion, the conclusion is *probably* true if the premises are true.

How Can We Tell Whether an Argument Is Deductive or Inductive?

We have seen that an argument is deductive if its premises are *intended* to provide conclusive grounds for the truth of its conclusion, and inductive if its premises are *intended* to provide merely probable grounds for the truth of its conclusion. But it is not always easy to know what a given speaker or writer intends. For that reason, it is sometimes difficult to tell whether a particular argument is deductive or inductive.

Fortunately, there are four tests that greatly simplify the task of determining whether an argument should be regarded as deductive or inductive. These tests are

- the indicator word test
- the strict necessity test
- the common pattern test
- the principle of charity test

The Indicator Word Test

Just as we use indicator words to signal the assertion of premises or conclusions, so we use indicator words to signal that our arguments are deductive or inductive. For example, a phrase such as "it necessarily follows that" almost always indicates that an argument is deductive. Here are some other common **deduction indicator words:**

certainly

definitely

absolutely

conclusively

it logically follows that

it is logical to conclude that

this logically implies that

this entails that

it must be the case that

These are some common **induction indicator words:**

probably

likely

it is plausible to suppose that

it is reasonable to assume that

one would expect that

it is a good bet that

chances are that

odds are that

The **indicator word test** is often extremely helpful. Nevertheless, two limitations of the test should be noted.

First, many arguments contain no deduction or induction indicator words. Here are three examples:

> Capital punishment should be abolished, because innocent persons may be mistakenly executed.

> Don't put that screwdriver in the electrical outlet! You might electrocute yourself!

> It makes sense for younger workers to save for retirement, because Social Security may not be around when they reach retirement age.

None of these arguments contains any indicator words that would help us decide whether it is deductive or inductive. For arguments such as these, we must rely on one or more of the other tests discussed in this section.

Second, arguers often use indicator words loosely or improperly. For example, it is common to hear speakers use strong phrases such as "it must be the case that" and "it is logical to assume that" when the context makes clear that the argument is not intended to be strictly deductive. For these reasons, the indicator word test must be used with some caution.

The Strict Necessity Test

All deductive arguments claim, explicitly or implicitly, that their conclusions follow necessarily from their premises. Moreover, we know from experience (1) that most arguers don't offer *obviously bad* deductive arguments and (2) that most arguers don't offer logically conclusive arguments unless they *mean* to offer logically conclusive arguments. From these simple facts, we can usually determine whether an argument is meant to be deductive or inductive.

The **strict necessity test** can be stated as follows:

> Either an argument's conclusion follows with strict logical necessity from its premises or it does not.

If the argument's conclusion *does* follow with strict logical necessity from its premises, then the argument should always be treated as deductive.[6]

If the argument's conclusion does *not* follow with strict logical necessity from its premises, then the argument should normally be treated as inductive. (The few exceptions to this rule will be discussed on pages 00–00.)

Now let's apply this test to a few examples. Consider the following arguments:

Alan is a father. Therefore, Alan is a male.

Jill is a six-year-old girl. Therefore, Jill cannot run a mile in one minute flat.

If Abe Lincoln was eaten by a dinosaur, then Abe Lincoln is dead. Abe Lincoln is dead. Therefore, Abe Lincoln was eaten by a dinosaur.

Does the conclusion of the first argument ("Alan is a male") follow with strict necessity from the premise ("Alan is a father")? Could it be possibly be true that Alan is a father yet false that he is a male? Clearly not, for by definition all fathers are male. According to the strict necessity test, therefore, the first argument is deductive.

What about the second argument? Could it be true that Jill is a six-year-old girl yet false that she cannot run a mile in one minute flat? Yes. Of course, it is not *physically possible* for a six-year-old girl to run a mile in one minute flat. Six-year-old girls (and human beings in general) just lack the physical equipment to be able to do that. But there is no *logical contradiction* in thinking that there could be a six-year-old girl who could run that fast. It is logically possible, therefore, that the premise is true and the conclusion false. Thus, the conclusion does not follow with strict logical necessity from the premises. Therefore, the argument should be treated as inductive.

The third argument is a little trickier. It is clear that the conclusion ("Abe Lincoln was eaten by a dinosaur") doesn't strictly follow from the premises, for the premises are both true and the conclusion is false. Normally, this would mean that the argument should be treated as inductive. In this case, however, the arguer has employed a pattern of reasoning that is almost invariably deductive.[7] As we shall see, cases like this are exceptions to the general rule about when an argument should be treated as inductive. A fuller discussion of such exceptions is provided on page 61.

The Common Pattern Test

Because deductive and inductive arguments often occur in characteristic, telltale patterns of reasoning, we can apply the **common pattern test** to determine which kind of reasoning we are dealing with.

Consider this argument:

If we are in Brussels, then we are in Belgium.
We are in Brussels.
Therefore, we are in Belgium.

This argument has a particular pattern or form that occurs frequently in deductive reasoning. The general pattern of the argument is this:

If [*the first statement*] is true, then [*the second statement*] is true.

[*The first statement*] is true.

Therefore, [*the second statement*] is true.

Because it is awkward and wordy to talk about "the first statement," "the second statement," and so on, logicians generally use *letters* to stand for the various parts of an argument. Suppose we let the letter A stand for the statement "We are in Brussels" and the letter B stand for the statement "We are in Belgium." Then we can state the general pattern of the argument as follows:

If A then B.

A.

Therefore, B.

This is an argument pattern that logicians call *modus ponens,* a Latin expression that means "affirmative mode." Because it is obvious that this is a logically reliable pattern of reasoning, arguments of this pattern should always be treated as deductive.

Modus ponens is one very common pattern of deductive reasoning. Later in this chapter we shall discuss several other common patterns of deductive and inductive reasoning. Once you have learned to recognize such patterns, you will be surprised at how simple it is to identify everyday examples of deductive and inductive reasoning.

The Principle of Charity Test

Suppose you have tried each of the three tests we have discussed and you are still not sure whether a particular argument should be treated as deductive or inductive. In that case, it is time to fall back on the important principle discussed at the end of the last chapter: *the principle of charity.* Let's recall what that principle says: When interpreting an unclear argument or passage, always give the speaker or writer the benefit of the doubt. Never attribute to an arguer a weaker argument when the evidence reasonably permits us to attribute to him or her a stronger one. And never interpret a passage as a bad argument when the evidence reasonably permits us to interpret it as not an argument at all.

The principle of charity serves two important goals in critical thinking. First, it fosters goodwill and mutual understanding in argument by demanding that we treat the arguments of others with the same generous and respectful spirit with which we would like others to treat our own arguments. Even more important, it promotes the discovery of truth by insisting that we confront arguments that we ourselves admit to be the strongest and most plausible versions of those arguments.

Let's apply the **principle of charity test** to an actual example. Consider the following:

> Andy told me that he ate at Maxine's Restaurant yesterday. But Maxine's was destroyed by fire less than a month ago. It is certain, therefore, that Andy is either lying or mistaken.

Should this argument be regarded as deductive or inductive? Let's apply our various tests.

First, are there any deduction or induction indicator words? Yes. We have seen that the phrase "it is certain that" is often used as a deduction indicator. But we have also seen that people often use indicator words—especially deduction indicator words—loosely or improperly. So this first test, though it clearly *suggests* that the argument is meant to be deductive, shouldn't be treated as conclusive.

Second, does the conclusion follow with strict necessity from the premises? No. Although it seems quite unlikely, it is certainly conceivable that the restaurant has been quickly rebuilt and has reopened for business. This suggests that the argument should be regarded as inductive.

Third, does the argument have a pattern of reasoning that is either characteristically deductive or characteristically inductive? Not really, as we shall see. Thus, the third test doesn't apply in this case.

In short, the first test suggests that the argument is deductive, the second test suggests that the argument is inductive, and the third test doesn't apply. So where does that leave us? Up the proverbial creek without a paddle?

No, because this is where the principle of charity comes to the rescue. According to that principle, we should always interpret a doubtful argument *in the way most favorable to the arguer.* In this case, we are in doubt as to whether the argument should be treated as deductive or inductive. But consider: If we treat the argument as deductive, it is clearly a bad deductive argument, since the conclusion plainly does not follow necessarily from the premises. On the other hand, if we treat the argument as inductive, then the argument is clearly a good inductive argument, since the premises, if true, do clearly make the conclusion likely. Thus, the most charitable way to interpret the argument is to interpret it as inductive. This is what the principle of charity requires that we do.

A word of caution about the principle of charity, however: *The principle should never be used to reinterpret bad arguments as good ones.* The principle of charity is a principle of interpretation, not a principle of argument repair. Its basic purpose, like that of the other three tests, is to help us decide what arguments are actually being offered, not to replace bad arguments with ones we think are better. Thus, the principle should be used only when there is genuine uncertainty about how an argument should be interpreted. It should not be used when it is clear what argument has actually been put forward.

Exceptions to the Strict Necessity Test

We saw earlier that an argument should generally be treated as inductive if its conclusion does not follow necessarily from its premises. We also saw, however, that there are exceptions to this general rule. Two broad exceptions should be noted.

An argument in which the conclusion does not follow necessarily from the premises should nonetheless be treated as deductive if either

1. the *language* or the *context* makes clear that the arguer has *intended* to offer a logically conclusive argument, but the argument, in fact, is not logically conclusive;

or

2. the argument has a *pattern of reasoning* that is characteristically deductive, and nothing else about the argument indicates clearly that the argument is meant to be inductive.

Here is an example of the first exception:

Magellan's ships sailed around the world. It necessarily follows, therefore, that the earth is a sphere.

Here the phrase "it necessarily follows that" indicates that the argument is meant to be deductive. However, in this case it is clear that the conclusion does not follow necessarily from the premise, because it would still be possible for a ship to sail around the world if the earth were, say, egg-shaped or cylindrical rather than spherical.

Here is an example of the second exception:

If I'm Bill Gates, then I'm mortal.
I'm not Bill Gates.
Therefore, I'm not mortal.

This is a terrible argument. The premises provide no support whatever for the conclusion, much less logically conclusive support. Nevertheless, the argument is rightly regarded as deductive because it employs a pattern of reasoning that is almost invariably deductive.

This has been a rather complex discussion. The following list is the simplest and clearest way we know to sum up the basic guidelines for distinguishing deductive from inductive arguments.

Guidelines for Distinguishing Deductive from Inductive Arguments
1. If the conclusion follows necessarily from the premises, then the argument should always be treated as deductive.
2. If the conclusion does not follow necessarily from the premises, then the argument should be treated as inductive unless (a) the language or the context of the argument makes clear that the argument

> ## Critical Thinking Lapse
>
> There is one recorded instance of a woman smearing honey on her toddler's fingers so that a national park bear would lick it off for the video camera. Failing to understand this, the bear ate the baby's hand.[8]

is deductive or (b) the argument has a pattern of reasoning that is characteristically deductive.

3. If the argument has a pattern of reasoning that is characteristically deductive, then the argument should be treated as deductive unless there is clear evidence that the argument is intended to be inductive.

4. If the argument has a pattern of reasoning that is characteristically inductive, then the argument should be treated as inductive unless there is clear evidence that the argument is intended to be deductive.

5. Arguments often contain indicator words—words such as *probably, necessarily,* and *certainly*—that provide helpful clues in determining whether an argument is deductive or inductive. Keep in mind, however, that indicator words are often used loosely or improperly.

6. If there is significant doubt about whether an argument is deductive or inductive, always interpret the argument in the way most favorable to the arguer.

COMMON PATTERNS OF DEDUCTIVE REASONING[9]

Often, the quickest way to determine whether an argument is deductive or inductive is to note whether it has a pattern of reasoning that is characteristically deductive or inductive. In this section we shall discuss five common patterns of deductive reasoning:

- Hypothetical syllogism
- Categorical syllogism
- Argument by elimination
- Argument based on mathematics
- Argument from definition

Hypothetical Syllogism

A *syllogism* is simply a three-line argument—that is, an argument that consists of exactly two premises and a conclusion. A **hypothetical syllogism** is a syllogism that contains at least one hypothetical or conditional (i.e., if–then) premise.[10]

Here are two examples of hypothetical syllogisms:

If the Tigers beat the Yankees, then the Tigers will make the play-offs.
The Tigers will beat the Yankees.
So, the Tigers will make the play-offs.

If I want to keep my financial aid, I'd better study hard.
I do want to keep my financial aid.
Therefore, I'd better study hard.

Notice that these two arguments have the same logical pattern or form:

If A then B.
A.
Therefore, B.

This pattern, as we have seen, is called *modus ponens*. Arguments with this pattern consist of one conditional premise, a second premise that asserts as true the antecedent (the "if" part) of the conditional, and a conclusion that asserts as true the consequent (the "then" part) of the conditional. Other common varieties of hypothetical syllogisms include the following:

- Chain argument
- *Modus tollens* (denying the consequent)
- Denying the antecedent
- Affirming the consequent

Chain arguments consist of three conditional statements that link together in the following way:

If A then B.
If B then C.
Therefore, if A then C.

Here is an example of a chain argument:

If we don't stop for gas soon, then we'll run out of gas.
If we run out of gas, then we'll be late for the wedding.
Therefore, if we don't stop for gas soon, then we'll be late for the wedding.

Modus tollens[11] arguments have the following pattern:

If A then B.
Not B.
Therefore, not A.

Arguments of this pattern are sometimes called "denying the consequent" because they consist of one conditional premise, a second premise that denies (i.e., asserts to be false) the consequent of the conditional, and a conclusion that denies the antecedent of the conditional. Here is an example:

> If we're in Sacramento, then we're in California.
> We're not in California.
> Therefore, we're not in Sacramento.

Modus ponens, chain argument, and *modus tollens* are all logically reliable patterns of deductive reasoning. That is, any argument that has one of these patterns is absolutely guaranteed to have a true conclusion if the premises are also true. But not all patterns of deductive reasoning are completely reliable in this way. Two patterns that are *not* logically reliable are denying the antecedent and affirming the consequent.

Denying the antecedent arguments have the following pattern:

> If A then B.
> Not A.
> Therefore, not B.

Here are two examples:

> If Shakespeare wrote *War and Peace,* then he's a great writer.
> Shakespeare didn't write *War and Peace.*
> Therefore, Shakespeare is not a great writer.

> If President Kennedy was assassinated in 1987, then he died in the twentieth century.
> President Kennedy wasn't assassinated in 1987.
> Therefore, President Kennedy didn't die in the twentieth century.

Notice that in each of these examples the premises are true and the conclusion is false. This shows straightaway that the pattern of reasoning of these arguments is not a logically reliable pattern of reasoning.

Another faulty pattern of deductive reasoning is *affirming the consequent.* Its pattern is as follows:

> If A then B.
> B.
> Therefore, A.

Here are two examples:

> If we're on Neptune, then we're in the solar system.
> We're in the solar system.
> Therefore, we're on Neptune.

> If Tom Cruise is a woman, then he is a human being.
> Tom Cruise is a human being.
> Therefore, Tom Cruise is a woman.

Given that these arguments have true premises and false conclusions, it is clear that affirming the consequent is not a logically reliable pattern of reasoning.

Because *modus ponens, modus tollens,* and chain argument are logically reliable patterns of reasoning, they should always be treated as deductive. Denying the antecedent and affirming the consequent are not logically reliable patterns of reasoning. Nevertheless, they should normally be treated as deductive, because they have a pattern of reasoning that is characteristically deductive.

Categorical Syllogism

Another common pattern of deductive reasoning is categorical syllogism. For present purposes, a **categorical syllogism** may be defined as a three-line argument in which each statement begins with the word "all," "some," or "no."[12] Here are three examples:

> All tigers are carnivores.
> All carnivores eat meat.
> Therefore, all tigers eat meat.

> No fish are mammals.
> All sharks are fish.
> Therefore, no sharks are mammals.

> Some Democrats are elected officials.
> All elected officials are politicians.
> Therefore, some Democrats are politicians.

Because categorical reasoning like this is such a familiar form of rigorous logical reasoning, such arguments should nearly always be treated as deductive.

Argument by Elimination

An **argument by elimination** is an argument that seeks to logically rule out various possibilities until only a single possibility remains. Here are two examples:

> Either Joe walked to the library or he drove.
> But Joe didn't drive to the library.
> Therefore, Joe walked to the library.[13]

> Either Dutch committed the murder, or Jack committed the murder, or Celia committed the murder.
> If Dutch or Jack committed the murder, then the weapon was a rope.
> The weapon was not a rope.
> So, neither Dutch nor Jack committed the murder.
> Therefore, Celia committed the murder.

Since the aim of such arguments is to logically exclude every possible outcome except one, such arguments are always deductive.

Argument Based on Mathematics

Mathematics is a model of logical, step-by-step reasoning. Mathematicians don't claim that their conclusions are merely likely or probable. They claim to *demonstrate or prove* their conclusions on the basis of precise mathematical concepts and reasoning. An **argument based on mathematics** is an argument in which the conclusion is claimed to depend largely or entirely on some mathematical calculation or measurement (perhaps in conjunction with one or more nonmathematical premises).[14] Here are three examples:

Eight is greater than four.
Four is greater than two.
Therefore, eight is greater than two.

Norm cannot run faster than ten miles per hour.
Norm is fifteen miles from downtown Denver.
Therefore, Norm cannot run to downtown Denver in less than an hour.

Light travels at a rate of 186,000 miles per second.
The sun is over 93 million miles distant from the earth.
Therefore, it takes over 8 minutes for the sun's light to reach the earth.

Because mathematical arguments are generally models of precise logical reasoning, arguments based on mathematics are usually best treated as deductive. However, arguments based on mathematics can be inductive, as this example shows:

My blind uncle told me that there were eight men, six women, and twelve kids at the party.
By simple addition, therefore, it follows that there were twenty-six people at the party.

Here, the conclusion clearly does *not* follow from the premise, since it is possible for the premise to be true and the conclusion false. (Maybe my blind uncle miscounted, for example.) For that reason, the argument is best treated as inductive.

Argument from Definition

An **argument from definition** is an argument in which the conclusion is presented as being "true by definition"—that is, as following simply by definition from some key word or phrase used in the argument. Here are some examples:

Janelle is a cardiologist. Therefore, Janelle is a doctor.
Bertha is an aunt. It follows that she is a woman.

> God, by definition, is the greatest conceivable being. Nothing can be the great-est conceivable being unless it exists. Therefore, God, by definition, exists.

Since a statement that follows by definition is necessarily true if the relevant definition is true, arguments from definition are always deductive.

Our discussion of common patterns of deductive reasoning can be summarized as follows:

> Arguments by elimination and arguments from definition should always be treated as deductive.

> Logically reliable hypothetical syllogisms, categorical syllogisms, and arguments based on mathematics should always be treated as deductive.

> Logically unreliable hypothetical syllogisms, categorical syllogisms, and arguments based on mathematics should be treated as deductive unless there is clear evidence that they are intended to be inductive.

COMMON PATTERNS OF INDUCTIVE REASONING

In this section we shall look at six characteristic patterns of inductive reasoning:

- Inductive generalization
- Predictive argument
- Argument from authority
- Causal argument
- Statistical argument
- Argument from analogy

Inductive Generalization

A *generalization,* as that term is used in critical thinking, is a statement that attributes some characteristic to *all, most,* or *some* members of a given set. Here are some examples of generalizations:

> All wild grizzly bears in the United States live west of the Mississippi River.
> Many college students work full-time.
> Men are so unromantic!
> Stealing is wrong.
> Twenty-five percent of Americans believe in astrology.

An **inductive generalization** is an argument in which a generalization is claimed to be probably true on the basis of information about some members of a particular class. Here are three examples:

> All dinosaur bones so far discovered have been more than 65 million years old.
> Therefore, probably all dinosaur bones are more than 65 million years old.

Six months ago I met a farmer from Iowa, and he was friendly.

Four months ago I met an insurance salesman from Iowa, and he was friendly.

Two months ago I met a dentist from Iowa, and she was friendly.

I guess most people from Iowa are friendly.

In a random survey of 1,000 registered voters, 398 said they support Senator Porkbarrel.

Therefore, approximately 40 percent of voters do support Senator Porkbarrel.

Life is the art of drawing sufficient conclusions from insufficient premises.

—Samuel Butler

Since all inductive generalizations claim that their conclusions are probable rather than certain, such arguments are always inductive.

Predictive Argument

A *prediction* is a statement about what may or will happen in the future. A **predictive argument** is an argument in which a prediction is defended with reasons. Predictive arguments are among the most common patterns of inductive reasoning. Here are two examples:

It has rained in Vancouver every February since weather records have been kept.

Therefore, it will probably rain in Vancouver next February.

Most U.S. presidents have been tall.

Therefore, probably the next U.S. president will be tall.

Since nothing in the future (including death and taxes) is absolutely certain, arguments containing predictions are usually inductive. It should be noted, however, that predictions can be argued for deductively. For example:

If Pete comes to the party, then Laurel will come to the party.

Pete will come to the party.

Therefore, Laurel will come to the party.

Even though this argument contains a prediction, it is clearly deductive, since the conclusion must be true if the premises are true.

Argument from Authority

An **argument from authority** asserts that a claim is true, and then supports that claim by citing some presumed authority or witness who has said that the claim is true. Here are three examples:

More Americans die of skin cancer each year than die in car accidents. How do I know? My doctor told me.

The *Encyclopaedia Britannica* says that parts of Virginia are farther west than Detroit. In general, the *Encyclopaedia Britannica* is a highly reliable source of information. Therefore, it is probably true that parts of Virginia are farther west than Detroit.

There are bears in these woods. My neighbor Frank said he saw one last week.

Because we can never be absolutely certain that a presumed authority or witness is accurate or reliable, arguments from authority should normally be treated as inductive. However, arguments from authority are sometimes deductive. For example:

Whatever the Bible teaches is true.

The Bible teaches that we should love our neighbors.

Therefore, we should love our neighbors.

Because the conclusion of this argument follows with strict necessity from the premises, the argument should be regarded as deductive.

Causal Argument

A **causal argument** is an argument that asserts or denies that something causes, has caused, or will cause something else. Here are three examples:

Shoot! I left my lights on. I bet the battery is dead.

I can't log-in. The network must be down.

Medical care is the number-one cause of sudden rapid aging among middle-aged people. Ask yourself how many times you have heard somebody tell you a story like this: "Ralph was feeling fine, no problems at all, and then he went in for a routine physical checkup, and the next thing we heard he was in critical condition with the majority of his internal organs sitting in a freezer in an entirely different building."[15]

As we shall see in Chapter 11, we can rarely, if ever, be 100 percent certain that one thing causes, or does not cause, something else. For that reason, causal arguments are usually best treated as inductive.

It cannot be assumed, however, that causal arguments are always inductive. The following causal arguments, for example, are clearly deductive:

If I left my headlights on all weekend, then my battery must be dead.

I did leave my headlights on all weekend.

Therefore, my battery must be dead.

Whenever iron is exposed to oxygen, it rusts.

This iron pipe has been exposed to oxygen.

Therefore, it will rust.

Statistical Argument

A **statistical argument** is an argument that rests on statistical evidence—that is, evidence that some percentage of some group has some particular characteristic. Here are some examples:

> Eighty-three percent of St. Stephen's students are Episcopalian.
> Beatrice is a St. Stephen's student.
> So, Beatrice is probably Episcopalian.

> Nearly all freshmen at North Dakota Tech own their own computers.
> Mark is a freshman at North Dakota Tech.
> Therefore, it is likely that Mark owns his own computer.

> Twenty-seven percent of scholarship athletes in Dr. Abelson's biology class at Wexford College wear baseball hats to class.
> Therefore, approximately 27 percent of scholarship athletes at Wexford College wear baseball hats to class.

Because statistical evidence is generally used to support claims that are presented as probable rather than certain, statistical arguments are usually inductive. It should be noted, however, that statistical evidence can be used in deductive reasoning. For example:

> If 65 percent of likely voters polled support Senator Beltway, then Senator Beltway will win in a landslide.
> Sixty-five percent of likely voters polled do support Senator Beltway.
> Therefore, Senator Beltway will win in a landslide.

Argument from Analogy

An *analogy* is a comparison of two (or more) things that are claimed to be alike in some relevant respect. Here are three examples of analogies:

> The atom is like a miniature solar system.

> The human eye works much like a sophisticated camera.

> Habits are like a cable. We weave a strand of it every day and soon it cannot be broken. (Horace Mann)

An **argument from analogy** is an argument in which the conclusion is claimed to depend on an analogy (i.e., a comparison or a similarity) between two or more things. Here are three examples:

> Hershey Park has a thrilling roller-coaster ride.
> Dorney Park, like Hershey Park, is a great amusement park.
> Therefore, probably Dorney Park also has a thrilling roller-coaster ride.

> Bill is a graduate of Central University, and he is bright, energetic, and dependable.

Mary is a graduate of Central University, and she is bright, energetic, and dependable.

Paula is a graduate of Central University.

Therefore, Paula is probably bright, energetic, and dependable, too.

On Monday, I ate at the Sizzling Tenderloin Restaurant in Cleveland, and the food was good.

On Tuesday, I ate at the Sizzling Tenderloin Restaurant in Detroit, and the food was good.

On Wednesday, I ate at the Sizzling Tenderloin Restaurant in Chicago, and the food was good.

Therefore, if I eat at the Sizzling Tenderloin Restaurant in Milwaukee today, the food will probably also be good.

Note the basic logical pattern of these arguments:

These things are similar in such-and-such ways.

Therefore, they're probably similar in some further way.

Since the conclusions of arguments of this pattern are claimed to follow only probably from the premises, such arguments are clearly inductive.

However, not all analogical arguments are inductive. For example:

1. Automobiles cause thousands of deaths each year and produce noxious and offensive fumes.
2. Smoking causes thousands of deaths each year and produces noxious and offensive fumes.
3. Thus, if smoking is heavily regulated, automobiles should also be heavily regulated.
4. But automobiles shouldn't be heavily regulated.
5. Therefore, smoking shouldn't be heavily regulated either.

This is an analogical argument because the main conclusion, statement 5, is claimed to depend on an analogy between automobiles and smoking. Nevertheless, the argument is deductive because it would be logically inconsistent to assert all the premises and deny the conclusion.

Our discussion of common patterns of inductive reasoning can be summarized as follows:

Inductive generalizations, by definition, are always inductive.

Predictive arguments, arguments from authority, causal arguments, statistical arguments, and arguments from analogy are generally, but not always, inductive.

It takes practice to be able to recognize the various common patterns of deductive and inductive reasoning we have discussed. However, it is important to be able to do so, because such patterns often provide the best clue available to whether an argument is deductive or inductive.

EXERCISE 3.2

I. Determine whether the following arguments are best regarded as deductive or inductive. For each argument, state which test(s) you used in reaching your decision (i.e., the indicator word test, the strict necessity test, the common pattern test, and/or the principle of charity test). If you used the common pattern test, indicate which specific pattern the argument exemplifies (causal argument, argument from authority, etc.).

1. If $x = 3$ and $y = 5$, then $x + y = 8$.

2. According to the *New York Public Library Desk Reference,* the pop-up toaster was invented by Charles Strite in 1927. The *New York Library Desk Reference* is a highly reliable reference work. Therefore, it is reasonable to believe that Charles Strite did invent the pop-up toaster in 1927.

3. Seventy-three percent of Ft. Gibson residents enjoy fishing. Lonnie is a Ft. Gibson resident. So, Lonnie probably enjoys fishing.

4. Either Elmo will win the election or Schlomo will win the election. But Elmo won't win the election. Therefore, Schlomo will win the election.

5. The burglar was tall and thin. Duncan is short and fat. Obviously, therefore, Duncan isn't the burglar.

6. There are no visible signs of forced entry. It seems certain, therefore, that the burglar had a key.

7. The sign says it is eleven miles to Lake Lily. Therefore, it is approximately eleven miles to Lake Lily.

8. Joan is an extravert. It follows that she is outgoing.

9. All inductive generalizations are inductive. Some inductive generalizations are unreliable. Therefore, some inductive arguments are unreliable.

10. If it rains, the game will be postponed until next Saturday. According to the National Weather Service, there is a 90 percent chance of rain. Therefore, probably the game will be postponed until next Saturday.

11. If the batter bunts in this situation, then he'll move the runner over to second base. But the batter won't bunt in this situation. Therefore, the runner will never be moved over to second base.

12. Hughie is the father of Louie. It follows that Hughie is the grandfather of Dewey, since Louie is the father of Dewey.

13. Mandatory school uniforms are a good idea, because they keep students' minds focused on their schoolwork rather than on what the kid sitting next to them is wearing.

14. Klaus ingested a large dose of rat poison just before he died. Therefore, the rat poison must have caused Klaus's death.

15. All previously observed polar bears have weighed less than 1,500 pounds. Therefore, all polar bears probably weigh less than 1,500 pounds.

16. Kevin said he can lift 1,000 pounds over his head. A full-grown cow weighs less than 1,000 pounds. Therefore, Kevin can lift a full-grown cow over his head.

17. If my car is out of gas, then it won't start. My car won't start. Therefore, it is out of gas.

18. Yale is an Ivy League school, and it has a good library. Harvard is an Ivy League school, and it has a good library. Therefore, since Brown is an Ivy League school, it must have a good library, too.

19. I wouldn't swim in that water if I were you. It might be polluted.

20. This tree is deciduous. It must be the case, therefore, that it periodically sheds its leaves.

21. Whatever the church teaches as infallible doctrine is true. The church teaches as infallible doctrine that God is eternal. Therefore, God is eternal.

22. Every argument is either deductive or inductive. Since this argument isn't deductive, it must be inductive.

23. Five alleged eyewitnesses have testified that they saw Frank Lane stab Melissa Jenkins. So, Frank Lane did stab Melissa Jenkins.

24. Tiger Woods is one of the best golfers in the world. Melvin Rumsley has never played golf in his life. It is certain, therefore, that Melvin Rumsley could never beat Tiger Woods in a round of golf.

25. If Steve is 48 years old and Pam is exactly 19 years younger than Steve, it necessarily follows that Pam is 29 years old.

26. Some college students love pizza. Some college students love ice cream. It stands to reason, therefore, that some college students who love pizza are college students who love ice cream.

27. Wexford College won the NCAA Division III national championship in football last year, and eighteen of their twenty-two starting players are returning this year. It's a good bet, therefore, that they will win the national championship again this year.

28. Dogs are put to sleep when they become too old or too sick to enjoy life further. Similarly, human beings should be mercifully put to death when they become too old or too sick to enjoy life further.

29. In a random survey of 100 students at Eastern State University, 63 said they believe in angels. Therefore, approximately 63 percent of students at Eastern State University do believe in angels.

30. The sun has risen every morning from time immemorial. Therefore, you can bet your bottom dollar that the sun will rise tomorrow.

31. Where life is possible, then it is possible to live the right life; life is possible in a palace; so it is possible to live the right life in a palace. (Marcus Aurelius, *Meditations,* c. A.D. 180)

32. Boxing is the toughest sport. It teaches self-defense and attacking skills. The risk of head injury is prevalent. And you have to deal with Don King. (Mark Fitzhenry, "And the Toughest Sport Is . . . ," *Wilkes-Barre Times Leader,* June 17, 1999)

33. I am not a sports-minded person, but I object to the hunters being called sportsmen. There is no sport in hunting. Sport is where the other person or the opponent has a chance. There is no way these hunters can be hurt in the woods unless they shoot themselves, which I hope all of them do. But the deer, the birds, the rabbits, everybody else out there are just targets. (From a newspaper call-in column, *Wilkes-Barre Times Leader,* September 17, 2000)

34. Studies indicate that high school graduates are more tolerant of political and social nonconformity than those who did not complete high school. College graduates are more tolerant than high school graduates. Thus, education has a positive effect on such values as egalitarianism, democratic principles, and tolerance of minority and opposition views. (John A. Perry and Erna K. Perry, *Contemporary Society: An Introduction to Social Science,* 6th ed., 1991)

35. Get a job that lets you "analyze" or "evaluate" something as opposed to actually "doing" something. When you evaluate something you get to criticize the work of others. If you do something, other people get to criticize *you.* (Scott Adams, *The Dilbert Principle,* 1996)

DEDUCTIVE VALIDITY

In this section we shall introduce the most important concept in deductive logic: the concept of deductive validity.

We have seen that all deductive arguments *claim,* implicitly or explicitly, that their conclusions follow necessarily from their premises. A logically reliable deductive argument is an argument in which the conclusion *really does* follow necessarily from the premises. In logic, a logically reliable deductive argument is called a *valid* deductive argument.

More formally, a **valid deductive argument** is an argument in which it is impossible for all the premises to be true and the conclusion false. Put another way, a valid deductive argument (or valid argument for short) is an argument in which these conditions apply:

If the premises are true, then the conclusion *must* be true.

The conclusion follows *necessarily* from the premises.

The premises provide logically *conclusive* grounds for the truth of the conclusion.

The truth of the premises *guarantees* the truth of the conclusion.

It is logically *inconsistent* to assert all the premises as true and deny the conclusion.

In everyday language, "valid" often means "good" or "true." We say, for instance, that a person makes a "valid point" or offers a "valid suggestion." In logic, however, "valid" *never* means simply "good" or "true." It is always used in the precise technical sense indicated above.

EXERCISE 3.3

Difficult as it is to explain the notion of deductive validity, we have found that most students already have a good intuitive grasp of the concept. Working individually, see if you can determine what statement follows validly from the statements provided. When you are finished, discuss your answers with a partner.

1. If alpha, then beta.
   Alpha.
   Therefore, _____.

2. Either alpha or beta.
   Not beta.
   Therefore, _____.

3. All alphas are betas.
   Delta is an alpha.
   Therefore, _____.

4. If Delta is an alpha, then Delta is a beta.
   Delta is not a beta.
   Therefore, _____.

5. No alphas are betas.
   Delta is an alpha.
   Therefore, _____.

6. All alphas are betas.
   Delta is not a beta.
   Therefore, _____.

7. If Delta is an alpha, then Delta is a beta.
   If Delta is a beta, then Delta is a theta.
   Therefore, _____.

8. If Delta is an alpha, then Delta is a beta.
   If Delta is a theta, then Delta is a beta.
   Either Delta is an alpha or Delta is a theta.
   Therefore, _____.

9. Either Delta is an alpha or Delta is a beta.
   If Delta is an alpha, then Delta is a theta.
   If Delta is a beta, then Delta is a sigma.
   Therefore, _____.

10. Some alphas are betas.
    All betas are thetas.
    Therefore, _____.

As the preceding exercise makes clear, it is not necessary to know whether an argument's premises or conclusion are true to know whether the argument is valid. In fact, some valid arguments have obviously *false premises* and a *false conclusion*. For example:

All squares are circles.
All circles are triangles.
Therefore, all squares are triangles.

Some valid arguments have *false premises* and a *true conclusion*. For example:

All fruits are vegetables.
Spinach is a fruit.
Therefore, spinach is a vegetable.

Some valid arguments have *true premises* and a *true conclusion*. For example:

If you are reading this, then you are alive.
You are reading this.
Therefore, you are alive.

However, there is one combination of truth or falsity that no valid argument can have. No valid argument can have *all true premises* and *a false conclusion*. This important truth follows from the very definition of a valid argument. Since a valid argument, by definition, is an argument in which the conclusion *must* be true if the premises are true, no valid argument can have all true premises and a false conclusion.

A deductive argument in which the conclusion does *not* follow necessarily from the premises is said to be an **invalid deductive argument.** Here are four examples:

All dogs are animals.
Lassie is an animal.
Therefore, Lassie is a dog.

If I'm a monkey's uncle, then I'm a mammal.
I'm not a monkey's uncle.
So, I'm not a mammal.

All pears are vegetables.
All fruits are vegetables.
Therefore, all pears are fruits.

All dogs are cats.
All cats are whales.
Therefore, all whales are dogs.

Each of these arguments is invalid. The first argument has true premises and a true conclusion. The second argument has true premises and a false conclusion. The third argument has false premises and a true conclusion. The fourth argument has false premises and a false conclusion.

To recap: An invalid argument can have any combination of truth or falsity in the premises and conclusion. A valid argument can have any combination except one: no valid argument can have true premises and a false conclusion.

Since an argument's conclusion either does or does not follow necessarily from its premises, it follows that all deductive arguments are either valid or invalid. For the same reason, all deductive arguments are either 100 percent valid or 100 percent invalid. Either a deductive argument provides logically conclusive grounds for its conclusion or it does not. If it does, then the argument is valid. If it does not, then the argument is invalid. Thus, no deductive argument can be "sort of valid" or "mostly valid." Deductive validity, by definition, doesn't come in degrees.

The most common mistake students make when they are first introduced to the concept of deductive validity is to think that "valid" means "true." Remember: *"Valid" does not mean "true."* "Valid" means that the argument is well reasoned, that the *pattern* of reasoning is a logically reliable pattern of reasoning, that the conclusion follows necessarily from the premises. Thus, the basic test of deductive validity is not whether the premises are actually true. Instead, the basic question is this: *If the argument's premises were true, would the conclusion also have to be true?* If the answer is yes, then the argument is valid. If the answer is no, then the argument is invalid.

Now let's apply this basic test of validity to a few examples. Here's one:

The Eiffel Tower is in Paris.

Paris is in France.

Therefore, the Eiffel Tower is in France.

If the premises of this argument were true (as they are, of course), would the conclusion also have to be true? Yes; it would be contradictory to assert that the Eiffel Tower is in Paris and that Paris is in France and yet deny that the Eiffel Tower is in France. Thus, the argument is deductively valid.

Here is a second example:

All pigs are sheep.

All sheep are goats.

Therefore, all pigs are goats.

Here both the premises and the conclusion are false. Does this mean that the argument is invalid? No, because if the premises were true, then the conclusion would also have to be true. Thus, the argument is valid.

Here is a third example:

Some people like spinach.

Some people like anchovies.

Therefore, some people who like spinach also like anchovies.

Here the premises and the conclusion are all true. Does the conclusion follow with strict necessity from the premises? No; it is logically possible that the class of people who like spinach doesn't overlap at all with the class of people who like anchovies. Thus, there is no contradiction involved in asserting the premises and denying the conclusion. Hence, the argument is invalid.

Consider a final example:

No dogs are cats.

Some dogs are not housebroken.

Therefore, some things that are housebroken are not cats.

> Valid deductive arguments are like steel traps. Once a person walks into the trap by accepting the premises, there is no escape; the conclusion follows necessarily.
>
> —Kathleen Dean Moore

Critical Thinking Lapse

A small-town emergency squad was summoned to a house where smoke was pouring from an upstairs window. The crew broke in and found a man in a smoldering bed. After the man was rescued and the mattress doused, the obvious question was asked: "How did this happen?"

"I don't know," the man replied. "It was on fire when I lay down on it." [16]

Is this argument valid? Does the conclusion follow necessarily from the premises? In this case, the logic of the argument is complex, so it is not easy to say. In fact, the argument is *invalid,* but most of us have trouble seeing that using just our seat-of-the-pants logical intuitions. Fortunately, there are several ways of testing whether arguments are valid or invalid. We shall discuss some of these methods later in this chapter.

Why is the concept of validity the most important concept in deductive logic? Because validity is the basis of all exact, rigorous reasoning directed at the discovery of truth. Much as a leakproof pipe perfectly preserves whatever fluids flow through it, so a valid argument perfectly preserves whatever truth is contained in the argument's premises. In short, validity is important because *validity preserves truth.* Only by reasoning validly can we reason rigorously from truth to truth.

Important as the concept of validity is, however, we should not presume that every valid argument is a *good* argument. Consider the following:

All heavenly bodies are made of green cheese.
The moon is a heavenly body.
Therefore, the moon is made of green cheese.

This is a valid argument. It is also clearly a very *bad* argument. What examples like this show is that we don't merely want our deductive arguments to be valid; we also want them to have *true premises.* Deductive arguments that combine these desirable features—that is, deductive arguments that both are *valid* and have *all true premises*—are called **sound deductive arguments.** Deductive arguments that either are invalid or have at least one false premise, or both, are called **unsound deductive arguments.**

INDUCTIVE STRENGTH

Inductive arguments, like deductive arguments, can be well reasoned or poorly reasoned. A well-reasoned inductive argument is called a *strong* inductive argument. More precisely, a **strong inductive argument** is an inductive argument in which the conclusion follows probably from the premises. Put otherwise, a strong inductive argument is an argument in which the following conditions apply:

> If the premises are true, then the conclusion is probably true.
>
> The premises provide probable, but not logically conclusive, grounds for the truth of the conclusion.
>
> The premises, if true, make the conclusion likely.

Here are several examples of strong inductive arguments:

> Most college students own CD players.
> Andy is a college student.
> So, Andy probably owns a CD player.

> Sixty-five percent of Kingston residents don't smoke.
> Joel is a Kingston resident.
> So, Joel probably doesn't smoke.

> All recent U.S. presidents have been college graduates.
> Therefore, it is reasonable to think that the next U.S. president will be a college graduate.

An inductive argument that is not strong is said to be *weak*. A **weak inductive argument** is an inductive argument in which the conclusion does *not* follow probably from the premises. In other words, an inductively weak argument is an inductive argument in which the premises, even if they are assumed to be true, do not make the conclusion probable. Here are some examples:

> Fifty-five percent of students at East Laredo State University are Hispanic.
> Li Fang Wang, owner of Wang's Chinese Restaurant, is a student at East Laredo State University.
> Therefore, Li Fang Wang is probably Hispanic.

> All previous Speakers of the House have been men.
> Therefore, it is reasonable to assume that the next Speaker of the House will be a woman.

> After sniffing glue, Andrea said she saw a polka-dotted elephant in Feeny's Bar.
> Andrea is normally a pretty reliable and level-headed person.
> Therefore, it is likely that Andrea did see a polka-dotted elephant in Feeny's Bar.

Because the conclusions of these arguments are not probably true even if we assume that the premises are true, the arguments are inductively weak.

Like deductively valid arguments, inductively strong arguments can have various combinations of truth or falsity in the premises and conclusion. Some inductively strong arguments have *false premises* and a *probably false conclusion*. For example:

> All previous U.S. vice presidents have been women.
> Therefore, it is likely that the next U.S. vice president will be a woman.

Some inductively strong arguments have *false premises* and a *probably true conclusion*. For example:

> Every previous U.S. president has been either a Republican or a Democrat.
> Therefore, it is likely that the next U.S. president will be a Republican or a Democrat.

And some inductively strong arguments have *true premises* and a *probably true conclusion*. For example:

> Every previous U.S. president has been over forty years old.
> Therefore, probably the next U.S. president will be over forty years old.

As with valid deductive arguments, however, there is one combination of truth or falsity no strong inductive argument can ever have. Since, by definition, a strong inductive argument is an argument in which the conclusion follows probably from the premises, *no strong inductive argument can have true premises and a probably false conclusion.*

Weak inductive arguments, on the other hand, like invalid deductive arguments, can have any combination of truth or falsity in the premises and conclusion. Here are some examples:

> Most U.S. presidents have been married.
> Therefore, probably the next U.S. president will be a man.

> Most U.S. presidents have been over fifty years old.
> Therefore, probably the next U.S. president will be single.

> Most U.S. presidents have been women.
> Therefore, probably the next U.S. president will be married.

> Most U.S. presidents have been less than five feet tall.
> Therefore, probably the next U.S. president will be single.

Each of these inductive arguments is weak. That is, each has a conclusion that does not follow probably from the premise, even if we assume that the premise is true. The first argument has a true premise and a probably true conclusion. The second argument has a true premise and a probably false conclusion. The third argument has a false premise and a probably true conclusion. The fourth argument has a false premise and a probably false conclusion.

As these examples make clear, whether an inductive argument is strong or weak generally does not depend on the actual truth or falsity of the premises and the conclusion. Rather, it depends on whether the conclusion *would be* probably true if the premises *were* true. Thus, the basic test of inductive strength asks: *If the argument's premises were all true, would the conclusion be probably true?* If the answer is yes, then the argument is inductively strong. If the answer is no, then the argument is inductively weak.

The concept of inductive strength is similar in many ways to the concept of deductive validity. However, there are two important differences. First, inductive strength, unlike deductive validity, does come in degrees. Deductive arguments, as we have seen, are either 100 percent valid or 100 percent invalid. Inductive arguments, by contrast, can be more or less inductively strong or weak. Consider the following examples:

> According to the National Weather Service, there is a 60 percent chance of rain today.
> Therefore, probably it will rain today.

> According to the National Weather Service, there is a 90 percent chance of rain today.
> Therefore, probably it will rain today.

> According to the National Weather Service, there is a 40 percent chance of rain today.
> Therefore, probably it will rain today.

> According to the National Weather Service, there is a 10 percent chance of rain today.
> Therefore, probably it will rain today.

The first and second arguments are both strong inductive arguments, since the conclusions are probably true if the premises are true. However, the second argument is a stronger argument than the first, since its premise provides greater support for its conclusion than the premise of the first argument provides for its conclusion. Similarly, the third and fourth arguments are both weak inductive arguments, since the conclusions do not follow probably from the premises. However, the fourth argument is a weaker argument than the third, since its premise provides less support for its conclusion than the premise of the third argument provides for its conclusion.

Thus, whereas no deductive argument can be more or less valid, an inductive argument can be more or less strong or weak.

A second important difference between the notions of deductive validity and inductive strength is that whereas deductively valid arguments remain 100 percent valid no matter what new premises are added, inductively strong arguments can be strengthened or weakened by the addition of new premises. Consider the following example:

> Eighty percent of students at Wexford College graduate in four years.
> Quentin is a student at Wexford College.
> Therefore, Quentin will probably graduate in four years.

This is a relatively strong inductive argument. However, we can make it stronger by adding a premise (indicated by brackets):

> Eighty percent of students at Wexford College graduate in four years.
> Quentin is a student at Wexford College.
> [Quentin is an excellent and highly motivated student.]
> Therefore, Quentin will probably graduate in four years.

Or we can make it weaker by adding a premise:

> Eighty percent of students at Wexford College graduate in four years.
> Quentin is a student at Wexford College.
> [Quentin is the biggest party animal on campus.]
> Therefore, Quentin will probably graduate in four years.

Deductively valid arguments, by contrast, remain valid no matter what premises are added.

An inductive argument may be inductively strong and still be a very poor argument. For example:

> All previous U.S. presidents have worn togas.
> Therefore, probably the next U.S. president will wear a toga.

Although this argument is inductively strong, it is a poor argument because the premise is obviously false. A good inductive argument must both be strong (i.e., inductively well reasoned) and have all true premises. If an argument both is inductively strong and has all true premises, it is said to be a **cogent argument.** If an argument either is inductively weak or has at least one false premise, it is said to be an **uncogent argument.** Consider these examples:

> All previous U.S. presidents have been men.
> Therefore, probably the next U.S. president will be a man.

> All previous U.S. presidents have been Democrats.
> Therefore, probably the next U.S. president will be a Democrat.

> All previous U.S. presidents have been clean-shaven.
> Therefore, probably the next U.S. president will wear a beard.

The first argument is cogent because it meets both conditions of a cogent argument: its premise is true and the argument is inductively strong. The second argument is uncogent because it fails one of the conditions of a cogent argument: its premise is false. The third argument is uncogent because it fails both conditions of a cogent argument: its premise is false and the argument is inductively weak.

Summary of Key Definitions

Argument: A set of statements in which a claim (called the *conclusion*) is put forward and defended with reasons (called the *premises*).

Deductive argument: An argument in which the conclusion is claimed or intended to follow necessarily from the premises.

Inductive argument: An argument in which the conclusion is claimed or intended to follow probably from the premises.

Valid argument: A deductive argument in which the conclusion follows necessarily from the premises—that is, a deductive argument in which it is impossible for the premises to be true and the conclusion false.

Invalid argument: A deductive argument in which the conclusion does not follow necessarily from the premises—that is, a deductive argument in which it is possible for the premises to be true and the conclusion false.

Sound argument: A deductive argument that both is valid and has all true premises.

Unsound argument: A deductive argument that either is invalid or has at least one false premise, or both.

Strong argument: An inductive argument in which the conclusion follows probably from the premises—that is, an inductive argument in which it is unlikely that its conclusion is false if its premises are true.

Weak argument: An inductive argument in which the conclusion does not follow probably from the premises—that is, an inductive argument in which it is not likely that if its premises are true, its conclusion is true.

Cogent argument: An inductive argument that both is strong and has all true premises.

Uncogent argument: An inductive argument that either is weak or has at least one false premise, or both.

In light of the preceding definitions, arguments may be diagrammed as follows:

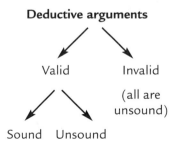

Deductive arguments

Valid   Invalid
                (all are
                unsound)

Sound   Unsound

Inductive arguments

Strong   Weak
                (all are
                uncogent)

Cogent   Uncogent

EXERCISE 3.4

I. The following arguments are deductive. Determine whether the arguments are valid or invalid. Explain your answer in each case.

1. If Flipper is a dolphin, then Flipper is a mammal. Flipper is a dolphin. So, Flipper is a mammal.

2. If anything is a trout, then it is a fish. A dolphin is not a fish. Therefore, a dolphin is not a trout.

3. If we're at the North Pole, then we're on Earth. We are on Earth. Therefore, we're at the North Pole.

4. If Bigfoot is human, then Bigfoot has a heart. Bigfoot is not human. So, Bigfoot doesn't have a heart.

5. Some people like ice cream. Some people like cake. So, some people who like ice cream must also like cake.

6. *Science student:* Science is often defined as the organized arrangement of facts. But that cannot be the correct definition, since a phone book is an organized arrangement of facts, and a phone book is not science.

7. *Frank:* I'm going to bring my cell phone with me when I take the logic test tomorrow. Whenever I don't know the answer, I'll just call my roommate, Ted. He aced logic last semester.
Maria: Are you crazy? Professor Hardy will never allow you to cheat like that.
Frank: Sure he will. I distinctly heard him say, "No notes or books are allowed during the test," and phone calls, my friend, qualify as neither. It's simple logic: "No notes or books may be used during the test; phone calls aren't notes or books; so, they are allowed."
Maria: Clearly, you're going to need all the help you can get.

8. *Maggie:* I heard Marge pledged a sorority. I wonder which one.
Lisa: Well, let's deduce from some simple premises: Every one of the girls in Sigma Snooty Snu is a snob, and Marge is one of the snobbiest girls I know. So, Marge definitely pledged Sigma Snu.

9. *Brad:* I thought that freshmen weren't eligible for the Campus Events Committee, but I guess I was wrong. The entire committee registered early for next year's classes, and some freshmen registered early, so it just stands to reason that the committee has some freshmen on it.

10. *Bill:* I guess some of the seniors were late to practice this morning.
Diane: How do you know?
Bill: Because the coach said that anyone late to practice this morning would have to do wind sprints, and I just saw some of the seniors doing wind sprints. That'll teach them.

II. The following arguments are deductive. Determine whether the arguments are sound or unsound. Explain your answer in each case.

1. All mosquitoes are insects. All insects are animals. So, all mosquitoes are animals.

2. Either dogs are cats, or dogs are fish. Dogs are not fish. So, dogs are cats.

3. If Rome is in Italy, then Rome is in Europe. Rome is in Italy. So, Rome is in Europe.

4. If Bill Gates is a billionaire, then he's rich. Bill Gates is rich. So, he's a billionaire.

5. No Democrats are women. Hillary Rodham Clinton is a Democrat. So, Hillary Rodham Clinton isn't a woman.

6. California has a larger population than Ohio. Ohio has a larger population than Vermont. So, California has a larger population than Vermont.

7. If the pope is a Southern Baptist, then he's Protestant. The pope is not a Southern Baptist. So, the pope is not Protestant.

8. Some apples are red. Some apples are delicious. So, some apples are red and delicious.

9. Los Angeles is west of Chicago. Hence, Atlanta is east of Chicago, since Atlanta is east of Los Angeles.

10. Halloween is always on a Friday. Therefore, the day after Halloween is always a Saturday.

III. The following arguments are inductive. Determine whether the arguments are cogent or uncogent. Explain your answer in each case.

1. It tends to be cold in Minneapolis in January. So, probably it will be cold in Minneapolis next January.

2. Cigarette smoking causes lung cancer. Therefore, if you have been a heavy cigarette smoker for many years, you will probably die of lung cancer.

3. The vast majority of popes have been Americans. Therefore, the next pope will probably be an American.

4. Detroit is a large, ethnically diverse North American city, and it has a serious problem with gun violence. Miami is a large, ethnically diverse North American city, and it has a serious problem with gun violence. Houston is a large, ethnically diverse North American city, and it has a serious problem with gun violence. Montreal is a large, ethnically diverse North American city. Therefore, probably Montreal also has a serious problem with gun violence.

5. Billions of men around the world shave daily. Therefore, somewhere in the world, someone must be shaving right now.

6. Shakespeare was English, and he was a great poet. Milton was English, and he was a great poet. Wordsworth was English, and he was a great poet. I guess most great poets were English.

7. Harvard University has been a leading American university for many years. Therefore, probably Harvard University will be a leading American university ten years from now.

8. Ninety percent of Americans jog daily. Al Gore is an American. So, Al Gore probably jogs daily.

9. Very few people in this country are named Obadiah. Therefore, the next person I meet is unlikely to be named Obadiah.

10. John F. Kennedy was a Democratic president, and he cheated on his wife. Bill Clinton was a Democratic president, and he cheated on his wife. I suppose all Democratic presidents have cheated on their wives.

IV. Determine whether the following arguments are deductive or inductive. If an argument is deductive, determine whether it is valid or invalid. If an argument is inductive, determine whether it is strong or weak. Explain your answer in each case.

⬡ 1. If Boston loses, then Cleveland will make the play-offs. If Cleveland makes the play-offs, then the first play-off game will be played in Seattle. Therefore, if Boston loses, then the first play-off game will be played in Seattle.

2. All birds can fly. Penguins are birds. So, penguins can fly.

3. Most college students sleep late on Sunday mornings. Wes is a college student. So, Wes probably sleeps late on Sunday mornings.

⬡ 4. Exercise is good for the vast majority of people. Therefore, it would be good for my ninety-five-year-old grandfather to run in next year's Boston Marathon.

5. John's home address is 47 Riverside Drive. It follows that he must live near a river.

6. It is totally dark in here, but I know the only things in the drawer are socks, ten black, ten white. I had better take out eleven socks to be sure I get a matched pair.[17]

⬡ 7. According to the *Cambridge Dictionary of Philosophy,* philosopher William James was born in New York City in 1842. So, William James was born in New York City in 1842.

8. If it rained, then the streets are wet. The streets are wet. So, it rained.

9. This bath water is tepid. It follows that it is neither extremely hot nor extremely cold.

⬡ 10. States were justified in suing tobacco companies to recover the health-care costs associated with smoking. Similarly, states would be justified in suing McDonald's and Burger King to recover the health-care costs associated with eating fatty foods.

11. There are more than fifty students in this class. It must be the case, therefore, that at least one of them is a Capricorn.

12. In a recent Gallup poll, 72 percent of Americans said they favored the death penalty. Therefore, approximately 72 percent of Americans do favor the death penalty.

⬡ 13. On Monday I drank ten rum and Cokes, and the next morning I woke up with a headache. On Wednesday I drank eight gin and Cokes, and the next morning I woke up with a headache. On Friday I drank nine bourbon and Cokes, and the next morning I woke up with a headache. Obviously, to prevent further headaches I must give up Coke.[18]

14. If we're in Cleveland, we're in Ohio. Hence, we're not in Cleveland, since we're not in Ohio.

15. Some Native Americans are Democrats. Some Democrats are Supreme Court justices. So, some Supreme Court justices must be Native Americans.

⬡ 16. All but two U.S. presidents (Clinton and George W. Bush) were born before 1925. It stands to reason, therefore, that the next U.S. president will have been born before 1925.

17. The Empire State Building is taller than the Sears Tower. Therefore, since the World Trade Center is shorter than the Empire State Building, it follows that the Sears Tower is taller than the World Trade Center.

18. Do most Americans like rap music? Apparently not. In a random survey of 10,000 nursing home patients around the country, fewer than 5 percent said they enjoyed listening to rap.

Critical Thinking Lapse

Dwayne Carver was a maintenance man at the Cedar Wood Apartments in Virginia Beach, Virginia. He had a good job, his own tools, and a blue uniform that read "Cedar Wood" on the back and "Dwayne" on the front.

Now, if you were going to rob a 7-Eleven store, as Dwayne did, you would probably wear a ski mask, as Dwayne did. But you probably wouldn't wear your work uniform . . . yes, as Dwayne did.

When he approached the clerk, his face was completely covered. He even made his voice sound deeper as he ordered, "Give me all the money." The clerk stared at Dwayne and his name tag and handed over several hundred dollars. Dwayne fled to a carefully concealed rental car that he had rented just for the day so that he couldn't be traced.

The police arrived shortly, and the clerk was asked to give a description of the robber. "All I can tell you is that he was wearing a ski mask and a blue maintenance uniform with 'Cedar Wood' on the back and 'Dwayne' on the front."

The two officers looked at each other. Surely not . . . no, this was too easy. Maybe the thief stole the uniform or purchased it at Goodwill. . . .

But it was Dwayne, all right. When the officers appeared at his apartment, he hadn't even changed clothes. The gun, the ski mask, and the money were all found in his pockets.[19]

19. Carl Sagan, the famous astronomer, has said that the heavy elements like iron and zinc that compose human bodies were created billions of years ago in the interiors of long-extinct stars. Moreover, virtually all astronomers agree with Sagan on this point. Therefore, it is probably true that the heavy elements like iron and zinc that compose human bodies were created billions of years ago in the interiors of long-extinct stars.

20. Jerry was born on Easter Sunday. It necessarily follows, therefore, that his birthday always falls on a Sunday.

21. Whatever Rush Limbaugh says is true. Rush Limbaugh has said that there are more trees in America now than when Columbus discovered America in 1492. Therefore, it is true that there are more trees in America now than when Columbus discovered America in 1492.

22. Wally weighs 200 pounds. Hence, Joyce weighs 150 pounds, since she weighs exactly 25 percent less than Wally does.

23. Fifty-five percent of Americans favor Social Security reform. Wilma is a seventy-five-year-old American. Hence, Wilma probably favors Social Security reform.

24. If the moon is made of green cheese, then pigs can fly. Pigs can fly. So, the moon is made of green cheese.

25. If Sturdley fails all his classes, then he won't graduate. Hence, Sturdley will graduate, since he won't fail all his classes.

TESTING FOR VALIDITY

Deciding whether an argument is valid or not can sometimes be a tricky business. In this section we present an informal three-part test that can be used to test arguments for validity.[20] We call it the *Three C's Test*.

The Three C's Test for Validity

Step 1: *Check* to see whether the premises are actually true and the conclusion is actually false. If they are, then the argument is invalid. If they are not, or if you can't determine whether the premises and the conclusion are actually true or false, then go on to step 2.

Step 2: See if you can *conceive* a possible scenario in which the premises would be true and the conclusion false. If you can, then the argument is invalid. If you can't, and it is not obvious that the conclusion follows validly from the premises, then go on to step 3.

Step 3: Try to construct a *counterexample*—a special kind of parallel argument—that proves that the argument is invalid. If you can construct such a counterexample, then the argument is invalid. If you can't, then it is usually safe to conclude that the argument is valid.

Let's look at each of these steps in turn.

Step 1   A valid argument is an argument in which it is impossible for the conclusion to be false if the premises are true. Thus, the simplest test for validity is to check to see whether the premises are actually true and the conclusion is actually false. If they are, then the argument is invalid. For example:

> If Michael Jordan was the world's greatest baseball player, then he was a great athlete.
>
> Michael Jordan was a great athlete.
>
> Therefore, Michael Jordan was the world's greatest baseball player.

Here the two premises are, in fact, true and the conclusion is, in fact, false. Thus, we know immediately that the argument is invalid.

Unfortunately, since invalid arguments can have any combination of truth or falsity and valid arguments can have any combination except true premises and a false conclusion, step 1 tells us nothing about the validity or invalidity of arguments that do not have the particular combination of true premises and a false conclusion. For such arguments, we must turn to step 2.

Step 2   Step 2 involves a kind of thought experiment. Since a valid argument is an argument in which it is impossible for the conclusion to be false if the premises are true, we can show that an argument is invalid if we can imagine any logically possible circumstances in which the premises are all true and the conclusion is false. Consider this example:

> Professor Butterfingers was working on a hydrogen bomb when it accidentally exploded in his face.
>
> Therefore, Professor Butterfingers is dead.

All our dignity lies in thought. Let us strive, then, to think well.

—Blaise Pascal

Can we imagine any situation, however unlikely or improbable, in which the premise of this argument is true and the conclusion is false? Sure. Perhaps Professor Butterfingers is actually an indestructible robot in disguise. Or maybe some orbiting extraterrestrials decide to beam him up to their spacecraft just as the bomb explodes. Many things could conceivably happen that would cause the premise to be true and the conclusion false. Thus, the conclusion does not follow logically from the premise. Hence, the argument is not deductively valid.

Here is a second example:

Millions of Americans are Democrats.

Millions of Americans are blondes.

Therefore, at least some American Democrats must be blondes.

Here again, it is not difficult to imagine circumstances in which the premises are true and the conclusion is false. (Imagine a world, for instance, in which, for some strange reason, it is illegal for blondes to be Democrats.) The mere fact that we can imagine such a world shows that the conclusion does not follow necessarily from the premises.

Unfortunately, thought experiments of this kind work only when one can clearly imagine a set of circumstances in which the premises are all true and the conclusion is false. Sometimes, however, we encounter arguments (e.g., logically complex arguments) for which it is difficult to do that. For arguments of this sort, we must turn to step 3.

Step 3   Step 3 also involves a kind of thought experiment, but one that is slightly more elaborate than the kind of thought experiment described in step 2. In step 2 we ask: Is there any conceivable way that *this particular argument* could have all true premises and a false conclusion? In step 3 we ask: Is there any conceivable way that *any argument with this particular logical pattern* could have all true premises and a false conclusion? If the answer to either question is yes, then the argument is invalid.

Step 3 involves use of a procedure known as the *counterexample method of proving invalidity*. This method requires some ingenuity but is basically very simple once you get the hang of it.

Counterexample Method of Proving Invalidity

Step 1: Determine the logical pattern, or *form,* of the argument that you are testing for invalidity, using letters (A, B, C, etc.) to represent the various terms in the argument.

Step 2: Construct a *second argument* that has exactly the same form as the argument you are testing but that has premises that are obviously true and a conclusion that is obviously false.

The method works because a valid argument never has true premises and a false conclusion. Thus, any time you find an argument that has true premises and a false conclusion, you know immediately that it is invalid. Because validity is determined by the logical *form* of an argument rather than by the actual truth or falsity of the premises and the conclusion,[21] you also know immediately that any argument that has that form must also be invalid. Thus, if you can find just one counterexample (i.e., one argument of that form that has all true premises and a false conclusion), then you can prove that all arguments that have that form are invalid.

Let's now apply the counterexample method to a few simple examples. Suppose we want to determine whether the following argument is valid or invalid:

Example 1

Some Republicans are conservatives, and some Republicans are pro-choice. Therefore, some conservatives are pro-choice.

The first step in the counterexample method is to determine the logical form of the argument. To make sure that we are representing the form of the argument correctly, we begin by *numbering* the steps in the argument, with the conclusion stated last. We thus get this:

1. Some Republicans are conservatives.
2. Some Republicans are pro-choice.
3. Therefore, some conservatives are pro-choice.

(Note that in logic, "some" always means "at least one"—that is, "some and perhaps all." "Some" never means "some but not all." Thus, in logic, when we say "Some dogs are animals," we mean "At least one dog is an animal" [which is true], not "Some but not all dogs are animals" [which is false].)

Next, we assign *letters* to represent the various terms in the argument. Using "A's" to represent "Republicans," "B's" to represent "conservatives," and "C's" to represent "people who are pro-choice," we get the following:

1. Some A's are B's.
2. Some A's are C's.
3. Therefore, some B's are C's.

This is the logical form of the argument in example 1. Having determined this form, we have completed the first step of the counterexample method.

The second step in the counterexample method involves attempting to construct a *second argument* that has exactly the same form as the argument being tested but that (unlike the first) has obviously true premises and an obviously false conclusion. With most invalid argument forms, it is possible to construct such a counterexample using a few stock terms, such as "dogs," "cats," "animals," "men," "women," "people," "apples," "pears," and "fruit." Using "animals" as a substitute for "A's," "dogs" as a substitute for "B's," and "cats" as a substitute for "C's," we can construct an argument that has the same form as the argument in example 1, but that has clearly true premises and a clearly false conclusion:

1. Some animals are dogs. (true)
2. Some animals are cats. (true)
3. Therefore, some dogs are cats. (false)

We have thus constructed a counterexample to the argument in example 1. Other counterexamples would work equally well; here are two:

1. Some fruits are apples. (true)
2. Some fruits are pears. (true)
3. Therefore, some apples are pears. (false)
1. Some politicians are Democrats. (true)
2. Some politicians are Republicans. (true)
3. Therefore, some Democrats are Republicans. (false)

Let's try another example.

Example 2

If God exists, then life has meaning. Hence, God does exist, since life has meaning.

We begin by numbering the premises and the conclusion:

1. If God exists, then life has meaning.
2. Life has meaning.
3. Therefore, God exists.

We next identify the form of the argument. Using "A" to represent the statement "God exists," and "B" to represent the statement "Life has meaning," we get this form:

1. If A then B.
2. B.
3. Therefore, A.

Finally, we attempt to find an argument that has exactly the same form but obviously true premises and an obviously false conclusion.

For starters, we might try this:

1. If Lassie is a dog, then Lassie is an animal. (true)
2. Lassie is an animal. (true)
3. Therefore, Lassie is a dog. (true)

That won't work, because we need a *false* conclusion to get a good counter-example.

Next, we might try this:

1. If JFK was killed by a lone assassin, then JFK is dead. (true)
2. JFK is dead. (true)
3. Therefore, JFK was killed by a lone assassin. (true? false?)

That won't work, either, because for an effective counterexample we need a conclusion that is *obviously* false (i.e., one that is known to be false by practically everyone), and it is far from obviously false that JFK was killed by a lone assassin.[22] So, back to the drawing board one more time:

1. If Kansas City is in California, then Kansas City is in the United States. (true)
2. Kansas City is in the United States. (true)
3. Therefore, Kansas City is in California. (false)

Bingo! This gives us the counterexample we're looking for. Now we have proven that example 2 does not have a valid argument form and thus is invalid. Here is another counterexample:

1. If George Washington died in a car crash, then George Washington is dead. (true)
2. George Washington is dead. (true)
3. Therefore, George Washington died in a car crash. (false)

Consider a third example:

Example 3

Some senators are Republicans. Hence, some Republicans are politicians, since all senators are politicians.

First, we number the premises and the conclusion:

1. Some senators are Republicans.
2. All senators are politicians.
3. Therefore, some Republicans are politicians.

Next, we identify the form of the argument:

1. Some A's are B's.
2. All A's are C's.
3. Therefore, some B's are C's.

Finally, we try to create a counterexample. First, we might try this:

1. Some dogs are animals. (true)
2. All dogs are mammals. (true)
3. Therefore, some animals are mammals. (true)

That won't work, since the conclusion is true. Next, we might try this:

1. Some apples are red. (true)
2. All apples are fruits. (true)
3. Therefore, some red things are fruits. (true)

That won't work, either, since again the conclusion is true. Finally, we might try this:

1. Some students love jazz (true)
2. All students love hot wings. (false)
3. Therefore, some people who love jazz are people who like hot wings. (true)

That fails, too, because not only is the conclusion true but also one of the premises is false. At this point, we might begin to suspect that the reason we can't find a counterexample is that there is no counterexample to be found, because the blessed thing is *valid*. And that is, in fact, the case. One could work until doomsday trying to come up with a counterexample to the argument in example 3 and never succeed, since the form of the argument is such that it *guarantees* a true conclusion if you plug in true premises. This raises an urgent question: At what point should you throw in the towel? At what point is it safe to conclude that the reason you can't find a good counterexample to a particular argument is not that you have been insufficiently imaginative or persevering in your attempts but, rather, that the argument is simply valid?

Alas, there is no such perfect security with the counterexample method. As a rule, however, it is generally safe to assume after three or four unsuccessful tries that no counterexample can be found. On exams, however, the rule is always: Try as many attempted counterexamples as time permits.

> *People with untrained minds should no more expect to think clearly and logically than people who have never learnt and never practiced can expect to find themselves good carpenters, golfers, bridge players, and pianists.*
>
> —A. E. Mander

EXERCISE 3.5

Use the counterexample method to determine whether the following arguments are valid or invalid.

1. All Anglicans are believers. Therefore, since all Calvinists are believers, all Anglicans are Calvinists.
2. If Josef is an anarchist, then he's a bolshevik. Hence, Josef is not a bolshevik, since he's not an anarchist.
3. No ales are brandies. Some ales are not champagnes. Therefore, some champagnes are not brandies.
4. If Ophelia is an Australian, then she's a beach-lover. Hence, since Ophelia is not a beach-lover, she's not an Australian.
5. Allen is a big spender, since Allen is a Californian, and all Californians are big spenders.
6. If Alice is a Presbyterian, then she believes in God. Hence, Alice is a Presbyterian, since she believes in God.
7. No Argentinians are Bolivians. Therefore, some Cubans are not Bolivians, since some Argentinians are not Cubans.
8. Some animals are brown. Some animals are cows. So, some animals are brown cows.
9. No Alsatians are Burgundians. Some Channel-watchers are not Alsatians. So, some Burgundians are not Channel-watchers.

10. All aphids are bugs. Some aphids are cranky. So, some cranky things are not bugs.
11. No apple pickers are broncobusters. Some broncobusters are cellists. So, some cellists are apple pickers.
12. No artichokes are carrots, because no artichokes are beets, and no carrots are beets.

Summary

1. This chapter has introduced you to some of the most basic and important concepts in logic.

2. All arguments are either deductive or inductive. A *deductive argument* is an argument in which the conclusion is claimed to follow necessarily from the premises. An *inductive argument* is an argument in which the conclusion is claimed to follow only probably from the premises.

3. In deciding whether an argument is deductive or inductive, one should apply four simple tests: the indicator word test, the strict necessity test, the common pattern test, and the principle of charity test. The *indicator word test* asks: Are there any indicator words—words such as "probably," "necessarily," and "likely"—that signal whether the argument is intended to be deductive or inductive? The *strict necessity test* asks: Does the conclusion follow with strict necessity from the premises? The *common pattern test* asks: Does the argument have a pattern that is characteristically deductive or inductive? The *principle of charity test* urges us to treat doubtful arguments in whatever way is most favorable to the arguer.

4. Common patterns of deductive reasoning include hypothetical syllogism, categorical syllogism, argument by elimination, argument based on mathematics, and argument from definition. A *hypothetical syllogism* is a three-line argument that contains at least one conditional (if-then) statement. A *categorical syllogism* is a three-line argument in which each statement in the argument begins with "all," "some," or "no." An *argument by elimination* is an argument that seeks to logically rule out various possibilities until only a single possibility remains. An *argument based on mathematics* is an argument in which the conclusion is claimed to depend largely or entirely on some mathematical calculation or measurement (perhaps in conjunction with one or more nonmathematical premises). An *argument from definition* is an argument in which the conclusion is presented as being true by definition.

5. Common patterns of inductive reasoning include inductive generalization, predictive argument, argument from authority, causal argument, sta-

tistical argument, and argument from analogy. An *inductive generalization* is an argument in which a generalization is claimed to be likely on the basis of information about some members of a particular class. A *predictive argument* is an argument in which a prediction is defended with reasons. An *argument from authority* asserts that a claim is true, and then supports that claim by alleging that some presumed authority or witness has said that the claim is true. A *causal argument* is an argument that asserts or denies that something causes, has caused, or will cause something else. A *statistical argument* is an argument that rests on statistical evidence—that is, evidence that some percentage of some group has some particular characteristic. An *argument from analogy* is an argument in which the conclusion is claimed to depend on an analogy (i.e., a comparison or a similarity) between two or more things.

6. Deductive arguments are either valid or invalid. A *valid deductive argument* is a deductive argument in which the conclusion follows necessarily from the premises. In other words, it is an argument in which it is impossible for all the premises to be true and the conclusion false. An *invalid deductive argument* is a deductive argument in which the conclusion does not follow necessarily from the premises.

7. A *sound argument* is a deductive argument that both is valid and has all true premises. An *unsound argument* is a deductive argument that either is invalid or has at least one false premise, or both.

8. Inductive arguments are either strong or weak. A *strong inductive argument* is an inductive argument in which the conclusion follows probably from the premises. In other words, it is an inductive argument in which, if the premises are (or were) true, the conclusion would probably be true. A *weak inductive argument* is an inductive argument in which the conclusion does not follow probably from the premises.

9. A *cogent argument* is an inductive argument that both is strong and has all true premises. An *uncogent argument* is an inductive argument that either is weak or has at least one false premise, or both.

10. This chapter presented an informal three-step test to check whether an argument is valid or invalid *(the Three C's Test of Validity)*:

    Step 1: Check to see whether the premises are actually true and the conclusion is actually false. If they are, then the argument is invalid. If they are not, or if you can't determine whether the premises and the conclusion are actually true or false, then go on to step 2.

    Step 2: See if you can *conceive* a possible scenario in which the premises would be true and the conclusion false. If you can, then the argument is invalid. If you can't, and it is not obvious to you that the argument is valid, then go on to step 3.

Step 3: Try to construct a *counterexample* to the argument—that is, a second argument that has exactly the same form as the first argument, but whose premises are obviously true and whose conclusion is obviously false. If you can construct such a counterexample, then the argument is invalid. If you can't, then it is usually safe to assume that the argument is valid.

CHAPTER 4

LANGUAGE

THE ROLE OF LANGUAGE IN THE ASSESSMENT OF ARGUMENTS

We take our language for granted. Seldom do we think about our dependence on the ability to use words and to put them together in phrases and sentences. With language we plan the day's events, curse the television, proclaim our surprise or frustration ("Damn!"), express pain ("Ouch!"), scribble reminders on scraps of paper, record thoughts and feelings in diaries and journals, recall past conversations and events, talk to ourselves in anxious moments, pray, wonder, and worry. We could, perhaps, think in other ways—with images, for example—but that would be very limiting. Because we can put words to our experiences and not just recall them as images, when we know what things are called, we are able to gain some measure of control over our world. In fact, until we know the words for some things, we often fail to even notice them.

As children, we pointed at things and shouted their names and labels ("Puppy!") or appraised their worth ("Yuk!"). As adults, we name our possessions—pets, boats, cars, homes, ranches, and estates. We pass final judgment on a "worthless piece of junk" before we toss it out or assure ourselves that we have spent our money wisely on a "bargain" or a "real find." We decide serious matters by writing out our options and weighing the pros and cons. We paraphrase the ideas of others, putting what we have learned into our own words to take possession of new knowledge. We decide what language best fits people we have met, actions we have performed, and our feelings: it was a "mistake" to date that "loser"; I am "concerned," not "worried." Unfortunately, we also often abuse our ability to use language—employing racial slurs, for example, to assert our dominance over people different from us—but without the ability to label and name the things of our world and to express our judgment about them, we would feel a loss of control, much as we do when we have forgotten someone's name, when a word is "on the tip of our tongue," or when we are in a foreign country and don't speak the

> Only where there is language is there world.
> —Adrienne Rich

97

language. Things without names seem unusual and intimidating. Before we eat something we have never seen before, we want to know what it is called.

It is when we are among others, and not alone, that we realize how indispensable language is, since it allows us to communicate with one another. Through language, we build linguistic bridges and connect ourselves to the world's community. The desire to communicate through language is very strong, even overpowering: We ask people, "How are you?" or "What's up?" and wish them "a nice day" or a "great weekend." We share secrets, express our love, apologize, make promises, confess our faults, and confide in friends. We run up excessive phone bills, write countless e-mails, and spend hours in chat rooms. Although we can communicate without words—with gestures, facial expressions, touches, and grunts, for example—our language allows us to connect with one another in more complicated ways and satisfies a need in us to belong.

Although we often speak or write to others for our own benefit—putting jumbled feelings into words can be very therapeutic, for example—usually we communicate with the purpose of influencing or affecting our readers and listeners in some way: to entertain, console, inform, persuade, request, command, educate, sell something, solicit a vote, frighten, win someone's approval, gain a friend, and so forth. The list of objectives that can be accomplished through communication is almost endless, but in every case, the person doing the writing or speaking attempts to influence his or her audience.

To think critically about communication, we need to remind ourselves constantly that language is not something that just happens, that in almost every act of communication some*one* is, through language, attempting to find the words that accurately name the things, ideas, and events of the world, and that express opinions and feelings about those things, and to communicate those words in the hope of influencing someone else. It seems like a simple point, but it is one we tend to forget. For example, we too often read newspapers, advertisements, encyclopedias, and textbooks as if the words assembled themselves on the pages in neat rows with justified margins, and we forget that someone has designs on our attention, our beliefs, our opinions, and our actions. We forget at our peril that the arguments we listen to and the information we collect have been carefully constructed by someone who wants to influence and affect us in some way.

When we read or listen to an argument or gather information, we are being asked to believe that the writer's or speaker's statements are correct and that the conclusions are built on true premises, so we need to be able to tell if those premises are indeed true. And before we build our own arguments on information, we need to know if that information is true. As you saw in the previous chapter, we can sometimes rely on personal experience, background beliefs, and our knowledge about a source to decide whether it is reasonable to accept a claim. One of the most important additional ways to determine truth is by analyzing language.

> *The basic agreement between human beings, indeed what makes them human and makes them social, is language.*
>
> —Monique Wittig

DECIDING WHETHER A PREMISE IS TRUE OR FALSE

As a way of demonstrating how the truth of a claim is assessed through language, let us remind you of what for many students is a painful moment in their academic careers—the dreaded "True/False" test. Is the following statement true or false?

> In June of 2000, George W. Bush, the ultraconservative governor of Texas and a son of the former and much admired President George H. W. Bush, was a strong candidate for the presidency of the United States.

If you're like most students, you're thinking hard about that sentence and you may even be wondering if this is a trick question. In trying to determine the truth of the statement, you are looking at the factual content of the sentence and deciding if the statement has any correspondence to real life-events. Does the writer's language accurately reflect the actual occurrence of a certain person's being in a certain position at a particular time? You might be wondering about the accuracy of "H. W." in Bush Sr.'s name or whether Bush Jr. was governor of Texas. Or was it Florida? Was Bush a "candidate" in June of 2000, or did he declare his candidacy later than that? You are most likely weighing the facts, and you are hesitant to call the statement true if any of the language doesn't correspond to reality. To answer your questions and determine whether the facts are correct, you might have to do a little research— look up Bush Sr.'s middle names, for example.

You are probably also wondering exactly what "ultraconservative" and "strong" mean and whether they alter the truth or falsity of the statement. By "strong," does the writer mean that Bush was physically powerful or that his chances for election were good? Does "ultraconservative" mean precisely the same thing to the writer of the sentence as it does to each reader? Does "ultraconservative" here refer to all Bush's views or just to his economic, his foreign, or his social policies? And what about that word "admired"? How *true* is that? How does one define "admired"? By whom was Bush Sr. admired? By how many people? Was Bush Sr. actually "admired," or is the writer subtly encouraging us to admire the former president?

Certainly, we don't need to dissect every claim we come across as we have done here. We must allow writers—and ourselves—the freedom to speak metaphorically or passionately on a topic. We can also make some assumptions about words without becoming too petty; the word "strong" in the example most likely refers to Bush's chances of winning. Besides, overanalysis can be maddening and stifling to the point that we never get to the important step of determining the author's overall meaning and presenting our own arguments.

But before we agree to accept the claims in an argument of serious consequence or decide to alter our beliefs or to take action, we need to scrutinize rigorously the language of those claims in the same way we customarily analyze the questions on True/False tests.

As the analysis of the Bush example illustrates, when attempting to determine whether a claim is true, we usually ask two kinds of questions about the language of the claim:

1. Is the language an accurate or factual reflection of the real, historical events, things, ideas, people, and so forth, to which the claim refers? In other words, has the writer or speaker correctly called things what they are?
2. Is the language a *reflection of the writer's point of view (including attitude, opinions, beliefs, evaluations, judgments, and feelings)* toward the events, objects, ideas, people, and so forth to which the claim refers? If so, has the writer or speaker defended that point of view, or has he or she merely *slanted* reality in an apparent effort to evoke a particular response from us?

Elements of language besides words can be used to slant an argument. Sentence structure, for example, can be used to emphasize one point over another:

Although lazy, Susan is naturally talented.

Although naturally talented, Susan is lazy.

The two sentences make the same point, but the first emphasizes Susan's talent and the second her laziness.

Punctuation can also indicate a bias; quotation marks around a word, for example, can suggest the opposite of what is stated:

Mr. Anderson will read from his "poetry" this afternoon at the bookstore.

Our concern in this chapter, however, is with the way writers and speakers use words to inform and influence readers. As you will see in the rest of this chapter, the ability to tell when language is being used to express a writer's personal feelings, attitude, opinion, and assessment is necessary for determining the truth of claims. This isn't to suggest that neutral language makes a claim true, or that language that expresses a personal viewpoint makes a claim false. In fact, a writer can use neutral language in obviously false statements ("Bill Clinton was elected president in 1880") and can tell the truth in statements that contain a personal judgment ("Bill Clinton's impeachment damaged his presidency"). The word "damaged" contains the writer's assessment of Clinton's presidency, but the assessment could be made factual with a definition of "damaged" and supporting evidence.

We must be able to distinguish language intended to present factual information from language that presents an arguer's viewpoint so that we can tell whether we are responding to the content, facts, and information contained in an argument or merely reacting to the writer's attitude and feelings. We should reserve our approval or agreement for arguments in which the claims are expressed in precise, accurate, well-defined language, and in which personal viewpoints are defended rather than merely presented in emotionally charged and manipulative language.

PRECISION AND PERSONAL VIEWPOINT IN OUR OWN ARGUMENTS

The language we use to defend our opinions in our own arguments should be as precise as possible. Anyone who has struggled, perhaps futilely, for the perfect, exact, unambiguous word to make herself understood knows how elusive precision can be. A physician might ask about your pain, "Is it a stabbing pain or a dull pain? Is it a twinge or a constant ache? Is it a throbbing pain?" In fact, you could draw a distinction between an ache, a spasm, a crick, a cramp, a contraction, a tingle, a twinge, a pinch, a pang, and so on. What is it *exactly* that you feel? Frustrated by your inability to pin it down and speak accurately, you settle for a word that's "close enough," or you select vague and general terms. "Basically, I just don't feel good," you end up saying.

We know, too, the confusion that can result from the misuse of words or from a failure to define terms. You say about a heartless man, "He's so cold," and your listener imagines a man shivering. Or take the word "liberal." It can cause all sorts of confusion, since its definition can depend on the audience and on the context. In fact, this word—with its various meanings—has caused more damage to the political discourse in our country over the past few years than is, perhaps, measurable. Writing "Ms. Jones, a liberal congresswoman from the Midwest," will evoke enough diverse reactions to make the statement meaningless. Some people hear a derisive term denoting a person who believes in raising taxes and increasing government spending. To others "liberal" describes someone who approves of governmental intervention in economic and social matters. To some it indicates a person who is open to new ideas and tolerant of the differences in other people. To still others, it describes someone who supports the rights of the individual. Some people cringe at the word; others cheer.

Our choice of words is greatly influenced by such factors as where we grew up, our reading habits, our political views, and our religious beliefs, and we may fail to communicate if we assume that everyone around us uses words in the same way we do. In college we often meet students whose words for things differ from our own. In some parts of the country, for example, a certain type of sandwich is called a submarine sandwich or "sub;" in others it is called a hoagie, a hero sandwich, a poor boy, a bomber, or a grinder. On a more serious level, political views can creep into word choices. What do you call those who have pledged themselves to fight vigorously, even to the death, for the freedom of citizens in their country? If they are fighting for us, we might call them "soldiers." If they are fighting against us, we may call them "terrorists." The fight for independence in Northern Ireland provides an excellent example: members of the Irish Republican Army are often called terrorists by the British press, whereas the press in the Republic of Ireland often refers to them as soldiers.

What you call a sandwich might depend on where you live or what you were taught growing up, but what you call a member of a military or political organization also depends on where you live, what you were taught, what you believe, what you value. You reveal much about yourself when you use certain terms, and because not everyone will agree with those terms, you might have to defend your use of them. If you call a big sandwich a "hoagie," no one might care. If you call a member of the Irish Republican Army a terrorist, or abortion "murder," or spanking "child abuse," you might be asked to defend your use of those words. Someone claiming that "abusing a child by spanking him causes not only physical harm but psychological damage as well" cannot assume that the reader or listener will agree that spanking is abusive—he or she may prefer to call it "discipline," "punishment," "instruction," or even "education."

We control our world by labeling its contents, and we express our opinion of those contents in language that is sometimes private and often very subjective: I named my cat Aslan; I scream at the TV when the Mets lose; I call it a "hoagie"; and spanking, as far as I'm concerned, is "abuse." But when language is used for the purpose of influencing others—to present claims in an argument or facts in a source of information—listeners or readers need to know when language is precise and when it is personal. The rest of this chapter will show you how to recognize imprecise language and how to define the words you use in an argument so that your readers and listeners will better understand your claims, and will alert you to the ways language can be used by those who would manipulate you into agreement or action. Thinking critically depends on a sensitivity to language and on a willingness to think hard about words, look up their meanings, use them correctly, define them carefully, and consider how one's words might be interpreted by others. The following exercises will help you think about your language in ways you may not have thought about before.

> All words are prejudices.
> —Friedrich Nietzsche

EXERCISE 4.1

I. In groups of three, four, or five, use the following questions to guide a discussion about language.

1. Since you arrived at college, have you recognized that some of your words or expressions are unique to the area where you come from? Are there any words—for foods or activities popular among people in your hometown, for example—that might not be recognizable to outsiders or that might be called by different names elsewhere? What words or expressions have you heard among your classmates that seem unusual or odd to you?

2. What is the term generally given to a promiscuous young woman? Is there a term for a promiscuous young man? What does the difference in terms say about our cultural attitudes toward sexual behavior? Give your opinion of the following quotations: "Language is not neutral. It is not merely a vehicle which carries ideas. It is a shaper of ideas" (Dale Spender, *Man Made Language,* 1980); "Conventional English usage, including the generic use of masculine-gender words, often obscures the actions, the contributions, and sometimes the very presence of women (Casey Miller and Kate Swift, *The Handbook of Nonsexist Writing,* 1980).

3. Think of a time (or several, if you can) when you were involved in a misunderstanding with someone else because each of you assumed that the other defined a word in the same way. As an example, consider this case: "An older, married friend of mine excused himself to leave for a 'date' with the principal, a married woman. I was shocked and upset until I realized he had not a 'date' as I use that term, but an appointment."

4. What do you mean by _____? Work individually to define the following words without using a dictionary. Try to define the words as you have heard them used or used them yourself. You may use synonyms or use the words in a sentence to indicate their meaning. When you are done, group members should compare answers and discuss any differences. Is one definition "more correct" than the others? What do the similarities and differences suggest? After you have recorded and discussed your definitions, use a dictionary to determine the standard definition.

imply	unique	prejudice
postpone	nauseous	dilemma
disinterested	aggravate	hysterical
feminist	decimate	anxious
flaunt	allusion	verbal
exotic	adverse	ironically

II. Words and Pictures

A picture is worth a thousand words, it is often said. But which of those words describe the picture and which describe the person perceiving the picture? Look at the photographs on pages 104 and 105. What words would you use to describe what you see? Divide your language into two categories: words that accurately describe what the pictures contain and words that express your impressions of the picture or the feelings that the picture evokes. Think about the words you chose for the first category. Did you reject some words because they weren't precise enough? In the second category, your words will describe only how *you* see the picture. A scene may be disturbing to you, for example, but not at all disturbing to someone else. After you have listed several descriptive and impressionistic words, compare your list with the lists of other members of the class. Did you use the same descriptive language? Are your impressions comparable?

Words are made for a certain exactness of thought, as tears are for a certain degree of pain.
—René Daumal

Walker Evans, *Bethlehem graveyard and steel mill, Pennsylvania*, 1935. Courtesy of the Library of Congress.

FINDING THE RIGHT WORDS: THE NEED FOR PRECISION

Failure to be precise in communicating can result in confusion and misunderstanding. What makes perfectly good sense to one person might be confusing to someone else. "My father is a painter," you tell a friend, but does your father paint houses or canvases? A professor writes "vague" in the margins of what you consider your best paper. Whose fault is it that your professor didn't "get it"? (Hint: Not your professor's.) To communicate clearly, to defend our claims without confusing or misleading anyone, and to assess the truth of premises presented to us in the arguments of others, we must insist that language in the context of argumentation be clear and precise.

Say, for example, that as support for the claim that college bookstores should stop selling clothes manufactured in foreign sweatshops, the following were offered as premises:

Dorothea Lange, *Migrant Mother: Nipomo, California*, 1936. Courtesy of the Library of Congress.

> Sweatshop laborers earn minimal pay working in suffocating conditions in factories owned by American corporations. They claim that economic realities force them to participate in this practice.

To the writer, that may be clear, but the reader will question what is meant by "sweatshop" and "minimal pay" and may wonder if "suffocating" is a literal description of the factory (limited fresh air to breathe) or a metaphorical description of the oppressive working conditions. The reader might also wonder if "they" in the second sentence refers to the corporations or to the laborers, both of which could conceivably feel "forced" into such practices. Thinking critically and arguing effectively often depends on recognizing imprecise language—that is, is vague, overgeneral, and ambiguous language.

Vagueness

Vagueness refers to a lack of clarity or precision. A word (or a group of words) is vague when its meaning is fuzzy or inexact. The phrase "minimal pay" in our example is vague, since it does not indicate precisely how much money is paid to laborers. Or consider the word "rich." It is clear that Bill Gates is rich. It is equally clear that most welfare recipients are not rich. But what about an NBA benchwarmer who earns $400,000 a year? Or a plastic surgeon who earns $1,000,000 a year but has large gambling debts? Are they rich? It is hard to say, because the word "rich" isn't precise enough to yield a clear, determinate answer. The term "middle-aged" is also vague. Everyone would agree that President Bush is middle-aged. Everyone would also agree that Leonardo DiCaprio and former President Reagan are not middle-aged. But what about Madonna, or Mick Jagger? No definite answer can be given, because the word "middle-aged" has no clear and distinct meaning.

As these examples suggest, a vague word typically divides things into three classes: those things to which the word clearly applies, those things to which it clearly does not apply, and those things to which it may or may not apply. In such "borderline" cases, it is hard to say whether the word applies to those things or not.

Nearly all words are vague to some degree. Some words, such as "indecent" and "obscene," are extremely vague: they create lots of difficult borderline cases. Other words, such as "vehicle," are moderately vague. (Ordinary cars and trucks are clearly vehicles, but what about bicycles, roller skates, baby carriages, and motorized wheelchairs?) Still other words, such as "triangle" and "prime number," have very precise meanings, with little or no vagueness.

Vague language is useful and appropriate in many contexts. It lets us speak with suitable caution when we lack precise information. ("I think I did pretty well on the exam.") It frequently adds richness, subtlety, and complexity to poetry and other literary forms ("a slumber did my spirit seal"). In diplomacy, a certain deliberate vagueness may be needed to avoid revealing important information. ("If you invade, there will be severe consequences.") And vague language is useful—indeed, probably indispensable—in formulating suitably broad legal standards ("freedom of speech") in contexts in which it would be unwise to attempt to enact a detailed code of laws.

Generally speaking, however, vagueness should be avoided, since it frustrates clear thinking and communication. Imagine, for example, living in a police state in which the following laws were enforced:

> Anyone dressing *inappropriately* will be imprisoned.
>
> Anyone acting *immorally* will be severely punished.
>
> Anyone speaking *disloyally* will be shot.

Would you have any clear idea what kinds of conduct were permitted or prohibited by such vague laws?

Overgenerality

Vagueness is often confused with **overgenerality.** There is, however, an important distinction between the two. Words are vague if they have fuzzy boundaries, and thus give rise to borderline cases. By contrast, words are *over-general* if they are *not specific enough* in a given context.

Consider the following brief dialogues:

Teacher: Johnny, what is 7 + 5?
Johnny: More than 2.

Dean of Students: What were you drinking at this keg party?
Freshman: A beverage.

Mother: Where are you going?
Teenager: Out.
Mother: When will you be back?
Teenager: Later.

None of these replies is particularly vague. The phrase "More than 2," for example, gives rise to no troublesome borderline cases. The problem with these answers is not vagueness but overgenerality. The answers are not specific enough to count as satisfactory answers in the context indicated.

Whether an expression is overly general usually depends upon the context. Thus, "He's human" may be a perfectly adequate response to the question "Is your chess opponent human or a machine?" But it is a very poor response to the question "Can you describe the robbery suspect?"

Sometimes, of course, words may be both vague and overgeneral. Thus, if I describe my lost luggage simply as "a large black bag," my description is both too vague (since "large," "black," and "bag" all have fuzzy meanings) and too general (since the phrase "large black bag" isn't specific enough to distinguish my bag from many others).

Attempting to evaluate an argument built on language that is overgeneral can be very frustrating, since the claims will contain very little information for us to get a grip on. Say, for example, that a government official argues for military intervention in a foreign country, and that when pressed for specifics, the official claims that the Air Force will be deployed. The response is not vague since the Air Force is a definable and limited group, but the answer is overgeneral, since it says nothing about the specific actions that will be undertaken by the Air Force. Likewise, politicians sometimes try to defend a claim by speaking in generalities. A politician, asked for his or her thoughts on higher taxes, says, "I'm opposed to them," giving us no idea of what he or she intends to do about taxes.

Ambiguity

Ambiguity refers to a doubtful sense of a word. Many words have more than one meaning. The word "star," for example, can mean, among other things, a Hollywood celebrity and a twinkling celestial object. A word or expression is *ambiguous* if it has two or more distinct meanings and if the context does not make clear which meaning is intended. Ambiguity is what makes puns and many jokes funny, but used unintentionally it can destroy the effectiveness of an argument.

Ambiguity, like overgenerality, is often confused with vagueness. The basic difference between ambiguity and vagueness is this: A vague expression is imprecise because it has blurry boundaries. An ambiguous expression is imprecise because it is unclear which of two or more *distinct* meanings (each of which may be quite precise) is the one intended by the author. A handy way to remember the distinction is to keep in mind that *ambi-* means "both," as in "ambidextrous": able to use both hands with equal skill.

Some expressions are ambiguous because it is not clear what a single word or phrase in the expression refers to:

Joe went to the bank. ["Bank" in the sense of a financial institution or "bank" in the sense of a slope bordering a river? Or could it be a sperm bank?]

John called. [John Smith or John Brown?]

Margie sold out. [Did Margie sell her possessions or did she surrender her ideals?]

Ambiguities that result from uncertainty about the meaning of an individual word or phrase are called **semantic ambiguities.**

Other expressions are ambiguous because of a faulty sentence structure:

As a young girl, her grandfather often told her stories about the Wild West. [Her grandfather was never a young girl.][1]

One morning Bill shot an elephant in his pajamas. [Those must have been big pajamas!]

Jennifer told her mother she was jealous. [Whom does "she" refer to? Jennifer or her mother?]

Newspaper ad: Dog for sale. Eats anything and is especially fond of children.

Billboard for Planned Parenthood: Come to us for unwanted pregnancies.[2]

Church sign: What is hell? Come to church next Sunday and listen to our new minister.[3]

Newspaper headline: Prostitutes Appeal to Pope.

Headline: Two Sisters Reunited after 18 Years in Checkout Line.

Headline: Drunk Gets Nine Months in Violin Case.

Sign in laundromat: Customers are required to remove their clothes when the machine stops.[4]

Ambiguities that result from faulty grammar or word order are called **syntactical ambiguities** or *amphibolies.*

Some phrases that on their own appear ambiguous are clarified in the context of an argument, so that, for instance, "Joe went to the bank" creates no confusion in the sentence "Joe went to the bank to complain to the manager about the increase in ATM fees." But confusion and miscommunication result when a term in an argument has more than one meaning and the intended meaning is not clarified by definition or by context. In some cases, this failure results in what is known as a **verbal dispute,** which occurs when two people appear to disagree on an issue but in actuality have simply not resolved the ambiguity of a key term. Suppose two people were asked the same question: "Is the suspect arrested last night *guilty* of the crime?" The first person answers, "No, a person is innocent until proved guilty." The second person disagrees: "I say he is guilty; he confessed when he was picked up." There is really no disagreement here on the whether or not the suspect *committed* the crime, since the first person is defining "guilt" in a legal sense (the suspect can't be sentenced yet), and the second is defining it to mean that the suspect did the crime of which he or she is accused. A **factual dispute,** on the other hand, occurs when opponents disagree not over the terms but over the actual facts of the case. Person A might say, "That man did not commit the crime; he has an alibi." Person B might respond, "He did commit the crime; I saw him do it."

In other cases, though, assessing the truth of a claim that hinges on an ambiguous term can be nearly impossible. If someone claimed that, on average, "men are more powerful than women," we would have no way of assessing that claim, since "powerful" has several meanings, and whereas one of those meanings (physical strength) may be defensible, the others are not.

EXERCISE 4.2

Identify problems of vagueness, overgenerality, and ambiguity in the following passages. You will notice that many of the examples are comical, whether the writer intended them to be so or not. See if you can determine which of the comical passages contain some clever and deliberate use of imprecision and which are unintentionally funny.

1. Headline: Stud Tires Out.
2. As a member of Parliament, Anglo-Irish playwright Richard Brinsley Sheridan (1751–1816) had been asked to apologize for insulting a fellow member of Parliament. "Mr. Speaker," replied Sheridan, "I said the honorable member was a liar it is true and I am sorry for it. The honorable member may place the punctuation where he pleases."[5]
3. No cruising on this street.
4. Headline: Need Plain Clothes Security: Must Have Shoplifting Experience.[6]
5. Aristotle: The good is what all things desire.
6. Men are such slobs!
7. In his will, Uncle Henry left his diamond watch and his Rolls-Royce to his nephews Peter and John.
8. When one of the [Columbine High School] gunmen asked Cassie Bernall if she believed in God, she said "yes." Then he killed her. Elementary school teacher Kathi Cossey of Houston said Bernall's death "made me really think,

what would I say, knowing that you're going to go to heaven and someone is sitting there with a gun."[7]

9. *Headline:* Advice to Teachers and Parents on Drugs.

10. He ate his cheesecake with relish.

11. With her enormous bottom exposed to the sky, Ellen watched *Titanic* slowly sink.

12. On returning from church one day, President Coolidge was asked on what topic the minister had preached. After a moment's thought he replied, "Sin." "And what did he say about the sin?" his interlocutor asked. "He was against it," Coolidge replied.[8]

13. Always do the loving thing.

14. Only men have immortal souls.

15. *Headline:* Former Concentration Camp Guard Helps Burn Victims.

16. $3 + 5 \times 3 = ?$

17. *Politician:* We need a tax code that is fair to working families. I intend to introduce appropriate legislation that achieves this end.

18. She cannot bear children.

19. *Headline:* British Left Waffles on Falkland Islands.

20. *Sign:* Get fat free. Call me.

21. British Prime Minister Benjamin Disraeli had a standard acknowledgment for people who sent him unsolicited manuscripts for his opinion: "Thank you for the manuscript; I shall lose no time in reading it."[9]

22. Lost: Small brown dog with black collar. Generous reward for return.

23. *Headline:* Teacher Strikes Idle Kids.

24. Jana told her sister she was envious.

25. Never withhold herpes infection from loved one.

26. *Sign:* Wanted: 50 girls for stripping machine operators in factory.

27. *From a student paper:* The German Emperor's lower passage was blocked by the French for years and years.[10]

28. *From the U.S. Bill of Rights:* Congress shall make no law respecting an establishment of religion, or prohibiting the free exercise thereof.

29. *Headline:* Astronaut Apologizes for Gas in Spacecraft.

30. *Headline:* Panda Mating Fails; Veterinarian Takes Over.

> *The difference between the almost right word and the right word is really a large matter—'tis the difference between the lightning and the lightning bug.*
>
> —Mark Twain

THE IMPORTANCE OF PRECISE DEFINITIONS

A convincing argument can often depend upon the clear and accurate definition of language. The failure to define terms carefully and completely can result in a messy battle, with some participants struggling to find the truth and others fighting to avoid it. President Clinton's entire political career nearly came to a crashing halt because he and investigators looking into an alleged affair disagreed on the definition of the term "sexual relations." Prosecutors provided a legal definition of the phrase, a definition Clinton believed excluded the specific behavior he had engaged in. He denied the affair on the grounds that the term was inaccurate. Whereas many observers might argue that Clinton, knowing full well the meaning of "sexual relations," played games with the meaning of the phrase, others might claim that, like any good lawyer, Clinton held the prosecutor's language to the highest standard: it wasn't as precise as it should have been or defined as carefully as it might have been. In some respects, Clinton's looking for an escape hatch is understandable. You would be very aware of the need for clarity if, for example, you were arrested and charged with an offense. Our radar for undefined terms seems to kick in quickest when we are on the defensive: "What exactly," you might ask, "is 'reckless driving'?" Good defense lawyers usually start by considering whether or not the actions a client has committed actually fit the definition of the charge. Politicians, similarly, when attacked, will often challenge the term rather than the accusation.

In many discussions of significant topics, terms may need to be defined before a position can be advanced. Take, for example, the issue of whether or not Congress should propose an amendment outlawing desecration of the American flag. Such an amendment would make it a crime to deliberately deface or destroy the flag in certain circumstances. Of course, if such an amendment passes, individual cases of "desecration" will be decided on the basis of the courts' definition of the term. Clearly, "desecration" would require defining: Would tying the flag to your bumper and dragging it through the streets be considered desecration? How about using a small flag as a handkerchief or a bandana? What about sewing an old flag into a T-shirt or a bathing suit? Using it as a tablecloth? Flying it upside down? But the word "flag" would also need defining. What is a "flag"? Is it only the cloth banner that flies or hangs from a pole? What if, after a law against desecration has been passed, someone using a slide projector projects the image of a flag onto a white wall and throws paint or blood or eggs against the wall and shouts obscenities at the "flag"? What if the same person projects the image not against a white wall but against a wall spray-painted with antigovernment slogans? Certainly this person intends to protest the country or its policies, and he may indeed start a fight or a riot if he stages his protest among more patriotic citizens. But has he "desecrated" the American "flag" by his actions? Clearly, the interpretation of such documents as the Constitution can depend heavily on our definitions of key terms, and whereas an amendment might be deliberately left vague, it is up to the courts to decide on a case-by-case basis whether individual actions fall under the amendment.

Take another example from the Constitution. Many people in the United States believe that American citizens have a right to possess handguns in their homes, citing in their defense the second amendment to the Constitution: "A well regulated militia, being necessary to the security of a free state, the right of the people to keep and bear arms, shall not be infringed." To assert that this amendment applies to the types of guns available for purchase in the twenty-first century, proponents of gun ownership have insisted that the phrase "keep and bear arms" means precisely now what it did in 1791, when the first ten amendments were ratified, or that the writers of the Constitution clearly would have approved of the current application of the amendment. Those who argue that the language of the Constitution is outdated claim that the founders of the United States would have used the phrase "keep and bear" to mean a specific action different from possessing guns for personal use. Furthermore, they ask, what, in 1791, was considered an "arm"? Would the framers of the Constitution have been more specific in their language had they been able to foresee the invention of repeating pistols? Whereas some broad legal standards, such as "freedom of speech," have allowed for interpretation, the "right to bear arms" seems to be one that cries out for a more precise definition. Indeed, some advocates of strict gun control have proposed repealing the amendment.

In almost any argument, the definition of words can be at the heart of the debate. In fact, whereas some arguments take place over the truth or falseness of a claim ("The death penalty should be abolished"), other arguments center on the meaning of the words used to express the claim. Suppose that your former high school proposes to begin testing students for drug use. Even if you agree that this is a good idea, you need to know what school officials mean by "drug." What specific drugs do they intend to test for? Or suppose that a local PTA petitions the school board to ban violent movies from classrooms. Because many of us disagree on the definition of "violence," those parents making the suggestion must clearly define what they mean by "violent movie." If the PTA's proposition were accepted without a clear definition, teachers would never know whether a film they intended to show fit the category "violent movie" or not. Driver-education teachers could be charged with violating the rule if, in an effort to encourage safer driving, they were to show their students films depicting the aftermath of traffic accidents.

He who defines the terms wins the argument.

—Chinese Proverb

Types of Definitions

The trick to using language correctly in an argument is to remain aware that not everyone reading or listening to your claims has the same background, experience, and values that you do. Your audience, therefore, might not understand completely how you are using certain terms or what you mean by them. In fact, your audience may have very different definitions of the terms you are using. Therefore, you need to present definitions. There are several kinds of definitions that you can provide in an argument, some of which are subjective.

"When I use a word," Humpty Dumpty said in a rather scornful tone, "it means just what I choose it to mean— neither more nor less."

—Lewis Carroll

Stipulative   If you have ever created a new word or used an old word in an entirely new way, then you have provided a **stipulative definition,** in which you stipulate a definition; that is, you tell your readers or listeners what *you* mean by the term. A stipulative definition is among the most subjective of definitions, since the definition is one you have determined. In other words, a stipulative definition cannot be true or false; no one can disagree with you. Writers frequently stipulate definitions when they give labels to cultural trends, political movements, schools of thought, and so forth. Stipulative

> ## Critical Thinking Lapse
>
> How would a mouse define the term "animal"?
>
> "The Agriculture Department, interpreting the Animal Welfare Act, decreed that rats, mice and birds are not animals. As such, they are exempt from strict rules governing the treatment of laboratory creatures. The Humane Society of the United States and the Animal Defense Fund objected to their exclusion and sued. They won, but the department appealed.
>
> "The U.S. Court of Appeals decided in favor of the Agriculture Department on a technicality: Only those directly injured by the Animal Welfare Act can sue to change it. Martin Stephens, HSUS vice president, said further appeals would be hard, 'unless we can teach these animals to represent themselves.'"[11]

definitions create problems only when a writer fails to explain what he or she means by a word or a phrase that is not in common usage and that may be unfamiliar to a reader or listener.

Persuasive   Another kind of subjective definition is a **persuasive definition,** in which an arguer defines a term in an effort to persuade the reader to agree with the arguer's point of view regarding the thing being defined. Persuasive definitions usually contain emotional appeals and slanted terms and are often given in arguments over highly charged political and social topics on which people have firm views. For example, someone providing a persuasive definition of capital punishment might claim that "capital punishment means the state-sanctioned, vengeful murder of helpless prisoners," whereas someone else might claim that "capital punishment means the enactment of appropriate punishment for murderous cowards who have no regard for life." Either way, the writer provides a definition intended to persuade the reader toward a particular attitude. Although persuasive definitions are often presented as objective and authentic, they are convincing only if they are very well defended. Someone claiming that capital punishment is "vengeful murder" would have to provide support for that statement.

Lexical   Less personal definitions include lexical definitions and precising definitions (see next paragraph). In **lexical definitions,** words are defined in the way they are generally used in the language. For example: "A rug is a heavy fabric used to cover a floor." In the United States, most people would define the term *rug* that way. In England, however, a rug can also mean a type of blanket that is used to cover the legs of a passenger in a car or carriage. Notice that the definition of "rug" reflects its general usage, not one person's use of the word.

Precising   In a **precising definition,** the arguer attempts to qualify a vague word so that its meaning is not left to the interpretation of the reader or listener. For example, a college professor who says that students "participating" in class will receive extra points at the end of the semester might make that word more precise by listing the behaviors that "participating" entails: attending class, answering and asking questions, contributing relevant illustrations to help clarify points, and so forth. In giving a precising definition, the arguer must be careful to avoid attaching fanciful, persuasive or personal qualities to the meaning of the vague word. A professor could not, for example, claim that bringing gifts was part of "participating." Finally, a precising definition must be appropriate for the particular context. Whereas shouting out the answer might be appropriate behavior for "participating" in a game show, it would not fit the definition of "participation" in a classroom. Other terms that might need to be qualified or "precised" include those discussed earlier under the heading "Vagueness": "rich," "middle-aged," "indecent," "inappropriate," "unnatural," and so forth. Notice that there is a touch of subjectivity in a precising definition, since a reader or listener could disagree with the definition, arguing, for example, that "contributing relevant illustrations to help clarify points" should not be included in the definition of "participation." But a precising definition at least allows both parties to engage in the more productive activity of arguing over the definition rather than confusing the issue with vague and abstract terms.

Strategies for Defining

Writers rely on a number of strategies for helping readers understand exactly what is meant by important terms in an argument. Many of the techniques are quite complicated and specialized (how would a scientist define "motion," for example?), but critical thinking students can make use of several possible strategies, all of which are helpful, but all of which have shortcomings to be aware of.

Give Illustrations   One of the simplest ways to indicate what you mean by a particular word is to provide illustrations or examples of exactly what the word refers to. For example, you could employ an **ostensive definition,** which entails simply pointing to the object named. If a visitor from a foreign country were trying to learn English and asked what you meant by "door," you could simply point to a door. You could also illustrate a word's meaning in an **enumerative definition**—that is, by listing, or enumerating, members of the class to which a term refers. For example, to help someone understand the meaning of "baseball player," you could list some famous baseball players: Babe Ruth, Lou Gehrig, Joe DiMaggio, Andy Pettitte. To define "river," you could mention the Mississippi, the Ohio, the Rio Grande, the Susquehanna, and other rivers. Finally, you could help define a word by indicating what **subclasses** the word contains. To define "poetry," for example, you could say "sonnet, limerick, haiku, epic, ode, and the like," adding the last phrase to show that the list is incomplete.

Defining by pointing to the object, listing the members of a class, or providing subclasses is useful, but definitions of this type tend to be partial rather than complete. Your foreign visitor might conclude that a "door" must be made of wood or that anything with hinges is a "door" (lids can have hinges). You could take your visitor on a tour and point to every type of door you come across (elevator doors, sliding glass doors, car doors, and so forth) to provide a complete ostensive definition, but such an exercise is obviously time-consuming. Enumerating can also be partial. Your list of baseball players might give the impression that "baseball player" is synonymous with "Yankee," and your list of categories under "poetry" is likely to be incomplete given the many types of poetry that exist. You could, of course, provide complete lists, and at times it may be possible to do so. Keep in mind, though, that these methods are most helpful not in providing exhaustive lists but in helping you better connect the word to the concrete thing it denotes.

Use a Dictionary   A good dictionary tells what part of speech a word is, how it is commonly pronounced, and where it came from—its ancestry, or **etymology.** Since the meanings of words can change over time, knowing a word's etymology is not always useful, but it will often help us define the word correctly and use it properly. "Automobile," for example, comes from the Greek *autos,* meaning "self," and the French *mobile* (from the Latin *mobilis*), meaning "move." An "automobile" is self-moving or self-propelled. The name "Jeep," a particular automobile, comes from "GP," meaning General Purpose, which was the original Army designation for the now-famous vehicle. Some people say "ambivalent" when they really mean to say "apathetic" (unconcerned). "Ambivalent" comes from the Latin for "both" (*ambi-*) and "vigor" (*valentia*); so to be "ambivalent" is to feel strongly both ways. "Apathy" comes from the Latin prefix *a-*, meaning "not," and from the Greek *pathos,* meaning "suffering" or, more commonly, "feeling." So "apathy" means a lack of feeling. You might feel ambivalent about abortion, but you are probably not apathetic about it.

A final example can be taken from the title of this book. Some people wrongly assume that to be "critical" means to comment negatively or harshly, as in "a parent who is critical of his child." And, in fact, the word has come to mean harsh or severe judgment. But the etymology of "critical" shows that it comes from the Latin *criticus,* which, in turn, comes from the Greek *kritikos,* meaning "able to discern or judge." The same root is found in "criterion," a standard or rule upon which one bases a judgment. A critical thinker must be a discerning judge who applies rules and standards to make a decision. The final verdict does not necessarily have to be harsh or even negative. Parents who are critical might be very pleased with the behavior of their children.

Besides pronunciation and etymology, dictionaries also, obviously, provide definitions. But because they are written in a particular time and place, dictionaries cannot contain all the meanings for each word in our language. Meanings change over time, and new words are added as they become popular. "Gay," for example, means something different today from what it meant fifty years ago, and "Internet" is difficult to find in even the most recent dictionaries, including those published for access on a computer. Dictionaries are best considered history books that describe the way words were used when the dictionary was being written rather than prescribe how we should or must define a word. Furthermore, because dictionaries are written by people, they can show the bias of a particular person or group. A dictionary can also be incomplete, limited in the number of definitions it gives for a word, or just plain incorrect. Considered the best dictionary in English, *The Oxford English Dictionary (OED)* overcomes many of the deficiencies inherent in dictionaries by providing extensive definitions, etymologies, and examples of a word's use throughout history.

Provide a Synonym   You might try defining your terms by supplying **synonyms** that your readers or listeners are more familiar with. The confusion caused by technical jargon, for example, can be lessened if the jargon is accompanied by a synonymous definition. An apprentice carpenter might be puzzled to hear about a chisel's "bezel" until he or she discovers that the bezel is more commonly known as the "bevel," or even more commonly as the "edge," or imprecisely as the "point." Speaking among themselves, teachers might use words such as "assessment" or "inventory." When speaking to parents, teachers might refer instead to "tests." In an argument, a writer could define the word "morality" as meaning "virtuous behavior." Of course, "virtuous" would also have to be defined, a point that shows how careful we must be in using synonyms. There are very few true synonyms in the English language, and the subtle differences between words such as "rob" and "steal" or "excuse" and "justification" prevent us from substituting one for the other without regard to our real intentions. Robbers threaten or use violence to get what they want; someone could steal from you without your knowing it. And although poverty might be an excuse for robbing someone, it is certainly no justification.

Define by Genus and Difference   One of the most useful methods of providing precise definitions is to define by **genus and difference,** a method that lexicographers (dictionary writers) often use to create definitions. One of the ways that words get their meanings is through their differences from other words. We know what "life" means because we know what death is and vice versa; we know what darkness is because we know about light. Imagine that you lived in a world where the sun shone constantly overhead, never rising or setting. You would never know what "night" was simply because no such thing would exist. Interestingly, you would never know what "day" was, either, because it would have no opposite. In fact, the idea of "dayness" wouldn't occur to you. In defining by genus and difference, keep in mind that many of the things of our world have meaning in their distinction, their difference.

In other words, you could define an automobile by describing everything in the world that is not an automobile—furniture, clothes, trees, animals, Pluto, your sister, this book, and on and on. The thing that remains would be an automobile. Obviously, such an exercise would take forever, so the first step in defining by genus and difference is to place your term into a class—the genus—that helps eliminate furniture, clothes, trees, planets, people, and other classes in one fell swoop. An "automobile" belongs not in the class of furniture, and so on, but in the class of vehicles. Now you are left with the much easier task of listing characteristics—the differences—that distinguish an automobile from other objects in the class of vehicles—trucks, golf carts, motorcycles, and so forth. To distinguish an automobile from a truck, you might say that an automobile is intended for the transportation of passengers. Unlike a motorcycle, an automobile usually has four wheels. An internal-combustion engine separates an automobile from a golf cart. Your definition now looks like this: *An automobile is a vehicle that is used to transport passengers and that usually has four wheels and an internal-combustion engine.* You can edit your definition for style: *An automobile is a passenger vehicle that usually has four wheels and an internal-combustion engine.*

Next, ask if your definition could apply to anything that is not an automobile. In other words, is there any thing that *is* a passenger vehicle with four wheels and an internal-combustion engine but is *not* an automobile? You might argue that a gas-powered, four-wheeled car used to transport coal miners (passengers) satisfies the definition, but it is certainly not an automobile, since it travels along rails into the mine. To separate automobiles from coal cars, you could add a distinguishing characteristic to your definition: *An automobile is a passenger vehicle that usually has four wheels and an internal-combustion engine and that is used for transportation on streets, roads, and highways.*

Defining by Genus and Difference

Term	Genus	Difference
Automobile	Vehicle [and so are buses, trucks, bicycles, motorcycles, airplanes, golf carts, the space shuttle, and so on]	To transport passengers [distinguishes an automobile from a truck] Usually has four wheels [distinguishes an automobile from a bicycle, a bus and a motorcycle] With an internal combustion engine [further distinguishes an automobile from bicycles and from other four-wheeled vehicles, such as golf carts] Used for transportation on streets, roadways, and highways [distinguishes an automobile from such things as cars that run on rails]

Smart readers are starting to wonder how long these definitions can become. You may have noticed some other possible problems as well: Does a three-wheeled electric car no longer qualify under my definition? What if I add "with four doors" to the definition, since many cars have four doors? What if I discover that "automobile" has other meanings in other contexts? Keeping a few simple rules in mind will help resolve these issues:

Don't make the definition too broad. A definition of automobile as "*any* vehicle that has four wheels" would be too broad, since it would include golf carts and even wheelchairs; "*any* self-propelled vehicle" could include the space shuttle, and so on.

Don't make the definition too narrow. Giving attributes that are not shared by a large number of the things being defined could mislead the reader. Using words and phrases such as "four-door" or "made of metal" to define "automobile" would exclude cars such as Corvettes, which have two doors and are made in part of fiberglass. Often, adding words such as "usually" or "commonly" allows for the possibility that the definition will not fit every case and helps avoid making the definition too narrow or too broad.

Provide a context. Often, adding a context to your definition narrows your classifications even further. An "error" in mathematics is different from an "error" in baseball. An "apron" in the theater means the part of the stage that extends in front of the curtain, which is different from the apron worn by a cook, the apron at an airport, or the apron of a table.

Try to be objective. Don't let personal preferences or attitudes interfere with your definition. Don't use metaphorical language ("An automobile is a tin can") or emotionally charged language ("An automobile is a smog-producing death trap"). Try to capture the essential attributes of the thing being defined without filtering those attributes through your own personal viewpoint. An objective definition of "socialist" or "capitalist" should not reveal the definition-writer's political beliefs.

Remember your reader or listener. Don't use technical jargon that your reader might not understand or write circular definitions that only confuse the reader. Look at your definition through the eyes of someone who is unfamiliar with the term and who is truly trying to determine its meaning.

It should be noted that one limitation of the genus and difference method is that it can define a word without capturing the true essence of the thing being denoted. One famous example is this definition of a human being: A human being is an *animal* (excludes all inanimate objects and plants) that *walks on two legs* (excludes all four-legged animals, but birds, such as chickens, walk on two legs) and that *has no feathers.* That definition is correct: a human being is, in fact, the only featherless animal that walks on two legs. But it is incomplete and unfair to human beings since it doesn't really capture the essence of being human. Besides their upright stature and lack of feathers, what essential attributes separate humans from all other animals? The capacity for language? The ability to laugh? Critical thinking skills? How would you define "human being"?

The Final Word on Definitions

A good definition can combine several of the methods we have discussed—ostensive, enumerative, etymological, synonymous, and genus and difference—in a complete definition. The following definition includes a synonym, a reference to the word's history, a definition by genus and difference, a list of classes, and several illustrations or examples.

> *Automobile: A motorcar; a self-propelled passenger vehicle that usually has four wheels and an internal-combustion engine and that is used for transportation on streets, roads, and highways. Automobiles include, among others, sedans, coupes, limousines, and sports cars such as the Mazda Miata and the Ford Mustang.*

See the box on the following page for a summary of our discussion of definitions.

Types of Definitions and Strategies for Defining

TYPES

Stipulative: A definition that the writer or speaker has assigned to a term or that has been assigned to a term for the first time. Example: "'The Wild Bunch' means our intramural football team." "I call my little sister 'the gnat.'"

Persuasive: A definition given to a term in an effort to persuade the reader or listener to agree with the writer's or speaker's point of view. Example: "Advertising is the means by which companies persuade unsuspecting consumers to buy defective or unnecessary products."

Lexical: A definition in which terms are defined in the way they are generally used in the language. Example: "Blue jeans are pants made of blue denim."

Precising: A definition in which the writer or speaker qualifies a vague term so that the word's meaning is not left to the interpretation of the reader or listener. Example: "The newly elected governor wants to raise taxes on the rich, which he defines as anyone making over $100,000 dollars a year in take-home pay."

STRATEGIES

Give Illustrations: Define a term by providing illustrations or examples of exactly what the word refers to. An ostensive definition provides a concrete example of the term.

Example: "The capital letter 'a' looks like this: A." An enumerative definition lists members of the class to which the term refers. Example: "The term 'country' refers to France, England, Iraq, Mexico, and so on." Or you can indicate what subclasses the word contains. Example: "Fiction includes short stories, novellas, and novels."

Use a Dictionary: Dictionaries tell what part of speech a word is, how it is commonly pronounced, and where the word comes from—its etymology. Example: "A playwright is not one who writes plays, but one who makes a play the way a wheelwright makes a wheel. The term 'wright' comes from an Old English word, *wryhta,* meaning 'work.'"

Provide a Synonym: Synonyms are words that have the same meaning or nearly the same meaning as the term being defined. Example: "A playwright is a dramatist."

Define by Genus and Difference: Place the term in a class that helps narrow its meaning, and then provide characteristics that distinguish the term from other terms in the same class. Example: "A pen is an instrument that dispenses ink, that is used for writing, and that is held in the hand. A pen, then, is a handheld writing instrument that uses ink."

EXERCISE 4.3

I. In groups of three or four, choose from the list below eight words to define. Using any of the methods we have discussed, or a combination of them, define your chosen words on your own; then, in groups of three or four, compare your definitions. What do your definitions have in common? What makes them unique? Could you come to some agreement on a definition for each of the terms? How important is it that you agree as a group on the definition of some of these terms?

chair	poet	self-defense
sofa	basketball	democracy
pencil	rock and roll	advertising
coat	pop music	racism
jacket	Grunge	patriotism
mother	blues	justice
actor	horror novel	knowledge
sports star	drunk	environmentally
fan (sports)	heart	responsible person
fanatic	missing person	good politician

II. As a group, read and respond to each situation given below. Your answer will depend on how you define the key word in the question. Group members might debate the definitions and the application of the definition to the given situation. Use any strategy for defining terms, or use a combination of strategies. You may have to consult outside sources in deciding on your definitions, and you may want to agree on some contextual details that are not provided in the question. Some students, for example, might argue that the first question depends on how long the couple has been dating.

1. You just caught your boyfriend or girlfriend carrying on a sexually explicit dialogue with someone in an electronic chat room. Has your mate "cheated" on you?

2. As a "computer genius," you can access the college's computer files anytime you like. You can review your transcript, check your medical records, read what your high school guidance counselor said about you, and so forth. All of this information would be provided to you if you asked, but you don't. Can you be accused of "stealing"?

3. A sign posted outside the auditorium reads, "No food or drink in the auditorium." During a lecture, your neighbor is loudly sucking on a lollipop. You remind him that food is not allowed. He tells you he doesn't have "food." Who is right?

4. Jack knows that the college to which he is applying gives preference to minorities. He argues in his application letter that his being a second-generation Irish immigrant distinguishes him from other people applying to the college. Is he a "minority"?

5. Nancy has a paper due tomorrow morning. She has written a very rough, undeveloped draft. Last semester Nancy's roommate, Sharon, wrote a paper on the very same topic. Sharon gives Nancy the paper and tells her to "take as much of it as you want." With Sharon's permission and help, Nancy uses Sharon's paper to develop her own. Is Nancy guilty of "plagiarizing"?

6. An acquaintance of yours was just seen leaving your room with one of your favorite CDs, which you did not give him permission to take. Can he be charged with "robbery"? With "larceny"?

7. Your professor thinks women are far superior to men in every way—intellectually, morally, emotionally, and so forth. Is your professor a "feminist"?

8. The cheerleaders at your school have petitioned to have cheerleading listed as one of the school's sports teams. Is cheerleading a "sport"?

9. One day, out of frustration, your roommate throws a full plate of mashed potatoes against the wall of the room, where, amazingly, it sticks. You get up to remove the plate and potatoes from the wall. "Leave it," your roommate insists. "It says something. It's art." "It's garbage," you reply. Who is right?

10. One day, Professor Smith tells the class a joke he heard on a popular late-night talk show. The joke involves a sexual situation and the punch line is quite offensive. Several students in the room, including a number of women, are clearly shocked by the joke. Could Smith be accused of "sexual harassment?" Does it make a difference if Smith is male or female?

11. Recently a third-grader (age 8) told several off-color jokes to a female classmate. Is this an example of "sexual harassment"?

12. A high school football coach in Florida, upset at the behavior of one of his black players, warned the student not to "act like a street nigger." Many of the coaches, players, parents, and community members have accepted the coach's apology and pointed out that the incident is not typical of the coach, but others insist that the coach's remark indicates that he is "racist." What do you think? Does it make a difference if the coach is white or black?

13. After meeting Brad at a party, Sarah accompanies him to his apartment. After several minutes of kissing on his bed, Brad asks Sarah if she'd like to have sex. She says no, but as they continue to kiss and touch, Brad is persistent in his efforts to persuade Sarah and she finally consents, even though she is not entirely sure she is doing the right thing. Has a "rape" occurred?

14. You are standing in line of about one hundred people of varying ages waiting to buy movie tickets at a multiscreen cinema. Your attention is drawn to a woman who is speaking very loudly to a child of about six who is pleading with the woman to take him to the bathroom. She tells him to "quiet down" several times before slapping him firmly once on the cheek. The force of the slap is equivalent to what you would use to swat a mosquito on your own skin. Has this child been "abused"?

15. In the last three seconds of a professional hockey game, Team A is losing by two goals. A member of Team A skates up behind a player from Team B and swings his stick at the player, hitting him on the side of the head and knocking him unconscious. The player is removed from the rink on a stretcher and taken to the hospital, where doctors find that he has sustained a concussion. His wound requires twenty stitches to close. He is hospitalized for several days. Should the player from Team A be charged with "assault"? (You may wish to consult a dictionary of legal terms.)

EMOTIVE LANGUAGE: SLANTING THE TRUTH

So far in this chapter we have seen how language is used to convey information and defend claims in an argument. We have seen that clarity, precision, objectivity, and clear definitions go a long way toward making ideas comprehensible and claims more convincing. But although we may be careful to avoid vague and ambiguous terms and to define our terms, we aren't always as cautious as we should be when claims are presented to us, and we sometimes find ourselves falling under the sway of those whose masterful use of language we find hard to resist. Consider the way college brochures are written. What follows is a fictional illustration assembled from the brochures of several colleges and universities; you might recognize some of the language.

> Most people, when visiting our campus, say Wexford feels like a college should feel: warm and welcoming—a community atmosphere. Wexford's faculty and staff form the kind of close relationships with students that challenge them to their full potential. Students appreciate the personal attention in the classroom, the relatively small classes, and the dedicated faculty. Our residence halls provide a sense of family from your first days here. You will find activities to suit your personal style, from the performing arts to competitive sports, from volunteer service to student-run organizations.
>
> Students are involved and enjoy being at Wexford. Nearly nine of every ten freshmen return for their sophomore year—well above the national average. Parents and students comment frequently on how friendly and professional the people are at Wexford.
>
> From the innovative freshman orientation program to the ongoing support for planning a career, you will find your four years at Wexford marked by a sincere interest in both your personal and your academic growth.

A "dedicated faculty," "close relationships," a "sense of family," the "relatively small classes," "well above the national average," "innovative"—all these words and phrases have been carefully chosen for their intended impact on the reader beyond their literal meaning. The words are selected not so much for the information they convey as for their **emotive force,** the appeal they make to readers' feelings, desires, and needs. Emotive language more overtly reveals a writer's attitude and feelings toward the subject than precise, neutral, and more objective language does, and is intended to create in the reader those same *feelings and attitude* toward the subject rather than to increase the reader's *knowledge* about it. "Emotive" is the adjective form of "emotion," which comes from the same Latin word, *movere,* from which we get "motion" and "move." You have no doubt heard the expressions "moved to tears" and "moved by your kind words." Emotive language in an argument is intended to rile up, to *move* readers by agitating, disturbing, angering or exciting them. This is usually accomplished by creating strong feelings such as fear, rage, disgust, joy, and desire. Sometimes readers are literally moved to pound the table or write their congressperson. Sometimes the language is overt and obvious: "You should write to your idiotic, insane, corrupt senator and tell him . . .". Such language is easy to recognize as unfair, and intelligent people are seldom persuaded by such appeals. But emotive appeals in arguments are often far less overt and contain subtle evaluative comments that can trick us out of critical thought.

Look again at the college brochure. The phrase "relatively small classes," for example, suggests that such small classes are a desirable thing. Instead of telling us precisely how many students are in an average class, the writer assures us that the classes are "relatively small," which in this case gives us no information whatsoever. Relative to what? The Los Angeles Coliseum? The writer doesn't exactly lie about the college; he or she just slants the truth to a degree that makes the college more attractive. The writer could easily have said that the "faculty do the jobs they are paid for," or that "the orientation program was created by the staff," but "dedicated" and "innovative" sound so much better and are almost guaranteed to create a warm feeling in the receptive reader and to move him or her to approve of the college and perhaps apply. The danger is that we might believe that information has been conveyed, when in truth we have learned nothing factual.

In some cases, the slant is so pronounced that the truth is bent to its breaking point. What if the faculty in the next brochure are "devoted" to the students, or "passionate" or even "fanatical" about their teaching? Assessing the truth of premises and claims—a routine practice for those thinking critically—requires that we be on the lookout for language clearly intended to evoke our emotions, encourage our business, or ensure our passive acceptance of the claim.

The Emotive Power of Words

The emotive power of a word can come from what the word *denotes* (or literally means). If someone tells you that a child was "punched," you might find yourself moved to disgust or even action at hearing a word that means "hit forcefully with the closed fist." But emotive meaning also comes from the word's *connotation*—the images and feelings that are associated with the word. The word "waterfall," for example, denotes (or means literally) the steep descent of water from a high point, but it also connotes (or suggests) power, strength, the beauty of nature, island paradises, and so forth. Connotations of words come from many sources, including people's experiences, the use of the word in the culture (in poems, for instance, or in advertisements), the way the word is used as a symbol or a metaphor in various religions, and even the word's sound.

To see just how language can generate feelings and reactions by connotation and sound, consider the names of any number of motor vehicles currently on the market: Aurora, Blazer, Bravado, Breeze, Camaro, Catera, Concorde, Crown Victoria, Expedition, Explorer, Integra, Intrigue, Mustang, Ranger, Regency, Sebring, Sierra, Sonoma, Taurus, Voyager, Windstar. Several of those names are chosen for what they might suggest. The names Ranger or Explorer or Blazer, for example, let the prospective buyer know what the vehicle can best be used for and suggest a feeling of strength and adventure. Other names suggest wealth and status (Crown Victoria and Regency), speed and privilege (Concorde), wild independence (Mustang), or youthful freedom (Breeze). Other names though, are chosen entirely for their sound. Because there is no conventional meaning for Sebring or Catera, consumers are simply expected to associate those words with something positive. "Sebring" has a luxurious sound and so might suggest elegance and refinement. What does "Catera" suggest?

People's names also evoke certain reactions independent of the names' meanings. Some names become more common simply because of the connotations—the suggested meanings—they carry. The name "Tiffany," for example, is associated with beauty, courtliness, or artistry that probably results from its association with the jewelry store founded in 1837 by Charles Tiffany or the decorative glass designed by Louis Comfort Tiffany. But "Tiffany" as a first name has nothing to do with those two individuals. The *word* "tiffany" means transparent gauze made of silk or muslin. The *name* "Tiffany" probably comes from an obsolete French word, *tiphanie,* which comes from a Latin word, *theophanie,* meaning the appearance of a god to a human being, a meaning we still see in the word "epiphany." If anything, the name Tiffany has more to do with religious inspiration and divine manifestation than with watches, earrings, or lamp shades. Similarly, two names very popular among children born in the late 1990s—Taylor and Tyler—though they seem unusual and distinguished, come from "tailor" (one who sews clothing) and from "tiler" (one who tiles, or shingles, roofs). Surely, parents who give their children these names don't do so because of the literal meanings of the words.

EXERCISE 4.4

I. In groups of three, come up with names for several new cars—a massive luxury sedan, an SUV for the family, an off-road vehicle for the sports-minded, an affordable four-door, and a sleek, sporty coupe. Then choose one of your new cars and write an ad to sell the car

II. You have probably noticed that the builders of shopping malls and housing developments often use emotive language when naming their facilities. It is not uncommon to see such names as "Meadowbrook Farms Shopping Plaza" and "Sunnydale Apartments" in the most unlikely places. Even cemeteries get in on the emotive act ("Riverview Memorial Gardens"). Discuss with a group of your classmates some of the names you have seen on housing complexes, shopping malls, and cemeteries in your hometown or college area. You might want to discuss the reasons for these names and perhaps even the irony involved in their creation—how, for example, a deer hasn't been seen alive in "Deer Run Community Acres" for over twenty years.

Let's look now at more sophisticated examples of the use of words to slant the truth and evoke predictable responses from a reader. Whereas advertisers use words deliberately to get us to buy their products or services, not everyone is so aggressively manipulative. It is up to critical readers to keep their eyes and minds open to the use of connotative language (language that evokes certain images or emotions) in all forums, including supposedly neutral sources such as newspapers, magazines, and encyclopedias. Read the following passages from *Time* magazine and *The Philadelphia Inquirer,* both of which describe the launch of a space shuttle.

Time describes the launch of *Discovery,* the first shuttle to be launched after the *Challenger* disaster in January of 1986. The *Inquirer* describes the launch of the former Soviet Union's first shuttle.

From *Time*

As the countdown clock flashed out the number of seconds until lift-off, the eyes of an entire nation focused on Launch Pad 39-B and the gleaming white shuttle Discovery, flanked by its two solid rocket boosters and clinging to the side of a giant, rust-colored external fuel tank. . . .

Finally, spectators joined in for the last 15 seconds of countdown, the engines ignited and the shuttle rose majestically from the pad, carrying its crew of five veteran astronauts. Over the space center's loud-speakers came the triumphant announcement: "Americans return to space, as Discovery clears the tower." But the cheers were muted as the crowd—many with clenched fists, gritted teeth and teary eyes—nervously watched the spacecraft rise on its pillar of flame, then begin its roll out over the Atlantic.[12]

From *The Philadelphia Inquirer*

For the 6 a.m. launch, Buran could be seen piggy-backed on the white Energia rocket, towering against the pre-dawn sky at the Baikonur Cosmodrome in the central Asian republic of Kazakhstan. As the countdown neared zero, the rocket was enveloped first in smoke and then in a giant ball of flame as it lumbered off the launch pad and into the dark blue sky.

Three and a half hours and two orbits later, the gleaming white Buran with its black underbelly came back into the television camera's view. Buran glided on automatic pilot until it bumped onto the specially built runway stretching across the vast, flat steppes a few miles from Baikonur.[13]

The difference in the language used in these two accounts is obvious. Whereas the American shuttle rises "majestically" on a "pillar of flame," the Soviet shuttle "lumber[s] off the launch pad," on "a giant ball of flame." The American shuttle, "gleaming white," "cling[s]" to its fuel tank; the Soviet shuttle "can be seen piggy-backed" on its white rocket, and we are reminded of the "black underbelly" when it lands. The differences in these two descriptions are truly amazing because the Soviet space shuttle, aside from the national markings it carried and the fact that it was imperceptibly smaller, looked precisely the same as the American space shuttle and lifted off in an identical manner. In other words, if the two shuttles had had no flags and such to indicate their countries of origin, an observer would have seen no difference between them. Why, then, does NASA's shuttle "rise majestically," whereas the Soviets' "lumbers"? Because both of these launches took place during the

Cold War, and because *Discovery* marked a return to space after a national tragedy, the shuttle lifting off from Cape Canaveral appeared to an American writer much more thrilling than the liftoff of the shuttle from the Baikonur Cosmodrome. The way language is used to direct our perceptions and influence our reactions is clear in these two passages. In fact, although no description is given of the landing of the American shuttle, we know that, whereas the Soviet shuttle "bumped" onto the runway, ours surely _____ (fill in the blank).

The test for emotive language is not whether a reader or listener is emotionally moved by the words in an argument. Some words have inescapable connotations, and an audience's reactions are often individual and unpredictable. The word "mother," for example, which means, simply and precisely, a female parent, will stir up positive images and feelings in many people and may evoke negative reactions in others. But even though these associations are inescapable, a writer who uses the word "mother" in an argument may have no intention of evoking the reader's emotions and may simply be denoting a female parent—nothing more or less: "Single mothers returning to work have difficulty finding affordable day care."

The test for emotive words is, instead, whether the writer or speaker *appears* to be using the word unfairly to generate predictable feelings in an audience or to manipulate the audience into either agreeing with the argument or overlooking its flaws. Much depends, of course, on the context and the tone of the argument. For example, a young man who says to his girlfriend, "Don't mother me," intends the word in a negative sense and appears to be claiming that his girlfriend's attention diminishes his independence. One way to distinguish between fair and unfair use of an emotive word is to ask whether the use of the word needs to be defended. No one would challenge the use of "mother" in the first example, since a woman (whether single or married) with a child is, in fact, a mother. On the other hand, the girlfriend in the second example might say, "How do I 'mother' you?" or "What do you mean by 'mother'?"

The best and simplest way to determine whether words in an argument are unfairly emotive is to ask whether the words could be replaced with neutral words and phrases with no damage to whatever information is being conveyed. Good examples often come from the sports world. A writer will claim that one team "slaughtered"—or "annihilated," "destroyed," "crushed," "embarrassed," and so forth—another team that in a more neutral sentence simply "lost" or was "beaten." A writer who chooses "slaughtered" for "beat" is slanting the statement to evoke the reader's emotions.

Just as "slaughtered" could be replaced by "beat" in a sports report, emotive words in an argument can often be replaced by neutral ones. Consider the following statement:

Rush Limbaugh's daily monologues are little more than repetitive recitations that reveal his blind adherence to a regressive political agenda.

"Monologue" (connoting selfishness and boredom), "recitations" (suggesting that little original thinking goes into the commentary), "blind adherence" (connoting a failure to see clearly and independently), and "regressive" (moving backward) are all examples of emotive language. The writer clearly hopes that the reader will accept this unflattering description of Limbaugh.

But the statement could be written in a less emotive, nearly neutral manner:

> In his daily comments, Rush Limbaugh voices his support of a conservative political philosophy.

In fact, the point of the sentence could be expressed in very positive terms:

> In his daily observations, Rush Limbaugh reaffirms his faith in traditional values and social relationships.

The writer of the first example would certainly be unhappy with our revisions, since the writer's anger has been diluted in the first one and turned into approval in the second. Clearly, the revisions say something other than what the writer intended, and since writers must be allowed to voice their opinions, we can't expect that they will speak only in factual, nonevaluative, nonemotive language. Besides, it would be very boring if they did. It is important to remember that it is the job of the *reader* to remain wary of emotive appeals, to determine whether the emotive language is substituting for a reasoned support of the claims made in the argument and whether further support would be necessary before the claim should be accepted. Before we accept the argument made by the writer of the first sentence above, we might ask, "Why do you say that Limbaugh's adherence is 'blind'?" "Why do you use the word 'regressive' in reference to conservative politics?" and so forth. In presenting our own arguments, we can stem our tendency to use overly inflated emotive language and recognize evaluative language when we use it, being sure to defend our judgments and opinions.

As you will recall from the beginning of this chapter, we all differ in the way we perceive the world and the people around us. I might report to you that "a government bureaucrat was cold and officious toward the persistent taxpayer," whereas you might have seen "a public servant treat a belligerent citizen with calm, objective professionalism." When it is important to know *exactly, factually* how the worker acted, a reader or listener must get beyond the reactions to "cold and officious" or "calm and objective." In fact, when assessing the truth of claims couched in emotive terms, we need to be especially wary of personal attacks accomplished through subtle emotive language. The philosopher Bertrand Russell demonstrated our tendency to use emotive rather than neutral language when we compare ourselves with others, so that about ourselves we say, "I am firm," whereas someone else, we claim, "is obstinate." If we really don't like the person, he's "pigheaded." We generally spend very little time defining or precising those terms. We usually hope that our listeners will simply agree with us.

When determining whether language is emotive or not, ask the following questions:

1. Is the term—even though it may have emotive power—actually an accurate and precise way to describe an event, an idea, a person, and so forth? "Slaughter" is not always manipulative if it is used correctly—to describe events in warfare, for example.
2. Does the writer appear to be manipulating the reader's reactions or attempting to move the reader toward feelings of rage, fear, joy, desire, and so forth? What other evidence in the context of the argument supports the conclusion that the writer's language is unfairly emotive? Be sure to separate your personal reactions to certain words from reactions that the writer appears to be aiming at.
3. Should the writer be expected to defend the term? A political candidate who calls his opponent a "fascist" would have to define the term and show how the opponent's words and actions fit that definition.
4. Is there a more neutral way to make the same point?
5. How important to the argument, information, or explanation is the suspected emotive language? We don't usually quibble over the emotive naming of cars. Nor should we deny a writer some leeway in an argument for the expression of feelings and attitudes.

EXERCISE 4.5

I. Look at the underlined words in the following sentences and think of three or four words you could use to describe the action. Then discuss what differences are suggested by the words you have listed. The first is done as an example.

1. Bill used a blunt instrument to <u>make contact with</u> Bob. (hit, strike, bash, bludgeon) "Hit" and "strike" suggest less force and aggression; "bash" and "bludgeon" connote a greater impact.
2. She <u>said</u>, "I don't love you."
3. "I want ice cream," the child <u>said</u>.
4. "Do this, please," she <u>asked</u>.
5. "Did you <u>look at</u> that woman?"
6. Out of anger, he <u>damaged</u> the CD player.
7. He <u>held on to</u> her arm.
8. You were <u>not rational</u> to do that.
9. I am a <u>firm believer</u> in that cause.
10. He is a man <u>without feeling</u>.
11. She is a woman of <u>inaction</u>.
12. He became <u>angry</u>.
13. The boss <u>approved of</u> her work.

14. You're <u>thinking only of yourself</u>.
15. His actions were <u>inappropriate</u>.

II. For each of the emotive words and phrases below, first determine what re-action (positive or negative) the emotive language would produce in a reader or listener. Then supply a word (or a phrase) that is more neutral than the under-lined language, or a word (or a phrase) that would evoke a reaction *opposite* to the intended one, or both a neutral and an opposite word if possible. It may not be possible in some cases to provide both a neutral word and an opposite word.

> **Example**
>
> "My sister is <u>skinny</u>." The word "skinny" would probably evoke a negative reac-tion, since it might suggest poor health or malnourishment. A more neutral word would be "thin." "Slender" might produce a positive reaction.

> **Example**
>
> "My opponent always <u>wraps himself in the flag</u> on issues concerning veterans." The phrase sounds very negative, since it suggests that the opponent is insin-cere or that he is playing to the crowd's prejudices. A more neutral or even pos-tive word might be "patriotic": "My opponent is very patriotic when it comes to issues concerning veterans."

> **Example**
>
> "My uncle has decided to <u>take a chance</u> on the stock market." The phrase "take a chance" shows that the speaker has a positive attitude toward the uncle and apparently wants others to feel the same way. But what if the speaker had said, "My uncle decided to risk everything on the stock market"? The reaction would be less positive and perhaps even negative.

1. He's a <u>dreamer</u>.
2. I can't believe they're <u>forcing these contracts down our throats</u>.
3. That's the <u>stench</u> of his cooking.
4. He <u>dresses well</u>.
5. My son <u>tries to avoid confrontations</u>.
6. The dorm room is filled with <u>cheap</u> furniture.
7. My father picked up a few <u>old treasures</u> at the flea market.
8. The driver was clearly <u>perturbed</u>.
9. She decided to <u>think for a week or two</u> before deciding.
10. The student <u>stood up for himself</u> when questioned by the security guard.
11. He <u>applied a liberal amount</u> of cologne in preparation for his date.
12. I was a <u>bit of a radical</u> when I was young.
13. The new employee was <u>assertive</u> with her boss.
14. Microsoft <u>cornered the market</u> on software.
15. Salespeople often <u>take advantage of</u> my grandmother because she <u>trusts everyone</u> so much.
16. The Democrats' new tax <u>scheme</u> will never work.
17. I feel sorry for people living under such a <u>regime</u>.
18. The <u>activists targeted</u> several key political figures with antismoking <u>protests</u>.
19. Their <u>tactics</u> are not going to win them much support.
20. I'm sorry, sir, but that's our <u>policy</u>.

III. Identify the emotive language in the following passages. Indicate which emotive terms you feel are manipulative and which you feel are appropriate.

1. *From an ad for a home:* Charming, cozy three-bedroom Cape Cod in an older neighborhood, wall-to-wall carpeting throughout, lower-level recreation room opening onto large deck, modern kitchen, new roof, garage, needs some tender loving care.

2. *From a personal ad:* DWF, mature, petite, attractive, spiritual, intelligent business professional, occasional drinker, enjoys quiet evenings, serious movies, and long novels.

3. Most Canadian physicians who are themselves in need of surgery, for example, scurry across the border to get it done right: the American way. They have found, through experience, that state medical care is too expensive, too slow and inefficient, and, most important, it doesn't provide adequate care for most people. (Rush Limbaugh, *See, I Told You So,* p.153)

4. *Q.* What chance of success do you give the union of Angelina Jolie and Billy Bob Thornton? (J. Klugge, San Antonio, Texas)
   A. If we were bookmakers in Las Vegas, where the two tied the knot on May 5, we'd set the odds at 1000 to 1. The wedding was scheduled just two hours in advance by Jolie, 24, an admitted bisexual, and Thornton, 44, an oddball who publicly praised actress Laura Dern, his longtime lover, then dumped her for Jolie. Thornton is a four-time loser at the altar whose previous wife, Pietra, told us in 1997 that he was guilty of spousal abuse. (He denied the charges.) And Jolie already has walked away from one brief marriage, to actor Jonny Lee Miller *(Trainspotting).* Incidentally, Jolie's brother, Jamie Haven—whose on-the-mouth kisses with her at the Oscars spawned rumors of incest—didn't attend the nuptials. ("Walter Scott's Personality Parade," *Parade Magazine,* June 18 2000)

5. Leave it to the People for the Ethical Treatment of Animals (PETA) to try and spoil the party for all of us fishing families.
   The animal rights group traipsed across the country last week in an attempt to disrupt National Fishing Week activities and indoctrinate school children. Circumventing parents and teachers, PETA members stood outside schoolyards and distributed "Look, Don't Hook" toy binoculars to kids. A 6-foot-tall, antifishing mascot, "Gill the Fish," hovered nearby while activists spread the animal rights' gospel.
   . . . Kids, take note: This kind of self-indulgent terrorism by animal rights activists is truly "cruel – not cool." (Michelle Malkin, "PETA, Go Jump in the Lake," *Philadelphia Daily News,* June 19, 2000)

6. Many of the problems of our schools derive from the kind of people who are teaching in them. Throughout the 20th century, there has been a tug of war between the public, who want their children taught intellectual skills, and "educators" who want to do fun things, manipulate children's emotions, indoctrinate them with political correctness or do other things that make the teachers' job easier and make them feel important in saving the world or shaping society. (Thomas Sowell, "Why Most Teachers Are Failures at Their Job," Wilkes-Barre *Times Leader,* June 18, 2000)

7. . . . " Big Daddy" is easily the laziest, most slapdash and altogether crummy picture Sandler's done to date. The writing—by Sandler, Tim Herlihy, and Steve Franks—is so cornball and comically feeble it makes "The Waterboy" play like a lost masterpiece of Shavian wit.

And the way this film treats children is contemptible. . . .

[W]hen "Big Daddy" attempts to leaven the gross jokes with Sandler's ingratiating, aw-shucks smarm, it loses what little appeal it has.

A perfunctory love interest for Sonny pops up in the person of a lawyer, played by Joey Lauren Adams. It all ends up before a judge, of course, with Sandler delivering a maudlin courtroom soliloquy that's impressive only in that grown-ups get paid big bucks to write dialogue this lame. (Rod Dreher, "Big Daddy A Big Dud," *New York Post Online*. Accessed May 5, 2000; available online at http://208.248.87.252/062599/9858.htm).

8. Women, unless they were quite wealthy, have always worked: in the house and out of the house, on the farm, in factories, sometimes caring for other people's kids, often leaving their own with the family herd under grandma's practiced eye. I've read that early in this century, when desperate families flooded into cities seeking work, leaving their rural support systems behind, female factory workers had to bundle their toddlers up on boards and hang them on hooks on the walls. At break time they'd unswaddle the kids and feed them. I like to mention this to anyone who suggests that modern day care is degrading the species." (Barbara Kingsolver, "The Household Zen," *High Tide in Tucson: Essays from Now or Never,* 1996).

9. Five years after a world war has been won, men's hearts should anticipate a long peace, and men's minds should be free from the heavy weight that comes with war. But this is not such a period—for this is not a period of peace. This is a time of the "cold war." This is a time when all the world is split into two vast, increasingly hostile armed camps—a time of a great armaments race. . . .

The reason why we find ourselves in a position of impotency is not because our only powerful potential enemy has sent men to invade our shores, but rather because of the traitorous actions of those who have been treated so well by this Nation. It has not been the less fortunate or members of minority groups who have been selling this Nation out, but rather those who have had all the benefits that the wealthiest nation on earth has had to offer—the finest homes, the finest college education, and the finest jobs in Government we can give.

This is glaringly true in the State Department. There the bright young men who are born with silver spoons in their mouths are the ones who have been the worst. . . . In my opinion the State Department, which is one of the most important government departments, is thoroughly infested with Communists.

I have in my hand 57 cases of individuals who would appear to be either card carrying members or certainly loyal to the Communist Party, but who nevertheless are still helping to shape our foreign policy. . . .

I know that you are saying to yourself, "Well, why doesn't the Congress

do something about it?" Actually, ladies and gentlemen, one of the important reasons for the graft, the corruption, the dishonesty, the disloyalty,
the treason in high Government positions—one of the most important
reasons why this continues is a lack of moral uprising on the part of the
140,000,000 American people. In the light of history, however, this is not
hard to explain.

It is the result of an emotional hang-over and a temporary moral lapse
which follows every war. It is the apathy to evil which people who have
been subjected to the tremendous evils of war feel. As the people of the
world see mass murder, the destruction of defenseless and innocent people,
and all of the crime and lack of morals which go with war, they become
numb and apathetic. It has always been thus after war.

However, the morals of our people have not been destroyed. They still
exist. This cloak of numbness and apathy has only needed a spark to re-
kindle them. Happily, this spark has finally been supplied. . . .

[This] moral uprising . . . will end only when the whole sorry mess of
twisted, warped thinkers are swept from the national scene so that we may
have a new birth of national honesty and decency in government." (Senator
Joseph McCarthy, Remarks, *Congressional Record*. Originally "Speech Delivered to the Women's Club of Wheeling, West Virginia, 1950)

10. We have waited for more than 340 years for our constitutional and God-
    given rights. The nations of Asia and Africa are moving with jetlike speed
    toward gaining political independence, but we still creep at horse-and-
    buggy pace toward gaining a cup of coffee at a lunch counter. Perhaps it is
    easy for those who have never felt the stinging darts of segregation to say,
    "Wait." But when you have seen vicious mobs lynch your mothers and fa-
    thers at will and drown your sisters and brothers at whim, when you have
    seen hate-filled policemen curse, kick, and even kill your black brothers
    and sisters; when you see the vast majority of your twenty million Negro
    brothers smothering in an airtight cage of poverty in the midst of an
    affluent society; when you suddenly find your tongue twisted and your
    speech stammering as you seek to explain to your six-year-old daughter
    why she can't go to the public amusement park that has just been advertised
    on television, and see tears welling up in her eyes when she is told that
    Funtown is closed to colored children, and see ominous clouds of inferior-
    ity beginning to form in her little mental sky, and see her beginning to dis-
    tort her personality by developing an unconscious bitterness toward white
    people; when you have to concoct an answer for a five-year-old son who
    is asking, "Daddy, why do white people treat colored people so mean?";
    when you take a cross-country drive and find it necessary to sleep night
    after night in the uncomfortable corners of your automobile because no
    motel will accept you; when you are humiliated day in and day out by nag-
    ging signs reading "white" and "colored"; when your first name becomes
    "nigger," your middle name becomes "boy" (however old you are) and
    your last name becomes "John," and your wife and mother are never given
    the respected title "Mrs."; when you are harried by day and haunted by

night by the fact that you are a Negro, living constantly at tiptoe stance, never quite knowing what to expect next, and are plagued with inner fears and outer resentments; when you are forever fighting a degenerating sense of "nobodiness"—then you will understand why we find it difficult to wait. There comes a time when the cup of endurance runs over, and men are no longer willing to be plunged into the abyss of despair. I hope, sirs, you can understand our legitimate and unavoidable impatience." (Martin Luther King, Jr., "Letter from Birmingham Jail," 1963)

IV.   Divide into groups of four. Each group is to select a name from the following list, and each member of the group is to look up the name in an encyclopedia, making sure that no two members of a single group use the same encyclopedia. After the group members have done their research, the group reassembles and compares notes on how the various encyclopedias portrayed their topic. Compare, especially, the language used by the writers of the encyclopedia entries. Some writers may focus on different aspects of the person's life, but does the language reveal anything about the attitude of the writer toward the subject?

> John Kennedy
> John Brown
> Malcolm X
> Benedict Arnold
> Elizabeth Cady Stanton
> Martin Luther King, Jr.

Now do the same with newspapers. Choose a contemporary issue and read about it in four different newspapers. What differences in language can you find? Many daily papers can be found on the Internet. You can find them by starting at http://www.ajr.newslink.org, an index of almost 4,000 newspapers and magazines on the Internet.

EUPHEMISMS AND POLITICAL CORRECTNESS

Very often in our communications with one another, we avoid language that might offend, upset, or insult our listeners or readers. For example, when consoling a friend who has suffered a death in the family, we might refer to that death as a "passing away" or "passing on": "I'm sorry your uncle has passed on," we say, because "I'm sorry your uncle died" seems too blunt or because "died" seems so final, whereas "passing" connotes moving to another place. Whatever our reasons, when we choose a more gentle and less negative word over those we feel would be offensive or too direct, we are speaking in **euphemisms:** mild, comforting or evasive words that take the place of harsh, blunt, or taboo words. Many euphemisms exist to describe actions and places associated with bodily functions. "Bodily function" is itself a euphemism, and so are words and phrases such as "the facilities," "restroom," "bathroom," and "powder room." In a strange place, we would hesitate to ask for the "toilet," but in England, asking for the "restroom" will bring you strange looks and an unwelcome delay in the response. When you have "to go" (a euphemism) in London, ask for the "toilet," a word that is itself a euphemism that still exists in American usage in such phrases as "toilet water." It is no surprise that many everyday euphemisms are used to cover up our most private actions; perhaps we believe we lend some measure of dignity to our lives if we talk about our instincts, drives, and needs in more refined and civilized language.

There is nothing wrong with using euphemisms to make us more comfortable in "polite society." But a critical thinker should be aware that pleasant or vague language is often used to hide reality or to avoid facing the truth. For example, knowing that the word "downsizing"—itself a euphemism for "firing"—can evoke fear and anger from workers or citizens, corporations and the United States government often substitute language that, because it is confusing or overly technical, does not immediately generate negative responses. Sometimes the word is a clear synonym for "downsizing." For example, "rightsizing" has been used by executives in many firms to suggest that the number of employees had grown to an excessive number and that trimming that number would return the workforce to its "right size." So although these companies were, in fact, downsizing, they avoided, at least momentarily, the negative results of using that word. Other companies have used even more creative euphemisms. General Motors instituted a "career transition program"; Wal-Mart began a "normal payroll adjustment"; National Semiconductor called its efforts at downsizing "reshaping"; Tandem Computers called it "reducing duplication"; and Procter and Gamble, in perhaps the most pleasant-sounding euphemism, called it "strengthening global effectiveness."[14] In all these cases, the companies were scaling back their workforce. They were downsizing.

One of the discoveries of the twentieth century is the enormous variety of ways of compelling language to lie.
—Jules Henry

Government employees and politicians are notorious for using euphemisms. The military of the United States, for example, has referred to civilian casualties as "collateral damage" and has labeled soldiers "expendable resources." Enemy troops are sometimes called "soft targets." Soldiers who die by "friendly fire" have been accidentally killed by their own forces. The word "retreat" would never be uttered among the military elite, but "strategic redeployment" would be. When President Jimmy Carter authorized an attempt to rescue hostages being held in Iran, an attempt that failed miserably and resulted in the death of several soldiers, he announced to the nation that the mission had been an "incomplete success." After President Bush raised taxes, in violation of his famous "read my lips" promise not to, he explained that the new taxes were not taxes at all but "revenue enhancements." Not every euphemism is used in an effort to hide the truth or to bamboozle audiences, and some writers simply use synonyms to avoid repetition. But when euphemisms are used in a deliberate effort to confuse the audience or evade the truth, a critical thinker can call the lie what it is.

> ## Critical Thinking Lapse
>
> After his election to the highest Texas court that hears criminal appeals, Steve Mansfield admitted to *Texas Lawyer* a host of campaign lies, among them his vast criminal-court experience (he is an insurance and tax lawyer), that he was born in Texas (Massachusetts) and that he dated a woman who died (she is still alive). Mansfield called these and other claims "puffery" and "exaggerations" and promised to stop now that he is one of the state's highest-ranking judges.[15]

In the past several years, euphemisms for various people and groups have proliferated. It is not unusual to hear that the school has hired several "custodial engineers" or that the local market is looking to hire "meat cutters." It seems that no one wants to be a janitor or a butcher any longer. In many cases, this use of euphemisms has been an attempt to find language more precise than the words commonly used. For example, although someone confined to a wheelchair may face some difficulty getting around, the term "crippled" or "disabled" strikes many people as inaccurate in describing the wheelchair-bound, who are often very resourceful in overcoming common obstacles and who can lead lives as productive as anyone else's provided that their needs are considered in the design of buildings and transportation. In other words, "disability" might be more the result of obstacles placed in the way than a quality inherent in those people, who because of their circumstances, must attempt to negotiate those obstacles. For some people, then, the word "challenged" more accurately describes the condition of the wheelchair-bound. Because we often begin to perceive people by the words we use to describe them, calling someone "challenged" rather than "disabled" can have the positive result of changing our perceptions.

Other attempts have been made to use more precise language in describing human beings. The phrase "people of color" has gained some popularity among those who consider it more exact than "black" to denote the diverse groups of nonwhites in the United States, and "Native American" is more accurate than "Indian." "Firefighter" is more precise than "fireman" if that fire-fighting human being's name is Barbara. There is little danger in using words such as these, and, in fact, doing so only improves our way of communicating and may even help keep the peace.

But perhaps we have gone too far in some regards. What was once an effort at accuracy has in some respects become excessive. The term "political correctness" was coined to indicate the almost ridiculous extremes to which some people have gone to avoid using language that might offend or insult. In this case, politically correct language can be euphemistic. Take, for example, the term "urban," which is used by some contemporary writers in place of "black" or "African American." Reviews now often refer to "urban" films or

THE WIZARD OF ID   Brant parker and Johnny hart

By permission of Johnny Hart and Creators Syndicate, Inc.

"urban" themes rather than saying that the film portrays an African American cast of characters confronting racial issues. The use of the term "urban" betrays an effort on the writer's part to remain politically correct. Similarly, writers often refer to the "economically disadvantaged" rather than the "poor," or say that someone is "chemically dependent" rather than a "drug addict." Such use of euphemisms, however, may hide the real tragedy of poverty or addiction. Critical thinkers should strive to remain aware of euphemisms that conceal reality and should make every effort in their own writing to use words that are accurate and precise.

EXERCISE 4.6

In groups of three or more, discuss which word from each of the following pairs you think is more accurate. Which word in the pair would you prefer to use? Which would you prefer to see used by writers and speakers? How would the context of the word influence your answers to the previous questions? How would the context influence your judgment? The words in the right column might be considered euphemisms or politically correct terms.

convict	socially separated
retarded	mentally challenged
learning-disabled	self-paced cognitive ability
old, elderly	senior citizen
used car	pre-owned car
Oriental	Asian
stewardess	flight attendant
mankind	humanity
fat	full-figured
deaf	hearing impaired
chairman	chairperson

cheating	academic dishonesty
ghetto	culturally deprived area
sweat	perspiration
false teeth	dentures
job	career
musician	recording artist
lying	creating a credibility gap
undertaker/mortician	funeral director
pimples	blemishes
pornography	adult entertainment
tooth pulled	tooth extracted
blockaded	quarantined
bombed	pacified
secretary	administrative assistant

Summary

1. We use language to label and control our world, to reveal to others how we see things, and to influence others to see the world the way we do. When we read arguments we need to remember that a writer is trying both to inform us and to influence us.

2. In assessing claims, we need to ask two sets of questions:
   a. Is the language an accurate or factual reflection of the real, historical events, things, ideas, people, and so forth to which the claim refers? In other words, has the writer or speaker correctly called things what they are?
   b. Is the language a *reflection of the writer's point of view (including attitude, opinions, beliefs, evaluations, judgments, and feelings)* toward the events, objects, ideas, people, and so forth to which the claim refers? Has the writer or speaker defended a point of view, or has he or she merely slanted reality in an apparent effort to evoke a particular response from us?

3. How we use certain words can depend on many factors: where we are from, our attitudes and values, our experiences, our audience, the context in which we are writing or speaking. In some cases, our words are very subjective, revealing something about ourselves. In other cases, we struggle to find language that more objectively denotes experience. Often, we use language that contains a personal judgment.

4. Failing to be precise can lead to miscommunication. *Vague* words are fuzzy or inexact and have no distinct meaning. *Overgenerality* occurs when our language is unspecific in certain contexts. *Ambiguous* words have two or more distinct meanings in a particular context, making it difficult if

not impossible for the reader or listener to decide which is intended. Ambiguity can also be caused by faulty sentence structure.

5. Very often, good arguments will depend on the precise definition of words and phrases that opponents might define differently.

6. Definitions can be *stipulative* (a word's meaning is determined by the writer), *persuasive* (the writer reveals a point of view in the definition), *lexical* (the word is defined in the way it is generally used), and *precising* (a vague word is clarified). A writer might provide concrete examples of what is meant by a word by pointing to the object being defined *(ostensive),* by listing members of the class *(enumerative),* or by indicating what *subclasses* the word contains. Etymological definitions give a word's history, whereas synonymous definitions provide more familiar equivalent terms. A definition by genus and difference records the characteristics that distinguish one thing from the other things in its class.

7. Good critical thinkers are careful to avoid vague language and to define terms, but they are also aware of the manipulations of language, especially language intended to evoke emotional responses that trick us out of attention and skepticism. Even sources we expect to be objective may contain language that subtly edges us toward a particular, predictable feeling or attitude.

8. Euphemisms are mild or evasive words that take the place of harsh, negative words. Some euphemisms are perfectly acceptable. Euphemisms are unacceptable when they are used in an effort to hide the truth. The effort to label people and groups more precisely has led to creations such as "Native American" in place of "Indian." Although this is seen by some people as an example of "political correctness," that term is better applied to efforts to dress up reality with euphemistic language.

LOGICAL FALLACIES—1

We encounter arguments all over the place: in books, advertisements, TV talk shows, political speeches, newspaper editorials, class discussions, and late-night "bull sessions" with our friends. Some of those arguments are sound and convincing, but many are fallacious. An argument is *fallacious* when it contains one or more logical fallacies. A **logical fallacy**—or *fallacy,* for short—is an argument that contains a mistake in reasoning.[1] In this chapter and the next we discuss many of the most common logical fallacies.[2] In general, these are fallacies that are both frequently committed and often psychologically persuasive.

There are many common logical fallacies, and they can be classified in many ways. The simplest way—and the one we shall adopt in this text—is to divide such fallacies into two broad groups: fallacies of relevance and fallacies of insufficient evidence. **Fallacies of relevance** are fallacies that occur because the premises are *logically irrelevant* to the conclusion. *Fallacies of insufficient evidence* are fallacies that occur because the premises, though logically relevant to the conclusion, *fail to provide sufficient evidence* to support the conclusion. In this chapter we discuss fallacies of relevance. Fallacies of insufficient evidence will be discussed in Chapter 6.

THE CONCEPT OF RELEVANCE

Before we consider the fallacies of relevance, we must first get clear about the concept of relevance itself.

To say that one statement is *relevant* to another is to say that *it counts either for or against that other statement.* In other words, a statement is relevant to another statement if it provides at least some evidence or reason for thinking that the second statement is true or false.

There are three ways in which a statement can be relevant or irrelevant to another. A statement can be positively relevant, negatively relevant, or logically irrelevant to another statement.[3]

A statement is *positively relevant* to another statement if it counts in favor of that statement. Here are several examples:

> *First argument:* Dogs are cats. Cats are felines. So dogs are felines.
>
> *Second argument:* All dogs have five legs. Rover is a dog. So Rover has five legs.
>
> *Third argument:* Most Penn State students are residents of Pennsylvania. Joyce is a Penn State student. So, Joyce is probably a resident of Pennsylvania.
>
> *Fourth argument:* Chris is a woman. Therefore, Chris enjoys knitting.

Each of these premises is positively relevant to its conclusion. That is, each provides at least some evidence or reason for thinking that the conclusion is true. In the first and second arguments, the premises provide logically conclusive reasons for accepting the conclusion. In the third argument, the premises provide probable reasons for accepting the conclusion.[4] In the fourth argument, the premise ("Chris is a woman") provides neither probable nor conclusive reasons for accepting the conclusion ("Chris enjoys knitting"). However, the premise does make the conclusion slightly more probable than it would be if the conclusion were considered independently of that premise. Thus, the premise does provide some evidence for the conclusion, and hence is positively relevant to it.

These examples highlight two important lessons about the concept of relevance. First, a statement can be relevant to another statement even if the first statement is completely false. Thus, in the first example, the statement "Dogs are cats" is clearly false. Nevertheless, it is relevant to the statement "Dogs are felines" because *if it were true,* then the latter statement would have to be true as well.

Second, whether a statement is relevant to another usually depends on the *context* in which the statements are made. Thus, in the second example, the statement "All dogs have five legs" is positively relevant to the statement "Rover has five legs" only because it is conjoined with the statement "Rover is a dog."

Statements that count *against* other statements are said to be *negatively relevant* to those statements. Here are some examples:

> Joe is an uncle. Therefore, Joe is a female.
>
> Althea is two years old. Thus, Althea probably goes to college.
>
> Mark is a staunch Republican. Therefore, Mark probably favors higher taxes.

In each of these examples, the premises are negatively relevant to the conclusion. Each premise, if true, makes the conclusion at least somewhat less likely.

Finally, statements can be logically irrelevant to other statements. A statement is *logically irrelevant* to another statement if it counts neither for nor against that statement. Here are three examples:

> Last night I dreamed that the Yankees will win the pennant. Therefore, the Yankees will win the pennant.

Critical Thinking Lapse

Kodak introduced a single-use camera called The Weekender. Customers have called the support line to ask if it's okay to use it during the week.[5]

The earth revolves around the sun. Therefore, marijuana should be legalized.

Julie is a woman. Therefore, Julie should not be permitted to attend medical school.

None of these premises provides even the slightest reason for thinking that its conclusion is either true or false. Thus, they are logically irrelevant to those conclusions.

Exercise 5.1

Determine whether the premises in the following arguments are positively relevant to the conclusion, negatively relevant to the conclusion, or logically irrelevant to the conclusion.

1. Carlos recently gave Amy an engagement ring. Therefore, Carlos loves Amy.
2. Marcos lives in Costa Rica. Therefore, Marcos probably speaks German.
3. The sky is blue. Hence, the next president will be a Democrat.
4. Thousands of tobacco farm workers will lose their jobs if cigarette taxes are doubled. Therefore, smoking does not cause cancer.
5. Thousands of tobacco farm workers will lose their jobs if cigarette taxes are doubled. Therefore, cigarette taxes should not be doubled.
6. Emily is CEO of a Fortune 500 Company. Thus, it is likely that Emily earns more than $50,000 a year.
7. Mel lives in Pittsburgh. Hence, Mel lives in Ohio.
8. Sue lives in Ohio. Hence, Sue lives in Cleveland.
9. The last three coin tosses have been heads. So, the next coin toss will probably be tails.
10. You should believe in God. You have everything to gain if God does exist, and little to lose if He doesn't.
11. Peter and his wife are both over six feet tall. Therefore, their daughter is likely to be over six feet tall, too.
12. The anonymous organ donor is eighty years old. Hence, the anonymous organ donor is probably a man rather than a woman.
13. Martina partied all night last night. However, Martina was valedictorian of her high school class. Therefore, she will do well on her critical thinking test this morning.

14. Xu is a five-year-old child living in China. Therefore, Xu is probably a boy.
15. Most Americans believe that abortion should be legal. Therefore, abortion should be legal.

FALLACIES OF RELEVANCE

A *fallacy of relevance* occurs when an arguer offers reasons that are logically irrelevant to his or her conclusion. Like most popular fallacies, fallacies of relevance often *seem* to be good arguments but aren't. In this chapter we shall look at eleven fallacies of relevance.

Personal Attack (*Ad Hominem*)

We commit the **fallacy of personal attack**[6] when we reject a person's argument or claim by attacking the person rather than the person's argument or claim. Here is an example:

> Hugh Hefner, founder of *Playboy* magazine, has argued against censorship of pornography. But Hefner is an immature, self-indulgent millionaire who never outgrew the adolescent fantasies of his youth. His argument isn't worth a plugged nickel.

Notice what is going on here. The arguer makes no attempt to show why Hefner's arguments against the censorship of pornography are flawed. Instead, he simply attacks Hefner's character. In effect, he argues this way:

1. Hugh Hefner is a bad person.
2. Therefore, Hugh Hefner's argument must be bad.

But the pattern of reasoning is clearly fallacious. Even if it is true that Hefner is a bad person, that doesn't mean he is incapable of offering good arguments on the topic of censorship. The attack on Hefner's character is simply irrelevant to the point at issue, which is the strength of Hefner's case against the censorship of pornography.

It is important to bear in mind, however, that not every personal attack is a fallacy. The fallacy of personal attack occurs only if (1) an arguer rejects another person's argument or claim and (2) the arguer attacks the person who offers the argument or claim, rather than considering the merits of that argument or claim.

Consider some examples of personal attacks that *aren't* fallacies but might easily be mistaken for fallacies. Here is one example:

> My opponent in this election is a low-down mangy dog!

This statement is not a fallacy, because it is simply a statement, not an argument. Mere name-calling, however unfair or inappropriate, is not a fallacy.

One Good *Ad Hominem* Deserves Another

In one of his famous debates with Abraham Lincoln, Stephen Douglas spoke disparagingly of Lincoln's humble origins and in particular of Lincoln's brief career as a storekeeper. Lincoln responded: "Many a time I have been on one side of the counter and sold whiskey to Mr. Douglas on the other side. But now there's a difference between us: I've left my side of the counter, but he sticks to his as tenaciously as ever."[7]

Here is another example:

> Millions of innocent people died in Stalin's ruthless ideological purges. Clearly, Stalin was one of the most brutal dictators of the twentieth century.

This personal attack is not a fallacy, because no *argument* offered by Stalin is rejected on irrelevant personal grounds. There is no fallacious claim that any particular argument of Stalin's must be bad because Stalin himself was a bad person. The argument, in fact, is a good one.

Here is a final example:

> Ima Liar has testified that she saw my client rob the First National Bank. But Ms. Liar has twice been convicted of perjury. In addition, you've heard Ms. Liar's own mother testify that Ms. Liar is a pathological liar. Therefore, you should not believe Ms. Liar's testimony against my client.

Here the issue is whether Ms. Liar is or is not a credible witness. Because the arguer's personal attack is relevant to this issue, no fallacy is committed.

Attacking the Motive

Closely related to the fallacy of personal attack is the fallacy of attacking the motive. **Attacking the motive**[8] is the error of criticizing a person's motivation for offering a particular argument or claim, rather than examining the worth of the argument or claim itself. Here are several examples:

> Ned James claims that he can prove that Mayor Babcock has embezzled city funds. But James is just trying to get back at the mayor for firing him from his job as city controller. Clearly, James's accusation is a lot of hot air.
>
> Professor Michaelson has argued in favor of academic tenure. But why should we even listen to Professor Michaelson? As a tenured professor, of course he supports tenure.
>
> Barbara Simmons, President of the American Trial Lawyers Association, has argued that punitive damage awards resulting from tobacco litigation

should not be limited. But this is exactly what you would expect her to say. Trial lawyers stand to lose billions if such punitive damage awards are limited. Therefore, we should ignore Ms. Simmons's argument.

Note that these examples share a common pattern:

1. X is biased or has questionable motives.
2. Therefore, X's argument or claim should be rejected.

This pattern of reasoning is fallacious because people with biases or questionable motives do sometimes offer good arguments. You cannot simply assume that because a person has a vested interest in an issue, any position he or she takes on the issue must be false or weakly supported.

It is important to realize, however, that not all attacks on an arguer's motives are fallacious. Here are two examples:

Burton Wexler, spokesperson for the American Tobacco Growers Association, has argued that there is no credible scientific evidence that cigarette smoking causes cancer. Given Wexler's obvious bias in the matter, his arguments should be taken with a grain of salt.

"Crusher" Castellano has testified that mob hit man Sam Milano was at the movies at the time mob informer Piero Roselli was gunned down. But Castellano was paid $30,000 by the mob for his testimony. Therefore, Castellano's testimony should not be believed.

Both of these arguments include attacks on an arguer's motives. However, neither of the arguments is fallacious. Both simply reflect the commonsense assumption that arguments put forward by arguers with obvious biases or motivations to lie need to be scrutinized with particular care. Thus, the fallacy of attacking the motive does not consist in simply criticizing another arguer's motives. Instead, it consists in criticizing an arguer's motives rather than offering a rational critique of the argument itself.

Look Who's Talking (*Tu Quoque*)

The **fallacy of look who's talking**[9] is committed when an arguer rejects another person's argument or claim because that person fails to practice what he or she preaches. Here are several examples:

Doctor: You should quit smoking.
Patient: Look who's talking! I'll quit when you do, Dr. Smokestack!

President Clinton: We need to restore family values in the American entertainment industry. Our children's futures depend on it.
Joe Q. Public: What incredible chutzpah! Why should we listen to anything that hypocrite has to say about "family values"?

Parent: Honey, I don't want you to skip school on senior skip day. You don't want to jeopardize your chances of being class valedictorian, do you?

> Some people will take every other kind of trouble in the world, if they are saved the trouble of thinking.
> —G. K. Chesterton

Daughter: But Mom, you told me you skipped out on senior skip day! Why do you always get to have all the fun?

Presidential candidate Bill Bradley: When Al [Gore] accuses me of negative campaigning, that reminds me of the story about Richard Nixon, the kind of politician who would chop down a tree, then stand on the stump and give a speech about conservation.[10]

The logical pattern of these arguments is this:

1. X fails to follow his or her own advice.
2. Therefore, X's claim or argument should be rejected.

But this reasoning is clearly fallacious. Arguments are good or bad not because of who offers them but because of their own intrinsic strengths or weaknesses. You cannot refute a person's argument simply by pointing out that he or she fails to practice what he or she preaches.

However, it should be noted that there is nothing fallacious as such in criticizing a person's hypocritical behavior. For example:

Jim: Our neighbor Joe gave me a hard time again yesterday about washing our car during this drought emergency.

Patty: Well, he's right. But I wish that hypocrite would live up to his own advice. Just last week I saw him watering his lawn in the middle of the afternoon.

Here, Patty is simply pointing out, justifiably, that their neighbor is a hypocrite. However, because she does not reject any argument or claim offered by the neighbor, no fallacy is committed.

Two Wrongs Make a Right

Closely related to the fallacy of look who's talking is the fallacy of two wrongs make a right. The **fallacy of two wrongs make a right** occurs when an arguer attempts to justify a wrongful act by claiming that some other act is just as bad or worse. Here are some examples:

I don't feel guilty about cheating on Dr. Boyer's test. Half the class cheats on his tests.

You can't blame Clinton for being unfaithful to his wife. Many presidents have had extramarital affairs.

Why pick on me, officer? Nobody comes to a complete stop at that stop sign.

Parent: Bart, quit hitting your brother.

Child: Well, he pinched me.

We have all offered our share of such excuses. But however tempting such excuses may be, we know that they can never truly justify our misdeeds.

Of course, there are times when an act that would *otherwise* be wrong can be justified by citing the wrongful actions of others. Here are two examples:

How to Distinguish the Look Who's Talking Fallacy from the Two Wrongs Make a Right Fallacy

1. The look who's talking fallacy *always* involves a charge of hypocrisy or failing to practice what one preaches; the two wrongs make a right fallacy often does not. Here is an example of an argument that commits the fallacy of look who's talking but does not commit the fallacy of two wrongs make a right:

   I can't believe our pastor told us that wives should stay home and not work! What a crock! I happen to know his own wife worked to put him through college.

2. The two wrongs make a right fallacy *always* involves an attempt to justify an apparently wrongful act; the look who's talking fallacy often does not. Here is an example of an argument that commits the two wrongs make a right fallacy but does not commit the fallacy of look who's talking:

   I don't feel any obligation to report all my waitressing tips to the IRS. I don't know a single waitress who does.

Police officer: Why did you spray this man with pepper spray?
You: Because he attacked me with a knife. I did it in self-defense.

Father: Why did you go swimming when the pool was closed?
Son: Because my friend Joe jumped in and was drowning. I did it to save his life.

In these cases, the justifications offered do, in fact, serve to justify what would otherwise be wrongful behavior. Not all cases, however, are so clear. Here are two cases that are more debatable:

Jedediah Smith murdered three people in cold blood. Therefore, Jedediah Smith should be put to death.

Umpire: Why did you throw at the opposing pitcher?
Pitcher: Because he threw at three of our players. I have an obligation to protect my teammates if you guys won't.

Do these arguments commit the fallacy of two wrongs make a right? They do just in case the justifications offered are insufficient to justify the apparently wrongful behavior. Whether that is so or not is, of course, an open question.

The fallacy of two wrongs make a right is frequently confused with the fallacy of look who's talking. This is easy to understand, because it is easy to think of examples of arguments that commit *both* fallacies. For example:

Mother: Honey, it's wrong to steal. How would you feel if someone stole your favorite doll?
Child: But you told me you stole your friend's teddy bear when you were a little girl. So stealing *isn't* really wrong.

This argument commits the fallacy of two wrongs make a right because it attempts to justify a wrongful act by citing another wrongful act. It also commits the fallacy of look who's talking because it dismisses an argument on the basis of the arguer's failure to practice what she preaches.

In fact, however, the fallacy of two wrongs make a right is distinct from the fallacy of look who's talking. The key differences between the two fallacies are summarized in the box on page 147.

Appeal to Force (FEAR)

Fear is a powerful motivator—so powerful that it often causes us to think and behave irrationally. The **fallacy of appeal to force**[11] is committed when an arguer threatens harm to a reader or listener and this threat is irrelevant to the truth of the arguer's conclusion. Here are three examples:

> *Racketeer to store owner:* It's good business to pay protection money to our organization. If you don't agree, I'm sure my friends Rocko and Bruiser here can convince you.

> *Diplomat to diplomat:* I'm sure you'll agree that we are the rightful rulers of the San Marcos Islands. It would be regrettable if we had to send armed forces to demonstrate the validity of our claim.

> *Gun lobbyist to politician:* This gun control bill is wrong for America, and any politician who supports it will discover how wrong they were at the next election.[12]

In each of these examples, the scare tactics employed provide no relevant evidence that supports the stated conclusion.[13]

Of course, not all threats involve fallacies. Here are two examples:

> *Parent to teen:* If you come home late one more time, then your allowance will be cut.

> *President Kennedy to Soviet Premier Kruschchev:* If you don't remove your nuclear missiles from Cuba, then we will have no choice but to remove them by force. If we use force to remove the missiles, that may provoke an all-out nuclear war. Neither of us wants an all-out nuclear war. Therefore, you should remove your missiles from Cuba. (paraphrased)

The first example is not fallacy because it is simply a statement, not an argument. The second example is not a fallacy because the premises are logically relevant to the conclusion.

Appeal to Pity (GUILTY)

The **fallacy of appeal to pity**[14] occurs when an arguer attempts to evoke feelings of pity or compassion, when such feelings, however understandable, are not logically relevant to the arguer's conclusion. Here are two examples:

> *Student to professor:* I know I missed half your classes and failed all my exams. But I had a really tough semester. First my pet boa constrictor died. Then

Force or Reason?

Once, while giving a speech, Catholic historian Hilaire Belloc was repeatedly heckled by a member of the audience. Belloc, who was built like a boxer, bore these interruptions patiently for some time. Finally, however, he could endure no more. Fixing the heckler with a glare he said, "I should prefer, sir, to settle this question by physical encounter, but since the rules of this club do not permit that method, I am compelled to attempt the task of teaching you how to think."[15]

my girl friend told me she wants a sex-change operation. With all I went through this semester, I don't think I really deserved an F. Any chance you might cut me some slack and change my grade to a C or a D?

Parent to high school football coach: I admit my son Billy can't run, pass, kick, catch, block, or tackle. But he deserves to make the high school football team. If he doesn't make the team, he's going to be an emotional wreck, and he may even drop out of school.

These arguments may or may not be effective in arousing our sympathies. Logically, however, the arguments are clearly fallacious, for the premises provide no relevant reasons to accept the conclusions.

Are all arguments that contain emotional appeals fallacious? No, as the following examples illustrate:

Mother to daughter: Nana was asking about you the other day. She's so lonely and depressed since Grandpa passed away, and her Alzheimer's seems to get worse every day. She's done so much for you over the years. Don't you think you should pay her a visit?[16]

High school softball coach: Girls, this state championship softball game is the biggest game of your lives. This is what you've been working for all year. Your parents are counting on you, your school is counting on you, and your community is counting on you. Make them proud! Play like the champions you are!

In these examples, the appeals to emotion are both appropriate and relevant to the arguers' legitimate purposes. Too often, however, people use emotional appeals to hinder or obscure rational thinking. When emotional appeals are used in this way, the appeals are fallacious.

Bandwagon Argument

We all like to feel loved, admired, recognized, valued, and accepted by others. A **bandwagon argument** is an argument that plays on a person's desire to be

It is never too late to give up our prejudices. No way of thinking or doing, however ancient, can be trusted without proof.

—Henry David Thoreau

popular, accepted, or valued, rather than appealing to logically relevant reasons or evidence. Here are three examples:

> All the really cool kids in East Jefferson High School smoke cigarettes. Therefore, you should, too.
>
> I can't believe you're going to the library on a Friday night! You don't want people to think you're a nerd, do you?
>
> There must be something to astrology. Millions of Americans can't be wrong.

The basic pattern of these arguments is this:

1. Everybody (or a select group of people) believes or does X.
2. Therefore, you should believe or do X, too.

This pattern is fallacious, because the fact that a belief or a practice is popular usually provides little or no evidence that the belief is true or that the practice is good.

Bandwagon arguments are especially common in advertising. Here are three examples:

> I'm a Pepper, he's a Pepper, she's a Pepper. Wouldn't you like to be a Pepper, too?
>
> Join the Pepsi generation.
>
> *Hudson Bay Furs:* For the discerning few, only the best will do.

The first two examples appeal to our desire not to be left out of the group. The third example is a kind of "snob appeal" that plays on our desire to belong to the "exclusive" bandwagon of the select or superior few.

Not all appeals to popular beliefs or practices are fallacious, however, as these examples illustrate:

> All the villagers I've talked to say that the water is safe to drink. Therefore, the water probably is safe to drink.
>
> Lots of my friends recommend the Back Street Deli. So it's probably a good place to eat.
>
> In this country, it's considered rude to stand right next to a person on an elevator when there's nobody else in it. Therefore, if you don't want to be considered rude, you should move over next time that situation occurs.

These bandwagon appeals are not fallacious, because the premises are relevant to the conclusions.

Straw Man

The **straw man fallacy** is committed when an arguer distorts an opponent's argument or claim in order to make it easier to attack. For example:

> Pete has argued that the New York Yankees are a better baseball team than the Atlanta Braves. But the Braves aren't a bad team. They have a great

Neither believe nor reject anything, because any other person, or description of persons, have rejected or believed it. Your own reason is the only oracle given you by heaven, and you are answerable, not for the rightness, but the uprightness of the decision.

—Thomas Jefferson

pitching staff, and they consistently finish at or near the top of their division. Obviously, Pete doesn't know what he's talking about.

This argument misrepresents Pete's view. Pete hasn't claimed that the *Braves are a bad team*—merely that the *Yankees are a better team than the Braves.* By mischaracterizing Pete's view—making it seem weaker or less plausible than it really is—the arguer has committed the straw man fallacy.

Straw man fallacies are extremely common in politics. For example:

> Senator Biddle has argued that we should outlaw violent pornography. Obviously, the Senator favors complete governmental censorship of books, magazines, and films. Frankly, I'm shocked that such a view should be expressed on the floor of the United States Senate. It runs counter to everything this great nation stands for. No senator should listen seriously to such an outrageous proposal.

This argument distorts the senator's view. His claim is that violent pornography should be outlawed, not that there should be complete governmental censorship of books, magazines, and films. By misrepresenting the senator's position and then attacking the misrepresentation rather than the senator's actual position, the arguer commits the straw man fallacy.

The logical pattern of straw man arguments is this:

1. X's view is false or unjustified [but where X's view has been unfairly characterized or misrepresented].
2. Therefore, X's view should be rejected.

Clearly, arguments of this pattern provide no logically relevant support for their conclusions.

Red Herring

The **red herring fallacy** is committed when an arguer tries to sidetrack his or her audience by raising an irrelevant issue and then claims that the original issue has effectively been settled by the irrelevant diversion. The fallacy apparently gets its name from a technique used to train English foxhounds.[17] A sack of red (i.e., smoked) herrings was dragged across the trail of a fox to train the foxhounds to follow the fox's scent rather than the powerful distracting smell of the fish. In a similar way, an arguer commits the red herring fallacy when he seeks to distract his audience by raising an irrelevant issue and then claims or implies that the irrelevant diversion has settled the original point at issue. Here is an example:

> Many people criticize Thomas Jefferson for being an owner of slaves. But Jefferson was one of our greatest presidents, and his Declaration of Independence is one of the most eloquent pleas for freedom and democracy ever written. Clearly, these criticisms are unwarranted.

The issue here is whether Jefferson can rightly be criticized for owning slaves, not whether he was one of America's greatest presidents or whether he deserves

How to Distinguish the Straw Man Fallacy from the Red Herring Fallacy

1. The straw man fallacy *always* involves misrepresenting another person's argument or claim; the red herring fallacy often does not. Here is an example of an argument that commits the straw man fallacy but does not commit the red herring fallacy:

   I overheard my friend Hal say that democracy isn't always the best form of government. Funny, I never figured Hal for a communist.

2. The red herring fallacy *always* involves changing or evading the issue; the straw man fallacy often does not. Here is an example of an argument that commits the red herring fallacy but does not commit the straw man fallacy:

   Jessica Wu has argued that immediate steps should be taken to reduce global warming. However, the most serious environmental problem isn't global warming, it's overpopulation. Unless something is done to reduce population growth in the third world, mass starvation and irreversible environmental devastation will result. Frankly, I think Jessica's view is ridiculous.

---

credit for writing the Declaration of Independence. By diverting the reader's attention from the original argument and then claiming that the original argument has been effectively refuted by the irrelevant diversion, the arguer commits the red herring fallacy.

Red herring fallacies are also extremely common in politics. For example:

> Critics have accused my administration of doing too little to save the family farm. These critics forget that I grew up on a farm. I know what it's like to get up at the crack of dawn to milk the cows. I know what it's like to work in the field all day in the blazing sun. Family farms are what made this country great, and those who criticize my farm policies simply don't know what they're talking about.

The issue here is whether the speaker's administration is doing enough to save the family farm. The fact that the speaker grew up on a farm is simply a smokescreen used to distract attention from this issue.

It should be noted, however, that it is *not* a fallacy simply to change the subject or to evade an issue. For example:

> My opponent in this election has accused me of accepting illegal campaign contributions. But this election isn't about campaign finances—it's about lower taxes, safer neighborhoods, and better schools for our children. That's what I'm fighting for in this election, and that's why I deserve your vote in November.

Here the speaker doesn't deny the accusation or pretend it is refuted by discussing irrelevant issues; rather, he or she simply evades the issue. Because there is no mistake in reasoning in the argument, no fallacy is committed.

The straw man fallacy is often confused with the red herring fallacy. The key differences between the two fallacies are summarized in the box on page 152.

Equivocation

We saw in the last chapter that words often have more than one meaning. The **fallacy of equivocation** is committed when a key word is used in two or more senses in the same argument and the apparent success of the argument depends on the shift in meaning. Here are several examples:

> It's a crime to smoke grass. Kentucky bluegrass is a grass. Therefore, it's a crime to smoke Kentucky blue grass.

> A star is a heavenly body. Roseanne is a star. Thus, Roseanne is a heavenly body.

> Any law can be repealed by the proper legal authority. The law of gravity is a law. Therefore, the law of gravity can be repealed by the proper legal authority.[18]

In each of these arguments a key word is used *ambiguously* or *equivocally*— that is, with two or more distinct senses. The first argument equivocates on the word "grass." In the first premise it means marijuana; in the second it means ordinary lawn grass. The second argument uses "star" in two different senses. In the first premise it means a star in the sky; in the second it means a celebrity. The third argument equivocates on the word "law." In the first premise it refers to a law regulating human conduct; in the second it refers to an observed uniformity of nature.

Fallacies of equivocation can be difficult to spot because they often *appear* valid, but aren't. The third example above appears to have the following logical pattern:

1. All A's are B's. [All laws are things that can be repealed by the proper legal authority.]
2. C is an A. [The law of gravity is a law.]
3. Therefore, C is a B. [Therefore, the law of gravity is a thing that can be repealed by the proper legal authority.]

Such a pattern is, of course, valid. Moreover, the premises appear to be true. Nevertheless, the argument is clearly fallacious. Why?

The argument is fallacious because it only *appears* to have a valid argument form. This becomes clear if we make explicit the two different senses in which the word "law" is used in the argument.

1. All A's are B's. [All laws regulating human conduct are things that can be repealed by proper legal authority.]
2. C is a D. [The law of gravity is an observed uniformity of nature.]
3. Therefore, C is a B. [Therefore, the law of gravity is a thing that can be repealed by the proper legal authority.]

When the two senses of the word "law" are distinguished in this way, it is clear that the premises provide no relevant support for the conclusion.

> ### Critical Thinking Lapse
>
> I've been told by a friend of a friend of a great mathematician that this genius cannot remember where he lives, although his house is only a short distance from the campus of the university where he works. The story, sworn to be true, is that this man must count each day the number of streets away from campus, and the number of houses down the street on the right, as he walks home. Three streets down, take a right, twelve houses on the right. One day, I am told, as he was walking home he was deep in thought about a mathematical problem and lost count. Utterly confused and totally lost, he saw a little boy playing at the side of the road. He called out, "Young man, can you tell me where the mathematician lives?" The boy looked up and said, "What's wrong with you, Daddy?" [19]

Begging the Question

The **fallacy of begging the question** is committed when an arguer states or assumes as a premise the very thing he or she is trying to prove as a conclusion. There are two common ways to commit this fallacy.

The most obvious way is to simply *restate* the conclusion in slightly different words. Here are two examples:

> Bungee-jumping is dangerous, because it's unsafe.
> Capital punishment is morally wrong, because it is ethically impermissible to inflict death as punishment for a crime.

In the first example, the premise basically just repeats the conclusion, since saying that bungee-jumping is "unsafe" is another way of saying that it is "dangerous." In the second example, the conclusion is begged, because saying that it is "ethically impermissible" to inflict death as punishment for a crime is equivalent to saying that capital punishment is "morally wrong."

The second common form of the begging the question fallacy involves "circular reasoning" or "arguing in a circle." This occurs when an arguer offers a chain of reasons for a conclusion, where the conclusion of the argument is stated or assumed as one of the premises. For example:

> *Kylie:* God wrote the Bible.
> *Ned:* How do you know?
> *Kylie:* Because it says so in the Bible, and what the Bible says is true.
> *Ned:* How do you know what the Bible says is true?
> *Kylie:* Because God wrote the Bible.

Notice the tight circle of reasoning here: A because B, B because A. In more complex arguments, the circular reasoning may be more difficult to spot, as in this example:

Summary of Fallacies of Relevance

Personal attack: Arguer attacks the character of another arguer.

Attacking the motive: Arguer attacks the motive of another arguer.

Look who's talking: Arguer attacks the hypocrisy of another arguer.

Two wrongs make a right: Arguer tries to justify a wrong by citing another wrong.

Appeal to force: Arguer threatens a reader or listener.

Appeal to pity: Arguer tries to evoke pity from a reader or listener.

Bandwagon argument: Arguer appeals to a reader's or listener's desire to be accepted or valued.

Straw man: Arguer misrepresents an opponent's view.

Red herring: Arguer tries to distract the attention of the audience by raising an irrelevant issue.

Equivocation: Arguer uses a key word in two or more senses.

Begging the question: Arguer assumes the point to be proven.

Wexford College is a better college than Aggie Tech. Wexford is a better college because it has better students. It has better students because it has better faculty. It has better faculty because it pays higher faculty salaries. It pays higher faculty salaries because it has a larger endowment. It has a larger endowment because it has more generous and loyal alumni. It has more generous and loyal alumni because it is a better college.

Here the chain of reasoning is so lengthy that it is easy to overlook the fact that the statement "Wexford College is a better college than Aggie Tech" appears both as a premise and as a conclusion in the argument.

EXERCISE 5.2

I. Identify the fallacies of relevance committed by the following arguments. There may be more than one. If no fallacy is committed, write "no fallacy."

1. The new Volkswagen Beetle is the coolest car around. It's selling like hotcakes. You should ask your parents to buy you one.

2. *Jason:* Did you hear Andrew's class presentation on senior-class rights and privileges?
   Kyle: Yeah, but I don't buy any of his arguments. He's just a rich snob who likes to hear himself talk.

3. Bill Baxter deserves to be promoted to vice president. He has three small children, and just last week his wife was diagnosed with breast cancer.

4. School superintendent Kate Duncan has argued that children in public schools should be allowed to participate in a voluntary moment of silence at the beginning of each school day. But it's wrong to allow teachers to indoctrinate

children with their own religious views. Duncan's argument must be firmly rejected.

5. My driving instructor, Mr. Peterson, told me that it's dangerous to drive without a seat belt. But why should I listen to him? Last week I saw him driving without a seat belt.

6. Jeff and Maribeth slept together on prom night. Sleep is a state of unconscious or semiconscious rest or repose. It follows that Jeff and Maribeth must have spent a very restful night together.

7. Paper is combustible, because it burns.

8. Jesse Jackson has argued that last week's police shooting was racially motivated. But this is exactly what you would expect Jackson to say. After all, he's black.

9. *Child to playmate:* Admit it! Admit that *Scooby-Doo* is a better cartoon show than *Pokemon*! If you don't, my big brother is going to beat you up!

10. *Al:* I can't believe it! My bank made a mistake on my account balance. There's an extra $3,000 in my checking account.
    Joe: Are you going to report the mistake?
    Al: Why should I? They've been ripping me off for years with their high ATM fees.

11. Opponents of capital punishment have argued that the death penalty is unfair and discriminatory. But it's ridiculous to suggest that cold-blooded murderers should not have to pay for their crimes. How is that fair to the victims or their families?

12. Malcolm Cox isn't qualified to be a kindergarten teacher. He's lazy and incompetent and has twice been convicted of child abuse.

13. Only man has an immortal soul. No woman is a man. Therefore, no woman has an immortal soul.

14. *Blenheim cufflinks:* As elegant and refined as you are.

15. I almost lost it when I heard the Maharishi condemn Western materialism and consumerism. What a crock! Did you see the Rolls Royce he drove up in?

16. *Dean of Students to student:* Mr. Boosely, you've twice been cited for violating the college's alcoholic beverage policy. If you commit a third violation, I'll have no choice but to suspend you from school.

17. You often hear people say that the French are rude, especially to people who don't speak their language. But France is a wonderful country! The wine, the food, the museums! There's no country in Europe I'd rather visit.

18. I wish I could take my four basset hounds with me when I move, but I just can't. I know you only have a small apartment, but won't you consider adopting them? I hate to think of them starving in the street or winding up in the dog pound.

19. Recently, a scientific study found that eating large amounts of jamoca almond fudge ice cream is actually good for you. However, we shouldn't be too quick to accept this conclusion, because the study was funded entirely by Baskin-Robbins and other leading ice cream makers.

20. Dear Mr. Ferguson, I'm sure you'll agree that after three years working as head of company security I'm long overdue for a raise. By the way, may I

respectfully suggest that you make sure the surveillance cameras are turned off next time you and your secretary need to "catch up on some paperwork"?

21. Convicted murderer Johnny Palko has argued that he did not receive a fair trial. But Palko is a vicious thug who's spent most of his adult life behind bars. Why should we even listen to such a parasite?

22. Rachel Nussbaum has argued that assault weapons should be outlawed. Apparently, Rachel believes that no one has the right to own firearms for purposes of self-protection. But such a view is completely indefensible. It would leave law-abiding citizens defenseless against predatory criminals.

23. Baseball owners have argued that baseball should continue to be exempt from antitrust laws. But the owners stand to lose millions if baseball's antitrust exemption is revoked. No sensible person should be taken in by the owners' obviously self-serving arguments.

24. I see nothing unethical in paying bribes to foreign officials to obtain business favors. That's the way business is done in many parts of the world. As they say, "When in Rome, do as the Romans do."

25. Karen has argued that the secretaries at Acme Steel will get more respect if they change their titles from "secretaries" to "office assistants." But everyone knows that Acme Steel has a bottom-line mentality. They'll let you call yourself anything you want, but they won't raise your salary a nickel.

26. Hi, Mrs. Bowman, this is Debbie at Little Tykes Daycare. Sorry to bother you at work. I know you asked us not to give Petey any more candy or desserts at day care, but there's a birthday party today and all the kids are having chocolate cupcakes. Petey feels so left out. He's the only one without a cupcake, and he's just bawling his little eyes out. Wouldn't it be okay if I gave him a dessert just this once?

27. You're home alone. You've just heard on the radio that a homicidal maniac has escaped from the state penitentiary. Suddenly you hear the sound of breaking glass. What do you do? What *do* you do? Don't let this happen to you. Give your family the peace of mind they deserve. Call Allied Security today!

28. At the global warming conference at Kyoto in 1997, many developing nations argued against setting strict emissions standards, claiming that this would put them at a competitive disadvantage against rich industrialized nations that have already benefited from lax environmental standards. But these developing nations are just jealous of the high standard of living industrialized nations have achieved. Sour grapes, that's all their arguments amount to.

29. Sigrid is an illegal alien. An alien is a creature from outer space. Therefore, Sigrid is a creature from outer space.

30. Wellington's is a classier bar than Jake's. It's a classier bar because it has a more upscale clientele. It has a more upscale clientele because it has a nicer décor. It has a nicer décor because it's a classier bar.

31. Flag-burning is unconstitutional. Just ask anybody.

32. My doctor told me I need to eat right and lose weight. What a laugh! You know where that tub o' lard was when he gave me this great advice? He was a contestant in the banana-split-eating contest at the county fair.

33. I can't believe these convicted murderers have the gall to claim that their rights have been violated by prison officials. They didn't respect the rights of their victims. Why should we respect theirs?

34. *Beef industry slogan:* "Beef: Real food for real people."

35. Mr. Martin claims that boys tend to be better at math than girls. What a ridiculous overgeneralization! My friend Alice is the best math student in her class. So, it's clear that boys are not always better at math than girls.

36. Penicillin is a miracle of modern medicine. A miracle is a divinely produced violation of a law of nature. Therefore, penicillin is a divinely produced violation of a law of nature.

37. Dr. Christina Sparks has argued that the morning-after pill is an effective contraceptive. But the morning-after pill simply encourages sexual promiscuity. Sexual promiscuity is the reason we have such high rates of abortion and out-of-wedlock births in this country. Obviously, Dr. Sparks's argument is flawed.

38. Mrs. Devlin, your right rear tire is practically bald. I recommend you replace it. I know you do a lot of driving at night on backcountry roads, and I'm sure you wouldn't want to get stranded.

39. Professor Douglas has argued that marijuana should be legalized. But Douglas is radical ex-hippie whose brains were fried at Woodstock. No sensible person should listen to such a fruitcake.

40. *Al:* Doc Miller told me I've been working too hard. He said I need a vacation.
    Deb: He's a fine one to talk! I bet Doc hasn't taken a vacation in forty years. But you know he's probably right. You have been working awfully hard lately.

II. Write an original example of each of the fallacies of relevance discussed in this chapter. Be prepared to share your examples with the class.

III. Find examples of the fallacies discussed in this chapter from everyday life (newspapers, magazines, TV, radio, class discussions, etc.). Collect your examples in a notebook or portfolio. For each example, indicate where you found the fallacy and explain briefly why you think it commits the fallacy you claim. Be prepared to share your examples with the class.

Summary

1. A *logical fallacy* is an argument that contains a mistake in reasoning. Fallacies can be divided into two broad groups: fallacies of relevance and fallacies of insufficient evidence. *Fallacies of relevance* are arguments in which the premises are logically irrelevant to the conclusion. *Fallacies of insufficient evidence* are arguments in which the premises, though logically

relevant to the conclusion, fail to provide sufficient evidence for the conclusion. In this chapter we discussed fallacies of relevance. Fallacies of insufficient evidence will be discussed in the next chapter.

2. A statement is *relevant* to another statement if it provides at least some evidence or reason for thinking that the second statement is true or false. There are three ways in which a statement can be relevant or irrelevant to another. A statement can be positively relevant, negatively relevant, or logically irrelevant to another statement. A statement is *positively relevant* to another statement if it provides at least some reason for thinking that the second statement is true. A statement is *negatively relevant* to another statement if it provides at least some reason for thinking that the second statement is false. A statement is *logically irrelevant* to another statement if it provides no reason for thinking that the second statement is either true or false.

3. In this chapter we studied eleven common fallacies of relevance:
   a. Personal attack (*ad hominem*): The rejection of a person's argument or claim by means of an attack on the person's character rather than the person's argument or claim.

   Example

   Professor Snodblatt has argued against the theory of evolution. But Snodblatt is a pompous, egotistical windbag, and a card-carrying member of the Communist Bikers' Association. I absolutely refuse to listen to him.

   b. Attacking the motive: Criticizing a person's motivation for offering a particular argument or claim, rather than examining the worth of the argument or claim itself.

   Example

   Jim Gibson has argued that we need to build a new middle school. But Gibson is the owner of Gibson's Construction Company. He'll make a fortune if his company is picked to build the new school. Obviously, Gibson's argument is a lot of self-serving baloney.

   c. Look who's talking (*tu quoque*): The rejection of another person's argument or claim because that person is a hypocrite.

   Example

   My opponent, Bill Peters, has accused me of running a negative political campaign. But Peters has run a much more negative campaign than I have. Just last week he ran television ads falsely accusing me of incest, child abuse, and cruelty to animals. Clearly, Peters's charge that I'm guilty of mudslinging is untrue.

   d. Two wrongs make a right: Attempting to justify a wrongful act by claiming that some other act is just as bad or worse.

   Example

   I admit we plied Olympic officials with booze, prostitutes, free ski vacations, and millions of dollars in outright bribes in order to be selected as the site of the next winter Olympics. But everybody does it. That's the way the process works. Therefore, paying those bribes wasn't really wrong.

e. Appeal to force: Threatening harm to a reader or listener, when the threat is irrelevant to the truth of the arguer's conclusion.

Example

You've argued that Coach Bubba should be fired because he's twice been arrested for starting barroom brawls. But Coach Bubba is the winningest football coach we've ever had at Culmbank High. He doesn't deserve to be fired. And if you can't understand that, maybe these boys with baseball bats can change your mind.

f. Appeal to pity: Attempting to evoke feelings of pity or compassion, when such feelings, however understandable, are not relevant to the truth of the arguer's conclusion.

Example

Officer, I know I was going 80 mph in a 15-mph school zone. But I don't deserve a speeding ticket. I've had a really tough week. Yesterday, I got fired from my job, and last Monday my Chihuahua got eaten by a Great Dane.

g. Bandwagon argument: An appeal to a person's desire to be popular, accepted, or valued rather than to logically relevant reasons or evidence.

Example

All the popular, cool kids at Westmont Middle School wear Mohawk haircuts. Therefore, you should, too.

h. Straw man: The misrepresentation of another person's position in order to make that position easier to attack.

Example

Professor Strinberg has argued that the Bible should not be read literally. Obviously, Strinberg believes that any reading of the Bible is as good as any other. But this would mean that there is no difference between a true interpretation of Scripture and a false interpretation. Such a view is absurd.

i. Red herring: An attempt to sidetrack an audience by raising an irrelevant issue and then claiming that the original issue has been effectively settled by the irrelevant diversion.

Example

Frank has argued that Volvos are safer cars than Ford Mustang convertibles. But Volvos are clunky, boxlike cars, whereas Mustang convertibles are sleek, powerful, and sexy. Clearly, Frank doesn't know what he's talking about.

j. Equivocation: The use of a key word in an argument in two (or more) different senses.

Example

In the summer of 1940, Londoners were bombed almost every night. To be bombed is to be intoxicated. Therefore, in the summer of 1940, Londoners were intoxicated almost every night.

k. Begging the question: Stating or assuming as a premise the very thing one is seeking to prove as a conclusion.

Example

I am entitled to say whatever I choose, because I have a right to say whatever I please.

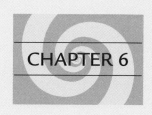

CHAPTER 6

LOGICAL FALLACIES—2

FALLACIES OF INSUFFICIENT EVIDENCE

In the last chapter we looked at fallacies of relevance, fallacies that occur when the premises are logically irrelevant to the truth of the conclusion. In this chapter we discuss fallacies of insufficient evidence. **Fallacies of insufficient evidence** are fallacies in which the premises, though relevant to the conclusion, fail to provide sufficient evidence for the conclusion. We shall discuss nine such fallacies.

Inappropriate Appeal to Authority

All of us depend upon things that other people tell us. Children rely on their parents and teachers for basic guidance and instruction. Scientists rely on other scientists to report their findings accurately. Historians depend on primary sources and other historians for reliable information about the past. Indeed, it is hard to see how any stable and cohesive society could exist without a great deal of shared trust in its members' basic honesty and reliability. For that reason, trust in authority has aptly been described as "the very foundation of civilization."[1]

Too often, however, people rely *uncritically* on the authority of others. Throughout history, blind faith in authority has bred superstition, dogmatism, and humbug. Consequently, it is of great importance to be able to distinguish legitimate appeals to authority from those that are fallacious.

The **fallacy of inappropriate appeal to authority** is committed when an arguer cites a witness or an authority who, there is good reason to believe, is unreliable. But when, in general, is it reasonable to believe that a witness or an authority is unreliable? Here are some relevant circumstances:

- When the source is not a genuine authority on the subject at issue
- When the source is biased or has some other reason to lie or mislead
- When the accuracy of the source's personal observations or experiences is doubtful

- When we have reason to believe that a media source, a reference work, or an Internet source is generally unreliable
- When we have reason to believe that the source has not been cited correctly
- When the source's claim conflicts with expert opinion
- When the issue is not one that can be settled by expert opinion
- When the claim made by the source is in itself highly improbable

Let's look briefly at each of these reasons for questioning the reliability of a source.

Is the Source an Authority on the Subject at Issue?   An *authority* is a person who possesses special knowledge, competence, or expertise in a particular field. The most obvious way to commit the fallacy of inappropriate appeal to authority is to appeal to a person who is not a genuine authority on the subject at issue. For example:

> My barber told me that Einstein's general theory of relativity is a lot of hogwash. I guess Einstein wasn't as smart as everybody thinks he was.

Because the arguer's barber presumably is not an authority on Einstein's general theory of relativity, this argument commits the fallacy of unreliable authority.

Fallacies of this sort are particularly common in advertising. Consider this example:

> Hi! I'm heavyweight boxing champ Buster Brawler. After a tough night in the ring, my face needs some tender loving care. Lather-X Sensitive Skin Shaving Gel. You can't get a smoother, closer shave.

The arguer may be an expert on knocking out opponents in the boxing ring, but because he is no expert on the comparative virtues of shaving products, the argument is fallacious.

Is the Source Biased?   Common sense tells us that we should be cautious about accepting a claim when the person making the claim is biased or has some other obvious motive to lie or mislead. Here are two examples:

> Ned Bumpley has been paid $100,000 by the *Sensational Enquirer* tabloid for his story that he is Bill Gates's illegitimate son. Given Mr. Bumpley's reputation for honesty, I think we should believe him, even though he has produced no corroborating evidence and DNA tests fail to support his claim.

> Mrs. Cox has testified that her son Willie was home with her at the time when Willie is alleged to have shot Steve Wilson. Even though Willie's fingerprints were found on the murder weapon and six witnesses have identified Willie as the assailant, I can't believe that a good woman like Mrs. Cox would lie to protect her son. I think Willy is innocent.

In both of these examples, the testifier has an obvious motive to lie (financial gain in the first example, maternal love in the second). Given these motivations, together with other information contained in the examples, these appeals to authority are fallacious.[2]

Is the Accuracy of the Source's Personal Observations or Experiences Doubtful?   A source may also be unreliable if we have reason to doubt the accuracy of his or her observations or experiences. Here are two examples:

> Jerry (who was playing heavy metal music at full blast on his boom box) claims he heard the victim whisper his name from more than 100 feet away. Jerry has always struck me as a straight shooter. So, I have to believe that Jerry really did hear the victim whisper his name.

> After taking LSD and drinking seven beers, Jill claims she had a conversation with Elvis's ghost in the alley behind McDearmon's Bar. I've never known Jill to lie. So, I think we should believe her.

In these examples, there are obvious reasons for doubting the reliability of the witnesses' observations or experiences. Consequently, these appeals to authority are fallacious.

Do We Have Reason to Believe That a Media Source, a Reference Work, or an Internet Source Is Unreliable?   Generally speaking, it is reasonable to accept claims made in reputable newspapers, magazines, encyclopedias, television news programs, and Internet web sites. But we must be cautious about accepting claims found in sources that we have reason to believe are generally unreliable. Here is an example from a recent issue of the *Weekly World News,* a popular supermarket tabloid.

> ### Scientists' Research Reveals . . . It Takes 3 Million Years For a Human Soul to Reach Heaven . . . And No One from Earth Has Arrived There Yet!
>
> Heaven is a mind-boggling 3 billion light-years from earth, space scientists have recently determined—a distance so vast that not a single person who's died in all of recorded history has yet reached the Pearly Gates! . . .
>
> Startling photos taken by the Hubble Space Telescope and the Mars Pathfinder have pinpointed a shining white city suspended in the blackness of space, roughly 3 billion light-years away.
>
> Those secret NASA photos, leaked by an insider and published in the *Weekly World News,* are widely believed to depict Heaven itself.
>
> And the implication of the great distance is staggering.
>
> "Even a single light year, the distance light travels in one year, is enormous—5.8 trillion miles," said [French astrophysicist Antoinne] Letelier.
>
> "Presumably, the human soul has zero mass, allowing it to travel at the speed of light—the fastest any natural object can move.
>
> "In fact, let's assume that because of its supernatural nature, a soul can travel 1,000 times faster than light.

"Even at that breakneck rate, the earliest cavemen would just now be arriving at Heaven's gates . . . and if you died today, you wouldn't get there until the year 2998003 A.D."[3]

Given the obvious weaknesses of the reported argument and the fact that tabloids such as the *Weekly World News* are known to concoct outlandish stories, an argument based on an appeal to the authority of the *Weekly World News* would be fallacious.

Do We Have Reason to Believe That the Source Has Not Been Cited Correctly?   The fallacy of inappropriate appeal to authority can also be committed if the arguer has not cited a source correctly. For example:

> It states in the Constitution that there must be a "wall of separation" between church and state. Publicly funded school vouchers clearly violate this wall of separation. Therefore, publicly funded school vouchers are unconstitutional.

Though many people believe that the phrase "wall of separation" is found in the Constitution, it actually appears in a letter Thomas Jefferson wrote to the Danbury Connecticut Baptist Association on January 1, 1802. For that reason, this appeal to authority is fallacious.

Does the Source's Claim Conflict with Expert Opinion?   Damon Runyon once said, "The race is not always to the swift, nor the battle to the strong, but that's the way to bet."[4] Much the same can be said about expert opinion. Though experts are often wrong (sometimes spectacularly so), it is generally unwise to accept a claim that conflicts with a clear expert consensus. For example:

> Dr. Duane Gish, a biochemist with a Ph.D. from Berkeley and Senior Vice President of the Institute for Creation Research, has argued that there is no credible evidence supporting the theory of evolution. In view of Dr. Gish's expertise on this subject, we should conclude that evolution is a myth.

Since an overwhelming majority of scientists disagree with this view, it would be unwise to accept this conclusion simply on the authority of Dr. Gish.

Can the Source's Claim Be Settled by an Appeal to Expert Opinion? Some issues are so inherently controversial that they cannot be settled by appeals to expert opinion. Here are two examples:

> Dr. Stanford P. Higginbotham, a leading social philosopher, has argued that capital punishment is always morally wrong. Given Dr. Higginbotham's impressive professional credentials, we should conclude that capital punishment is always morally wrong.
>
> Swami Krishnamurti Chakrabarti, spiritual leader of the Worldwide Church of Cognitive Enlightenment, has said that the meaning of life lies in achieving mystical unity with the Great I Am. In view of the Swami's deep spiritual insight, it's clear that this is indeed the meaning of life.

> *Testimony is like an arrow shot from a long bow; the force of it depends on the strength of the hand that draws it. Argument is like an arrow shot from a crossbow, which has equal force though shot by a child.*
>
> —Samuel Johnson

Would You Believe . . . ?

Here are some more wacky headlines from the *Weekly World News:*

Haunted Toilet Claims Third Plumber in Eight Years!

Adolf Hitler Was a Woman!

Abe Lincoln's Corpse Revived!

UFOs Are Piloted by Angels and Demons—And They're Planning a Dogfight That Could Destroy Us All!

Your Internet Dream Girl Could Be a CHIMP!

Ghost Pours Ice Water on Couple—Every Time They Have Sex!

I Had Bigfoot's Baby!

3,600-lb. Mystery Sphere Is Hairball from Space Alien!

Olympic Broad Jumpers Using Gas Pills to Boost Athletic Performance!

> *In discussion it is not so much weight of authority as force of argument that should be demanded.*
>
> —Cicero

Topics such as the morality of capital punishment and the meaning of life are issues on which no expert consensus exists or is likely to exist. For that reason, debates on these issues cannot be settled by appeals to authority.

Is the Claim in Itself Highly Improbable?   The more improbable a claim is in itself, the less willing we should be to accept it merely on the say-so of a witness or an authority. If we accept an extraordinary claim on authority and it is more likely that the alleged authority is lying or mistaken than it is that the claim is true, we commit the fallacy of inappropriate appeal to authority. For example:

> Old Doc Perkins claims he has an eighty-year-old friend who can run a 100-yard dash in less than ten seconds. Old Doc is one of the most trusted members of this community. So, if Old Doc says he has an eighty-year-old friend who can run a 100-yard dash in less than ten seconds, I, for one, believe him.

> *Extraordinary claims require extraordinary evidence.*
>
> —Carl Sagan

This claim, considered independently of Old Doc's report, is so improbable that it should be rejected unless strong additional evidence is provided.

Appeal to Ignorance

When we lack evidence for or against a claim, it is usually best to suspend judgment—to admit that we just don't know. When an arguer treats a *lack* of evidence as positive evidence that a claim is true or false, he or she commits the fallacy of appeal to ignorance. More precisely, the **fallacy of appeal to ignorance** occurs when an arguer asserts that a claim must be true because no one has proven it false, or, conversely, that a claim must be false because no one has proven it true. Here are several examples:

> There must be intelligent life on other planets. No one has proven that there isn't.

> There isn't any intelligent life on other planets. No one has proven that there is.

> No one has proven that global warming is occurring. Therefore, we must conclude that it is not occurring.

> No one has proven that global warming is not occurring. Therefore, we must conclude that it is occurring.

Each of these examples suffers from the same basic flaw: it assumes that the lack of evidence for (or against) a claim is good reason to believe that the claim is false (or true). If such reasoning were allowed, we could "prove" almost any conclusion:

> No one has proven that three-eyed, four-armed, polka-dotted gremlins don't exist deep in the interior of the moon. Therefore, it's reasonable to believe that three-eyed, four-armed, polka-dotted gremlins do exist deep in the interior of the moon.

> There is no evidence that it was cloudy in Rome on September 8, A.D. 643. Therefore, we must conclude that it wasn't.

Not ignorance, but ignorance of ignorance, is the death of knowledge.
—Alfred North Whitehead

Is it ever legitimate to treat a lack of evidence for a claim as evidence that the claim is false? In some cases, yes. Two exceptions, in particular, should be noted.

First, sometimes the fact that a search *hasn't* found something is good evidence that the thing isn't there to be found. Here are two examples:

> We've searched this car from top to bottom looking for the stolen jewels and no trace of the jewels has been found. Therefore, probably the jewels aren't in the car.

> After years of extensive scientific testing, there is no evidence that substance XYZ is toxic to rodents. Therefore, it's reasonable to conclude that substance XYZ is not toxic to rodents.

It is important to keep in mind, however, that this "fruitless search" exception applies only when (1) a careful search has been conducted, and (2) it is likely that the search would have found something if there had been anything there to be found.

The second exception applies to cases in which special rules require that a claim be rejected as false unless a certain burden of proof is met. Here are two examples:

> In the American legal system, a criminal defendant is legally guilty only if his or her guilt is proved beyond a reasonable doubt. My client has not been proven guilty beyond a reasonable doubt. Therefore, my client is not legally guilty.

> Under Wildebeest club rules, a member is guilty of "conduct unbecoming a Wildebeest" only if his or her guilt is proved by clear and convincing evidence. Elmo Hurlburt's guilt has not been proved by clear and convincing evidence. Therefore, Elmo Hurlburt is not guilty of conduct unbecoming a Wildebeest.

Critical Thinking Lapse

Joseph Pileggi thought he knew the woman he was marrying. But the woman he wed three years ago apparently wasn't 83-year-old Ducile Palermo. It was her 61-year-old daughter, Carli Buchanan. Pileggi, 69, says he was shocked when he came across the marriage license that Buchanan had signed as the bride and Palermo as a witness. He says he thought he married Palermo, with whom he'd lived since 1992. But the daughter claims Pileggi knew he was marrying her and that they consummated the wedding the same day. "He truly is in a state of disbelief," said Russell Pry, Pileggi's attorney. Pry said much of the confusion may be traced to Palermo's tendency to use her daughter's name. "I'm not sure what names were used in the wedding ceremony. I'm not even sure Joe knows," Pry said.[5]

In these examples, special rules of evidence require that a claim be rejected as false unless it is proven to be true by some elevated standard of proof. Because these special rules mandate the inference "not proven, therefore false," no fallacy is committed.

False Alternatives

The **fallacy of false alternatives** is committed when an arguer poses a false either/or choice.[6] Here are two examples:

> Look, the choice is simple. Either you support a pure free-market economy or you support a communist police state. Surely you don't support a communist police state. Therefore, you should support a pure free-market economy.

> Either we elect a Republican as president or crime rates will skyrocket. Obviously, we don't want crime rates to skyrocket. Therefore, we should elect a Republican as president.

Mankind likes to think in terms of extreme opposites. It is given to formulating its beliefs in terms of Either-Ors.

—John Dewey

In these examples, the arguers claim that there are only two relevant choices, when, in fact, there are more than two.[7] The first arguer poses a false choice by ignoring a wide range of political and economic systems that lie somewhere between a pure free-market economy on the one hand and a communist police state on the other. The second arguer poses a false choice by assuming, implausibly, that the only way to avoid rapidly rising crime rates is to elect a Republican as president.

Note that the fallacy of false alternatives need not involve just *two* false choices. For example:

> There are just three types of base hits in baseball: a single, a double, and a triple. Slugger got a base hit but didn't get a single or a double. Therefore, Slugger must have gotten a triple.

Doonesbury   BY GARRY TRUDEAU

Panel 1: YOU LOOK LIKE YOU'RE CHEWING ON SOMETHING, NEPHEW...

Panel 2: I AM, UNCLE ZONKER—I FIND MYSELF IN A QUANDARY!

Panel 3: I CAN'T DECIDE WHETHER TO JOIN A DRY FRAT OR A WET ONE! / WELL, LAY IT OUT. WHAT'S THE NUB?

Panel 4: BEING BORED TO TEARS VS. WAKING UP IN MY OWN VOMIT. / THAT *IS* A TOUGH CALL. WANT TO BE ALONE?

DOONESBURY © G. B. Trudeau. Reprinted with permission of Universal Press Syndicate. All rights reserved.

This argument poses a false choice between three alternatives: single, double, or triple. This is a false choice because it ignores the possibility that Slugger may have hit a home run.

Note also that the fallacy of false alternatives need not be explicitly expressed in "either . . . or" form. Often, for instance, a false choice is expressed as a conditional (if-then) statement, as in this example:

> If we don't elect a Democrat as president, then the economy will go down the tubes. Obviously, we don't want the economy to go down the tubes. So, we should elect a Democrat as president.

Here, the first sentence is equivalent to saying, "*Either* we elect a Democrat as president *or* the economy will go down the tubes."

It should also be noted that fallacies of false alternatives are often expressed as incomplete arguments. Here are two examples:

> Either buy me some candy, Daddy, or I'll hold my breath until I die.

> Dad, I know a new BMW is expensive, but you wouldn't want me riding around in this old rust bucket all winter long, would you?

It is not difficult to fill in the missing parts of these arguments.

Finally, it is important to keep in mind that merely posing a false choice is not a fallacy. Here are two examples:

> *Tabloid headline:* Bigfoot: Gentle Woodland Creature or Satan's Slave?[8]

> *Chapter title:* Children: Big Mistake, or Bad Idea?[9]

Although these questions certainly pose false choices, they are simply questions, not arguments. Because only arguments can be fallacies, these passages are not fallacies.

Loaded Question

A loaded question is a question that contains an unfair or questionable assumption. For example, "Do you still steal from your boss?" is a loaded question if it presupposes, without justification, that you once did steal from your boss. The **loaded question fallacy** occurs when an arguer asks a question that contains an unfair or unwarranted presupposition. Here is a particularly blatant example:

> *Joe:* Have you stopped cheating on exams?
>
> *Pete:* No!
>
> *Joe:* Oh, so you admit that you still cheat on exams?
>
> *Pete:* No, I meant to say yes!
>
> *Joe:* Oh, so you admit that you used to cheat on exams?

It is easy to spot the trick here. Joe's question, "Have you stopped cheating on exams?" is a loaded question because any direct yes or no answer to it will force Pete to admit something that he does not want to admit. Joe's apparently single question is really two questions rolled into one.

> *Question 1:* Did you cheat on exams in the past?
>
> *Question 2:* If you did cheat on exams in the past, have you stopped now?

By applying Pete's single yes or no answers to both questions, Joe commits the fallacy of the loaded question.

Here is a more realistic example:

> *Hon. Flora MacDonald (Kingston and the Islands)* [speaking in the Canadian House of Commons]: Madam Speaker, my question is also directed to the Minister of Finance. I would like to say to him that his policies are directly responsible for the fact that 1,185 more Canadians are without jobs every single day, 1,185 more Canadians with families to feed and mortgages to pay. How long is the minister prepared to condemn 1,200 more Canadians every day to job loss and insecurity because he is too stubborn and too uncaring to change his policies? [10]

This question is loaded because it unfairly rolls *three* questions into one.

> *Question 1:* Are the Minister of Finance's policies directly responsible for the fact that 1,185 Canadians lose their jobs every single day?
>
> *Question 2:* If so, are these policies allowed to continue because the Minister is too stubborn and uncaring to change his policies?
>
> *Question 3:* If the Minister is too stubborn and uncaring to change his policies, how much longer will this stubborn and uncaring attitude continue?

To respond to a loaded question effectively, you must often distinguish the different questions being asked and respond to each individually.

Are all loaded questions fallacies? No, strictly speaking, a loaded question is fallacious only if it is used unfairly in an argumentative context. For purposes of this text, however, it can be assumed that all loaded questions are fallacious. Thus, for example, the following questions may be regarded as fallacious:

> When are you going to stop acting so immature?
>
> Tell me, how long have you been embezzling money from the firm?
>
> Where did you hide the body?
>
> How long had you planned this bank robbery before you carried it out?
>
> Why do you always act like a total jerk when you're around my ex-boyfriend?
>
> Are you still in favor of this fiscally irresponsible bill?
>
> Did you write this immoral trash?

Questionable Cause

We live in a complex and mysterious world. Often, it is hard to know what has caused some event to occur. When an arguer claims, without sufficient evidence, that one thing is the cause of something else, he commits the **fallacy of questionable cause.**

There are three common varieties of the questionable cause fallacy: the *post hoc* fallacy, the mere correlation fallacy, and the oversimplified cause fallacy.

The *post hoc fallacy* (from the Latin *post hoc ergo propter hoc* ["after this, therefore because of this"]) is committed when an arguer assumes, without adequate evidence, that because one event, A, occurred before another event, B, A is the cause of B. Here are two examples:

> How do I know that ginseng tea is a cure for the common cold? Last week I had a bad case of the sniffles. I drank a cup of ginseng tea, and the next morning my sniffles were gone.
>
> *Medieval villager:* Two days after that old hag Jezebel Taylor moved into the village, my cow died. That witch must have put a hex on my cow!

In the first example, the arguer assumes that because her sniffles disappeared after she drank ginseng tea, drinking the tea must have caused her sniffles to disappear. This is precisely the kind of *post hoc* reasoning that underlies almost all quack cures. It is much more reasonable to suppose that the arguer never really had a cold or that the cold simply got better on its own.[11]

The second example illustrates how superstitions often have their origin in *post hoc* thinking. It is a fallacy to think that because something bad happened to you after a black cat crossed your path, black cats are bad luck.

Another common variety of the false cause fallacy is the mere correlation fallacy. The *mere correlation fallacy* is committed when an arguer assumes, without sufficient evidence, that because A and B regularly occur together, A must be the cause of B (or vice versa). Here are two examples:

> On Monday I stayed up all night partying, had eggs for breakfast, and failed my calculus test. On Wednesday I stayed up all night partying, had eggs for breakfast, and failed my biology test. On Thursday I stayed up all night partying, had eggs for breakfast, and failed my history test. Obviously, to do better on tests, I must stop eating eggs for breakfast.[12]

> *Aztec high priest:* Every spring we sacrifice a virgin to the sun god, and every spring the life-giving rains come. Therefore, sacrificing a virgin to the sun god causes the life-giving rains to come.

In these examples, the arguers have mistakenly assumed that because two events are regularly correlated (i.e., go together), there must be a cause-and-effect relationship between the two. But correlation does not imply causation. The rooster may crow every morning just before sunrise, but that doesn't mean that the rooster's crowing causes the sun to rise.

Perhaps the most common form of the questionable cause fallacy is the *oversimplified cause fallacy.* This fallacy is committed when we assume, without sufficient evidence, that A is the sole cause of B, when, in fact, there are several causes of B. Here are two examples:

> Violent crime has declined steadily in recent years. Obviously, tougher imprisonment policies are working.

> SAT scores have fallen sharply since the 1960s. Clearly, students are watching too much TV.[13]

The first argument oversimplifies the situation by ignoring other causes that have likely contributed to falling crimes rates (new policing strategies, changing demographics, reduced use of crack cocaine, etc.). In the second argument, the arguer correctly identifies one likely cause of declining SAT scores: kids today watch too much TV. However, he fails to mention other important causes that have also contributed to the decline (e.g., the fact that a much larger number of average and below-average students now take the SAT than was true in the past). For those reasons, these arguments commit the fallacy of questionable cause.

Hasty Generalization

A *generalization* is a statement that asserts that *all* or *most* things of a certain kind have a certain property or characteristic. Here are some examples of generalizations:

> All emeralds are green.
>
> Most college students receive financial aid.
>
> Most dogs are not dangerous.
>
> Plays are boring! [All plays? Most plays?]
>
> Germans are very methodical. [All Germans? Most Germans?]

We commit the **fallacy of hasty generalization** when we draw a general conclusion from a sample that is biased or too small. Here are two examples:

> Do most Americans still believe in God? To find out, we asked over 10,000 scientists at colleges and universities throughout America. Less than 40 percent said they believed in God. The conclusion is obvious: Most Americans no longer believe in God.

> *Small-business owner:* I've hired three San Pedrans in the last six months, and all three were lazy and shiftless. I guess most San Pedrans are lazy and shiftless.

The first argument is fallacious because it draws a general conclusion from a sample that is *biased* (i.e., not representative of the target population as a whole). Surveys indicate that scientists tend to be far more skeptical of religious beliefs than average Americans.[14]

The second argument illustrates how hasty generalizations can give rise to harmful stereotypes and prejudices. In this example, a general conclusion is drawn from a sample that is too small to support a reliable generalization. It is unfair, as well as illogical, to stigmatize an entire people on the basis of the perceived faults of a few.

It should be noted that not every argument that "jumps to a conclusion" is a hasty generalization. For example:

> That large biker with the swastika tattoo and the brass knuckles looks friendly enough. I bet he wouldn't mind if I introduced myself with a joy buzzer handshake.

This is certainly a hasty conclusion. But it is not a hasty generalization, because it is not a generalization at all. The conclusion is a particular statement about one particular biker, not a general statement about bikers in general. A hasty generalization must have a general statement (i.e., a statement about all or most members of a group) as its conclusion. Hence, this argument does not commit the fallacy of hasty generalization.[15]

Those sweeping judgements which are so common are meaningless. They are like men who salute a whole crowd of people in the mass. Those who really know them salute and take notice of them individually and by name.

—Montaigne

Slippery Slope

We often hear arguments of this sort: "We can't allow A, because A will lead to B, and B will lead to C, and we sure as heck don't want C!" Arguments of this sort are called slippery-slope arguments. Often, such arguments are fallacious. We commit the **slippery-slope fallacy** when we claim, without sufficient evidence, that a seemingly harmless action, if taken, will lead to a disastrous outcome. Here are several examples:

> Senator Walker has argued that we should outlaw terrorist threats on the Internet. This proposal is dangerous, and must be strongly resisted. If we allow the government to outlaw terrorist threats on the Internet, next it will want to ban "hate speech" and other allegedly "harmful" speech on the Internet. Next, the government will want to censor "harmful" ideas on television, on

radio, and in newspapers. Eventually, everything you see, hear or read will be totally controlled by the government.

Bans on so-called "assault weapons" must be vigorously opposed. Once the gun-grabbing liberals have outlawed "assault weapons," next they'll go after handguns. After that, it will be shotguns and semiautomatic hunting rifles. In the end, law-abiding citizens will be left totally defenseless against predatory criminals and a tyrannical government.

In a recent letter to the editor, Stella Davis argued that we should legalize same-sex marriages. But allowing same-sex marriages would undermine respect for traditional marriage. Traditional marriage is the very foundation of our society. If that foundation is destroyed, our whole society will collapse. Thus, if we want to prevent the complete disintegration of our society, we must oppose the legalization of same-sex marriage.

Notice that each of these arguments has the same basic pattern:

1. The arguer claims that if a certain seemingly harmless action, A, is permitted, A will lead to B, B will lead to C, and so on to D.
2. The arguer holds that D is a terrible thing and therefore should not be permitted.
3. In fact, there is no good reason to believe that A will actually lead to D.[16]

It should be noted that many slippery–slope arguments leave out some or all of the intermediate steps that an arguer believes will occur. Here are two examples:

Dr. Perry has proposed that we legalize physician-assisted suicide. No sensible person should listen to such a proposal. If we allow physician-assisted suicide, eventually there will be no respect for human life.

Socialized medicine really frightens me. Once you start down that road, there's no turning back. A complete socialist dictatorship is the inevitable result.

In general terms, it is not difficult to imagine what sorts of intermediate steps these arguers fear will occur.

It is important to note that not all slippery–slope arguments are fallacious. Sometimes there are good reasons for thinking that an undesirable or even catastrophic series of events may result from a seemingly harmless first step. For example:

Brad, I know you've been shootin' up heroin. Man, don't you know what that stuff can do to you? First, you shoot up "just when you need a rush." After a while, you become addicted to the stuff. You lose your job, your apartment, even steal from your best friend to feed the habit. Eventually you wind up dead in some alley or strung out in some detox center. Listen to me, I'm your best friend. Think about what you're doing.

In this case, there are perfectly sound reasons for avoiding an all-too-genuine slippery slope.

Weak Analogy

We have all heard the expression "That's like comparing apples and oranges." This saying points to a mistake that critical thinkers call the fallacy of weak analogy. The **fallacy of weak analogy** occurs when an arguer compares two (or more) things that aren't really comparable in relevant respects. Here are two examples:

> Teachers of false religions are like carriers of a deadly plague. Just as we rightly quarantine plague victims to prevent them from infecting others, so we should quarantine teachers of false religions to prevent them from spreading their spiritual poison.

> Lettuce is leafy and green and tastes great with a baloney sandwich. Poison ivy is also leafy and green. Therefore, poison ivy probably tastes great with a baloney sandwich, too.

In these examples, there are obvious and important differences, or "disanalogies," between the things being compared. Because of these disanalogies, the premises don't provide good reasons to accept the conclusion.

Fallacies of weak analogy occur in many different forms. However, three patterns are particularly common.

One common pattern is a comparison of two things that have several identified similarities. For example:

> Alan is tall, dark, and handsome, and has blue eyes. Bill is also tall, dark, and handsome. Therefore, Bill probably has blue eyes, too.

The basic pattern here is this:

1. A has characteristics w, x, y, and z.
2. B has characteristics w, x, and y.
3. Therefore, B probably has characteristic z, too.

Many arguments with this pattern are perfectly good arguments. For example:

> Alice lives in a mansion, drives a Rolls Royce, wears expensive jewelry, and is rich. Beatrice also lives in a mansion, drives a Rolls Royce, and wears expensive jewelry. Therefore, Beatrice probably is rich, too.

This is a good argument from analogy because people who live in a mansion, drive a Rolls Royce, and wear expensive jewelry are usually rich. However, there is no relevant connection between being tall, dark, and handsome on the one hand, and having blue eyes on the other. For that reason, the first example is fallacious.

Another common pattern of reasoning by analogy is a comparison of several things that have only one or two identified similarities. For example:

> Jake is a member of the Wexford College Football Fanatics, and he goes bare-chested to all the home football games. Kyle is a member of the

Wexford College Football Football Fanatics, and he goes bare-chested to all the home football games. Brad is a member of the Wexford College Football Fanatics, and he goes bare-chested to all the home football games. Jennifer is also a member of the Wexford College Football Fanatics. So, she probably goes bare-chested to the home football games, too.

The pattern of the argument is this:

1. A is an x, and A is a y.
2. B is an x, and B is a y.
3. C is an x, and C is a y.
4. D is an x.
5. Therefore, D is probably a y, too.

This argument is clearly fallacious because it ignores an obvious difference between the things being compared (the fact that Jennifer is a woman). However, some arguments with this logical pattern are good arguments from analogy. For example:

Steven Spielberg directed *Jaws,* and that was a good movie. Spielberg directed *Schindler's List,* and that was a good movie. Spielberg directed *Saving Private Ryan,* and that was a good movie. In fact, I've seen almost all of Spielberg's movies, and almost all of them have been good. Therefore, Spielberg's next movie will probably also be good.

This is a good argument from analogy, because there is good reason to think that the things being compared are, in fact, relevantly similar.

A third common pattern of argument by analogy is simply an assertion, without further elaboration, that two cases are relevantly similar. For example:

Why does a family who has no children in a school district have to pay school taxes? This is like paying cigarette taxes even though you don't smoke.[17]

Here, the arguer doesn't bother to spell out why he thinks these two cases are analogous. To critically evaluate an argument like this, we need to do three things: List all important similarities between the two cases; list all important dissimilarities between the two cases; and decide whether, on balance, the similarities are strong enough to support the conclusion.

Let's apply this three-step method to the school taxes argument.

Step 1: List important similarities.
   How making families that have no children in a public school system pay school taxes is *like making people who don't smoke pay cigarette taxes:*
   Both are taxes that you are required to pay regardless of whether you or your family derives any immediate benefit from them.

Step 2: List important dissimilarities.
   How making families that have no children in a public school system pay school taxes is not *like making people who don't smoke pay cigarette taxes:*

Imposing school taxes on all property owners benefits society by promoting equal educational opportunities and helping to create an educated and informed citizenry. Imposing cigarette taxes on nonsmokers would harm society by subsidizing an activity that is harmful and addictive.

Imposing school taxes on all property owners provides significant indirect benefits even to families without school-aged children, because the taxes help to create a better-educated workforce and citizenry. Imposing cigarette taxes on nonsmokers would provide few, if any, indirect benefits to people who don't smoke.

It is fair to require cigarette smokers to pay cigarette taxes, because smokers impose economic and health costs on the rest of society in the form of higher insurance premiums, increased Medicare costs, lost workdays, health risks of second-hand smoke, and so on. It would *not* be fair to require nonsmokers to pay cigarette taxes, because this would force nonsmokers to subsidize a costly and unhealthy activity that doesn't benefit them and for which they bear no personal responsibility.

Step 3: Decide whether the similarities or the dissimilarities are more important.

In this case, the relevant differences between the two cases are too great to support the conclusion. For that reason, the argument commits the fallacy of weak analogy.[18]

Inconsistency

Two statements are inconsistent when they both can't be true. The **fallacy of inconsistency** occurs when an arguer asserts inconsistent premises, asserts a premise that is inconsistent with his or her conclusion, or argues for inconsistent conclusions. Here are several examples:

Philosophy professor: Error doesn't exist.
Student: I deny that.
Philosophy professor: Well, then you're dead wrong.

Mickey Mantle: Hey, Yogi, what do you say we eat at Toots's tonight?
Yogi Berra: That place is old news. Nobody goes there anymore. It's too crowded.[19]

Pearson Q. Legacy: Preferential treatment is unfair and discriminatory. It has no place in college admissions.
Roommate: But didn't you say a minute ago that you got into this college only because your father was a rich alumnus?
Pearson Q. Legacy: Well, yeah. But what's wrong with that?
Roommate: Just checking, man.

> ### Critical Thinking Lapse
>
> SALT LAKE CITY—It wouldn't be surprising if Johnny Lee Miller got upset at the mention of his anger-management course. FBI agents seeking a man who took $34,804 from First Utah Bank on New Year's Eve caught up with Miller after finding his course graduation certificate in the bank's vault, said U.S. Attorney Paul Warner. The FBI said Miller slid a gun out from an envelope and demanded of a teller, "Where is the money?" The suspect took the gun with him but left behind the envelope, which also contained the certificate. It was issued by the Utah Department of Corrections.[20]

The foolish and the dead alone never change their opinion.

—James Russell Lowell

In the first example, the arguer asserts a claim that conflicts with her conclusion. In the second and third examples, the arguers assert inconsistent premises. For those reasons, these arguments commit the fallacy of inconsistency.

Inconsistency is a logical fault that critical thinkers are careful to avoid. We should remember, however, that it is also a mistake to cling stubbornly to an old idea when new information suggests that the idea is false. No real learning takes place without an openness to new ideas.

EXERCISE 6.1

I. Identify the fallacies of insufficient evidence in the following arguments. If no fallacy is committed, write "no fallacy."

1. I better eat my Wheaties. Michael Jordan says that it's the breakfast of champions.
2. I can't believe I failed my chemistry test. I knew I should have worn my lucky sweatshirt to take the test.
3. When is the CIA going to quit stonewalling about its involvement in the Kennedy assassination?
4. Podunk State University is a better university than Harvard University. I've been assured of this by Dr. Bigelow Hype, Dean of Admissions at Podunk State University.
5. Skeptics have tried for centuries to prove that reincarnation is a myth, and no one has ever succeeded. Therefore, we must conclude that reincarnation is a fact.
6. I've long been convinced that nothing exists outside my own mind. Indeed, the arguments for this seem so obvious to me that I can't understand why everybody else doesn't believe it, too.[21]
7. Ford cars are lemons. I've owned two, and they gave me nothing but trouble.
8. *Police detective:* Did you get a good look at the bank robber?
   Witness: Yes, I saw his face clearly. It was Willie, the night watchman.
   Police detective: And were you also able to recognize his voice?

Witness: No, I couldn't really hear what he said very well. His voice was muffled by the full ski mask he wore.

9. Either you support preferential treatment for disadvantaged minorities in university admissions or you're a racist. But surely you're not a racist. Therefore, you support preferential treatment for disadvantaged minorities in university admissions.

10. Old Mr. Ferguson (who resides at the Burnside Home for the Blind) claims he could read the car's license plate from over 150 feet away. I've never known Mr. Ferguson to be deliberately dishonest. Therefore, we should conclude that Mr. Ferguson really did read the car's license plate from over 150 feet away.

11. Students have asked that we extend residence hall visitation hours by one hour on Friday and Saturday nights. This request will have to be denied. If we give students an extra visitation hour on weekends, next they'll be asking us to allow their boyfriends and girlfriends to stay over all night. Eventually, we'll have students shacking up in every room.

12. There is no information in Private Wilson's service record that indicates that he is not a homosexual. Consequently, I can only assume that he is.

13. A Saint Bernard is large, cuddly, and furry, and makes a great house pet. A grizzly bear is also large, cuddly, and furry. Therefore, a grizzly bear would make a great house pet, too.

14. I've searched my car carefully and I haven't found my lost car keys there. It's reasonable to conclude, therefore, that my car keys aren't in the car.

15. You're not seriously thinking of voting for that bum, are you? Why don't you wake up and smell the coffee?

16. Most of the immigrants who enter this country wind up in jail or on welfare. I know this because I read it on a White Power Web site.

17. It would be a much greater wrong to destroy the last remaining copy of Shakespeare's *Macbeth* than it would be to destroy an individual copy of *Macbeth*. Similarly, it is a much greater wrong to cause the extinction of an entire animal species than it is to destroy an individual member of that species.

18. In golf, there's nothing wrong with taking a mulligan (i.e., a do-over shot) if you hit a bad shot on the first tee. Similarly, there's nothing wrong with getting an abortion if you discover that the child is not going to be of the desired sex.

19. It says in the *Encyclopaedia Britannica* that the Bermejo River is a western tributary of the Paraguay River, in south-central South America. This is probably true, because the *Encyclopaedia Britannica* is a highly reliable reference source.

20. The volcano erupted shortly after the king abandoned worship of the ancient tribal spirits. Obviously, the tribal spirits must be angry.

21. Strong measures must be taken to halt the flood of Mexican immigrants into the United States. If we allow this immigration to continue, soon Spanish will become the official language of California and Texas. Eventually, the entire United States will be just a cultural offshoot of Mexico.

22. I once hired a blonde, and you know what? They are a little slow on the uptake.

23. Only two U.S. states border on California: Nevada and Arizona. Therefore, if we wish to leave California and drive to another U.S. state by car, we can drive to either Nevada or Arizona.

24. Why all the fuss about preserving old-growth redwood forests? Redwood trees are like Motel 6's. Once you've seen one, you've seen them all.[22]

25. My taxicab driver this morning told me he once drove from New York to Los Angeles in less than eighteen hours at an average speed of 165 mph. I hate to think how many speeding tickets he must have gotten along the way!

26. If a large asteroid had struck China in A.D. 1200, it's likely that some historical records of the disaster would have been preserved. But there is absolutely no mention of any such catastrophe in any of the numerous Chinese historical records that survive from that period. Therefore, it's reasonable to conclude that a large asteroid did not strike China in A.D. 1200.

27. Why do you find it so difficult to be fair and impartial?

28. I'm prejudiced only if I hold irrational biases. But I don't hold any irrational biases. I just think this country's being overrun by Catholics and Jews.

29. Since the 1960s, promiscuity, divorce, abortion, teen suicide, and out-of-wedlock births have all risen sharply. The cause-and-effect relationship is clear. Plainly, we need to restore prayer in public schools.

30. Dr. Leonard Vesey, Chief of Pediatrics at Boston Children's Hospital, has argued that abortion is always immoral. Given Dr. Vesey's impressive professional credentials, we must conclude that abortion is always immoral.

31. President Clinton: One of our best presidents or one of our worst?

32. Rich Kowalski is a young, successful CEO of an Internet start-up company, and his parents come from Poland. Kelly Yablonski is a young, successful CEO of an Internet start-up company, and her parents come from Poland. Matt Golembeski is a young, successful CEO of an Internet start-up company, and his parents come from Poland. Miguel Gonzalez is also a young, successful CEO of an Internet start-up company. So, his parents probably come from Poland, too.

33. A benevolent, all-powerful Creator may exist. On the other hand, a benevolent, all-powerful Creator may not exist. No one knows for certain which of these claims is true. But one thing is certain: one of these claims must be true.

34. There's nothing wrong with segregating restrooms on the basis of race. After all, we've always had separate restrooms for men and women, and no one seems to complain about that.

35. Which sport is more popular: sailing or snow skiing? To find out, we asked more than 500 people on the streets of Miami, Florida. The result? Americans prefer sailing by a margin of more than 3 to 1.

36. I have no proof that my refrigerator light goes off when I close the refrigerator door. Therefore, it's reasonable to believe that it doesn't.

37. Most women from California believe in astrology. I know because I've dated three women from California, and they all believed in astrology.

38. I don't understand why you have to wear a helmet to play football. Soccer is a dangerous sport, and they don't make soccer players wear helmets.

39. Carl Sagan, the world-famous astronomer, has argued that Venus is too hot to support life. Moreover, I've consulted three astronomy textbooks, and they all agree with Dr. Sagan on this point. Therefore, it's reasonable to believe that Venus is too hot to support life.

40. If we don't dramatically increase defense spending, the Chinese will soon surpass us as a military power. If the Chinese surpass us as a military power, it's only a matter of time before we'll all be speaking Chinese and eating chop suey.

II. Most of the following passages were taken from letters to the editor and newspaper call-in columns. Identify any fallacies discussed in this chapter or in the previous chapter that you find. If no fallacy is committed, write "no fallacy."

1. When will the American people finally realize that the Democrats are leading this country straight into socialism? (From a newspaper call-in column)

2. Nasrudin was throwing handfuls of crumbs around his house. "What are you doing?" someone asked him. "Keeping the tigers away." "But there are no tigers in these parts." "That's right. Effective, isn't it." (Idries Shah, *The Exploits of the Incomparable Mulla Nasrudin,* 1972 [slightly adapted])

3. I'd like to make a comment on the boy who wore the KKK outfit to school. I think it was blown way out of proportion. You have other organizations, the KKK is an organization, the Knights of Columbus is an organization, the Shriners are an organization, the Masons are an organization, they all have uniforms. This is a uniform of something that is all over the United States, the KKK. Now, I don't see anything wrong with it. (From a newspaper call-in column)

4. You're either a feminist or you're a complete idiot. (Susan Powter)[23]

5. See it or be un-American! (Ad for *Rocky and Bullwinkle* movie)

6. This is for the person that thinks school board relatives are smarter than everybody else. Prove it, and until you do, they're still stupid. (From a newspaper call-in column)

7. This is for the youngster who writes that he is paying the bills for the oldsters. Years ago my wife and I took the family out of the area to find better jobs. . . . Now, in our 70s and retired, we are back and in somewhat good health, but on about 12 different medications. Our drug co-pay this year will probably be $1,100 and the supplemental insurance that covers this co-pay is over $500 a month. Medicare payments are deducted from Social Security and some Social Security is even taxed. . . . This whiner who [called in] probably doesn't have the guts it would take to get any amount of schooling and leave the area to improve his situation. Ignorance is curable by learning, but stupidity is forever. (From a newspaper call-in column)

8. Party labels don't mean anything anymore. You can draw a line right down the middle. On the one side are the Americans, on the other are the Communists and Socialists. (George Murphy, Speech to a Republican Fundraiser, 1946)[24]

9. In regards to Thursday's paper: To have a gay lead a Boy Scout troop. Isn't that like putting the fox in the hen house? What a travesty of common sense. (From a newspaper call-in column)

10. I'm calling in regards to that person in California that used his car to run into the fence and kill those two children. Now I hope the anti-gunners out there will now take up a cry to ban automobiles. (From a newspaper call-in column)

11. To the caller that talked about [college basketball player] Dave Januzzi and said the only way he was going to see Europe is as a traveler. Well, I'd like to see you play him one-on-one. (From a newspaper call-in column)

12. After nine years at Pacific Bell I learned just about everything there was to know about *looking* busy without actually being busy. During that time the stock price of Pacific Bell climbed steadily, so I think I can conclude that my avoidance of work was in the best interest of the company and something to be proud of. (Scott Adams, *The Dilbert Principle,* 1996)

13. Your opinion that Puerto Rican citizens should vote in an election is entirely wrong. Puerto Rico is not a state in the United States, it has never been a state, and only states in the United States have a right to let their people vote. If you start with Puerto Rico, why not the Virgin Islands, why not Cuba, why not Panama? (From a newspaper call-in column)

14. *U.S. Army Captain Laughlin Waters:* "Well, you were supposed to have 1,500 prisoners. Where are they?"
    Polish captain: "They are dead. We shot them. These are all that are left."
    Captain Waters: "Then why don't you shoot these, too?" A pause, then Waters corrected himself: "No, you can't do that."
    Polish captain: "Oh, yes we can. They shot my countrymen." [25]

15. This is about the person who is concerned about McDonald Corporation's treatment of pigs and chickens. What about the poor potatoes? They gouge out their eyes, they rip off their skin, and they throw them in boiling oil. (From a newspaper call-in column)

16. I see where students in Lehman High School made death threats. They shouldn't show pictures like *Star Wars* for them kids to go see. Teenagers going to see *Star Wars* is a waste of money. That's where they get such silly ideas. (From a newspaper call-in column)

17. Miscarriages of justice are rare [in capital sentencing], but they do occur. Over a long enough time they lead to the execution of some innocents. Does this make irrevocable punishments morally wrong? Hardly. Our government employs trucks. They run over innocent bystanders more frequently than courts sentence innocents to death. We do not give up trucks because the benefits they produce outweigh the harm, including the death of innocents. (Ernest van den Haag, "The Death Penalty Once More," 1985)

18. The one point fixed by nature, and by God, is that there must be authority everywhere, and that the authority existent for the time being, under such and such a form, be under that form obeyed; for since there is no actual authority in the country except under that form, to refuse to obey that is to

refuse authority simply, and to revert to anarchy, which is against nature: just as a man having nothing but bread and cheese to eat, and refusing to eat his bread and cheese, under pretence that he much prefers mutton, condemns himself to starvation, which again is unnatural. (Joseph Rickaby, S.J., "Authority," 1913)

19. Boji stones. These miraculous stones were found at the bottom of a natural earth pyramid at North America's geographical center. Paired as male (angular projections on surface) and female (smooth), their balanced energy alleviates pain by closing holes in the human energy field. (Advertisement in *The Pyramid Collection: A Catalog of Personal Growth and Exploration,* 1998)

20. In regards to the teachers working on the Dallas [Pennsylvania] curriculum. That's a joke. I had two daughters nine years apart in the Dallas Middle School. Both had the same two science teachers, they used the same exact questions and lesson plans nine years later. Come on guys, wake up. Science changes on a daily basis. Dallas teachers are a joke and an embarrassment. (From a newspaper call-in column)

21. One of your readers suggested we should ban smoking [in public places] like California does. I'm from New York and New York State tried to do something similar, but think about this. You might be concerned with the filthy smoke that streams over to the nonsmoking section, but realize this: When your state starts to control your actions that's just the beginning, and soon everything else will be controlled. You might want to think about that. If you don't like places that allow smoking, try going somewhere that does not allow it. (From a newspaper call-in column)

22. School uniforms are effective in promoting safety in schools, because they do cut down on crime and violence. (From a student paper)

23. The callers who oppose the sport of hunting are entitled to their opinions. Career welfare recipients are also entitled to their opinions. When you contribute to the purchase of game lands, the restoration of the deer herd, the restocking of turkeys, pheasants, etc., then your opinion might mean something. When you support the economy of this area through the numerous purchases of firearms, ammunition, boots, clothing, etc., used in our fine sport, then your uninformed and short-sighted opinion might carry some weight. (From a newspaper call-in column)

24. I hope that you understand why it would be wrong to allow a club for homosexuals in school. It would only encourage a lifestyle that is destructive and immoral.

    If you still believe there should be a gay club, then you should insist on there being a club for thieves and robbers and a club for murderers including abortionists. (Letter to the Editor, *Scranton Times,* April 2, 1996)

25. I read your editorial concerning the helmet law for motorcycle riders (Dec. 3). This opinion sounds like it comes from a draft-dodging yuppie who probably drives an imported car, has never been on a motorcycle, and is proud to call himself an American. . . .

    The real issue here is "personal freedom." A lot of things we do in life are dangerous. Have you ever driven on bad roads to return a video rental before you get a late charge? What risks we take! Where do you draw the line? . . .

You editors should be careful: You may stab yourself with a pen, get carpal tunnel syndrome from clicking your mouse, or worse yet—get a paper cut. Then we would have to legislate a ban on these items and that might endanger your livelihood. (Letter to the Editor, *Wilkes-Barre Times Leader,* December 20, 1998)

26. A savings certificate for the *New York Review of Books* asked respondents to place one of two stickers on the reply card. The first sticker read: "Yes! I'm an intellectual and proud of it. Send me 3 free issues!" The second one read: "No! I don't like to think. Give my 3 free issues to someone who does."

27. I have been noticing recently and have also read in the local newspapers that there are probably more and more young women between the ages of 18 and 29 involved in automobile accidents.

These young women drive their vehicles with complete disregard for the legal speed limits. Usually when someone is passing you on the highway, and you are going the allowed speed limit, it will be a young woman driver passing at an incredible rate of speed. (Letter to the Editor, *Wilkes-Barre Times Leader,* January 15, 2000)

28. I found the editorial Other Opinion, "Decreasing crime rates in U.S. envy of the Brits" (Nov. 11), very interesting. I find it hard to believe the Brits don't really know the cause of the increased crime.

It's very simple. It's the failure of that nation's gun-control laws. Britain is in the company of locales like Washington, D.C., New York City, Chicago, Los Angeles and South Carolina.

In 1976, Washington enacted a virtual ban on handguns. By 1991, that city's homicide rate had tripled, while the U.S. rate rose 12 percent. New York City, Chicago, Los Angeles and Washington—all having very restrictive gun laws—make up only 5 percent of the U.S. population, yet account for 15 percent of U.S. murders.

Why all the fuss about gun control and registration? Quite simply, gun registration has been used—even in this country—to later confiscate firearms. (Letter to the Editor, *Wilkes-Barre Times Leader,* November 21, 1998)

29. Judges make the decision to return children to an abusive home once the Department of Human Services has investigated a home and have presented their findings to the judge. Unfortunately most judges are incompetent to make a decision.

I have watched three cases in which judges in Pawhuska [Oklahoma] have allowed access of their children to abusive parents. (Letter to the Editor, *Tulsa World,* May 17, 1994)

30. I just want to say about this President Clinton, how he could go to Arlington Cemetery, the draft dodger, go to Arlington Cemetery and make a speech in front of these guys that fought for our country. Oh, it just burns me up. I wish I could, I feel like calling him a SOB, and I hope you put that in the paper, that he is a SOB, to go and make a speech in front of that Arlington Cemetery. (From a newspaper call-in column)

31. Yeah, this is for the person who called in and said that he likes enjoying cold weather football and there are sissy teams in the dome and down in Florida. I have one question for this macho man. Was he sitting outside in his yard with his TV and cold beer out in the snow? Or was he in his warm, warm living room? Who's the real sissy, pal? (From a newspaper call-in column)

32. We seem to have a one-sided society today. Men and women trying to be like men, that's why our kids have gone bonkers today. (From a newspaper call-in column)

33. Maybe my hearing is going bad, but I didn't hear one weather person attributing the recent storms to "Mother Nature." Did they finally realize there is no such person?

     This fictional being was created by radical feminists who want to overthrow any kind of male leadership.

     They want "God the Father" to become "Mother of Us All."

     They want the fathers in the house to become effeminate, limp-wristed sweeties. And they want to call all the shots.

     These feminists aren't after equal rights for women but are trying to change things in a negative way. They want to pressure Democrats into putting more gay men into public office. They want to show movies of lesbians kissing to pre-school girls. (Letter to the Editor, *Wilkes-Barre Times Leader,* June 6, 1998)

34. I would like to comment on the woman who says kids don't have anything to do. Well, lady, when we were kids, we all worked doing something, we didn't have everything handed to us. Today's kids, most of them, are all a bunch of arrogant, spoiled jerks. They have no respect for the law or anybody else. They're mostly all on drugs, their parents don't give a damn, either. . . . This is a disgusted citizen. Might as well move out in Bullfrog County someplace. (From a newspaper call-in column)

35. Amid cries that there is too much violence on TV, members of Congress are moving to censor network programming. Congress should mind its own dang business. . . .

     Rep. Edward Markey, D-Mass., wants to require new TV sets to include a computer chip that will allow parents to block violent programs.

     That's not as harmless as it seems. What's next? A computer chip to block antigovernment programs? (Editorial, "On TV Censorship," *Charleston (W. Va.) Daily Mail,* August 13, 1993)

36. The Democratic Party makes victims out of all taxpaying Americans. For 40 years they had control of Congress and the money. The results? We've had an out-of-control illegitimacy rate, out-of-control entitlements for illegal immigrants, a public education system that's broken. There's [sic] more people in prison than any other nation. We've had moral decay. It seems that the Democratic Congress's objective was to keep everybody uneducated, overweight, drugged and drunk, and charge responsible taxpayers for the cost. (From a newspaper call-in column)

37. We can have a free country or a socialistic one. We cannot have both. Our economic system cannot be half free and half socialistic. . . . There is no

middle ground between governing and being governed, between absolute sovereignty and liberty, between tyranny and freedom. (Ogden Mills, *Liberalism Fights On,* 1936)

38. To the person that feels a methadone clinic is way overdue in this area, you must be a heroin addict as well. Why don't you ask the people that supplied you with the heroin to help you out here? We don't need a methadone clinic here. (From a newspaper call-in column)

39. You know who's pushing [the right to abortion]. You saw some of those women out there. I mean those women aren't ever going to have a baby by anybody. I mean, these are primarily lesbians, and lesbians don't have babies. And it's the one thing a mother has—that a lesbian can never have—is this femininity, and they can never achieve that. And so, in order to level the field, they say, "Hey, let you abort your baby so you'll be like us, because we don't have them." (Pat Robertson, Statement on the *700 Club*[26]

40. It is a proven scientific fact that video games are . . . corrupting American youth. In a recent experiment, scientific researchers exposed a group of teenaged boys to an arcade game, and found all of them had unclean thoughts. Of course, the researchers got the same result when they exposed the boys to coleslaw, an alpaca sweater, and "The McNeil-Lehrer News Hour" but that is beside the point. The point is that we should all write letters to our elected officials to urge them to ban video games. (Dave Barry, *Dave Barry's Bad Habits,* 1985)

III. Write an offbeat or amusing example of each of the fallacies of insufficient evidence discussed in this chapter. Be prepared to share your examples with the class.

IV. Find examples of the fallacies discussed in this chapter from everyday life (newspapers, magazines, TV, radio, etc.). Collect your examples in a notebook or portfolio. For each example, indicate where you found the fallacy and explain briefly why you think it commits the fallacy you allege. Be prepared to share your examples with the class.

V. Watch the classic 1957 film *12 Angry Men* in class. As you do so, keep the following questions in mind for class discussion.

1. What evidence initially points to the guilt of the defendant? How was this evidence later undermined or called into question by good critical thinking?

2. What fallacies were committed by individual jurors? (Hint: There are lots of them.)

3. In your opinion, was the final verdict correct or incorrect? Defend your answer.

4. What do you see as the basic "message" of the film?

5. Why aren't there any women on the jury?

6. Does the film lower your confidence in the jury system? Why or why not?

7. How does the film underscore the practical value of critical thinking skills and dispositions?

VI. This exercise is a game we call "Name That Fallacy!" Here's how the game is played: The instructor divides the class into teams of four or five students.

The instructor reads an example of a fallacy (or puts it on an overhead). The first team to raise a hand gets a chance to identify the fallacy. Before the instructor reveals the correct answer, the other teams are given the opportunity to challenge the first team's answer. Scoring is as follows:

Correct answer: 5 points
Incorrect answer: −5 points
Correct challenge: 5 points
Incorrect challenge: −5 points

The first team to reach 40 points wins.[27]

Summary

1. In this chapter we studied fallacies of insufficient evidence. *Fallacies of insufficient evidence* are arguments in which the premises, though logically relevant to the conclusion, fail to provide sufficient evidence to support the conclusion.

2. In this chapter we studied nine common fallacies of insufficient evidence:

   a. *Inappropriate appeal to authority:* Citing a witness or an authority that is untrustworthy.

      Example

      My hairdresser told me that extraterrestrials built the lost city of Atlantis. So, it's reasonable to believe that extraterrestrials did build the lost city of Atlantis.

   b. *Appeal to ignorance:* Claiming that something is true because no one has proven it false, or vice versa.

      Example

      Bigfoot must exist. No one has proved that it doesn't.

   c. *False alternatives:* Posing a false either/or choice.

      Example

      The choice in this election is clear. Either we elect a staunch conservative as our next president, or we watch as our country slides into anarchy and economic depression. Clearly, we don't want our country to slide into anarchy and economic depression. Therefore, we should elect a staunch conservative as our next president.

   d. *Loaded question:* Posing a question that contains an unfair or unwarranted presupposition.

      Example

      Al: Are you still dating that total loser Phil?

      Mary: Yes.

      Al: Well, at least you admit he's a total loser.

e. *Questionable cause:* Claiming, without sufficient evidence, that one thing is the cause of something else.

Example

Two days after I drank lemon tea, my head cold cleared up completely. Try it. It works.

f. *Hasty generalization:* Drawing a general conclusion from a sample that is biased or too small.

Example

BMWs are a pile of junk. I have two friends who drive BMWs, and both of them have had nothing but trouble from those cars.

g. *Slippery slope:* Claiming, without sufficient evidence, that a seemingly harmless action, if taken, will lead to a disastrous outcome.

Example

Immediate steps should be taken to reduce violence in children's television programming. If this violent programming is allowed to continue, this will almost certainly lead to fights and acts of bullying in school playgrounds. This in turn will lead to an increase in juvenile delinquency and gang violence. Eventually, our entire society will become engulfed in an orgy of lawlessness and brutality.

h. *Weak analogy:* Comparing things that aren't really comparable.

Example

Nobody would buy a car without first taking it for a test drive. Why then shouldn't two mature high school juniors live together before they decide whether to get married?

i. *Inconsistency:* Asserting inconsistent premises, asserting a premise that is inconsistent with the conclusion, or arguing for inconsistent conclusions.

Example

Note found in a Forest Service suggestion box: Park visitors need to know how important it is to keep this wilderness area completely pristine and undisturbed. So why not put up a few signs to remind people of this fact?

CHAPTER 7

ANALYZING ARGUMENTS

One of the most important critical thinking skills is that of analyzing arguments. To *analyze* an argument means to break it down into its various parts to see clearly what conclusion is being defended and on what grounds. Learning to analyze arguments is important, because to evaluate an argument, we need to understand clearly what the argument is saying. In this chapter we discuss two methods for analyzing arguments, one for short arguments and one for longer arguments.

> *One can deal with no problem until one has analyzed its nature.*
>
> —Hilaire Belloc

DIAGRAMMING SHORT ARGUMENTS

Diagramming is a quick and easy way to analyze relatively short arguments (i.e., arguments that are roughly a paragraph in length or shorter). Here is how the diagramming method works:

First, read through the argument and circle any premise or conclusion indicators you see. For example:

> The death penalty should be abolished, (because) it's racially discriminatory, there's no evidence that it's a more effective deterrent than life imprisonment, and innocent people may be executed by mistake.

Second, number the statements consecutively as they appear in the argument:

> ① The death penalty should be abolished, because ② it's racially discriminatory, ③ there's no evidence that it's a more effective deterrent than life imprisonment, and ④ innocent people may be executed by mistake.

Third, arrange the numbers on a page with premises placed above the conclusion(s) they are claimed to support:

②   ③   ④

①

Fourth, omit any logically irrelevant statements—that is, statements that don't function as either premises or conclusions in the argument. In this particular example, there are no logically irrelevant statements.

Finally, using arrows to mean "therefore" (or "is offered as evidence for"), create a kind of flowchart that indicates relationships of argumentative support:

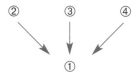

In this argument, each of the three premises provides *independent support* for the conclusion. A premise provides independent support for a conclusion when it provides a separate, freestanding reason for accepting the conclusion. More precisely, a premise provides **independent support** for a conclusion when the support it provides would not be canceled or weakened by the removal of any other premise in the argument. We symbolize this relationship of independent support by drawing arrows from each of the three premises to the conclusion.

In some arguments, the premises work cooperatively, rather than independently, to support the argument's conclusion. For example:

① Every member of the Applewood Association is more than fifty years old. Hence, ② Bob is more than fifty years old, since ③ Bob is a member of the Applewood Association.

Here, the argument's premises provide *linked support* for the conclusion. A premise provides linked support when it works conjointly with another premise to support the conclusion. More precisely, a premise provides **linked support** for a conclusion when the amount of support it provides *would* be weakened or destroyed by the removal of some other premise in the argument.[1] We symbolize relationships of linked support by underlining the linked premises and putting a plus sign between them. Thus, the preceding argument can be diagrammed as follows:

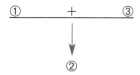

The basic distinction between linked and independent premises isn't hard to understand. Two premises are *linked* if the omission of one of the premises would reduce the amount of support provided by the other. For example:

① No members of the Mill City High School marching band are Yankee fans. ② Allan is a member of the Mill City High School marching band. So, ③ Allan isn't a Yankee fan.

In this example, neither premise provides any support for the conclusion without the other. Taken together, however, the premises validly imply the conclusion. Thus, the premises are linked, because the amount of support provided by at least one of the premises would be reduced if another premise were omitted.

Similarly, two premises are *independent* if neither premise would lose any power to support the conclusion if the other premise were removed. Here are two examples:

> ① Ten witnesses say they saw Blotto rob the bank. ② The stolen bank money was found in Blotto's apartment. ③ Blotto's fingerprints were found on the note the robber handed to the bank teller. Therefore, ④ probably Blotto robbed the bank.

> ① Agatha is a mother. ② Agatha is an aunt. Therefore, ③ Agatha is a female.

In the first example, the premises work independently to build a cumulative case to support the conclusion. In the second example, each of the premises independently provides complete logical support for the conclusion. In both examples, the premises are independent, because the amount of support each provides individually would not be weakened or destroyed even if every other premise in the argument were omitted.

Let's practice this diagramming technique with a few examples.

> If Amy runs marathons, then she's probably very fit. Amy does run marathons. She's also an A student. Therefore, Amy probably is very fit.

First, we circle all the premise and conclusion indicators:

> If Amy runs marathons, then she's probably very fit. Amy does run marathons. She's also an A student. (Therefore,) Amy probably is very fit.

Next, we number the statements in the argument consecutively:

> ① If Amy runs marathons, then she's probably very fit. ② Amy does run marathons. ③ She's also an A student. Therefore, ④ Amy probably is very fit.

Next, we check to see if there are any logically irrelevant statements in the argument. In this case, statement ③ is clearly irrelevant. It is simply an aside that provides no support whatsoever for the conclusion. Thus, we omit it from our diagram.

Finally, we diagram the argument by arranging the numbers on a page with premises placed above the conclusion(s) they are claimed to support. In this argument, the conclusion indicator "therefore" indicates that ④ is the conclusion. Since ① supports ④ only if it is conjoined with ②, ① and ② provide linked support for ④. Thus, the argument can be diagrammed as follows:

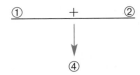

How to Decide Whether Premises Are Linked or Independent

Two premises are *linked* when the omission of one of the premises would cancel or reduce the amount of support provided by the other.

Example:

No student at Wexford College is a Rhodes Scholar.

Melissa is a Rhodes Scholar.

Therefore, Melissa is not a student at Wexford College.

Two premises are *independent* when neither premise would provide less support for the conclusion if the other premise were omitted.

Example:

Tenure protects faculty members who express unpopular views from hostile reactions from colleagues and university officials.

Tenure allows faculty members to engage in long-term research projects without the constant pressure to "publish or perish."

Therefore, tenure should be preserved.

Here is a second example:

Most Democrats are liberals, and Senator Dumdiddle is a Democrat. Thus, Senator Dumdiddle is probably a liberal. Therefore, Senator Dumdiddle probably supports affirmative action in higher education, since most liberals support affirmative action in higher education.

First, we circle all premise and conclusion indicators:

Most Democrats are liberals, and Senator Dumdiddle is a Democrat. (Thus,) Senator Dumdiddle is probably a liberal. (Therefore,) Senator Dumdiddle probably supports affirmative action in higher education, (since) most liberals support affirmative action in higher education.

Next, we number the statements consecutively:

① Most Democrats are liberals, and ② Senator Dumdiddle is a Democrat. Thus, ③ Senator Dumdiddle is probably a liberal. Therefore, ④ Senator Dumdiddle probably supports affirmative action in higher education, since ⑤ most liberals support affirmative action in higher education.

Next, we check to see whether any of the numbered statements are irrelevant to the argument. In this case, none are.

Finally, we diagram the argument by arranging the numbers on a page with premises placed above the conclusion(s) they allegedly support. ① and ② clearly work conjointly to support ③. Thus, they provide linked support for ③. We therefore diagram this part of the argument as follows:

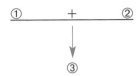

③ and ⑤ likewise provide linked support for ④. Thus, the entire argument can be diagrammed as follows:

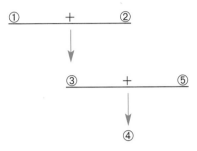

Here is a third example:

Cheating is wrong for several reasons. First, it will ultimately lower your self-respect, because you can never be proud of anything you got by cheating. Second, cheating is a lie, because it deceives other people into thinking you know more than you do. Third, cheating violates the teacher's trust that you will do your own work. Fourth, cheating is unfair to all the people who aren't cheating. Finally, if you cheat in school now, you'll find it easier to cheat in other situations later in life—perhaps even in your closest personal relationships.[2]

First, we circle the premise and conclusion indicators:

Cheating is wrong for several reasons. First, it will ultimately lower your self-respect, (because) you can never be proud of anything you got by cheating. Second, cheating is a lie, (because) it deceives other people into thinking you know more than you do. Third, cheating violates the teacher's trust that you will do your own work. Fourth, cheating is unfair to all the people who aren't cheating. Finally, if you cheat in school now, you'll find it easier to cheat in other situations later in life—perhaps even in your closest personal relationships.

Next, we number the statements consecutively, as follows:

① Cheating is wrong for several reasons. First, ② it will ultimately lower your self-respect, because ③ you can never be proud of anything you got by cheating. Second, ④ cheating is a lie, because ⑤ it deceives other people into thinking you know more than you do. Third, ⑥ cheating violates the teacher's trust that you will do your own work. Fourth, ⑦ cheating is unfair to all the people who aren't cheating. Finally, ⑧ if you cheat in school now, you'll find it easier to cheat in other situations later in life—perhaps even in your closest personal relationships.

Next, we decide whether any of the numbered statements are logically irrelevant to the argument. In this argument, none are.

Finally, we diagram the argument using the method presented above. As the premise indicator "because" indicates, ③ is offered as support for ②, and ⑤ is offered as support for ④. We thus get

Finally, we note that ②, ④, ⑥, ⑦, and ⑧ all provide independent support for the main conclusion ①. Thus, the complete diagram of the argument is as follows:

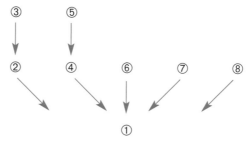

Consider a final example:

Either Knuckles was the murderer, or Sluggo was the murderer, or Bruiser was the murderer. If Bruiser was the murderer, then the murder took place on a Tuesday. If Sluggo was the murderer or Bruiser was the murderer, then the murder took place in the saloon. Hence, Knuckles was the murderer, since the murder did not take place in the saloon.

First, we circle all the premise and conclusion indicators:

Either Knuckles was the murderer, or Sluggo was the murderer, or Bruiser was the murderer. If Bruiser was the murderer, then the murder took place on a Tuesday. If Sluggo was the murderer or Bruiser was the murderer, then the murder took place in the saloon. (Hence,) Knuckles was the murderer, (since) the murder did not take place in the saloon.

Next, we number the statements consecutively:

① Either Knuckles was the murderer, or Sluggo was the murderer, or Bruiser was the murderer. ② If Bruiser was the murderer, then the murder took place on a Tuesday. ③ If Sluggo was the murderer or Bruiser was the murderer, then the murder took place in the saloon. Hence, ④ Knuckles was the murderer, since ⑤ the murder did not take place in the saloon.

Next, we check to see whether any of the statements are irrelevant to the conclusion. In this case, ② is irrelevant, since it functions as neither a premise nor a conclusion in the argument. Thus, we omit it from the diagram.

Finally, we diagram the argument's logical structure. In this argument, ①, ③, and ⑤ all work together to support ④. None provides any real support for the conclusion without the others. Thus, the premises provide linked support for the conclusion. Hence, the argument can be diagrammed as follows:

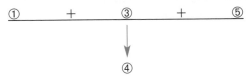

Tips on Diagramming Arguments

Diagramming arguments is a little like learning to play golf: difficult at first, but challenging and fun once you get the hang of it. This section provides a few tips on how to diagram arguments like a pro.[3]

1. *Find the main conclusion first.* It is easy to get lost if you don't have a clear idea where you are going. For that reason, it is often a good idea, especially when diagramming complex arguments, to start by locating the main conclusion and then work back through the passage to see how the argument as a whole works together to support the conclusion. (For help in locating the main conclusion of an argument, review "Tips on Finding the Conclusion of an Argument" on pages 31–32.)

2. *Pay close attention to premise and conclusion indicators.* One of the most common mistakes students make in diagramming arguments is to overlook premise and conclusion indicators such as "since," "as," "so," and "because." Pay especially close attention to premise indicators such as "since" or "because" that precede independent clauses. Here are two examples:

    All dogs go to heaven. So, Sparky will go to heaven, *since* Sparky is a dog.

    If Boxwood is a senator, then Boxwood is a politician. Hence, *because* Boxwood is a senator, he is a politician.

    In these two examples, the premise indicators "since" and "because" signal that the sentences in which they appear express two statements (a premise and a conclusion) rather than one. These two statements must be distinguished for purposes of argument analysis.

3. *Remember that sentences containing the word "and" often contain two or more separate statements.* We have seen that a single sentence frequently expresses two or more distinct statements. Sometimes these distinct statements are separated by the word "and." For example:

    Never fly Cattle Car Airlines. They're never on time, and the food tastes like warmed-over cardboard.

Analysis is a skill you need everywhere in life. Lawyers analyze complex claims and sort out the issues; physicians analyze symptoms; detectives look for patterns in the evidence; business people sort through the parts of an intricate deal; parents try to untangle and get a grip on the issues troubling a family.

—Tom Morris

Here, the second sentence is a compound sentence that expresses two logically distinct premises separated by the word "and." These distinct premises should be diagrammed separately.

4. *Treat conditional statements (if-then statements) and disjunctive statements (either/or statements) as single statements.* As we saw in Chapter 2, conditional statements should always be treated as a single logical unit, since they assert a single complete thought. For example, the conditional sentence

If I win the lottery, then I'll move to Tahiti

doesn't assert that I'll win the lottery, nor does it assert that I'll move to Tahiti. Rather, it asserts a single conditional statement: that one event will occur (I'll move to Tahiti) *if* another event occurs (I win the lottery). Since conditional sentences assert only a single statement, they should always be treated as a single logical unit for purposes of argument analysis.

For similar reasons, disjunctions (either/or statements) should also be diagrammed as single statements. Notice that if I say

Either Boston will win the pennant or Cleveland will win the pennant

I am not saying that Boston will win the pennant or that Cleveland will win the pennant. Rather, I am asserting a single (disjunctive) statement: that one of two events will occur—*either* Boston will win the pennant *or* Cleveland will win the pennant (but not both). Because disjunctive statements, like conditional statements, express a single complete thought, they should always be diagrammed as single statements.

5. *Don't number or diagram anything that is not a statement.* Arguments, by definition, consist entirely of statements—that is, sentences that it makes sense to regard as either true or false. For that reason, questions, suggestions, exclamations, and other nonstatements should be omitted from argument diagrams.

6. *Don't diagram irrelevant statements.* In real life, most lengthy and complex arguments contain logically irrelevant statements—that is, statements that don't support the conclusion in any way. Since the purpose of an argument diagram is simply to map the logical structure of an argument, such statements should be omitted.

7. *Don't diagram redundant statements.* Many arguments contain redundant statements—that is, statements that basically repeat what has already been said. Such statements are often useful for rhetorical purposes, but they should be omitted in argument diagrams, since they merely clutter the argument.

How to Diagram an Argument

1. Read through the argument carefully, circling any premise or conclusion indicators you see.
2. Number the statements consecutively as they appear in the argument. Don't number any sentences that are not statements.
3. Arrange the numbers on a page with premises placed above the conclusion(s) they are claimed to support. Omit any irrelevant statements—that is, statements that don't function as either premises or conclusions in the argument.
4. Using arrows to mean "therefore," create a kind of flowchart that shows which premises are intended to support which conclusions.
5. Indicate independent premises by drawing arrows directly from the premises to the conclusion they are claimed to support. Indicate linked premises by placing a plus sign between each of the premises, underlining the premises, and drawing an arrow from the underlined premises to the conclusion they allegedly support.
6. Put the argument's main conclusion at the bottom of the diagram.

EXERCISE 7.1

Diagram the following arguments using the method presented in the preceding section.

1. All humans are mortal. Socrates is a human. Therefore, Socrates is mortal.
2. No members of the volleyball team like hip-hop. Andrea is a member of the volleyball team. So, Andrea doesn't like hip-hop.
3. School uniforms reduce violence and theft, improve discipline, make it easier for kids to resist peer pressure, help prevent gang symbols in school, and make it easier for school officials to recognize intruders. For those reasons, school uniforms should be adopted in our nation's public schools.
4. Affirmative action in higher education is morally justifiable, because it compensates for past discrimination, provides valuable role models for women and minorities, and promotes multicultural understanding.
5. Only three people could have stolen the CD: Danny, Stacy, or Patrick. But Stacy couldn't have stolen the CD, because she was out riding her bike. Patrick couldn't have stolen the CD, because he was at a friend's house. Therefore, Danny must have stolen the CD.
6. If it rains, then the concert will be moved indoors. Hence, the concert probably will be moved indoors, since there's a 70 percent chance of rain.
7. Several states have abolished the insanity defense as a defense against criminal responsibility. This may be popular with voters, but it is morally indefensible. Insanity removes moral responsibility, and it is wrong to punish someone who is not morally responsible for his crime. Moreover, it is pointless to

punish the insane, because punishment has no deterrent effect on a person who cannot appreciate the wrongfulness or criminality of his or her actions.

8. All Republicans are either moderates or conservatives, and Senator Hornswaggle is not a moderate. Since Senator Hornswaggle is a Republican, it follows that he is a conservative. All conservatives oppose socialized medicine. Thus, Senator Hornswaggle opposes socialized medicine.

9. It's foolish to smoke cigarettes. Smoking is expensive, unhealthy, and obnoxious to many nonsmokers. I wouldn't date anyone who smokes cigarettes.

10. If today is Saturday, then tomorrow is Sunday. If tomorrow is Sunday, then we'll be having pasta for dinner. If we'll be having pasta for dinner, then I should pick up some red wine today, since in this state wine can be purchased only at liquor stores, and the liquor stores are closed on Sundays. Today is Saturday. Therefore, I should pick up some red wine today.

11. Chris rides a motorcycle. Most people who ride motorcycles are males. Hence, Chris is probably a male. Hence, Chris probably doesn't carry a purse. Whoever stole the necklace was carrying a purse. Hence, Chris probably didn't steal the necklace.

12. It makes no sense to ask God for things in prayer. Either the thing you ask for is good or it is not. If it is good, then God will do it anyway. If it is not, then He won't. In neither case can your prayer make any difference.[4]

13. Most drugs should be legalized. Since drugs such as heroin and cocaine are literally worth more than their weight in gold, it's foolish to think that we can ever prevent drugs from being smuggled into this country. Moreover, the drug war is extremely expensive to fight. According to a recent FBI report, local, state, and federal governments spent over $20 billion last year enforcing our nation's drug laws. In addition, it distracts police from the task of fighting more serious crimes, clogs our courts, and leads to grossly overcrowded prisons. Finally, just as in the days of Prohibition, making drugs illegal funnels huge profits into the hands of a dangerous criminal underground.

14. Since our feelings, desires, and preferences can be either beneficial or harmful, noble or ignoble, praiseworthy or damnable, and since they can be either in harmony or in conflict with other people's feelings, desires, and preferences, they are obviously not accurate tools for analysis of moral issues or trustworthy guidelines to action. (Vincent Ryan Ruggiero, *The Moral Imperative,* 2nd ed., 1984)

15. Whatever fate befalls you, do not give way to great rejoicings or great lamentations; partly because all things are full of change, and your fortune may turn at any moment; partly because men are so apt to be deceived in their judgments as to what is good or bad for them. (Arthur Schopenhauer, *Parerga and Paralipomena,* 1851)

16. Brute beasts, not having understanding and therefore not being persons, cannot have rights. (Joseph Rickaby, *Moral Philosophy of Ethics and Natural Law,* 1889)

17. All change is either change for the better or change for the worse. But God is necessarily a greatest possible being. So he cannot change for the better,

since if he did, he would not have been the greatest possible being prior to the change. And he cannot change for the worse, since if he did, he would not be the greatest possible being subsequent to the change. Therefore, God cannot change. (Thomas V. Morris, *Our Idea of God,* 1991)[5]

18. Education implies teaching. Teaching implies knowledge. Knowledge is truth. The truth is everywhere the same. Hence education should be everywhere the same. (Robert Maynard Hutchins, *The Higher Learning in the United States,* 1936)

19. All humans have equal positive value. There is no morally relevant difference between humans and some animals (such as mammals). Therefore, some animals have equal positive worth with humans. Moral rights derive from the possession of value. Since humans have rights (to life, not to be harmed, and so forth), animals have those same rights. (Louis P. Pojman, *Global Environmental Ethics,* 2000)

20. True/false and multiple-choice tests have well-known limits. No matter how carefully questions are worded, some ambiguities will remain. The format of the questions prohibits in-depth testing of important analytic skills. Students can become so "test savvy" that objective tests measure test-taking skill as much as subject-matter content. (Douglas J. Soccio, *Instructor's Manual for Archetypes of Wisdom: An Introduction to Philosophy,* 3rd ed., 1998)

21. We have ideas of many things. These ideas must arise either from ourselves or from things outside us. One of these ideas we have is the idea of God—an infinite, all-perfect being. This idea could not have been caused by ourselves, because we know ourselves to be limited and imperfect, and no effect can be greater than its cause. Therefore, the idea must have been caused by something outside us which has nothing less than the qualities contained in the idea of God. But only God himself has those qualities. Therefore, God himself must be the cause of the idea we have of him. Therefore, God exists. (Peter Kreeft and Ronald K. Tacelli, *Handbook of Christian Apologetics,* 1994 [slightly adapted])[6]

22. Planetary exploration has many virtues. It permits us to refine insights derived from such Earth-bound sciences as meteorology, climatology, geology and biology, to broaden their powers and improve their practical applications here on Earth. It provides cautionary tales on the alternative fates of worlds. It is an aperture to future high technologies important for life here on Earth. It provides an outlet for the traditional human zest for exploration and discovery, our passion to find out, which has been to a very large degree responsible for our success as a species. And it permits us, for the first time in history, to approach with rigor, with a significant chance of finding out the true answers, questions on the origins and destinies of worlds, the beginnings and ends of life, and the possibilities of other beings who live in the skies—questions as basic to the human enterprise as thinking is, as natural as breathing. (Carl Sagan, *Broca's Brain: Reflections on the Romance of Science,* 1979)

23. Creation has no place in a science class because it is not science. Why not? Because creationism cannot offer a scientific hypothesis that is capable of

Critical Thinking Lapse

Police in Fort Smith, Ark., charged James Newsome, 37, with robbing a Gas Well convenience store after the cashier provided a key identifying detail: The robber had entered the store wearing an orange hard hat with the name "James Newsome" printed on it.[7]

being shown wrong. Creationism cannot describe a single possible experiment that could elucidate the mechanics of creation. Creationism cannot point to a single prediction that has turned out to be right, and supports the creationist case. Creationism cannot offer a single instance of research that has followed the normal course of scientific inquiry, namely, independent testing and verification by skeptical researchers. (Douglas J. Futuyma, *Science on Trial: The Case for Evolution,* 1983)

> *The better off you become at analyzing complex problems, the better off you are for solving them.*
>
> —Tom Morris

24. Nonhuman animals lack linguistic capacity, and, for this reason, lack a mental or psychological life. Thus, animals are not sentient. If so, of course, they cannot be caused pain, appearances to the contrary. Hence, there can be no duty not to cause them pain. (Christine Pierce and Donald VanDeveer, "General Introduction," in Christine Pierce and Donald VanDeveer, eds., *People, Penguins, and Plastic Trees: Basic Issues in Environmental Ethics,* 2nd ed., 1995 [slightly paraphrased])[8]

25. Here is a gentleman of a medical type, but with the air of a military man. Clearly an army doctor, then. He has just come from the tropics, for his face is dark, and that is not the natural tint of his skin, as his wrists are fair. He has undergone hardship and sickness, as his haggard face says clearly. His left arm has been injured. He holds it in a stiff and unnatural manner. Where in the tropics could an English doctor have seen much hardship and get his arm wounded? Clearly in Afghanistan. (Sherlock Holmes, in Sir Arthur Conan Doyle's *A Study in Scarlet,* 1887)

SUMMARIZING LONGER ARGUMENTS

Diagramming works well with relatively short arguments, but with longer arguments it quickly becomes tedious and confusing. For that reason, it is usually better to *summarize* lengthy arguments than to diagram them. In summarizing an argument, we don't try to identify every step in the argument. Instead, the goal of an **argument summary** is to provide a brief synopsis of the argument that accurately restates the main points of the argument in the summarizer's own words. In this section, we introduce a relatively formal and precise method for summarizing longer arguments known as **standardization.** Later, in Chapter 12, we present a more informal method for summarizing passages of various types and lengths.

Summarizing involves two skills of argument analysis that are not generally used in argument diagramming, namely, paraphrasing and finding missing premises and conclusions. Let's look briefly at these two skills before we introduce our general method for summarizing extended arguments.

Paraphrasing

The purpose of an argument summary is to clarify an argument's structure by restating its main points as briefly, clearly, and accurately as possible. Because many arguments are expressed in ways that are needlessly wordy, complex, or obscure, it is often necessary to *paraphrase* arguments in order to restate them in ways that are simpler and easier to understand.

> *Don't criticize what you don't understand.*
> —Bob Dylan

A **paraphrase** is a detailed restatement of a passage using different words and phrases. A good paraphrase is *accurate, clear, concise,* and *charitable.* Let's look briefly at each of these four qualities.

A Good Paraphrase Is Accurate   The first virtue of a good paraphrase is that it is accurate. An accurate paraphrase is faithful to an author's intended meaning; it reproduces that meaning fairly and without bias or distortion. For example:

Original passage
Europe has a set of primary interests, which to us have none, or a very remote relation.—Hence, she must be engaged in frequent controversies, the causes of which are essentially foreign to our concerns.—Hence, therefore, it must be unwise in us to implicate ourselves, by artificial ties in the ordinary vicissitudes of her politics, or the ordinary combinations and collisions of her friendships or enmities. (George Washington, "Farewell Address," 1796)

Paraphrase 1
Europe's vital interests are totally different from ours. For that reason, European nations will often become embroiled in conflicts that don't concern us. Therefore, we shouldn't become involved in Europe's political affairs.

Paraphrase 2
Europe has a set of vital interests that are of little or no concern to us. For that reason, European nations will often become embroiled in conflicts for reasons that don't really concern us. Therefore, we shouldn't form artificial ties that would get us involved in the ordinary ups and downs of European politics.

The first paraphrase clearly distorts Washington's argument, making it easier to attack. Washington does not say, for example, that Europe's vital interests are *totally* different from ours. Nor does he say flatly that we shouldn't become involved in Europe's political affairs. The second paraphrase is more faithful to Washington's intent.

A Good Paraphrase Is Clear　Arguments are often expressed in language that is needlessly wordy or confusing. Since one of the basic aims of an argument summary is to help us get clear about what an argument is saying, it is often necessary to translate (i.e., paraphrase) complex or confusing language into language that is easier to understand. Here are several examples:

Original passage

The patient exhibited symptoms of an edema in the occipital-parietal region and an abrasion on the left patella.

Paraphrase

The patient had a bump on the back of his head and a scrape on his left knee.

Original passage

High-quality learning environments are a necessary precondition for facilitation and enhancement of the ongoing learning process.

Paraphrase

Children need good schools if they are to learn properly.[9]

Original passage

'Twas the nocturnal segment of the diurnal period preceding the annual Yuletide celebration and throughout our place of residence, kinetic activity was not in evidence among the organic possessors of this potential, including the species of diminutive rodent known as Mus musculus.[10]

Paraphrase

'Twas the night before Christmas, when all through the house, not a creature was stirring, not even a mouse.

In short, anytime you can say something more simply and clearly than the author himself has, by all means do so.

Beware of and eschew pompous prolixity.

—Charles A. Beardsley

A Good Paraphrase Is Concise　A good summary captures the *essence* of an argument. It strips away all the irrelevant or unimportant details and puts the key points of the argument in a nutshell. To lay bare the essence of an argument, it is often necessary to paraphrase portions of the argument that can be stated more briefly than they are by the author. Here are some examples:

Original passage

The office wasn't open at that point in time, owing to the fact that there was no electrical power in the building. (22 words)

Paraphrase

The office was closed then, because there was no electricity in the building. (13 words)

Original passage

Macbeth was very ambitious. This led him to wish to become king of Scotland. The witches told him that this wish of his would come true. The king of Scotland at this time was Duncan. Encouraged by his wife, Macbeth murdered Duncan. He was thus enabled to succeed Duncan as king. (51 words)

Paraphrase

Encouraged by his wife, Macbeth achieved his ambition and realized the prediction of the witches by murdering Duncan and becoming king of Scotland in his place. (26 words)[11]

Original passage

Look round the world: Contemplate the whole and every part of it: You will find it to be nothing but one great machine, subdivided into an infinite number of lesser machines, which again admit of subdivisions, to a degree beyond what human senses and faculties can trace and explain. All these various machines, and even their most minute parts, are adjusted to each other with an accuracy, which ravishes into admiration all men, who have ever contemplated them. The curious adapting of means to ends, throughout all nature, resembles exactly, though it much exceeds, the productions of human contrivance; of human design, thought, wisdom, and intelligence. Since therefore the effects resemble each other, we are led to infer, by all the rules of analogy, that the causes also resemble; and that the Author of Nature is somewhat similar to the mind of man; though possessed of much larger faculties, proportioned to the grandeur of the work, which he has executed.[12] (160 words)

Paraphrase

The universe is like a giant machine, made up of an infinite number of smaller machines. These machines are similar to human artifacts, though far more complicated and impressive. Since human artifacts are made by intelligent beings, the universe is probably also made by an Intelligent Being, though one far wiser and more powerful than human beings are. (58 words)

As these examples show, a paraphrase can be significantly shorter than the original but still remain faithful to the author's intent.

A Good Paraphrase Is Charitable   It is often possible to interpret a passage in more than one way. In such cases, the principle of charity requires that we interpret the passage as charitably as the evidence reasonably permits.[13] Here are two examples:

Genius is the ability to reduce the complicated to the simple.

—C. W. Cernan

Original passage

You know as well as I do that you can't get a good job today unless you have a college degree. So, I hope you'll rethink your decision not to go to college.

First paraphrase

No one can get a good job today unless they have a college degree. So, I hope you'll rethink your decision not to go to college.

Second paraphrase

It's very difficult to get a good job today unless one has a college degree. So, I hope you'll rethink your decision not to go to college.

Original passage

Cigarette smoking causes lung cancer. Therefore, if you continue to smoke, you are endangering your health.

First paraphrase

Cigarette smoking invariably produces lung cancer. Therefore, if you continue to smoke, you are endangering your health.

Second paraphrase

Cigarette smoking is a positive causal factor that greatly increases the risk of getting lung cancer. Therefore, if you continue to smoke, you are endangering your health.

In these examples, the second paraphrases are better than the first, since they clarify the arguer's intent in ways that make the arguments stronger and less easy to attack.

EXERCISE 7.2

Paraphrase the following passages. Be prepared to share your answers with the class as a whole. (*Note:* You'll probably need a dictionary for this exercise.)

1. Californians are friendly.
2. Thou shalt not kill. (Exodus 20:13)
3. Only man is rational.
4. Money can't buy happiness.
5. All men are created equal. (Declaration of Independence)
6. A well-regulated Militia, being necessary to the security of a free State, the right of the people to keep and bear Arms, shall not be infringed. (Second Amendment)
7. He jests at scars that never felt a wound. (Shakespeare)
8. With reference to yesterday's electronic-mail communication from you, I would urge you to take into consideration that at this point in time there are no parking facilities within close proximity to the convention center, due to the fact that the Jefferson Street Parking Garage is currently closed for repairs.
9. Prudence, indeed, will dictate that Governments long established should not be changed for light and transient causes; and accordingly all experience hath shown, that mankind are more disposed to suffer, while evils are sufferable, than to right themselves by abolishing the forms to which they are accustomed. But when a long train of abuses and usurpations, pursuing invariably the same Object evinces a design to reduce them under absolute Despotism, it is their right, it is their duty, to throw off such Government and to provide new Guards for their future security. (Declaration of Independence)

10. Not every man should have the knowledge of his duty left to his own judgment; he should have it prescribed to him, and not be allowed to choose at his discretion. Otherwise, seeing the imbecility and infinite variety of our reasons and opinions, we should in the end forge for ourselves duties that would set us on devouring one another. (Montaigne)

11. Read the following article. What does this law, read literally, actually prohibit? How would you paraphrase it to express more accurately and clearly the lawmakers' intent?

> No Sex in the Show Me State?
>
> In 1994, Missouri lawmakers passed a law intended, according to a later Missouri Supreme Court interpretation, to outlaw nonconsensual sex. The law read as follows: "A person commits the crime of sexual misconduct in the first degree if he has deviate sexual intercourse with another person of the same sex, or he purposely subjects another person to sexual contact or engages in conduct which would constitute sexual contact except that the touching occurs through the clothing without that person's consent."[14]

Finding Missing Premises and Conclusions

In real life, people often leave parts of their arguments unstated. Sometimes they leave a premise unstated.

> *Store clerk:* I'm sorry, I can't sell you any beer; you're under twenty-one.

Implied here is the premise, "I can't sell beer to anyone under twenty-one." In other cases, people leave a conclusion unstated.

> *Advertisement:* The bigger the burger, the better the burger. Burgers are bigger at Burger King.

Implied here is the conclusion, "Burgers are better at Burger King."

There are many reasons why a premise or a conclusion might be implied rather than stated. Sometimes the missing statement is something so obvious and familiar that it would be tedious to state it explicitly. For example:

> Sally can't drive, because she doesn't have a driver's license.

Understood here is the premise, "No one can drive without a driver's license." This is something so widely known that in most contexts, it can simply be assumed.

At other times, an arguer may leave a premise or a conclusion unstated because she wishes to conceal a weak or questionable step in her argument. For example:

> She's Cuban, so she's probably hot-tempered.

Here the unstated premise is "Most Cubans are hot-tempered." By leaving this questionable premise unstated, the arguer makes the argument appear stronger than it actually is.

An argument with a missing premise or conclusion is called an **enthymeme.** There are two basic rules in filling in missing steps in enthymemes: [15]

1. *Faithfully interpret the arguer's intentions.* The most important rule in filling in missing premises and conclusions is to be as accurate as possible in interpreting an arguer's intent. A missing premise or conclusion is a genuine part of an argument only if it was implicitly understood to be part of the argument by the arguer himself. Consequently, we should always try to fill in a missing step in an argument in a way that the arguer himself would recognize as expressing his own thought. One way to determine this is to ask *what else the arguer must assume—that he does not say—to reach his conclusion.* All assumptions you add to the argument must be consistent with everything the arguer says.

2. *Be charitable.* Sometimes it is difficult or impossible to know what unstated premise or conclusion an arguer had implicitly in mind. In such cases, the principle of charity requires that we interpret the argument as generously as possible. In general, this means that we should search for a way of completing the argument that (1) is a plausible way of interpreting the arguer's uncertain intent and (2) makes the argument as good an argument as it can be. Such judgments require practice and skill. But you'll seldom be far off the mark if you remember this simple golden rule: *Be as generous in interpreting other people's incompletely stated arguments as you would like them to be in interpreting your own.*

EXERCISE 7.3

I. Assume that the following arguments are deductive. Identify the missing premises or conclusions that are needed to make the arguments deductively valid.

1. Since this is a Mazda Miata, it's a convertible.
2. All Volkswagens are fuel efficient, and this Beetle is a Volkswagen.
3. Either Blazers are made by Chevy, or Blazers are made by Ford. Therefore, Blazers are made by Chevy.
4. This is a Civic only if it's a Honda. Therefore, this is not a Civic.
5. If this is a Camaro, then it's a Chevy. If this is a Firebird, then it's a Pontiac. Therefore, this is either a Chevy or a Pontiac.
6. Ford Windstars are roomy; after all, Windstars are minivans.
7. If this is a Camry or a Corolla, then it's a Toyota. If this is a Toyota, then it gets good gas mileage. This is a Corolla. Therefore, it gets good gas mileage.
8. If this car gets good gas mileage, then it's good for the environment. If this car doesn't get good gas mileage, then I don't want it. This car isn't good for the environment. Therefore, I don't want it.

9. Either this is a Contour or it's a Mystique. If this is a Contour, then it's a Ford. If this is Mystique, then it's a Mercury.

10. Some Fords are trucks, because all Rangers are trucks.

II. Identify the missing premises or conclusions in the following enthymemes. Some of the arguments are deductive and some are inductive.

1. Li Fong is from Singapore, so she probably speaks English.

2. No one who has committed murder deserves to live. Casey has confessed that he murdered O'Brien.

3. Boxing should be banned because it's dangerous.

4. Abortion is wrong, because it's wrong to intentionally kill an innocent human person.

5. Angela is blonde, so she's probably dumb.

6. If it's snowing, then it's cold. My car won't start if it's cold. My car will start. If it's not snowing, then Uncle Fred will be coming over for dinner.

7. Kevin graduated from Princeton, so he must be smart. Therefore, he should be able to solve this logic puzzle in the time allotted.

8. If I'm Bill Gates, then I'm rich. Hence, I'm not Bill Gates. Hence, I'm not the chairman of Microsoft.

9. If today is Thursday, then Zoe is either at work or on the golf course. Therefore, Zoe is at work.

10. Everything in this world will come to an end. So, my life will come to an end, and all the consequences of my life will come to an end. Thus, my life is meaningless, and so is everything else.[16]

11. If Sparky committed the robbery, then he was working for Curley. If Sparky was working for Curley, then Bugsy drove the getaway car. But Bugsy became totally blind last year. So, I guess we can cross Sparky off our list of suspects.

12. Most Hampton College students are Republicans. Therefore, Jay is probably a Republican. I know he voted the straight Republican ticket in the last election. I also know he has a large poster of Republican presidential candidate George W. Bush in his dorm room. Since Jay is probably a Republican, it's likely that he favors a constitutional amendment banning abortion.

13. Since ethical statements—statements about what is right or wrong—are not part of the subject matter of any science, it follows that there are no ethical facts. (Elliot Sober, *Philosophy of Biology,* 2nd ed., 2000)

Summarizing Extended Arguments

Now that we have learned how to paraphrase passages and fill in missing premises and conclusions, it is time to introduce our method for summarizing extended arguments. The method is called **argument standardization,** because it consists in restating an argument in standard logical form. An argument is said to be in *standard logical form* when each step in the argument is listed consecutively, premises are stated above the conclusions they are claimed to support, and justifications are provided for each conclusion in the argument.

The following list shows the steps in argument standardization.

How to Standardize an Extended Argument

1. Read through the argument carefully. As you do so, try to identify the main conclusion of the argument (it may only be implied). Once you have identified the main conclusion, go back through the argument to identify major premises and subconclusions offered in support of the main conclusion. Paraphrase as needed to clarify meaning.

2. Omit any unnecessary or irrelevant material. Focus only on the key points in the argument. Omit any statements that provide little or no direct support for the main conclusion.

3. Number the steps in the argument and stack them in correct logical order (i.e., with the premises placed above the conclusions they are intended to support). State the main conclusion last.

4. Fill in any key missing premises or conclusions. Don't worry about filling in all missing premises or conclusions. Include only those missing statements that are important in understanding and evaluating the central argument. Place brackets around implied statements to indicate that they have been added to the argument.

5. Add parenthetical justifications for each conclusion in the argument. In other words, for each conclusion or subconclusion in the argument, indicate in parentheses which previous lines in the argument the conclusion or subconclusion is claimed to directly follow from.

Let's practice this technique for summarizing extended arguments with a few examples. First, a very brief example will provide a quick illustration of how the method works.

> [The] desire for perfect happiness is inborn in all of us, it is a universal human longing, it is rooted in human nature. But everything that is in human nature has been put there by God. In His Wisdom and Goodness, he could not have implanted a natural longing that was impossible to fulfill. Therefore, there must exist, somehow, a real perfect happiness which is within the capacity of struggling men to attain.[17]

In this simple argument, there are four statements: three premises and a conclusion (here stated last and indicated by the word "therefore"). To standardize the argument, we first number the statements and list them in logical order:

1. The desire for perfect happiness is a natural longing, inborn in all human beings.

2. Everything that is in human nature has been put there by God.

3. In His Wisdom and Goodness, God could not have implanted a natural longing that was impossible to fulfill.

4. Therefore, it must be possible for human beings to achieve perfect happiness.

Next, we check to see whether any of the steps in the argument are unnecessary or irrelevant. In this short argument, none are.

Next, we check to see whether there are any crucial premises or conclusions missing in the argument. In this case, no statements need to be added, because the argument is deductively valid as it stands.

Finally, we add justifications to indicate which premises are intended to support which conclusions. In this case, there are three premises that support the conclusion. The complete argument summary is thus as follows:

1. The desire for perfect happiness is a natural longing, inborn in all human beings.
2. Everything that is in human nature has been put there by God
3. In His Wisdom and Goodness, God could not have implanted a natural longing that was impossible to fulfill.
4. Therefore, it must be possible for human beings to achieve perfect happiness. (from 1–3)

Here is a second and slightly more complex example:

Destroying a little brain tissue in a living subject can eliminate a whole range of mental functions, including thought, emotion, and sensation. Therefore, it is a natural inference to conclude that the permanent death of all brain tissue amounts to the permanent cessation of all mental function, including thought, emotion, and sensation. But this just amounts to the annihilation of the conscious person, which means that none of us will survive bodily death.[18]

Reading this argument carefully, we can see that it contains two stated premises, a subconclusion, and a main conclusion (here stated last). First, we number the statements and list them in logical order:

1. Destroying a little brain tissue in a living subject can eliminate a whole range of mental functions, including thought, emotion, and sensation.
2. Thus, it is reasonable to conclude that the permanent death of all brain tissue amounts to the permanent cessation of all mental function.
3. The permanent cessation of all mental function amounts to the annihilation of the conscious person.
4. Therefore, none of us will survive bodily death.

Second, we check to see whether the argument contains any unnecessary or irrelevant steps. In this case, none of the statements are unnecessary or irrelevant.

Third, we look to see if there are any important premises or conclusions missing in the argument. If we examine the argument closely, we can see that there are. Statement 2 follows from statement 1 only if we add something like the following implied premise:

If destroying a little brain tissue in a living subject can eliminate a whole range of mental functions, then it is reasonable to conclude that the permanent death of all brain tissue amounts to the permanent cessation of all mental function.

This is an important, and questionable, assumption that needs to be made explicit. Thus, we add it to the argument, using brackets to indicate that the statement is implied rather than stated. We thus get the following:

1. Destroying a little brain tissue in a living subject can eliminate a whole range of mental functions, including thought, emotion, and sensation.
2. [If destroying a little brain tissue in a living subject can eliminate a whole range of mental functions, then it is reasonable to conclude that the permanent death of all brain tissue amounts to the permanent cessation of all mental function.]
3. Thus, it is reasonable to conclude that the permanent death of all brain tissue amounts to the permanent cessation of all mental function.
4. The permanent cessation of all mental function amounts to the annihilation of the conscious person.
5. Therefore, none of us will survive bodily death.

Finally, we add parenthetical justifications to indicate which premises are claimed to support which conclusions. The complete argument summary, then, is this:

1. Destroying a little brain tissue in a living subject can eliminate a whole range of mental functions, including thought, emotion, and sensation.
2. [If destroying a little brain tissue in a living subject can eliminate a whole range of mental functions, then it is reasonable to conclude that the permanent death of all brain tissue amounts to the permanent cessation of all mental function.]
3. Thus, it is reasonable to conclude that the permanent death of all brain tissue amounts to the permanent cessation of all mental function. (from 1–2)
4. The permanent cessation of all mental function amounts to the annihilation of the conscious person.
5. Therefore, none of us will survive bodily death. (from 3–4)[19]

Here is a third and slightly longer example:

EBR's Students Need Your Vote

Students in East Baton Rouge Parish schools need your help today. Please vote to extend, for 10 years, a 4.98-mill property tax that helps operate the public school system.

The School Board has been strapped for funds for several years. State aid is stagnant, property tax revenue has grown more slowly than inflation and the board has trimmed considerable fat from its budget.

Losing the $6.7 million a year generated by the tax would force budget cuts that could affect the quality of learning in a school system already struggling to improve academic achievement.

This tax should not be confused with the School Board's past or potential proposals to raise taxes for school improvements. This tax is modest, amounting to less than 3 percent of the system's general revenue. It already is on the books; voting "for" won't raise anyone's taxes, but just keep them from dropping slightly. And the money will keep going to day-to-day operations, not new buildings or programs.

We understand why some people are less than satisfied with the School Board and might be eager to send a message. But a negative vote today will not hurt the board; it will hurt the 56,000 students who rely on the public schools for an education.

Voters probably will have a chance to vote for or against another tax-increase plan this summer. They definitely will have a chance to vote on School Board members when all the board seats come up for election this fall.

Today, vote for the students.[20]

Here is one reader's standardization of the argument:

1. The school board has been short of money for several years because state aid has not increased, inflation has outstripped increases in property tax revenue, and the board has cut spending.

2. Losing the $6.7 million a year generated by the tax would force budget cuts that could harm the quality of learning at a time when schools are struggling to improve academic achievement.

3. [Voters should not place the quality of learning at risk by depriving the school system of money.]

4. The tax is not a large one, but amounts to less than 3 percent of the school system's general revenue.

5. The tax is already in effect, meaning that taxes will stay as they are now rather than going up.

6. The money will be used to fund the daily operation of the schools, not to build new buildings or add programs.

7. Voting against the tax will hurt the 56,000 students who rely on the public schools.

8. Therefore, voters in East Baton Rouge should vote for the 4.98-mill property tax which funds public school operation. (from 1–7)

This standardization, though somewhat lengthy, is relatively straightforward, since little paraphrasing is required and there are few missing premises or conclusions. Not all arguments, however, can be reconstructed so straightforwardly. Here is an argument that requires more radical surgery:

Editor:

Regarding your editorial (Sept. 7), "Give us better SAT scores," that's the last thing we need! It is common knowledge that many successful entrepreneurs and inventors were not high honor students. In fact, many were high school and college dropouts, and many did not get outstanding SAT scores.

Professional speaker Jim Rohn states: "Formal education will earn you a living. Self-education will earn you a fortune. You determine how much of a fortune you will earn by how much self-education you decide to get."

So, there must be better predictors of success than grades and standardized tests. As a business owner, I want to hire people who have excellent people skills and positive attitudes and are committed to doing quality work. These skills are a million times more important to me, as well as to other employers in the long run, than perfect SAT scores.

In my opinion, our country is in the shape it's in because of our illiteracy in human relations. Memorization-based education does not teach our children how to find answers, solve problems, deal with difficulties in their personal or professional lives, take responsibility for their actions, or develop their skills and talents. It does encourage people to seek the easy way out. And it destroys our children's ability to use their common sense. The United States has more people in prison, in terms of percentage of population, than any other nation. They're not there because they didn't memorize easily looked-up information.

The political and power structures of the medical community as well as our legal system damage our country with their lack of common sense. Throughout history, mainstream organizations have always resisted change. The most educated people believed the earth was flat. It was the so-called dumbbell who proved them wrong.

If we want high scores, let's get them in kindness. In the words of Theodore Roosevelt, "The most important single ingredient in the formula of success is knowing how to get along with people."

So tell me about the schools where our kids get great grades in kindness and consideration. You can build a life on those traits. We can build bombs and prisons when we focus on the opposite.[21]

This argument is neither as clear nor as well organized as the previous argument we examined. Here is one reader's[22] attempt to summarize the writer's central argument:

1. Memorization-based education does not teach our children how to find answers, solve problems, deal with difficulties in their personal or professional lives, take responsibility for their actions, or develop their skills and talents.

2. Memorization-based education encourages people to take the easy way out and destroys our children's ability to use their common sense.

3. Memorization-based education is largely responsible for the bad shape this country is in today, including the high prison population and the lack of basic common sense in our medical and legal communities.

4. [Thus, memorization-based education is a mistake. (from 1–3)]

5. [The SAT is mainly a test of memorized information.]

6. Many successful entrepreneurs and inventors were high school or college dropouts and did not get outstanding SAT scores.

7. Good people skills are a million times more important to employers than perfect SAT scores.

8. Thus, success in life depends much more on good people skills than it does on good grades or high SAT scores. (from 6–7)

9. [Therefore, contrary to the September 7 editorial, it is much more important for schools to teach good people skills than it is for them to teach the kinds of memorized information tested on the SAT. (from 4–5, 8)]

This argument is fairly typical of arguments encountered in letters to the editor, radio talk shows, and other popular forums. Key parts of the argument are left unstated (including the main conclusion), some statements appear to have little or no relevance to the main conclusion, and a fair amount of paraphrasing and "reading between the lines" is needed to clarify the author's apparent intent. The standardization we have offered is an example of the kind of major reconstruction that is sometimes needed to summarize an argument briefly and accurately.

Common Mistakes to Avoid in Standardizing Arguments It takes practice to become good at standardizing arguments. Here are some common mistakes to watch out for.

1. *Don't write in incomplete sentences.*

   Example 1
   1. Because animals can experience pain and suffering **(incorrect)**
   2. Therefore, it's wrong to kill or mistreat animals. (from 1)

   Line 1 is a sentence fragment, not a complete sentence. Since arguments are composed entirely of statements (i.e., sentences that can sensibly be regarded as true or false), only complete sentences should be included in argument standardizations. In this argument, the standardization can be repaired simply by deleting the word "because" in the first line. The correct version is thus:

   Example 2
   1. Animals can experience pain and suffering. **(correct)**
   2. Therefore, it's wrong to kill or mistreat animals. (from 1)

2. *Don't include more than one statement per line.*

   Example 3
   1. The president should resign, since he no longer enjoys the confidence of the Board of Trustees. **(incorrect)**

   There are two statements on this line: a premise ("he no longer enjoys the confidence of the Board of Trustees") and a conclusion ("The president should resign"). These two statements should be placed on separate lines as follows:

   Example 4
   1. The president no longer enjoys the confidence of the Board of Trustees.
   2. Therefore, he should resign. (from 1) **(correct)**

3. *Don't include anything that is not a statement.*

Example 5

1. It's all the same whether there's a Democrat or a Republican in the White House.
2. Therefore, why should I care about presidential politics? (from 1) **(incorrect)**

Here, the second line is phrased as a rhetorical question rather than as a statement. Since only statements are included in arguments, this question must be rephrased as a statement in order for the argument to be standardized. This can be done as follows:

Example 6

1. It's all the same whether there's a Democrat or a Republican in the White House.
2. Therefore, I have no reason to care about presidential politics. (from 1) **(correct)**

4. *Don't include anything that is not a premise or a conclusion.*

Example 7

1. Many people today argue that capital punishment is morally wrong. **(incorrect)**
2. But the Good Book says "an eye for an eye, a tooth for a tooth."
3. What the Good Book says is true.
4. Therefore, capital punishment is not morally wrong. (from 2–3)

Arguments are composed entirely of premises and conclusions. In this argument, the first line is neither a premise nor a conclusion. Therefore, it should be omitted.

The following exercises will give you practice in standardizing arguments.

EXERCISE 7.4

Standardize the following essays using the method presented in the preceding section.

Why Teachers Shouldn't Assign Homework

My opinion regarding the amount of homework a child receives is basically threefold. I don't believe the children should receive any homework whatsoever. One, because the teacher has seven or eight hours during the course of the school day to instruct children and do work assignments with them, to review material for tests. They do not need to be sending work home. To me, homework is an excuse for a teacher's lack of ability to do their job properly. Two, there are too many children that come home with either no adult there or no adult with the ability to help them with their homework. That places too many children at a disadvantage compared to other children who have their parents there to help them with their homework. Three, an adult spends eight hours at work, comes home and has the rest of the day to enjoy themselves. That is a luxury that a child should definitely be afforded. They don't need to spend time after school. Teacher, it is time to wake up.*

Don't Rush to Adopt Mail Voting System

The recent use of mail ballots in Oregon's election of a U.S. senator has led some people to hail this as the wave of the future in our democratic republic.

We do not share that enthusiasm.

The primary advantage of the mail ballot is that it requires little time and effort on the part of the voter. We think that also is a primary shortcoming of this process.

It is worth a little of both our time and our energy to exercise the right to vote, and that personal investment should serve to make us a bit more conscious of the value of that opportunity.

Another negative aspect for the electorate is that a mail election necessarily must take place over a relatively long time frame, rather than a single day that is the culmination of an election campaign process.

That means voters who cast their ballots near the end of the designated voting period might have a larger volume of information, and perhaps more accurate information, than those who vote early in the process.

We also are seriously concerned about the potential for voter fraud in elections conducted by mail. A state with Louisiana's political history would be fertile ground for that.

Finally, we take note of one of the more ironic potential shortcomings of this procedure, and that is the very fact that this process involves using the mail, rather than a voting machine.

Many of us, at one time or another, have sent or received mail that, through no fault of our own, did not arrive on time or was lost altogether.

We would prefer not to risk having that happen to our ballots in any local, federal or state election.†

The Dangers of Genetic Engineering

Genetic engineering is a dangerous experiment with nature and one that we may live to regret. When you mess around with nature in ways that you don't fully understand, nature has a nasty habit of biting back. The most common way of using genetic engineering, to make proteins that we want or new vaccines, is to take genes out of animals or plants and *switch* them into the DNA of bacteria or viruses. We are told that only harmless bacteria or viruses are used, but how can we be sure? There is a danger that we will accidentally create dangerous new bacteria and viruses, and these things are so hard to contain they could escape and multiply out of control. Even seemingly harmless tinkering with plants holds potential hazards. If we start growing vast quantities of crops that are resistant to certain insect "pests," we could upset the "balance of nature" by starving . . . beneficial birds and insects that live on these pests. We just don't know enough about the complex ecology of the natural world to go messing around with it by genetic engineering.

Then there is the whole issue of the misuse of genetic engineering; the creation of deadly new biological and chemical weapons, for example. We might

---

*Anonymous newspaper call-in column, *Wilkes-Barre Times Leader,* September 11, 2000.

†Editorial, *Baton Rouge Advocate,* February 8, 1996.

approve the techniques of genetic engineering for use in beneficial medicinal or agricultural applications only to find other people and nations adapting these techniques to create selective weapons of mass destruction. Humanity has already made too many mistakes when trying to become masters of nature. Just think about nuclear waste, global warming, and the destruction of the ozone layer. Genetic engineering could eventually prove to be our biggest mistake yet, because the fact that altered animals and plants reproduce and evolve means that we might change things very badly for the worse, and forever.*

Nation Isn't Ready for Same-Sex Marriages

President Clinton's announced opposition to gay marriage may be largely a case of pragmatic politics, an attempt to preempt a campaign debate he cannot win. But his stance also reflects a deep, national reluctance to tamper with a beleaguered institution that, for now, is best left alone.

For all its frailties, marriage still lends much-needed stability to individuals and the community. But the frailty of the institution is precisely why the nation, from Congress to the courts, should be very careful and very sure before tampering with its social fabric.

Seattle prides itself in its civil-rights protections. This is a place where citizens believe that the rights of a majority are only as secure as the rights of the minority next door. Just last weekend, a gay couple's commitment was celebrated at St. Mark's Episcopal Cathedral here. Clearly, government has no business in anyone's bedroom, nor in telling any of its citizens with whom they should or should not share their lives.

But marriage introduces a conflict of rights—the right of gays to share in an important legal status, and the right of society to decide when and how to legally recognize that status. A Hawaii court has ruled that marriages between people of the same sex are legal in that state. If that decision is upheld on appeal, other states may be required to recognize those marriages.

The nation doesn't need this debate. For all the turmoil that swirls around marriage, its basic definition has remained unchanged for centuries. Most people continue to see it as a legal and/or religious bond between a man and a woman.

This does not prevent other people from forming deep, positive lifelong relationships. But marriage is about legal recognition of one specific type of relationship, with all the attendant rights and responsibilities of property, taxes, employee benefits, inheritance and child-rearing. Government should not attempt to expand its definition of marriage until a substantial portion of its body politic is ready to do so.

Clearly, most Americans are not ready. A recent Gallup Poll indicates people oppose gay marriage by 68 to 27 percent—more than a 2-to-1 ratio.

These attitudes have changed and will continue to change. People over 50 overwhelmingly oppose same-sex marriage, but people under 30 are far more comfortable with the idea. A generation from now, the question may not even be controversial.

But for now, it is controversial—so much so that the battle threatens to destabilize a troubled institution while undermining hard-won victories in gay

---

*Paul B. Kelter, James D. Carr, and Andrew Scott, *Chemistry: A World of Choices* (New York: WCB/McGraw-Hill, 1999), p. 544. The selection is included as one side of a "pro/con discussion" and does not necessarily reflect the views of the authors.

rights to housing, employment and other areas.

A proposal to redefine marriage would offend millions of Americans and go nowhere in Congress. The gay community would be wise to follow Clinton's election-year prudence and avoid a divisive battle that promises to do little more than fuel the cause of its opponents.*

Legalizing Drugs Spawns Many Problems, Solves None

I am hoping that you're as fed up as I am with all this pro-legalization of drugs nonsense. It is offensive to those of us who have dedicated our lives to helping the addicted and their families.

Some people might say I have a self-serving reason for writing this article, because I work in the drug treatment and prevention/education field.

Well, consider this: If I was selfish, I'd say legalize drugs because, without doubt, all drug treatment professionals would have an abundance of work. Rather, we treatment professionals are dedicated to significantly reducing and eventually eliminating America's No. 1 health problem.

I would welcome the day when our drug problem will be so insignificant that there would no longer be a need for professional drug and alcohol treatment agencies.

With this said, let me set the record straight, because you won't get the full picture from these pro-legalizing drug advocates.

Fact 1: Legalization advocates always use the argument that legalizing drugs will take the profit motive away from the street or clandestine manufacturers. They never tell you, however, that the economic cost of legal drugs is 2½ times greater than that of illicit drugs.

Additionally, these advocates never use the argument that legalization will reduce hospitalizations, crimes, car accidents, addicted babies, industrial accidents, family breakups, etc. The reason they don't is, if the drugs were legalized, every one of these problems would worsen significantly.

Common sense should tell us when there are fewer controls, there will be more incidents.

For example, between 1972 and 1978, 11 states decriminalized marijuana, and marijuana use escalated to unprecedented levels.

Fact 2: Drug use is not a right and should never be. People who proclaim, "It's my body, and I have a right to do with it what I want," need to re-examine this naïve statement. Drug use not only impacts on the user, but has serious implications for families, community, consumers and others.

Legalizing drugs would open the floodgates of access to these mood-altering chemicals and would send a message that drugs are not harmful.

Think about flying to Disney World and having to depend on a pilot or an air-traffic controller who is high. Or having your child's surgery being performed by a surgeon who has just ingested mood-altering chemicals. Or entrusting your children to school bus drivers who fire up a joint of marijuana before their daily run. . . .

Legalizing drugs is not a solution; in fact, it is a ridiculous option. It's like saying our child abuse laws are not effective because abuse of children is escalating, therefore we should do away with these child protection laws.

Fact 3: If we still don't believe that legalizing drugs will make the problems worse, then I would ask you to examine two of America's favorite legal drugs:

---

*Editorial, *The Seattle Times,* May 21, 1996.

alcohol and nicotine. I don't think much more needs to be said about the epidemic use of these two chemicals and the tremendous negative impact they have had on the physiological, social, psychological, economic and spiritual aspects of our lives.

By legalizing illicit drugs that are proven harmful, you'd better be ready to hire thousands of police officers, physicians, counselors and other medical personnel to respond to the human carnage.

Some could argue that I am very emotional when I write or lecture about this topic.

You bet I am.

When legalization proponents have seen 24 years of human misery in the form of suicide, homicides, overdoses, psychiatric institutionalizations, medical emergencies, etc., then you'll qualify to be emotional as well.

I took a pledge in 1973 to use my God-given energies to help people to find the joys that come with living a drug-free life.

I am confident that our public will reject any effort that might be made by a small minority who have, unfortunately, chosen not to get all the facts before they talk.

If you want the facts, talk with recovering addicts and families who have lost their loved ones to a chemical that some want to legalize.*

The Toilet Police

If you call yourself an American, you need to know about a crucial issue that is now confronting the U.S. Congress (motto: "Remaining Firmly in Office Since 1798"). This is an issue that affects every American, regardless of race or gender or religion or briefs or boxers; this is an issue that is fundamental to the whole entire Cherished American Way of Life.

This issue is toilets.

I'm talking about the toilets now being manufactured for home use. They stink. Literally. You have to flush them two or three times to get the job done. It has become very embarrassing to be a guest at a party in a newer home, because if you need to use the toilet, you have to lurk in the bathroom for what seems (to you) like several presidential administrations, flushing, checking, waiting, flushing, checking, while the other guests are whispering: "What is (your name) DOING in there? The laundry?"

I know this because I live in a home with three new toilets, and I estimate that I spend 23 percent of my waking hours flushing them. This is going on all over America, and it's causing a serious loss in national productivity that could really hurt us as we try to compete in the global economy against nations such as Japan, where top commode scientists are developing super-efficient, totally automated household models so high-tech that they make the Space Shuttle look like a doorstop.

The weird thing is, the old American toilets flushed just fine. So why did we change? What force would cause an entire nation to do something so stupid? Here's a hint: It's the same force that from time to time gets a bee in its gigantic federal bonnet and decides to spend millions of dollars on some scheme to

---

*Carmen F. Ambrosino, "Legalizing Drugs Spawns Many Problems, Solves None," *Wilkes-Barre Times Leader,* February 17, 1997.

convert us all to the metric system, or give us all Swine Flu shots, or outlaw tricycles, or whatever. You guessed it! Our government!

What happened was, in 1992, Congress passed the Energy Policy and Conservation Act, which declared that, to save water, all U.S. consumer toilets would henceforth use 1.6 gallons of water per flush. That is WAY less water than was used by the older 3.5-gallon models—the toilets that made this nation great; the toilets that our Founding Fathers fought and died for—which are now prohibited for new installations. The public was not consulted about the toilet change, of course; the public has to go to work, so it never gets consulted about anything going on in Washington.

But it's the public that has been stuck with these new toilets, which are saving water by requiring everybody to flush them enough times to drain Lake Erie on an hourly basis. The new toilets are so bad that there is now—I am not making this up—a black market in 3.5-gallon toilets. People are sneaking them into new homes, despite the fact that the Energy Policy and Conservation Act provides for—I am not making this up, either—a $2,500 fine for procuring and installing an illegal toilet. . . .

The public—and this is why I love this nation—is not taking this sitting down. There has been a grass-roots campaign, led by commode activists, to change the toilet law, and a bill that would do that (H.R. 859—The Plumbing Standards Act) has been introduced in Congress by Rep. Joe Knollenberg of Michigan. I talked to Rep. Knollenberg's press secretary, Frank Maisano, who told me that the public response has been very positive. But the bill has two strikes against it:

1. It makes sense.
2. People want it.

These are huge liabilities in Washington. The toilet bill will probably face lengthy hearings and organized opposition from paid lobbyists; for all we know it will get linked to Whitewater and wind up getting investigated by up to four special prosecutors. So it may not be passed in your lifetime. But I urge you to do what you can. Write to your congresshumans, and tell them to support Rep. Knollenberg's bill. While you're at it, tell them you'd like to see a constitutional amendment stating that if any federal agency has so much spare time that it's regulating toilets, that agency will immediately be eliminated, and its buildings will be used for some activity that has some measurable public benefit, such as laser tag.

So come on, America! This is your chance to make a difference! Stand up to these morons! Join the movement!

Speaking of which, I have to go flush.*

Summary

1. In this chapter we learned how to analyze arguments. To *analyze* an argument means to break it up into its various parts in order to see clearly what conclusion is being defended and on what grounds.

---

*Dave Barry, "The Toilet Police," *Wilkes-Barre Times Leader,* July 20, 1997.

2. To analyze short arguments, we use a method called *diagramming*. Diagramming involves six basic steps:

    a. Read through the argument carefully, circling any premise or conclusion indicators you see.

    b. Number the statements consecutively as they appear in the argument. (Don't number any sentences that are not statements.)

    c. Arrange the numbers spatially on a page with the premises placed above the conclusion(s) they are alleged to support.

    d. Using arrows to mean "therefore," create a kind of flowchart that shows which premises are intended to support which conclusions.

    e. Indicate independent premises by drawing arrows directly from the premises to the conclusions they are claimed to support. Indicate linked premises by placing a plus sign between each of the linked premises, underlining the premises, and drawing an arrow from the underlined premises to the conclusions they are claimed to support. (Two premises are *independent* if neither premise would provide less support for the conclusion if the other premise were removed. Two premises are *linked* if at least one of the premises would provide less support for the conclusion if the other premise were removed.)

    f. Put the argument's main conclusion last.

3. To analyze longer arguments, we use a method called *standardizing*. There are five basic steps in standardizing arguments:

    a. Read through the argument carefully. Identify the main conclusion (it may only be implied) and any major premises and subconclusions. Paraphrase as needed to clarify meaning. (A *paraphrase* is a restatement of a passage using different words and phrases. A good paraphrase is clear, concise, accurate, and charitable.)

    b. Omit any unnecessary or irrelevant material.

    c. Number the steps in the argument and list them in correct logical order (i.e., with the premises placed above the conclusions they are intended to support).

    d. Fill in any key missing premises and conclusions.

    e. Add justifications for each conclusion in the argument. In other words, for each conclusion or subconclusion in the argument, indicate which previous lines in the argument the conclusion or subconclusion is claimed to directly follow from.

CHAPTER 8

EVALUATING ARGUMENTS

People don't analyze arguments just for the fun of it; they analyze them because they want to understand and *evaluate* the arguments, to see whether the arguments provide good reasons to accept a conclusion or not. In this chapter we present some general guidelines for evaluating arguments. Our focus will be primarily on two questions: When is an argument a good one? and When is it reasonable to accept a premise?

WHEN IS AN ARGUMENT A GOOD ONE?

Arguments, like people, can be good or bad in many ways. To help us get clear on what a good argument *is* from the standpoint of critical thinking, let's begin by spelling out a few things that a good argument is *not*.

What "Good Argument" Does *Not* Mean

"Good Argument" Does Not Mean "Agrees With My Views" One of the most serious mistakes in critical thinking is to confuse "good argument" with "argument whose conclusion I agree with." To suppose that an argument is good only if it agrees with your own preexisting opinions is the epitome of closemindedness. It reflects the mind-set of someone who thinks, "I have a monopoly on the truth. Anyone who disagrees with me must be wrong." Such an attitude makes it impossible to learn from viewpoints that differ from one's own. For that reason, it is completely opposed to the spirit of critical thinking.

"Good Argument" Does Not Mean "Persuasive Argument" A good archery shot hits the bull's-eye. A good putt goes in the hole. A good pair of scissors cuts the paper efficiently. In many contexts, a thing is said to be good if it does successfully what it was intended to do.[1] Does this hold true of arguments as well? Is a good argument a *persuasive* argument—that is, an argument that actually succeeds in persuading an audience to accept a conclusion?

Not necessarily, for two major reasons. First, not all arguments are meant to persuade. Sometimes, the arguer is just "playing devil's advocate," or "preaching to the choir," or "going through the motions," or "thinking out loud," or giving examples without any thought of persuading anybody. Second, bad arguments often persuade, whereas good arguments often fall on deaf ears. In the years leading up to World War II, for example, Hitler's demagogic ravings convinced millions, whereas Churchill's well-founded warnings were largely ignored. Yet no critical thinker would suggest that Hitler's arguments were, therefore, "better" than Churchill's.

"Good Argument" Does Not Mean "Well-Written or Well-Spoken Argument"   We sometimes praise arguments for their *literary or rhetorical merit*—their clarity, verve, organization, imaginativeness, and the like. Does it follow that a good argument is, or must be, a well-written or well-spoken argument?

No, because some obviously bad arguments possess literary merit, whereas some obviously good ones do not. A subtly deceptive political speech may be a masterpiece of rhetorical skill and still be seriously flawed from the standpoint of critical reasoning. By the same token, an argument in, say, science or mathematics may be a perfectly good argument but possess little or no literary merit.

What "Good Argument" *Does* Mean

What, then, *is* a good argument from the standpoint of critical thinking? To answer this question, we need to review some things we learned in previous chapters.

In Chapter 3 we learned that a good argument is basically an argument in which two conditions are met: All the premises are true,[2] and the premises provide good reasons to accept the conclusion.

We also learned in Chapter 3 that a set of premises provides good reasons to accept a conclusion when the argument is either deductively valid or inductively strong. (Remember: An argument is *deductively valid* if the conclusion *must* be true if the premises are true. An argument is *inductively strong* if the conclusion is *probably* true if the premises are true.) Arguments that both are deductively valid and have all true premises are said to be deductively *sound*. Arguments that both are inductively strong and have all true premises are said to be inductively *cogent*. Thus, *a good argument is fundamentally an argument that is either deductively sound or inductively cogent.*

That definition, however, is not fully adequate. For as we saw in Chapter 1, there are certain basic critical thinking standards that all good thinking and argumentation must meet. Among the most important of these standards are clarity, precision, accuracy, relevance, consistency, logical correctness, completeness, and fairness. An argument that was deeply obscure, full of irrelevant statements, and grossly incomplete in its examination of the relevant evidence clearly wouldn't count as a "good" argument, even if it were deductively sound. Thus, it is not enough for an argument merely to be a "logically good" argument (i.e., deductively sound or inductively cogent). It must also satisfy (at least up to a certain threshold) the basic critical thinking standards we discussed in Chapter 1.

Now that we have combined these insights from Chapters 1 and 3, we are ready to answer the question "When is an argument a good one?"

A good argument, from the standpoint of critical thinking, *is an argument that satisfies the relevant critical thinking standards that apply in a particular context.* The most important of these standards are accuracy (Are all the premises true?) and logical correctness (Is the reasoning correct? Is the argument deductively valid or inductively strong?). But other critical thinking standards must also be taken into account, including clarity, precision, relevance, consistency,[3] completeness, and fairness.

Given this broad definition of "good argument," we can offer the following general guidelines on evaluating arguments.

Evaluating Arguments: Some General Guidelines

- Are the premises true?
- Is the reasoning correct? Is the argument deductively valid or inductively strong?
- Does the arguer commit any logical fallacies?
- Does the arguer express his points clearly and precisely?
- Are the premises relevant to the conclusion?
- Are the arguer's claims logically consistent? Do any of the arguer's claims contradict other claims made in the argument?
- Is the argument complete? Is all relevant evidence taken into account (given understandable limitations of time, space, etc.)?
- Is the argument fair? Is the arguer fair in her presentation of the evidence? Is she fair in her treatment of opposing arguments and views?[4]

WHEN IS IT REASONABLE TO ACCEPT A PREMISE?

All good arguments, as we have seen, have true premises. But when is it *reasonable* or *rational* to accept a premise as true? This is a notoriously complicated issue, and only a few general suggestions can be offered here. A more detailed discussion of some of these issues is presented in later chapters.

Let's suppose that somebody asserts a claim—for example, that *women are more superstitious than men* or that *I saw Elvis at a Dunkin' Donuts in Lubbock.* For

The possession of truth is the ultimate good of the human mind.
—Mortimer Adler

simplicity, let's suppose that the claim is unsupported (i.e., no argument is given for it) and that for some reason it is either impossible or not worthwhile to try to verify the claim for ourselves. Under what conditions is it reasonable to accept such a claim?

The most general principle can be summed up in the following **principle of rational acceptance:** Generally speaking, it is reasonable to accept a claim if (1) the claim does not conflict with personal experiences that we have no good reason to doubt, (2) the claim does not conflict with background beliefs that we have no good reason to doubt, and (3) the claim comes from a credible source that we have no good reason to doubt.[5]

Let's briefly discuss these three conditions.

You can observe a lot just by watching.

—Yogi Berra

Does the Claim Conflict with Our Personal Experiences?   Sometimes people assert claims that conflict with our own personal observations and experiences. When this happens, it is usually best to trust our own experiences. Thus, if your neighbor's Doberman pinscher is snarling, foaming at the mouth, and chewing on the tattered remnants of a mail carrier's bag, it is probably a good idea to trust your own eyes rather than your neighbor's assurance that his dog is "as gentle as a kitten."

The problem is that people often place too much trust in their own observations and experiences. As Brooke Moore and Richard Parker point out, we often overestimate the reliability of our observations by failing to take into account factors such as poor physical conditions for making observations (e.g., bad lighting, excessive noise, frequent distractions); sensory impairment (e.g., poor vision or hearing); poor physical condition of the observer (e.g., fatigue, stress, intoxication); unreliable measuring instruments; and failures of memory.[6] Indeed, studies show that even under good observational conditions, people are often much less accurate in their observations than they generally assume.[7]

Our own opinion and our own sense do often deceive us, and they discern but little.

—Thomas à Kempis

Critical thinkers also recognize that their beliefs, hopes, fears, expectations, and biases can affect their observations. Children, for example, "see" monsters in the closet. Sports fans perceive referees as partial to the other team. Coffee drinkers who unwittingly drink decaffeinated coffee typically feel more alert. Teachers who expect improvement from their students often "perceive" better performance even when none exists. And love, as the adage says, is blind.

In short, personal experiences are often much less reliable than we think. We need to be aware that "believing" is often "seeing" and that things are not always as they appear.

Does the Claim Conflict with Our Background Beliefs?   Sometimes, a claim doesn't conflict with any of our personal observations or experiences, but does conflict with certain background beliefs we hold. By "background beliefs" we mean that vast network of conscious and unconscious beliefs we

How Many *F's*?

Here's a quick observation exercise. Reading at normal speed, count the number of times the letter *f* appears in the following sentence:

These functional fuses have been developed after years of scientific investigation of elec-

tric phenomena, combined with the fruit of long experience on the part of the two investigators who have come forward with them for our meeting today.

How many *f*s did you count? Check endnote 8 to see if your answer is correct.[8]

use as a framework to assess the credibility of claims that can't be verified directly. In general, if a claim fits well with our background beliefs, then it is reasonable for us to accept it. Thus, for example, the claim "It was hot in Las Vegas last Fourth of July" is quite believable given background information most of us share about midsummer weather conditions in the Nevada desert. However, the claim "It snowed in Las Vegas last Fourth of July" would rightly be rejected out of hand unless it was accompanied by strong supporting evidence.

The problem is that most of us place too much confidence in the accuracy of our background beliefs. A chain is only as strong as its weakest link. Consequently, if our backgrounds beliefs are unwarranted, any beliefs based entirely on those background beliefs will also be unwarranted. Suppose, for example, I believe that

Al Gore is a cleverly disguised Martian robot.

And suppose I believe this based entirely on my background belief that

All politicians are cleverly disguised Martian robots.

Clearly, it would be unreasonable for me to believe the first statement if the only reason I have for believing the second statement is that I read it in a supermarket tabloid.

Because critical thinkers know how important it is to have accurate and well-grounded background beliefs, they think very carefully about the beliefs they accept. *Never believe without sufficient evidence* and *Never believe more strongly than the evidence warrants* are the watchwords of the wise.

> *A healthy garden of beliefs requires well-nourished roots and tireless pruning.*
> —W. V. O. Quine and J. S. Ullian

EXERCISE 8.1

For each of the claims in this exercise, indicate whether you think the claim is

Completely believable ("I know this is the case")
Somewhat believable ("I am somewhat confident that this is the case")

Somewhat unbelievable ("I am somewhat confident that this is not the case")
Completely unbelievable ("I know this is not the case")

Then for each claim, list several important background beliefs that led you to as-sign the claim the degree of confidence you did. Be prepared to discuss your re-sponses in small groups.

1. Your astrological sign strongly influences your personality.
2. The biblical story of Noah's Ark is literally true.
3. The Loch Ness monster really exists.
4. After people die, their souls are reincarnated in other human bodies.
5. Extraterrestrials have visited the earth in some form.[9]

Does the Claim Come from a Credible Source?   Much of what we be-lieve about the world is based on testimony or authority. All of us believe, for example, that George Washington was the first president of the United States, that the earth revolves around the sun, that there is such a place as the Sahara Desert, and that it is cold at the North Pole in January. Yet few of us have per-sonally verified any of this information for ourselves. Thus, a crucial question for critical thinkers is: When is it reasonable or justifiable to accept a claim based simply on the testimony or authority of another?

This is a complex topic that we discussed in Chapter 6 and will examine further in Chapter 12. Here, we'll just remind you of some of the highlights of our discussion in Chapter 6.

Generally speaking, we should accept a claim on authority if it comes from a credible source that we have no good reason to doubt. Good reasons to doubt the credibility of a source may include the following:

- The source is not a genuine expert or authority.
- The source is speaking outside the area of his or her expertise.
- The source is biased or has some other motive to lie or mislead.
- The accuracy of the source's personal observations or experiences is doubtful.
- The source is a media source, a reference work, or an Internet source that is generally unreliable.
- It is likely that the source has not been cited correctly.
- The issue cannot be settled by expert opinion.
- The claim made by the source is, in itself, highly implausible or unlikely.

Finally, it is important to remember that the principle of rational accept-ance applies only to claims that are unsupported by arguments or evidence and that are either impossible or not worthwhile to verify for ourselves. If the claim *is* supported by reasons, then of course we must consider the strength of those

Critical Thinking Lapse

A Houston man learned a succinct lesson in gun safety when he played Russian roulette with a .45-caliber semiautomatic pistol. The nineteen-year-old man was visiting friends when he announced his intention to play the deadly game. He apparently did not realize that a semiautomatic pistol, unlike a revolver, automatically inserts a cartridge into the firing chamber when the gun is cocked. His chance of winning a round of Russian roulette was zero, as he quickly discovered.[10]

reasons in deciding whether we should accept the claim. Specifically, we must ask, "Are all the premises are true?" and "Do the premises provide good reasons to accept the conclusion?" (That is, is the argument deductively valid or inductively strong?)

Moreover, if the claim is an important one, and one that we can reasonably investigate for ourselves, then we have an intellectual responsibility to do so. Indeed, a willingness to seek out evidence and then to proportion one's belief to that evidence lies at the very heart of what it means to be a critical thinker.

The foundation of morality is to . . . give up pretending to believe that for which there is no evidence.

—Thomas Henry Huxley

EXERCISE 8.2

I. How good are your powers of observation and recollection? Answer the following questions outside class. Then bring your answers to class and be prepared to compare your responses with those of your classmates.

Remember the last time the class met? Answer the following questions about your instructor.

a. Approximate height _____
b. Approximate weight _____
c. Hair color _____
d. Eye color _____
e. Was he or she wearing a jacket? _____
f. If so, what color? _____
g. Was he or she wearing slacks? Jeans? A skirt? _____
h. If so, what color? _____
i. Was he or she wearing a tie or scarf? _____
j. If so, what color? _____
k. Was he or she wearing a ring? _____
l. Was he or she wearing a watch? _____
m. Was he or she carrying a briefcase or backpack? _____ If so, describe it.

n. Was he or she wearing a hat? _____ If so, describe it.
o. Did the instructor end class early? _____ [11]

II. For each of the following unsupported claims, indicate whether it would be reasonable to accept the claim or not. Also state the criteria you use in reaching your decision.

1. Kangaroos live in Australia.
2. The South won the American Civil War.
3. Smoking causes cancer.
4. Black cats bring bad luck.
5. I saw the bank robber clearly. (said by an elderly man wearing dark glasses, walking with a cane, and being led by a Seeing Eye dog)
6. Lying is always wrong. (overheard in the school cafeteria)
7. 98 percent of statistics are just made up.
8. Dunleavy Ford: *Nobody* sells for less. (heard on the radio)
9. World War II Bomber Found on the Moon! (tabloid headline) [12]
10. The closest star to the earth, other than the sun, is Proxima Centauri. (said by your astronomy instructor)
11. I fought in World War II. (said by a man who appears to be about forty years old)
12. There is no clear scientific evidence that smoking is addictive. (said by a tobacco company executive)
13. Parts of Alaska are farther west than Hawaii. (overheard on the bus)
14. Parts of Alaska are farther west than Hawaii. (said by your geography instructor)
15. Analgex brand aspirin: Nothing works stronger or faster on your tough headaches. (said by a paid sports celebrity)
16. I read the entire *Encyclopaedia Britannica* last summer. (said by a stranger at a party)
17. Most hate crimes in this country are not committed against African Americans or Jews. They are committed against evangelical Christians. (said by TV evangelist Jerry Falwell)
18. Free will is a myth. (said by your accounting instructor)
19. Did you know that gun control laws *actually increase* the violent crime rate? (statement on anti-gun-control Web page)
20. A Space Alien Tried to Mate with My Harley! (tabloid headline) [13]

III. **Writing a Critical Essay**   A *critical essay* is an essay in which you analyze and critically evaluate another person's argument. Write an 800– to 1,000– word critical essay on one of the following selections on pages 229–237. Your essay should include the four elements:

Introduction: Identify the title, author, and context of the essay you are critically evaluating. Summarize briefly the writer's basic position, and state in general terms your overall evaluation of the argument.

Argument summary: Standardize the writer's argument using the five-step method presented in Chapter 7.

Critical evaluation: Evaluate the argument; that is, explain whether you think the argument is a good, convincing argument or not. As you do so, keep in mind the following general guidelines on evaluating arguments discussed earlier in this chapter:

- Are the premises true? (*Note:* You may need to do some research to make an informed judgment on this issue.)
- Is the reasoning good? Is the argument deductively valid or inductively strong?
- Does the arguer commit any logical fallacies?
- Does the writer express his points clearly and precisely?
- Are the arguer's claims logically consistent?
- Is the argument complete? Is all relevant evidence taken into account?
- Is the argument fair? Is the arguer fair in her presentation of the evidence? Is she fair in her treatment of opposing arguments and views?

Conclusion: Briefly restate the key points of your critical response to reinforce them in the reader's mind. If possible, end with a strong concluding line (e.g., an apt quotation) that nicely sums up your response or puts the issue in a larger context.

A sample critical essay is included in an appendix to this chapter.

The Myth of School Choice

You hear a lot these days about the supposed benefits of "school choice." Supporters of school choice claim that parents should be given government-funded vouchers so that they can pull their kids out of schools that don't work and put them in public or private schools that do work. Forcing schools to compete for students and for funding will improve education, it is claimed, because it will make good schools even better and force bad schools to improve—or go out of business. In fact, however, school vouchers are bad for public education and bad for America.

Studies show that parents of poor, disadvantaged students are less likely to take advantage of school choice alternatives than parents of more affluent, higher-performing students. Consequently, vouchers will drain money and good students out of troubled inner-city schools, leaving the poorest and neediest students behind.

Studies also show that voucher programs don't work. For example, children who participated in the much-touted Milwaukee Parental Choice Program showed no significant improvement in reading or math scores after three years.

Moreover, school vouchers violate the constitutional separation of church and state. As interpreted by courts, the First Amendment establishment clause prohibits the use of taxpayer money to support religious education. It also prohibits "excessive entanglement" between government and religion. Forcing private schools to compete for government money would create such an entanglement, because it would pit different religious groups against one another and would threaten the independence of parochial schools, since those schools would become increasingly subject to government regulation.

Vouchers are undemocratic and unconstitutional. Let's tackle the real problems that afflict America's schools, not settle for quick fixes that would leave our poorest and most disadvantaged students behind.*

Helmet Laws Discriminate against Bikers

Freedom is a most valued and cherished possession. People are willing to fight, and even die, for it.

Isn't it great to live in the United States of America where we can choose to live the sort of life we care to live, choose any religion, decide which schools to attend, and choose our own livelihood?

As an avid motorcyclist, I wonder why the governments of some states, including Pennsylvania, target me and other riders with discriminatory legislation such as mandatory helmet laws.

There is no discernible difference in motorcycle injuries or fatalities among those states where helmet use is voluntary.

Motorcycles represent just 2 percent of total vehicles in the United States and account for less than 1 percent of all vehicle accidents. Trucks and buses account for 28 percent of accidents, and pedestrians account for 15 percent of total vehicle fatalities. Maybe they, too, should have been required to wear helmets, although I believe it wouldn't have mattered.

For me, this is an issue of personal freedom.

Mandatory helmet laws are annoying and unnecessary to an extremely small minority of citizens who would prefer to make their own decision on an issue which has no effect on anyone else.

To the average citizen who does not share an affection for motorcycles, this may not seem important. But what if the government decided to discriminate against your small group?

Would golfers enjoy a sunny afternoon on the greens sporting helmets to protect them from a stray golf ball, or would hunters care to wear bullet-proof vests in the woods?

Recently, a local television station conducted a telephone poll asking if the state should repeal its current mandatory helmet law. The results were 82 percent in favor of repealing the existing law.

I believe that the time has come for the government to allow responsible citizens to choose what safety measures best suit their particular needs.†

A Slap on the Wrist to Crusaders against Spanking

America has lots of problems. Drugs are a problem. Crime is a problem. The fact that less than half of American adults understand the earth takes a year to orbit the sun, as a National Science Foundation survey revealed Thursday, is a problem enough to make you weep for a once-great civilization.

But spanking?

Spanking is not a problem. In fact, spanking is so far from being a problem, you really have to marvel at the fretting it's getting from courts, psychologists and other "experts" alike.

Where, exactly, are the hospital wards that should be overflowing with victims of this abuse? How did we miss the National Crime Commission Report on Bottomwarming, the Harvard School of Public Health conference titled

---

*Adapted from a student essay.
†Stan Daniels, Letter to the Editor, *Wilkes-Barre Times Leader,* June 10, 1996.

"Knick, Knack, Paddywhack: Anatomy of a Public School Menace," the grade-schoolers standing against the wall of the classroom because they're too sore to sit down?

In other words, where is the science and the evidence driving the . . . [current crusade against spanking]?

They're getting darned hard to find. That's because spanking is, as usually practiced, a reasonable, effective and benign practice of child rearing, one with almost none of the ill-effects critics decry.

Want proof? OK: World War II. The Great Depression. World War I. Even the Civil War and the American Revolution, since we'd be surprised to learn parents of those hardscrabble eras used "time out" as a child-raising tool.

One way or another, Americans won wars, amassed wealth and built theirs into the most powerful and respected nation on earth, despite growing up in centuries in which spanking was the norm.

If they were physically impaired, psychologically scarred or emotionally twisted by the practice, they sure hid it well. And if you can find the closet hatred in historic America's numberless testimonials to Mom and Dad—such as the tender Civil War ballad that began, "Just before the battle, Mother/I am thinking most of you"—you've got sharper eyes than we have. . . .

Millions of parents have raised good kids without spanking. But millions of parents over hundreds of years have raised good kids by occasionally spanking them, too.

And in our terror over our cities' rising cacophony of gunfire, let's not try to outlaw a practice that for centuries helped keep the peace.*

Don't Use God's Law to Beat up on Gays

This is for those who hated my recent column about Ellen DeGeneres and Jerry Falwell—the lesbian comic and the preacher who finds her disgusting. It's for the ones who pointed me to the Bible, specifically Leviticus 20:13, which calls homosexuality an "abomination" worthy of death. . . .

Let me begin by saying that I have no answer.

When it comes to reconciling the words in the ancient book with the conundrums of modern life, such is often the case.

The same chapter of Leviticus, for instance, also mandates death for cursing your parents (Leviticus 20:9) or committing adultery (Leviticus 20:10).

Why aren't those who quote Leviticus as literal law rushing to obey this injunction? Why aren't the streets running red with the blood of sluttish spouses and spoiled brats?

I have no answer.

It is emphatically not my intention to ridicule God's Book. However, I do mean to challenge those who seem to take their faith as an excuse for spurning two of His greatest gifts. Meaning a heart that knows compassion and a mind that entertains questions.

They claim there's nothing personal in their persecution of gays. They are, they say, just following God's law.

But we seldom hear of anyone getting this hot and bothered over faithless spouses or ill-mannered children, both worthy of capital punishment according to the Bible.

---

*Editorial, *Wilkes-Barre Times Leader,* May 25, 1996.

For that matter, you seldom hear rage over men with long hair (I Corinthians 11:14) or women who speak out in church (I Corinthians 11:34–35)—both also scorned by the Bible. And so, if these people are honest with themselves, they must admit that their antipathy toward gays has less to do with God's law than with human aversion—the visceral shudder of revulsion many feel at the thought of all things homosexual. . . .

What's this say about us that so many are willing to interpret the Bible only to the limits of their own narrow-mindedness and bigotry? That so many are inclined to ignore passages that say men ought not to judge? Or that so many seem to disregard what happened when the scribes and Pharisees brought before Jesus a woman caught in the act of adultery and demanded that she be stoned in accordance with God's law. Instead, Jesus faced them and said the one who was without sin should cast the first stone.

Why is it so few ever take that literally?

I have no answer.

Is homosexuality an abomination?

No answer for that, either, except that if I was given heart and mind, the giver must have wanted me to use them. No answer except that my heart and mind find it difficult to justify loathing or impeding people who have done me no harm. No answer except to note that God is mercy. And, of course, He is love.

So it doesn't bother me to have no answers.

But I fear the man who has no questions.*

Buying Notes Makes Sense at Lost-in-Crowd Campuses

Higher education got a message last week from a jury in Gainesville, Fla.: Its customers, the students across the nation, deserve better service.

The jury found entrepreneurs are free to sell notes from college professors' lectures. And Ken Brickman is an example of good, old free enterprise, even if his services encourage students to skip class.

Brickman is a businessman who pays students to take notes in classes at the University of Florida. From a storefront a block off campus, he resells the notes to other students with a markup.

Professors and deans bemoan Brickman's lack of morals. They even use the word "cheating." They'd be more credible if their complaints—and the university's legal resources—were directed equally at Brickman's competitor in the note-selling business a few blocks away.

The difference: The competition pays professors for their notes; Brickman pays students. Morals are absent, it seems, only when professors aren't getting their cut.

The deeper issue is why Brickman has found a lucrative market. It's easy to say that uninspired students would rather read someone else's notes than spend time in class, but that's not the point.

Why are students uninspired? Why are they required to learn in auditorium-size classes where personal attention is non-existent, taking attendance impossible, and students can "cut" an entire semester with no one noticing.

Why are students increasingly subjected to teaching assistants—graduate students who know little more than they do—who control classes while profes-

---

*Leonard Pitts, Jr., "Don't Use God's Law to Beat Up on Gays," *Wilkes-Barre Times Leader*, June 8, 1997.

sors are off writing articles for esoteric journals that not even their peers
will read?

Why are there not more professors—every student can remember one—who
transmit knowledge of and enthusiasm for a subject with a fluency and flair
that make students eager to show up? No one would prefer to stay away and
buy that professor's notes.

The debate over professorial priorities—students vs. research—is old. But so
long as students come in second, they'll have good reasons to go to Ken Brickman for their notes.*

Making the Grade

It was a rookie error. After 10 years I should have known better, but I went to
my office the day after final grades were posted. There was a tentative knock on
the door. "Professor Wiesenfeld? I took your Physics 2121 class? I flunked it? I
wonder if there's anything I can do to improve my grade?" I thought: "Why are
you asking me? Isn't it too late to worry about it? Do you dislike making declarative statements?"

After the student gave his tale of woe and left, the phone rang. "I got a D in
your class. Is there any way you can change it to 'Incomplete'?" Then the e-mail
assault began: "I'm shy about coming in to talk to you, but I'm not shy about
asking for a better grade. Anyway, it's worth a try." The next day I had three
phone messages from students asking *me* to call *them*. I didn't.

Time was, when you received a grade, that was it. You might groan and
moan, but you accepted it as the outcome of your efforts or lack thereof (and,
yes, sometimes a tough grader). In the last few years, however, some students
have developed a disgruntled-consumer approach. If they don't like their grade,
they go to the "return" counter to trade it for something better.

What alarms me is their indifference toward grades as an indication of personal effort and performance. Many, when pressed about why they think they
deserve a better grade, admit they don't deserve one but would like one anyway. Having been raised on gold stars for effort and smiley faces for self-esteem, they've learned that they can get by without hard work and real talent if
they can talk the professor into giving them a break. This attitude is beyond
cynicism. There's a weird innocence to the assumption that one expects (even
deserves) a better grade simply by begging for it. With that outlook, I guess I
shouldn't be as flabbergasted as I was that 12 students asked me to change
their grades *after* final grades were posted.

That's 10 percent of my class who let three months of midterms, quizzes
and lab reports slide until long past remedy. My graduate student calls it hyper-
rational thinking: if effort and intelligence don't matter, why should deadlines?
What matters is getting a better grade through an unearned bonus, the academic equivalent of a freebie T-shirt or toaster giveaway. Rewards are disconnected from the quality of one's work. An act and its consequences are
unrelated, random events. . . .

In a society saturated with surface values, love of knowledge for its own
sake does sound eccentric. The benefits of fame and wealth are more obvious.
So is it right to blame students for reflecting the superficial values saturating
our society?

---

*Editorial, *USA Today,* December 17, 1993.

Yes, of course it's right. These guys had better take themselves seriously now, because our country will be forced to take them seriously later, when the stakes are much higher. They must recognize that their attitude is not only self-destructive, but socially destructive. . . .

Most of my students are science and engineering majors. If they're good at getting partial credit but not at getting the answer right, then the new bridge breaks or the new drug doesn't work. One finds examples here in Atlanta. Last year a light tower in the Olympic Stadium collapsed, killing a worker. It collapsed because an engineer miscalculated how much weight it could hold. . . . Two 10,000-pound steel beams at the new natatorium collapsed in March, crashing into the student athletic complex. (Should we give partial credit since no one was hurt?) Those are real-world consequences of errors and lack of expertise.

But the lesson is lost on the grade-grousing 10 percent. Say that you won't (not can't but won't) change the grade they deserve to what they want, and they're frequently bewildered or angry. They don't think it's fair that they're judged according to their performance, not their desires or their "potential." They don't think it's fair that they should jeopardize their scholarships or be in danger of flunking out simply because they could not or did not do their work. But it's more than fair; it's necessary to help preserve a minimum standard of quality that our society needs to maintain safety and integrity. I don't know if the 13th-hour students will learn that lesson, but I've learned mine. From now on, after final grades are posted, I'll lie low until the next quarter starts.*

End the Death Penalty; Use Life without Parole

The evidence is in: the verdict is beyond dispute. The death penalty is a failure as a tool of law, justice or public safety. . . .

You need not be a legal scholar to see the death penalty's many flaws. Nor do you need to be "soft on crime." Other punishments are more meaningful and just as satisfying. Indeed, the death penalty actually makes our society more violent and our persons less secure.

Capital punishment has a "brutalizing effect" that actually seems to incite killers. The phenomenon has been documented as far back as the 1850s, both here and in Europe. One famous study found that in New York between 1907 and 1963, the murder rate increased, on average, by two in every month following a public execution.

There's a simpler way to prove the death penalty doesn't work: Look at the crime stats. In 1992, the average murder rate in death-penalty states was 7.8 per 100,000 people. In states without: 4.9 per 100,000. Where do you want to live? . . .

Capital punishment satisfies a natural urge for revenge that is complete and final. And, certainly, the courts should impose lasting punishments that truly punish.

But the death penalty dooms the innocent along with the guilty. Since 1900, as many as 23 people have been put to death for crimes they did not commit. Even now, death-row inmates scheduled for execution are regularly reprieved. In 1993 alone, five death-row inmates were found to be completely innocent.

The risk of error has a companion: The taint of racism.

On the federal level, 75% of those convicted under the Drug Kingpin Act

---

*Kurt Wiesenfeld, "Making the Grade," *Newsweek*, June 17, 1996, p. 16.

have been white, but 90% of those who face capital prosecutions under the same statute are minorities. In the states, only one white in 18 years has been executed for killing a black. A black murderer is twice as likely to be executed if his victim was white than if his victim was a minority.

Make no mistake. Opposition to capital punishment is not opposition to swift and certain punishment. An alternative that meets both standards is available: Life in prison with no possibility of parole, now available in at least 33 states.

This sentence means what it says. A convict will not get out in seven years, or 12 years or 15 years. *There is no parole.*

Many jurors, like most Americans, think there's no such thing as a life sentence. They fear a killer will get out and kill again. But in California, for instance, not one person sentenced to life without parole has been freed. This is life in a cage—forever.

The only problem is that this sentence isn't more common. Life without parole:

- Is easier to win than the death penalty, and cheaper by one-third or one-half. . . .
- Is indisputably constitutional.
- And may actually deter crime, especially for those in communities where the prospect of death may be more tolerable than the prospect of life in a cage.

The death penalty offers no certainty of justice. It is arbitrary. It wastes money. It makes us less safe. It cannot be reconciled with the Constitution. It bogs down the courts. It encourages legalistic manipulation, and it erodes the system's integrity.

So why bother with it? Life in prison without any possibility of parole will put the bad guys where it hurts the most and improve our judicial system at the same time. . . . Abolish the death penalty.*

Improve Way We Educate Teachers and Kids' Education Will Improve

Headlines were made by the latest results of the Third International Mathematics and Science Study. Yet nobody should have been surprised, since our students have been doing badly on international tests for decades.

American 12th graders fell below the international average in general mathematics and general science. In advanced mathematics, our students were tied for last place and in physics they had sole possession of last place.

Students from Asian nations, who usually do very well on such tests, did not take part in these particular tests. So American students are trailing the pack among the also-rans.

While the American education system is falling behind academically, it is leading the world in excuses. One of these excuses is that more of our students reach the 12th grade, so that we are comparing our average with other countries' elites.

While that may be true for some countries, there are other countries that have as high a percentage of their students finish secondary school as we do—and some have a higher percentage completing secondary education. Both kinds of countries beat out our students.

---

*Editorial, *USA Today,* April 8, 1994.

Critical Thinking Lapse

Wayne Roth, 38, of Pittston, Pennsylvania, was bitten by a cobra belonging to his friend, Roger Croteau, after playfully reaching into the tank and picking up the snake. Wayne subsequently refused to go to a hospital, telling Roger, "I'm a man, I can handle it." Falser words have seldom been spoken. Instead of a hospital, Wayne reported to a bar. He had three drinks and enjoyed bragging that he had just been bitten by a cobra. Cobra venom is a slow-acting central nervous system toxin. He died within a few hours in Jenkins Township, Pennsylvania.[14]

Another excuse is that our population has so many disadvantaged minorities that this drags down the average. But when you compare our very top students with the top students from other countries, ours still get clobbered. . . .

U.S. Secretary of Education Richard Riley has responded to the sad results from these international tests by calling them "unacceptable." Nonsense! Such dismal results have been accepted for years and will be accepted for years to come, so long as the National Education Association continues to contribute millions of dollars to political campaigns.

From the standpoint of the NEA, the American public schools are not a failure but a great big success. These schools provide NEA members with jobs where they have iron-clad tenure, automatic raises, and no accountability for bad performances by their students or themselves.

The public schools also have a virtual monopoly on the supply of school-children, except for those whose parents are affluent enough to be able to afford private schools or dedicated enough to homeschool their children. What this all adds up to is that the public schools can pretty much do whatever they want to, including avoiding academic training and indulging in all sorts of fads and psychobabble, including "self-esteem." . . .

While there are many particular things than can be criticized in our public schools, even the critics often miss the point when they fail to see that the key to all these counterproductive policies are the people who make them. If we purged the public schools of all the time-wasting silliness there today, we would have accomplished little if the same kinds of people were left in place to bring in new non-academic nonsense tomorrow.

Innumerable tests over many decades have shown that the mental test scores of people who specialize in education are among the lowest of any college students. This is not an accident. Given the incredibly bad courses in education that abound, in even the top universities, intelligent people are repelled, while mediocrities sail through.

If you are not going to change that, then you are not going to change the low quality of American public schools. Education courses are a filter. They filter out intelligent students and let mediocrities pass through.

Just as you are not going to catch ocean fish in mountain lakes, no matter how expensive your fishing equipment, so you are not going to get an academically proficient or even academically oriented class of people coming out of education schools and education courses. First-rate people do not come out of such places because they do not go into such places or do not stay if they do.

Raising teachers' salaries will not do it. You will just get more expensive mediocrities in the classroom and more expensive incompetents being graduated from our schools.*

SUMMARY

1. In critical thinking, a *good argument* is an argument that satisfies the relevant critical thinking standards that apply in a particular context. The two most important critical thinking standards are accuracy (Are the premises true?) and logical correctness (Do the premises, if true, provide good reasons to accept the conclusion?). However, there are other critical thinking standards that should also be considered in evaluating arguments. Among these standards are clarity, precision, relevance, consistency, completeness, and fairness.

2. In general, it is reasonable to accept an unsupported claim as true when the claim does not conflict with personal experiences that we have no good reason to doubt; the claim does not conflict with background beliefs that we have no good reason to doubt; and the claim comes from a credible source that we have no good reason to doubt.

3. Key questions we should ask in evaluating arguments include the following:

   • Are the premises true?

   • Is the reasoning correct? Is the argument deductively valid or inductively strong?

   • Does the arguer commit any logical fallacies?

   • Does the arguer express his points clearly and precisely?

   • Are the premises relevant to the conclusion?

   • Are the arguer's claims logically consistent? Do any of the arguer's claims contradict other claims made in the argument?

   • Is the argument complete? Is all relevant evidence taken into account (given understandable limitations of time, space, context, etc.)?

   • Is the argument fair? Is the arguer fair in her presentation of the evidence? Is she fair in her treatment of opposing arguments and views?

---

*Thomas Sowell, "Improve Way We Educate Teachers and Kids' Education Will Improve," *Wilkes-Barre Times Leader,* February 28, 1998.

Appendix: Sample Critical Essay

Below is a sample critical essay. The essay is a critical analysis of a guest editorial by Jack Pytleski that appeared in the *Wilkes-Barre Times Leader* on July 10, 1997. First, an edited and abridged version of Pytleski's editorial is given, followed by the critical essay itself.

Defending My Right to Claim My "Steak" in the Animal Kingdom

. . . [A recent caller to a newspaper call-in column] opined that the "healthiest way to prepare and eat meat is not to eat it at all."

Who cares!

I love a good steak. . . . But I'm not about to start carrying a sign that promotes a carnivorous diet. Your health is your business, not mine. If you wish to clog your arteries with cholesterol, saturated fat and other toxins, go right ahead. Just make sure you've made plenty of room at your table for me. And pass the butter for that ear of roast corn while you're at it, OK?

Let's quickly examine two of the three popular reasons for vegetarianism, the health aspect and the animal rights point of view. . . . The third reason, the use of edible grain and arable land for animal feed, is worth an entire column at another time.

I freely admit that excessive consumption of meat is probably not the best thing for your body. I contend, however, that gastronomic preference is a highly personal choice, and claim refuge under my "constitutional right to privacy" (feminists, take note) and the privilege of doing whatever I please with my body.

Once you're born, death is inevitable. Since I'll die no matter what I eat, I plan to enjoy every minute of my allotted time on earth, including consuming my favorite foods. Am I killing myself? Possibly, but I'm as good as dead anyway, aren't I?

Now some of you might say that eating meat shortens my natural life span. Maybe. But given the choice of sitting around drooling all over myself in something euphemistically called a "personal care home" and punching out earlier with a massive thrombosis, guess which deal I'll take, Monty? You've got it—the one behind Door Number Two. . . .

Pass the sour cream, please. . . .

There are just some things I take on faith. One of those is that some animals, like it or not, have another purpose besides wandering around doing animal-like things in the weeds. This includes everything from guide and companion duties to gracing the body on the table. Unfortunately for most herbivores and some carnivores, . . . they haven't yet become accepted as caregivers or companions. So we eat 'em or wear 'em. At least I do. What you do is your business. . . .

Don't misunderstand. I'm on the side of a certain degree of animal rights. I believe that all animals deserve humane treatment. . . . Companion animals should be spayed or neutered and properly fed, loved and sheltered.

Some animals shouldn't be kept as companions, and even animals used for food or clothing ought to be kept in clean and compassionate surroundings—until that final two hundred and thirty grains catches them between the running lights.

As I stated at the outset, what you eat is your business. What I eat is mine. But whoever you are, if you feel you have the right to dictate something so fundamental as my diet I reserve the privilege to answer accordingly.

Stick that in your Brussels sprouts! And pass the bacon.

Sample Critical Essay

Kendall 1

Jamie Kendall

Critical Thinking 101

Professor Lewis

March 25, 2001

Animal Rights and Human Health

For a variety of reasons, more and more people today are choosing to become vegetarians. Two of the most common reasons given for adopting a vegetarian diet are that it is healthier than a meat-based diet, and that eating animals is wrong because it inflicts suffering on sentient creatures without good reason. In a column titled "Defending My Right to Claim My 'Steak' in the Animal Kingdom" that appeared in the *Wilkes-Barre Times Leader* on July 10, 1997, Jack Pytleski argues that neither of these two popular arguments for vegetarianism is convincing. In this essay I will argue that Pytleski's argument for this conclusion is weak.

Pytleski's basic argument can be summarized as follows:

1. I'm going to die no matter what I eat.

Kendall 2

2. I want to enjoy every minute of my allotted time on earth.

3. If given a choice between sitting around drooling in a "personal care center" or checking out earlier from a massive heart attack, I would choose the latter.

4. I have a right to do as I please with my own body.

5. I have a constitutional right of privacy that gives me the right to eat the kinds of foods I enjoy.

6. [Thus, contrary to one popular argument for vegetarianism, the fact that eating a balanced vegetarian diet tends to be healthier than a meat-based diet is not a good reason for me to switch to a vegetarian diet. (from 1–5)]

7. I believe on faith that animals were put on earth to provide food, clothing and other benefits to humans.

8. [Thus, contrary to a second popular argument for vegetarianism, animals have no right not to be killed and eaten by humans. (from 7)]

9. [Therefore, two popular arguments for vegetarianism—the health benefits argument and the animal rights argument—do not provide good reasons for adopting a vegetarian diet. (from 6 and 8)]

Pytleski's essay, while it raises some interesting issues, is flawed for a number of reasons.

First, much of Pytleski's argument in lines 1–6 misses the point of what his opponents are arguing. In this part of his argument, Pytleski seems to be arguing for two things: first, that people have both a moral and a constitutional right to eat unhealthy foods, and second, that it is reasonable, given certain personal preferences, to prefer a less healthy meat-based diet to a more healthy vegetarian diet. But both these claims rest on a misunderstanding of what the health benefits argument asserts. As it is typically formulated, all that the health benefits argument asserts is that it is *prudent* to eat a balanced vegetarian diet, *if* one wants to live a long, healthy life.[1] Nothing in Pytleski's argument shows that this claim is false. At best what Pytleski shows is that he personally is unmoved by the health benefits argument, because he prefers eating foods he enjoys rather than living a long, healthy life.

Some of Pytleski's arguments are shaky on other grounds as well. Let's examine two of these arguments: the "drooling" argument in lines 3 and 6, and the animal rights argument in lines 7 and 8.

Pytleski says he has good reasons for not adopting a vegetarian diet, and that one of these reasons is that he'd rather die earlier of a

---

[1] See, for example, William O. Stephens, "Five Arguments for Vegetarianism," *Philosophy and the Contemporary World* 1, No. 4 (Winter 1994), pp. 25–39; reprinted in Joseph DesJardins, ed., *Environmental Ethics: Concepts, Policy, Theory* (Mountain View, CA: Mayfield, 1999), pp. 288–301. The health benefits argument is discussed on pp. 294–95 in the DesJardins text.

Kendall 4

massive heart attack than sit around drooling in a
personal care center. This argument is weak because
it falsely assumes that there are only two relevant
possibilities: dying of a sudden massive heart
attack or vegetating in a personal care center.
This overlooks the fact there are many adverse
health effects other than heart disease that are
linked to diets high in animal fat, including
kidney disease, osteoporosis, diverticulitis, food
poisoning, hypertension, and, most significantly,
stroke and many kinds of cancer. The possibility of
stroke is particularly relevant in this context,
because many of the 570,000 stroke victims in the
United States each year do suffer from precisely
the kind of severe long-term mental impairment that
Pytleski fears.

Furthermore, Pytleski's response to the animal
rights argument is also very weak. Boiled down to
essentials, the animal rights argument is this:

1. Practices which inflict suffering on sentient
   beings without good reason are morally wrong.

2. Thus, sentient beings have a right not to be
   made to suffer without good reason. (from 1)

3. For humans to kill and eat sentient animals
   inflicts suffering on them without good
   reason.

4. Therefore, sentient animals have a right not
   to be killed and eaten by humans. (from 2-3)[2]

---

[2]Some of the language in this formulation of the argument
is borrowed from Stephens, p. 293 in the DesJardins text.

Kendall 5

Pytleski's response to this argument is simply to state that he believes "on faith" that animals exist for the purpose of providing food and other benefits to humans. But of course this is precisely what animal rights supporters deny. So this isn't so much an "argument" against the animal rights view as it is simply a denial of that view.

Finally, it should be noted that Pytleski's argument is unclear at key points. In fact, as the argument summary reveals, Pytleski leaves it to his readers to formulate every major conclusion in the argument.

In sum, Pytleski offers a very weak argument for his conclusion. Several of his arguments against the health benefits argument misfire because they are based on a misunderstanding of what that argument claims. His "drooling" argument is faulty because it poses a false either/or choice between dying early from a massive heart attack and sitting around drooling in a personal care center. His "argument" against the animal rights view basically boils down to just a denial of that view. And Pytleski's argument as a whole is neither as clear nor as explicit as it should be.

Albert Einstein once said, "Our task must be to free ourselves . . . by widening our circle of compassion to embrace all living creatures and the whole of nature and its beauty." It may be that a strong case can be made against widening this circle of moral concern, but Pytleski's argument against doing so is not persuasive.

CHAPTER 9

GETTING DEEPER INTO LOGIC: CATEGORICAL REASONING

To help us make sense of our experience, we humans constantly group things into *classes* or *categories*. These classifications are reflected in our everyday language. For instance, we often encounter statements like these:

> All donuts are fattening.
> No minors are permitted in the store.
> Some mushrooms are poisonous.
> Some Republicans are not conservatives.

The first statement says that anything included in the class of donuts is also included in the class of things that are fattening. The second statement says that no member of the class of minors is included in the class of persons permitted in the store. The third statement says that some members of the class of mushrooms are also members of the class of things that are poisonous. And the fourth statement says that some members of the class of Republicans are not members of the class of conservatives.

These are examples of what logicians call *categorical statements*. In this chapter we introduce a simple yet powerful technique for testing the validity of simple arguments made up of categorical statements.

CATEGORICAL STATEMENTS

A **categorical statement** is a statement that makes a claim about the relationship between two or more classes or categories of things. In this chapter we shall focus on what are called **standard-form categorical statements**. These are categorical statements that have one of the following four forms:

> All *S* are *P*. (*Example:* All Democrats are liberals.)
> No *S* are *P*. (*Example:* No Democrats are liberals.)
> Some *S* are *P*. (*Example:* Some Democrats are liberals.)
> Some *S* are not *P*. (*Example:* Some Democrats are not liberals.)

Logicians have discovered a number of techniques to test the validity of simple categorical arguments. The easiest method involves drawing a series of overlapping circles and associated markings called **Venn diagrams.**[1] Let's start with a few simple examples to see how the method works.

Suppose we wish to draw a Venn diagram of the statement "All Democrats are liberals." We start by drawing a circle to stand for the class of Democrats:

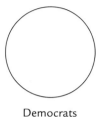

Democrats

Next, we draw a circle to stand for the class of liberals:

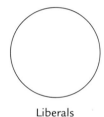

Liberals

The first circle includes anyone who is a Democrat; the second circle includes anyone who is a liberal.

Next, we need to connect the two circles to indicate that the two classes are being related to each other in the statement. We do this by drawing the circles so that they partially overlap, as follows:

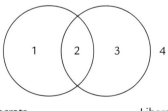

Democrats   Liberals

Anything in area 1 is a Democrat but not a liberal. Anything in area 2 is both a Democrat and a liberal. Anything in area 3 is a liberal but not a Democrat. And anything in area 4, the area outside the two circles, is neither a Democrat nor a liberal.[2]

Finally, we need some way to depict the asserted relationship between these two classes, namely, that all members of the class of Democrats are also members of the class of liberals. To do this, we shade that part of the Democrats circle that does not overlap with the Liberals circle, as follows:

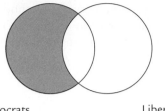

Democrats   Liberals

The shading means that that part of the Democrats circle that does not overlap with the liberals circle is *empty;* that is, it contains no members.[3] The diagram thus asserts that there are *no* Democrats who are not liberals. This is what we mean when we say that all Democrats are liberals.

Next, let's diagram the statement "No Democrats are liberals." Once again we start by drawing two overlapping circles, one to represent Democrats and the other to represent liberals:

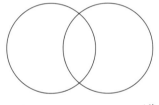

Democrats   Liberals

To say that no Democrats are liberals is to say that no members of the class of Democrats are members of the class of liberals—that is, that there is *no overlap* between the two classes. To represent this claim, we shade that portion of the two circles that overlaps, as follows:

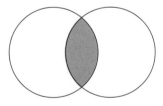

Democrats   Liberals

The diagram now tells us that anyone who is a Democrat is *not* a liberal—that is, that the class of people who are both Democrats and liberals is empty. And that is what it means to say that no Democrats are liberals.

Categorical statements that begin with "some" must be treated differently from categorical statements that begin with "all" or "no." "Some" is often ambiguous in ordinary usage. Does it mean "one," "two," "a few," "at

Two Important Things to Remember about "Some" Statements

1. In categorical logic, "some" always means "at least one."
2. "Some" statements are understood to assert that something actually exists. Thus, "Some mammals are cats" is understood to assert that at least one mammal exists and that that mammal is a cat. By contrast, "all" or

"no" statements are not interpreted as asserting the existence of anything. Instead, they are treated as purely conditional statements. Thus, "All snakes are reptiles" asserts that *if* anything is a snake, then it is a reptile, not that there *are* snakes and that all of them are reptiles.

least a few," "at least one but not all," "at least one and maybe all," "at least a few but not all," "lots," "many"? To avoid such confusions, logicians always use "some" with the same consistent meaning. In logic, *"some" always means "at least one."* Thus, for example,

Some dogs are animals.

means "At least one dog is an animal" (which is true), not "At least one dog is an animal, but not all" (which is false).

There is another important difference between "some" statements and "all" or "no" statements. In modern logic, "all" or "no" statements are treated as purely *conditional* (if-then) statements. Thus, the statement "All Cyclopes are one-eyed monsters" doesn't say that there *are* any Cyclopes or one-eyed monsters. Rather, it says that *if* anything is a Cyclops, then it is a one-eyed monster. By contrast, the statement "Some Cyclopes are one-eyed monsters" *does* assert that something exists. Specifically, it asserts that at least one Cyclops exists and that that Cyclops is a one-eyed monster. This difference between the two kinds of quantifiers isn't very intuitive, but it causes few problems as long as the special meanings assigned to these expressions are kept firmly in mind.

In logic, therefore, the statement "Some Democrats are liberals" means "There exists at least one Democrat and that Democrat is a liberal." To diagram this statement, we place an X in that part of the Democrats circle that overlaps with the Liberals circle, as follows:

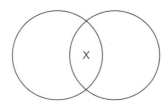

Democrats   Liberals

The *X* here stands for that at-least-one-Democrat who is definitely asserted to be a liberal.

A similar strategy is used with statements of the form "Some *S* are not *P*." In logic, the statement "Some Democrats are not liberals" means "At least one Democrat is not a liberal." To diagram this statement we place an *X* in that part of the Democrats circle that lies outside the Liberals circle, as follows:

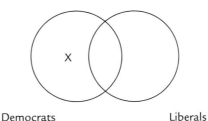

Democrats   Liberals

The diagram now asserts that at least one member of the class of Democrats is not a member of the class of liberals. And that is what it means, in logic, to say that some Democrats are not liberals.

In summary, the four kinds of standard-form categorical statements are diagrammed as follows:

All *S* are *P*.

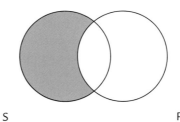

S   P

No *S* are *P*.

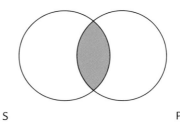

S   P

Some *S* are *P*.

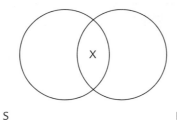

Some *S* are not *P*.

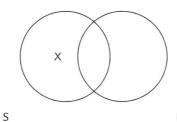

EXERCISE 9.1

Draw Venn diagrams of the following statements. In some cases, you may need to rephrase the statements slightly to put them in one of the four standard forms (i.e., All *S* are *P*, No *S* are *P*, Some *S* are *P*, or Some *S* are not *P*).

1. No apples are fruits.
2. Some fruits are apples.
3. All apples are fruits.
4. Some apples are not fruits.
5. No fruits are apples.
6. Some fruits are not apples.
7. All fruits are apples.
8. Some apples are fruits.
9. No apples are nonfruits.
10. Some fruits are nonapples.
11. Anything that is an apple is a fruit.
12. Only apples are fruits.

Critical Thinking Lapse

TACOMA, Wash.—Kerry Bingham had been drinking with several friends when one of them said they knew a person who had bungee-jumped from the Tacoma Narrows Bridge in the middle of traffic. The conversation grew more heated and at least 10 men trooped along the walkway of the bridge at 4:30 a.m. Upon arrival at the midpoint of the bridge they discovered that no one had brought bungee rope. Bingham, who had continued drinking, volunteered and pointed out that a coil of lineman's cable lay nearby. One end of the cable was secured around Bingham's leg and the other end was tied to the bridge. His fall lasted 40 feet before the cable tightened and tore his foot off at the ankle. He miraculously survived his fall into the icy river water and was rescued by two nearby fishermen. "All I can say," said Bingham, "is that God was watching out for me on that night. There's just no other explanation for it." Bingham's foot was never located.[4]

The main practical value of logic to one who wants to distinguish between straight and crooked thinking is that it introduces him to the device of reducing arguments to their skeleton form as a means of judging whether or not they give sound support to their conclusions.

—Robert H. Thouless

TRANSLATING INTO STANDARD CATEGORICAL FORM

Do people really go around saying things like "Some fruits are not apples"? Not very often. But although relatively few of our everyday statements are *explicitly* in standard categorical form, a surprisingly large number of those statements can be *translated* into standard categorical form. That is why Venn diagrams are so useful in testing everyday arguments.

Before we discuss ways to translate ordinary English sentences into standard-form categorical statements, let's take a closer look at what such statements involve.

Standard-form categorical statements have a very simple logical structure. Here, once again, are the four standard categorical forms:

All *S* are *P*.

No *S* are *P*.

Some *S* are *P*.

Some *S* are not *P*.

Notice that each of these statement forms has four basic parts:

1. They all begin with the word "all," "no," or "some." These words are called **quantifiers,** because they are used to express a quantity or a number.
2. They all have a **subject term.** The subject term is a word or a phrase that names a class and that serves as the grammatical subject of the sentence. In these statement forms, the subject term is represented by "*S*."
3. They all have a **predicate term.** The predicate term is a word or a phrase that names a class and that serves as the subject complement

of the sentence. In these statement forms, the predicate term is represented by "*P.*"

4. They all have a **copula,** or linking verb, which is some form of the verb "to be." The copula serves to link, or join, the subject term with the predicate term.

With this helpful terminology in mind, we can now offer the following tips on how to translate ordinary English sentences into standard categorical form.

Tip 1: Rephrase all nonstandard subject and predicate terms so that they refer to classes.

Many everyday English sentences have adjectives as their grammatical predicates. Because adjectives name attributes rather than classes, they must be rewritten as nouns, pronouns, or noun phrases that refer to classes. Here are two examples:

All actors are vain.	All actors are vain *people.*
Some puppies are cute.	Some puppies are cute *animals.*

Tip 2: Rephrase all nonstandard verbs.

For the sake of consistency, only two linking verbs (copulas) are allowed in standard-form categorical statements: "are" and "are not." Sentences that contain linking verbs other than "are" or "are not" must be rewritten in standard form. Here are three examples:

Some students walk to school.	Some students *are persons who* walk to school.
No animal should be mistreated.	No *animals are things that* should be mistreated.
All the northern counties were flooded.	All the northern counties *are places that* were flooded.

Tip 3: Fill in any unexpressed quantifiers.

Often, categorical statements have no stated quantifier. In such cases, the unexpressed quantifier must be added. Here are two examples:

Koalas are marsupials.	*All* koalas are marsupials.
Californians are health nuts.	*Some* Californians are health nuts.

Sometimes it is hard to know what quantifier a speaker or writer may have had implicitly in mind. In such cases, we should interpret the speaker's or writer's intent as charitably as possible. Here are two examples:

Bankers are conservatives.	*Some* bankers are conservatives. (*Not: All* bankers are conservatives.)
Politicians are liars.	*Some* politicians are liars (*Not: All* politicians are liars.) [5]

Tip 4: Translate singular statements as "all" or "no" statements.

A *singular statement* is a statement that makes a claim about a particular person, place, or thing. Often, with a little ingenuity, such statements can be translated into "all" or "no" statements. Here are several examples:

Caesar crossed the Rubicon.	*All persons identical with* Caesar *are persons that* crossed the Rubicon.
Joe wasn't born in Kansas.	*No persons identical with* Joe *are persons who were* born in Kansas.
Paris is the capital of France.	*All places identical with* Paris *are places that are* the capital of France.
This flower is blooming.	*All things identical with* this flower *are things that are* blooming.
Tomorrow is my birthday.	*All days identical with* tomorrow *are days that are* my birthday.

Such translations, however artificial, are useful because they greatly increase the number of everyday arguments that can be tested by means of Venn diagrams.

Tip 5: Translate stylistic variants into the appropriate categorical form.

Each of the four standard categorical forms has numerous *stylistic variants*— that is, different ways of saying essentially the same thing.[6] For instance, the statement

Mary is loved by John.

is a stylistic variant of the statement

John loves Mary.

Following is a list of some of the most common stylistic variants of statements of the form "All *S* are *P*."

Common Stylistic Variants of "All *S* are *P*"

Every *S* is a *P.*	*Example:* Every dog is an animal.
Whoever is an *S* is a *P.*	*Example:* Whoever is a bachelor is a male.
Whatever is an *S* is a *P.*	*Example:* Whatever is a lemon is a fruit.
If anything is an *S,* then it is a *P.*	*Example:* If anything is a lizard, then it is a reptile.
If something is not a *P,* then it is not an *S.*	*Example:* If something is not a bird, then it is not a sparrow.
Any *S* is a *P.*	*Example:* Any triangle is a geometrical figure.
Each *S* is a *P.*	*Example:* Each monkey is a primate.
S are all *P.*	*Example:* Senators are all politicians.
S are always *P.*	Examples: Racists are always bigots.

Only *P* are *S*.	*Example:* Only Catholics are popes.
Only if something is a *P* is it an *S*.	*Example:* Only if something is a fish is it a salmon.
The only S are *P*.	*Example:* The only seats available are seats in the upper deck.
Something is an *S* only if it is a *P*.	*Example:* Something is an elm only if it is a tree.

Pay special attention to the phrases containing the word "only" in that list. ("Only" is one of the trickiest words in the English language.) Note, in particular, that as a rule the subject and predicate terms must be *reversed* if the statement begins with the words "only" or "only if." Thus, "Only citizens are voters" must be rewritten as "All voters are citizens," *not* "All citizens are voters." And "Only if a thing is an insect is it a bee" must be rewritten as "All bees are insects," *not* "All insects are bees."

EXERCISE 9.2

Translate the following sentences into standard categorical form.

1. Only hotel guests may use the Jacuzzi.
2. Only doctors are psychiatrists.
3. Something is a bluejay only if it is a bird.
4. Only if something is an insect is it a ladybug.
5. None but the brave deserve the fair.
6. No one is allowed in the hall without a pass.
7. None except faculty members are permitted in the faculty locker room.
8. Employees alone may use the side entry.
9. The only people at the party are company employees.
10. No dogs except Seeing Eye dogs are allowed in the store.

Following is a list of some of the most common stylistic variants of statements of the form "No *S* are *P*."

Common Stylistic Variants of "No *S* are *P*"

No *P* are *S*.	*Example:* No vegetables are fruits.
S are not *P*.	*Example:* Oaks are not conifers.
Nothing that is an *S* is a *P*.	*Example:* Nothing that is a known fact is a mere opinion.
No one who is an *S* is a *P*.	*Example:* No one who is a Democrat is a Republican.
None of the *S* are *P*.	*Example:* None of the students are registered Independents.

Not a single *S* is *P*.	*Example:* Not a single U.S. president is a woman.
If anything is an *S*, then it is not a *P*.	*Example:* If anything is a plant, then it is not a mineral.
All *S* are non-*P*.	*Example:* All robots are nonhumans.

Following is a list of some common stylistic variants of statements of the form "Some *S* are *P*."

Common Stylistic Variants of "Some *S* are *P*"

Some *P* are *S*.	*Example:* Some Democrats are women.
A few *S* are *P*.	*Example:* A few mathematicians are poets.
There are *S* that are *P*.	*Example:* There are monkeys that are carnivores.
Several *S* are *P*.	*Example:* Several planets in the solar system are gas giants.
Many *S* are *P*.	*Example:* Many billionaires are Internet tycoons.
Most *S* are *P*.	*Example:* Most high school principals are men.
Nearly all *S* are *P*.	*Example:* Nearly all Hollywood producers are liberals.[7]

Following is a list of some common stylistic variants of statements of the form "Some *S* are not *P*."

Common Stylistic Variants of "Some *S* are not *P*"

Not all *S* are *P*.	*Example:* Not all mammals are quadrupeds.
Not everyone who is an *S* is a *P*.	*Example:* Not everyone who is a used-car dealer is a crook.
S are not always *P*.	*Example:* Sailors are not always swimmers.
Some *S* are non-*P*.	*Example:* Some theologians are nonbelievers.
There are *S* that are not *P*.	*Example:* There are bears that are not carnivores.
A few *S* are not *P*.	*Example:* A few logicians are not eccentrics.
Several *S* are not *P*.	*Example:* Several of the world's most famous sports celebrities are not good role models.

Most *S* are not *P*.   *Example:* Most students are not binge drinkers.

Nearly all *S* are not *P*.   *Example:* Nearly all physicists are not sharp dressers.

It should be emphasized that these translation tips are not intended as hard-and-fast rules. Language is far too subtle an instrument ever to be reduced to any mechanical set of "do's" and "don'ts." The best general advice we can give is this: *Always try to restate the speaker's or writer's intended meaning as accurately as possible.* Don't assume that because two sentences look alike they can be translated alike. In the final analysis, as William Halverson remarks, there is no safe route to accurate categorical translation except "through the brain of an alert restater."[8]

EXERCISE 9.3

I. Translate the following sentences into standard-form categorical statements.

1. Maples are trees.
2. Roses are red.
3. Some bats are nocturnal.
4. Each insect is an animal.
5. If anything is an igloo, then it is made of ice.
6. All that glitters is not gold.
7. Cheaters never prosper.
8. Every cloud has a silver lining.
9. World War II began in 1939.
10. If something is not a vehicle, then it is not a car.
11. There are birds that cannot fly.
12. Almost all Wessex College students graduate in four years.
13. Not every sheep is white.
14. Some persons are nonhumans.
15. Nothing is a mammal unless it is not a reptile.
16. Polar bears live in Canada.
17. Every man prefers belief to the exercise of judgment. (Seneca)
18. Success has ruined many a man. (Benjamin Franklin)
19. Only the educated are free. (Epictetus)
20. Anybody who goes to see a psychiatrist ought to have his head examined. (Samuel Goldwyn)
21. The mass of men lead lives of quiet desperation. (Thoreau)
22. The questions that can be answered are not worth asking. (Milton Mayer)
23. What's not worth doing is not worth doing well. (Don Hebb)
24. Only the fool perseveres in error. (Cicero)
25. The unexamined life is not worth living. (Socrates)
26. Every calling is great when greatly pursued. (Oliver Wendell Holmes, Jr.)
27. The only certainty is that nothing is certain. (Pliny the Elder)

Critical Thinking Lapse

Paul Stiller, 47, was hospitalized in Andover Township, N.J., and his wife Bonnie was also injured, by a quarter-stick of dynamite that blew up in their car. While driving around at 2 a.m., the bored couple lit the dynamite and tried to toss it out the window to see what would happen, but they apparently failed to notice that the window was closed.[9]

28. Anybody who is any good is different from anybody else. (Felix Frankfurter)
29. He who has a why to live can bear with almost any how. (Nietzsche)
30. Without some goal and some effort to reach it no man can live. (Dostoevsky)

II. Arrange the chairs in the class into a circle. Your instructor will give each student a three-by-five-inch index card. On one side of the card, write your own original example of a stylistic variant of a standard-form categorical statement. On the other side of the card, write the correct standard-form translation of your example. (For example, you might write "Only men are uncles" on one side, and the correct translation—"All uncles are men"—on the other. Check the lists of stylistic variants for ideas.) When everyone has finished, pass your card to the student sitting to your right. Read the card you have received and decide what you think is the correct translation. Then check your answer with the answer indicated on the back of the card. If your answer was wrong, place a checkmark on the back of the card. Continue passing the cards until each card has been read. The instructor will then collect the cards and go over the examples that gave students the most problems.

CATEGORICAL SYLLOGISMS

I consider the invention of the form of syllogisms one of the most beautiful, and also one of the most important, made by the human mind.
—Gottfried Leibniz

A **syllogism** is simply a three-line deductive argument—that is, a deductive argument that consists of two premises and a conclusion. A **categorical syllogism** is a syllogism in which all the statements in the argument are categorical statements. Here are several examples of categorical syllogisms:

No doctors are professional wrestlers.

All cardiologists are doctors.

So, no cardiologists are professional wrestlers.

All snakes are reptiles.

All reptiles are cold-blooded animals.

So, all snakes are cold-blooded animals.

Some Baptists are coffee-lovers.

All Baptists are Protestants.

So, some Protestants are coffee-lovers.

No Democrats are Republicans.

Some lifeguards are Republicans.

So, some lifeguards are not Democrats.

In this section we shall see how Venn diagrams can be used to test the validity of categorical syllogisms.

Let's start with the first example above:

No doctors are professional wrestlers.

All cardiologists are doctors.

So, no cardiologists are professional wrestlers.

Since this argument, like all standard-form categorical syllogisms, has three category-terms (in this case, "cardiologists," "professional wrestlers," and "doctors"), we need three interlocking circles rather than two to represent the three categories. By convention, the two circles for the conclusion are placed at the bottom. Thus, the diagram for our example is as follows:

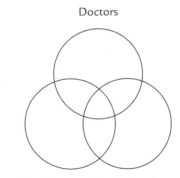

The first premise states that no doctors are professional wrestlers. To represent this claim, we shade that part of the Doctors circle that overlaps with the Professional wrestlers circle, as follows:

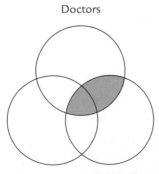

The second premise states that all cardiologists are doctors. To represent this claim, we shade that part of the Cardiologists circle that does not overlap with the Doctors circle:

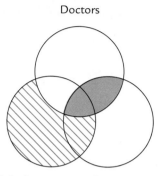

Doctors

Cardiologists   Professional wrestlers

We now have all the information we need to see whether the argument is valid. The conclusion tells us that no cardiologists are professional wrestlers. This means that the area where the Cardiologists and Professional wrestlers circles overlap is shaded, that is, empty. We look at the diagram to see if this area is shaded, and we see that it is indeed shaded. That means that the conclusion is implicitly "contained in" (i.e., follows logically from) the premises. Thus, the argument is shown to be valid.

Now, let's look at the second example:

All snakes are reptiles.

All reptiles are cold-blooded animals.

So, all snakes are cold-blooded animals.

First, we draw and label our three circles, placing the circles for the conclusion at the bottom:

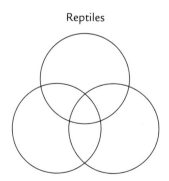

Reptiles

Snakes   Cold-blooded animals

Next, we diagram the first premise. That premise states that all snakes are reptiles. We represent this information by shading the area of the Snakes circle that does not overlap with the Reptiles circle.

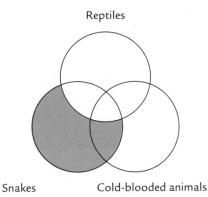

Reptiles

Snakes   Cold-blooded animals

Next, we diagram the second premise. The second premise states that all reptiles are cold-blooded animals. We represent this claim by shading that part of the Reptiles circle that does not overlap with the Cold-blooded animals circle.

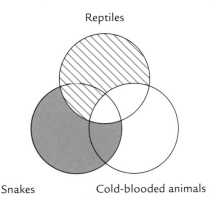

Reptiles

Snakes   Cold-blooded animals

Finally, we look to see if the information contained in the conclusion is depicted in the diagram. The conclusion tells us that all snakes are cold-blooded animals. This means that the part of the Snakes circle that does not overlap with the Cold-blooded animals circle should be completely shaded. Inspection of the diagram shows that this is indeed the case. So, the argument is valid.

Let's turn to the third example:

Some Baptists are coffee-lovers.

All Baptists are Protestants.

So, some Protestants are coffee-lovers.

Notice that this example includes two "some" statements. Diagramming "some" statements is a little trickier than diagramming "all" or "no" statements. As we have seen, "some" statements are diagrammed by placing *X*s rather than by shading. Most mistakes in Venn diagramming involve incorrect placement of an *X*.

To avoid such mistakes, remember the following rules:

1. If the argument contains one "all" or "no" statement, this statement should be diagrammed first. In other words, *always do any necessary shading before placing an X.* If the argument contains two "all" or "no" statements, either statement can be done first.

2. When placing an X in an area, if one part of the area has been shaded, place the X in the unshaded part. *Examples:*

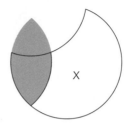

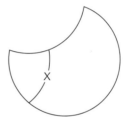

3. When placing an X in an area, if one part of the area has *not* been shaded, place the X precisely on the line separating the two parts. *Examples:*

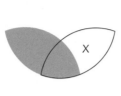

The rationales for these rules will be explained in the following discussion. Now, let's return to our third example:

Some Baptists are coffee-lovers.

All Baptists are Protestants.

So, some Protestants are coffee-lovers.

First, we draw and label our three circles:

Baptists

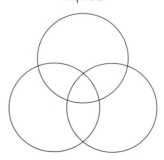

Protestants   Coffee-lovers

Next, we need to decide which premise to diagram first. Should it be the "some" premise or the "all" premise? Suppose we start with the "some" premise. Right away we see that we have a problem: Where exactly in the overlap between the Baptists and Coffee-lovers circles do we put the X? Any choice at this point would be a sheer guess (and a guess that might later be shown to be wrong by additional information contained in the argument). To avoid this problem, *it is always a good idea to diagram an "all" or a "no" premise before diagramming a "some" premise.*

So we begin by diagramming the second premise. That premise states that all Baptists are Protestants. This means that the class of Baptists that are not Protestants is empty. To represent this claim, we shade that area of the Baptists circle that does not overlap with the Protestants circle:

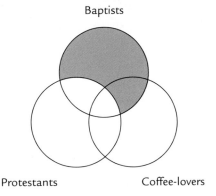

Baptists

Protestants   Coffee-lovers

Now we can diagram the first premise, which states that some Baptists are coffee-lovers. To represent this claim, we place an X in the area of the Baptists circle that overlaps with the Coffee-lovers circle. Part of this area, however, is shaded. This means that there is nothing in that area. For that reason, we place the X in the unshaded portion of the Baptists circle that overlaps with the Coffee-lovers circle, as follows:

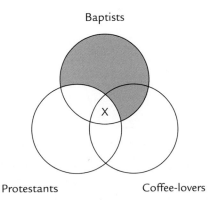

Baptists

Protestants   Coffee-lovers

Finally, we inspect the completed diagram to see if the information contained in the conclusion is represented in the diagram. The conclusion states that some Protestants are coffee-lovers. This means that there should be an X in the area of the Protestants circle that overlaps with the Coffee-lovers circle. A glance at the diagram shows that there is an X in this area. Thus, the argument is valid.

Let's turn to the fourth example:

No Democrats are Republicans.

Some lifeguards are Republicans.

So, some lifeguards are not Democrats.

First, we draw and label our three circles:

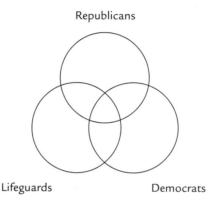

Since one premise begins with "no" and one begins with "some," we start by diagramming the premise that begins with "no." That premise states that no Democrats are Republicans. To represent this information, we shade that part of the Democrats circle that overlaps with the Republicans circle:

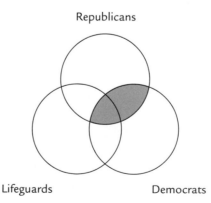

The second premise states that some lifeguards are Republicans. To diagram this claim, we place an X in the area of the Lifeguards circle that overlaps with the Republicans circle. Since part of this area is shaded, we place the X in that part of the area that is not shaded:

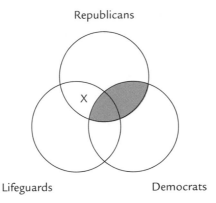

Republicans

Lifeguards   Democrats

Finally, we look at the completed diagram to see if the claim made in the conclusion is represented in the diagram. The conclusion states that some lifeguards are not Democrats. This means that there should be an *X* in that part of the Lifeguards circle that does not intersect with the Democrats circle. Inspection of the diagram shows that there is an *X* in this area. Thus, the argument is shown to be valid.

So far, all the categorical syllogisms we have looked at have been valid. But Venn diagrams can also show when a categorical syllogism is invalid. Here is one example:

All painters are artists.

Some magicians are artists.

So, some magicians are painters.

First, we draw and label our three circles:

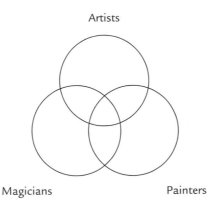

Artists

Magicians   Painters

Since the first premise begins with "all" and the second premise begins with "some," we diagram the first premise first. The first premise states that all painters are artists. To depict this claim, we shade that part of the Painters circle that does not overlap with the Artists circle:

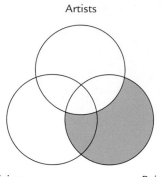

Next, we enter the information of the second premise, the claim that some magicians are artists. To represent this claim, we place an X in that portion of the Magicians circle that overlaps with the Artists circle. That area, however, is divided into two parts (the areas here marked "1" and "2"), and we have no information that warrants placing the X in one of these areas rather than the other. In such cases, we place the X *precisely on the line* between the two sections, as follows:

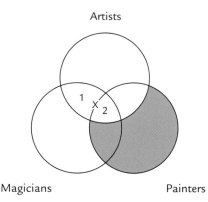

The X on the line means that we have no way of knowing from the information given whether the magician-who-is-an-artist is also a magician-who-is-a-painter.

The conclusion states that some magicians are painters. This means that there should be an X that is definitely in the area where the Magicians and Painters circles overlap. There is an X in the Magicians circle, but it dangles on the line between the Artists circle and the Painters circle. We don't know whether it is inside or outside the Painters circle. For that reason, the argument is invalid.

Let's look at a final example:

No scientists are toddlers.

All physicists are scientists.

So, some physicists are not toddlers.

First, we draw and label our circles:

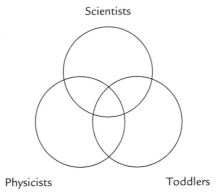

Since both of the premises are "all" or "no" statements, it doesn't matter which premise we diagram first. Let's start with the first. That premise states that no scientists are toddlers. To diagram this information, we shade that portion of the Scientists circle that intersects with the Toddlers circle:

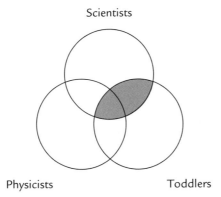

Next, we diagram the second premise, the claim that all physicists are scientists. To represent this claim, we shade that part of the Physicists circle that does not overlap with the Scientists circle:

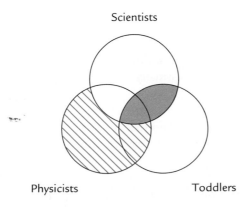

Finally, we look at the diagram to see if the information contained in the conclusion is represented in the diagram. The conclusion states that some physicists are not toddlers. This means that there should be an *X* in the part of the Physicists circle that does not overlap with the Toddlers circle. Inspection of the diagram shows that there are no *X*s at all in the diagram. Hence, the argument is invalid.

The following list summarizes the basic steps to be followed in Venn diagramming.

Using Venn Diagrams to Test the Validity of Categorical Syllogisms

Step 1: Translate all statements in the argument (if necessary) into standard-form categorical statements.

Step 2: Draw and label three overlapping circles, one for each term (class name) in the argument, with the two circles for the conclusion placed on the bottom.

Step 3: Use shading to represent the information in "all" or "no" statements. To diagram statements of the form "All *S* are *P*," shade that portion of the *S* circle that does not overlap with the *P* circle. To diagram statements of the form "No *S* are *P*," shade that portion of the *S* circle that overlaps with the *P* circle.

Use *X*s to represent the information in "some" statements. To diagram statements of the form "Some *S* are *P*," place an *X* in that portion of the *S* circle that overlaps with the *P* circle. To diagram statements of the form "Some *S* are not *P*," place an *X* in that portion of the *S* circle that does not overlap with the *P* circle.

Step 4: Diagram the two premises. (No marks should be entered for the conclusion.) If the argument contains one "all" or "no" premise and one "some" premise, diagram the "all" or "no" premise first. Otherwise, diagram either premise first.

Step 5: When placing an *X* in a two-part area, if one part of the area has been shaded, place the *X* in the unshaded part. If neither part of the area has been shaded, place the *X* squarely on the line separating the two parts.

Step 6: Look to see if the diagram contains all the information presented in the conclusion. If it does, the argument is formally valid. If it doesn't, the argument is formally invalid.

It takes practice to become skilled at Venn diagramming. Once you get the hang of it, however, you'll find that it is a neat way to check the validity of a surprisingly wide range of everyday arguments.

EXERCISE 9.4

I. Use Venn diagrams to test the validity of the following arguments.

1. Some bankers are vegetarians. No anarchists are bankers. So, some anarchists are not vegetarians.

2. All violinists are musicians. Therefore, since some bookworms are violinists, some bookworms are musicians.

3. All curmudgeons are pessimists. All pessimists are party poopers. So, some party poopers are curmudgeons.

4. No sharks are pets, since no barracuda are pets, and no sharks are barracuda.

5. No beach bums are workaholics. Some beach bums are rollerbladers. So, some rollerbladers are not workaholics.

6. No farmers are city-dwellers. Hence, since all city-dwellers are urbanites, no urbanites are farmers.

7. No poker players are early risers. Some firefighters are early risers. So, some firefighters are not poker players.

8. Some dot.com millionaires are philanthropists. All philanthropists are altruists. Hence, some altruists are dot.com millionaires.

9. Some telemarketers are Methodists. Some Methodists are Democrats. So, some Democrats are telemarketers.

10. No Fords are Pontiacs. All Escorts are Fords. So, some Escorts are not Pontiacs.

11. No mockingbirds are cardinals. Some cardinals are songbirds. So, some songbirds are not mockingbirds.

12. All Green Party members are environmentalists. Hence, since all Green Party members are wilderness-lovers, all wilderness-lovers are environmentalists.

13. No landlubbers are sailors. Some sailors are not pirates. So, some pirates are not landlubbers.

14. All cats are carnivores. All tigers are cats. So, all tigers are carnivores.

15. All sound arguments are valid arguments. Therefore, since some sound arguments are mathematical arguments, some mathematical arguments are not valid arguments.

16. No fish are reptiles. All trout are fish. So, some trout are not reptiles.

17. Some dreamers are not romantics, because some idealists are not romantics, and all idealists are dreamers.

18. Some stockbrokers are couch potatoes. Hence, since all stockbrokers are e-traders, some e-traders are couch potatoes.

19. Some butchers are not bakers. No butchers are candlestick makers. Therefore, some candlestick makers are not bakers.

20. All meteorologists are forecasters. Hence, since some forecasters are psychics, some psychics are meteorologists.

II. Translate the following into standard categorical form. Then use Venn diagrams to test the arguments for validity.

1. No one who is a Nobel Prize winner is a rock star. A number of astrophysicists are Nobel Prize winners. Therefore, a number of astrophysicists are not rock stars.

2. Many philosophers are determinists. Anyone who is a fatalist is a determinist. So, many fatalists are philosophers.

3. If anything is a maple, then it's a tree. Hence, since nothing that is a bush is a tree, nothing that is a bush is a maple.

4. Everybody who is a liberal is a big spender. Therefore, since Senator Crumley is a big spender, Senator Crumley is a liberal.

5. Many tarot-readers are lottery players. Every tarot-reader is a fraud. So, many frauds are not lottery players.

6. Only poems are sonnets. No mathematical treatise is a poem. Therefore, no mathematical treatise is a sonnet.

7. At least one lawyer is not a golfer. Only persons who have attended law school are lawyers. So, at least one person who has attended law school is not a golfer.

8. No one who is a cardsharp is a psychic. Someone is a cardsharp only if he is a poker player. Therefore, some poker players are not psychics.

9. Whatever is a pterosaur is a nondinosaur. Each pterodactylus is a pterosaur. So, no pterodactylus is a dinosaur.

10. Only social scientists are political scientists. Many political scientists are persons who favor campaign finance reform. Accordingly, many persons who favor campaign finance reform are social scientists.

11. Egoists are not humanitarians. Not a single humanitarian is a sweatshop owner. So, not a single sweatshop owner is an egoist.

12. There are e-mail messages that are not spell-checked. There are interoffice memos that are e-mail messages. Therefore, there are interoffice memos that are not spell-checked.

13. Every tax evader is a lawbreaker. Hence, since no one who is a lawbreaker is a model citizen, no one that is a model citizen is a tax evader.

14. If anything is a truck, then it is not a car. There are Mazdas that are trucks. It follows that there are Mazdas that are not cars.

15. Only the good die young. James Dean was good. So, James Dean died young.

16. Not every lie is immoral, for no harmless acts are immoral and some lies are harmless.

17. Mystics are always religious. At least one religious person is not greedy. Consequently, at least one mystic is not greedy.

18. Every person who drinks and drives is an irresponsible person. Not every person who talks on a car phone is an irresponsible person. Hence, not every person who talks on a car phone is a person who drinks and drives.

19. Anyone who eats pizza every night is at risk for heart disease. Some people who are at risk for heart disease are cab drivers. So, some cab drivers are people who eat pizza every night.

20. Joey is in kindergarten. Only children in kindergarten fingerpaint in school. So, Joey fingerpaints in school.

SUMMARY

1. A *categorical statement* is a statement that makes a claim about the relationship between two or more classes or categories of things. In this chapter we focused mainly on standard-form categorical statements. *Standard-form categorical statements* are statements that have one of the following four forms: All S are P, No S are P, Some S are P, Some S are not P.

2. Standard-form categorical statements have four basic parts:
   - They all begin with the word "all," "no," or "some." These words are called *quantifiers,* because they are used to express a quantity or a number.
   - They all have a *subject term.* The subject term is a word or a phrase that names a class and that serves as the grammatical subject of the sentence. In the four statement forms listed above, the subject term is represented by "S."
   - They all have a *predicate term.* The predicate term is a word or a phrase that names a class and that serves as the subject complement of the sentence. In the statement forms listed above, the predicate term is represented by "P."
   - They all have a *copula,* or linking verb, which is some form of the verb "to be." The copula serves to link, or join, the subject term with the predicate term.

3. With a little ingenuity, many ordinary English sentences can be translated into standard-form categorical statements. When translating into standard categorical form, keep in mind the following tips:

   Tip 1: Rephrase all nonstandard subject and predicate terms so that they refer to classes.
   Tip 2: Rephrase all nonstandard verbs so that the statement includes the linking verb "are" or "are not."
   Tip 3: Fill in any unexpressed quantifiers.
   Tip 4: Translate singular statements as "all" or "no" statements.
   Tip 5: Translate stylistic variants into the appropriate categorical form.

4. A *categorical syllogism* is a three-line deductive argument in which all three statements in the argument are categorical statements. A simple way to test the formal validity of categorical syllogisms is to use *Venn diagrams,* in which overlapping circles are used to represent relationships between

classes. The Venn diagram technique for checking the validity of categorical syllogisms involves six basic steps:

Step 1: Translate all statements in the argument (if necessary) into
standard-form categorical statements.

Step 2: Draw and label three overlapping circles, one for each term (class
name) in the argument, with the two circles for the conclusion placed on
the bottom.

Step 3: Use shading to represent the information in "all" or "no" statements. To diagram statements of the form "All *S* are *P*," shade that portion of the *S* circle that does not overlap with the *P* circle. To diagram
statements of the form "No *S* are *P*," shade that portion of the *S* circle
that overlaps with the *P* circle.

Use *X*s to represent the information in "some" statements. To diagram
statements of the form "Some *S* are *P*," place an X in that portion of the
S circle that overlaps with the *P* circle. To diagram statements of the form
"Some *S* are not *P*," place an X in that portion of the *S* circle that does
not overlap with the *P* circle.

Step 4: Diagram the two premises. (No marks should be entered for the
conclusion.) If the argument contains one "all" or "no" premise and one
"some" premise, diagram the "all" or "no" premise first. If the argument
contains two "some" or two "all" or "no" premises, diagram either
premise first.

Step 5: When placing an *X* in a two-part area, if one part of the area has
been shaded, place the *X* in the unshaded part. If neither part of the area
has been shaded, place the *X* squarely on the line separating the two
parts.

Step 6: Look to see if the completed diagram contains all the information
presented in the conclusion. If it does, the argument is formally valid. If it
does not, the argument is formally invalid.

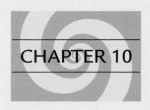

CHAPTER 10

GETTING DEEPER INTO LOGIC: PROPOSITIONAL LOGIC

It is often difficult to determine whether a long and complex argument is valid or invalid just by reading it. Consider the following example:

> If the Democrat loses the Senate race, then the Republicans will have a majority in the Senate.
>
> If the Republicans have a majority in the Senate, then the Senate will vote down the new bill.
>
> It is not the case that the Senate will vote down the new bill or the Democrat will lose the Senate race.
>
> So it is not the case that if the Democrat does not lose, then the Senate will not vote down the new bill.

Can you tell whether that argument is valid or invalid? Most people can't. In this chapter we learn the basics of **propositional logic,** a way to symbolize the parts of arguments so that we can analyze whole arguments for validity. By the end of the chapter, difficult examples, such as the one above, will be easy to analyze.

The method we present for analyzing arguments for validity involves assigning variables to the different parts of the argument, much as we do in algebra. For example, if $a = 3$ and $b = 7$, then $a + b = 10$. With the same variables, we can solve for an unknown: $a + c = b,$ so $3 + c = 7$. We know that c must equal 4. We won't be solving equations or crunching numbers in this chapter, but we will be using variables to consider arguments in a more abstract and more manageable way. In algebra, we start with variables whose values we know and solve for variables whose values we don't know. Similarly, in propositional logic, we start by assigning variables to the parts of the argument that are given and "solve for" what we don't know, namely, whether the argument is valid or invalid.

Propositional logic is nothing to be afraid of. In fact, some students find it to be the most enjoyable and interesting part of their critical thinking course. With some practice, anyone can become a master of propositional

> *The object of reasoning is to find out, from the consideration of what we already know, something else which we do not know.*
>
> —C. S. Peirce

271

logic. This chapter is full of exercises, so you'll get all the practice you need. We start with simple arguments and gradually build up to more complex arguments.

CONJUNCTION

As we learned in Chapter 2, arguments are composed of statements. A statement is a sentence that can sensibly be regarded as either true or false. A **simple statement** consists of just one sentence that sensibly can be regarded as either true or false—for example, "Tina is tall." A **compound statement** consists of two or more statements, each of which can separately be considered either true or false—for example, "Tina is tall, and Sarah is tall."

Sometimes, the premise or the conclusion of an argument is a simple statement, such as "Tina is tall." We can easily symbolize a simple statement by assigning it a variable. Let's assign "Tina is tall" the variable p. If the argument contains a second simple statement—for example, "Sarah is tall"—we can symbolize it by assigning it a different variable. Let's assign "Sarah is tall" the variable q.

Let's assume that we do not know whether our premises are true or false. In that case, each of the variables has two possible **truth values**; that is, each variable could be true or it could be false. With that in mind, we can now set up a **truth table** for each variable. A truth table is just a listing of all possible truth values.

The truth table for p is

$$\frac{p}{\begin{array}{c} \text{T} \\ \text{F} \end{array}}$$

The truth table displays the information that p is either true or false.

We can do the same now for our second variable, q:

$$\frac{q}{\begin{array}{c} \text{T} \\ \text{F} \end{array}}$$

This displays the information that q is either true or false.

Let's consider the compound statement "Tina is tall, and Sarah is tall." This compound statement consists of two simple statements joined by the word "and." In grammar, the word "and" is a **conjunction**; that is, it "conjoins," or joins together, two elements. In propositional logic, the word "conjunction" refers to a compound statement. Notice that the conjunction "Tina is tall, and Sarah is tall" consists of two simple statements to which we have already assigned variables, p and q, joined by the word "and." In propositional logic, we symbolize the word "and" with the ampersand, &. Thus, we symbolize the conjunction "Tina is tall, and Sarah is tall" as p & q.

Now we are ready to determine the truth values for p & q. The compound statement p & q is true only when both of its variables stand for true simple statements. Put another way, only when p is true and q is true is the statement p & q true. If either p or q is false, the statement p & q is false. If both p and q are false, the whole statement p & q is false. To set up the truth table for p & q, we need to account for all four possible combinations of p & q. We do this as follows:

p	q	p & q
T	T	T
T	F	F
F	T	F
F	F	F

In a truth table that includes two variables, the first two columns will follow the pattern of the two columns in the truth table shown above. The first variable is true in the first and second lines and false in the third and fourth. The second variable alternates between true and false. Although all four possible combinations of the two variables can be obtained in other ways, this is the conventional way of setting up a truth table with two variables and is the easiest to remember.

We used p & q to stand for "Tina is tall, and Sarah is tall," but p & q can be used to stand for other compound statements as well. The compound statement "Winter is cold, and summer is warm" could also be represented by p & q, where p stands for "winter is cold" and q stands for "summer is warm." In fact, p & q is a propositional form that can stand for an infinite number of compound statements: "The train is late, and the bus is on time"; "The sky is blue, and the grass is green"; and so on.

A word of caution: Not every use of the word "and" indicates a compound statement that can be represented by p & q. That makes sense, given the fact that the word "and" does not always join two simple statements. Sometimes "and" joins two things within the same simple statement—for example, "The Knicks and the Bulls are playing each other tonight." This is one simple statement, not two, and is properly symbolized by a single variable, say, p. To determine whether a statement is simple or compound, we must ask ourselves what the statement means. Our example does not consist of two simple statements: "The Knicks are playing each other tonight" and "The Bulls are playing each other tonight." Rather, it is one simple statement: "The Knicks and the Bulls are playing each other tonight." Take another example: "Peanut butter and jelly is my favorite lunch." This, too, is a single simple statement and is properly symbolized by a single variable, say, q. To see the contrast, consider a compound statement: "I like peanut butter, and she likes jelly." This compound statement consists of two simple statements joined by the word "and."

Thus, it is properly symbolized by the conjunction of two variables, say, *r* & *s*. If we are ever unsure whether a statement is simple or compound, we should ask ourselves, "What does the statement mean?" Does the statement consist of two simple statements? If it does, then it is compound. If it doesn't, then it is simple.

Don't get too hung up on the variables *p, q, r,* and *s*. Any letters will do. Be careful, however, that you don't repeat variables when you symbolize an argument. Once a variable has been used to represent one statement, it cannot be used again to represent a different statement in the same argument. We'll discuss this more when we get deeper into analyzing argument forms for validity.

Propositional logic has many advantages when it comes to dealing with arguments, but it also has one important disadvantage: it does not capture the richness of everyday language. For example, there may be a big difference in emphasis between "He likes Fords, and she likes Chevys" and "He likes Fords, *but* she likes Chevys." The first statement may simply be pointing out the likes of two different people, whereas the second may be contrasting their different likes. The fact is, though, that each of the two compound statements is true only when both of its simple statements are true—that is, when it is true that he likes Fords and it is true that she likes Chevys. In every other case, it is false. Since in propositional logic there is no difference in logical significance between the words "but" and "and," they are treated as interchangeable for the purposes of determining truth value. So, both of our compound statements fit the propositional form *p* & *q,* and both can be analyzed by the following truth table:

p	*q*	*p* & *q*
T	T	T
T	F	F
F	T	F
F	F	F

In propositional logic, any word that conjoins two simple statements is symbolized by the ampersand, &. For the purposes of propositional logic, then, all these words are equivalent and can be symbolized by the ampersand: *and, but, yet, while, whereas, although, though, however*. The following compound statements are all correctly symbolized as *p* & *q*.

Tony had steak, *and* Theresa had chicken.

Tony had steak, *but* Theresa had chicken.

Tony had steak, *yet* Theresa had chicken.

Tony had steak, *while* Theresa had chicken.

Tony had steak, *whereas* Theresa had chicken.

Tony had steak, *although* Theresa had chicken.

Tony had steak, *though* Theresa had chicken.

Tony had steak; *however* Theresa had chicken.

Each of these compound statements has a slightly different emphasis, but each is true only when it is true that Tony had steak and it is also true that Theresa had chicken.

Exercise 10.1

I. Put the following statements in symbolic form.

1. Ken hit a home run.
2. Hank went fishing, and Dirk went hunting.
3. Hank and Dirk went fishing.
4. Hank went fishing, but Dirk went hunting.
5. The train was late, and the bus was on time.
6. The train was late, though the bus was on time.
7. France is in Europe, and China is in Asia.
8. France is in Europe, but China is in Asia.
9. France and Germany are in Europe.
10. Sally ate a peanut butter and jelly sandwich, whereas Nancy ate a salad.

II. Let the following variables stand for the following statements:

a = December is cold. x = February is sunny.
b = June is warm. y = July is cold.
c = March is windy. z = August is snowy.

Assume that a, b, and c are true, and x, y, and z are false. Determine whether each of the following is true or false.

1. $a \& b$ 6. $c \& a$
2. $b \& z$ 7. $c \& z$
3. $z \& y$ 8. $x \& y$
4. $c \& b$ 9. $a \& c$
5. $x \& z$ 10. $y \& a$

III. Without knowing what they stand for, assume for the sake of this exercise that p, q, and r are true, and w, x, and y are false. Determine whether each of the following is true or false.

1. $p \& q$ 6. $y \& w$
2. $p \& w$ 7. $x \& w$
3. $x \& y$ 8. $q \& r$
4. $r \& q$ 9. $p \& y$
5. $r \& y$ 10. $r \& p$

CONJUNCTION AND VALIDITY

Now we are ready to symbolize arguments and analyze them for validity. We already know enough to deal with some very basic arguments. Consider this one:

Tina is tall.

Sarah is tall.

So, Tina is tall, and Sarah is tall.

We can symbolize the argument as follows (in propositional logic, the symbol ∴ simply indicates that the conclusion follows):

p

q

$\therefore p \mathbin{\&} q$

It should be clear to you just by reading it that this argument is valid, but it is a handy example for illustrating the truth table method for establishing validity. In the previous section we learned how to set up truth tables for statements; now we'll see how truth tables can be used to determine the validity or the invalidity of arguments.

First, we must set up the truth table:

p	q	$p \mathbin{\&} q$
T	T	T
T	F	F
F	T	F
F	F	F

The truth table above starts with columns for our basic building blocks, the two variables p and q, and ends with a column for their conjunction, $p \mathbin{\&} q$. In this case, the three columns represent the two premises of the argument and the conclusion. To analyze the truth table for validity or invalidity, we have to recall one very important piece of information about validity. *In a valid argument, it is impossible for all the premises to be true and the conclusion false. So, in examining the truth table, we look for instances in which all the premises are true. If any instance of all true premises is followed by a false conclusion, an F under the conclusion column, the argument is invalid.* It doesn't matter if there are instances in the truth table in which all the premises are true and the conclusion is true, too. If it is even possible for an argument's conclusion to be false while all the premises are true, the argument is invalid.

Let's reconsider the truth table for the argument form we have been examining:

p	q	p & q
T	T	T
T	F	F
F	T	F
F	F	F

There is only one case, the first line across, in which both of the premises are true. And in this case, the conclusion is true as well. This tells us that the argument form for "Tina is tall. Sarah is tall. Therefore, Tina is tall, and Sarah is tall" is valid. That is, the argument form

> p
>
> q
>
> ∴ p & q

is valid. Any two arguments that share the same argument form are either both valid or both invalid. When we know that an argument form is valid, we know that any argument that fits that form is valid.

Thus, we know, for example, that the argument

> The sky is blue.
>
> The grass is green.
>
> Therefore, the sky is blue, and the grass is green.

is valid, because it fits the valid argument form

> p
>
> q
>
> ∴ p & q

Consider another argument:

> Grass is green.
>
> So, grass is green, and the sky is blue.

We hope that it is obvious to you that this argument is invalid. Its conclusion may be true, but it doesn't follow from its premise. We can symbolize this argument in the following way:

> p
>
> ∴ p & q

The truth table set up for the argument is familiar to us by now:

p	q	p & q
T	T	T
T	F	F
F	T	F
F	F	F

We now must examine the truth table to see if there are any cases in which all the premises are true (this argument has only one premise) and the conclusion is false. In other words, are there any cases in which we get a T under the p column and an F under the p & q column?

Examining truth tables for validity takes a careful eye. In this book we will mark premises with an asterisk, *, and conclusions with a capital C. This method isn't pretty, but it helps us remember which columns we are concerned with. Since you don't have to be a graphic designer to make an asterisk or a capital C, you can do the same in making your own truth tables for homework exercises. (It isn't *necessary* to use the asterisk and capital C, but it may help you to avoid careless mistakes at first.) In our examples, the line across that ultimately allows us to determine validity or invalidity will be circled. Circles are easy to draw and are helpful in focusing attention on lines that are crucial for determining validity.

Here is our truth table appropriately marked:

p*	q	p & qC
T	T	T
T	F	F
F	T	F
F	F	F

There are two relevant lines across, two cases in which the premise is true. In the first line, the premise is true and the conclusion is true as well. But in the second line, the premise is true and the conclusion is false. This second line allows us to determine that the argument form is invalid. Our examination of the truth table has established that the argument "Grass is green. So, grass is green, and the sky is blue" is invalid. Even more important, it has established that any argument that has the form

p

∴ p & q

is invalid.

Consider one more argument:

Franklin is short and stout.

So, Franklin is short.

We must recognize that the first statement is a compound statement. It is an abbreviated way of saying "Franklin is short, and Franklin is stout." Clearly, we can symbolize the argument as follows:

p & q

∴ p

In setting up the truth table for analyzing this argument form, we start with the basics:

p	q	p & q
T	T	T
T	F	F
F	T	F
F	F	F

All the information we need to determine the validity or the invalidity of the argument form is in the truth table as it stands. To make it easier to examine, though, we can mark the premise and the conclusion:

p C	q	p & q*
T	T	T
T	F	F
F	T	F
F	F	F

To make it even easier and to minimize the chances of making a careless mistake in looking at the argument, we can treat the first two columns as "guide columns" and line up our premises and conclusion from left to right. It isn't necessary to do this, but it is never wrong to repeat information in a truth table, especially if it helps you see the columns and analyze for validity.

p	q	p & q*	p C
T	T	T	T
T	F	F	T
F	T	F	F
F	F	F	F

As the truth table shows, in the only case in which the single premise is true, the conclusion is true as well. So, the argument form is valid.

EXERCISE 10.2

I. Determine the validity of the following argument forms using truth tables.

1. p

    q

    ∴ p & q

2. p & q

    ∴ q

3. r

    ∴ r & s

4.   *r*

  ∴ *s*

5.   *r & s*

  ∴ *r*

II. Put the following arguments in symbolic form and then test them for validity using a truth table.

1. The train was on time. The bus was late. So, the train was on time, and the bus was late.
2. The train was on time. So, the train was on time, but the bus was late.
3. The train was on time. So, the bus was late.

NEGATION

The next element of propositional logic we need to learn is **negation.** Negation is simply the use of the word "not" (or an equivalent word or phrase) to deny a statement. Let's return to the simple statement "Tina is tall." The negation of this simple statement would be "Tina is *not* tall." If we symbolize "Tina is tall" by assigning it the variable *p,* then we need a convenient way of symbolizing the negation of *p,* "not *p*." The conventional symbol for negation is the tilde, ~. So, we can symbolize "Tina is not tall" with ~*p.*

As you might expect, the truth values for the negation of a statement are just the opposite of those for the original statement. When *p* is true, ~*p* is false. This just makes sense when you consider that when "Tina is tall" is true, "Tina is not tall" must be false. The following, then, are the truth tables for *p* and ~*p.*

p	~*p*
T	F
F	T

The same pattern holds true for all other variables. If we assign "Sarah is tall" the variable *q,* then we symbolize "Sarah is *not* tall" with ~*q.*

q	~*q*
T	F
F	T

Now let's use negation and conjunction together. Consider the statement "Tina is tall, and Sarah is not tall." We can symbolize this as *p* & ~*q.* To get the truth table for this statement, we first set up the four possible combinations of *p*'s and *q*'s.

> *[I]t is impossible for anything at the same time to be and not to be . . . this is the most indisputable of all principles.*
>
> —Aristotle

p	q
T	T
T	F
F	T
F	F

Next, we add the column for ~q, determining the truth value for ~q in each case by taking the opposite of the corresponding truth value for q.

p	q	~q
T	T	F
T	F	T
F	T	F
F	F	T

Finally, we add the column for p & ~q. We determine the truth values for p & ~q by examining the p column and the ~q column. Remember: A conjunction is true only when both of its statements are true. So, in this case, p & ~q will be true only when there is a T in the p column and a T in the ~q column for the same line across.

p	q	~q	p & ~q
T	T	F	F
T	F	T	T
F	T	F	F
F	F	T	F

Now we are ready to examine an argument that involves both negation and conjunction: "Tina is not tall, but Sarah is tall. So, Tina is not tall." The symbolic form for the argument is

~p & q

∴ ~p

Let's set up the truth table for the argument:

p	q	~p	~p & q*	~p C
T	T	F	F	F
T	F	F	F	F
F	T	T	T	T
F	F	T	F	T

Our argument has one premise and a conclusion. We have set up the premise and the conclusion so that they read from left to right and have marked them accordingly, to keep our attention focused and prevent careless mistakes. Now we must see if there are any cases in which all the premises are true (this argument has only one premise, ~p & q) and the conclusion is false. We find that our premise is true only under one condition, represented in the third line of the column. And we find that in that third line the conclusion is also true. There are no cases in which all the premises are true and the conclusion is false, so we know that the argument form is valid.

Consider another argument:

Frank does not drive a truck.

So, Frank does not drive a truck, and Vinny does not drive a minivan.

The symbolic form for the argument is

~p

∴ ~p & ~q

Let's set up the truth table for the argument:

p	q	~p	~q	~p*	~p & ~q C
T	T	F	F	F	F
T	F	F	T	F	F
F	T	T	F	T	F
F	F	T	T	T	T

The first two columns are "guide columns," which lay out the truth values for the four possible occurrences of p and q. The third column lays out the truth values for ~p, and the fourth column lays out the truth values of ~q. (~q isn't an independent statement in the argument, but we need it as a building block in forming ~p & ~q.) The final column lays out the truth values for ~p & ~q. Remember that this conjunction is true only when there is a T in the ~p column and a T in the ~q column. This occurs once, in the fourth line across.

To determine whether the argument is valid or invalid, we examine the truth table to see if there are any cases in which the premise is true and the conclusion is false. In the third line across, the premise is true and the conclusion is false. This alone tells us that the argument form is invalid. In the fourth line across, the premise is true and so is the conclusion, but that doesn't matter. We already know the argument form is invalid from the third line.

Be careful in dealing with negation. Sometimes a negation applies only to a single simple statement, as in "Lisa does not drive a Jeep," symbolized as ~p. Sometimes there are two negations applying to both elements of a compound statement, as in "Lisa does not drive a Jeep, and Jennifer does not drive a Jeep," symbolized as ~p & ~q. At other times, one negation applies to a whole compound statement. For example, "It is not the case that Lisa drives a Jeep and Jennifer drives a Jeep," symbolized as ~(p & q). We need to be clear about what this statement means in order to symbolize it properly. When we consider it carefully, we realize that this statement isn't necessarily saying that Lisa does *not* drive a Jeep *and* Jennifer does *not* drive a Jeep. Rather, it is claiming that it is *not true* that *both* of them drive a Jeep. One of them may drive a

Jeep, or neither of them may drive a Jeep. It is just claiming that it isn't the case that both of them drive a Jeep.

To symbolize the statement "It is not the case that Lisa drives a Jeep and Jennifer drives a Jeep," we need a way of showing that the negation applies to the whole statement rather than to just a specific part. To make this distinction we use parentheses. So, we symbolize "It is not the case that Lisa drives a Jeep and Jennifer drives a Jeep" as $\sim(p \& q)$. As in mathematics, we do the work inside the parentheses first. If there is more than one set of parentheses, we start with the innermost set and work our way outward. So, first we determine if p & q is true or false, and then we negate our answer. So, for example, if p & q is true, then we know that $\sim(p \& q)$ is false. Thus, in forming our truth table for $\sim(p \& q)$, we first list the truth values for p & q. Then we assign the opposite truth values to $\sim(p \& q)$.

p	q	$p \& q$	$\sim(p \& q)$
T	T	T	F
T	F	F	T
F	T	F	T
F	F	F	T

Accuracy in the placement of the negation is not an insignificant detail. It affects the meaning of a statement. Consider the following argument:

It is not the case that Tina is tall and Sarah is tall

So, Tina is not tall, and Sarah is not tall.

Is the argument valid? If the premise and the conclusion really mean the same thing, the argument would have to be valid.

The symbolic form of the argument is

$\sim(p \& q)$

$\therefore \sim p \& \sim q$

Now let's look at the truth table for the argument:

p	q	$p \& q$	$\sim p$	$\sim q$	$\sim(p \& q)$*	$\sim p \& \sim q$ C
T	T	T	F	F	F	F
T	F	F	F	T	T	F
F	T	F	T	F	T	F
F	F	F	T	T	T	T

By examining the truth table we can easily see that the argument form is not valid. In the second line, the premise is true and the conclusion is false. On that basis alone, we know that the argument form is invalid. This should make it clear that placement of the negation makes a big difference to what a statement means and to whether the argument it is a part of is valid or invalid.

EXERCISE 10.3

I. Assume *a*, *b*, and *c* are true, and *x*, *y*, and *z* are false. Then determine whether each of the following is true or false.

▢ 1. ~a & b   6. c & ~z
    2. ~x & ~y   ▢ 7. ~(c & ~z)
    3. ~(x & y)   8. y & x
▢ 4. ~(a & b)   9. ~(y & x)
    5. ~z & ~c   ▢ 10. ~x & ~z

II. Translate each of the symbolic statements in Exercise I into a statement in English.

III. Put the following statements in symbolic form.

▢ 1. The bus was on time, but the train was not.
    2. The bus was not on time, and the train was not on time.
    3. It's not the case that the bus and the train were on time.
▢ 4. Lemons are not sweet, but sugar is.
    5. It's not the case that lemons and sugar are sweet.
    6. Her friends don't care, and her parents don't, either.
▢ 7. Her friends care, but her parents don't.
    8. It's not the case that her friends and her parents care.
    9. Intentions don't matter, though actions do.
▢ 10. It's not the case that intentions and actions matter.

IV. Determine the validity of the following arguments using truth tables.

▢ 1. ~p

   q

   ∴ ~p & q

   2. ~p

   ~q

   ∴ ~(p & q)

   3. ~p & ~q

   ∴ ~(p & q)

▢ 4. ~(p & q)

   p

   ∴ ~q

   5. ~(p & q)

   ~p

   ∴ ~q

V. Put the following arguments in symbolic form. Then test them for validity using a truth table.

▢ 1. Vegas Jack didn't commit the crime, and the Weasel didn't commit the crime. So, it is not the case that Vegas Jack and the Weasel committed the crime.

2. It's not the case that Vegas Jack and the Weasel committed the crime. So, the Weasel didn't commit the crime.

3. It's not the case that John failed calculus and chemistry. John didn't fail calculus. So, he didn't fail chemistry.

4. It's not the case that John failed calculus and chemistry. John failed calculus. So, he didn't fail chemistry.

5. It's not the case that John failed calculus and chemistry. So, John didn't fail calculus and didn't fail chemistry.

DEEPER ANALYSIS OF NEGATION AND CONJUNCTION

In learning propositional logic, we need to start with simple building blocks and gradually erect a more complex structure. So far, all the arguments we have examined have had only two variables, but now we are ready to work with arguments that have three variables.[1] Everything we have learned so far holds true. The process just gets a little lengthier and more involved.

Consider this example:

Tina is tall.

Sarah is not tall, but Missy is tall.

So, Tina is tall, and Missy is tall.

Let p = Tina is tall, q = Sarah is tall, and r = Missy is tall. The symbolic form of the argument is

p

$\sim q \ \& \ r$

$\therefore p \ \& \ r$

Before analyzing the argument, let's see how to set up our three guide columns for the basic three variables. With two variables, there are only four possible combinations of truth values; with three variables, there are eight. The conventional way to set up the truth table for three variables is as follows: The first column contains four "trues" followed by four "falses." The second column contains alternating pairs of "true" and "false." The third column contains an alternation of "true" and "false."

	p	q	r
1.	T	T	T
2.	T	T	F
3.	T	F	T
4.	T	F	F
5.	F	T	T
6.	F	T	F
7.	F	F	T
8.	F	F	F

When working with three variables, we can keep things in order by numbering the lines 1 through 8. Once we have our three guide columns set up, everything else follows naturally. All the rules we have learned so far apply. For a conjunction to be true, both its variables must be true. The truth value of a negation is just the opposite of the truth value of the statement it negates.

Now let's form the truth table for the argument form

p

$\sim q \And r$

$\therefore p \And r$

	p	q	r	$\sim q$	p^*	$\sim q \And r^*$	$p \And r\,$C
1.	T	T	T	F	T	F	T
2.	T	T	F	F	T	F	F
3.	T	F	T	T	T	T	T
4.	T	F	F	T	T	F	F
5.	F	T	T	F	F	F	F
6.	F	T	F	F	F	F	F
7.	F	F	T	T	F	T	F
8.	F	F	F	T	F	F	F

The columns for p, q, and r are set up in the conventional way. The truth values in the $\sim q$ column are just the opposite of the corresponding truth values in the q column. The truth values for the $\sim q \And r$ column are determined by consulting the $\sim q$ column and the r column. Only in lines 3 and 7 is there a T in both columns, so only lines 3 and 7 are true under the $\sim q \And r$ column. All other lines under $\sim q \And r$ are false. The truth values for the $p \And r$ column are determined by consulting the p column and the r column. Only in lines 1 and 3 are both true, so only in lines 1 and 3 is $p \And r$ true.

The validity of an argument with three variables is determined in the same way as the validity of an argument with two variables. We just have eight lines to check instead of four. *If there is any line in which all the premises are true and the conclusion is false, we know the argument is invalid. If there is no such line, then we know the argument is valid.* Look at the table again.

	p	q	r	$\sim q$	p^*	$\sim q \And r^*$	$p \And r\,$C
1.	T	T	T	F	T	F	T
2.	T	T	F	F	T	F	F
3.	T	F	T	T	T	T	T
4.	T	F	F	T	T	F	F
5.	F	T	T	F	F	F	F
6.	F	T	F	F	F	F	F
7.	F	F	T	T	F	T	F
8.	F	F	F	T	F	F	F

Only in line 3 are both premises true, and in line 3 the conclusion is true as well. There are no cases in which both premises are true and the conclusion is false. So, the argument is valid.

Consider another three-variable example:

$\sim(p \& q)$

$\sim q \& r$

$\therefore \sim p$

First we set up the truth table, starting with our three basic variables and building from there. Then we examine the table to determine validity.

	p	q	r	$\sim q$	$p \& q$	$\sim(p \& q)*$	$\sim q \& r*$	$\sim p$ C
1.	T	T	T	F	T	F	F	F
2.	T	T	F	F	T	F	F	F
3.	T	F	T	T	F	T	T	F
4.	T	F	F	T	F	T	F	F
5.	F	T	T	F	F	T	F	T
6.	F	T	F	F	F	T	F	T
7.	F	F	T	T	F	T	T	T
8.	F	F	F	T	F	T	F	T

To set up the truth table, we follow the familiar pattern. We derive the truth values for our first premise, $\sim(p \& q)$, by constructing a column for $p \& q$ and then taking the negation of each line's corresponding truth value. We assign truth values to $\sim q \& r$ by consulting the column for $\sim q$ and the column for r. We derive the truth values for the conclusion, $\sim p$, by taking the negation of the truth values in the p column.

To determine the validity of the argument, we look for any cases in which both of the premises are true and the conclusion is false. In line 3, both of the premises are true and the conclusion is false. From this line alone we know that the argument is invalid. It does not matter that in line 7 both of the premises are true and the conclusion is true.

Sometimes it makes things easier to assign a variable to a statement that will help us remember what the variable stands for. Consider the following argument:

The train was on time, but the bus was not on time.

The plane was on time.

$\therefore$ It's not the case that the bus and the plane were on time.

To symbolize the argument, let $t =$ The train was on time, $b =$ The bus was on time, and $p =$ The plane was on time. So, our argument form is

$t \& \sim b$

p

$\therefore \sim(b \& p)$

Now let's set up the truth table:

	t	b	p	$\sim b$	$b \mathbin{\&} p$	$t \mathbin{\&} \sim b$*	p*	$\sim(b \mathbin{\&} p)$ C
1	T	T	T	F	T	F	T	F
2.	T	T	F	F	F	F	F	T
3.	T	F	T	T	F	T	T	T
4.	T	F	F	T	F	T	F	T
5.	F	T	T	F	T	F	T	F
6.	F	T	F	F	F	F	F	T
7.	F	F	T	T	F	F	T	T
8.	F	F	F	T	F	F	F	T

We set up the truth table just as we would if the variables were p, q, and r. All the rules for determining the truth values assigned to the columns for the various statements remain the same. And we set up our premises and conclusion so that they read from left to right, marking them accordingly.

Now let's examine the truth table to determine the validity of the argument. Are there any cases in which all the premises are true and the conclusion is false?

	t	b	p	$\sim b$	$b \mathbin{\&} p$	$t \mathbin{\&} \sim b$*	p*	$\sim(b \mathbin{\&} p)$ C
1.	T	T	T	F	T	F	T	F
2.	T	T	F	F	F	F	F	T
3.	T	F	T	T	F	T	T	T
4.	T	F	F	T	F	T	F	T
5.	F	T	T	F	T	F	T	F
6.	F	T	F	F	F	F	F	T
7.	F	F	T	T	F	F	T	T
8.	F	F	F	T	F	F	F	T

There is only one case in which the premises are both true, and in this case the conclusion is true as well. So, we know that the argument is valid.

Consider this argument:

> Bill Clinton didn't serve two terms in office, but Jimmy Carter did.
>
> George H. W. Bush served two terms in office.
>
> So, it is not the case that both Carter and Bush did not serve two terms in office.

You may notice that all the statements in the argument are false, but remember that an argument's validity does not necessarily depend on the truth of its statements.

To symbolize this argument, let b = Bill Clinton served two terms in office; let j = Jimmy Carter served two terms in office; and let g = George H. W. Bush served two terms in office. We can symbolize our argument in the following way:

~b & j

g

∴ ~(~j & ~g)

Let's set up the truth table.

	b	j	g	~b	~j	~g	~j & ~g	~b & j*	g*	~(~j & ~g) C
1.	T	T	T	F	F	F	F	F	T	T
2.	T	T	F	F	F	T	F	F	F	T
3.	T	F	T	F	T	F	F	F	T	T
4.	T	F	F	F	T	T	T	F	F	F
5.	F	T	T	T	F	F	F	T	T	T
6.	F	T	F	T	F	T	F	T	F	T
7.	F	F	T	T	T	F	F	F	T	T
8.	F	F	F	T	T	T	T	F	F	F

We use b, j, and g as our guide variables and assign their truth values in the conventional way, just as we would if we were using p, q, and r. Next, we build up gradually, assembling the parts we need to state the truth values of our premises and conclusion. Finally, we line up our premises and conclusion from left to right, marking them accordingly.

Now let's examine the truth table to determine the validity of the argument. Are there any cases in which all the premises are true and the conclusion is false?

	b	j	g	~b	~j	~g	~j & ~g	~b & j*	g*	~(~j & ~g) C
1.	T	T	T	F	F	F	F	F	T	T
2.	T	T	F	F	F	T	F	F	F	T
3.	T	F	T	F	T	F	F	F	T	T
4.	T	F	F	F	T	T	T	F	F	F
5.	F	T	T	T	F	F	F	T	T	T
6.	F	T	F	T	F	T	F	T	F	T
7.	F	F	T	T	T	F	F	F	T	T
8.	F	F	F	T	T	T	T	F	F	F

There is only one case in which the premises are both true, and in this case the conclusion is true as well. So, we know that the argument is valid, even though we know that the premises are false. Remember that an argument can have all false premises and a false conclusion and still be valid. Such an argument is not sound, however.

EXERCISE 10.4

I. Assume that a, b, and c are true, and x, y, and z are false. Determine whether each of the following is true or false. Remember to start with the innermost parentheses.

1. *a* & *b* & *c*
2. ~(*a* & *b*) & *c*
3. (*a* & *b*) & ~*c*
4. (*b* & *x*) & *a*
5. *b* & ~(*x* & *y*)

6. ~*z* & ~(*a* & *c*)
7. ~*x* & ~(~*b* & ~*c*)
8. ~*y* & ~(*a* & ~*c*)
9. ~[~*y* & ~(*a* & ~*c*)]
10. ~[~(~*a* & ~*b*) & (*x* & ~*a*)]

II. Translate each of the symbolic statements in Exercise I into a statement in English.

III. Put the following statements in symbolic form.

1. Cats and dogs are mammals, but kangaroos are not mammals.
2. Cats, dogs, and humans are mammals.
3. It's not the case that cats, dogs, and humans are mammals.
4. Tuna and bass are fish, but whales are not.
5. It's not the case that tuna and bass are fish but whales are not.

IV. Determine the validity of the following arguments using truth tables.

1. *p* & *q*

   ~(*q* & *r*)

   ∴ ~*r*

2. ~(*a* & *x*)

   ~*y*

   ∴ ~*x* & ~*y*

3. ~(~*b* & *f*)

   g

   ∴ *g* & *f*

4. (*b* & ~*t*)

   ~(*m* & *b*)

   ∴ ~*m* & ~*t*

5. ~(~*k* & ~*h*)

   z

   ∴ ~(~*z* & *h*)

V. Put the following arguments in symbolic form. Then test them for validity using a truth table.

1. Frogs hop, and toads hop. Snakes don't hop. So, it is not the case that frogs and snakes hop.
2. Freshman take required core courses, and so do sophomores. Seniors do not take required core courses. So, it's not the case that sophomores and seniors take required core courses.
3. It's not the case that fish is fattening and beef is fattening. Vegetables are not fattening. So, fish and vegetables are not fattening.

4. Students can raise their grades by studying hard, but not by doing extra-credit work. It's not the case that students can raise their grades by doing extra-credit work and getting a tutor. So, students can raise their grades by working hard and by getting a tutor.

5. It's not the case that France and Japan are in Europe. China is not in Europe. So, Japan is not in Europe, and China is not in Europe.

DISJUNCTION

We have seen how to symbolize conjunctions, two statements joined together. Now we are ready to discuss disjunctions, two statements set apart, usually by the word "or." For example, "Frank is angry *or* Hank is tired." The symbol for disjunction is the lowercase v, also called the wedge. So, we can symbolize "Frank is angry or Hank is tired" in the following way: $p \vee q$.

It is important to note that the word "or" has two possible senses. In its **exclusive sense,** the word "or" eliminates or excludes one of the possibilities. For example, if a waiter tells you, "You can have the soup *or* the salad," he usually means that you can have either soup or salad *but not both.* In its **non-exclusive sense,** the word "or" does not exclude either possibility. For example, your advisor may inform you, "To fulfill the science requirement, you can take biology *or* chemistry." In all likelihood, what your advisor means is that you can take biology, *or* chemistry, *or both.*

In which sense are we supposed to understand the word "or" for the purposes of propositional logic? The convention is to take the word "or" in its nonexclusive sense. This is the safest way to proceed. (Of course, outside our use of propositional logic, we should use the principle of charity to interpret an "or" statement to the best of our ability in accord with the intention of the speaker or writer.)

A disjunction, such as "Frank is angry or Hank is tired," is true if either Frank is angry, or Hank is tired, or both. We can symbolize the disjunction as $p \vee q$, and the truth table for the disjunction is as follows:

p	q	$p \vee q$
T	T	T
T	F	T
F	T	T
F	F	F

The truth table shows that the only case in which $p \vee q$ is false is the final line, in which both p is false and q is false.

Consider a simple argument that includes a disjunction:

Frank is angry or Hank is tired.

So, Frank is angry.

Because language is misleading, as well as because it is diffuse and inexact when applied to logic (for which it was never intended), logical symbolism is absolutely necessary to any exact or thorough treatment of our subject.

—Bertrand Russell

Let's put our argument in symbolic form:

$p \vee q$

$\therefore p$

Now we set up the truth table for the argument:

p	q	$p \vee q$*	p C
T	T	T	T
T	F	T	T
F	T	T	F
F	F	F	F

Examining the truth table to determine validity, we notice that there are three cases in which the single premise is true. In the first two cases, the conclusion is true as well, but in the third case, the conclusion is false. On that basis we know that the argument is invalid, since one instance of all true premises and a false conclusion establishes that an argument is invalid, no matter what else we may find.

Just as conjunctions can involve negations, so too can disjunctions. And as with conjunctions, we must be careful to note what is being negated. Consider the following disjunctions. Each has the same subject matter, but each has a different truth table resulting from the differences in what is negated.

Frank is not angry or Hank is tired.

p	q	$\sim p$	$\sim p \vee q$
T	T	F	T
T	F	F	F
F	T	T	T
F	F	T	T

Frank is not angry or Hank is not tired.

p	q	$\sim p$	$\sim q$	$\sim p \vee \sim q$
T	T	F	F	F
T	F	F	T	T
F	T	T	F	T
F	F	T	T	T

It's not the case that Frank is angry or Hank is tired.

p	q	$p \vee q$	$\sim(p \vee q)$
T	T	T	F
T	F	T	F
F	T	T	F
F	F	F	T

Now consider a simple argument that involves disjunction, negation, and conjunction:

It's not the case that Frank is angry or Hank is tired.

So, Frank is angry and Hank is tired.

The argument form is

$\sim(p \vee q)$

$\therefore \sim p \And \sim q$

The truth table looks like this:

p	q	$\sim p$	$\sim q$	$p \vee q$	$\sim(p \vee q)$*	$\sim p \And \sim q$ C
T	T	F	F	T	F	F
T	F	F	T	T	F	F
F	T	T	F	T	F	F
F	F	T	T	F	T	T

Examining the truth table to determine validity, we find that only in the final line is the premise true. And in that line the conclusion is true as well. On that basis we know the argument is valid.

Consider an argument with three variables that involves disjunction, negation, and conjunction.

Frank is angry or Hank is tired.

It's not the case that Hank is tired and Larry is lonely.

So, Hank is tired.

The argument form is

$p \vee q$

$\sim(q \And r)$

$\therefore q$

Here is the truth table:

	p	q	r	$q \And r$	$p \vee q$*	$\sim(q \And r)$*	q C
1.	T	T	T	T	T	F	T
2.	T	T	F	F	T	T	T
3.	T	F	T	F	T	T	F
4.	T	F	F	F	T	T	F
5.	F	T	T	T	T	F	T
6.	F	T	F	F	T	T	T
7.	F	F	T	F	F	T	F
8.	F	F	F	F	F	T	F

The only thing new to us in the truth table is the disjunction, $p \vee q$, with eight lines rather than four. There is nothing surprising about the truth values in this column, however. The disjunction is true in every case except lines 7 and 8, in which p and q are both false. Examining the truth table to determine validity, we find that both our premises are true in lines 2, 3, 4, and 6. In addition, however, we find that the conclusion is false in line 3; thus, we know that the argument is invalid.

EXERCISE 10.5

I. Assume that a, b, and c are true, and x, y, and z are false. Determine whether each of the following is true or false.

1. $a \lor x$
2. $\sim a \lor \sim x$
3. $\sim(a \lor x)$
4. $(x \lor \sim y) \& a$
5. $(x \lor y) \lor b$

6. $\sim(x \lor y) \lor z$
7. $(y \lor z) \lor (a \lor b)$
8. $\sim(y \lor z) \lor \sim(a \lor b)$
9. $(c \lor z) \& (b \lor \sim x)$
10. $\sim(\sim c \lor \sim z) \& (\sim b \lor x)$

II. Translate each of the symbolic statements in Exercise I into a statement in English.

III. Put the following statements in symbolic form.

1. The Democrat or the Republican won the election.
2. The Democrat or the Republican won the election, but not the Socialist.
3. It's not the case that the Democrat or the Republican won the election.
4. A whale is a mammal or a dolphin is a fish.
5. A whale is a mammal or a dolphin is not a fish.
6. A whale is a mammal or a dolphin is not a fish, but a dog is not a marsupial.
7. Lance passed the exam or he failed the course.
8. It's not the case that Lance passed the exam or he failed the course.
9. Sheila is a soprano or an alto, but she is not both.
10. It's not the case that Tim is a handyman or Al is a tailor, but Wilson is a neighbor.

IV. Determine the validity of the following arguments using truth tables.

1. $p \lor q$

   $\sim p$

   $\therefore q$

2. $\sim(p \lor q)$

   q

   $\therefore \sim p$

3. $\sim(t \lor a)$

   w

   $\therefore \sim a \& w$

4. ~(t & a)

    a ∨ w

    ∴ ~t & a

5. ~((j ∨ m) & z)

    z ∨ m

    ∴ ~(j & z)

V. Put the following arguments in symbolic form. Then test them for validity using a truth table.

1. The Democrat or the Republican won the election. The Republican did not win. So the Democrat did win.
2. The Democrat or the Republican won the election, but not the Socialist. So, it's not the case that the Socialist or the Democrat won.
3. It's not the case that Lance passed the exam or he failed the course. Lance failed the course. So, Lance did not pass the exam.
4. Sheila is a soprano or an alto. Sheila is not both a soprano and an alto. Sheila is an alto. So, Sheila is a soprano.
5. It's not the case that Tim is a handyman or Al is a tailor. Al is a tailor or Wilson is a neighbor. So, Tim is not a handyman.

CONDITIONAL STATEMENTS

The final element of propositional logic that we need to consider is the conditional statement. We discussed conditional statements in Chapter 2. As you recall, a conditional statement is an if-then statement consisting of two parts. The first part of the statement, which follows "if" and precedes "then," is called the *antecedent*. The second part of the statement, which follows "then," is called the *consequent*.

In the conditional statement "If it rained, then the ground is wet," "it rained" is the antecedent and "the ground is wet" is the consequent. In symbolizing the conditional, we assign one variable to the antecedent and another variable to the consequent. For example, we can let p = it rained and q = the ground is wet. The symbol for the implication involved in an if-then statement is the arrow, →.[2] We therefore symbolize "If it rained, then the ground is wet" as $p \rightarrow q$.

The truth table for conditional statements can be a little tricky. The only time a conditional is false is when the antecedent is true and the conclusion is false.[3] So, the truth table for $p \rightarrow q$ is as follows:

	p	q	$p \rightarrow q$
1.	T	T	T
2.	T	F	F
3.	F	T	T
4.	F	F	T

Clearly, the conditional should be assumed to be true in line 1. If the antecedent is true and the consequent is true, the conditional is true. Even more clearly, the conditional must be false in line 2, where the antecedent is true and the conditional is false. Line 3 might seem strange at first: a false antecedent and a true consequent gives us a true conditional. It might seem even stranger, in line 4, that a false antecedent and a false consequent gives us a true conditional. We can make sense of these peculiarities if we consider each of the four possibilities for our original example, "If it rained, then the ground is wet."

1. If it is true that "it rained" and it is true that "the ground is wet," we have no reason to think that the conditional is false. So, the truth value for the conditional is true.
2. If it is true that "it rained" but it is false that "the ground is wet," we know that the conditional is false. Our information clearly demonstrates it.
3. If it is false that "it rained" but true that the ground is wet, we have no reason to think that the conditional is false. It didn't rain, but the ground is wet. Our conditional doesn't suggest that the ground can become wet *only* as a result of rain. It is perfectly possible that someone wet the ground while washing his car or watering her lawn. So, the conditional is assumed to be true.
4. If it is false that "it rained" and false that "the ground is wet," we have no reason to think that the conditional is false. It didn't rain and the ground isn't wet. This information doesn't contradict our conditional in any way. Without any reason to think the conditional is false, we assume it is true.

It may be helpful to think of the truth table for conditional statements in terms of the guiding legal principle that a person is presumed innocent until proven guilty. In a similar way, a conditional is presumed true until proven false. The only thing that can definitively show that a conditional is false is a true antecedent followed by a false consequent.

Let's consider a basic argument using a conditional statement:

If it rained, then the ground is wet.

It rained.

So, the ground is wet.

We can symbolize this argument form, known as *modus ponens,* in the following way:

$p \rightarrow q$

p

$\therefore q$

Now let's set up the truth table:

Few persons care to study logic, because everybody conceives himself to be proficient enough in the art of reasoning already. But I observe that this satisfaction is limited to one's own ratiocination, and does not extend to that of other men.

—C. S. Peirce

	p	q	$p \rightarrow q$*	p*	q C
1.	T	T	T	T	T
2.	T	F	F	T	F
3.	F	T	T	F	T
4.	F	F	T	F	F

We encounter no surprises in setting up the truth table. We begin with our columns for p, q, and $p \rightarrow q$. Then we move left to right, adding our second premise, p, and our conclusion, q. Examining the table to determine validity, we discover that only in line 1 are both of the premises true. In line 1 the conclusion is also true, so we know that the argument is valid.

Let's consider another basic argument using a conditional statement:

If it rained, then the ground is wet.

The ground is not wet.

So, it did not rain.

We can symbolize this argument form, known as *modus tollens,* in the following way:

$p \rightarrow q$

$\sim q$

$\therefore \sim p$

Now let's set up the truth table:

	p	q	$p \rightarrow q$*	$\sim q$*	$\sim p$ C
1.	T	T	T	F	F
2.	T	F	F	T	F
3.	F	T	T	F	T
4.	F	F	T	T	T

Again, we encounter no surprises in setting up the truth table. We begin with our columns for p, q, and $p \rightarrow q$. Then we move left to right, adding our second premise, $\sim q$, and our conclusion, $\sim p$. Examining the table to determine validity, we discover that only in line 4 are both of the premises true. In line 4 the conclusion is also true, so we know that the argument is valid.

As in symbolizing conjunction and disjunction, we must be careful in placing the negation sign in symbolizing a conditional statement. The place of the negation makes a big difference in the setup for the truth table. To illustrate that point, let's look at present three different possibilities.

Consider the first conditional:

If it did *not* rain, then the game was played.

$\sim p \rightarrow q$

	p	q	$\sim p$	$\sim p \rightarrow q$
1.	T	T	F	T
2.	T	F	F	T
3.	F	T	T	T
4.	F	F	T	F

To determine the truth values for $\sim p \rightarrow q$, we set up the truth table as you would expect. Keep in mind here that $\sim p$ is the antecedent and q is the consequent. So, to determine the truth values for the conditional, we must look from right to left, and we can remind ourselves of that by drawing an arrow from the $\sim p$ to the q. The truth table shows that the only case in which the truth value for the conditional is false is in the fourth line, where the $\sim p$ is true and the q is false.

Now consider the second conditional:

If it did *not* rain, then the game was *not* played.

$\sim p \rightarrow \sim q$

	p	q	$\sim p$	$\sim q$	$\sim p \rightarrow \sim q$
1.	T	T	F	F	T
2.	T	F	F	T	T
3.	F	T	T	F	F
4.	F	F	T	T	T

To determine the truth values for $\sim p \rightarrow \sim q$, we set up the truth table as you would expect. We use the $\sim p$ column and the $\sim q$ column to determine our truth values. The only case in which the truth value for the conditional is false is in the third line, where the antecedent, $\sim p$, is true and the consequent, $\sim q$, is false.

Finally, consider this conditional:

It is not the case that if it rained then the game was played.

$\sim(p \rightarrow q)$

	p	q	$p \rightarrow q$	$\sim(p \rightarrow q)$
1.	T	T	T	F
2.	T	F	F	T
3.	F	T	T	F
4.	F	F	T	F

To determine the truth values for $\sim(p \rightarrow q)$, we set up the truth table as you would expect. We build up to $p \rightarrow q$ and derive the truth values for $\sim(p \rightarrow q)$ by simply taking the opposite of what is in the $p \rightarrow q$ column for each corresponding line. The only time the conditional is true is when its opposite, $p \rightarrow q$, is false.

To analyze a three-variable argument involving a conditional, we simply follow what we have learned so far. We build the truth table by setting up the first three columns in the conventional way and representing the premises and the conclusion of the argument accordingly. With three variables, there will be two cases in which the antecedent is true and the conclusion is false, and thus the conditional will be false in two cases.

Consider the following example:

$p \rightarrow q$

$p \& r$

$\therefore q$

	p	q	r	$p \rightarrow q$*	$p \& r$*	q C
1.	T	T	T	T	T	T
2.	T	T	F	T	F	T
3.	T	F	T	F	T	F
4.	T	F	F	F	F	F
5.	F	T	T	T	F	T
6.	F	T	F	T	F	T
7.	F	F	T	T	F	F
8.	F	F	F	T	F	F

Having set up the columns for our three variables, we set up the column for our first premise, $p \rightarrow q$. There are two cases, lines 3 and 4, in which the antecedent, p, is true and the consequent, q, is false. In those cases, $p \rightarrow q$ is false. We set up the column for $p \& q$ by consulting the p column and the q column, and to facilitate reading the table we repeat the q column for our conclusion. Scanning the table, we see that only in line 1 are both of the premises true. The conclusion is also true in line 1, so we know that the argument is valid.

Let's consider a slightly more complicated argument:

$\sim(p \rightarrow q)$

$q \vee r$

$\therefore q \rightarrow p$

	p	q	r	$p \rightarrow q$	$\sim(p \rightarrow q)$*	$q \vee r$*	$q \rightarrow p$ C
1.	T	T	T	T	F	T	T
2.	T	T	F	T	F	T	T
3.	T	F	T	F	T	T	T
4.	T	F	F	F	T	F	T
5.	F	T	T	T	F	T	F
6.	F	T	F	T	F	T	F
7.	F	F	T	T	F	T	T
8.	F	F	F	T	F	F	T

Having set up the columns for our three variables, we build up to our first premise, $\sim(p \rightarrow q)$. To set up the column for $\sim(p \rightarrow q)$, we set up the column for $p \rightarrow q$ and take the negation of it. We set up the column for $q \vee r$ simply by consulting the q column and the r column. Finally, we set up the column for our conclusion, $q \rightarrow p$, by looking from right to left at our first two columns. Only in lines 5 and 6 is our antecedent, q, true and our consequent, p, false, so only in lines 5 and 6 is $q \rightarrow p$ false. Now looking at the table to determine validity, we see that only in line 3 are both of our premises true. In line 3 the conclusion is also true, so we know that the argument is valid.

Consider the following argument:

If the Democrat wins the election, then she will raise taxes.

If taxes are raised, then individual savings will decrease.

So, if the Democrat wins, individual savings will decrease.

Is this argument valid? Let's symbolize it and test it for validity using a truth table.

$d \rightarrow t$

$t \rightarrow s$

$\therefore d \rightarrow s$

	d	t	s	$d \rightarrow t$*	$t \rightarrow s$*	$d \rightarrow s$ C
1.	T	T	T	T	T	T
2.	T	T	F	T	F	F
3.	T	F	T	F	T	T
4.	T	F	F	F	T	F
5.	F	T	T	T	T	T
6.	F	T	F	T	F	T
7.	F	F	T	T	T	T
8.	F	F	F	T	T	T

In lines 1, 5, 7, and 8 both of the premises are true. In each of these lines, the conclusion is true as well, so we know that the argument is valid. In fact, of course, this means that any argument fitting this pattern, known as the *hypothetical syllogism*, is valid.

Finally, recall the following argument from the beginning of this chapter:

If the Democrat loses the Senate race, then the Republicans will have a majority in the Senate.

If the Republicans have a majority in the Senate, then the Senate will vote down the new bill.

It's not the case that the Senate will vote down the new bill or the Democrat will lose the Senate race.

So, it's not the case that if the Democrat does not lose, then the Senate will not vote down the new bill.

Let's test it for validity, symbolizing the argument and checking the truth table.

$$d \rightarrow r$$
$$r \rightarrow s$$
$$\sim(s \lor d)$$
$$\therefore \sim(\sim d \rightarrow \sim s)$$

	d	r	s	$\sim d$	$\sim s$	$\sim d \rightarrow \sim s$	$s \lor d$	$d \rightarrow r$*	$r \rightarrow s$*	$\sim(s \lor d)$*	$\sim(\sim d \rightarrow \sim s)$C
1.	T	T	T	F	F	T	T	T	T	F	F
2.	T	T	F	F	T	T	T	T	F	F	F
3.	T	F	T	F	F	T	T	F	T	F	F
4.	T	F	F	F	T	T	T	F	T	F	F
5.	F	T	T	T	F	F	T	T	T	F	T
6.	F	T	F	T	T	T	F	T	F	T	F
7.	F	F	T	T	F	F	T	T	T	F	T
8.	F	F	F	T	T	T	F	T	T	T	F

Line 8 is the only line in which all three premises are true. In line 8 the conclusion is false, so the argument is invalid.

EXERCISE 10.6

I. Assume that *a, b,* and *c* are true, and *x, y,* and *z* are false. Determine whether each of the following is true or false.

1. $a \rightarrow y$
2. $y \rightarrow a$
3. $\sim(x \rightarrow y)$
4. $(z \rightarrow b) \lor \sim c$
5. $(z \rightarrow \sim x) \lor y$
6. $(c \rightarrow a) \lor (z \rightarrow c)$
7. $\sim(b \rightarrow c) \& (\sim x \rightarrow \sim a)$
8. $(a \rightarrow y) \rightarrow y$
9. $(\sim z \rightarrow x) \rightarrow (\sim a \rightarrow \sim c)$
10. $\sim(\sim c \rightarrow y) \rightarrow \sim(\sim b \rightarrow \sim z)$

II. Translate each of the symbolic statements in Exercise I into a statement in English.

III. Put the following statements in symbolic form.

1. If Bert is taking a bath, then Ernie is taking a bath.
2. It's not the case that if Hank is taking a bath, then Tiffany is taking a bath.
3. If Bert is not taking a bath, then Ernie is not taking a bath.
4. If there is helium in the balloon, then it can float.
5. If the balloon can't float, then there is no helium in the balloon.
6. If Lisa passed the final exam, then she passed the course.
7. If Lisa did not pass the course, then she did not pass the final exam.
8. If the groundhog doesn't see his shadow, then spring is not coming in six weeks.
9. It's not the case that if the groundhog doesn't see his shadow, then spring is not coming in six weeks.
10. If it is the case that if the sun shines then the game is on, then if the storm doesn't hit I'll be at the park.

IV. Determine the validity of the following arguments using truth tables.

⬚   1.

$p \rightarrow q$

$\sim p$

$\therefore \sim q$

2.

$\sim(p \rightarrow q)$

q

$\therefore \sim p$

3.

$\sim p \rightarrow q$

$\sim p \& r$

$\therefore q \& r$

⬚   4.

$p \rightarrow q$

$\sim q \vee r$

$\therefore \sim p \& r$

5.

$\sim p \rightarrow q$

$\sim r \vee \sim p$

$\therefore r \rightarrow q$

V. Put the following arguments in symbolic form. Then test them for validity using a truth table.

⬚   1. If Bert is taking a bath, then Ernie is taking a bath. Ernie is not taking a bath. So, Bert is not taking a bath.

2. If the balloon can't float, then there is no helium in the balloon. The balloon can float. So, there is helium in the balloon.

3. If Lisa passed the final exam, then she passed the course. Lisa did not pass the final exam. So, she did not pass the course.

⬚   4. If the groundhog sees his shadow, then spring is coming in six weeks. So, if the groundhog doesn't see his shadow, then spring isn't coming in six weeks.

5. The game is on if the sun shines. The game is on and the team is excited. So, the sun must be shining.

Summary

1. In propositional logic, the word *conjunction* refers to a compound statement. A compound statement, such as "This chapter was stimulating, and I learned a lot," is symbolized by two variables joined by the ampersand, & (for example, *p* & *q*).

2. If in any case we are unsure whether a statement is simple or compound, we must ask, "What does the statement mean?" Does the statement consist of two simple statements? If it does, then it is compound. If it doesn't, then it is simple.

3. *Truth values* for a variable are indicated as true, T, or false, F. A *truth table* is a listing of all possible truth values for the variables in an argument form.

4. For the purposes of propositional logic, the following words are all equivalent and can be symbolized by the ampersand: *and, but, yet, while, whereas, although, though, however.*

5. In a valid argument it is impossible for all of the premises to be true and the conclusion false. So in examining the truth table, we look for instances in which all the premises are true. If there is any instance of all true premises followed by a false conclusion, an F under the conclusion column, the argument is invalid. It doesn't matter if there are other instances in the truth table where all the premises are true and the conclusion is true, too.

6. Any two arguments that share the same argument form are either both valid or both invalid. When we know that an argument form is valid, we know that any argument that fits that form is valid.

7. Negation is the use of the word "not" (or an equivalent word or phrase) to deny a statement. The conventional symbol for negation is the tilde, ~. So, we can symbolize "Shaq is not short" with ~*p*.

8. Sometimes a negation applies only to a single simple statement—for example, "Sam is not a shortstop," symbolized as ~*p*. Sometimes two negations apply to both elements of a compound statement—for example, "Sam is not a shortstop, and Diane is not an intellectual," symbolized as ~*p* & ~*q*. At other times one negation applies to a whole compound statement—for example, "It's not the case that Sam is a bartender and Woody is a mailman," symbolized as ~(*p* & *q*).

9. The setup and analysis for three variables is lengthier and more complex, but all the same rules apply.

10. A *disjunction* is an "or" statement—that is, a statement that consists of two (or more) statements set apart, usually by the word "or." For

example, "Norm is an accountant or Norm is unemployed." The symbol for disjunction is the lowercase v, also called the wedge. We can symbolize the previous disjunction as p v q.

11. The word "or" has two possible senses. The *exclusive sense* eliminates one of the possibilities. For example, a flight attendant may tell you, "For dinner you may have chicken or fish." The *nonexclusive sense* does not exclude either possibility. For example, a coach may advise you that "when you're feeling dehydrated, you should drink water or Gatorade." It is true when either of the two statements is true, and it is also true when both statements are true. For the purposes of propositional logic, it is conventional to take the word "or" in its nonexclusive sense.

12. A conditional statement is an if-then statement consisting of two parts. The first part of the statement, which follows "if" and precedes "then," is called the *antecedent*. The symbol for the implication involved in an if-then statement is the arrow, $\rightarrow$. We therefore symbolize "If he loves me, then he will call" as, $p \rightarrow q$.

13. The only time a conditional is false is when the antecedent is true and the conclusion is false. It may be helpful to think of the truth table for conditional statements in terms of the guiding legal principle that a person is presumed innocent until proven guilty. In a similar way, a conditional is presumed true until proven false. The only thing that can definitively show that a conditional is false is a true antecedent followed by a false consequent.

CHAPTER 11

INDUCTIVE REASONING

INTRODUCTION TO INDUCTION

The topic of inductive reasoning is familiar to us from the discussion of deductive and inductive arguments in Chapter 3. Now it's time to take a closer look at inductive arguments. *Inductive arguments* are those in which the premises are intended to provide support, but not conclusive evidence, for the conclusion. Because inductive arguments do not guarantee that their conclusions are true, we evaluate them according to the strength of the support they provide for their conclusions. An inductive argument is *strong* when its premises provide evidence that its conclusion is more likely true than false. An inductive argument is *weak* when its premises do *not* provide evidence that its conclusion is more likely true than false. As we shall see, arguments have varying degrees of strength or weakness.

As we saw in Chapter 3, not all inductive arguments move from specific premises to a general conclusion. Here is an example of an inductive argument that moves from a general premise to a more specific conclusion:

> Most critical thinking students improve greatly in their ability to analyze arguments.
>
> So, *you* will probably improve greatly in your ability to analyze arguments.

This is an inductive argument that has a single premise dealing with a general group, "most students," and a conclusion about a single specific student, *you*. Notice that it is inductive because the premise provides support for the conclusion but the premise is not intended to guarantee the conclusion. You may recall that in Chapter 3 we spoke about *the strict necessity test:* Either an argument's conclusion follows with strict necessity from its premises or it does not. If the argument's conclusion *does* follow with strict logical necessity from its premises, then the argument should always be treated as deductive. If the argument's conclusion does not follow with strict logical necessity from its premises, then the argument should normally be treated as inductive. Clearly, in the argument above, the conclusion is not meant to follow, and does not follow, with strict necessity from its premises. The argument is inductive.

Another important clue that this is an inductive argument is the word "probably." In Chapter 3 we called such words *induction indicator words*. Among the important indicator words and phrases for inductive arguments are *likely, probably, it's plausible to suppose that, it's reasonable to believe that, one would expect that, it's a good bet that, chances are that,* and *odds are that.* Notice that most of these phrases can be, and often are, used in making predictions. When an argument makes a prediction, that is a good, but not foolproof, indication that the argument is inductive. Of course, the presence of one or more of these indicator words in an argument does not guarantee that the argument is inductive, but chances are that it is.

Another way to identify inductive arguments is to look for their common patterns. Four[1] of these are *inductive generalizations, statistical arguments, arguments from analogy,* and *causal arguments.* We shall look at each of these inductive argument forms in turn.

INDUCTIVE GENERALIZATIONS

A generalization is a statement made about all or most members of a group. Inductive generalization is one of the most important kinds of inductive arguments. An *inductive generalization* is an argument that relies on characteristics of a sample population to make a claim about the population as a whole. In other words, it is an argument that uses evidence about a limited number of people or things of a certain type, the **sample population**, to make a claim about a larger group of people or things of that type, the **population as a whole.**

Let's consider an example:

> All the bass Hank has caught in the Susquehanna River have weighed less than one pound.
>
> So, most of the bass in the Susquehanna River weigh less than one pound.

The sample population is the bass Hank has caught in the Susquehanna River. The population as a whole is all the bass in the Susquehanna River. Inductive generalizations, such as our example, fit the stereotype of induction. The argument moves from a specific premise to a more general conclusion. But remember that the important thing about inductive arguments is that the truth of their premises is not intended to guarantee the truth of their conclusions. At best, the premises provide strong support for the conclusion.

A good inductive argument should reach a conclusion that is appropriate to the evidence offered by its premises. The conclusion should not claim more than its premises can support. In the preceding example, the conclusion claims that most of the bass in the Susquehanna River weigh less than one pound. The degree of support that the premise lends will depend in part on how much fishing Hank has done and how many bass Hank has caught, but it is unlikely that this will be enough support to make this a strong argument. We could make the argument stronger by making our conclusion less *sweeping*, that is, the conclusion could cover less ground. For example, if we concluded that *many* of the bass in the Susquehanna River weigh less than one pound, the argument would be stronger. Given our premise, the conclusion is more likely to be true if its claim is more limited, restricting itself to *many* rather than *most* bass. If we concluded that *all* the bass in the Susquehanna River weigh less than one pound, the argument would be far weaker. Other phrases that could soften the conclusion are *possibly, probably,* and *likely.* If we soften the conclusion by saying, "So, it is *possible* (or *probable* or *likely*) that most of the bass in the Susquehanna River weigh less than one pound," our argument is stronger because its conclusion is less forcefully asserted.

Inductive generalizations should not overstate their conclusions. For example:

> No rabbit Alan has come across has tried to attack him.
>
> So, most rabbits are not inclined to attack human beings.

This is a strong inductive generalization. Given its premise, it seems very likely that its conclusion is true. Let's assume that Alan has come across thousands of rabbits and has yet to be attacked by one. The sample population, then, is the rabbits Alan has come across. The conclusion is about the population of rabbits as a whole. Notice that the conclusion is modest. It doesn't go too far by claiming that all rabbits are not inclined to attack human beings. It recognizes that there could be an exception to the rule.

Here is another example:

> None of the medical doctors Joe has ever met smoked cigarettes while examining him.
>
> So, no doctor smokes cigarettes while examining patients.

Let's assume Joe has been examined by six medical doctors over the course of his life. We know that cigarette smoking causes cancer and that doctors in general have been outspoken about the dangers of smoking. This common knowledge aids the argument. However, the conclusion is so sweeping that the argument is not strong. After all, if there is just one doctor somewhere who smokes cigarettes while examining his or her patients, the conclusion is false. To play it safe, then, we might conclude instead that "Very few, if any, doctors smoke cigarettes while examining patients." This is still a sweeping conclusion, but it allows for the possibility of the occasional exception. Given the revised premise, it is likely that the conclusion is true, and thus the argument is strong.

Here is a third example:

> Tom has visited Cocoa Beach, Florida, in October several times, and the weather was always great—sunny skies and temperatures in the 80s. So, there's a good chance that Cocoa Beach usually has great weather in October.

THE FAR SIDE © Farworks, Inc. All rights reserved.

The sample population is Tom's experience of the weather in Cocoa Beach in October, based on several visits. The population as a whole is the weather in Cocoa Beach in October, in general. Tom's several visits do not guarantee the conclusion about the weather in general, but they do lend it some support. The conclusion reflects the fact that the evidence is limited. The conclusion does not say that the weather is always great, but only that it *usually* is. Given the premise, it is likely that the conclusion is true, and thus the argument is strong.

EXERCISE 11.1

In each case, decide if the example is a strong inductive generalization or a weak inductive generalization. Be ready to explain and justify your answers.

1. All the hunters Ted knows eat the meat from the animals they kill. So, it is possible that many hunters eat the animals they kill.

2. All the blond men Sarah knows are exceedingly intelligent. So, it must be that all blond men are exceedingly intelligent.

3. Some students sell back this textbook at the end of the semester. So, it is likely that all students sell back most of their textbooks at the end of the semester.

4. The fifteen winters Eric spent in New York City were cold. So, it may be that most winters in New York City are cold.

5. Many of the children in Ms. Santuzzi's first-grade class can read. So, most children in the first grade can read.

6. Many of the unemployed steelworkers who hang out at the Dew Drop Inn are actively looking for work. So, it must be that many unemployed steelworkers are actively looking for work.

7. All the unemployed steelworkers who hang out at the Dew Drop Inn are not looking for work. So, it could be that most unemployed steelworkers are not looking for work.

8. None of the many students Lisa knows at State College are majoring in anthropology. So, it may be that not many students at State are majoring in anthropology.

9. Many of the women on the swim team are majoring in women's studies. So, it is possible that some of the women on the swim team consider themselves feminists.

10. None of the players on the New York Knicks is Serbian. So, there must not be any Serbian players in the NBA.

Evaluating Inductive Generalizations

So far, we have been relying on our innate logical abilities and common sense to determine whether an inductive generalization is strong or weak. To a great extent, that is what we will continue to do. Although there are standard tests for determining whether a deductive argument is valid or invalid, there is no standard test for determining whether an inductive argument is strong or weak. Still, we are not totally lost when it comes to evaluating inductive generalizations we examine.

- Are the premises true?
- Is the sample large enough?
- Is the sample representative?

Are the Premises True?   One thing that inductive arguments have in common with deductive arguments is the need for true premises. "Garbage in, garbage out" applies just as well to inductive generalizations as it does to deductive arguments. As you know, a deductive argument that is valid and has all true premises leading to a true conclusion is called a *sound* argument. A deductive argument can have good—that is, valid—argumentation and still be unsound if the premises are not all true. In the same way, the premises of an inductive generalization can provide strong support for its conclusion, but if the premises are not all true, it is not a cogent inductive argument. A *cogent* inductive argument is one that has all true premises and supplies strong support for its conclusion. One or more false premises makes an inductive argument *uncogent*, even if its argumentation, its support for the conclusion, is strong.

Consider this example:

Most CEOs of Fortune 500 companies are women.

So, the CEOs of most big businesses are probably women.

The premise in this argument provides strong support for the conclusion. After all, if most of the CEOs of the most financially successful big businesses are women, it would seem likely that the CEOs of most big businesses are women. However, the premise is false (most CEOs are men), so it cannot legitimately be used to support the conclusion. The argument is not cogent.

Is the Sample Large Enough?   Common sense prompts us to ask that obvious question about an inductive generalization. The size of the sample population must be sufficient to justify the conclusion about the population as a whole. A sample is "large enough" when it is clear that we have not rushed to judgment, that we have not formed a *hasty generalization*. Admittedly, this business of specifying what we mean by "enough" is not easy. For the moment, we shall rely on common sense to determine whether the sample is large enough. In the next section of this chapter we'll take a look at the mathematical determination of sample size.

Let's begin with a familiar example:

None of the thousands of rabbits Alan has come across has tried to attack him.

So, most rabbits are not inclined to attack human beings.

Thousands of encounters with rabbits seems like a large enough sample size to support the modest conclusion that *most* rabbits are not inclined to attack human beings. No inductive argument can guarantee the truth of its conclusion, but you don't have to be an expert in statistics to see that this one is a pretty good bet.

On the other hand, consider this example:

Brooke taught three students with purple hair last semester, and all of them were A students.

So, all students with purple hair must be A students.

Considering the thousands of students with purple hair, three students is clearly not a large enough sample on which to base this conclusion. The conclusion may or may not be true, but given the small sample, the premise is not strong enough support for it.

Consider this example:

> Two nuclear bombs were dropped on Japan, and today Japan has one of the strongest economies in the world.
>
> So, all the concern about nuclear warfare and the end of humankind is a bunch of nonsense.

The two nuclear bombs dropped on Japan devastated that country, but the Japanese have recovered well. However, the use of two nuclear bombs is not enough to tell us what would result from the use of more nuclear bombs; they are not a large enough sample. Beyond that, those two nuclear bombs may not be like other nuclear bombs that could be used. That leads us to the third question.

Is the Sample Representative?   An inductive generalization is weak if the sample population it draws on is not enough like the population as a whole that it makes its claims about. In technical terms, we want the sample population to be *representative*. A **representative sample** is like the population as a whole in all relevant ways. It should be a miniversion of the population as a whole.

Let's examine the previous example:

> Two nuclear bombs were dropped on Japan, and today Japan has one of the strongest economies in the world.
>
> So, all the concern about nuclear warfare and the end of humankind is a bunch of nonsense.

The sample population is the two nuclear bombs dropped on Japan. Not only is this sample too small, but it is also not representative. The two bombs dropped on Japan were not nearly as powerful as the nuclear bombs of today. Japan's ability to recover after the bombing cannot be generalized correctly to humankind's ability to survive and recover from the devastation that would be caused by the current generation of nuclear bombs.

Recall the first inductive generalization we considered:

> All the bass Hank has caught in the Susquehanna River have weighed less than one pound.
>
> So, most of the bass in the Susquehanna River weigh less than one pound.

Let's assume for the sake of argument that Hank has caught hundreds of bass in the Susquehanna River and that they all weighed less than one pound. That would seem to be a large enough sample, but the argument could still be weak. How? It could be that the hundreds of bass Hank caught were not truly representative of the population of bass in the Susquehanna River as a whole. Why? There are many possible reasons. Perhaps Hank has fished only a short stretch of the river, and there are actually much larger bass twenty miles north. Perhaps Hank has fished only with artificial lures, but if he used live bait he could catch three-pound bass right under the Market Street Bridge, where he usually fishes. Can you think of other reasons?

Terminology Recap

A *strong inductive argument* has premises that provide evidence that its conclusion is more likely true than false.

A *weak inductive argument* has premises that do not provide evidence that its conclusion is more likely true than false.

A *cogent inductive argument* has all true premises and supplies strong support for its conclusion.

An *uncogent inductive argument* has one or more false premises or weak support for its conclusion.

Often, the size of the sample is closely connected to how representative it is. But, as we just saw, a large sample is no guarantee of a representative sample. It is also possible, though less common, for a sample to be representative but not large enough. If, for example, Hank has fished every mile of the mighty Susquehanna with both artificial lures and live bait but has caught only a dozen bass—all under one pound—the sample might be representative, in a sense. After all, he varied methods and locations. Still, a dozen bass would not be a large enough sample on which to base the conclusion that most of the bass in the Susquehanna River weigh less than one pound. Maybe there are many three pounders but Hank is just a poor fisherman.

EXERCISE 11.2

I. Determine whether the following inductive generalizations are strong or weak. For the sake of this exercise, assume that all the information given is true. In each case, answer these questions: Is the sample large enough? Is the sample representative?

1. All the millions of rubies gemologists have gathered from around the world are red. So, the chances are good that most of the rubies in the world are red.
2. All the guys who live in Jim's dorm room on the first floor and Fred's dorm room on the third floor heard the fire alarm ring last night. So, it is plausible that many of the guys in the three-story dormitory heard it.
3. Most guys who watch the Super Bowl at Wexford College are unprepared for class the next day. So, most students who watch the Super Bowl are probably unprepared for class the next day.
4. Based on a survey of one hundred thousand American high school students, approximately half of all American high school students go on to attend college. So, it is probably the case that about half the people in the world have attended college.
5. There has been at least some snowfall in New York City every January for the past one hundred years. So, the chances are good that there will be at

least some snowfall in New York City every January for the next two hundred years.

II. Consider each of the following weak inductive generalizations. Each is flawed in at least one way. For the sake of this exercise, assume that all the information given is true. In each case, answer these questions: Is the sample large enough? Is the sample representative? Explain and defend your answers.

1. Chicago, Los Angeles, and Houston are all big cities with big crime problems. So, all big cities must have big crime problems.

2. All former presidents of the United States have either died in office or died within fifty years of leaving office. So, it is likely that all future presidents will either die in office or die within fifty years of leaving office.

3. All one thousand of the frogs in Springfield Pond, next to the nuclear plant, have only three legs. So, it is reasonable to believe that many other ponds in Springfield have at least some three-legged frogs as well.

4. All four of the biology professors at Wexford College who were considered for tenure over the last twelve years received tenure. So, it is likely that almost all professors at Wexford who are considered for tenure receive tenure.

5. All one hundred children who saw the advance screening of the latest Disney movie said it was great. So, chances are that nearly everyone who sees the movie will think it is great.

Opinion Polls and Inductive Generalizations

Opinion polls are an excellent source of inductive generalizations. In recent years, polling has become an increasingly large part of the political process. Gallup and Harris polls are often very accurate in predicting the outcomes of national elections, for example. The aim of a poll is to determine what a large population thinks or believes about a certain issue. To make that determination, it is not necessary to ask every member of that population. Rather, the preferred method is to ask a question of a sample of the population that is both large enough and representative of the population as a whole.

In the case of a presidential election, the population would be those who are eligible to vote and intend to vote in the election in question. Obviously, this is a very large population, usually consisting of hundreds of millions. Do we need to survey a million people or more to have a large enough sample? Your inclination might be to answer yes, but in actuality the number of people in the sample population does not have to be nearly that large.

No sample, no matter how large, will ever guarantee that our poll results will be accurate. Still, we can use polls to arrive at a level of 95 percent[2] certainty that our sample population will mirror the population as a whole within a small margin of error. The margin of error is usually indicated by a combination of the plus and minus signs, $\pm$. This means that the results will be within a range of plus or minus the amount indicated. For example, let's say the latest poll shows that Sacamano leads Lomez by a margin of 60 to 40 with a margin of error of ± 3. This suggests that there is a 95 percent chance that if the population as a whole voted, the result would be somewhere between 63%–37% and 57%–43% in favor of Sacamano. Not bad. So how large does the sample have to be to yield these kinds of results? The following table gives the breakdown.[3]

Number Polled	Margin of Error
4,000	±2
1,500	±3
1,000	±4
750	±4
600	±5
400	±6
200	±8
100	±11

As you can see, it doesn't take a huge sample to yield a reasonable margin of error. With a sample of just 1,500, we get a margin of error of ± 3. We can add 2,500 more people to our sample and the margin of error decreases only slightly to ± 2. So, we can produce a fairly accurate poll on a presidential election with millions of voters with a sample population of only 1,500 voters, but there's a catch: *The sample must be representative, too.* The millions of voters represent a great diversity of people, and somehow our sample must be representative of this larger group. To get an idea of what kinds of things can cause a sample to fail in its attempt to be representative, let's consider a classic case.

A well-respected periodical, *The Literary Digest*, conducted a telephone poll to predict the winner of the 1936 presidential election. The pollsters for the magazine understood that the sample had to be large enough. In fact, they went overboard, gathering over two million responses. They also understood that the sample had to be representative, so they randomly picked names from phone books all over the country. Having gathered and tabulated all the responses, *The Literary Digest* predicted a landslide victory for Alf Landon over Franklin Delano Roosevelt. As it turned out, Roosevelt won by an even greater landslide. Although the sample was more than large enough, it was not representative, despite the effort to select the sample population randomly.

Why was the sample not representative? Because in 1936 many people did not have, and could not afford, a telephone in their home, and these people without telephones were mostly members of the lower and middle classes who voted in droves for Roosevelt. Despite their efforts, the pollsters at *The Literary Digest* failed to draw upon a representative sample. They thought they had selected participants in the survey randomly, but in reality they had allowed a bias in favor of wealthier voters to creep into their sample population. To have a truly representative sample, we must select subjects at random from within the appropriate pool. This means nothing is done at the outset of the selection process that would automatically eliminate any segment of the population. The selection is random only if each member of the population has an equal chance of being selected as a member of the sample population. As we shall see, many things can prevent random selection.

Some polls do not even attempt to utilize a truly random sample. Instead, they use *self-selecting samples*. Television talk shows and news broadcasts that invite you to call a certain phone number to cast your vote and register your opinion are prime examples of self-selecting samples. The question of the day might be, for example, "Should flag burning be protected under the First Amendment?" Although this is a controversial issue, it would not be surprising to find a large majority of votes against the protection and legality of flag burning. Why? There could be many reasons. Perhaps the show during which this issue was raised has an overwhelming and nonrepresentative percentage of conservative viewers. Perhaps those against flag burning are just more vocal and outspoken about their position and so more inclined to call in to register their opinion.

Such call-in polls face another problem: they have a significant percentage of *nonresponses*. The nonresponses leave us with the problem of a sample population that is not likely to be representative of the population as a whole. The bias introduced by nonresponses will be even greater if the polling is done using an Internet Web site for people to register their votes. Those who respond to an Internet poll will likely be, on average, younger, better educated, and wealthier than the population as a whole. In fact, most people realize that such call-in polls and Internet surveys are not reliable. The shows responsible for them usually make clear that the results are not the product of "a scientific poll." In other words, aside from entertainment value, they have little value at all.

What might seem random often isn't. Choosing names out of a phone book will not necessarily produce a representative sample, but what about approaching people on the street? This could work, but there are potential pitfalls here, too. The pollster, the person taking the poll, might introduce bias into the sample because of a tendency to approach certain kinds of people and not others. Perhaps the pollster is not even aware that he is doing it. For example, he might have a tendency to approach only people who look "friendly." This may mean that he is more inclined to approach a well-dressed businesswoman and much less inclined to approach a disheveled man. This may introduce a gender bias and a socioeconomic bias into the sample population, automatically eliminating a significant portion of the population, namely, lower-class males. Perhaps the problem could be solved by randomly selecting the people on the street to be approached. For example, our pollster could be given instructions to approach every tenth person who walks down the block. This would certainly be a better strategy than simply allowing the

pollster to approach the people he chooses on the basis of his own whims. Still, there can be problems. For example, if the New York Yankees wanted to know what the reaction would be to tearing down their stadium in the Bronx and building a new one in New Jersey, they would find strong opposition to this plan if they did all their polling in the Bronx. People in the Bronx take pride in their borough as the home of Yankee Stadium, and many residents depend on the stadium, directly or indirectly, for their livelihood. In the same way, if you asked every tenth high school student who walked down the street in Scarsdale, New York, if he or she was planning to go to college, you would get some uncharacteristic results. Perhaps 90 percent of the high school students in this wealthy suburb would indicate that they were planning to go to college, whereas the national average is closer to 60 percent.

Still another factor that may affect the reliability of polls is *dishonesty*. We all like to give the "right answer" to a question, even when the question does not have a right answer but is simply a matter of opinion or an attempt to collect information. The result is that some people actually lie in response to anonymous polls. For example, in response to the question "Do you consider yourself racially prejudiced?" we can expect more people to respond "No" than is actually the case. People think that the "right answer" is "No," so some will answer "No" even if they do indeed consider themselves racially prejudiced. Polling agencies often take advantage of this tendency of people to try to give the "right answer" by asking slanted questions. That is to say, polling agencies may not be interested in gathering objective data and so ask questions that clearly point toward one response as the "right answer." For example, depending on the answer that a polling agency wants respondents to consider the "right answer," they might ask two very different questions. On the subject of whether or not the United States should decrease the size of its nuclear arsenal, a polling agency might ask, "Are you in favor of peaceful multilateral nuclear disarmament?" Or alternatively, "Are you against the weakening of the ability of the United States of America to offer a sufficient nuclear deterrent against foreign attack?" There is not much need to wonder what is the "right answer" in each case. Polling is big business, and those who hire polling agencies often have a vested interest in getting results that confirm their own position on an issue.

Another potential pitfall for objective polling is the person who is doing the poll. Even without intending to, he or she may clue the respondents in to what the "right answer" is, or respondents may answer differently depending on the person doing the polling. A white male is much less likely to admit that he considers himself racially prejudiced if he is polled in person by a black male. A woman is much less likely to admit that she has had a venereal disease when polled by a man rather than by a woman. If the polling question is "Do you believe in God?" we would expect a higher number of "Yes" responses if the person taking the poll is dressed in the garb of a priest or minister. What is the solution? Polling should be *double-blind*. The person taking the poll and the person responding should have no information about each other, or at least as little as possible. And neither the person taking the poll nor the person responding should have any indication of the "right answer."

EXERCISE 11.3

Put together your own plans for a campus poll on the death penalty. What questions will you ask? How will you phrase them so as to avoid pointing to a "right answer"? How will you gather your responses? How many people will you include in the sample population? How will you ensure that the sample is representative? Be prepared to present your plans and defend them against possible objections.

STATISTICAL ARGUMENTS

Closely related to inductive generalization is another type of inductive argument, the statistical argument. A *statistical argument* argues from premises regarding a percentage of a population to a conclusion about an individual member of that population or some part of that population.[4] For example:

> Ninety percent of college students are in favor of not having a cumulative final exam in their critical thinking class.
>
> Vera Peterson is a college student.
>
> So, Vera Peterson is in favor of not having a cumulative final exam in her critical thinking class.

Like other inductive arguments, statistical arguments are evaluated along a continuum of strong to weak. A statistical argument is strong when it

There are three kinds of lies: lies, damned lies, and statistics.
—Benjamin Disraeli

provides evidence that its conclusion is more likely true than false—that is, when the chances that the conclusion is true are greater than 50 percent. A statistical argument is weak when it provides evidence that its conclusion is more likely false than true—that is, when the chances that the conclusion being true are less than 50 percent. The preceding example is thus a strong argument, providing evidence that there is a 90 percent chance that its conclusion is true. The evidence does not logically guarantee that the conclusion is true, but the evidence in inductive arguments never does.

Let's look at another example:

> Only 3 percent of Wexford College students are against building the new gymnasium.
>
> Johnny Z is a Wexford College student.
>
> So, Johnny Z is not against building the new gymnasium.

Again, this is a strong argument, offering evidence that there is a 97 percent chance that the conclusion is true. The argument could be made even stronger by softening the conclusion so that the argument would say instead:

> Only 3 percent of Wexford College students are against building the new gymnasium.
>
> Johnny Z is a Wexford College student.
>
> So, Johnny Z is *probably* not against building the new gymnasium

The word "probably" safeguards this conclusion by claiming less than the conclusion in the original formulation did. Although there might be some doubt about the conclusion as originally stated, "So, Johnny Z is not against building the new gymnasium," it would be tough to deny the softened version of the conclusion, "So, Johnny Z is *probably* not against building the new gymnasium." Given the evidence, Johnny Z "probably" is not against building the new gymnasium. Even if 49 percent of Wexford College students were against building the new gymnasium, it would still follow that "Johnny Z is *probably* not against building the new gymnasium."

Let's consider a different version of the argument:

> Only 3 percent of Wexford College students are against building the new gymnasium.
>
> Johnny Z is a Wexford College student.
>
> So, Johnny Z is against building the new gymnasium.

The evidence that this argument provides makes it unlikely that the conclusion is true. In fact, there is a 97 percent chance it is false. The argument, then, is weak. What if we soften the conclusion with the word "probably"?

> Only 3 percent of Wexford College students are against building the new gymnasium.
>
> Johnny Z is a Wexford College student.
>
> So, Johnny Z is *probably* against building the new gymnasium

The argument is still weak, since the evidence overwhelmingly suggests that "Johnny Z is *probably not* against building the new gymnasium."

Statistical arguments that approach 50 percent, and that offer evidence that that their conclusion is more likely true than false are strong but *unreliable*. There is no specific percentage point at which a statistical argument is judged unreliable. The best way to determine whether a statistical argument is reliable or not is to be practical. Ask yourself, would a reasonable person act or bet on it? If the answer is yes, then the argument is *reliable*. If the answer is no, then the argument is unreliable. For example:

> 55 percent of Wexford students voted for Watkins as "Teacher of the Year."
>
> Eileen is a Wexford student.
>
> So, Eileen voted for Watkins.

Although it is true that a majority of students voted for Watkins, it would be going out on a limb to say Eileen voted for Watkins. A reasonable person certainly wouldn't bet on it. It would be safer to say that "Eileen *probably* voted for Watkins," but even that would be relatively unreliable. After all, there is a 45 percent chance that she didn't vote for Watkins.

Consider another example:

> Just 42 percent of Wexford students come from out of state.
>
> Gloria is a Wexford student.
>
> So, Gloria doesn't come from out of state.

This, too, is a relatively unreliable argument. The fact that only 42 percent of Wexford students come from out of state that doesn't make it very likely that Gloria doesn't come from out of state.

Of course, we can have statistical arguments that are stronger than those in the 50 percent range but not as strong as those that approach the extreme of 100 percent. Their strength and reliability will depend, in part, on how much the conclusion claims. Consider this example:

> 76 percent of new businesses in this state go out of business within the first year.
>
> Dan the Man's Hot Dog Stand is a new business in this state.
>
> So, Dan the Man's Hot Dog Stand will go out of business within the first year.

This argument is strong but not very reliable. In fact, the numbers tell us there is a 24 percent chance that its conclusion is false.

Let's consider a slightly different version of the argument:

> 76 percent of new businesses in this state go out of business within the first year.
>
> Dan the Man's Hot Dog Stand is a new business in this state.
>
> So Dan the Man's Hot Dog Stand will *probably* go out of business within the first year.

This argument makes use of the same information as the previous one, but the word "probably" softens the conclusion, thus increasing the strength of the argument.

Reference Class

In examining opinion polls, we saw that the sample on which the conclusion is based must be representative. Similarly, in statistical arguments, the subject of the premise should be as much like the subject of the conclusion as possible. Let's return to our first example:

> Ninety percent of college students are in favor of not having a cumulative final exam in their critical thinking class.
>
> Vera Peterson is a college student.
>
> So, Vera Peterson is in favor of not having a cumulative final exam in her critical thinking class.

All we know about Vera Peterson is that she is a college student, but surely there is more to know about her than that. And who are the students who want the cumulative final? Suppose we discovered that 85 percent of students who like writing essays want a cumulative final because there will be an essay on the cumulative final—and that Vera is a student who likes writing essays. That would change things. Now our argument is as follows:

> Eighty-five percent of college students who like writing essays want the cumulative final because it will have an essay.
>
> Vera Peterson is a college student who likes writing essays.
>
> So, Vera Peterson probably wants the cumulative final.

Now we have a strong argument that contradicts the conclusion of the original version of the argument. With our added information we have changed our reference class. The **reference class** is the group to which our statistics apply. As a rule, the more specific the reference class is, the better the argument is. In changing the reference class from "college students" to "college students who like writing essays," we found that our conclusion about Vera changed. Adding new information to an inductive argument can change its strength. In our case, changing reference classes called for a different conclusion.

Let's return to another familiar example:

> Fifty-five percent of Wexford students voted for Watkins as "Teacher of the Year."
>
> Eileen is a Wexford student.
>
> So, Eileen probably voted for Watkins.

Now let's add more information to arrive at a different argument:

> Eighty-nine percent of Wexford students who took Watkins's critical thinking course voted for Watkins as "Teacher of the Year."

Terminology Recap

A *strong argument* has premises that provide evidence that its conclusion is more likely true than false.

A *strong and reliable argument* has premises that provide evidence that its conclusion is more likely true than false, *and* it is an argument that a reasonable person *would* act or bet on.

A *strong but unreliable argument* has premises that provide evidence that its conclusion is more likely true than false, *but* it is an argument that a reasonable person *would not* act or bet on.

Eileen took Watkins's critical thinking course.

So, Eileen probably voted for Watkins as "Teacher of the Year."

We have changed our reference class, becoming more specific in the second argument. Now we are no longer talking simply about "Wexford students" but about "Wexford students who took Watkins's critical thinking course." The change in reference class in this case changes the argument (though the conclusion remains the same) from a moderately strong but unreliable one to a stronger and more reliable one.

We should also note that a statistical argument can be used to support a conclusion about a group rather than an individual. For example:

Ninety percent of college students are in favor of not having a cumulative final exam in their critical thinking class

So, ninety percent of Wexford College students are in favor of not having a cumulative final exam in their critical thinking class.

Notice that the conclusion does not necessarily follow from the premises. The premise concerns all college students, whereas the conclusion concerns a limited group of college students, those who attend Wexford. Wexford students in general could be very much like the population of college students as a whole, or they could be quite different in significant ways. As in other inductive arguments, the argument could be strengthened by softening the conclusion with the word "probably." The argument is strong, but it might be stronger if the reference class were more specific.

> *Statistics are like a bikini. What they reveal is suggestive, but what they conceal is vital.*
>
> —Aaron Levenstein

EXERCISE 11.4

I. Decide whether each of the following statistical arguments is (a) weak, (b) strong but unreliable, or (c) strong and reliable. Then rewrite each argument, changing the reference class to make weak arguments strong and strong arguments weak.

1. Only 5 percent of registered Republicans voted for the Democratic candidate in the last presidential election.
Larry is a registered Republican.
So, Larry probably did not vote for the Democratic candidate in the last presidential election.

2. Fifty-two percent of independent voters voted for the Republican candidate in the last presidential election.
Shane is an independent voter.
So, Shane probably voted for the Republican candidate in the last presidential election.

3. Thirty percent of senior biology majors at Wexford College applied to medical school last year.
Catherine was a senior biology major at Wexford College last year.
So, Catherine probably applied to medical school.

4. Ninety-five percent of people who lose weight on a diet gain most or all of it back within three years.
Ray lost fifty pounds on a diet five years ago.
So, Ray has probably gained most or all of the weight back by now.

5. Only 5 percent of the students in Watkins's critical thinking course receive a grade of D or F.
Sheila was a student in Watkins's critical thinking course.
So, Sheila probably received a D.

6. Forty-eight percent of graduating seniors at Wexford College have a grade point average of 2.9 or higher.
Dean is a graduating senior at Wexford.
So, Dean probably does not have a grade point average of 2.9 or higher.

7. Eighty-eight percent of freshmen at Wexford College return for their sophomore year.
Lindsey was a freshman at Wexford last year.
So, chances are that Lindsey is back for her sophomore year.

8. Only 5 percent of the population of Springfield is unemployed.
Barney lives in Springfield.
So, Barney is probably unemployed.

9. Forty-nine percent of marriages end in divorce.
Beth and Keith just got married.
So, Beth and Keith will probably end up getting divorced.

10. Less than 1 percent of female high school students try out for their high school football team.
Patty is a female high school student.
So, Patty probably did not try out for her high school football team.

II. Construct your own statistical arguments according to the following directions.

1. Give your own example of a strong statistical argument.
2. Give your own example of a strong but unreliable statistical argument.
3. Give your own example of a strong but unreliable statistical argument. Then change the reference class and give a stronger version of the argument.

4. Give your own example of a weak statistical argument. Then change the reference class and give a strong version of the argument.

5. Give your own example of a strong but unreliable statistical argument with a conclusion dealing with a group rather than an individual. Then change the reference class and give a stronger version of the argument.

INDUCTION AND ANALOGY
What Is an Analogy?

Up is to down as right is to ?

Understanding analogies and arguments that use analogies is essential to critical thinking. Analogies are not just the stuff of nightmares and entrance exams; they have a useful purpose. As you probably knew right away, the word "left" is the correct answer to the analogy question above. Why? Because the relationship is one of opposites. Up is the opposite of down, and right is the opposite of left.

An **analogy** is a comparison of things based on similarities those things share. Analogies, then, depend on what is similar or the same in two or more cases. Analogies are everywhere: on exams, in arguments, in newspapers, in poems and songs. In literature in general, and poetry in particular, analogies are common. Similes, which are comparisons using *like* or *as*, are actually a type of analogy. In literature, similes can be quite moving even though they might not stand up well to critical analysis. For example, when a poet says, "My love is like the sun," the comparison is a limited one. The poet may simply want to stress the beauty, warmth, and centrality of his beloved by comparing her to something else that is beautiful, warm, and central. The analogy stops there, however. The poet's love does not dwell in the sky or give off radiation, and so on. Most often, poets intend these analogies to make us look at things differently, not to pass muster in a critical thinking textbook.

How Can We Argue by Analogy?

Although analogies are interesting and important for many reasons, including their use in poetry, we shall focus on one: their importance in constructing inductive arguments. Arguments from analogy depend upon an analogy or a similarity between two or more things. Analogies compare two or more things; arguments from analogy go one step further. They often claim that another similarity exists, given the similarities already recognized. Whereas analogies simply point out a similarity, arguments from analogy claim that certain similarities are evidence that there is another similarity (or other similarities).[5]

Let's look at an example:

The Post Office is a government agency.

The Department of Motor Vehicles is a government agency.

The Post Office is closed for Martin Luther King, Jr., Day.

So, the Department of Motor Vehicles must be closed for Martin Luther King, Jr., Day.

Our example first notes a similarity between the Post Office and the Department of Motor Vehicles. Then it states something additional about the Post Office. Last, it claims that the same thing is true of the Department of Motor Vehicles.

Our example, in fact, is a general form of an argument from analogy. Rather than speak about specific examples, we can give the general form of arguments from analogy by using letters as symbols.

A has characteristic X.

B has characteristic X.

A has characteristic Y.

Therefore, B has characteristic Y.

That is the basic form, though we can expand it to include even more details. For example:

The Post Office and the Department of Motor Vehicles are both government agencies, and both were closed on Veterans Day.

The Post Office is closed for Martin Luther King, Jr., Day.

So the Department of Motor Vehicles must be closed for Martin Luther King, Jr., Day.

This is also an argument from analogy, but this version of the argument includes one additional detail, that both the Post Office and the Department of Motor Vehicles were closed on Veterans Day. Now the form just reflects the additional detail:

> A has characteristics X and Y.
>
> B has characteristics X and Y.
>
> A has characteristic Z.
>
> Therefore, B has characteristic Z.

We could continue to add details represented by variables, but the basic form of the arguments from analogy would remain the same.

Evaluating Arguments from Analogy

Critical thinking involves more than just recognizing arguments from analogy; it also involves evaluating those arguments. All analogies break down . . . eventually. They wouldn't be analogies otherwise, since we make analogies only between things that are similar but not the same. If you claim, "A squirrel is just like a squirrel!" people will look at you funny. On the other hand, people may disagree, but they will want to know more, if you claim, "Squirrels, which are like suburban rats, should be exterminated."

In other words, there are good and bad analogies, and there are also good and bad arguments from analogy. Sometimes the points of similarity warrant a certain conclusion and sometimes they don't. Most arguments from analogy are inductive arguments, so they are neither valid nor invalid. Rather, they are either strong or weak. Whereas there are cut-and-dried ways to test whether a deductive argument is valid or invalid, there are no such direct methods for determining whether inductive arguments are strong or weak. There are, though, some good questions to ask to help determine whether a particular argument from analogy is a strong or weak inductive argument. Consider the statement "Squirrels, which are like suburban rats, should be exterminated." There must be some reason that you claimed this. Let's suppose that it is the conclusion of the following argument:

> Squirrels and rats are rodents of similar size and appearance.
>
> Rats cause problems in the city, and squirrels cause problems in the suburbs.
>
> Rats should be exterminated.
>
> So, squirrels should be exterminated.

Is that a good argument?

EXERCISE 11.5

Before we go further in discussing how to determine whether an argument from analogy is a good one, test your logical instincts. Decide whether you think the preceding argument is a good argument by deciding whether the analogy is a good one. Don't focus on whether or not you agree with the conclusion. Just focus on how well or how poorly the premises support the conclusion.

Evaluating arguments from analogy is not totally new to you. Probably, you have done it for years without realizing it. In Chapter 6 you looked at arguments from analogy in a more formal way in the discussion of logical fallacies. Remember the *fallacy of weak analogy*? It's the fallacy that results from comparing two (or more) things that aren't really comparable. It is a matter of claiming that two things share a certain similarity on the basis of other similarities, while overlooking important dissimilarities. For example:

> Tiffany and Heather are both tall and play basketball.
>
> Tiffany also plays volleyball.
>
> So, Heather must also play volleyball.

Not necessarily, right? Clearly, we have come to recognize this kind of argument as a fallacy, but where exactly does the reasoning go wrong? Let's return to this example after we look at what to consider in evaluating an argument from analogy.

The first thing we want in an argument from analogy is what we want in all arguments, whether they are inductive or deductive: *true premises*. Remember: Garbage in, garbage out! In our example, if Tiffany and Heather are not both tall or don't both play basketball, the argument is doomed from the start. So, we must always ask if our premises are true. Assuming that the premises are true, at least as far as we can tell, we must move on to consider other things.

The second thing we must consider is the *relevance of the similarities*. In the case of Heather and Tiffany, the similarities are relevant because they make a difference to whether the conclusion is likely to be true. Both women are tall, and height is an advantage in volleyball. They both play basketball, and this shows they each have some interest in an athletic activity in which height is an advantage. Still, the similarities are not overwhelming. Some other similarities would not be relevant at all. For example, they are both women and have seven letters in their names. These similarities are irrelevant, meaning that they make no difference to whether the conclusion is true. There is no causal or statistical connection between one's sex or the number of letters in one's name and one's athletic ability or interest. By contrast, a truly relevant similarity might be that they both play basketball for a coach who insists that his players also play volleyball. Another might be that they are best friends who rarely do anything without each other; or that they are sisters whose mother insists that they play every sport they possibly can.

The third thing to consider is the *number of relevant similarities*. In our example, there are only two relevant similarities between Tiffany and Heather: they are tall and they play basketball. If additional relevant similarities could be noted, the strength of the argument would increase. For example, if it was noted that they are best friends, rarely do anything apart, have a coach who insists that his basketball players also play volleyball, and attend a college that gives scholarships only to athletes who play more than one sport, the argument would certainly be stronger, because these similarities are directly related to Heather's being a volleyball player.

A potential pitfall for all inductive arguments, including arguments from analogy, is "the unknown." No information, no premise, can ever be added to a valid deductive argument to make it invalid. By contrast, information, premises, can be added to a strong inductive argument to make it weak. With regard to arguments from analogy, one important *unknown* or neglected area of information can be relevant differences or dissimilarities. We need to consider both the *relevance and the number of dissimilarities*.

Not all differences or dissimilarities are important or relevant. For example, Tiffany may have blonde hair and Heather may have black hair; Tiffany may be studying philosophy and Heather may be studying accounting; Tiffany may be left-handed and Heather may be right-handed. None of these dissimilarities is relevant in arguing that Heather, like Tiffany, plays volleyball. However, there are possible dissimilarities that would weaken the argument. For example, Heather may have to work at a part-time job, whereas Tiffany may not; Heather may have a medical condition that limits her physical activity, and Tiffany may not; or Heather may not like volleyball, whereas Tiffany thinks it's great. All these dissimilarities are relevant to the argument, some perhaps more than others. If any of these dissimilarities were actually true, the argument would be weaker. If more than one were true it would be even weaker; if all were true, it would be weaker still.

In the example we have been discussing, there is a sample of only two, Tiffany and Heather. A larger sample would strengthen the argument, just as increasing the number of similarities increases the strength of the argument. Consider the following increase in the size of the sample of our original argument:

> Tiffany, Heather, Amber, and Krissy are all tall and play basketball.
>
> Tiffany, Amber, and Krissy also play volleyball.
>
> So, Heather must also play volleyball.

This argument, with its increased sample size, is stronger than the original argument.

Still, there is another potential pitfall resulting from "the unknown." This pitfall has to do with diversity in the sample. In the original argument, we were concerned with the similarities between just two people, Tiffany and Heather. What happens when we increase the size of the sample? *With increased sample size, diversity becomes a mark of strength.* If Tiffany, Amber, and Krissy were a diverse group in many ways, the argument would be strengthened. If these three had nothing much in common aside from being tall and playing both basketball and volleyball, there would be greater support for the conclusion that Heather must also play volleyball. If these three were very much alike in other ways—for example, all being A students and coming from the same high school, whereas Heather is a C student who comes from a different high school—the argument would be weakened.

Let's look at another example to highlight the importance of diversity with increased sample size.

> Jason's German car was a lemon and so was Fred's.
>
> So, Dirk's German car is probably a lemon, too.

If Fred and Jason both owned Volkswagens and Dirk owned a BMW, the argument is very weak. If Jason owned a Volkswagen and Fred owned a BMW, the argument is stronger (though still weak), because we have a slightly better case and more evidence for our claim about Dirk's German car.

If we increase the sample size, the importance of diversity becomes all the more apparent.

> Jason's German car was a lemon and so was Fred's, Joe's, Roy's, and Bob's.
>
> So, Dirk's German car is probably a lemon.

If they all owned Volkswagens, the argument is very weak. If Jason owned a Volkswagen, Fred owned a BMW, Roy owned a Mercedes, and Bob owned a Porsche, the argument would be stronger (though still perhaps weak, since the number of individual cars is still small). The argument would be stronger because the diversity of German cars in the sample makes the claim about a particular German car more likely.

A final consideration in evaluating the strength of an argument from analogy is the *specificity of the conclusion relative to the premises.* That is, we don't want to claim too much. The broader and less specific the conclusion is, the stronger the argument is. In our volleyball example, the conclusion, "Heather must also play volleyball," is narrow and specific, particularly considering the evidence offered by the premises. We could increase the strength of the argument by instead concluding, "Heather must have played a game of volleyball at some time," or "Heather may also play volleyball," or, even better, "Heather may have played a game of volleyball at some time."

To sum up, consider these things in evaluating the strength of an argument from analogy:

1. The truth of the premises
2. The relevance of the similarities
3. The number of relevant similarities
4. The relevance of dissimilarities
5. The number of relevant dissimilarities
6. The diversity of the sample, especially with increased sample size
7. The specificity of the conclusion relative to the premises

EXERCISE 11.6

Consider each of the following arguments from analogy. For the purposes of this exercise, assume that all the information is true. In each case, rank the argument along a continuum from weak to strong. Use numbers from 1 to 10 for your ranking, with 1 being extremely weak and 10 being extremely strong. Be prepared to justify your rankings.

1. If you can learn to hit a baseball, you can learn to speak a foreign language fluently. They both take practice.
2. Life is just like chess. It's a complicated game, but you can win if you learn the rules and cheat a little.
3. Taking care of your body is like taking care of your car. Preventive maintenance and a yearly inspection are required.
4. My father did an excellent job of balancing the family budget, so they should let him try to balance the city budget.
5. My brother changed the oil in my Chevy, so he can probably change the oil in your Ford.
6. My brother changed the oil in my Chevy, so he can probably change the brakes on your BMW.
7. Michael Jordan is a gifted athlete and a great basketball player who is interested in tennis. So, with a lot of practice, he could probably play tennis fairly well.
8. You like lobster and other seafood, and king crab legs taste like lobster. So, you would probably like king crab legs.
9. When car dealers charge a lot of money for an automobile, people often assume it must be of higher quality than less expensive models. So, if Wexford College raises its tuition, people will think it's a better school.
10. In "real life" Jerry Seinfeld must be just like the character Jerry Seinfeld on the show *Seinfeld*. After all, the character is based on the person and they have the same name. (Think carefully about this one.)

Common Areas of Argument from Analogy

Arguments from analogy are found in many areas of study and have numerous practical applications. Let's briefly consider two, law and ethics. American law has its roots in English common law, so legal decisions are often made on the basis of precedent. That is to say, a judge may often support a current decision by appealing to a decision made in a similar case at an earlier date. For example, in deciding whether or not the free speech guaranteed by the First Amendment applies to cyberspace communications, a judge would be expected to appeal to earlier and analogous free speech cases. Of course, in deciding whether an earlier case is truly analogous, we apply our criteria for evaluation. Are there a good number of relevant similarities? Are there few, if any, relevant dissimilarities? Is the conclusion of the judicial ruling properly specific?

Arguments from analogy are particularly effective in matters of ethics. On the most basic level, the Golden Rule instructs, "Do unto others as you would have others do unto you." In a sense, the message is that you should treat others in a way analogous to the way you would like to be treated. A more involved strategy in moral reasoning is to argue that a controversial issue is analogous to one that is not controversial. Capital punishment is certainly a controversial moral issue. Someone who is against capital punishment might argue that it is about as moral, and about as effective, to put murderers to death as it is to beat a child who hits his sister. In her article "A Defense of Abortion," Judith Jarvis Thomson argues from analogy in favor of the morality of abortion. Using a creative scenario, Thomson argues that a person would have no moral obligation to stay connected to a famous violinist who was linked to her kidneys without her knowledge or consent. She then argues by analogy that a woman similarly has no moral duty to carry her pregnancy to term. There are some similarities here. Neither the pregnant woman nor the woman hooked to the violinist may have wanted to be in their respective situations. In fact, they may have done everything to prevent it. Both have someone of great potential dependent upon them. There are also dissimilarities. The question is, How relevant are they? Does the analogy work? If we accept that the woman involuntarily linked to the violinist has no moral obligation to continue that way, does it follow by analogy that a pregnant woman has no moral obligation to continue her pregnancy?

EXERCISE 11.7

1. Read Judith Jarvis Thomson's article "A Defense of Abortion" in *Philosophy and Public Affairs* 1 (1971), pp. 47–66. Evaluate the argument from analogy that she offers. Is it weak, strong, or somewhere in between? Be prepared to give reasons in support of your evaluation.

2. The First Amendment to the United States Constitution says: "Congress shall make no law respecting an establishment of religion, or prohibiting the free exercise thereof; or abridging the freedom of speech, or of the press; or the right of the people peaceably to assemble, and to petition the Government for a redress of grievances." Construct an argument from analogy either for or against free speech in cyberspace on the basis of the First Amendment. Does your argument apply to pornography? Does it apply to "hate speech"?

3. Construct your own argument from analogy for or against the death penalty.

EXERCISE 11.8

I. Consider the following arguments from analogy. In each case, decide whether the argument is weak or strong. If the argument is weak, what makes it weak? Are there any ways to add to, or otherwise change, the argument to make it stronger?

1. An umpire won't give you first base for swinging hard in baseball. So, a teacher shouldn't give you a passing grade just for trying hard.
2. Animals are like human beings. They feel pain and pleasure and are part of the same chain of evolution. It is wrong to eat human beings, so it must be wrong to eat animals.
3. Flag burning is, or can be, a form of political protest. Verbal political protest is protected and allowed as free speech. Free speech can be nonverbal, as is the case with dance. So, flag burning, as a nonverbal form of political protest, should be allowed and protected as free speech.
4. A man who carries a fat wallet in his back pocket while strolling through a tough neighborhood at night should not be surprised if he is robbed. So, a woman who wears tight and revealing clothes in a bar filled with men should not be surprised if she is raped.

II. Read each of the following arguments from analogy. Each is followed by four additional pieces of information. In each case, decide which of the individual pieces of information if added would strengthen the argument and which if added would weaken the argument.

1. Luke and Frank are both students at Jefferson High School in a rural area of Indiana. Luke and Frank each live on their families' farms. Luke plans to work full-time on the family farm after graduation and has no plans to go to college. So, Frank probably has no plans to go to college, either.

   Consider whether each of the following would strengthen or weaken the argument:
   a. Both Luke and Frank have no close relatives who have gone to college.
   b. Neither Luke nor Frank has ever traveled outside his home state.
   c. Luke is a C student, but Frank is an A student.
   d. Luke does not like farming, but Frank does.

2. Lisa and Lauren are identical twins who were separated at birth. Lisa has been in trouble with the law most of her life. So, it's a good bet that Lauren has been in trouble with the law most of her life.

   Consider whether each of the following would strengthen or weaken the argument:
   a. Lisa and Lauren were both shuffled from one foster home to another for the first eighteen years of their lives.
   b. Lisa was adopted and raised by a family in which the parents later divorced. Lauren was adopted and raised by a distant relative whose family unit stayed together.
   c. Lisa and Lauren have each sought help for substance abuse.

    d. Lisa went to elite private schools, whereas Lauren went to public schools.

3. Spartansville and Loyalton are both small cities in the northeastern part of the United States with populations under one hundred thousand people. Spartansville has a museum. So there's a good chance that Loyalton has a museum.

    Consider whether each of the following would strengthen or weaken the argument:

    a. Spartansville is home to a major university, whereas Loyalton is not.

    b. Both cities have a symphony orchestra.

    c. Loyalton is having difficulty in obtaining funding for its libraries.

    d. Spartansville and Loyalton compete for tourists.

4. Al and Dave are both unemployed steelworkers. Al has given up looking for work. So, Dave has probably given up looking for work.

    Consider whether each of the following would strengthen or weaken the argument:

    a. Al and Dave are the same age.

    b. Al has no family to support, whereas Dave has a sick wife and three children.

    c. Al recently won the lottery.

    d. Al and Dave are both union members.

5. Capital City and Metropolis are both cities of two million people located in the southern United States. Capital City has a terrible crime problem. So, it's a good bet that Metropolis has a terrible crime problem, too.

    Consider whether each of the following would strengthen or weaken the argument:

    a. Both cities have high rates of unemployment.

    b. Capital City is known as the center of the drug trade in the South.

    c. Metropolis has a tough police commissioner and a well-respected police force.

    d. Neither city has affordable public housing.

Arguing by Analogy

So far, we have been looking at how to evaluate arguments from analogy, but we should also consider how to construct arguments from analogy. As you might expect, the criteria for constructing a good argument from analogy are the same as those for evaluating an argument from analogy. A strong argument from analogy can be very effective. People like comparisons, particularly when the comparison relates something difficult or foreign to something they consider easy or familiar. Still, not every position can be defended by an argument from analogy. Offering a weak argument from analogy will do more harm than good.

    Here's an example: If Parker wanted to explain to a group of students why they should study critical thinking, he might argue his point by using an analogy to karate. There are many ways in which learning karate and learning critical thinking are similar. They both require patience and discipline but result in greater confidence and increased self-esteem. They are both used for defense and offense. With karate you can defend yourself against attack and you can attack others (though you should do so only when appropriate). With critical thinking you can defend your positions against the attacks of those who hold other positions and you can attack the positions of others (though you should do so only when appropriate) or put forward a new position. Learning karate builds on your native abilities but is hard work. You may not always understand the reasons for everything involved in the training, even though it pays off in the end. In a similar way, learning critical thinking builds on your native abilities but is hard work. You may not always understand the reasons for everything involved in the training—the concepts, the terminology, the exercises, and so on. Most serious students of karate agree that there is much to gain and that your effort will be rewarded if you study karate. Therefore, if you are serious about studying critical thinking, you will find that there is much to gain and that your effort will be rewarded.

Here is the argument in more standard form:

> There are important similarities between learning karate and learning critical thinking. They both require patience and discipline and result in increased confidence and self-esteem. They both build on native abilities but involve hard work, which you may not always immediately see the point of. They are both of use for offense and defense.

> Most serious students of karate agree that there is much to gain and your effort will be rewarded if you study karate.

> Therefore, if you are serious about studying critical thinking you will find that there is much to gain and your effort will be rewarded.

Is this a good argument from analogy? Let's see if it meets the criteria we have established. Are the premises true? Yes. Are the similarities relevant? Yes. Just consider the difficulties involved in learning the skills of both critical thinking and karate, and the parallels in the way they are used for defense and offense. There are also a good number of similarities, not merely one or two. How about dissimilarities? Well, karate is a physical activity used for physical defense and offense, whereas critical thinking is an intellectual activity. That is a big difference, but it is not relevant to the point we are making. Another difference is that learning karate can actually be good for your cardiovascular system, whereas we cannot say the same thing about learning critical thinking. What about the specificity of the conclusion with regard to the premises? Does it claim too much? "If you are serious about studying critical thinking, you will find that there is much to gain and your effort will be rewarded." The conclusion is not overly specific nor does it claim too much. In fact, it is somewhat vague, though not to the point of being a fault. It only claims that *if* you are *serious* about studying critical thinking, your effort will be *rewarded*. In other words, if you expend a good deal of effort in studying critical thinking, you will find that there is some payback. This is, then, a good argument from analogy.

EXERCISE 11.9

Construct your own argument from analogy for each of the following. Decide and explain whether it is a good or bad argument.

1. Argue that Bob would be a good mayor of his small town because he is a good employer.
2. Argue that Mr. Sanders would be a good health teacher because he is a good football coach.
3. Argue that Jezebel would be a good actress because she lives a life based on lies and deceit.
4. Argue that Warren Beatty would be a good president because he is a good actor.
5. Argue that Sam would be a bad police officer because he was a bad marine.

INDUCTION AND CAUSAL ARGUMENTS

Human beings are a curious life form. Our very nature drives us to search for knowledge. One of the most basic, most common, and most important kinds of knowledge we seek is knowledge of **cause and effect**. Why didn't my alarm clock go off when it was supposed to? Why is there no hot water left for my shower? We tend to look for causal connections when we are surprised (pleasantly or unpleasantly) by what occurs. We want to know the cause of what happened. In the absence of a good account, we will often accept a bad one — as in the case of superstition and mythology. By contrast, cats don't care about cause and effect. If a ball rolls by a cat, she'll chase after it if she's in the mood, but she'll never look to see where it came from. On the other hand, if a ball unexpectedly rolled by you, you'd first look to see where it came from.[6]

Roughly speaking, a *cause* is that which brings about a change, that which produces an effect. The relationship of cause and effect doesn't come into play only when we're surprised by something, though. We count on it all the time without realizing it. For example, you may rarely think much about the law of gravity, the law that tells us there is a cause-and-effect relationship making heavy objects fall to the ground. Something might have to unexpectedly float upward to get you thinking about gravity. You may count on your car starting up every morning. But how often do you think about all the cause-and-effect relationships involved in that occurring?

Our focus here will be on inductive arguments that try to identify a cause-and-effect relationship. This kind of argument is notoriously difficult. When we search for the cause of a certain effect, we are looking to identify a certain relationship between two things or events. What is that relationship, though? Certainly the cause has to come before the effect, but, as we learned in Chapter 6 with the fallacy of questionable cause, not every event that comes

before another causes the other. To a certain extent, that is just common sense; yet, it is surprising how prone we are to commit the fallacy anyway. One piece of supporting evidence for a cause-and-effect relationship between two things or events is that one thing regularly comes before the other. For example, every time you let go of your coffee mug, the coffee mug falls to the floor. So, you assume there is a cause-and-effect relationship at work between the release of the heavy object and its falling to the ground. To take another example, one that the philosopher David Hume was fond of, every time you have seen one billiard ball strike another, it has caused the other to move. So, you assume there is a cause-and-effect relationship there. You have witnessed the same pairing of events over and over again—it is no mere coincidence. But, Hume asks us, when you think about it, what have you really witnessed? Just the pairing of two events, one billiard ball striking the other and then the other billiard ball moving. You have witnessed what Hume called "constant conjunction." The two events always happen one before the other—they are "constantly conjoined." You never really see any separate things that you could call "cause" and "effect." You never see "necessary connection" or "causal power."

We don't have to fully agree with Hume to get his point; it is tough to be certain about the cause-and-effect relationships you take for granted. They could simply be the result of coincidence. To make this same point, the philosopher Bertrand Russell asks you to consider yourself in the position of a chicken on a farm. Every day that you can remember, the farmer's wife has approached you and then fed you. You have come to associate the two in terms of cause and effect (even though chickens don't really think this way). But then comes the day when the farmer's wife approaches you and doesn't feed you. Instead, she wrings your neck. The moral of the story is that we need to be careful in assuming a cause-and-effect relationship between two things.

THE FAR SIDE   By GARY LARSON

© 1983 FarWorks, Inc. All Rights Reserved

FREEZER

THE FAR SIDE © Farworks, Inc. All rights reserved.

While Farmer Brown was away, the cows got into the kitchen and were having the time of their lives — until Betsy's unwitting discovery.

As we saw, Hume introduced the issue of trying to understand the relationship of cause and effect. That's a tough issue to settle, and, thankfully, it is not our concern to settle it here. Instead, we want to look at arguments about particular relationships of cause and effect and learn how to evaluate them. As it turns out, it is easier to show that something *couldn't be* the cause of a certain effect than it is to prove what *is* the cause.

Let's take a look at arguments of cause and effect. We should note that not all causal arguments contain the word "cause." Other causal terms include *produce, is responsible for, affects, makes, changes,* and *contributes to.* Such arguments come in two broad types: arguments about the cause of a single instance, and arguments about a general relationship.

Here's an example of an argument about a single instance:

Megan's car wouldn't start this morning and she hasn't replaced the battery since she bought the car six years ago.

So, it is probably a dead battery that caused the car not to start.

Here's an example of an argument about a general relationship:

> The Surgeon General has found that there is a strong link between smoking cigarettes and getting lung cancer.
>
> So, smoking cigarettes causes lung cancer.

In each case, it should be clear that the argument is inductive. The premise provides evidence (strong evidence) for the conclusion. The conclusion does not follow with strict necessity from the premises. It is always at least possible that the premises are true and the conclusion is false. Given what the argument says, it is at least possible that the car's alternator is shot and the battery is fine. Of course, there would be ways to investigate the matter further, but the argument, as it stands, does not do so. Given only what the second argument says, there is no guarantee that smoking is the cause of lung cancer. Two things can be linked without one causing the other.

There is a very practical reason why most causal arguments are inductive. It is very difficult to take every conceivable possibility into account when attempting to form an argument concerning cause and effect. Still, some causal arguments are intended to be deductive. Here is one that we mentioned in Chapter 3:

> Whenever iron is exposed to oxygen, it rusts.
>
> This iron pipe has been exposed to oxygen.
>
> Therefore, it will rust.

Certain relationships of cause and effect have been well established. Not only has iron exposed to oxygen rusted repeatedly, but also there is sound scientific understanding of why this occurs. Aside from Hume's skeptical concerns about observing cause and effect, this is a very well established causal relationship.

Let's consider arguments about general causal relationships. When speaking about causality in a population, we usually mean that X causes a higher rate of Y in the population. We do not usually mean that every individual who uses X will get Y. Consider, for example, the argument that smoking cigarettes causes cancer. This does not mean, or intend to claim, that everyone who smokes will get cancer. Rather, it means that smoking cigarettes results in a higher rate of cancer in people who smoke as opposed to people who don't smoke. Some people who do not smoke do get cancer. And some rare individuals may smoke cigarettes every day until they die at one hundred years old without ever getting cancer.

As is the case with all arguments, deductive and inductive, we need true premises for our causal arguments to be of any value. In arguing for a cause-and-effect relationship, we should base our premises on careful observation. *Selective attention and memory* can be problems here. That is, focusing attention on, or recalling from memory, only certain examples distorts our sample. Consider the following example:

> Every time we have a full moon, people behave strangely.
>
> So, the full moon must cause the strange behavior.

How might a person be mistaken in this conclusion as a result of selective attention or memory? It could be that he is very alert for any signs of strange behavior every time the moon is full and is quick to interpret behavior as "strange" at those times. But if he thought about it more carefully, he would recall that there were many times that the moon was full and yet he observed no one behaving strangely. Thinking about it some more, he may realize that he has witnessed just as much strange behavior on nights when the moon was not full.

Another danger in forming premises for causal arguments is relying on anecdotal evidence—that is, what others tell us. As we just saw, sometimes we cannot trust our own observations as a result of selective attention or memory. This is all the more true when it comes to the observations of others. Others are also subject to misreporting observations on the basis of their own selective attention or memory. Others may also have reasons to distort the truth. They may have something to gain by deceiving us. As a general rule, we need to be careful and critical when basing causal arguments on the anecdotal evidence of others.

Of course, we must admit that we cannot observe everything for ourselves. Thankfully, though, there are experts who investigate the causal connections between things the rest of us do not have the time, money, or expertise to explore. Scientists, for example, make use of experimental and control groups for determining causality. To see if chemical X prevents disease Y, a scientist gives chemical X to group one—the *experimental group*—and does not give chemical X to group two—the *control group*. By keeping all conditions except the intake of chemical X the same for the two groups, the scientist can isolate the effects caused by chemical X. It is common for such experiments to initially be done on laboratory animals. Human subjects complicate the matter, because a human subject who believes that the drug she is given will prevent or cure her disease will actually have a better chance of prevention or cure. This is known as the *placebo effect*. A placebo is a pill that does not contain any actual drug (or active ingredient). Often, it is just a sugar pill. With human subjects, then, the experimental group is given the actual drug and the control group is given a placebo. To ensure that the results are not compromised, the study should be *double-blind*. In a double-blind study, neither the subjects nor the experimenters know who is receiving the treatment and who is receiving the placebo until the experiment is finished.

Correlation and Cause

Sometimes, two things or events are clearly "associated" or "linked." Where you find X, you will often find Y. A relationship such as this, in which two things are frequently, or even constantly, found together, is called **correlation**. In a correlation, two things share a mutual relationship; where one is found, the other is often, or always, found. By contrast, in the relationship of causation, one thing *produces* or brings about the other. Sometimes, a correlation is an indicator of a cause-and-effect relationship. For example, the high rate of lung cancer deaths among smokers led to the investigation and discovery of a causal link between them. We must be careful, though. Most correlations do not indicate a causal relationship between the two things or events correlated. For example, there is a strong correlation between shoe size and average ability in math among children. The higher the shoe size, the greater the average ability in math. For example, on average, children who wear a size 8 shoe score higher on the same exam than those who wear a size 6 shoe. Does this imply that having large feet causes an increase in mathematical ability? Or does it suggest that mathematical ability causes feet to grow? Of course not. There is an underlying explanation for this phenomenon. A child's age is correlated with both shoe size and mathematical ability. As a child grows older, both shoe size and mathematical ability tend to increase, but neither one causes the other.

Maybe the previous example was obvious, but there are correlations that are more easily and more convincingly mistaken as cause and effect. In fact, one of the biggest problems with popular news reports is their tendency to make a new study sound as if it proves a cause-and-effect relationship between two things when all the study actually does is report a significant correlation. To critically evaluate such reports, we must grasp the nature of correlation.

The correlation of two things or events, their mutual presence or absence, can be positive or negative. If the two things are found together to exactly the same extent as they are found apart, there is no correlation. A positive correlation, one which indicates that two things are found together more than 50 percent of the time, *may* indicate a causal connection between one thing and the other. A negative correlation, one which indicates that two things are found together less than 50 percent of the time, *may* indicate that one thing prevents the other. The important question, though, is this: Is the correlation significant? The answer will depend, in part, on the size of the sample.

The sample must be large enough to put our observations within an acceptable margin of error. For example, suppose we notice that of three people we know who took vitamin C all winter long, two never became sick. That is a strong correlation, nearly 67 percent, between taking vitamin C and remaining healthy through the winter. But our sample, of just three people, is much too small for the correlation to be significant. If we did a controlled study using 2,000 subjects and found that 67 percent of those who took vitamin C remained healthy through the winter, we might have a significant correlation. We would have to compare it with the correlation between not taking vitamin C and remaining healthy through the winter. If we found that 66 percent of those who did not take vitamin C remained healthy through the winter, then our correlation would no longer be useful as evidence for establishing cause and effect. Nearly the same percentage of people remained healthy without vitamin C.

Let's suppose, however, that our study revealed that only 52 percent of those who did not take vitamin C remained healthy through the winter. Then the correlation of 67 percent would be good evidence to support the claim

Summary of Key Points on Cause and Correlation

1. It is easier to show that something couldn't be the cause of a certain effect than it is to prove what is the cause.
2. Not all causal arguments contain the word "cause."
3. When speaking about causality in an entire population, we usually mean that X results in a higher rate of Y in the population, not that every individual who uses X will get Y.
4. When we are speaking of a cause, we do not always mean to suggest that is a necessary or a sufficient condition for bringing about the effect.
5. Sometimes, two things or events are clearly "associated" or "linked." Where you find X, you will often or always find Y. A mutual relationship such as this, in which two things are frequently or invariably found together, is called *correlation*.
6. Sometimes, but not always, a correlation is a sign of a cause-and-effect relationship.
7. The correlation of two things or events, their mutual presence or absence, can be positive or negative. Or, if they are found together to exactly the same extent as they are found apart, there is no correlation.
8. *Is the correlation significant?* The answer will depend, in part, on the size of the sample.
9. Correlation can always be a result of mere coincidence, and most of the time it is.

that vitamin C prevents illness. If the study was not properly controlled, this would not in itself, no matter how large and representative the sample, be conclusive evidence of a cause-and-effect relationship. Why? Because something else might be independently correlated with both the vitamin C intake and the good health. For example, the correlation between health and vitamin C intake could be the result of each being further correlated with proper rest. Perhaps proper rest promotes health and prevents illness, and people who get proper rest tend to do other things they think might promote health and prevent illness, such as taking vitamin C.

We must always be on our guard against arguments that base their conclusions about cause and effect on correlations. Correlation can always be a result of mere coincidence, and most of the time it is. When a correlation is not absolute, neither 0 percent nor 100 percent, we should be suspicious. The discovery of a significant correlation can be the beginning of an investigation, but it should never be the end of one, particularly when arguing about cause and effect.

EXERCISE 11.10

I. Examine the following claims. In each case, decide whether what is being reported is good or bad evidence for a cause-and-effect relationship.

1. Most people who are over the age of seventy do not feel comfortable with computers.

2. All ten of the people who ate the fish at the buffet were sick the next day.
3. Most National Hockey League Players are Caucasians.
4. Eighty percent of students who studied more than ten hours for the exam earned a grade of B or higher, whereas only 5 percent of students who studied less than 10 hours for the exam earned a grade of B or higher.
5. Most people who quit smoking report at least some weight gain.
6. All fifty-two Republicans in the Senate voted for the new bill.
7. Ninety-three out of one hundred people who cut down their calorie intake and exercised more lost weight.
8. All twelve of the students who went on the camping trip came back with a cold.
9. All fourteen players on the basketball team are over six feet tall.
10. None of the twenty experimental subjects who took the new flu shot caught the flu all season.

II. For each example, decide what questions you would ask and what additional information, if any, you would need to tell if there is a cause-and-effect relationship, a correlation, or no relationship.

1. Gomez became violently ill after eating the fish he caught under the Pierce Street Bridge.
2. Whenever the space shuttle is launched in Florida, we have nasty weather in Pennsylvania.
3. Chewing tobacco causes mouth cancer.
4. Silicon breast implants cause connective tissue disease.
5. People who drink vegetable juice every day never seem to get sick.
6. More acts of violence are committed by children who watch professional wrestling than by children who do not watch professional wrestling.
7. People who sit in the front row tend to get higher-than-average grades.
8. Minimizing salt in your diet can bring down high blood pressure.
9. Dioxin in the soil leads to cancer in the population.
10. Drinking two glasses of red wine per day will give you a healthier heart.

A Few Words about Probability

Why should we discuss probability in a chapter on inductive reasoning? The answer is that there is an important connection between probability and induction. All inductive arguments are a matter of probability because they are not certain. They do not guarantee the truth of their conclusions but only offer evidence that the conclusion is probably true.

> *Almost all human life depends on probabilities.*
> —Voltaire

We need to be clear about what we mean by probability because there are several different senses of the word. Consider these three examples.

There is a pretty high probability that I'll go to the beach some time this summer.

There is a 90 percent probability that the operation will be successful.

There is a 50 percent probability of getting tails on a fair coin toss.

The first example, "There is a pretty high probability that I'll go to the beach sometime this summer," illustrates **epistemic probability**. Epistemic probability expresses how likely we think an event is given other things we believe. This is the kind of probability we assign to statements we believe but to which we cannot assign a probability on any truly mathematical basis. Knowing that I want to go to the beach some time this summer and believing with good reason that I'll have time to do so, I can rationally assert that there is a high probability that I will indeed go to the beach. Along the same lines, we can also assign low probabilities to certain events. For example, "Considering the way Sid and Nancy were arguing last night, I'd say there's a pretty low probability that they will get married."

The second example, "There is a 90 percent probability that the operation will be successful," illustrates **relative frequency probability**. This kind of probability takes information about a group as a whole and applies it to an individual case. The application is based on accumulated data, derived from what has already been observed in the group. In this sense it is related to the statistical arguments we discussed earlier in this chapter. For example, a surgeon may inform her patient that ninety out of one hundred of her patients who had this surgery found it improved their condition. Of course, it is always possible to improve the accuracy of a prediction based on relative frequency probability by increasing the size of the sample or by being more specific about the group to which it applies. Perhaps the surgery has a 90 percent success rate with patients in general, but a 98 percent success rate for patients under thirty-five and only an 81 percent success rate for patients over eighty. What is the probability of an infant's surviving the first year of life? Over 99 percent in the United States in general, but less than that in some inner city areas. It is greater than 99 percent for infants with no apparent problems at birth, and far less than 99 percent for infants with certain kinds of congenital birth defects.

The third example, "There is a 50 percent probability of getting tails on a fair coin toss," illustrates **a priori probability**. Statements of a priori probability have odds that can be calculated previous to, and independent of, sensory observation. Even if I have never seen a coin before, you can explain the nature of the coin toss and I will be able to tell you that the probability of the coin coming up tails is 50 percent, and that the probability of its coming up heads is likewise 50 percent. The same would be true of a deck of cards. Even if I have never seen one, you can explain to me that there is a total of fifty-two cards with thirteen different values and four different suits. I can then tell you that the chances of any one particular card's being drawn are 1 in 52, or 1.92 percent. The chances of an ace's being drawn are 4 in 52, or 1 in 13, or 7.7 percent.

Probabilities direct the conduct of the wise man.
—Cicero

Could You Predict the Weather?

Some weather forecasters give a "five degree guarantee." They will "guarantee" they can predict tomorrow's high temperature within 5 degrees. This sounds impressive until you consider that this means within a range of 10. If the weather person predicts 51, then she is right if the high temperature falls anywhere within the range of 46 to 56. You don't have to be a weather forecaster to make that kind of prediction most days.

EXERCISE 11.11

Decide whether each of the following is an example of epistemic probability, relative frequency probability, or a priori probability.

1. The probability of a random student passing the next exam without studying
2. Your chances of picking the winning number in the state lottery
3. The probability of a hurricane hitting the Northeast in October
4. The probability of your mother going to a Marylyn Manson concert
5. The odds of the horse you bet on winning the Kentucky Derby
6. The probability of being dealt a royal flush in poker
7. The chances of a random student getting an A in this course
8. The likelihood of your getting a perfect score in bowling
9. The odds of your favorite team winning the Super Bowl
10. The chances of rolling a 6 with two standard dice

A Closer Look at A Priori Probability

Sometimes we want to know the probability of a situation involving two events. For example, let's say you need to draw *either* a 7 *or* a king from a full deck of fifty-two cards. What are the chances? The probability of either of two events occurring is the sum of their probabilities. In other words, add them: the odds of drawing a 7 are 1 in 13, or 7.7%, and the odds of drawing a king are also 1 in 13 or 7.7%. So the chances of drawing either a 7 or a king are: $\frac{1}{13} + \frac{1}{13} = \frac{2}{13}$, or 15.4 percent. The probability of *both* of two independent events occurring is substantially less, however. Let's say that this time you have to draw a 7 from a deck of fifty-two cards and then draw a king from another deck of fifty-two cards. What are the odds? The probability of both of two events occurring is the product of their probabilities. In other words, multiply them: the chances of drawing the 7 are 1 in 13 and the chances of drawing the king are also 1 in 13. So the chances of drawing the 7 from one deck and then

The rules of probable inference are the most difficult part of logic, but also the most useful.

—Bertrand Russell

drawing the king from the next deck are $\frac{1}{13} \times \frac{1}{13} = \frac{1}{169}$ or .59 percent—less than 1 percent.

What are the chances of drawing a 7 from a deck of fifty-two, if you have just drawn a 7 from the deck and randomly put it back. As we saw, the odds of drawing the 7 in the first case were 1 in 13, or 7.7 percent, but you may be surprised to find that the odds of randomly drawing the 7 again are also 1 in 13 or 7.7 percent. If you thought the odds were much worse, you committed the **gambler's fallacy**. The gambler's fallacy is the mistaken belief that a past event has an impact on a current random event. In our example, the past event was the first draw of the 7 and the current random event was the second draw. The question wasn't, What are the odds of getting a 7 on two successive draws of the cards? The question was only, What are the odds of getting a 7 on the second draw of the cards? The past draw has no causal effect on the present one. The cards are dumb. They don't know which one was drawn last. Consider the case of betting on a roulette wheel. On a standard roulette wheel there are thirty-eight spaces; eighteen of the spaces numbered 1–36 are black and eighteen are red. There are also two green spaces numbered 0 and 00. The chances of red coming in are 47.37 percent and the chances are the same for black, 47.37 percent. If you observe that red has come in twice in a row, should you then put your money on black for the next spin of the wheel? No, there is no good reason to, because there is no causal connection between one spin and another. The odds are not, as you might think, in your favor. There is still only a 47.37 percent chance of black coming in. Each spin of the wheel is a random event, unaffected by previous events—including previous spins of the wheel. What if you wanted to bet on your lucky number, say 15, but the wheel just came in 15 on the spin before you could get your bet down. Does that mean there is a good reason not to bet on 15 this time? Aside from the nonexistence of lucky numbers and the terrible odds of any one particular number coming in, only 2.63 percent, there is no reason not to bet on 15. The chances of 15 coming in are the same for every spin of the wheel, 2.63 percent—even when the number just came in.

"But what about the law of averages?" you might object! Don't things even out over the long run? Yes, they tend to do that. You might be surprised just how long the long run is, though. With thirty-eight different numbers, we're talking about a very large number of spins of the roulette wheel before we are likely to see an even distribution of the numbers that come in. It will be easier to grasp this if we stick with a simple example that has only two possible outcomes—for example, a coin toss. The toss of a fair coin will result in 50 percent heads and 50 percent tails over the long run. No one would be shocked to see 60 percent heads if we tossed the coin five times—that would mean three heads and two tails. We wouldn't be too surprised even if it were ten tosses—six heads and four tails—or twenty tosses—twelve heads and eight tails. It would be more surprising to toss the coin one hundred times and get sixty heads and forty tails, but this is not impossible or unheard of, even with a fair coin. The point is, though, that according to the **law of large num-**

YA SAY IT'S YOUR BIRTHDAY . . .

Surprising Odds—If you are sitting in a classroom with 23 other people, what are the odds you share the same birthday (excluding year) with another person in the room? Believe it or not, the odds are 1 in 2. Try it out.

bers, the proximity of theoretically predicted and actual percentages tends to increase as the sample grows. In other words, the bigger the sample, the closer the actual results are likely to be to the predicted results. If we tossed the coin ten thousand times, it would be surprising if we didn't have something very close to a 50–50 split. But it would also be surprising if we did have exactly that. An exact match between actual and theoretically predicted percentages is more likely with a smaller sample. This is easy to see, in that there is a better chance of having a 50–50 split after two coin tosses (there is a 50 percent chance of this) than there is after ten tosses. The same reasoning can be applied to spins of the roulette wheel. The chance of black coming in is just under 50 percent, at 47.37 percent, but strange things do happen. In 1918 in Monte Carlo black came up twenty-six consecutive times on the roulette wheel.

There are different ways to assess the value of making a bet, ranging from the objective to the subjective. **Expected value** is essentially the payoff or loss you can expect from making a bet. Without getting heavily into the mathematics of it, we can fairly easily eyeball the expected value of a particular bet to see if it is positive, negative, or neutral. For example, if five hundred $1 chances are being sold for a raffle in which the first and only prize is a bicycle worth $200, buying a raffle ticket is a pretty bad bet in terms of expected value. In fact, it has a negative expected value. How can you tell? Consider what would happen if you could somehow manage to buy all the raffle tickets. The good news is that you would be guaranteed to win! The bad news is that you would have spent $500 to win a $200 bicycle. If there were only two hundred $1 tickets sold for the raffle, then the bet would have a neutral expected value of 0. If you bought all two hundred tickets, you would win a $200 bicycle. If there were only one hundred $1 tickets sold for the raffle, this would be a good bet with a positive expected value. If you could manage to buy all the tickets you would have spent only $100 and be guaranteed to win a $200 bicycle. Unfortunately, bets with positive or even neutral expected values are rare. Most bets have a negative expected value. This gives "the house" the edge, making it profitable for them to offer the bet. That is no big secret. Most people know the odds are against them when they make a bet or buy a raffle ticket. But they do it anyway! Why?

They do it because it's fun and the bet is worth it to the person making it, even when she knows it is not a sound investment of her money. Perhaps

> ## Critical Thinking Lapse
>
> Out for some Italian food one night, Yogi Berra was asked if he wanted his pizza cut into four slices or eight slices. His response: "Better make it four. I don't think I could eat eight."

Wise venturing is the most commendable part of human prudence.

—Marquis of Halifax

she gets some thrill out of the possibility of turning her $1 into a $200 bicycle. Maybe the profits from the sale of the raffle tickets go to support a good cause, and that alone makes it worthwhile to her. What we see illustrated here is **relative value**, the value a bet has in relation to an individual's own needs, preferences, and resources. If spending $1 on a raffle ticket is not going to damage your personal finances and if you find it fun and worthwhile to have the chance of winning, it may make perfect sense for you to buy the ticket. The ticket represents a chance to win and has a high relative value. A second ticket, however, is not likely to have a relative value that is quite as high. The tenth ticket will likely have even less relative value. The more money you spend on tickets, the less relative value the tickets have. You had a chance to win with the purchase of the first ticket, and buying ten tickets hasn't increased your odds enough to warrant the purchase. The relative value of the first ticket was enough to override the negative expected value, but with each ticket you purchase, the ability for relative value to override expected value gets less and less. This is a phenomenon known as **diminishing marginal value**: As quantity increases, relative value tends to decrease. Diminishing marginal value (sometimes called diminishing marginal utility) is a basic economic concept, which your own experience will confirm. If you are hungry, one slice of pizza will have a very high relative value, probably making its cost worthwhile. But consider what happens as the number of slices you buy increases. The relative value tends to go down, doesn't it? The second slice and maybe the third will also have a moderately high relative value, but likely less than the first one, which calmed your rumbling stomach. If you get to a fifth, sixth, or seventh slice, not only will you be a glutton but you also will find that each slice has less and less value to you—less and less relative value.

Let's consider how these value concepts apply to the lottery. Multistate lotteries, such as Powerball, have become increasingly popular in recent years. It costs one dollar to play one game of Powerball. To win, you need to pick five numbers in any order and then pick one number exactly, the Powerball. The lottery officials tell us the chances of winning are 1 in 89,089,128. The implication is that there are just that many possible number combinations, given the rules of the game. So, does playing Powerball have a positive or negative expected value? That depends both on what the jackpot is and on how many tickets are sold. Let's say the jackpot reaches $50 million. That sounds pretty good, but there is a negative expected value, since you would have to spend over $89 million to play all possible combinations and guarantee a win.

THE PRISONERS' DILEMMA

Two thieves are taken into custody and held in separate areas. They are given the following options:

1. Confess and implicate your partner. If he does not confess, you will get only two years and he will get ten. If you confess and he also confesses, you will each get six years.
2. Don't confess. If neither one of you confesses, you will get four years, since we have enough evidence to tie you both to a different crime. If you don't confess and your partner does and implicates you, you will get ten years.

What is the more rational strategy for a prisoner in this situation to adopt? What would you do?

If the jackpot hits $100 million, the expected value could actually be positive. You could spend a little over $89 million and be guaranteed to hit the jackpot. Still, the expected value could be negative, depending on how many tickets are sold. If you are the only person allowed to buy tickets for this particular drawing (something not likely to happen), then you will be guaranteed to win and the expected value will be positive—it is a good bet. If others are playing, too (as you can be sure they will), the expected value will go down in proportion to the number of tickets sold. For example, if 180 million tickets are sold, there is a fair chance that there will be two winners who share the jackpot, that is, split it. Ugh! The bad news is that even if you alone hit the jackpot, you will have to split the prize money with the taxman. What was $100 million will soon be $50 million or less, and according to the rules of most lotteries, if you want it all at once rather than over a period of twenty years, you will get still less.

It looks like any way you slice it, Powerball is a bad bet in terms of expected value. Most people know this. Still, even many of those who know it's a bad bet will buy a ticket. Why? Because the relative value of one ticket is probably enough to override the negative expected value. For one dollar you can dream of winning a huge jackpot, telling off the boss, quitting your job, and dumping your husband for a Brad Pitt look-alike. Still, people don't generally buy tons of Powerball tickets, because the relative value goes down with each ticket purchased. Diminishing marginal value, remember? Unfortunately, not everyone gets the point. Many people travel for hours to a state where Powerball tickets are on sale and then proceed to buy hundreds or even thousands of tickets. The negative expected value tells us that with every ticket they purchase, they are in effect throwing money out the window. For some people it is an obsession, even an addiction. One Powerball ticket should be enough for anyone.

EXERCISE 11.12

I. Decide whether each of the following has a positive, negative, or neutral expected value.

1. Any 50-50 lottery, one in which first prize is half the amount collected from ticket sales
2. An even-money $100 bet on a single coin toss
3. Buying one ticket for a raffle in which there are ten tickets in total, each costing $1,000. The prize is a brand-new Mercedes
4. A $10 bet on red coming in on the next spin of the roulette wheel
5. Buying ten tickets for a raffle in which there are five hundred tickets in total, each costing $1. The prize is two tickets to a Broadway show.

II. Give your own evaluation of the relative value of the bets in the preceding exercise.

III. Give your own detailed example of a case of diminishing marginal value.

SUMMARY

1. This chapter focused on forming and critically evaluating inductive arguments. In particular, we examined four common types of inductive argument: *inductive generalizations, arguments from analogy, causal arguments,* and *statistical arguments.*

2. Inductive arguments do not guarantee their conclusions. We evaluate them according to the strength of the support they provide for their conclusions. An inductive argument is strong when its premises provide evidence that its conclusion is more likely true than false. An inductive argument is weak when its premises do *not* provide evidence that its conclusion is more likely true than false.

3. Among the important *indicator words and phrases* for inductive arguments are *likely, probably, it's plausible to suppose that, it's reasonable to believe that, one would expect that, it's a good bet that, chances are that,* and *odds are that.*

4. An *inductive generalization* is an argument that relies on characteristics of a sample population to make a claim about the population as a whole. In other words, it is an argument that uses evidence about a limited number of people or things of a certain type (the *sample population*) to make a claim about a larger group of people or things of that type (the *population as a whole).*

5. Ask these questions in evaluating an inductive generalization:
    • Are the premises true?

- Is the sample large enough? The size of the sample population must be sufficient to justify the conclusion about the population as a whole.
- Is the sample representative? A representative sample is like the population as a whole in all relevant ways. It should be a miniversion of the population as a whole.

6. A *strong argument* has premises that provide evidence that its conclusion is more likely true than false. A *cogent* inductive argument has all true premises and supplies strong support for its conclusion. A *strong and reliable argument* has premises that provide evidence that its conclusion is more likely true than false, *and* it is an argument that a reasonable person *would* act or bet on. A *strong but unreliable argument* has premises that provide evidence that its conclusion is more likely true than false, *but* it is an argument that a reasonable person *would not* act or bet on.

7. Polling should be *double-blind*. The person taking the poll and the person responding should have no information about each other, or at least as little as possible. And neither the person taking the poll nor the person responding should have any indication of the "right answer."

8. A *statistical argument* argues from premises regarding a percentage of a population to a conclusion about an individual member of that population or some part of that population.

9. Like other inductive arguments, statistical arguments are evaluated along a continuum of strong to weak.

10. Statistical arguments that approach 50 percent may be strong but are to be considered relatively unreliable.

11. The *reference class* is the group to which our statistics apply. As a rule, the more specific the reference class is, the better the argument is.

12. An *analogy* is a comparison of things based on similarities those things share. Whereas analogies simply point out a similarity, *arguments from analogy* claim that certain similarities are evidence that there is another similarity (or other similarities).

13. Things to consider in evaluating the strength of an argument from analogy include the truth of the premises; the relevance of the similarities; the number of relevant similarities; the relevance of dissimilarities; the number of relevant dissimilarities; the diversity of the sample (especially with increased sample size); and the specificity of the conclusion relative to the premises.

14. Not all causal arguments contain the word "cause." Other causal terms include *produce, is responsible for,* and *affects.* Such arguments come in two broad types; arguments about the cause of a single instance, and arguments about a general relationship.

15. Sometimes, two things or events are clearly "associated" or "linked." Where you find X, you will often find Y. A relationship such as this, in which two things are frequently found together, is called *correlation*. Sometimes, a correlation is an indicator of a cause-and-effect relationship. A positive correlation, one which indicates that two things are found together more than 50 percent of the time, may indicate a causal connection between one thing and the other. A negative correlation, one which indicates that two things are found together less than 50 percent of time, may indicate that one thing prevents the other. The important question, though, is this: Is the correlation significant? The answer will depend, in part, on the size of the sample.

16. *Epistemic probability* is the kind of probability we assign to things we have good reason to believe but to which we cannot assign a probability on any truly mathematical basis.

17. *Relative frequency probability* is the kind of probability that takes information about a group as a whole and applies it to an individual case, based on accumulated data derived from what has already been observed in the group.

18. Statements of *a priori probability* have odds that can be calculated previous to, and independent of, sensory observation.

19. The *gambler's fallacy* is the mistaken belief that a past event has an impact on a current random event.

20. According to the *law of large numbers*, the proximity of theoretically predicted and actual percentages tends to increase as the sample grows. In other words, the bigger the sample, the closer the actual results are likely to be to the predicted results.

21. *Expected value* is essentially the payoff or loss you can expect from making a bet.

22. *Relative value* is the value a bet has in relation to an individual's own needs, preferences, and resources.

23. *Diminishing marginal value* is the principle that as quantity increases relative value tends to decrease.

CHAPTER 12

FINDING, EVALUATING, AND USING SOURCES

In this chapter we tell you how to conduct research and use sources to defend your arguments. Other than "oral presentation required," perhaps no phrase on a syllabus throws students into more consternation than "research paper required." Few students look forward to the long, sometimes grueling, often frustrating process of finding information and incorporating it into a paper. Some are annoyed and ultimately deflated by finding their best thoughts expressed in better language, or irritated at the supposed lack of available information. Others are put off by having to adhere to all those conventions of research writing—accurate quoting and honest paraphrasing, proper documentation, correct listing of cited works, and so forth. In this chapter we show you that research does not have to be an intimidating academic exercise. Arguments are stronger and more credible when bolstered by support. And for a critical thinker—one committed to truth, fairness, and precision—research also develops the ability to find information, set the record straight, and advance the conversation.

It may be best to begin with some idea of *why* research work is assigned in colleges and universities. Obviously, in researching a topic, you discover data and opinions that you can use as evidence to support the claims in your argument. But conducting research well has implications beyond the immediate success of a single assignment, especially for someone studying critical thinking. Doing research lets you practice the skills of finding, evaluating, summarizing, and using information—skills necessary in just about every profession that requires a college degree. Accountants, physicians, lawyers, managers, computer experts, teachers—all must keep up with trends in the field, find causes and solutions, analyze precedent, collect data, and so forth. The good research habits developed in college will show up again in your nonprofessional life as well. Successfully running for local office, joining a civic committee such as the PTA, buying a house, hiring a contractor or a lawyer, investing in the stock market, voting, even deciding what movie to go to often depends on your ability to find and evaluate information. In fact, it is no exaggeration to say that many of the major decisions in our lives, and even

> *Research is formalized curiosity. It is poking and prying with a purpose.*
> —Zora Neal Hurston

some of the minor ones, would be more rewarding if we arrived at them only after investigation and study rather than on impulse and whim.

Good research can also help you set the record straight and avoid accepting at face value what you hear and read. A politician may convincingly argue that her commitment to the environment is above reproach, but simple research into her voting record on bills affecting clean water and air may suggest otherwise. Often in the search for truth, you need to go directly to the primary sources. If you want to know what the Constitution says about possessing firearms, it might be wise to read the Constitution and not just what has been written *about* it. Some secondhand sources are highly reliable, fair, and trustworthy, but others are sloppy, biased, or even unethical in their quoting, paraphrasing, and summarizing and, as a result, may relay distorted and inaccurate information. Reading the primary sources lets you set the record straight.

Just as returning to the primary source can help you see more clearly, research can help you correct your own misconceptions and shatter some long-cherished assumptions. Often what people have firmly accepted as true and unassailable has, upon further investigation, been shown to be baseless. What you believe, on just about any topic—welfare, culture, crime, religion, politics, education—might or might not hold up to objective and thorough investigation. Research can help clarify fuzzy, vague notions you may have about certain topics, and can help you analyze a complex issue, including what positions are held by others and what evidence is generally provided in support or rebuttal of claims. Research allows you to become something of an expert on a small issue and to speak with some authority as you attempt to correct misunderstanding, speak the truth, and set the record straight.

EXERCISE 12.1

In groups of four, complete the following test. Be sure to discuss each question or statement with your group members and to record only one answer that members of the group agree upon.

A. Decide whether the following are true or false.
   1. The first battle between ironclad ships took place between the *Monitor* and the *Merrimack*.
   2. "Yankee Doodle" was written as a patriotic song of the American Revolution.
   3. "The Star-Spangled Banner" was written during the American Revolution and has been our national anthem for almost two hundred years.
   4. Ferdinand Magellan was the first person to circumnavigate the globe.
   5. Charles Lindbergh was the first person to fly across the Atlantic.
   6. The Declaration of Independence was signed on July 4, 1776.
   7. You should never end a sentence with a preposition or start one with "and" or "but."

8. The United States has never fought a war with China.
9. A teacher with tenure can never be fired.
10. A Catholic priest can never be married.
11. Frankenstein was a monster.
12. Abbreviating Christmas to "Xmas" began as a way to insult Christians.
13. The Emancipation Proclamation freed the slaves.
14. Robert Fulton invented the steamboat, which he named the *Clermont*.
15. A number of women accused of being witches were burned in Salem, Massachusetts.
16. Benjamin Franklin discovered electricity.
17. The Immaculate Conception refers to Christ's having been born of a virgin.
18. Lightning never strikes the same place twice.

B. Answer the following questions.
1. Bagpipes were invented in what country?
2. What is "circumstantial evidence"?
3. Why is Los Angeles's baseball team called the Dodgers?
4. Who invented the sewing machine?
5. Mr. is an abbreviation for Mister. What is Mrs. an abbreviation for?
6. What was President Harry Truman's middle name?
7. What did Henry Ford invent?
8. Who invented the lightbulb?
9. Who invented the telephone?
10. What does the distress signal SOS stand for?
11. "Fourscore and seven years ago, our forefathers brought forth upon this continent a new nation" is the opening line of what famous document? Is the line quoted accurately?
12. In Nova Scotia, the sun rises in the _____, but on the west coast of Brazil, it rises in the _____.

After you have finished the test, divide up the thirty items among your group members. Each member of the group should research his or her items to determine if the group's response was correct.

Aside from teaching you how to find information and unveil the truth, researching a topic allows you to enter the debate on an issue, perhaps extending the conversation into new areas. Don't think of research *merely* as gathering and repeating everything you can find on a given topic. Gathering information is certainly part of the task, but well-researched arguments are not simply repetitions of previous arguments or collections of published data. Look carefully, respectfully, and skeptically at what others have said about the research topic. Pore over the data collected by other researchers; read the reactions and conclusions of other thinkers; accept, reject, or modify the claims of essayists, editorialists, and analysts; and ultimately add your own, perhaps innovative, thinking to the mix. Research provides the opportunity to discover

and learn, but also to infer and create, to go beyond what has already been said. In fact, if we thought of research as a chance not only to bolster our ideas but also to combine old ideas into new ones, and to propel us toward original thoughts, research would be less a boring chore and more an opportunity to increase our knowledge and to add something to the discourse. The great scientist and mathematician Sir Isaac Newton wrote in a letter to Robert Hooke, "If I have seen further, it is by standing on the shoulders of giants." Few of us will be Isaac Newtons, but our ability to see further than our predecessors depends entirely on our ability to find and to look carefully at what they have already seen.

Research, then, helps you develop the skills necessary to speak more intelligently, convincingly, and truthfully on your topics. It helps clear your thinking of false presuppositions, opens your mind to new ideas, and inspires you. And, of course, it can help you create powerful arguments. In fact, as a critical thinker, you'll most often research your arguments to give them strength, to provide a solid foundation of premises and data upon which to set your conclusions. We know from experience that arguments having the weight of authority behind them are far more powerful than arguments built solely on a writer's hunch or intuition. Although that is not always the case — you can make a good argument for the existence of God without mentioning Aristotle, Thomas Aquinas, or any of the current theological writing that seeks to confirm God's presence in the universe — your argument will probably be more convincing with help from authoritative sources and thinkers. Facts, too, can serve to strengthen your arguments. You increase the chances of persuading your readers to vote for a particular candidate if you can provide evidence of, for example, the candidate's voting record. In short, research is both necessary and rewarding.

All too often, however, especially at the undergraduate level, students conducting research become frustrated by the overwhelming amount of information available and select for their arguments whatever they discover first, assuming perhaps that *any* support is *good* support. That is understandable, given how time-consuming research can be: we are all reluctant to throw out the fruits of our labor, even what is sour and rotten. But an effective research project is based on reliable, accurate sources. When you use sources to support your own conclusions, you are saying to your readers, "Here is someone who agrees with what I am saying," or "Here is information that confirms what I have been claiming." It is vital to the success of the argument that those sources be good ones. The rest of this chapter will show you how to find sources, how to evaluate the sources you find so that only the most accurate and reliable information makes it into your arguments, and how to place those sources into an argumentative essay.

Finding Sources

In a famous twentieth-century short story called "The Library of Babel," the Argentine writer Jorge Luis Borges presented an image of the universe as a vast, seemingly infinite library of books. These books, all of one size and length, contained every conceivable combination of letters of the alphabet, commas, and periods that could be recorded in 410 pages. Most of the books in the library were unintelligible, one containing, for example, the letters MCV repeated over and over again, but occasionally a perfectly comprehensible book could be found among the unfathomable volumes. In fact, the library contained

> Everything: the minutely detailed history of the future, the archangel's autobiographies, the faithful catalogue of the Library, thousands and thousands of false catalogues, the demonstration of the fallacy of those catalogues, the demonstration of the fallacy of the true catalogue, the Gnostic gospel of Basilides, the commentary on that gospel, the commentary on the commentary on that gospel, the true story of your death, the translation of every book in all languages, the interpolations of every book in all books.[1]

Sound like your library? Surely not even the Library of Congress contains even a fraction of the immense number of books in Borges's mythical library, but to a researcher, any library can appear to be an enormous, impenetrable maze of books and periodicals. And with online databases, interlibrary loan, and Internet connections to other libraries and to resource centers all over the world, the walls of almost every college library expand far beyond those of the campus building. For today's researcher, the excuse that "our library doesn't have anything on this topic" is outdated and doubtful. In fact, the modern library has become so expansive and information so abundant that you are almost certain to find what you are looking for. But to conquer the modern library, you need help. This section will offer some basic instruction for locating sources of print and electronic information when researching an argumentative essay, but trying to provide an exhaustive research guidebook in a few pages would be like attempting to draw a map of New York City on a postage stamp. In fact, the closest thing to an exhaustive guide, the *Guide to Reference Books,* a list of general reference materials (encyclopedias, dictionaries, indexes, etc.), includes more than 16,000 entries in over 2,000 pages. The following advice is provided for the critical thinker preparing an argument, but anyone using a library today is strongly encouraged to seek the help of a reference librarian.

Refining Your Search

Most researchers approach the library with two types of questions in mind. The first is a simple, single question that requires the retrieval of specific data:

> What are the names of Jupiter's moons?
>
> Who was Basilides?
>
> Where is Skopje?
>
> When did Babe Ruth play for the Boston Red Sox?
>
> What does a hellgrammite look like?
>
> Why is the sky blue?
>
> Who said, "Freedom of the press belongs to those who own one?"

The second type of question requires a more complicated and intensive search:

> What started the Vietnam War?
>
> How dangerous is moshing?
>
> Was there a conspiracy to assassinate President Kennedy?
>
> What led to the arms race?
>
> Does the Loch Ness Monster exist?
>
> What were FDR's greatest contributions to the Democratic Party?

Sometimes the second type of question can indicate an extraordinary amount of research. Researching the nuclear arms race, for example, could lead you down many different paths as you collect information and interpretations from political figures, historians, scholars, and perhaps, depending on your purpose, even novelists and poets.

Before you begin searching for information, decide what specific questions you need to have answered and what general questions you have concerning areas you need to learn more about. For example, in researching workplace safety, you might list the following simple questions: How many workers are injured or killed each year on the job? How many in a specific industry, such as truck driving? What agencies oversee the trucking industry? What are the regulations governing truck transportation? What union representation do truck drivers have? What causes most accidents involving trucks? How many trucks were involved in accidents last year? More complicated questions might focus on recent improvements in truck safety or attempts to lower the number of accidents, or the recommendations proposed by state police, the AAA, state departments of transportation, OSHA, or the Federal Highway Administration. Often, these types of questions will occur to you if you have written a draft of an argument based only on your opinions and observations. At other times, you may be attempting to write about issues you know too little about to write a draft of more than a few sentences. As a way to guide your research, try writing down your questions, using them to direct but not restrict your search; you might find information you never thought to ask for. And remember that as you research and write, new questions will occur to you, requiring additional research for answers. The purpose of recording questions is to help guide your search and to prevent you from approaching the library with ill-defined needs and a sense of hopelessness.

Once you have determined what you are looking for, you can begin your search. Two kinds of library source material will be most helpful: material that will provide the information you are looking for, and material that will *direct* you toward the material you are looking for. Informational material includes encyclopedias, newspapers, journals, magazines, dictionaries, books, government documents, and Internet pages. Directional materials include indexes, bibliographies, card catalogues, guides to reference sources, and online databases. To use an example that almost every student is familiar with, *The Readers' Guide to Periodical Literature* provides direction toward information that is contained in magazines.

Knowledge is of two kinds. We know a subject ourselves, or we know where we can find information upon it.

—Samuel Johnson

Directional Information

The following are among the most popular and accessible reference works and search engines for pointing you in the direction of information located in books and periodicals and on Internet pages. To make the best use of these materials, consult the *Library of Congress Subject Headings* to determine how your topic is classified in reference works; otherwise, you might search in vain for books and articles on "free speech" and "religious tolerance" when your topics are listed in bibliographies and indexes under "freedom of speech" and "freedom of religion." On the other hand, online databases may permit keyword searches that will result in a number of hits whether you use your own terminology or the more "official" Library of Congress headings.

Bibliographies   Generally speaking, a bibliography is a list of books that provides for each book the name of the author, the title, the place and date of publication, the name of the publisher, and, in some cases, the price of the book. Bibliographies can also include recordings, films, photographs, and computer software programs. The most familiar bibliography to student researchers is the catalogue, available in every library in either print or electronic form and listing all the books held by the library and stored on the shelves (often called "stacks") or in special collections areas. Other bibliographies, less well known but available in most libraries in print or in electronic digital format, include the Library of Congress's *National Union Catalog,* which lists books published in the United States, and the *British National Bibliography,* which lists every work published in Great Britain since 1950. *Books in Print* lists all books currently available from publishers. Other bibliographies, more generally defined as "lists of publications," catalogue pamphlets, newspapers, and other periodicals. Such reference lists as *Urlich's International Periodical Directory, Gale Directory of Publications and Broadcast Media, Gale Directory of Databases,* and the *Vertical File Index* (for pamphlets) may be helpful in locating book titles, periodicals, and places of publication for a wide range of sources. Keep in mind that these bibliographies will usually provide only lists of what is available, with little additional information about the publication. One notable exception is *Magazines for Libraries,* which describes periodicals in some detail.

Periodical Indexes and Abstracting Services   Indexes and abstracting services allow you to search for articles, essays, editorials, and other items in periodicals. Many of these indexes and services are available electronically. Some indexes provide only the information you will need to locate a source (author's name, title, etc.), whereas others, especially databases, provide the full text of selected articles. Abstracting services provide a short description of the article, often including the thesis or central claim. Some of these indexes and abstracting services are extremely expensive and are not available in every library. For help in using these services, consult a reference librarian. Here are a few of the more popular indexes and abstracts:

- *Access: The Supplementary Index* (magazines not covered by the *Readers' Guide*)
- *Alternative Press Index* (alternative and radical press)
- *Business Periodicals Abstracts*
- *Business Source One* (indexes over 600 business-related journals)
- *Congressional Abstracts*
- ERIC (Educational Resources Information Center; indexes educational journal articles and documents)
- *General Science Index*
- *Historical Abstracts*
- *Humanities Index*
- InfoTrac (about 2,000 business, government, and education publications)
- LEXIS/NEXIS (NEXIS provides abstracts and full texts of newspapers, magazines, newsletters, industry reports, and broadcast transcripts; LEXIS indexes articles from law journals.)
- MasterFILE Premier (indexes about 3,000 periodicals)

- *MLA International Bibliography* (literature, language, linguistics, folklore)
- *Monthly Catalogue of U.S. Government Publications*
- *National Newspaper Index*
- *New York Times Index*
- *Periodical Abstracts* (over 1,000 periodicals in business, humanities, science, and social sciences)
- *Philosopher's Index*
- *Psychological Abstracts* and *PsycLIT*
- *Readers' Guide to Periodical Literature*
- *Social Sciences Index*
- *Times Index* (London *Times*)
- *Wall Street Journal Index*
- *Women's Studies Index*

Finally, a quick word about terminology. Occasionally you will hear words and acronyms such as EBSCOhost, DIALOG, and Wilson used at your library in discussions about indexes. These names refer to the companies, producers, vendors, and networks that oversee or control various indexes. Again, the complex world of academic research can be confusing enough to frustrate even the most seasoned researcher. Don't give up. Ask a librarian.

Internet Search Engines, Guides, and Directories   Nothing is more emblematic of the information age than the Internet, which has made millions of pages of text and illustrations available to us with only a few taps on the computer keyboard and a click of the mouse. But the blessing is also a curse: how do you sort through those millions upon millions of pages? It's like Borges's Library of Babel. Internet search engines (AltaVista, Lycos, HotBot, Excite, Yahoo, Google, to name a few) will help to provide some direction when you are looking for information, but entering a keyword can result in thousands of "hits," many of which are only marginally related to your interests. Most of the search engines have indexes for subject areas such as travel, games, movies, sports, and jokes, and these indexes do help reduce the number of pages you need to surf through; however, they are generally limited to popular interests. You may prefer to search the sports pages, but you are not likely to find much support there for a paper on religion and medicine.

Although there are many similarities among them, not all search engines are the same. Some search only the titles of pages, whereas others search entire texts. Some search engines (Magellan is the best example) review and rate the sites they search. One of the better sites for serious researchers, Alpha Search, sponsored by the Calvin Theological Seminary in Michigan (http://www.calvin.edu/library/searreso/internet/as/), allows visitors to search by discipline (Art, Archeology, Biology, English, etc.) and groups sites under helpful headings such as "databases," "full text documents," "gateways," and "journals." A short description of each site is provided. To make searching the Internet more rewarding, be sure to follow any guidelines provided by the search engine for narrowing or limiting the search. Many engines allow searches through Boolean operators, the use of "+" and "−" or "AND" and "NOT" to refine your search. Follow the instructions given by the search engine provider.

To broaden your search, use a "metasearch" such as Metacrawler (http://www.metacrawler.com), Dogpile (http://www.dogpile.com), or Savvysearch (http://www.savvysearch.com), three engines that search other engines. To search USENET discussions, use an engine designed for that purpose; Dejanews (http://www.deja.com) is among the best. Finally, there are sites that provide access to many specialized search engines. One of the best, All-In-One Search (http://www.allonesearch.com) will allow you to choose from "over 500 of the Internet's best search engines, databases, indexes, and directories in a single site." (For exhaustive advice on using search engines, visit the Thomas G. Carpenter Library page at the University of North Florida, http://www.unf.edu/library/guides/search.html.)

Although search engines help make some sense of the seemingly infinite Net, a researcher has an even better chance of finding helpful information by turning to noncommercial guides maintained by universities and the government to help students locate reliable Internet pages. Listed here is just a small fraction of the available guides for finding scholarly and other informational sites:

- Librarian's Index to the Internet: http://www.lii.org/
- The Virtual Library: http://vlib.org
- Library of Congress: http://lcweb.loc.gov/global/explore.html
- Cornell University Library: http://campusgw.library.cornell.edu/
- Internet Research Assistant: http://users.southeast.net/~drgwen/index.html
- The Internet Public Library: http://www.ipl.org/
- Thomas: Legislative Information on the Internet: http://thomas.loc.gov/
- AJR Newslink (newspapers and magazines on line): http://www.ajr.newslink.org
- Martindale's Reference Desk: http://www-sci.lib.uci.edu/HSG/Ref.html
- FedStats (statistical information): http://www.fedstats.gov/mod-perl/A2Z.cgi
- National Archives and Records Administration: http://www.nara.gov/

Web browsers (Netscape, Explorer) and search engines provide the easiest means to search the Internet, but other, older means are still available. Public files stored in host computers all over the world are often available through ftp (file transfer protocol), a method for connecting to a host computer and copying files ranging from entire books to one-page documents. The database "Archie" provides a means to search anonymous ftp sites and download their contents. Similarly, using Veronica and Jughead, you can conduct searches on Gopher, another system that allows you to locate files on the Internet through menus and submenus. Each Gopher server contains menus for local files and is linked to other servers in a seemingly limitless web of Gopher servers called Gopherspace. Another protocol (or set of procedures) known as Telnet allows computer users to connect through a telephone line directly to other computers provided the user has a password to get into the host computer. Some universities and colleges allow guests to access the library catalogue through the Telnet system. If all this talk about Archie, Gopher, and Telnet confuses you, don't worry. Most of the information available in cyberspace is currently accessible through the World Wide Web, and, in fact, other electronic means of retrieving information will most likely disappear very soon, leaving only the Web for you to use and master.

If you have only a broad topic and want to find what you can under that topic, try one of the more helpful directories, such as Yahoo! or About.com, which organize Web resources by categories such as "science," "culture," and "education." You can find links to useful sites by working your way through the subdirectories. For example, at Yahoo!, the path "Social Science—> Political Science—> Public Policy—> Institutes" will lead you to an annotated list of links to a great many of the various "think tanks" and policy research institutes that maintain Web sites.

Finally, through the Internet you can access information in discussion newsgroups and in listservs, discussion groups that operate by e-mail and that you must subscribe to. There are newsgroups and listservs on just about every subject imaginable (and some that are beyond what most of us can imagine). An earnest researcher may find helpful sources of information in some of the more academic and serious groups. Your search engine (AltaVista, Webcrawler, etc.) and your Web browser will help you locate discussion groups and listservs.

Bibliographies, indexes, and Internet search engines and guides will help point you in the right direction, though they will not provide the information you are seeking, whether your inquiry is simple or complex. What follows are some of the informational sources you will find in libraries and the kinds of informational sites you will find on the Internet.

Informational Sources

The directional resources listed in the preceding section (bibliographies, indexes, etc.) will guide you toward the books, articles, and Web pages that you are looking for. But you can find information in places other than the books in the stacks, the periodicals, and the Internet. When looking for information, consider the following reference materials and sources. Some of these sources can provide quick answers to simple questions or get you started in your attempt to familiarize yourself with a topic. Other sources will provide more in-depth analysis and information.

Encyclopedias   General encyclopedias such as *Encyclopaedia Britannica, Collier's, Encyclopedia Americana, Compton's,* and *Grolier* are excellent starting points for finding information about a topic, whether you are seeking specific answers or overviews and historical perspectives. Although encyclopedias don't always get the respect they deserve in colleges and universities, they can be helpful first steps toward understanding the basic concepts behind difficult subjects in disciplines such as psychology, philosophy, theology, science, and literature. In fact, many encyclopedia entries conclude with a short bibliography of reliable sources for further study. For more concentrated information about disciplines, you can consult subject encyclopedias, which contain information pertinent to specific topics: *Encyclopedia of Psychology, Encyclopedia of Philosophy, Encyclopedia of Religion,* the *McGraw-Hill Multimedia Encyclopedia of Science and Technology,* and *Benet's Reader's Encyclopedia* are just a very few of the subject encyclopedias available in most libraries. Additionally, the *Oxford Companion* series (*Oxford Companion to English Literature, Oxford Companion to Chess,* and so forth) provides an excellent starting place for researchers looking for basic information.

Almanacs, Yearbooks, Fact Books, Directories, Handbooks, Manuals, Atlases   These are the volumes you will most often consult when you need factual answers to uncomplicated questions such as "How many Americans are on Social Security?" or "Where is Mozambique?" or "Who said, 'Neither a borrower nor a lender be'?" As we noted earlier, people frequently assume that their basic knowledge is accurate, only to discover that they have been wrong all along. Ready-reference materials such as almanacs and fact books can help researchers find solid evidence to affirm or correct their assumptions and support their claims.

Some of the more popular sources of factual information include *The New York Public Library Desk Reference, The Guinness Book of World Records, Information Please Almanac, World Almanac and Book of Facts, Statistical Abstracts of the United States, Facts on File* (a weekly publication), *The New International World Atlas, Emily Post's Etiquette,* and *Bartlett's Familiar Quotations.* These and other books of factual information can usually be located in one area of the library, most often close to the reference desk.

Biographical Sources   When you need to find out who someone is or was, you can turn to a host of biographical sources, some of which are highly reliable sources of information about a person's life, accomplishments, contributions, publications, and even misdeeds or crimes. The well-regarded *Who's Who* series (*Who's Who of American Women, Who's Who among Black Americans, Who's Who in the World,* and so forth) is complemented by other sources, such as *Current Biography, The New York Times Biographical Service,* the *Dictionary of National Biography* (usually referred to as the *DNB* and devoted solely to British and Irish notables), the *Dictionary of American Biography (DAB), World Authors,* and *Contemporary Authors.* All these sources provide sketches of political figures, authors, scholars, dignitaries, executives, celebrities, socialites, and others whose contributions to their fields, to society, or to the culture have been noteworthy.

Dictionaries   When most students think of a dictionary, they think, sensibly, of a book that provides definitions of words, and there are plenty of such books in most college libraries. The best dictionaries for college use are unabridged, meaning that few English words have been excluded from the book no matter how colloquial, vulgar, esoteric, or obsolescent. *The Oxford English Dictionary* contains half a million words. *Webster's Third New International Dictionary* contains slightly fewer (roughly 460,000), and the *Random House Unabridged Electronic Dictionary* fewer still (about 315,00). These are available in most libraries, but for general use in college, smaller dictionaries, including *Merriam-Webster's Collegiate Dictionary, American Heritage Dictionary of the English Language,* and *Webster's New World Dictionary,* will serve.

But there are plenty of other "dictionaries" available in many libraries, including dictionaries of slang, legal terms, rhyming words, symbols, clichés, sign language, saints, theater, math, philosophy, film, names, music, ethics, archeology, politics, and myth. Many of these provide definitions for the terminology unique to the field, but others contain short, introductory passages and, in some cases, bibliographies. These dictionaries are a great place to start in your search for the kind of basic information necessary for a deeper understanding of an issue.

Several Internet dictionaries are convenient and reliable. Start with OneLook Dictionaries (http://www.onelook.com), which indexes over 600 general and specialized online dictionary Web sites. Because OneLook is so thorough, further searches are often unnecessary, but if you like, you can visit Merriam-Webster's home site (http://www.m-w.com/) and the Oxford English Dictionary if your school subscribes to it.

Government Documents   Many libraries have access to government documents through databases and online services, and a few libraries (at least one in every state) are depositories for government documents, meaning that hard copies are kept on hand. Government documents include everything published by the U.S. government, though, obviously, only unclassified documents are available to the public. Topics range from biographical information about members of Congress to advice on repairing a home. In collecting research for an argument, you might wish to look at government-supplied information such as census reports, labor statistics, or budget information. In looking on the Internet for government documents, start with GOVBOT (http://ciir2.cs.umass.edu/Govbot/), a large database of government Web sites.

Human Sources   Often overlooked in our dependence on the written word are human beings who could easily supply needed information. In looking for library sources, you would be wise to consult a librarian. Most librarians have advanced degrees and have had extensive, concentrated training in locating information, but for some reason, students will wander around for hours in a library before asking for help. Perhaps it's because we don't like to admit our shortcomings, and asking for someone's assistance is like asking for directions: we have to admit we're lost.

People besides librarians can be great sources of information, expert advice, and opinion, offering firsthand observations or even directing you toward resources you hadn't thought of. You might have a simple question that someone can answer quickly, or you might want to conduct an extended interview to collect an expert's thoughts on your topic. First consider the human sources close at hand—faculty members, local experts, government officials, members of the business and legal community, even other students who might have extensive experience or training in a particular area. Most faculty members and local authorities are willing to grant students interviews. Look, too, at the names that have appeared in your research. With e-mail, you might be able to contact an author or an editor for clarity on an issue or for additional information. Otherwise, of course, you can write or phone.

Before you interview someone (whether in person, by phone, or in writing), prepare a list of questions you would like the interviewee to answer. Divide your questions into simple, fact-based questions ("How much revenue does the city take in each year in taxes?") and questions that allow the interviewee to expand on an issue or to think out loud ("Should the city lower the tax rate?" or "What benefits do citizens enjoy because of taxes?"). Avoid vague questions or loaded ones ("What do you think of taxes?" or "Don't you think taxes are an unfair burden on the elderly?"). And don't let your questions restrict you; as long as the interviewee stays on track and doesn't digress into irrelevant areas, you might discover information and opinions that you hadn't anticipated.

Remember to be courteous in requesting and conducting an interview. Arrive promptly, finish the interview in a reasonable amount of time, and follow up with a thank you by e-mail or letter.

Evaluating Sources

It is no exaggeration to say that we live in an "information age": over 68,000 book titles were published in 1996 (that's almost 200 a day);[2] by some accounts, the Internet grows by three million pages a year; every day in the

United States, over fifteen hundred newspapers are published and over ten thousand radio stations broadcast programming around the country.[3] Information is so abundant that one edition of the *New York Times* contains more information than most of us could read in a week, let alone one day. But with all this information comes the difficulty of separating the truth from the lies, the useful and reliable information that helps advance our understanding of the world from the efforts to manipulate our thinking or control our spending. In evaluating all this information, we need to ask several questions about the *content,* the *author and the publisher* of the information, and the intended *audience.*

Content: Facts and Everything Else

The research you use to support your claims will generally come from books; essays, articles, letters, and editorials in periodicals such as journals and newspapers; interviews with experts; speeches; statistical abstracts; the Internet, and other sources in which writers and compilers inform or attempt to persuade their readers. Occasionally, you may also use creative literature—poems and stories—as references or sources of allusions and quotes, but nonliterary works will provide your primary supply of evidence and expert testimony. As you read and listen to your sources, keep in mind that you are seeking both factual answers and nonfactual, subjective opinions, judgments, interpretations, and so forth. Although both groups are important—facts and nonfacts—you must distinguish between them.

A fact is an item of information that is *objective* and *true.* The sun is about 93 million miles from the earth. That is a fact, whether you knew it or not, believe it or not, live in North or South America, and so forth. The claim is verifiable: you could measure the distance using instruments well calibrated to gauge so great a measurement, and any scientist using such instruments would come to the same conclusion.

Sometimes, facts cannot be authenticated. Say, for example, that while golfing alone you hit a hole-in-one. You know that you did, in fact, hit a hole-in-one, but you can't verify or document the occurrence, since no one else saw you and no cameras were rolling. In other words, some facts cannot be verified although they are *matters of fact.* You really did, cross your heart and hope to die, hit a hole-in-one; you just can't prove it. Or take as another example the statement "In my opinion, there is life on other planets." Whether or not extraterrestrial life exists is a matter of fact: either it does or it does not. If we had the means to verify existence in outer space, we could once and for all show this writer's statement to be either true or false. So although this writer's contention that life exists on other planets has not yet been verified, it would be wrong of us to claim that extraterrestrial life is not a fact. A writer's failure to verify a fact does not mean that his or her statement is nonfactual. And, obviously, some "facts" can never be verified. Is it a fact that Abraham Lincoln thought of his wife moments before he died? Who knows? So for the purposes of using sources to support your own arguments, it is best to separate *verified*

Critical Thinking Lapse

How much documentation do you need?

"The Idaho Department of Motor Vehicles denied a handicapped license plate to Jay Dula, even though he applied in person, because he didn't have a doctor's note verifying his condition. Dula has one leg, having lost all but six inches of the other to cancer at age 13. He does not wear an artificial leg and showed the DMV clerk his handicapped plates from California, from where he moved. Rules are rules, said the Transportation Department special plates supervisor Candy Smith, explaining, 'Even if he had an artificial limb and he took it off and slapped it on the counter, we'd still need a physician's statement stating what the disability is and whether it's permanent or temporary.'"[4]

---

and *documented* facts from everything else that a writer offers, including matters of fact that have yet to be verified.

Facts can be verified through eyewitness testimony, measurement, agreement among several sources, and documentation. If you tell a professor that you missed class because of illness, the professor might ask for a doctor's note, a document that helps verify your illness. If you tried to argue that a UFO appeared above your cornfield last night, you might want to prove it with a video or a snapshot. A driver's license proves your age. This isn't to say that apparent verifiability and documentation *always* prove a fact; documents can be altered or forged, and eyewitnesses lie. But the United States Golf Association will *record* the "fact" that you hit a hole-in-one only if at least one other person saw you do it.

To summarize, when looking for evidence to support your own claims, be careful to separate objective and verified facts from unverified facts, and all facts from everything else. When reading sources, it is essential that you separate facts in your source from the opinions, interpretations, and so forth offered by the writer. What makes this a difficult task is the manner, sometimes subtle, in which nonfacts are presented as fact. Consider the following sentences:

> The fact that women must be regarded as having little sense of justice is no doubt related to the predominance of envy in their mental life; for the demand for justice is a modification of envy and lays down the condition subject to which one can put envy aside. We also regard women as weaker in their social interests and as having less capacity for sublimating their instincts than men.[5]

Not everyone reading Freud's assessment of women's moral character will agree with these "facts," and despite Freud's promise that his lecture contained "nothing but observed facts, almost without speculative additions," some critics have taken him to task for the excess of speculation and assumption. What Freud claimed to be "fact" simply is not.

Here is perhaps a more subtle blend of fact and nonfact from a report in *Time* magazine thirty years ago:

> Forget the democratic processes, the judicial system and the talent for organization that have long been the distinctive marks of the U.S. Forget, too, the affluence (vast, if still not general enough) and the fundamental respect for law by most Americans. Remember, instead, the Gun.
>
> That is how much of the world beyond its borders feels about the U.S. today. All too widely, the country is regarded as a blood-drenched, continent-wide shooting range where toddlers blast off with real rifles, housewives pack pearl-handled revolvers, and political assassins stalk their victims at will.
>
> The image, of course, is wildly overblown, but America's own mythmakers are largely to blame. In U.S. folklore, nothing has been more romanticized than guns and the larger-than-life men who wielded them. From the nation's beginnings, in fact and fiction, the gun has been provider and protector. The Pilgrim gained a foothold with his harquebus. A legion of loners won the West with Colt .45 Peacemakers holstered at their hips or Winchester 73 repeaters cradled in their arms.[6]

How much of this is fact and how much is the writer's opinion? If while researching an argument on guns in America, you ran across this interesting and well-written essay, would you be able to draw any usable facts from it? Did "much of the world," in fact, view the United States as a "blood-drenched, continent-wide shooting range"? Because something is presented as fact does not necessarily mean that it is. If you wanted to use this quote from *Time* in your own argument, you might do well to find corroborating evidence of the world's view of the United States in 1968. Keep in mind that the author's contention, may, in fact, be true, but he offers no evidence, and you would only be repeating what he contends was the world's opinion of the United States. Your own careful study of history will show that his claim is either true or not.

Another problem can occur even when information is presented as fact *and* appears to be well documented and verified. The problem occurs most often in the reporting of the results of surveys. For example, you might read in an article that "75 percent of college students prefer to live in coed residence halls," a claim that is backed up in the article by a recent survey of students. Could you use such a statistic in your own argument? Is it a fact that 75 percent of college students prefer to live in coed dorms, or was the survey conducted in such a way that the results are not a reliable indicator of student opinion? It is not an easy call. When using such information in defense of your own claims, always inform your reader of the source of the "fact," and provide as much context as possible. You might write:

> According to a recent survey of 1,000 college students conducted for *Campus Harbinger* magazine, "75 percent of college students prefer to live in coed residence halls." The survey included students from all four classes in six colleges across the country.

In providing the context, you are saying to your reader, "The facts are that a survey was conducted and that the survey showed X." It is clear to your reader that you are presuming that the facts are true but that you are not stating with absolute certainty that they are.

Occasionally, the task of separating fact from opinion is simple: almanacs, indexes, and statistical abstracts provide bare-bones information, usually given numerically (the population of Rhode Island or the number of reported AIDS cases, for instance). But in reading essays, arguments, and articles from *any* source—even the most seemingly objective, such as encyclopedias, dictionaries, and government documents—you must be vigilant. Be sure that any facts you collect are objective and verifiable and that they could be documented. Find out what the writer's sources are. Remember that the facts you extract from a writer may not tell the whole story. The writer may have carefully selected certain facts and excluded others to defend a claim. Also remember that an inference drawn from facts is not necessarily the only or even the most logical conclusion. The same pieces of factual evidence might lead you to a conclusion very different from the one proposed by the writer. Be certain, too, that the facts are relevant to your purpose. Don't, for instance, assume that you can use facts about the popularity of jazz music in New York City to prove your contention that jazz has national appeal. Similarly, be certain that the facts are up-to-date. Innovations and new discoveries, especially in technology, medicine, and business, can quickly make facts obsolete. Check the dates of your sources and try to find the most recent information.

When you have separated the facts from the nonfacts, you will be in a better position to judge the value of an author's ideas. You can determine whether the opinions, judgments, interpretations, and so forth are backed by objective fact and, if so, whether those facts are presented in the essay or merely assumed. You can also evaluate the ideas on the basis of the writer's authority to speak on the issues.

> . . . [T]ruth or certainty is obtained only from facts. Every day of my life makes me feel more and more how seldom a fact is accurately stated; how almost invariably when a story has passed through the mind of a third person it becomes, so far as regards the impression it makes in further repetitions, little better than a falsehood.
>
> —Nathaniel Hawthorne

EXERCISE 12.2

I. Pay careful attention to what you read, watch, and hear in the next twenty-four hours and list between fifteen and twenty facts from your observations. Be sure that your facts are indeed factual. Then list between five and ten opinions that you have heard or read in the same time period.

II. In groups of four, read the following passages and individually list the verified facts and the matters of fact that appear in each passage. Remember to list only information that can be stated objectively and that has been verified or that is at least verifiable. When you are finished, compare your work. Do you and your group members agree on what is fact and what is not? What accounts for any differences you have?

1. The decline of broadcast journalism began in the late '60s when I worked for NBC News. The advertising department, which had been mostly kept out

of the news division during the tenure of NBC President Robert Kintner and his predecessor, Sylvester "Pat" Weaver, was allowed in. Ratings for news started to matter, as they did for entertainment. Stories were increasingly selected for the type of audience they would bring, especially women. The ratings declined anyway, along with the respect most people once had for the journalism profession. Add to story imbalance what many correctly perceive to be an ideological tilt to the left and you know why increasing numbers of people are looking elsewhere for real news. (Cal Thomas, "The Television People Kill Broadcast Journalism," *Jewish World Review,* July 28, 1999. Accessed August 10, 1999; available online at http://www.jewishworldreview.com/cols/thomas072899.asp.)

2. [Clint] Eastwood's unique ability to undermine and embrace myth at the same time reached its fullest fruition in his multiple Oscar-winning 1992 western "Unforgiven," but it's been part of his persona throughout his long, uneven but mostly honorable career. (Yeah, he did co-star with an orangutan twice, but in 41 films as a leading man—and 21 as a director—he's made only a few that are truly unwatchable.) It also helps explain why "True Crime" is so much wittier, more gripping and more honest than anything Eastwood-wannabes like Schwarzenegger, Stallone or Willis have made lately. Remember that Eastwood rose to stardom as a representative of the era of disillusionment, after the A-bomb, Sputnik and JFK. He was already well over 30, and the aquiline face around his piercing eyes was already scarred and weather-beaten. (Andrew O'Hehir, "True Prime," review of *True Crime,* in *Salon Magazine,* March 19, 1999. Accessed August 21, 1999; available online at http://www.salon.com/ent/movies/reviews/1999/03/19reviewc.html.)

3. There won't be many 50th [wedding] anniversary celebrations in the new millennium. Too many divorces. Too many marriages postponed till the career is launched. Too many cohabitors who never pledge their troth. . . .

   In recent years, we've been told there are many sorts of families, many sorts of relationships, all equally good. Except that heterosexual marriage isn't so good because it fosters dysfunctional families, domestic violence, child abuse and, of course, divorce.

   Divorce is bad if Dad doesn't pay child support, but it's otherwise all for the best because nobody should have to suppress their individual needs or wants for the good of others, and the kids adjust just fine.

   That's not true, but it sounds nice. In real life, children raised by two married parents do far better than kids growing up in any of those alternative forms of family, including stepfamilies. Married men and women are far happier and healthier than singles. Marriage works.

   Not perfectly. There are dreadful marriages, happy divorces and successful single moms. But, on average, marriage works better as a system for raising children than anything else we've come up with. (Joanne Jacobs, "Marital Milestones Will Be Sadly Missed in Coming Millenium," *Wilkes-Barre Times Leader,* September 3, 1999)

4. The grande dame [of colleges and universities in the Greater Boston area], of course, is Harvard University, the country's oldest institution of higher learning. Harvard grads are an impressive bunch: Among them are 33 Nobel Prize

winners, 30 Pulitzer Prize winners and six U.S. presidents. While living in a Cambridge dormitory, Bill Gates developed the programming language BASIC for the first microcomputer. Gates eventually dropped out of Harvard to found Microsoft, the world's leading provider of software for personal computers.

On the other side of Cambridge Common from the Harvard campus is Radcliffe College, founded in 1879 as a prestigious school for women. Co-ed since 1973, Radcliffe is indistinguishable from Harvard in terms of degrees and admission standards, and students share housing, classes and facilities. The former sister school does, however, function as an independent corporation and has its own president.

Sprawled along the Charles River in Cambridge is MIT, generally acknowledged to be the nation's top school for science and engineering. The demanding curriculum ensures a student body of "eggheads" who nevertheless are expanding the boundaries of the information age. Across the river in Boston itself is Boston University, founded in 1839. Nearly 26,000 graduates and undergraduates attend its various schools (Martin Luther King Jr. obtained his doctorate in theology there). BU was the first university in the nation to make all of its programs available to women and minorities, and the first to offer a school of music. (Automobile Association of America. *Boston Destination Guide,* 1999)

5. A widely used antibiotic that costs as little as 9 cents per dose could sharply alleviate suffering among millions of African AIDS patients by preventing pneumonia, toxoplasmosis and many of the other opportunistic infections that characterize full-blown AIDS, researchers said Tuesday.

"Other drugs that are far cheaper and easier to use than protease inhibitors can have a big effect," Dr. Kenneth Castro of the U.S. Centers for Disease Control and Prevention told the 13th International AIDS Conference in Durban, South Africa.

The antibiotic has no impact on the AIDS virus, which is killing 5,500 people a day in Africa, but is simply a means to minimize symptoms. "We are not going to cure HIV with our present drugs, so we need long-term strategies" to alleviate suffering, said Dr. Mauro Schechter of the British Columbia Center for Excellence in HIV/AIDS in Vancouver. Other reports delivered at the world conference indicated that brief interruptions in conventional AIDS therapy can make the drug regimen cheaper and more comfortable for patients and that some long-used drugs can help prevent mother-to-child transmission of the AIDS virus.

As protests about the high prices of AIDS drugs continued outside the conference center, another new report said that treating patients across the world could cost at least $60 billion a year. (Tomas H. Maugh II, "Inexpensive Antibiotic Could Help Millions of African AIDS Patients," *Los Angeles Times,* July 12, 2000. Accessed July 12, 2000; available online at http://www.latimes.com/news/state/updates/lat_aids000712.htm.)

6. The pungent aroma in a Los Angeles salon called Puncture is reminiscent of burnt popcorn. "That is a hell of a smell!" yelps Daren Gardner, 28, whose lanky body lies quivering on a medical-examination table. The odor is actu-

ally coming from Gardner's skin, as he submits to the latest trend catching on among tattoo and piercing devotees: branding. Body artist Todd Murray torches a small square of stainless steel using a propane flame, then lines up his shot like a pool shark with a cue, swiftly applying the red-hot metal in what's called a "kiss of fire," one of 10 strikes necessary to finish the job. "This is amazing," gasps Gardner, balling his fists while the scorching marks are applied. "If I could bottle this feeling up, I would give it away."

Welcome to the strange world of body modification, or "bod-mod," in which the human form serves as a personal canvas to be cut, poked, burned, stretched and adorned. It's a world in which terms like *journey* and *enlightenment* are used to describe acts of self-mutilation that would make even Quentin Tarantino cringe, a subculture combining tribal spirituality with kinky sex and a dash of circus sideshow. It may seem weird, but it has a long tradition: in November the American Museum of Natural History in New York City will present "Body Art: Marks of Identity," an exhibition surveying 4,000 years of skin decoration. (Jeffrey Ressner, "Brand New Bodies," *Time,* September 13, 1999)

The Author and the Publisher

Since we were young, we have been taught to rely on people more experienced, better educated, wiser, and stronger than we are to guide, protect, and nurture us. These authority figures—parents, guardians, grandparents, teachers, ministers, police officers, to name a few—have usually acted in our best interest, communicating the habits necessary for survival and the rules for success in a civil society. We have learned to trust authority figures and to respect their opinions and decisions. We would be lost without them.

But as critical thinkers, we must question and challenge the authorities we rely on for information and support. Not that we should become belligerent and suspicious. Constantly challenging the directives or recommendations of every authority becomes wearisome and could even be dangerous if we refused to accept the authority of, say, a crossing guard. But when looking to make our arguments more convincing, we should scrutinize our authoritative sources as carefully as we would an opponent's arguments. After all, our opponents will be scrutinizing us.

When it comes to gathering information, many of us do not question authority as often as we should. If you completed the group exercise mentioned early in this chapter, ask yourself how you regarded "authorities" in the group. Were you more likely to agree with someone who *seemed* to know what he or she was talking about? If someone in the group aggressively insisted that an item was true or false, were you more likely to agree because of the aggressive stance? Did you accept the authority of the group, accepting answers that were generally agreed upon?

Our best guide to truth is free and rational inquiry; we should therefore not be bound by the dictates of arbitrary authority, comfortable superstition, stifling tradition, or suffocating orthodoxy.

—*"Statement of Purpose," Free Inquiry Magazine*

Let's analyze the notion of an authority. The word "authority" contains, obviously, the word "author," and, sure enough, the two words derive from the same Latin word, *auctor,* which means "creator." An author creates, and an authority holds the power over that which he or she has created as fathers have authority over their children. Because of the similarity between the two words, it may seem safe to assume that authors (creators) are also authorities, and, in fact, that is often the case; many authors have spent countless years studying their subjects down to the finest detail and can speak with great expertise to even the most learned audiences. But not always. One does not have to be an expert to become an author. In fact, some authors speak with very little authority. Something's having been *written*—and written with all the appearances of objective truth—does not necessarily make it true. And although legitimate publishers of books, journals, and newspapers usually make every effort to ensure that their writers are knowledgeable and honest, publications often convey inaccurate and misleading information.

When you read or listen to someone, ask the following questions:

- What is the author's background?
- What are the author's bias and purpose?
- What are the author's sources?
- Who is the publisher or sponsor?

What Is the Author's Background?   What credentials does he or she have? What education and at what level? How much research went into the writer's own work? How much experience does the author have? Is the writer an expert in the topic at issue? Is the author recognized by others as an authority in the field? For information on authors, you can consult several biographical resources, including the *Who's Who* series and such works as the *Dictionary of American Biography.* When evaluating the background of an author, don't base your assessment on only one criterion. Don't assume, for instance, that the most highly educated writers speak with the greatest authority or that an uneducated person is ignorant. Be careful not to assume that only recognized authorities can speak knowledgeably on a subject. Fiction writers, for example, often exhaustively research their stories and seem to know as much about their topics as any recognized expert would. It is possible, too, that someone speaking outside his or her field may present a strikingly new and powerful idea. And the number of years that have gone into studying an issue can sometimes have relatively little to do with the writer's expertise. Albert Einstein was only in his mid-twenties when he published some of his most influential work. But overall, you should look for credible authors who have earned their right through careful study and sound analysis to speak on an issue. You may be tempted to argue that all opinions are equal, since they are merely opinions, but some opinions are dangerous or ridiculous and some are valuable, sensible, and well defended. Find authors who express opinions that have been carefully arrived at through intelligent inquiry. In fact, even those authors who represent the *opposing* side of the argument you intend to present should be the best representatives of that side.

What Are the Author's Bias and Purpose?   Writers and speakers may have a personal or professional interest in the information they are presenting. And although they may not lie outright (some might), they may hide contradictory information or carefully select language in which to present information most favorably. Perhaps the author is speaking for a company, a special interest group, an institute, a foundation, a "think tank," or a political party. He or she might be getting paid for an endorsement or for an opinion. When a writer has no special or personal interest in the topic, nothing to gain or lose by the audience's favorable or negative reaction to the topic, we say that the author is "disinterested," impartial, objective. That does not mean that the information provided by "interested" authors is to be discounted. Surely, even advertisers can occasionally present trustworthy information. But knowing what stake an author has in our reactions can be useful in our attempt to evaluate the information that has been filtered through that author's perspectives.

In the case of surveys or studies, the author may have worded the questions in such a way as to ensure the sought-after response. A corporation that sets out to prove that its product is better than everyone else's is likely to devise a method that will not produce disappointing results. And an industry trying to defend its product will most certainly put the best "spin" on its information. Take, for example, the following paragraph:

> Measurements of atmospheric cigarette smoke taken under realistic conditions indicate that the contribution of tobacco smoke to the air we breathe is minimal. One study at Harvard found only very small amounts of nicotine in the atmosphere of cocktail lounges, restaurants, bus stations and airline terminals. Based on those measurements of a substance specific to tobacco smoke, one astute reader of the literature estimated that a nonsmoker would have to spend 100 hours straight in the smokiest bar to inhale the equivalent of a single filter-tip cigarette.[7]

There may be truth in that statement, but because it is found in a pamphlet published by the Tobacco Institute, we should be highly skeptical. Although we should be careful to evaluate all the information we find, the fact that this information on secondhand smoke comes from an industry that profits from the sale of cigarettes should make us even more cautious of what we have read. When was the study done at Harvard? Was that the Harvard University in Cambridge, Massachusetts? What does "very small amounts" mean? "Small" by what standard? At what time of day were the tests done in the restaurants and lounges? Who is this mysterious "astute reader"? And so forth. If we were preparing an argument on, say, suspending anti-smoking laws in restaurants, we would be well advised to look elsewhere for support.

In attempting to uncover an author's point of view, try to determine the author's purpose in writing. If the writer is making a claim or trying to persuade the reader toward a particular belief or action, look at how he or she has dealt with opposing points of view or evidence. Does the writer seem fair and evenhanded, or does he or she dismiss opposing points of view without regard to their possible value? Does the writer commit the straw man fallacy, misrepresenting opposing views to more easily mow them down? Does the writer use slanted language or commit personal attacks? Does the writer make sweeping generalizations or demonstrate an either/or approach to complicated issues, thereby revealing a strong bias toward one side? Be wary, too, of writers who claim only to inform or who pretend to objectivity. The writer may be "stacking the deck" in an effort to subtly direct the reader toward some unstated goal. And remember: Biases and hidden agendas don't disqualify the source. You might find plenty of useful information—but useful only after a careful reading.

Finally, treat your sources fairly when judging bias and purpose. Perhaps the writer intended simply to amuse the reader or to comment casually on some inconsequential topic. If a writer intends to be ironic or satirical, if he or she is clearly exaggerating for effect, or if the writer admits to guesswork and speculation, be sure to fairly represent those intentions and admissions to your readers.

What Are the Author's Sources?   Writers seldom write in a vacuum. Most writers, as Isaac Newton suggested, respond to those who have preceded them, contributing in some sense to a long, ongoing conversation among thinkers. When you read someone's work, chances are that that writer has depended upon other sources for information, ideas, and inspiration. The original sources that a writer cites are called "primary sources." It may be important for the success of your work to consider how reliable the primary sources are and to uncover those sources if necessary to ensure that they have not been misquoted, or misrepresented. For example, in researching Thomas Jefferson's attitudes toward slavery, you might look at several books on the subject. In those "secondary sources," the authors will most likely cite Jefferson's own writings, his papers, letters, notebooks, and so forth, all of which are primary sources. Returning to the primary sources is especially necessary when an author uses statistical information in defending a claim, since statistics, like literature, can be interpreted in various, often contradictory, ways. You might want to see the numbers for yourself. As we noted before, although many authors are honest and trustworthy, not *all* writers are careful or ethical in their use of information, and others (careful *and* ethical) may simply be offering a subjective interpretation of the information. When in doubt, look up the primary, or original, source of information.

Be wary, too, of unnamed, undocumented, or completely unreliable sources in a writer's essay or argument. As we shall see later in the chapter on media, writers often attempt to give legitimacy to their work by referring to a well-known political figure or celebrity as the source of information.

> ### Critical Thinking Lapse
>
> The Princeton Dental Resource Center in Albany, New York, agreed to pay a $25,000 settlement for misleading consumers by claiming that a piece of chocolate a day might inhibit tooth decay. The center is funded by candy maker Mars Incorporated.[8]

Others allude to "an anonymous source" or "sources at the Pentagon" as the originators of important information. Other techniques include such phrases as "surveys have shown" or "according to recent studies." What surveys? What studies? The wise critical thinker is always wary of unnamed sources or those whose reliability cannot be checked.

Who Is the Publisher or Sponsor?   Most students know that not all publications are equal, which is why you don't usually find students using the *National Inquirer* or *Weekly World News* or even *People* magazine as a source of factual evidence. If we want to know whether or not Elvis is dead and, if so, when he died, we usually turn, instead, to the archives of the *New York Times* or *U.S. News and World Report*. In fact, most national publications employ respected editors whose reputations and job security depend on the quality and the veracity of the writing they publish. Mistakes can happen and unverified "facts" occasionally sneak by vigilant editors, but the information that appears in major newspapers and daily, weekly, and monthly magazines is *generally* reliable, although a critical reader, as always, would be wise to question even the most seemingly objective reports. Commercial interests often dictate editorial policy, and there have been several interesting cases of exceptional periodicals being the victims of hoaxes and sabotage, resulting in embarrassing retractions and even, in one famous case, the return of a Pulitzer Prize.[9]

Published opinions are another matter. Many periodicals have an editorial bias that governs not only the topics chosen but the perspective and slant of the writing as well. Although there is nothing wrong with a periodical's having a political slant, the careful reader should know what that slant is. *In These Times* and *Mother Jones,* for example, publish articles and arguments from a working class perspective, whereas *Commentary* usually takes a very conservative stance on labor issues. Scanning the table of contents and looking at the advertisements and any editorials will give you a good sense of the political and cultural biases of the periodical. Finally, a reference book called *Magazines for Libraries* provides brief descriptions, including the political dispositions, of periodicals available in libraries.

Publishers of academic books and journals are usually extremely careful to publish work of high quality, which is assured by a rigorous system of peer

Magazines for Libraries

5621. *The Nation.* [ISSN: 0027-8378] 1865. W. $52 (Foreign, $70). Katrina vanden Heuvel. Nation Co., L.P., 72 Fifth Ave., New York, NY 10011; http://www. TheNation.com. Index, adv. Sample. Circ: 95,000. Vol. ends: June & Dec. Microform: PMC, UMI. Reprint: Pub, UMI.

Indexed: API, MI, PAIS, PerO, RG. *Bk. rev:* 4, 1,000 words, signed. *Aud:* Ga, Ac.

The Nation was recently purchased by its longtime former editor, Victor Navasky, and a group of limited partners, including current editor Katrina vanden Heuvel and noted liberal Paul Newman. Under this new ownership, *The Nation,* which is the oldest continually published weekly in the United States, hopes to strengthen itself in its battle with *New Republic* for the hearts, minds, and pocketbooks of the liberal population in the United States. It remains an unabashedly liberal and left-wing publication, though it is not afraid to chide the Left as well. The writing is crisp and concise, a joy to read. The multiple short editorials at the beginning of each issue cover a wide range of topics, from the recent developments in cloning to the status of the publishing industry. *The Nation* is a valuable resource for any library.

The Nation's Web page currently includes an index to the current week's issue with some links to full-text articles. Searchable full-text archives are a planned addition to the site. One unique feature of *The Nation*'s Web page is the "Forums"— interactive online discussions of recent articles.

5608. *The American Spectator.* [ISSN: 0148-8414] 1967. m. $35. R. Emmett Tyrrell, Jr. 2020 N. 14th St., Suite 750, P.O. Box 549, Arlington, VA 22201; http://www. amspec.org:80. Illus., index, adv. Sample. Circ: 275,000. Vol. ends: Dec. CD-ROM: IA. Microform: UMI. Reprint: ISI, Pub. Online: IA.

Indexed: MI, PAIS, PerO, RG. *Bk. rev:* 6. 1,500 words, signed. *Aud:* Ga, Ac.

The American Spectator continues to feature excellent writing and to also place emphasis on investigative reporting. The articles are sharp, pungent, and definitely demonstrate a conservative bias, not unexpected from a publication that has included the Children's Defense Fund on its list of enemies. Its political slant allows this publication to tackle topics that more mainstream, nonpolitical sources may be cautious about taking on fully—such as the media's handling of the scandals revealed during President Clinton's reelection campaign. The "Presswatch" feature is of particular interest, especially when it skewers the mainstream media. This title remains a valuable one for libraries seeking to balance their collections. The online site has the current issue and archived issues back to June 1995. Not all articles are available full-text through this site. In addition to the print equivalent, there is an "Online Update" (updated on Tuesday), "Enemies of the Week" (updated on Wednesdays), and a new column by editor R. Emmett Tyrell each Friday. The site does not appear to have the capability to search.

review. Submissions to scholarly presses and journals (Oxford University Press or *The New England Journal of Medicine,* for example) are commonly sent to leading scholars familiar with the topic, who recommend the submission for publication, suggest revisions, or recommend that the submission be rejected. Ideally, the process helps guarantee that what gets published is trustworthy, although this does not release a critical thinker, as you can repeat now from memory, from the obligation to carefully evaluate even these sources of information.

In short, it is important to discover whatever you can, not only about the author of the piece, but about the publisher as well. Many publishers protect their well-deserved reputations by attempting to verify every statement they print. Some information makes it into print, however, without ever having passed through an exacting review process. Some presses (university presses, for example) publish only books of the highest caliber; others publish what they know will sell. Books can be published through "vanity presses," in which the author pays all costs associated with publication—printing, marketing, distributing, and so forth. Pamphlets and many newsletters are published without editing or review by disinterested parties. Some newspapers publish op-ed pieces that contain misinformation and distortions. In an effort to antagonize their listeners, radio commentators often say blatantly false things. Certainly, "published" (literally, "made public") is not synonymous with "truthful."

Where does the Internet fit into all of this? Honestly, it's a mess. Whereas most information in most traditional print sources (periodicals, books, newspapers) has passed through some sort of quality control to ensure its accuracy and value, anyone with a computer and access to a server can "publish" absolutely anything on the Internet. Surfing the Internet for information is like shopping blindfolded in the world's largest grocery store. You might come away with exquisite gourmet delicacies, spices you had no idea existed, and nutritious fruits and vegetables, or you might find sweets that taste good but are harmful to your health, bland cereals, or even deadly poisons for cleaning bathrooms or killing rats. Because of the excess of poison available, some students and their professors refuse to use the World Wide Web as a source of scholarly information; that is unfortunate given the riches a careful shopper can find there. When you shop around on the Internet, it is vital to your intellectual survival that you take off the blindfold.

Evaluating electronic sources is similar to evaluating print sources: ask a great many questions about the content and the author. When evaluating the site itself, give preference to those maintained by recognized and respected organizations and institutions such as universities (Cornell University Library or Purdue University's Online Writing Lab, for example), government agencies (the Library of Congress or the Smithsonian Institute), and noncommercial, service-oriented sites (the American Cancer Society). Often the URL, the address of the site, will provide some information about the sponsor of the site.

Distinguishing Scholarly from Nonscholarly Periodicals

There is no sure-fire method for distinguishing scholarly journals from other periodicals, but the characteristics listed below will offer some guidance. Generally speaking, scholarly journals are trustworthy, because the information they contain has undergone rigorous review by experts and scholars. But that in no way suggests that nonscholarly journals cannot be trusted or that scholarly journals are infallible. The following guidelines will help you categorize a journal, but you will still have to determine whether the information you collect is credible.

Scholarly Journals

- Have a serious and professional look; generally contain few visuals except for graphs and charts; carry very few advertisements, which are usually limited to announcements of upcoming conferences and recently published books and calls for papers.
- Contain articles based on research and experimentation, written by scholars who cite their sources in footnotes and bibliographies.
- Are written for other scholars, practitioners, and students who have some familiarity with the topic and the language used in the discipline.
- Are often, but not always, published by colleges and universities, and by professional and scientific societies, organizations, and associations.

Examples: *JAMA: The Journal of the American Medical Association; The New England Journal of Medicine; Philological Quarterly; The American Journal of Sociology; The Reading Teacher; Journal of Accountancy; Harvard Business Review; College English*

NONSCHOLARLY PERIODICALS

Nonscholarly periodicals include journals of opinion, news and general-interest magazines, popular magazines, trade publications, and sensational publications.

Journals of Opinion (also called policy journals)

- Appearance can range from a sober format to a glossier look; sometimes have the appearance of a newspaper; include few pictures, sometimes none; often contain political cartoons; contain limited and selective advertisements.
- Ususaly have a professed or easily inferred editorial policy that falls somewhere along the political spectrum, although some journals of opinion collect viewpoints from across the spectrum. The writers are often well-respected and educated experts, commentators, and journalists who write frequently on political and social topics. Political figures occasionally write for journals of opinion. Content is usually well researched; notes and bibliographies may appear with articles. Often contain book and movie reviews, and sometimes include original poetry.
- Are aimed at a broad, educated audience familiar with and interested in current social, political, economic, and cultural events. Tone and style are usually serious but not as academic as that found in scholarly journals.
- Published by think tanks, private organizations, political parties, policy institutions, and other groups who hope to foster a particular opinion.

Examples: *Dissent; Mother Jones; The Nation; Utne Reader; The New Republic; The American Spectator; Insight; Human Events; Commentary; National Review; Public Interest; Policy Review; The Progressive; Z Magazine; Reason Magazine; The Weekly Standard; Christian Century; In These Times*

News and General-Interest Magazines

- Glossy, attractive appearance; illustrated

Distinguishing Scholarly from Nonscholarly Periodicals (continued)

with colorful photographs, charts, and graphs; wide range of advertisements.

- Wide range of authors from freelance journalists, staff writers, scholars, editors, invited guests, and so forth. Sometimes contain articles and essays reprinted from other sources. Language is nontechnical. Topics covered range widely—from current events and social trends to politics, the economy, and art. Coverage also ranges from short and superficial to extensive and thoughtful. Most periodicals in this category contain movie and book reviews; some general-interest magazines contain original art, such as poetry and fiction.
- Audience is educated and interested in current news and issues but does not necessarily have extensive knowledge of the topics covered.
- Published almost entirely by for-profit corporations.

Examples: News: *Time; Maclean's* (Canada); *Newsweek; U.S. News and World Report.* General Interest: *New Yorker; Harper's; Atlantic Monthly; Scientific American; National Geographic*

Popular Magazines

- Glossy, attractive, colorful appearance with plenty of illustrations and advertisements geared toward specific groups.
- Written by staff and freelance writers. Some writers may know a great deal about their topics; others may simply be reporting what they have discovered. Topics are usually selected for specific consumer groups and often include such things as recipes and "how-to" essays. Ads are also geared toward specific groups.
- Audience is interested in topic of the magazine (sports, health, home decorating, and so forth); minimal reading skills necessary.
- Published for profit.

Examples: *People; Sports Illustrated; Rolling Stone; Ebony; Vanity Fair; Modern Maturity; Redbook; Southern Living; This Old House;* and most health, fitness, and fashion magazines

Trade Publications

- Similar in appearance to news and general-interest magazines: glossy appearance, many pictures and other illustrations, such as easy-to-read graphs and charts. Advertisements for a wide range of products and services and many specialized ads aimed at practitioners in a particular field.
- Articles are usually written by practitioners and educators, often in technical jargon common to the profession or industry. Focus on current trends and practical applications. Often include job announcements and personality profiles.
- Written for practitioners and students in particular field.
- Usually published through professional organizations but also by corporations.

Examples: *Industry Week; Advertising Age; Hotel and Motel Management; The Bookbag; Forbes; Fortune; Business Week; Publisher's Weekly; Broadcasting and Cable; Variety*

Sensational Publications

- Often look like tabloid newspapers; often contain shocking or attention-grabbing photographs and equally astonishing advertisements promoting products of questionable value.
- Articles are written by staff and freelance writers to hold reader's interest. Sources are seldom cited. Language is simple. Headlines often make outlandish claims.
- Audience is usually gullible and superstitious, interested in pseudoscience and the paranormal.
- Published for profit.

Examples: *National Enquirer; Globe; National Examiner; Weekly World News; Star*

Addresses with ".edu" (short for "education") usually originate at colleges and universities. Other current suffixes include the following:

.com or .cc (commercial site)

.gov (government agencies)

.mil (military sites)

.net (networks and service providers)

.org (nonprofit organizations)

Because the Web is growing so fast, new suffixes will most likely be added soon, including, possibly, .rec (recreation sites), .arts (cultural sites), and .store (merchants). A tilde (~) in the address usually indicates that the page is maintained by an individual who may be working independently of the school, organization, or agency that provides the Web address.

At a helpful Web site called Whois (http://www.network.solutions .com/cgi-bin/whois/whois), you can find limited information about a site, including contact information for the person who registered the domain name. Whois won't tell you whether the site is trustworthy, but it can get you started on finding more information about a site.

Appearance can sometimes help distinguish scholarly sites from the more commercial ones: scholarly sites are often the least flashy, looking more like electronic versions of typed pages—no banners, few pictures, dull graphics. But appearances, of course, can be deceiving, and some highly reliable sites are very attractive and user-friendly. All in all, it is difficult to make any general statements about Web sites, the designers of which are very clever indeed. If there were a clear indicator of a trustworthy site, Web masters at less legitimate sites would turn it to their advantage. In fact, some sites have managed to secure an ".edu" suffix even though the sites are not legitimate schools.

To determine whether to believe that "facts" you find on a site are reliable and whether the opinions expressed on a site are trustworthy, try the following:

- See if you can find out more about the author or the sponsoring site. Are there links on the site that will lead you to a résumé or biography of the author? Use a search engine to see what others have written about the author or the organization. Perhaps current news articles will provide helpful information, or even warnings.

- If an organization sponsors the site, see if you can find out more about the organization by following links to the home page, by clicking on any links labeled "About Us" or "Who We Are," or by looking at the part of the URL before the first "/". For example, an article found at the address http://www.guncite.com/ gun_control_gcbogus.html is housed at the site www.guncite.com, a site dedicated to preserving the right to bear arms. That bias should be taken into account when evaluating information and opinions collected from the site.

- What does your common sense tell you about the site? Does the author seem to have a pronounced bias? Are opposing views ridiculed or misrepresented? Is the author attempting to sell you something or solicit a donation? Is the site littered with banner advertisements?

- Consider how you found the site. Did you link to it from another, reliable site, or did you find it through a search engine?

- Follow the author's links to other sites. Do the linked sites reveal the same bias as that of the original site? Are the linked sites reliable and objective sources of information?

Assessing Web sites is a notoriously difficult task. It is probably no exaggeration to say that only researchers already well informed about a topic can know for certain whether the information on a site is reliable. Besides keeping your eyes open, the best method to determine whether a site is a legitimate source of information is to use some of the guides mentioned in the first section of this chapter, "Finding Sources," and to count on professors and librarians who can point you in the direction of trustworthy sites. If you have any doubts about what you find on the Internet, do your best to verify the information through other sources. Do not make the mistake of thinking that what you have found is any good just because you found it and just because it fits your purpose.

The Audience

Besides examining the content of your sources and asking a great many questions about the author and the publisher, inquiring about the intended audience and studying reader reactions can provide insight into the quality of a source.

Who Is the Intended Audience?   Knowing something about the author's intended audience can help you evaluate the information. In some cases, journals and books are aimed at readers far better versed than you are in the topic under study.[10] You may have to research a topic even more deeply than you at first expected to familiarize yourself more completely with an issue. On the other hand, writing intended for younger audiences, though accurate, may not contain the complete picture you are looking for. Certain encyclopedias—those published for use in a computer CD or DVD player, for example—are often written at levels that make them unreliable for research at the college level. They may be helpful in getting started, especially if you are completely unversed in a topic, but good research at the collegiate level must go beyond such sources. To help you decide what audience an encyclopedia is intended for, consult Kenneth Kister's *Kister's Best Encyclopedias* (2nd ed., Oryx

Press, 1994), which evaluates the reliability and objectivity of over eight hundred encyclopedias.

Finally, some authors write strictly for an audience that is predisposed to agree with the author's point of view. Newsletters published by radio-talk-show hosts and many pages published on the Internet, for example, are intended to provide data and opinions to readers who are merely looking to support long-held convictions. Pages devoted to "proving" that one race is superior to another, that one political viewpoint is uniquely correct, that religious beliefs are dangerous, that conspirators are stealing our freedoms, and so forth should be treated with suspicion. It is possible that these sites and sources contain some accurate or useful information, but the obviousness of the writer's objectives—to speak to like-minded readers, to "preach to the choir," as the cliché goes—can in some cases make the information nearly useless to a critical thinker. Knowing the intended audience, however, should not lead you to conclude automatically that the information in tainted. Several journals of opinion (*The Nation, Commentary, National Review,* to name a very few) have the highest editorial standards. Still, no critical thinker reads them with a closed mind.

How Has the Audience Responded?   Another part of the context of research is what has been written in *response* to the information you intend to use in your argument. Usually after the publication of a scholarly book, for example, reviews written by other scholars will appear in journals and on Internet sites. These reviews, although sometimes petty and personal (some reviewers are settling old scores or pushing their own agendas), can be helpful in alerting readers to the presence of misinformation or shoddy research. In doing research on a political, historical or literary figure, for example, you might consult reviews to determine if the biography you intend to quote from is considered by scholars to be accurate and fair to the subject. If it turns out that the biographer based the book on rumor and speculation, you are better off not using it. The methodology used in surveys and studies might be challenged in subsequent issues of a scholarly journal or even in the popular press. And the "letters" or "corrections" section of journals and magazines can rectify, or provide alternative interpretations of, information that appeared in previous editions. In a recent edition of *Harper's* magazine, a normally very reliable source of information, readers were notified in a "corrections" alert that the "2,000,000" Kurds killed by the Turkish government, as reported in an earlier issue of the magazine, should have read "37,000." Finally, even if you don't have access to comments made about a specific work, it can help to consider the writer's reputation in the community he or she writes for. Authors who are often cited by other writers or who show up often in bibliographies are usually considered experts in their fields.

EXERCISE 12.3

Suppose you want to use the following passages in an argument. How reliable do you judge them to be? Evaluate each passage according to the criteria outlined in this chapter: (1) author's background, (2) author's bias and purpose, (3) publisher or sponsor, (4) intended audience. (The author's sources will be unavailable as a criterion in these exercises.) In several cases, you may have to conduct a little research to determine something about the speaker, the author, or the organization.

1. Liberals tell kids in school all over America that the best way to protect themselves from AIDS is to wear condoms while engaging in sexual intercourse. It's a lie. They are imposing a death sentence on kids. The failure rate of condoms is around 17 percent. They're teaching kids to play Russian roulette. (Rush Limbaugh, *See, I Told You So,* 1993)

2. It's adequate for the time we use it, which is four to six weeks a year. We provide all the necessary things that are required by Federal, state and local standards: shower rooms, dishwashing rooms, smoke detectors, trash removal. (Dennett Butler, president of the Somerset County [Maryland] Growers Association speaking about Camp Somerset, a former prisoner of war camp used to house migrant farm workers. Quoted in Steven Greenhouse, "At Camp for Migrants, The Living Isn't Easy," *New York Times,* August 9, 1999)

3. Ever since the earliest days of the 17th century, at least some Americans have called for restricting immigration. And while many have framed their opposition in nakedly racist terms, others have always sought to dress up bigotry in high-minded concern for the common good. (Edward T. O'Donnell, Assistant Professor of History, Hunter College, Letter to *New York Times,* August 9, 1999)

4. "Over 80% of Americans support very little or no more immigration. Is anyone listening to us?" "Tired of sitting in traffic? Every day, another 6,000 immigrants arrive. Every day!!" (Billboards in Queens and Brooklyn, NYC, sponsored by Craig Nelsen, who maintains a Web site at ProjectUSA, an organization that claims that "the unprecedented level of foreigners arriving in the U.S. every day is eroding our quality of life and threatening the foundation of our country. We believe that immigration numbers should be returned to traditional levels." Available online at http://www.projectusa.org.)

5. Right now, there's little point to choosing a Pentium III computer unless you're a graphics designer or a devoted game player, or you rely heavily on speech-recognition software. There isn't enough software tailored for the Pentium III to justify spending extra for it instead of a fast Pentium II or the equivalent.

   Because even inexpensive machines can easily handle just about any software, you give up almost nothing in performance by shopping for computers in the lower end of the price spectrum. ("Computer Preview: How Fast? How Cheap?" *Consumer Reports,* July 1999.)

6. Milk paint "has a distinctive smell, but it is not disagreeable. There are no fumes during use, and it can be washed down the kitchen sink when it

comes time to clean up. The manufacturer warns that prolonged exposure to lime can burn wet skin and injure eyes. In 25 years of use, I have never experienced either of these problems. I think of the finish as perfectly safe." (Mike Dunbar, "Milk Paint: A Traditional Painted Finish That Improves with Age," *Fine Woodworking,* June 1999)

7. Sixty-seven percent of people would prefer that the races be separated. That's what a poll of my listeners is showing. (Mike Gallagher, radio-talk-show host, August 18, 1999)

8. There's no such thing as a bad Picasso. (Pablo Picasso)

9. Jon Benet was alive when Mom called 911. (Headline in *Weekly World News*)

10. President Clinton extolled the Constitution and rule of law yesterday in a speech to the American Bar Association, which was widely criticized for hosting the president 11 days after he was fined for lying under oath.

    "I understand he was the second choice because John Gotti wasn't available," said Mark Levin, president of Landmark Legal Foundation, a Washington public-interest law firm.

    "As a member of the ABA for more than four decades, I am ashamed," wrote lawyer Gerald Walpin in yesterday's *Wall Street Journal.* "[This] sends a message to lawyers that it is OK to lie and obstruct justice, so long as you maintain political allies in high places in the ABA."

    The Southeastern Legal Foundation, which is based in Atlanta, where the president addressed the ABA, said the association forfeited its "ethical authority over the legal profession" by hosting the president.

    Larry Klayman, chairman of the watchdog group Judicial Watch, excoriated the ABA for welcoming Mr. Clinton just days after it hosted convicted felon Webster L. Hubbell, whom the president once installed as the No. 3 official in the Justice Department. (Bill Shammon, "ABA Scolded Over Clinton Address," *Washington Times,* August 10, 1999) *Note:* How reliable are any of the sources in this article: the *Washington Times,* Landmark Legal Foundation, Gerald Walpin, The Southeastern Legal Foundation, and Judicial Watch?

11. . . . [O]ur popular culture has become not only offensive but deeply harmful. This is . . . largely because movies, popular music, and television have replaced schools and families as the "prime educational force" in America. There is now much consensus on this point from across the political spectrum.

    The relevant question is: How can we make things better? How can we convince movie producers, musicians, and television executives to cut the gratuitous violence and sexual depravity that, increasingly, are the hallmark of their craft? (William J. Bennett, Commentary, *The Weekly Standard,* August 23, 1999. Accessed August 30, 1999; available online at http://www.weeklystandard.com/censorship.html.)

12. No one in his right mind would argue that .50-caliber sniper rifles serve any "self-defense" purpose. By definition, they serve exactly the contrary purpose.

They are virtually useless in hunting. The handful of shooters in the Far West who use them for long range "target shooting" could still do so if they wished, just as machine-gun freaks get together to blast away in the woods with the NFA-registered guns.

What's left is the "slippery slope" argument that the National Rifle Association, its mouthpiece Charlton Heston and others in the gun lobby whine about.

In their view, any regulation, even President Clinton's mouse-size package of timid no-brainers, will lead inexorably to confiscation of every gun in America by jack-booted thugs.

This mechanistic argument seems to work for everybody in the gun-nut crowd, from the automatons in the trenches to the NRA's pocket lint in Congress—light-weight luminaries like Sens. Larry Craig and Trent Lott and the prolix Rep. Bob Barr.

Whether you buy that paranoid logic or not, one fact is clear. While Congress dithers and the president fiddles, the gun industry continues to run up the slope of killing power to make a buck. It blithely leaves the rest of us to slide down that bloody slope in a staggering epidemic of gun violence. (Tom Diaz, "Sniper-rifle Bargains Bump Threat to Society Up a Notch," *Wilkes-Barre Times Leader,* August 20, 1999) *Note:* Diaz is senior policy analyst at the Violence Policy Center, a think-tank in Washington, D.C.)

13. Modern American collegiate life is a surreal experience, completely unlike either the high school years that precede it or the adult world for which it ostensibly offers preparation. It resembles a sociological experiment gone wildly awry, in which young people of both sexes are crammed together in small rooms, relieved of adult supervision, and told that this is, somehow, an academic experience. These "students" inhabit a world of bizarre schedules, peculiar relationships, and frequent drinking, disturbed only by the occasional exam and the looming specter of a senior-year job search.

There is very little that can be said to prepare a fresh-faced member of the Class of 2003 for what awaits him during the next four years—like many creations of the liberal imagination, college must be seen to be believed. (Ross Douthat, "Advice to the Class of 2003," *The American Spectator,* August 19, 1999. Accessed August 21, 1999; available online at http://www .spectator.org/. *Note:* Douthat is a sophomore at Harvard and deputy editor of the *Harvard Salient.*)

14. Water is an important element in all our lives. Did you know that water makes up 65 percent of our bodies? And health experts recommend that we drink eight glasses of water a day? Safe, clean water is essential to our well being. That's why we want you to know that your water meets—and often surpasses—all the health and safety standards set by the United States Environmental Protection Agency (EPA) and the Pennsylvania Department of Environmental Protection (PADEP). At United Water we are dedicated to providing you and your family with water that is safe and healthy.

In 1998 we regularly tested water samples to be sure that your water met the safety standards. And we're proud to let you know that it did. All the test results are on file with the PADEP, the agency that monitors and regulates drinking water quality in our state. In all cases your water was as good as—or better than—the government requirements. (Letter to Customers, United Water Pennsylvania, Summer 1999)

TAKING NOTES

When reading, some college students, perhaps overwhelmed by the amount of new information they discover in college, tend to highlight an excessive number of sentences and paragraphs in their textbooks, waste hundreds of dimes at the photocopier, and attempt to write down every word a professor utters. That is an understandable reaction, especially since success on tests and projects often depends on the ability to recount what was read or heard. But the truth is that it is impossible to remember every detail, and trying to note every idea sinks the most important content in a sea of yellow highlighting and ink. Taking notes on what you have read, especially when researching a topic, means *carefully* selecting what is important and useful as you try to faithfully represent the opposing argument and support your own claims.

There are probably as many ways to take notes as there are writers, ranging from simple notations in a notebook to elaborate computer files, but the easiest and most effective method of note-taking is still the three-by-five-inch or six-by-four-inch index card. The process of recording information on cards is not difficult, and the use of cards can make the initial drafting of an essay much easier than using notes recorded in a notebook or even on a computer since the cards can be arranged and rearranged as you see fit. Arranging the cards will be easier if you record only a small amount of information on each card. And be sure to number your cards; you'll know why after you drop them all the first time. If you decide not to use note cards, be sure to devise a system that you can keep control over and that will serve you well when you begin to draft your essay. Some students prefer to photocopy or print out their sources on sheets of paper and then to highlight the important information or even cut and paste the quotes to their draft. Whatever system you use, your notes will be of two kinds, bibliographical and content. Although some of the following advice assumes that you will use cards, you can modify the advice to fit whatever system you prefer.

Bibliographical Information

Use one card to record the publication information for each work you will cite in your paper. Later in this chapter, you will see what publication information (author, title, place of publication, date, page numbers, and so forth) is needed in a works cited list or a bibliography. Be sure to devote one card to this information for each source, and remember to record everything you will need. There is nothing more frustrating than scrambling around the night before a paper is due looking for bibliographical information. (You're not the only person to have just thought to yourself, "I'll just make it up." Don't forget, your professors know the tricks and are usually on the lookout for them.)

Content Notes: Quotes, Summaries, and Paraphrases

Most of your cards will contain summaries, paraphrases, and quotations from your sources. You can decide how you want your cards to look, but be consistent in whatever format you choose. One possibility is to record a shortened form of the source (perhaps the author's last name), the page number of the source, and the note-card number at the top of the card. Then record your note.

Quotations   Obviously, the easiest note to record is a quotation. Select quotations carefully; as you will see shortly, it is far better for both you and your reader to paraphrase when possible. But when you do record a quotation, be very careful to place quotation marks around the material and to transcribe the quotation accurately. It is best not to omit anything if you copy a quotation, but if you do, replace the omission with ellipses points (three dots). If you add anything to the quotation, place the addition in brackets so that you don't later forget that it was not part of the original. Keep in mind that you will not have the original passage before you when you write your essay, so it is vitally important that you indicate clearly in your notes all the information you'll need to accurately cite your quotation. Finally, if you use index cards, be sure to organize them in a uniform manner. For example, you might give a shortened form of the author's name and the page number at the top of the card along with the number of the card. Below is a passage from an essay by William Carlos Williams, followed by several examples of cards with quotations.

> Hamilton had hounded him for years. At length he openly called Burr "politically dangerous." What did he mean? Burr wrote demanding an explanation. To the party in power, yes, dangerous he may have been, but to the country— How? Hamilton refused to answer. Then let it be pinned down. Either it must be one or the other. Burr was not angry. If any one feared it was not he. His head was clear, he slept well, he was refreshed and went to the place of the duel. Hamilton was fifty-seven. Burr somewhat younger.
>
> Hamilton fired first, the bullet clipping a twig above Burr's head. His hand was trembling. Did he fire wild, as his seconds say he did, on purpose? Burr's seconds said no, and stuck to it; the bullet came too close to their man's head to have been anything but a plain miss due to a shaking hand. Then Burr fired. He shot coolly, seriously and with conviction. He killed his man, logically and as he meant to do and knew he must. For a moment, as he saw his adversary fall, he was overcome with compassion, then he turned away. Hamilton, before he died, dictated his astonishing testament, in which he says—imagine the flimsy nature of his lifelong enmity toward the man—that, regarding Burr, he "might have been misinformed of his intentions." Good God, what an answer! Work till you are fifty-seven to ruin a man, insult him, malign him and then say, dying: I may have been misinformed.[11]

Williams, page 201   12

"He [Burr] shot coolly, seriously and with conviction. He killed his man, logically and as he meant to do and knew he must. For a moment, as he saw his adversary fall, he was overcome with compassion, then he turned away."

QUOTATION

Williams, page 201   13

"Hamilton, before he died, dictated his astonishing testament, in which he says—imagine the flimsy nature of his lifelong enmity toward the man—that, regarding Burr, he 'might have been misinformed of his intentions.' Good God, what an answer! Work till you are fifty-seven to ruin a man, insult him, malign him and then say, dying: I may have been misinformed."

QUOTATION

Summaries   In Chapter 7 we looked at methods for summarizing and paraphrasing arguments, and some of what we discuss here will help refresh your memory. But in using sources, you will often find that you need to summarize and paraphrase, in addition to arguments, essays, reports, explanations, and other materials that will aid in the defense of your own claim. A summary of an argument, essay, or article contains only the main idea (the thesis) or the claim and, depending on the purpose of the summary, the main premises or supporting points. A summary of an essay might contain the thesis sentence and the topic idea from each body paragraph. How much you summarize depends on how much of the original work you will need to remember and how much you intend to use. If you're simply going to refer to the article or argument or highlight its main idea, you can limit yourself to a sentence or two, perhaps to an outline, but if you hope to recall some of the author's evidence, you should record that evidence as well in your summary.

To write a summary, read the argument several times, underlining (if the book or periodical is your property) the main idea and subpoints on the second or third reading. Much of what you learned in Chapter 7 about analyzing arguments will come in handy here. Then try to write your summary without looking at the source. You can start with a sentence like "The author is saying that . . ." or "the author is arguing that . . ." or "the author is trying to prove that. . . ." If you are using cards, you can write this sentence on one card. Then try to recall the main developmental points, writing each on a separate card. After you have given the recall method your best shot, go back to the source to see how closely you have captured the author's ideas. Revise your cards if necessary, being very careful to use your own words when possible and to put quotation marks around any key words and phrases that appear in the original. At this point, you can also enter additional information under the main points. Sloppy cards full of crossouts and revisions should be rewritten to make the task of drafting your essay easier.

The following essay is summarized on index cards at the end of the essay.

Raised on Rock-and-Roll

Anna Quindlen

Mister Ed is back on television, indicating that, as most middle-of-the-road antique shops suggest, Americans cannot discriminate between things worth saving and things that simply exist. *The Donna Reed Show* is on, too, and *My Three Sons,* and those dopey folks from *Gilligan's Island.* There's *Leave It to Beaver* and *The Beverly Hillbillies* and even *Lassie,* whose plaintive theme song leaves my husband all mushy around the edges.

Social historians say these images, and those of Howdy Doody and Pinky Lee and Lamb Chop and Annette have forever shaped my consciousness. But I have memories far stronger than that. I remember sitting cross-legged in front of the tube, one of the console sets with the ersatz lamé netting over the speakers, but I was not watching puppets or pratfalls. I was born in Philadelphia, a city where if you can't dance you might as well stay home, and I was raised on rock-and-roll. My earliest television memory is of *American Bandstand,* and the central question of my childhood was: Can you dance to it?

When I was fifteen and a wild devotee of Mitch Ryder and the Detroit Wheels, it sometimes crossed my mind that when I was thirty-four years old, decrepit, wrinkled as a prune and near death, I would have moved on to some nameless kind of dreadful show music, something akin to Muzak. I did not think about the fact that my parents were still listening to the music that had been popular when they were kids; I only thought that they played "Pennsylvania 6-5000" to torment me and keep my friends away from the house.

But I know I'm never going to stop loving rock-and-roll, all kinds of rock-and-roll: the Beatles, the Rolling Stones, Hall and Oates, Talking Heads, the Doors, the Supremes, Tina Turner, Elvis Costello, Elvis Presley. I even like bad rock-and-roll, although I guess that's where my age shows; I don't have the tolerance for Bon Jovi that I once had for the Raspberries.

We have friends who, when their son was a baby, used to put a record on and say, "Drop your butt, Phillip." And Phillip did. That's what I love: drop-your-butt music. It's one of the few things left in my life that makes me feel good without even thinking about it. I can walk into any bookstore and find dozens of books about motherhood and love and human relations and so many other things that we once did through a combination of intuition and emotion. I even heard recently that some school is giving a course on kissing, which makes me wonder if I'm missing something. But rock-and-roll flows through my veins, not my brain. There's nothing else that feels the same to me as, say, the faint sound of the opening dum-doo-doo-doo-doo-doo of "My Girl" coming from a radio on a summer day. I feel the way I felt when I first heard it. I feel good, as James Brown says.

There are lots of people who don't feel this way about rock-and-roll. Some of them don't understand it, like the Senate wives who said that records should have rating stickers on them so that you would know whether the lyrics were dirty. The kids who hang out at Mr. Big's sub shop in my neighborhood thought this would make record shopping a lot easier, because you could choose albums by how bad the rating was. Most of the people who love rock-and-roll just thought the labeling idea was dumb. Lyrics, after all, are not the point of rock-and-roll, despite how beautifully people like Bruce Springsteen and Joni Mitchell write. Lyrics are the point only in the case of "Louie, Louie"; the words have never been deciphered, but it is widely understood that they are about sex. That's understandable, because rock-and-roll is a lot like sex: If you talk seriously about it, it takes a lot of the feeling away—and feeling is the point.

Some people over-analyze rock-and-roll, just as they over-analyze everything else. They say things like "Bruce Springsteen is the poet laureate of the American dream gone sour," when all I need to know about Bruce Springsteen is that the saxophone bridge on "Jungleland" makes the back of my neck feel exactly the way I felt the first time a boy kissed me, only over and over and over again. People write about Prince's "psychedelic masturbatory fantasies," but when I think about Prince, I don't really think, I just feel—feel the moment when, driving to the beach, I first heard "Kiss" on the radio and started bopping up and down in my seat like a seventeen-year-old on a day trip.

I've got precious few things in my life anymore that just make me feel, that make me jump up and dance, that make me forget the schedule and the job and the mortgage payments and just let me thrash around inside my skin. I've got precious few things I haven't studied and considered and reconsidered and studied some more. I don't know a chord change from a snare drum, but I know what I like, and I like feeling this way sometimes. I love rock-and-roll because in a time of talk, talk, talk, it's about action.

Here's a test: Get hold of a two-year-old, a person who has never read a single word about how heavy-metal musicians should be put in jail or about Tina Turner's "throaty alto range." Put "I Heard It Through the Grapevine" on the stereo. Stand the two-year-old in front of the stereo. The two-year-old will begin to dance. The two-year-old will drop his butt. Enough said.

Here is a one-card summary, highlighting only the main idea:

Quindlen   1

Rock and roll appeals to our feelings, not to our reason or understanding.

SUMMARY OF MAIN IDEA

Here is an additional card summarizing the main points of the entire article:

```
  Quindlen                                              2

      My consciousness was shaped not by television, but by
  rock-and-roll, and I'll never stop loving it. Rock-and-roll has an
  effect on me; it makes me feel good. I don't have to think about the
  music or analyze its deeper meaning the way some people have over-
  analyzed so much of what used to come naturally to us. I've studied
  and analyzed things too, but not rock-and-roll. For me, rock music
  lets me forget the pressures of life. I respond to rock-and-roll the way
  babies do: I just feel it.

  SUMMARY
```

Here is a card summarizing the central claim in Quindlen's argument and her supporting premises:

```
  Quindlen                                              3

  It's a dumb idea to put rating stickers on rock-and-roll albums.
        1. It would have the opposite effect. Kids could choose albums
  that got the lowest rating.
        2. The lyrics aren't the point of rock-and-roll. Rock music
  appeals to our feelings not our reasoning.

  SUMMARY
```

Notice how card 2 summarizes the essay, whereas card 3 summarizes Quindlen's argument. How you intend to use Quindlen's remarks will dictate how you summarize her work. Finally, keep in mind that if you intend to summarize an argument completely, including missing premises, you'll need to look again at Chapter 7.

Paraphrasing   Whereas a summary condenses an entire argument or article, a paraphrase restates a passage in different words. Just as explaining a complex process to someone else helps you better learn the process, recasting an idea into your own words helps you take possession of the idea. You still have to acknowledge your source, but you will be better able to use the idea for your own purposes if you have stated it in a manner that you understand. Consider, for example, the following passage, written by Francis Bacon in the seventeenth century:

> Studies serve for delight, for ornament, and for ability. Their chief use for de-light is in privateness and retiring; for ornament, is in discourse; and for ability, is in judgment and disposition of business. For expert men can execute and per-haps judge of particulars, one by one; but the general counsels, and the plots and marshaling of affairs, come best from those that are learned. To spend too much time in studies is sloth; to use them too much for ornament is affectation; to make judgment wholly by their rules is the humor of a scholler.[12]

Some modern readers, faced with this passage, might give up a few sentences into it. The expression appears alien to us; some words even seem to have been misspelled. But a close examination of the passage allows us to rephrase Bacon's Renaissance style and language and to take from the passage an interesting idea.

For the sake of comparison, the original passage is given on the left:

Studies serve for delight, for ornament, and for ability. Their chief use for delight is in privateness and retiring; for ornament, is in discourse; and for ability, is in judgment and disposition of business.	Reading and pursuing knowledge ("study") allows us to do three things: entertain ("delight") ourselves in private, adorn or embellish ("ornament") our speech ("discourse"), and increase our abilities to, for example, make better judgments and decisions (dispositions) in conducting our business.
For expert men can execute and perhaps judge of particulars, one by one; but the general counsels, and the plots and marshaling of affairs, come best from those that are learned.	Experts, those who excel at or specialize in one thing, are good at handling particular problems within their area of expertise, but the larger issues of life ("the general counsels," etc.) are handled best by those who have studied more widely, who are more "learned."
To spend too much time in studies is sloth; to use them too much for ornament is affectation; to make judgment wholly by their rules is the humor of a scholler.	Of course, spending too much time reading is laziness ("sloth"); referring too much to our reading, dropping quotes in everywhere, for example, is just showing off ("affectation"); and reacting to life according to the rules we've read is the characteristic ("humor" in the old sense) of a scholar, someone who spends too much time in school, someone who doesn't get out much into the real world.

You will notice that paraphrasing means more than just substituting synonyms for original words. Paraphrasing is almost like translating—looking up words to discover their meanings ("sloth" means "laziness"), using language you are more comfortable with, condensing phrases into words, turning words into phrases, adding details to help clarify the point. If necessary, you can break up sentences and rearrange the parts as long as you don't lose the original meaning. You don't have to replace every word of the original, struggling to find your own words for common expressions ("too much time" appears in both the original and the paraphrase). Nor do you have to "translate" every word, especially those that you believe are essential (our paraphrase retains the word "learned"). The goal of a good paraphrase is to capture the essence of the original passage and to repeat the original in your own voice, proving to the reader that you have full *possession* of the idea, even though you had to borrow it.

In other words, paraphrasing is not easy, primarily because it requires that you know what you are doing. You must actively, energetically engage the text you are reading, think about it, understand it. Your instinct may be to give up, to say to yourself, "WHAT?! I don't get it!" and to move on, or fall asleep, or order a pizza. Paraphrasing is harder than quoting because it requires greater understanding of the original so that the author's meaning is not misrepresented or distorted. When paraphrasing, imagine the original author looking over your shoulder, reading every word that you write. If he or she gives you a funny look or says, "Hey, I didn't mean that!" you must start again. If while recording your notes, you run out of energy trying to paraphrase, copy down the entire quotation (be sure to mark it as a quotation); you can always work on the paraphrase when you get to your draft.

EXERCISE 12.4

Split into groups of three or four and, working individually, paraphrase each of the following passages on an index card. (The passages get progressively more difficult.) Then compare your paraphrases. Are there any differences between individual cards? If so, what accounts for those differences: a misreading of the original, an ill-chosen synonym, a detail not warranted in the original?

1. College students dream of the clean sheets, good food and private bathroom that are home. Many schools have a long weekend break in October, and frosh who live nearby often come home for the first time then. They may bring along new friends, or arrive with only their dirty laundry and new ideas. Many other students don't make it home until Thanksgiving. Still others, who attend distant schools, first return at Christmas. That four-week or four-month absence feels like an eon, and the distance from school to home—even if it's only an hour—seems like travel from outer space to Earth or the other way around. (Linda Polland Puner, *Starting Out Suburban: A Frosh Year Survival Guide,* 1996, p. 121)

2. America is also the inventor of that most mythic individual hero, the cowboy, who again and again saves a society he can never completely fit into. The cowboy has a special talent—he can shoot straighter and faster than other men—and a special sense of justice. But these characteristics make him

so unique that he can never fully belong to society. His destiny is to defend society without ever really joining it. He rides off alone into the sunset like Shane, or like the Lone Ranger moves on accompanied only by his Indian companion. But the cowboy's importance is not that he is isolated or antisocial. Rather, his significance lies in his unique, individual virtue and special skill and it is because of those qualities that society needs and welcomes him. (Robert N. Bellah, et al., *Habits of the Heart: Individualism and Commitment in American Life,* 1985, p. 145)

3. The photograph—to narrow it down—reduces us to two dimensions and it makes us small enough to be represented on a piece of paper or a frame of film. We have been trained by the camera to see the external world. We look *at* and not *into,* as one philosopher has put it. We do not allow ourselves to be *drawn* into what we see. We have been trained to go by the externals. The camera shows us only those, and it is we who do the rest. What we do this *with* is the imagination. What photographs have to show us is the external appearance of objects or beings in the real world, and this is only a portion of their reality. It is after all a convention. (Saul Bellow, "Graven Images," 1998, p. 36)

4. One of many insights that individuals must gain along the path to literacy is phonemic awareness. Research has shown that phonemic awareness is a more potent predictor of success in reading than IQ or measures of vocabulary and listening comprehension and that if it is lacking, emergent readers are unlikely to gain mastery over print. However, teachers can provide activities that facilitate the acquisition of phonemic awareness. With an assessment device readily available, practitioners can quickly identify those children who may benefit most from phonemic awareness activities and reduce the role that one factor—phonemic awareness—plays in inhibiting their success in reading and spelling. (Hallie Kay Yopp, "A Test for Assessing Phonemic Awareness in Young Children," 1995)

5. It is of course undeniable that television is an example of Low Art, the sort of art that has to please people in order to get their money. Because of the economics of nationally broadcast, advertiser-subsidized entertainment, television's one goal—never denied by anybody in or around TV since RCA first authorized field tests in 1936—is to ensure as much watching as possible. TV is the epitome of Low Art in its desire to appeal to and enjoy the attention of unprecedented numbers of people. But it is not Low because it is vulgar or prurient or dumb. Television is often all these things, but this is a logical function of its need to attract and please Audience. And I'm not saying that television is vulgar and dumb because the people who compose Audience are vulgar and dumb. Television is the way it is simply because people tend to be extremely similar in their vulgar and prurient and dumb interests and wildly different in their refined and aesthetic and noble interests. It's all about syncretic diversity: neither medium nor Audience is faultable for quality. (David Foster Wallace, "E Unibus Pluram: Television and U.S. Fiction," 1997, p. 7)

If summarizing and paraphrasing are so difficult, why not just quote? For one thing, it can be very confusing for your reader to see so many quotations stitched together in a paper. Because you write, whether you know it or not, in a particular style and voice, your reader gets accustomed to that voice, which is interrupted by a different voice each time you drop in a quotation. Many inexperienced writers quote too often, creating a harsh blend of dissonant sounds and producing a paper that suggests that the writer is uncomfortable with his or her own voice and ideas. But more important, quoting should be saved for words that are truly worth quoting. If it is the writer's *idea* you want to use, then there is no reason to use the words, but if you want to analyze the writer's language, or if the words are particularly significant, then quoting is warranted. The last sentences of *The Communist Manifesto,* for instance, would lose their impact if translated into a paraphrase:

> *Quotation:* At the end of their manifesto, Marx and Engels must have terrified many of Europe's capitalists: "Let the ruling classes tremble at a communist revolution. The proletarians have nothing to lose but their chains. They have a world to win. Working men of all countries, unite!"

> *Paraphrase:* Marx and Engels must have terrified many of Europe's capitalists when they mentioned revolution in the last lines of their manifesto. They called on the world's workers to join together. After all, the workers had little to sacrifice and much to gain.

Although the paraphrase doesn't misrepresent the intent of the original, it washes it clean of any power or significance. In a case like this, it might be best to let the writers speak for themselves.

> I hate quotations. Tell me what you know.
> —Ralph Waldo Emerson

EXERCISE 12.5

Below are quotations from various sources. If you were using these sources in a paper, would you quote, summarize, or paraphrase? Explain your decision.

1. A player loses the point if in playing the ball he deliberately carries or catches it on his racket or deliberately touches it with his racket more than once. (Rule 20d, United States Tennis Association)

2. I am in awe of them, and I feel privileged to have been a witness to their lives and their sacrifices. There were so many other people whose stories could have been in this book, who embodied the standards of greatness in the everyday that the people in this book represent, and that give this generation its special quality and distinction. As I came to know many of them, and their stories, I became more convinced of my judgment on that day marking the fiftieth anniversary of D-Day. This is the greatest generation any society has produced. (Tom Brokaw, *The Greatest Generation,* 1998. Brokaw's book is about American men and women who came of age during the Great Depression and the World War II.)

3. Gym class was another brush with fascism. You line up in your squads, and you better be wearing your little gym suits. If your are not wearing the gym suit, you are not taking gym class. "Remember kids, exercise has no effect unless you're wearing these special suits." (Jerry Seinfeld, *SeinLanguage,* 1993)

4. American athletes tend to be an obsessed bunch, but the trend toward endurance extremes has sounded alarms in the medical community. In the short term, common consequences of prolonged, strenuous exercise include tendonitis, stress fractures and chronic fatigue syndrome. But research is beginning to show that by racing ever farther and longer, athletes may also be putting themselves at risk for a host of chronic diseases, even cancer. (Andrew Tabor, "Using Up Too Much Too Soon: Pushing the Body to Athletic Extremes May Be Harmful to Your Health," *Salon Magazine,* July 26, 1999. Accessed August 2, 1999; available online at http://www.salon.com/health/feature/1999/07/26/ultrathletics/index.html)

5. We hold these truths to be self-evident, that all men are created equal, that they are endowed by their Creator with certain unalienable rights, that among these are life, liberty and the pursuit of happiness. That to secure these rights, governments are instituted among men, deriving their just powers from the consent of the governed. That whenever any form of government becomes destructive to these ends, it is the right of the people to alter or to abolish it, and to institute new government, laying its foundation on such principles and organizing its powers in such form, as to them shall seem most likely to effect their safety and happiness. (Thomas Jefferson, *Declaration of Independence*)

A final word about taking notes: As you read—quoting, summarizing, and paraphrasing on your note cards or in your notebook, if that's what you're more comfortable with—you will inevitably have ideas of your own, reactions to what you have read or thoughts about where to place quotations and paraphrases in your final paper. If you are actively engaged with what you read, you will be shocked or upset to discover evidence contrary to your claims, thrilled to find supporting evidence, disturbed at the tone of a writer, incredulous at some author's outrageous assertions, puzzled over another's implausible conclusions. As we said earlier in this chapter, you will also be inspired toward your own inferences, and you will see connections previously unknown. Whenever these thoughts and reactions occur to you, write them down. We all know the frustration of being unable to recall the insights that pop like a soap bubble in our heads and are gone forever. Whenever you have a good idea, write it down! When you record these reactions and thoughts, be sure to indicate clearly that they are yours. If using cards, use a different color of card or give the card a distinguishing heading. But whatever you do, write it down.

USING SOURCES

So now you have a stack of note cards and a head full of ideas. In the next chapter, we talk about the process of drafting and revising essays, advice that is applicable to this chapter as well if you are going to assemble your thoughts and notes into an effective paper, so you might want to turn to Chapter 13 before you begin writing. Keep in mind that it is your paper that is being written—don't turn your essay over to your sources, allowing them to carry the weight or speak for you. Think of your paper as a conversation between you, the reader, and the various outsiders you have brought in to help you defend your viewpoint or represent your opponent. Your quotations, summaries, and paraphrases should flow naturally with your own writing, creating an almost seamless presentation from start to finish. What follows are recommendations on incorporating outside sources in your essay.

Acknowledging Sources

Plagiarism. It would be almost impossible to find a college student who hasn't heard that ugly word, and, honestly, it might be just as difficult to find one who hasn't committed some small act of plagiarism somewhere in his or her academic life—the lifted passages from the *World Book Encyclopedia* in fourth grade, the middle-school essay that a parent contributed more than a few sentences to, the fabricated bibliography entry in a high school research project. Although these actions may have been disregarded or gone unnoticed, plagiarism, especially plagiarism in college, is considered one of the most severe forms of academic dishonesty. Punishments for those who are caught range from failure on the specific paper to expulsion from school. Even those who get away with it suffer, primarily because the failure to develop research skills will inevitably show up at some point in the future.

There are probably as many reasons for cheating as there are cheaters. Students may panic because they have waited too long to begin a paper or because they can't find the best words to express their ideas. Some students lack the confidence to trust their own thoughts, or they argue to themselves, frustrated and defeated, that someone else has already expressed those thoughts in better language.

There may be students who simply feel overwhelmed by the course material, "in over their heads" to the point where it seems better to hand in someone else's paper than to submit a sure failure of one's own. Some students claim that cheating is a common practice and necessary to get ahead in the world, and others seem to believe that the goal of higher education is to receive a degree, not to learn skills or develop the dispositions and habits of an educated person. Whatever the reason, plagiarism is wrong. Period. It is theft: it violates the principles of academic integrity; it provides an unfair advantage over students who work hard at their own writing; it shows great disrespect

> ## Critical Thinking Lapse
>
> A student at a university in Kansas submitted a paper to a professor who immediately recognized the work. The professor himself had written the paper fifteen years earlier while a student at the same university. It had apparently ended up in a fraternity's files.

for the original author and contempt for the reader; it wastes tuition dollars; it cheapens the institution the student attends; it leaves the thief with no skills other than deception; it can be discovered, even years later, with dire consequences. And because most students know that plagiarism is wrong, it seems to us that *real* plagiarists—the ones who buy papers from the Internet or copy whole passages from obscure journals—are rare. Most plagiarism, we contend, occurs because students are not sure exactly what plagiarism is and how to avoid it.

Plagiarism comes from the Latin *plagium,* meaning "kidnapping." A plagiarist, in other words, is a kidnapper. Not only does the origin of the word show how serious the crime is considered to be, it also gives some idea of how authors feel when their words are stolen. To plagiarize means to kidnap, or, to be more modern about it, to take, the creations—thoughts, words, writings, inventions, charts, and tables—of another person, whether those creations have been published or not, and to pass them off as one's own creations. And even if you take those creations and dress them up a bit differently, using synonyms or rearranging the sentences, you are still guilty of plagiarism if you fail to tell your readers or listeners who the original creator is. Although most students haven't yet published their ideas, many of us know the feeling of having our creations stolen. Have you ever, in a moment of inspiration, produced a snappy one-liner, sending your friends into hysterical laughter, only to hear your line repeated later by someone else who fails to acknowledge you? Or have you ever proposed a truly insightful solution to a problem, only to have the solution repeated to you days later as if you had never heard it before? If so, you know the feeling of having your creations plagiarized.

When plagiarism appears in a scholarly work, it usually takes one of three forms:

- Material from an outside source is presented *word-for-word* or detail-for-detail as the student's original work with no acknowledgment whatsoever of the source. In this type of plagiarism, a student is taking credit for an author's words and ideas.

- Material from an outside source is *paraphrased* with no acknowledgment of the source. In this type of plagiarism, the student is taking credit for an author's idea.

- Material from an outside source is incorporated into a student's work and a weak effort is made to acknowledge the source. Usually, the student fails to use the conventional means of acknowledgment: introductions to quotations, quotation marks where necessary, parenthetical mention of page numbers, indentation of longer quotes, internal references ("the author goes on to argue . . ."), footnotes, and so forth. This kind of plagiarism is usually the result of indifference, uncertainty, carelessness, or ignorance.

It is this last sort of plagiarism—cheating from ignorance—that shows up most often in student papers. So let's assume that no student wants to plagiarize. No student wants to deliberately take credit for ideas that are not his or her own. How is plagiarism to be avoided?

First, know what *does not* have to be acknowledged. All writers owe a great debt to the millions of writers who have preceded them. Many of the ideas that we hold are the result of years of reading and thinking about what others have taught us. Much of what we know and think does not have to be credited. Any generally known fact, facts available in a wide variety of sources, and indisputable facts—Hemingway wrote *A Farewell to Arms;* the Great Depression began in 1929; Canada has ten provinces; Bill Clinton was born in 1946—need not be footnoted. Even if you are discovering the fact for the first time, it might not have to be cited. For example, in doing research for an argument on capital punishment, you might discover that capital punishment was suspended for several years in this country, from 1972 to 1976. Although that fact is new to you, it is one that many people are aware of or one that can be verified in many sources.

Some phrases and quotations do not have to be cited, but these are rare and usually amount to proverbs, clichés, and recognized literary quotations. If you started a paper with, for example, "The Lord is my shepherd," or "To err is human," or "To be or not to be," you would not necessarily have to mention the Bible, Alexander Pope, or Shakespeare. You could if you liked, but without acknowledgment, the reader would know that the saying is not your creation.

You *do* have to acknowledge the following and provide documentation:

- Direct quotations.
- Statistics and results of surveys. If you find in a paragraph, a table, or a chart, for example, that Americans watch an average of five hours of television a day, you must tell your reader who provided that information.
- Facts not currently widely known, especially new discoveries. If, for example, a writer has uncovered the truth about a historical event or person, you must give the writer credit. Eventually, the discovery may become extensively known, but until it does, acknowledge the source.
- Facts that have not yet gained acceptance, that are still considered controversial, or that you feel your reader might find hard to believe.

- Descriptions of events, and any plans, graphics, drawings, tables, charts, and other visual items that you reproduce in a paper.

- Unusual verbal illustrations. If a writer clarifies a point by providing an illustration that is unique, unusual, very creative, and so forth, give the writer credit if you borrow the illustration.

- Any ideas not your own. The judgments, opinions, interpretations, explanations, definitions, and claims made by other thinkers, including writers, speakers, and professors, must be cited.

Use your best judgment in deciding when to cite sources. It can be very discouraging to discover that our best thoughts have been expressed elsewhere. Many students who fail to give credit to their sources do so because they feel that if they attribute their ideas to someone else, the reader will think them ignorant for coming up with nothing new. There are ways to incorporate the ideas of other writers without turning your essay over to those writers. We will address these methods in the following section.

EXERCISE 12.6

In groups of four, individually examine the following facts, all of which are true. Which of these facts do you feel should be documented? Which do you feel could be placed in an essay without reference to a source? After you have decided, share your answers as a group. What differences do you note? Discuss those differences and try to reach agreement on what should be documented and what can appear without citation.

1. With the Gulf of Tonkin Resolution, the United States Congress authorized increased military action in Vietnam.
2. In 1764, Wolfgang Amadeus Mozart composed a symphony. He was eight years old.
3. In one Amish community in Pennsylvania, roughly three-quarters of all suicides that occurred in a 100-year period were in just four families.
4. The best-selling album of all time, as of August 1999, is Michael Jackson's *Thriller,* followed by The Eagles' *Their Greatest Hits,* Pink Floyd's *The Wall,* Led Zeppelin's *Untitled (IV),* and Billy Joel's *Greatest Hits: Volumes I & II.*
5. Alabama imports rocks from other states for prison chain gangs to crush.
6. Johnny Rotten, lead singer of the Sex Pistols, was born John Lydon.
7. Audrey Hepburn, not Julie Andrews, starred in the 1964 movie version of *My Fair Lady.*
8. The two most prevalent judicial systems in the world are the inquisitorial system and the adversarial system. The United States uses the latter.
9. The Bill of Rights originally applied only to the federal government, not to the states.
10. Charles Dickens's childhood experiences of humiliation, including his father's imprisonment for debt and Dickens's subsequent work in a shoe-polish factory, influenced his work as a novelist.

11. Hoping to become an artist, Adolf Hitler applied to the Vienna Academy of Fine Arts in October 1907 but was rejected. Later, penniless and unwilling to work, he ended up in a homeless shelter.

12. Because digital circuits operate in the binary number system, all circuit variables are either 1 or 0. Information in digital systems is processed through the use of Boolean algebra, which is based on the idea that logical propositions are either true or false. "True" corresponds to the digital value of 1; "false" corresponds to 0.

13. There is water on Mars.

14. Mark McGwire holds the record for home runs in a season: 70.

15. The rings of Jupiter are made up of dust created when Jupiter's four innermost moons collide with comets, asteroids, and other material.

16. Abraham Lincoln suffered from depression.

17. Abraham Lincoln was the tallest president.

18. On average, women in the 1950s first married at the age of twenty; now it's closer to twenty-five.

19. One way to distinguish a crocodile from an alligator is to look at their teeth. When its jaws are closed, you can still see a crocodile's teeth. Not so with an alligator.

20. The Pentateuch of the Old Testament includes five books.

21. The core of a nuclear reactor at Three Mile Island in Pennsylvania partially melted down in 1979.

22. Eugene Debs ran for the U.S. presidency five times. In 1920, while in jail and on the ballot for the Socialist Party, he received almost one million votes.

23. While George Bush was in the military during the Second World War, his plane was shot down. Two crewmen on the plane died, but Bush was rescued unharmed by a passing submarine.

24. During World War II, 350,000 women served in the military. Six and a half million women worked on the home front in war-related jobs.

25. In 1998, the Pentagon could not account for $22 billion in expenditures.

Incorporating Sources

A researched argument should be more than a collection of source material. The argument you write should present your conclusion, your point of view, your opinion, backed up by the evidence and arguments that you have collected. One method for ensuring that your paper is your own is to write the argument first without sources and then to plug in your sources where needed. If you use this method, be careful not to "accidentally" borrow some ideas that you fail to credit.

When you write, remember that the paper is yours: your name is on it; you will receive a grade for the work, including the quality of the writing, the strength of the argument, the caliber of your sources, and the appropriate use of those sources. Since it is your paper, let your sources serve you rather than the other way around. Present your case, and use your sources to bolster your argument. In other words, as you write think, "This is my argument and so-and-so agrees with me," or "This is my argument and here's the evidence I found to prove it." Don't think, "This is what everyone else said, and I agree with them."

The trick to using quoted material is to make the quotation fit gracefully and logically into your own writing. Even with quotations added, your sentences must make grammatical sense, and your paragraphs must be coherent. The quoted material cannot interrupt the flow of your prose. Following is some advice on incorporating sources into your writing. All documentation in this section accords with guidelines established by the Modern Language Association (the MLA). These guidelines are generally used by writers of research papers in the humanities (philosophy, literature, foreign languages, and so forth). Not all disciplines use MLA style; some use, for example, the American Psychological Association's (APA) guidelines. Your professor will tell you which he or she prefers.

Quoting Words and Phrases   Often, the passage you find useful will amount to no more than a word or a phrase. Even such short passages must be quoted if the word or phrase is unique to the writer or if it clearly indicates the writer's point of view or opinion. If you use a quoted word within a paraphrase, be sure to use quotation marks around the word.

> So great was essayist William Cobbett's hatred for cities and upper-class government officials that he often referred to London as "The Wen," which means pimple, and to Parliament as "The Thing."

> One especially poor customer saved a few pennies for "luxury" items, a packet of Kool-Aid and a small angel food cake for his children (Fetterman 117).

Notice how the quoted words fit neatly into each sentence. The same smooth effect can be accomplished when quoting longer passages.

Quoting and Paraphrasing Longer Passages   In quoting a sentence or two (usually under fifty words) from the original, provide an introduction to the sentence that helps to establish its context and that helps the reader understand its meaning and relevance to your point. Your introduction can include the author of the quote and, if necessary and applicable, the printed source of the quote. The following examples include a quoted sentence that follows from the introduction and the same quotation introduced with the author's name.

> Before the new student union is constructed, we should gather items to place in the foundation, in much the same way ancient builders "buried under cornerstones and posts and thresholds and inside walls and chimney piles these among other items: food, gems, coins, pottery, plants, statues, arrowheads, bottles of wine, carcasses of cattle and sheep, horses' heads and hoofs, and, as many legends have it, living human beings" (Kidder 304).

Before the new student union is constructed, we should gather items to place in the foundation, in much the same way ancient builders, as Tracey Kidder reminds us, "buried under cornerstones and posts . . ." (304).

You can introduce your quotation in a variety of ways. Use dialogue tags at the beginning of the sentence or within it, or use an introductory phrase and the word "that," or use an introductory phrase and a colon or a comma:

As Tracey Kidder points out, ". . ."

As Albert Camus once noted, ". . ."

As one author makes clear, ". . ."

According to Julia Kristeva, ". . ."

In fact, Einstein claims, ". . ."

Joyce said, ". . ."

From this evidence, concludes Caute, ". . ."

"I am certain of nothing," John Keats wrote, "but of the holiness of the heart's affections and the truth of Imagination."

"He's like an express train running through a tunnel," Virginia Woolf wrote of D. H. Lawrence, "—one shriek, sparks, smoke and gone."

In a recent lecture on John Donne's later poems, Professor Marian Williams pointed out that ". . ."

One look at the transcript of the trial reminds us that ". . ."

Churchill decided quickly: ". . ."

Darrow's argument seemed irrefutable: ". . ."

Occasionally, an introductory comment or phrase can be omitted, as when, for example, you want to start your essay with a quotation or when you want to segue into a quotation without announcing it. The transition between your words and the quoted passage must be very smooth so as not to jar the reader, and the connection between your words and the quotation must be apparent to the reader. Notice how in the following paragraph, John Kenneth Galbraith leads his reader gracefully to the quotation:

Economics, not entirely by accident, became a subject of serious study at an important turning point in the history of western man. This was when the wealth of national communities began, for the first time, to show a steady and persistent improvement. This change, which in advanced countries like England and Holland came some time in the eighteenth century, must be counted one of the momentous events in the history of the world. "From the earliest times of which we have record—back, say, to two thousand years before Christ—down to the beginning of the eighteenth century, there was no very great change in the standard of living of the average man living in the civilized centers of the earth. Ups and downs certainly. Visitations of plague, famine and war. Golden intervals. But no progressive violent change." [13]

If you are including a paraphrase in your paper, you must be sure to credit the source of the idea, which means you must be a bit more careful about your introduction, since there are no quotation marks to tell your reader where the borrowed idea begins. Compare, for example, the following two paragraphs:

> If we hope to cure some of the ills plaguing our system of education in America, we might do well to look to China, where the education system has produced children steeped in the basics and often capable of great accomplishments. China cannot solve all of our educational problems, but the fact that its children generally grow up happy may indicate something about the success of education there (Gardner 317–318).

> If we hope to cure some of the ills plaguing our system of education in America, we might take Howard Gardner's advice and look to China, where the education system has produced children steeped in the basics and often capable of great accomplishments. China cannot solve all of our educational problems, Gardner concedes, but the fact that its children generally grow up happy may indicate something about the success of education there (Gardner 317–318).

In the first paragraph, it is impossible to tell where Gardner's contribution begins and ends. The reader might assume that only the last sentence or even the last phrase has come from Gardner's book. In paraphrasing, be careful to provide a clear introduction and reminders along the way. Phrases like "Gardner continues," "He further notes that," "In a later passage, Gardner retracts his comments," and so forth will make your writing clear and keep you free from charges of plagiarism.

If you are following one quotation or paraphrase with another, be sure to let the reader know how the two passages relate to each other. Is the second a refutation, a clarification, a confirmation, or what? A simple transition might do the trick:

```
Shelley responded emphatically, ". . ."
```

Or you might need a somewhat more elaborate one:

```
Refusing to accept Peacock's definition of poetry, Shelley of-
fered his own: ". . ."
```

Block Quotations   If your quotation amounts to more than four or five lines of type in your text (generally fifty or more words), you should block the quotation, maintaining the double spacing of your paper, omitting quotation marks, and indenting the left margin five spaces.

```
It's difficult not to be moved by Lincoln's testament to the
fallen soldiers at Gettysburg:
        The world will little note nor long remember what we say
    here, but it can never forget what they did here. It is
    for us the living rather to be dedicated here to the
    unfinished work which they who fought here have thus far
```

```
so nobly advanced. It is rather for us to be here dedi-
cated to the great task remaining before us--that from
these honored dead we take increased devotion to that
cause for which they gave the last full measure of devo-
tion--that we here highly resolve that these dead shall
not have died in vain, that this nation under God shall
have a new birth of freedom, and that government of the
people, by the people, for the people shall not perish
from the earth.
```

Because of the indentation, readers know where the quotation begins and ends, which is why quotation marks are unnecessary, as are reminders or dialogue tags.

Conducting research, reading carefully and critically, taking notes, and coherently and accurately incorporating what you have found into your own work is not easy, but if you remember that it is your argument you are defending with the help of outside sources, not someone else's argument that you are repeating or copying, and if you approach research with the right attitude—that we can all learn a great deal from the giants whose shoulders we stand on—your work as a researcher and writer will be gratifying and rewarding. You can quote us on that.

Summary

1. Research does not have to be an intimidating task. Besides helping you to write more solid arguments, research can assist you in your effort as a critical thinker to correct misunderstandings, discover the truth, and set the record straight. If you approach research with the right attitude, treating it less as a chore and more as an opportunity, you will find yourself amply rewarded, not only with the skills necessary to speak more intelligently, convincingly, and truthfully on your topics, but also with the skills you will need for success in your career.

2. Modern libraries are astonishing and often confusing places. With the help of a reference librarian and the many directional sources available, you can find a wealth of information without ever leaving campus. Focus your search so that you don't waste time and effort chasing too much information. Consult bibliographies, indexes, and abstracting services to help locate information in the library and in databases. Use Internet search engines and guides to sort out the best information available on the Internet.

3. Use the books in the stacks and use periodicals for information on your topic, but also consult encyclopedias, almanacs, yearbooks, fact books,

directories, handbooks, manuals, atlases, biographies, dictionaries, and government documents both to get started and to provide in some cases advanced and specialized knowledge about a subject. Human sources of information—faculty members, business people, local experts, and so forth—are often overlooked but can often provide quick answers to simple questions and the kind of in-depth knowledge that comes from experience.

4. Evaluating sources means asking a great many questions about the information you uncover, including questions about the content, the author, the publisher, and the audience. Be sure to separate facts from opinions in a writer's work. Don't repeat a writer's opinions as if they were factual, and don't repeat a writer's facts without being certain that they are indeed true. Be sure that the facts are complete and up-to-date.

5. When evaluating an author and a publisher, ask the following questions: What is the author's background? What is the author's bias and purpose? What are the author's sources? Who is the publisher or sponsor?

6. Ask the following questions about the audience: Who is the intended audience? How has the audience responded?

7. Good research depends on good note-taking skills. Be sure to copy down all the bibliographical information you will need to cite your sources and document your research. When recording quotations, be accurate and careful. When summarizing an essay or argument for use in your own paper, decide how extensive your summary should be. When paraphrasing, be faithful to the intent of the original. Choose to paraphrase more than to quote. Be sure to separate your own impressions and reactions from the quotations, summaries, and paraphrases that you record. Whatever system you decide to use for note-keeping, be consistent, and remember that the extra effort put forth while taking notes will pay off when drafting your essay.

8. Be exceptionally careful when incorporating sources into your argument. Plagiarism is among the most serious of academic offenses and can result in severe consequences. Learn well what does and does not have to be acknowledged. Always err on the side of giving credit.

9. Make your researched material fit gracefully into your own writing. Keep your reader in mind as you write: introduce your quotes rather than just drop them into your paragraphs. Cite your sources in the text and provide a list of references.

CHAPTER 13

WRITING ARGUMENTATIVE ESSAYS

We have all been there. The Fight. The heart-pounding, teeth-clenching, name-calling, blood-boiling battle of words, from our first "You are!" "No, you are!" and "Did not," "Did too," to the more memorable and emotionally charged moments of our lives—

"Give me one reason why I should let you go to the ball game."

"Is that my sweater you're wearing?"

"It's my house, and while you're living in it. . . ."

"You spend too much time with your friends and not enough with me."

"Can't you see why we're meant to be together?"

—and a thousand other familiar lines that have been the catalyst for our most heated arguments with one another.

Some of us enjoy a good argument; others become tongue-tied, nervous, or even too angry to think clearly. Words fail us, and we end up growling or grunting like wild animals or, worse, acting aggressively or violently. If we manage to keep our cool, our creativity often fizzles out during the argument, leaving us murmuring later to ourselves or, too late, devising the most clever and profound retorts.

Of course, at this point in your reading of this text, you should be saying, "Wait a minute! An argument is not a quarrel or a fight; it's a _____," and you should fill in the blank without batting an eye. If we are honest, though, we all have to admit that even when we know we're supposed to coolly, rationally present evidence to support our claims, we often resort to the kinds of argument we are most familiar with—the kinds of no-holds-barred matches that take place between us and our families and friends. The "flaming" that goes on in some newsgroups and chat rooms is one example of the nasty combats we allow ourselves to engage in, so much so that many newsgroups have established "Netiquette" rules to help cool down the scorching rhetoric that participants throw at one another.

Why do so many of us become aggressive when we defend our point of view in an argument? Certainly, passionately defending ideals or beliefs is not always a bad thing, but name-calling or misrepresenting an opponent's argument is; yet, such tactics often appear in arguments. One reason may be that the current models of argumentation are not very helpful. Many of the "arguments" we see and hear today have the quality of combat: opponents facing off against one another, each armed with evidence to defend a position, sometimes resorting to excessive means (all's "fair" in war, after all) to win the battle. Many televised arguments about political or social issues seem more like verbal skirmishes, and some end in physical violence. Letters to the editor and calls to radio shows often contain vitriolic attacks on anyone who dares to disagree with the writer or speaker.

In some way, the language of argumentation encourages us to "fight" one another. In fact, it is the same language we use to discuss warfare: "attack," "defend," "positions," "opponents," and so forth. When speaking of people who are, we think, excessive in their commitment to a position, we often say they are "militant" or that they "have dug in," "have an ax to grind," and are "up in arms." Indeed, the two behaviors—verbal arguments and warfare—are not unrelated, since the failure to resolve conflicts through the language of diplomacy has often led to attempts to resolve them through gunfire.

But perhaps the major reason that we argue so aggressively, sometimes unfairly, and confuse supporting a claim with fighting for one is that our goal in both fights and arguments is the same—to win. A moment's reflection will show, however, that whereas a good fight—a boxing match, for example—usually ends with a "winner," the strength and success of an argument is not determined by whether the opponent loses or concedes or even agrees with the claim being made. Certainly, we should always hope to convince our readers and listeners that we are correct in our thinking and that we have truth on our side, but what if, after we have presented a solid argument, our readers and listeners refuse to accept our claim? An attorney may do a flawless job of defending his or her client to a jury and yet lose the case. The failure to gain converts to our cause does not mean we have failed to present a solid argument. We could ensure success, perhaps, by playing unfairly, by using only emotional appeals, attacking our opponents, fabricating evidence, but our "arguments" in that case become more like battles and less like civilized presentations. In fact, the objective of our "arguing" in a logical, rational manner should never be to beat or embarrass our listeners or readers into submissive acceptance of our claim. All arguments that we make should be judged solely on their qualities: consistency, coherence, relevance of premises, and so forth. In other words, the point is not to "win" the battle over who is right and who is wrong. It may very well be that someone is right, but if we make it our purpose to present a thoughtful, well-supported, carefully developed, fair, and honest argument, to concede to our listeners and readers their own good points, to admit when our evidence is weak or untrustworthy, to avoid abusing our readers

for their errors (spelling and otherwise), our arguments will be stronger, more civilized, and maybe more convincing.

The first rule of argument should be to consider logical discourse less as a battle for supremacy and more as an attempt to work as a community that *communi*cates in an effort to arrive at the truth, or at least, when it comes to practical matters and decision making, to arrive at compromises that make life easier and more enjoyable. As we have mentioned in several places throughout this book, thinking critically often depends on applying the principle of charity, which means that unless there is evidence to the contrary, you should assume that your opponents are rational people and that their arguments are sound and cogent. In other words, thinking critically does not mean intellectually beating people up or using your thinking skills to take advantage of others. Arguing, as opposed to fighting, means that you respect your opponents, accurately and fairly represent their points of view, and support your conclusions with true premises and sound reasoning. Writers who construct arguments merely to "win," who go for the jugular or manufacture evidence or appeal unfairly to the emotions of their readers, do little to advance knowledge or understanding. You should always strive to present a solid argument; if you convert others to your way of thinking, great. But if you have presented a powerful and sensible case, then you have done your job; even if someone says, "I don't agree with your position and I'm still voting Democrat" (or voting Republican, or supporting capital punishment, or getting married, or quitting my job, or whatever). Think of it this way: when you write an argument, make it your goal to be heard and listened to, to have your ideas considered and measured, to be regarded as an intelligent, rational, and sensitive person. If you win the argument in the process, congratulations; but the true measure of your success will be in what you have said or written and how you have said or written it, not in who agrees with you.

EXERCISE 13.1

We have been maintaining that your objective in writing an argument should be to present a rational, well-evidenced, solid defense of your claim. Blatant emotional appeals are, we claim, inappropriate in a good argument. What do you think? Is it always the case that you should choose a well-reasoned approach over an emotional one? Can you think of any occasions (real or imagined) when it would be appropriate to appeal to emotions to win your point?

WRITING A SUCCESSFUL ARGUMENT

Writing takes place in three very broad stages: what you do before you actually begin the first draft, what you do during the writing of your first draft, and what you do after you have completed the first draft. The following sections of this chapter will show you how to prepare and write an argument, but you should keep one important point in mind as you read: although the advice and information is arranged in a step-by-step fashion, writing an argumentative essay is *not* a linear process. You can't write a paper the way you follow a recipe, carefully adding one ingredient after the other until the dish is prepared. Writing a paper is more like decorating a room. You start with a vision of what you want the room to look like, but halfway through the process, you might change your mind and move the desk to another location or tack your favorite poster to a different wall. You try to move the bookcase, but it won't fit in its new location, so you return it to its original spot. Or you throw it out and buy one that does fit. Maybe you give up, buy all new furniture and decorations, and start again. Like decorating a room, writing a paper means thinking and rethinking, backing up, adding and subtracting, rearranging ideas, throwing out what doesn't fit, and bringing in new ideas to achieve the look you want. In the process of writing, you may discover an idea that changes the entire focus and point of your paper. You may throw everything out and start again.

The following outline will help you keep track of the steps in the process of writing an argument:

Before You Write

Know yourself

Know your audience

Choose and narrow your topic

Write a sentence that expresses your claim

Gather ideas: Brainstorm and research

Organize your ideas

Writing the First Draft

> Provide an interesting opening
>
> Include a thesis statement
>
> Develop your paragraphs
>
> Provide a satisfying conclusion

After the First Draft

> Read what you have written and revise
>
> Consider what you have not written and revise
>
> Show your work
>
> Edit your work
>
> Hand it in

BEFORE YOU WRITE

You should spend a great deal of time just preparing to write your first draft; in fact, the more time you spend preparing to write, the less frustrating the actual writing will be. Taking the time to think before you write will help prevent the panic that comes from plunging into a paper without any clear idea of how cold or deep the water is and then thrashing about without any idea of where you are going or how to get out. Before you write, take some time to think about how well you know your topic and who will be reading your argument. Decide what claim you would like to defend, and gather and organize your ideas for defending that claim.

Know Yourself

To write a good argument, you first must *want* to write a good argument, and you must be willing to inventory your critical thinking dispositions: Are you prepared to be precise and accurate, to offer only premises you believe to be true, to fairly represent opposing points of view, to credit your sources, and so forth? If you only want to win the fight, you can resort to sucker punches and taunting; but, to present a good argument, you must be willing to work hard at constructing a fair and honest case.

A healthy approach to writing arguments for a college class is to ask yourself *why* you are writing an argument. Of course, you are writing an argument because your professor wants you to; you are required to write an argument. That's true, but you will be in college only for a small fraction of your life. In the "real world," you may be called on to voice a claim and defend it on many occasions—at work, at the PTA meeting, as a member of the school board, in letters to editors or clients or constituents. Learning to argue well in writing allows you to use your talents for good purposes, to defend someone or some group that you feel is being maligned, to correct an injustice, to oppose what you believe to be an unethical or immoral act, to bring an end to a dangerous situation, or to prevent a disaster. It may sound trite or flattering, but you do have something to say, and you should be willing to take the time to say it well.

You must also be willing to ask yourself how well you know the issue you are going to address. We all have opinions, but we don't often stop to ask why we hold those opinions or how we arrived at them. If you have had a long-standing opinion on an issue, ask yourself where that opinion may have come from. It is possible that you can find many reasons to *explain* where a belief came from (perhaps from your parents, your church, or your studies), but if you are going to *argue* in support of your beliefs, you will have to provide justification and support that goes beyond explaining the origin of your beliefs. In other words, you may know how you *feel* about something, but what your readers want to know is what you *think*.

You may come to realize that you have inherited your views without honestly thinking about them or that you have absorbed them from your surroundings without realizing how sociocentric your thinking can be. That doesn't mean that you must abandon what you have inherited or absorbed, but you may discover that some beliefs are indefensible. An argument built on unexamined beliefs may be very weak. If you find that an opinion has little support, it is best to withhold that opinion until you have done enough research to back it up. Say, temporarily at least, "I don't know what I think about that issue." Because people find it difficult to say, "I don't know," especially on topics they feel they should know something about, they sometimes take a stand based only on what they have heard or what they assume. Trying to write a convincing argument on an issue about which you have only the vaguest notion is like trying to take an exam on material you have never seen before. It is not worth the embarrassment and frustration. If you remember that saying "I don't know" is often the smartest response to a request for an opinion, you will avoid the awful feeling of being trapped by someone insisting that you defend a claim you had little commitment to in the first place. If you want to write about a topic you don't know very well, take the time to learn as much as you can about it. If you feel strongly about an issue, you should be willing to defend it intelligently and rationally.

That doesn't mean, of course, that you must know all there is to know about an issue before you begin to formulate your opinion and take your stand, or that you must present your case in an absolute or exhaustive manner. Few of us can maintain that we know all there is to know on any issue or that we are absolutely, certifiably correct about our point of view, or that new evidence won't be discovered to prove us wrong, or that the opposing side is wholly without merit. It is no crime, when warranted, to use words such as "could be" and "possibly," to modify generalizations with "many" and "some," or to temper advice by saying, "I suggest" or "I recommend." We don't have to be overly humble, but we should be willing to grant our opponent his or her good points and to defend our own gracefully and considerately.

Know Your Audience

Many of us present arguments as if the reader either is an arch enemy who— if words could kill—would bleed to death after our first few sentences, or is someone madly in love with us who will nod in wild agreement with every- thing we say. Neither is usually the case, but let's suppose for a moment that one or the other is true. Take the first hypothetical reader, our enemy. If our purpose is to be understood and to present a well-reasoned argument in sup- port of our claim, does it make sense to antagonize the person we hope will judge us fairly? And if we actually do hope to "win" the argument, forget it! Jabbing at someone, taunting him, or hurling insults will almost always result in retaliation.

The second hypothetical reader—our loving champion—may agree with everything we say and, at the end of our presentation, tell us that we have presented a beautiful argument, full of truth and well structured, but there is very little to be gained from being evaluated by someone who is predisposed to compliment us. And what purpose is served, what progress is made, if our arguments are aimed at those who are ready to agree with everything we say? Certainly, we can find examples all around us of "arguments" presented to these two audiences. Listen, for instance, to any number of talk-show hosts on the radio, most of whom speak to an audience who is divided among the true believers and those who despise the host but listen, almost masochistically, be- cause they "can't believe what I'm hearing." Radio hosts know that their au- diences are divided this way; few people listen to popular talk radio for a keen analysis of complicated issues. For the sake of the show's sponsors, a radio host must keep the listeners tuned in, so he or she targets two audiences—the com- mitted fans and those who vehemently disagree.

Perhaps we shouldn't fault the talk-show hosts for targeting their audi- ence; that's what they are supposed to do. In fact, the first rule of all commu- nication is to know who your audience is and adjust your style (though not necessarily your point) accordingly. If you were to write a letter to your grand- mother telling her about your romantic weekend, you would most likely use language and a tone different from what you would use in a letter about the same topic written to your best friend. If you were asked to prepare a speech on the difficulties of being a first-year college student, how would that speech be different if you were speaking to seniors in high school, business leaders from the community, elementary students, parents with children in college, and so forth? When preparing an argument, you should try whenever possible to know who your audience is: Are you writing for the citizens of your com- munity, students of your age and background, professionals in the field, polit- ical figures, administrators in the school? Knowing who will be reading your argument will help you decide what tone to use, how sophisticated your word choices can be, how much background you must provide, and how much detail you need to go into. In the business world, even your position in a company or firm can dictate how you write your argument or proposal. Are your readers highly skeptical or open to even the riskiest proposals? Do they hate to spend a dime on new ideas, or do they enjoy taking a gamble on costly innovations? Are you in a position of some authority, so that your readers must implement your suggestions, or do you have to work hard at proving your case?

Anticipate Your Readers' Reactions   On the basis of what you know about your topic and your audience, try to determine how your audience might react to your claim and its defense. Perhaps your topic is very appealing and your audience will receive your argument graciously. Say, for example, that you are writing to your classmates urging them to oppose 7:00 A.M. classes. Some of your classmates—those who start work at 8:00 A.M.—might actually want early morning classes, but it's a safe bet that most will agree with your proposal. You will probably be facing an audience inclined to agree with your claim. If you were to present the same claim to the administration, on the other hand, you could probably assume that their reaction would differ from that of your classmates and that they would offer all sorts of reasons why 7:00 A.M. classes are a good idea. The administration would not necessarily act with hostility toward you or your ideas, but you might assume that they would not leap to embrace your idea without a very solid defense. You might find a more neutral audience in a group of people unaffiliated with the college. We often face neutral audiences when we address topics that our readers or listeners have little knowledge about or issues they are undecided about. You might find a largely neutral audience if, for example, you argued that life existed on other planets or that Pete Rose should be allowed into the Baseball Hall of Fame.

When you consider how your audience will react to your claim, you almost automatically begin thinking about their reasons for reacting that way. You begin considering their point of view, their claims, their counterarguments. Predicting what an audience might say in response to your claim will help you to create a stronger argument. You should argue courageously and never change your point of view to placate your audience; on the contrary, you will be better able to defend your claim if you are prepared for the reactions you will encounter. Anticipating some of the administration's primary reasons for beginning the class day at seven in the morning will help you head off some of those reasons when you present your case.

Often, you can predict your audience's reactions by considering how you would feel as a reader. For example, people generally don't like to be told that they are wrong about something; so, instead of telling your readers that they are wrong, try to discover what values you and they have in common and show that your approach is based on those values, not detrimental to them. If you want to correct what you believe to be dangerous behavior, point out what you see to be the terrible consequences to your readers of continuing to act as they are. If you hope to change their thinking on moral or ethical grounds, don't insult them or write in a haughty or superior tone. Showing an audience that you share their concerns, that you respect them, and that you believe there is merit in both your view and theirs can go a long way toward getting your viewpoint heard.

In the absence of information about your readers, or when writing for a general readership, there are a few things you can assume. First, assume that your readers are slightly skeptical, that they do not necessarily agree with everything you say, but that they are open-minded and fair. Believing that they are impartial and objective will prevent you from overstating your case. Assume that your readers are intelligent, rational, and humane. You don't necessarily have to prove that accepting your claim will benefit each reader individually, but you should try to show, when the topic warrants it, that your argument takes into consideration the lives of people other than yourself. Surely, you wouldn't argue that speed limits should be raised because you enjoy driving fast. How would you argue that claim to a slightly skeptical, open-minded, intelligent, rational, humane person? Always assume the best about your audience, but keep in mind, finally, that even if a close-minded, prejudicial audience refuses to listen to you, if you have defended your claim with solid evidence and clear reasoning, you have done your job.

EXERCISE 13.2

Look at the following letter, written to the editor of a newspaper. The paper had recently reported that Pennsylvania teachers were among the best paid in the country. Summarize the key points of the argument in a few sentences. Look for fallacies and examples of vague or slanted language. Then consider the overall effect of the argument. Determine as specifically as you can the writer's purpose. Does he seem to be writing to an audience inclined to agree with him, or is he trying to convince neutral readers and members of the opposition that he is correct in his thinking? How do you think the newspaper's readers would respond to this letter? How would a student of critical thinking evaluate this letter?

Editor:

Once again, the taxpayers of the Wyoming Area School District are being ordered to "open wide" and not for the purpose of checking for cavities. The dentist in this case is the Wyoming Area School Board and the order to open wide is directed to our wallets. With the passage of the 1998 budget, Wyoming Area has the dubious honor of joining the 200 and Above Club. The new budget includes a 15-mill tax hike, putting Wyoming Area's millage at 200.

When property owners are writing the check to pay that bill, they should remember that the largest part of that check, by far, is going into the pockets of members of the Wyoming Area "Education" Association. The current average cost per teacher to the taxpayers of Wyoming Area is $53 per hour.

To make matters worse, our school board is currently negotiating with the teachers union for a new contract. Unless we act now and let our board members know we will no longer accept big give-away contracts for the sake of peace, we will continue to pay for our silence and complacency with more big tax hikes in the future.

A mere 2 percent pay raise for one year for the $53-per-hour people will cost the taxpayers of Wyoming Area an additional $125,000, or 3.5 mills.

The teachers union is able to extort this money from the taxpayers of Pennsylvania; through their forced union dues, they are able to pour huge sums of money into the campaigns of their lap-dog political candidates. Under the guise of "doing it for the children," these teacher-union lackeys pass laws which make it very easy for the teachers union to get what it wants.

With the upcoming elections in November, taxpayers should know two things:

According to figures I have seen, approximately 40 percent of the delegates at the last Democratic National Convention were members of the teachers union. They apparently have plenty of time on their hands to corrupt our nation's political system.

Secondly, about 90 percent of all teacher union PAC money goes to Democratic candidates. They apparently have plenty of extra money with which they can corrupt our nation's political system. With figures like this, can there be any doubt about who controls the Democratic Party?

In my opinion, the teachers union is the taxpayers' greatest enemy, and a vote for a Democrat, generally speaking, is a vote for the enemy. Had it not been for a Republican governor and a Republican-controlled state House and Senate, we would never have had tenure reform, sabbatical leave reform, charter school legislation, or this meager but promising attempt at tax reform in Pennsylvania.

On the national level, the Democrats and President Clinton have stopped every single attempt made by Republicans to improve education in our country. As the cost of public education continues to sky-rocket with no corresponding improvement in results, the teachers union monopoly must not go on unchallenged.

As bad as things seem, they would be worse without the existence of taxpayer groups. Taxpayer groups are organized all around the state and every taxpayer who cares about fiscal responsibility in government functions should join and support their local group. We do make a difference.

George R. Race
President
Wyoming Area Taxpayers Association
Wyoming, Pennsylvania

Choose and Narrow Your Topic

If your professor has not assigned a topic to be investigated but has, instead, given you freedom to choose, decide on a topic that that is both controversial and interesting to you. It does not have to be one you are familiar with; in fact, you might want to select one that you have always been curious about or one that you have always wanted to learn more about so that you can argue your case more convincingly. Also, pick a topic that you can manage to cover completely in the space allowed for your paper. Often, the first question students ask is how long the essay should be. It's a fair question. If you are to write a 500- or 750-word essay, you are going to choose a different topic from the one you would select for a 10,000-word essay.

Say the required length is 750 words, or three double-spaced pages, and say you are interested in the topic of work or labor. List some of the controversial topics that fall under the heading "work":

- Are families harmed when both parents work?
- Do company perks such as on-site gyms and day care hurt employees more than help them?
- Does a booming economy actually have some negative effects on the job market?
- Should the minimum wage be increased?
- Should welfare recipients be required to work?
- Should employers be required to give advance notice to employees who are about to be laid off?
- How necessary (useful, outdated, etc.) are labor unions?
- Should child labor laws be relaxed?
- Should your college bookstore sell clothes made in sweatshops?
- Does the U.S. government interfere too much in overseeing workplace safety?
- How serious a problem is sexual harassment in the workplace?
- How far can companies go in "invading the privacy" of workers?
- Should employers be forced to hire a minimum number of minorities?
- Should the U.S. institute a four-day workweek?
- Should a law be passed mandating equal pay to both sexes for comparable work?
- Should companies offer benefits to same-sex partners?

Your list of controversial topics could go on for pages if you knew enough about the subject of work. Certainly, because you couldn't write about all these topics in a short argument, you would have to limit yourself to one. But you could also continue to narrow your focus by limiting one of the subtopics listed above. Take the invasion-of-privacy issue, which is narrower than the issue of work, but which could be further narrowed to something more manageable:

- How far can employers go in using surveillance cameras in the workplace?

- Should any employer be allowed to randomly test for drugs?
- How far can an employer go in conducting background checks on a potential employee?
- What questions should and should not be asked in a job interview?
- If an employee receives e-mail from outside the company, does the employer have a right to read it?
- Should an employer have unlimited access to an employee's desk, computer, and file cabinets?
- Does an employer have the right to know what an employee does in his or her off-hours?
- Does an employer have the right to know an employee's sexual preference?

Any one of these topics could be chosen for a short essay, but you could actually narrow the topic even further if, for example, you wanted to argue about surveillance cameras in a particular setting (the cabins of commercial airliners) or at a particular company. You may initially feel that if you narrow the topic down you won't have enough to say, but it is better to work at developing a focused topic than to leave a large issue undeveloped. And as you improve your writing and arguing skills, you will usually find that you have too much to say even about the most slender of topics.

Finally, keep in mind that the best arguments are often those that present an unusual point of view or a claim few people have considered. When deciding what to write about, don't hesitate to take a risk and choose a topic that is controversial or uncommon. Several of the topics in our first list—"Do company perks such as on-site gyms and day care hurt employees more than help them?" "Should child labor laws be relaxed?"—may strike you as unusual or absurd, but on second thought or after researching the topic, you might see some reason to answer yes to both.

EXERCISE 13.3

I. Choose one of the broad topics below and narrow the topic to one that could be addressed in a three-page (750-word) argument. Start by listing as many controversial issues as you can; then narrow even further until you have a workable topic.

The Environment	Birth Control	Television
AIDS	Domestic Violence	Professional Athletics
Alcoholism	Free Trade	NCAA
Gambling	Cuba	Genetic Testing
HMOs	Smoking	
Child Abuse	Cloning	

II. The following list of questions provides topics that can be used to practice the skills we will be discussing in this chapter. In a group of three or individually, choose a question from the list and use it to help you arrive at a narrow topic that you could address in a three- to four-page argument. As you proceed through the chapter, apply what you are learning to the topic you have selected.

1. Should the government be responsible for the unemployed?
2. Are minorities discriminated against in the media?
3. Should physician-assisted suicide be permitted?
4. Should the United States provide foreign aid to developing nations?
5. Is community service an appropriate punishment for criminals?
6. Isn't police brutality sometimes the only proper response to some situations?
7. Are beauty pageants harmful to those who participate in them?
8. Is feminism an outdated ideology?
9. Have historians been guilty recently of revising history?
10. Have environmentalists gone too far in their efforts to stop global warming?
11. Is there a date-rape crisis in society? On your campus?
12. Has racism diminished at all over the past fifty years in America?
13. Is the mainstream media liberal?
14. Do we need a return to family values?
15. Which does more damage, street crime or white-collar crime?
16. Should pornography be outlawed?
17. Can a businessperson be both successful and ethical?
18. Should Congress propose an amendment outlawing desecration of the American flag?
19. Should taxpayers receive vouchers to send their children to private schools?
20. Do you think marine mammals should be held in tanks to be used in shows?
21. Should public school students be required to pass through metal detectors each day?
22. Should school officials have the right to randomly search students' lockers or bookbags?
23. Should immigration laws be tightened?
24. Is competition always a good thing?
25. Should public school students be required to wear uniforms to school?
26. Do some of the questions on U.S. census forms constitute an invasion of privacy?
27. Do television commercials aimed at children exploit children's innocence and gullibility?
28. Should a public high school football team be allowed to pray as a team in the locker room before a game?
29. Should the states recognize same-sex marriages?
30. Should there be a national lottery?

Write a Sentence That Expresses Your Claim

Once you have decided what you want to write about, formulate a single sentence that presents the central claim of your argument and write it on a blank sheet of paper: "I think . . . ," "People should . . . ," "We must . . . ," "It's time for . . . ," "It is true that . . . ," and so forth. State your claim as forthrightly as you can, and be sure that your claim is debatable, something that could be disagreed with. You might write, for instance, "An employer has no right to read an employee's private e-mail messages," or "Lee Harvey Oswald was the lone assassin of JFK," or "The college should eliminate the football program." At this point, you are only focusing your argument, so don't worry about how clumsy or awkward your claim sounds. You can always revise it as your paper gets going.

Gather Ideas: Brainstorm and Research

Writers generally get their ideas from two sources: their own heads and the heads of other people, usually other writers. As with the larger process of writing, the process of gathering ideas does not proceed strictly step-by-step. Some writers do a great deal of reading and research before formulating ideas and approaches for a paper; other writers record their own thoughts first and then look for additional ideas and support; other writers combine the two approaches in a variety of ways. The approach you take will depend on your own habits, your familiarity with the topic, and your need for facts and expert opinion to back you up.

Brainstorming is a method for generating ideas for a paper. Like any other kind of storm, brainstorming is spontaneous and wild, but many writers make the mistake of trying to channel their creative thinking into grammatical sentences and coherent paragraphs. When you brainstorm, allow your ideas to flow freely. Write down whatever occurs to you, and don't censor any ideas as irrelevant or uninteresting. Don't worry about being incorrect or even sounding foolish. No one will judge your argument on your brainstorming. It is like a dialogue with yourself. You can always cut ideas after you have listed them.

You can brainstorm in several ways. Some writers like to freewrite, which entails writing for a measure of time, usually fifteen minutes, without stopping. Other writers favor a technique called "mapping," in which the writer freely associates ideas and connects them in a weblike fashion. The method we recommend here is slightly more structured than traditional methods of brainstorming, but it will better help you generate ideas for supporting an argument.

List Supporting Premises   First, when brainstorming for an argument, list as many reasons as you can to support the claim. For the claim that an employer should not read private e-mail, you might list the following premises:

> E-mail is like regular mail, and it's illegal to open someone else's regular mail, so it should be illegal to open someone's e-mail.
>
> Even if it weren't illegal to read e-mail, it's unfair to the recipient of the e-mail, who might be discussing personal matters, such as medical or family problems.
>
> If people know that their private correspondence might be read by someone else, they might be reluctant to speak freely, which would limit their ideas and perhaps encourage them to be dishonest.
>
> If an employee knows that his e-mail might be read by the boss, he could take advantage of the situation by telling his friends to send him e-mail about how great the boss is.

Some of these premises might not sound too convincing, and after consideration, you might eliminate one or two. That last premise, for example, sounds especially weak and may be impossible to defend.

If you find that you can't think of more than one or two premises, you may want to change your topic. But the inability to come up with premises is not always a sign that you should abandon your topic. If you believe in your claim but cannot think of support for it, you might have to seek help through research. In fact, reading more about your topic and examining the arguments made by other writers can bring on a storm of ideas that otherwise would not have arisen.

List Opposing Premises   Second, write down as many premises as you can think of to *oppose* your claim. What would someone who disagreed with you say?

> Employers have paid for the computer, the lines, and the service provider and therefore have a right to see how e-mail is being used.
>
> Employees waste time writing and reading personal e-mail.
>
> E-mail coming into the company or going out might contain sensitive material that the company needs to keep under wraps.

Like your own premises, some of these might be eliminated, and you might have to research your topic to determine if you have overlooked any opposing arguments. Sometimes it helps to get another mind involved at this point. Ask a friend, a family member, or a professor to "play devil's advocate" and tell you how someone might disagree with you.

Think Critically about Your Thinking   Think critically about your claim: Are you overgeneralizing in any way? Are there any exceptions to your claim? Maybe, for example, some employers (e.g., the Defense Department) must read all incoming e-mail. Are you creating a false alternative? Is there some middle ground you have overlooked? Are there solutions you have ignored? Has someone else already solved the problem or proposed a viable solution? Do you need to modify your claim to allow room for uncertainty?

Don't hesitate to get into an argument with yourself at this point. Remember, your reader is a critical thinker.

Think on Paper   Now write down what you know or think you know about your topic. In this part of brainstorming, you are simply trying to gather and create ideas from your own mind; in other words, you are thinking on paper. Some of the ideas you come up with will serve as additional premises to support your central claim; some ideas will serve to clarify, illustrate, and defend the premises themselves. You may find that in thinking on paper, you begin to conceive a structure for your argument, a structure that includes both central premises and subarguments.

If you have trouble coming up with ideas, ask yourself some questions: "Why did I choose this topic?" "Why does it bother me so much?" "What do I want my readers or listeners to do, to believe, to think?" "What are my experiences with this issue?"

Methods of Development   A very productive method for generating ideas is to think about the ways we usually develop and detail our communication with one another: we tell stories, describe people and places, compare and contrast events or things, give examples, define our words, and so on. These methods of development can be very useful both in discovering material to flesh out a paper and in prompting new thoughts in support of your claims.

Narration   A narration tells a *story* in *chronological* order. Are there any stories associated with your topic? Do you know of anyone whose experiences would be worth recounting? For example, perhaps you or someone you know has a story about working in a place where private e-mail is filtered or read by managers.

Description   A description gives *concrete details to paint a verbal picture* of a person, place, or thing. There may be in your topic something that can be described.

Cause   Causes are *reasons* for the occurrence of an event, a decision, an action, and so forth. Look at your topic and ask, "Why did this happen? "What caused this?" Ask why some companies began the practice of intercepting and opening private e-mail. Do employees, in fact, dislike the practice? If so, what reasons do they give? Be careful not to commit any of the fallacies that can result from arguing for causes where none may exist.

Effect   Effects are the *results* of an event, a decision, an action, and so forth. What effects are associated with your topic? Ask yourself, "What will happen if . . . ?" and "What has happened?" "What has the outcome been?" Ask what effect intercepting e-mail has had on companies. Has white-collar crime decreased? Have employees worked harder? Have employees revolted? Has production improved? What was the intended effect in the first place? What might happen if the practice continues? Be careful not to commit a slippery-slope fallacy.

Classification and Division   When we classify, we take a large group and break it down into smaller, more manageable groups. All the students in a college can be grouped by class (freshman, sophomore, etc.), major, living status, and so forth. When we divide, we take one thing (a car) and break it down into its various parts, such as systems (electrical, fuel, etc.) or individual items (seats, battery, rear bumper, etc.). Look at your topic to see if classification and division lead to any ideas. Perhaps you are grouping all private e-mail together, when, in fact, you could classify it by sender or where it comes from. Perhaps you could divide messages into header and text, leading to a compromise in your argument: managers could see from whom e-mail was coming but could not read the message. (Remember, you're just thinking on paper here; some of this—all of it, even—could end up on the cutting-room floor, as they say in the movie industry.)

Contrast   When we contrast two things, we show them to be *dissimilar* in important ways. Could you develop your topic through contrasts? Perhaps two companies have widely differing approaches to improving employee work habits and one of those companies does it without opening e-mail.

Comparison   When we compare two things, we discuss the *similarities* between them. Is there anything in your topic that calls for a comparison? Can you defend your claim by comparing the situation under study to something similar? If you were arguing that your workplace should not intercept e-mail, you might be able to point to other companies that have eliminated the practice without harmful consequences.

As you saw in Chapter 11, a comparison used to support a claim is called an analogy, a useful but tricky device when used in an argument. In fact, analogies must be used so carefully that it is sometimes wiser to avoid them. Any major weak spots in a comparison and the analogy—and the argument—falls apart. For example, if you tried to claim that students should always follow their teacher's advice and offered as support the fact that soldiers must always follow their leaders' orders and salespeople must always follow their managers' instructions, some reader is going to point out all the differences between soldiers, students, and salespeople and between teachers, generals, and managers. You can see why some analogies don't work.

But some do. Suppose you were trying to show that, despite what some misinformed people argue, a man who attacks a woman is guilty of a crime, no matter how provocatively she may be dressed. She may have been unwise for walking in a certain area, but she is the victim of a crime and should not be implicated in it. To prove this point, you argue that a man who cashes his paycheck and walks in an unsafe area with money visible in his pocket may not be a very smart man. But if he is mugged, the mugger cannot be excused. We should not accept an attacker's argument that the woman was tempting him any more than we would accept a mugger's that the money was irresistible. This may be an analogy that proves your point. Ask yourself if your argument could be supported with an analogy, but be careful.

Illustration   When we illustrate, we provide *examples* to help clarify a point and defend a general comment. If, for example, you said to someone, "My classmates are very bright," you might follow with, "Take Dawn, for example; she's double-majoring in neuroscience and English." To illustrate the claim that "that movie was terribly frightening," you would say, "In this one scene . . ."

In an argument, examples can be very helpful as you begin to build support for your conclusion, but keep in mind that examples have to be carefully chosen. Examples can come from personal experience or history, or they can be created, depending on your purpose and the topic. If you were trying to support the claim that noise in the dorms sometimes continues past the quiet hour, you might cite some examples of particular nights in the past month on which parties, music, fights, and so forth awakened you in the early hours of the morning. If you were trying to support the claim that United States presidents have often had extramarital affairs, you could refer to them by name. Both of those claims could be supported by real examples. Be cautious when you use either: your experiences may be unique, and you may be unable to generalize from your historical examples. Be sure that your examples are representative and that you have chosen as many as you need to establish your conclusion. Rarely are only a few examples sufficient. The best arguments from example usually combine examples with other support, such as expert opinion.

A hypothetical example is used to support a claim for which there may be no readily available real-life examples or for which a hypothetical example works just as well or better. Say the argument is over whether or not we are obligated to help someone who is in danger. If you were to argue that we are not, you would most likely begin your defense with "Well, suppose, for example, . . ." You are about to give a hypothetical example. The word "suppose" shows that the illustration is one you are creating, although it will serve your point: "Well, suppose, for example, that someone is drowning and I can't swim. Am I obligated to jump into the water, anyway?" Someone might respond that you are obligated to throw a flotation device or run for help, but your example has helped clarify the issue and your position. As you continue the discussion, you can further clarify both, perhaps reaching a more discerning position on when we are and are not obligated to help one another.

Definition   When we define a word, we tell our readers or listeners exactly *what we mean* by a word or a concept. In daily discourse with one another, we often use definitions to, for example, clarify our use of specific words ("He's not very *romantic;* he never brings me flowers"), or to persuade ("I wouldn't call her a friend; a 'friend' is someone who never judges you."). While brainstorming for ideas, look at your claim and your premises and ask if there are any words that should be defined for your reader. In the example on e-mail privacy, perhaps "private" could be defined, or even the larger concept of "privacy": What exactly is "private" in the context of the workplace?

Look Over Your Brainstorming   Look over your brainstorming and ask yourself the following questions:

- Should I refine my claim? Your brainstorming may lead you to reevaluate your claim. Decide if you need to modify what you intend to prove. For instance, you may want to limit the scope of your argument or qualify your generalizations: "With a few rare exceptions, employers should not have the right to intercept and read the private e-mails received by employees."

- Are there any additional premises in my rough collection of thoughts and ideas? Did my unstructured thinking on paper produce any additional reasons to support my claim? At this point, you should be able to revise your original list of premises.

- What do I still need to find out? Of your premises, ask, "Is that really true?" "Do I know that for a fact?" "Where did I hear that?" "Who told me that?" "When did I learn that or hear that?" "What evidence do I have that I'm right?" (I'm not exactly sure, for example, that it's illegal to open someone else's regular mail. I would need to find out.) Ask yourself what more you will need to do or to find out to make your premises acceptable to a reader. At this point, think long and hard about your audience. What questions might a reader have for you? What evidence might your reader challenge? You may have to conduct research at this point to fill in the gaps, supply more support for your argument, and so forth.

- What can I use and what do I need to exclude? Often, if you are lucky, your brainstorming will lead to more ideas than you can use in your argument. Your brainstorming may have led you off the track, or you may have gotten into areas (causes, for example) that are not immediately relevant to your claim. If you want to argue that plagiarism is a problem on campus that needs to be stopped, the causes of plagiarism may or may not be relevant to your argument. You, of course, have to decide. Use caution and be selective when deciding what will end up in your argument: more is not always better. It is also a good idea to file away the ideas you don't use; what doesn't make it into this argument could be useful in another.

EXERCISE 13.4

As a group, write out a claim and brainstorm ideas for an argument on the topic you chose in Exercise 13.3, Part II. When brainstorming, one member of the group should act as secretary while all members of the group provide premises, raise opposing premises, ask critical questions, "think on paper," and look over the ideas that have emerged.

Do Some Research   If you haven't already done so, you may at this point need to do research to support your claim and your premises. The support you seek will generally fall into two broad categories—facts and opinions. You can draw from a wide variety of reliable sources, including experts in the field, statistical abstracts, textbooks, encyclopedias, journals, and reliable Internet sites. Because Chapter 12 provided extensive advice for conducting research, we will just briefly remind you here of some key points.

Facts   Certainly, facts are very useful for supporting an argument, but determining what is and is not a "fact" can be tricky; what appears to be certain and indisputable may not be true at all or may actually be a matter of opinion. Loosely defined, a fact is something that has objective reality; it is not a matter of perception or opinion. Usually, a fact can be known with some measure of certainty and can be verified with data. Facts include statistical data, reports of observations, and examples of actual occurrences and events.

When using facts to support your argument, keep a few things in mind:

- You may be mistaken about what you believe to be fact. Don't always rely on your memory, on "conventional wisdom," or on what you have always assumed to be true. Spend the extra moments to verify your facts.

- For the most part, use facts that have been verified by reliable sources. If you are in any doubt about the truth of information, consult more than one source.

- Ask yourself how widely known your facts are. Some facts are generally agreed upon, but some are not. If you are using factual information that your audience is unfamiliar with or that they will have a hard time believing, you should give the source of your information.

Opinions   Yes, we are all entitled to our opinions, but that doesn't mean that we are rationally entitled to believe them or that all opinions are true. Unlike facts, opinions can be so subjective that they are sometimes based on nothing more than prejudice or wishful thinking. Or they can be based on a thorough examination of the facts, formed in a sensitive and reasonable mind, and backed by years of experience, study, and research. Clearly, you should choose to support your claims in the second way.

In seeking expert opinion to support your argument, look for opinions from experts who prove that they have the knowledge, fair-mindedness, and clear thinking skills necessary to offer informed opinions. Try to rely on disinterested authorities, and if your readers may be unfamiliar with your authority, be sure to tell who your expert is, providing the person's background to help make your citation more persuasive.

Finally, don't discount the authority of creative writers such as poets and novelists. You may be able to find some appropriate and useful thoughts from great writers who, although they may not have "studied" the topic you are addressing, may nonetheless have written eloquently and powerfully in defense of your claim. You may be able to use the insights of a writer to help support your argument—Henry James on privacy, or Joyce Carol Oates on boxing, for example—or your own thinking might be sparked by those insights.

Organize Your Ideas

Of all the difficulties faced by writers, organizing ideas seems to be the one that presents the most trouble. But the "block" that can occur from trying to organize ideas is actually a good sign that the writer is trying to communicate effectively with the reader. If we weren't worried about the reader, we could just blabber on in any way we liked. In setting up your organization, use your intuitive "audience-sense" to your advantage by looking at organization not so much from your point of view as from your reader's. Given the claim you are making, how would a reader want to see your evidence and defense presented? What would be the most logical or natural way to present the case? What would be the least confusing way to set up the presentation? You should be concerned not to bore your reader, but there is no need to get too creative or to impress the reader. Just present a good, solid, well-reasoned argument.

Once again, remember that the process of writing is nonlinear. New ideas may occur to you as you decide how to organize your essay. You may even change your entire approach. Be prepared to keep thinking and creating.

In deciding how to organize your argument, keep in mind that each body paragraph will be related somehow to your central claim. In most cases, the body paragraph will present a topic idea that is a premise for the claim made in the thesis. For example, if you were defending the claim that your hometown council should approve the placement of a traffic light at an intersection that currently has a four-way stop, you might organize your argument in the following manner:

Claim: Council should approve a stoplight for several reasons.

First body ¶: An average of six thousand cars pass through the intersection each day. Other equally busy intersections in the city have traffic lights.

Second body ¶: There has been a relatively high number of accidents at that intersection. Traffic lights have been shown to reduce the number of accidents at an intersection.

Third body ¶: A busy elementary school and a popular restaurant are located at the intersection.

Each paragraph helps to support the claim being made. You might decide to divide some ideas into two separate paragraphs. For example, the two ideas given in the second body paragraph—the number of accidents at the intersection and the study showing how lights reduce the number of accidents— could be divided into two paragraphs:

Claim: Council should approve a stoplight for several reasons.

First body ¶: An average of six thousand cars pass through the intersection each day. Other equally busy intersections in the city have traffic lights.

Second body ¶: There has been a relatively high number of accidents at that intersection. [The paragraph would give the number of accidents, perhaps collected from a study of police reports, and would compare that number with the number of accidents at other intersections in the city. The paragraph could also include a description of representative accidents that have occurred at the intersection under study.]

Third body ¶: Traffic lights have been shown to reduce the number of accidents at an intersection. [The paragraph would include statistics to show how many accidents occurred at intersections before and after a traffic light was installed. Examples might be provided for a number of representative intersections.]

Fourth body ¶: A busy elementary school and a popular restaurant are located at the intersection.

If you had a long list of facts and expert opinion to present in support of your claim, you could devote a paragraph to each fact and opinion. For example, if you were arguing that someone is guilty of a crime, you could organize in the following manner:

Claim: Colonel Mustard is guilty.

First body ¶: He was in the billiard room when the murder took place.

Second body ¶: His fingerprints are on the murder weapon, the lead pipe.

Third body ¶: He confessed to the police.

Fourth body ¶: All other suspects have been cleared.

Fifth body ¶: Experts from the Parker Brothers Crime Lab have all testified that only he could have committed the murder.

Sixth body ¶: The psychologist Professor Plum claims that Mustard is just crazy enough to do something like this.

Seventh body ¶: Ms. Scarlet saw him do it.

Eighth body ¶: Professor Plum heard him do it.

Well, you get the picture. Each one of the premises could be developed in its own paragraph, so that, for example, you would prove in the first body paragraph that Colonel Mustard was in the billiard room when the murder took place. You couldn't just assert it; you would have to prove it.

If you have too many short paragraphs, you may be able to combine several of them. For example, paragraphs seven (eyewitness) and eight (ear-witness) could be combined into one with a topic sentence about witnesses to the crime. Paragraphs five and six could be combined as well.

Using Methods of Development to Organize   In combining the two paragraphs on the basis of their similar content, you are applying another useful strategy for organizing, one taken from the list of methods for developing ideas, in this case *classification*. By combining the witnesses into one paragraph, you cut down on the amount of work the reader must do to keep your argument straight. In fact, you could combine other premises into one paragraph, namely, the premises referring to expert testimony.

In the writing of an argument, all the methods of development can come into play. Say, for example, you made the claim that citizens of the United States hate warfare. You could support your claim through **illustration,** calling on history to provide examples of how Americans have hesitated to go to war or have protested involvement in war. Of course, your generalization would need to be modified as you found examples showing that some Americans have supported the country's involvement in war. If you wanted to look at two possible causes for an event, you might organize your argument along the lines of a **contrast** or **comparison** essay, looking at one cause, then the other. You could argue that some decision or action would lead to particular **effects.** Recently, a group of citizens in a town in New Jersey argued before their city council that anyone using a laser pointer to "target" other people should be penalized. Such an argument would most likely be built on an analysis of the harmful effects of such devices, perhaps combining causal analysis with illustrations of the damage that has been done by people misusing laser pointers.

As a writer, you must select the pattern that best fits your purpose and point and combine patterns when appropriate to create the most effective paper.

Deductive Pattern   If you were writing a deductive argument, you could simply organize around the syllogisms that form your argument. Examine your claim closely to determine whether it follows from a set of premises that work together to prove the claim. Suppose, for instance, that you wanted to argue that radar detectors should be outlawed since they are designed for no purpose other than to break the law. Your argument would look like this:

Premise: Radar detectors are designed for no purpose other than to break the law.

Claim: Radar detectors should be outlawed.

As you know, deductive arguments often have missing or unstated premises. The missing premise in the argument above is

Any device designed for no other purpose than to break the law should be outlawed.

You could organize your argument around this syllogism, starting with the claim in the introductory paragraph and defending your stated premise (radar detectors have no purpose other than to break the law) in the paragraph immediately following. The third paragraph would then be used to show that anything made for the sole purpose of lawbreaking should be outlawed. Or you could start with the claim, followed by the "Any device" paragraph, and then the "Radar detectors" paragraph. You would have to decide as a writer which works better for your purpose and your audience.

Suppose you had several additional premises to contend with. The topic is the legalization of marijuana. You have four premises in support of its legalization:

1. It could be taxed.
2. It is not as harmful as some have contended.
3. Other, more dangerous drugs (alcohol, nicotine) are legal.
4. Some people use it for medicinal purposes.

Setting aside whether or not you had a good argument going here, you could defend each of these premises in its own paragraph. If there were unstated premises, you would not have to devote a single paragraph to each of the stated premises ("It could be taxed") *and* the assumption or unstated premise behind it ("Those things that can be taxed should be made legal"). You might, instead, deal with both of those premises in one paragraph (being sure, of course, to convince your readers that you wouldn't offer these two premises as the sole reason to support the legalization of marijuana, since something's being taxable doesn't mean it should be legal.)

Finally, if your claim were intended to show that a particular action or event does or does not fit the definition of a term, you could provide the definition in the first half of your argument and then discuss the event in the second half:

Claim: Buying a paper from an Internet supplier is plagiarism.

First body ¶: Definition of plagiarism: passing off the work of others as your own, etc.

Second body ¶: How buying a paper fits the definition of plagiarism.

If the definition were very complicated, you could devote a paragraph to showing how each component of the definition applies to the event.

Claim: Despite what some people claim, stock car racing is a sport.

First body ¶: A sport is competitive; stock car racing is competitive.

Second body ¶: A sport involves physical activity; stock car racing involves physical activity.

Third body ¶: A sport is governed by rules; stock car racing . . . , etc.

Problem-Solution Pattern   If you were proposing to solve a difficult problem, you might choose this pattern, which has three options. You could

1. State the problem and give the solution:
    Claim: Binge drinking could be reduced if the school provided more nonalcohol weekend events.
    First body ¶: The presence of binge drinking on campus (illustrations, perhaps).
    Second body ¶: How nonalcohol events could reduce binge drinking.

2. State the solution and then look at the problem that motivated you to discover a solution:
    Claim: The campus needs more security guards in the evening.
    First body ¶: Why more security is needed (to escort people to their dorms, to prevent uninvited visitors from getting into campus buildings, to stop drivers who speed through the campus, and so forth. Of course, each premise could receive its own paragraph.)
    Second body ¶: More security would prevent some of the problems we have seen in the last few months.

3. State the problem and consider alternative solutions before arguing for your own:
    Claim: Computer access on campus must be improved.
    First body ¶: We could give all students laptops (too expensive).
    Second body ¶: We could leave the computer labs open all night (not secure enough).
    Third body ¶: We could wire every room in the residence halls (cheaper, and security is not an issue).

Evaluative Pattern   This pattern works best when you are trying to determine the worth of something according to certain established criteria. For example, if a professor were to judge the value of a paper you had written, he or she might start by defining what a good paper is, laying out all the criteria for making a judgment: interesting topic and approach, clear organization, coherent paragraphs, and so forth. Then the professor would show how your essay does or does not meet those criteria. You will notice that this pattern makes use of definition in that "good essay" is defined before the question is asked whether or not your essay fits the definition.

Responding to Your Opponent's Arguments   Before you decide exactly how to organize your argument, consider what your opponent will say. If you have brainstormed ahead of time, you have given some consideration to your opponent's argument, and you may have even prepared some rebuttal comments. On the other hand, you may have realized that your opponent may have some points you simply cannot refute. Either way, you should work those opposing arguments into your paper somehow.

There are at least three ways to do so:

1. Start the paper with the opposing viewpoints and then organize your argument around a refutation of each point. This approach works well if you are proposing a claim that your reader might find upsetting. You can soften the ground a bit if you show your readers up front that you are familiar with their objections. You may, in fact, show that you share your audience's concerns and values.
2. Mention the opposition within each of your premise paragraphs. Some might argue that it is not a good idea to interrupt a paragraph with the opposing view, but most readers will not be disturbed by the interruption and would prefer that the opposition be dealt with on individual points rather than dealt with at the end.
3. Save the opposition for the end, showing that your opponent will raise some objections to your argument.

In any case, you have to decide how to deal with opposing views when you do raise them. If you have a stronger case, present it. If your opponent has a good point, don't overlook it. Your reader will consider you more intelligent and fair-minded if you acknowledge and even concede your opponent's strongest points or at least show that you and your adversary have something in common, perhaps a similar ethical code or a similar desire to do good.

Combining Patterns   Often, the most effective method for organizing an argument is to combine the patterns given above. An argument about the connection between advertisers' portrayal of beauty and eating disorders might be organized in the following manner:

> *Claim:* The advertising industry's exclusive use of slender models has contributed to the increase in eating disorders among young women.
>
> *First body ¶:* *Illustrations* of advertising's use of slender women; *descriptions* of some ads. (Be careful not to overgeneralize.)
>
> *Second body ¶:* *Facts* about the presence of eating disorders among young women; *comparison* with previous years; some *definition* of "eating disorder."

Critical Thinking Lapse

Try a different approach in your defense?

"After National Public Radio reported the existence of a top-secret list of 599 chemicals that U.S. cigarette companies add to cigarettes, including 13 chemicals that are so toxic they are not allowed in food, the six leading tobacco companies released the list, claiming redemption because it showed they add only eight of those chemicals, not 13, to their cigarettes."[1]

Third body ¶: Argument to show that advertisements have some *causal* connection to presence of eating disorders. (Be careful to avoid a questionable cause argument.)

Fourth body ¶: Opposing argument (there is no causal connection); response to opposing argument

Fifth body ¶: Possible *effects* if current advertising trends continue. (Be sure to avoid a slippery-slope argument.)

When you have decided how you want to proceed in your argument, draw up an outline to keep you on track. Your outline does not have to be elaborate; a few phrases and sentences should do the trick.

EXERCISE 13.5

Working individually, examine the brainstorming and research your topic has generated and produce an outline for the first draft of your argument. Your outline should indicate what you intend to do in each of the body paragraphs and what support (facts, examples, comparisons, expert opinion, and so forth) you will include in each paragraph. Do not write out long paragraphs; in other words, don't write a draft. Just outline one.

After you have completed your outline, compare it with the outlines of the others from your group. Discuss with one another why you chose the pattern you did. As a group, can you decide that any one pattern is better than the others? You should realize from doing this exercise that arguments can be organized in any number of ways. It is also true, however, that one pattern may occur more naturally given the topic, your purpose, and your audience.

WRITING THE FIRST DRAFT

The fact that you are more than three-quarters of the way through this chapter should indicate the importance of the activities that lead to the writing of an argument. If you have narrowed your topic, gathered your support, and organized your ideas, you will find writing the first draft of your argument to be much easier and more rewarding than if you had begun your paper with little idea of what you wanted to say or where you wanted to go.

Now it is time to write the first draft. You do not have to follow the advice chronologically. Depending on your own methods for writing papers, you might, for example, write your body paragraphs before you begin work on your introduction. But your readers will expect your finished product to look like a standard essay, and most successful essays (and arguments) have the following elements: an interesting and relevant opening, a clear thesis, a definition of key terms, well-organized ideas in coherent paragraphs, solidly defended topic ideas within those paragraphs, and a satisfying conclusion.

One more word of advice before you start: Writing the draft of an argument can lead you to more ideas than you discovered in your brainstorming, researching, and organizing. In fact, the act of writing can inspire such creativity that you may be surprised at the ideas you are "coming up with." Don't slavishly adhere to your outline if you find yourself discovering new and better support or if your writing takes you in new directions. Finally, remember that you are writing a draft; you can—and will!—revise it when you are finished.

Provide an Interesting Opening

You don't have to begin with your claim, but you can if it is startling, very controversial, or attention-grabbing. Otherwise, start with some background on your topic, or show why your issue is an important one. Start with some surprising statistics, an apt quote, a little-known fact, or an interesting story relevant to your topic. A personal account of an event can make a good opening. If you are writing to oppose an argument, you might begin with the point that you intend to oppose or with some mention of the values and ideals you hold in common with the opposing side.

Here are some examples for an argument claiming that boxing should be outlawed.

- STOP THE FIGHT! For good. The start of the twenty-first century is the perfect time to end one of the most brutal, deadliest sports on earth, boxing. [Opening with catchy sentence, followed immediately by the claim]

- In May of 1995, a young man named Jimmy Garcia was beaten to death in Las Vegas. Although such a violent act is not uncommon on American streets, this beating took place in front of thousands of people—during a boxing match at Caesar's Palace in Las Vegas, the site of another boxing fatality thirteen years earlier, when Korean boxer Duk Koo Kim died in a match with Ray Mancini. Unfortunately, Kim and Garcia are not alone. In the hundred years since boxing has been a sport, nearly 500 boxers have died as a result of injuries sustained in the ring. [Opening with facts and statistics]

- "Boxing is just show business with blood," once claimed Frank Bruno, the famed British boxer and sometime-actor. But, of course, actors don't often get killed on the job. [Opening with quote]

- Boxing is still among the most popular sports in the world. In fact, perhaps the most recognizable athlete in any country is Muhammad Ali, who, although he now suffers from a form of Parkinson's disease that may have been caused by a career of fighting, still draws huge crowds of fans wherever he goes and who had the honor of lighting the Olympic torch in the Atlanta games of 1996. For many people, Ali might represent what is best about boxing, a sport in which the smarter, more adroit, better-conditioned athlete prevails. Because it is in many ways a beautiful sport to watch—a dance in which the point is to avoid contact as much as to make it—it's hard to convince the sport's greatest fans that the sport should be banned. [Opening with concessions to the opposing argument]

Include a Thesis Statement

If you haven't already done so in the opening sentence or two, give a clear, carefully worded statement of your claim (sometimes called a thesis statement) somewhere in the opening paragraph. Not all writers place their thesis statement in the first paragraph, and some only imply their thesis. But it is always a good idea to state the claim early in the essay so that your readers know exactly what your point is and can therefore assess the relevance of your claims as they read your argument.

What form your thesis statement takes is up to you. You can give your statement in its own sentence or include it as part of a larger sentence: "Given the popularity of raves and the fact that few problems have been reported in the press, the citizens of Springfield may not realize just how *dangerous these dances can be.*" In the thesis statement of this long sentence, the writer is telling readers that this is the claim that will be defended.

Be sure to limit your thesis statement to the claim you are trying to defend. Say, for example, that you wanted to argue that public schools should not eliminate art and music courses from their curricula, but through brainstorming and research you narrowed your topic to public *elementary* schools and only *music* programs. You might have narrowed it even further to a particular school. Your thesis statement, then, would be "Kingston Elementary should not eliminate music courses from the curriculum."

Critical Thinking Lapse

Perhaps some arguments are best forgotten and not defended:

"Nikki Frey was ousted as editor of a Los Angeles Mensa chapter newsletter for publishing articles in the high-IQ group's publication proposing that people 'who are so mentally defective that they cannot live in society should, as soon as they are identified as defective, be humanely dispatched.' An article called for similar treatment for the homeless and infirm old people."

"Tennessee State Representative Frank Buck cited a report on the death penalty that put the cost of lethal injection at $46,000 per execution and a firing squad at $7,000. 'With figures like these, should we wonder why people don't trust government?' he commented. 'I believe I can figure out a way to shoot someone for less than $7,000.'"

"Anthony Yokley, serving 10 years for counterfeiting at the Federal Correctional Institution in Jefferson County, Colorado, appealed his sentence as unfair because it includes three leap years. He claimed that his punishment would be 'impermissibly enhanced by three days in violation of his equal protection and due process rights.' The 10th Circuit Court of Appeals ruled 'that this novel argument is without merit.'"[2]

If you like, your thesis statement can also give some idea of how you plan to defend your claim, or some idea of how your paper is organized. The following thesis sentence tells the reader what premises will be offered:

> Because music allows children to express their emotions, helps to keep them calm and relaxed, and teaches them to cooperate with one another, Kingston Elementary should not eliminate its music program.

In such a thesis statement, you are announcing your premises and your organization, since you will deal with your premises in the order you have presented them.

The following thesis statement also hints at the organization of the argument but does not give away the premises:

> Although music programs are expensive and often hard to staff, Kingston Elementary should retain its program for the benefits it brings to our community's children.

This thesis statement tells the readers that you intend to look at the reasons why the program is being eliminated and then to counter that argument with your own, better reasons to retain the program.

Of course, you are not required to mention either your reasons or the opposition in your thesis. However, your argument should never contradict the thesis statement or digress into areas you haven't prepared for. If your thesis concerns music programs at Kingston Elementary, you shouldn't start talking about art classes in high school.

Develop Your Body Paragraphs

Start each body paragraph with a topic sentence and develop the paragraph with details that support your topic sentence. Help your readers to better follow your line of thinking by organizing your ideas in a logical, fluid manner and, when necessary, by providing transitional words and phrases that link ideas together in a coherent flow.

The following paragraphs, both from Neil Postman's *Amusing Ourselves to Death,* are well developed, organized, and coherent. The first paragraph provides many examples, organized chronologically, to illustrate the idea given in the topic sentence. Coherency—or "flow"—is achieved through the use of parallel sentence structures. In the second paragraph, Postman lists several reasons for the popularity of *Sesame Street* among parents. In that paragraph, Postman uses several transitional words and phrases, which we have italicized.

> It is difficult to say exactly when politicians began to put themselves forward, intentionally, as sources of amusement. In the 1950's, Senator Everett Dirksen appeared as a guest on "What's My Line?" When he was running for office, John F. Kennedy allowed the television cameras of Ed Murrow's "Person to Person" to invade his home. When he was not running for office, Richard Nixon appeared for a few seconds on "Laugh-In," an hour-long comedy show based on the format of a television commercial. By the 1970's, the public had started to become accustomed to the notion that political figures were to be taken as part of the world of show business. In the 1980's came the deluge. Vice-presidential candidate William Miller did a commercial for American Express. So did the star of the Watergate Hearings, Senator Sam Ervin. Former President Gerald Ford joined with former Secretary of State Henry Kissinger for brief roles on "Dynasty." Massachusetts Governor Mike Dukakis appeared on "St. Elsewhere." Speaker of the House Tip O'Neill did a stint on "Cheers." Consumer advocate Ralph Nader, George McGovern and Mayor Edward Koch hosted "Saturday Night Live." Koch also played the role of a fight manager in a made-for-television movie starring James Cagney. Mrs. Nancy Reagan appeared on "Diff'rent Strokes." Would anyone be surprised if Gary Hart turned up on 'Hill Street Blues"? Or if Geraldine Ferraro played a small role as a Queens housewife in a Francis Coppola film? (pp. 132–33)

> Parents embraced "Sesame Street" for several reasons, *among them* that it assuaged their guilt over the fact that they could not or would not restrict their children's access to television. "Sesame Street" appeared to justify allowing a four- or five-year-old to sit transfixed in front of a television screen for unnatural periods of time. Parents were eager to hope that television could teach their children something other than which breakfast cereal has the most crackle. *At the same time,* "Sesame Street" relieved them of the responsibility of teaching their pre-school children how to read—no small matter in a culture where children are apt to be considered a nuisance. They could *also* plainly see that in spite

of its faults, "Sesame Street" was entirely consonant with the prevailing spirit of America. Its use of cute puppets, celebrities, catchy tunes, and rapid-fire editing was certain to give pleasure to the children and would *therefore* serve as adequate preparation for their entry into a fun-loving culture. (p. 142)

Just as your paragraphs should flow smoothly, so should the entire essay. Make sure that your reader can follow you from paragraph to paragraph. If the connection between topics is not immediately clear, give the reader some help with phrases such as "A second reason . . . ," "In contrast to [the reason just stated] . . . ," and "Finally . . .". Don't force transitional words to do the job that the content should do: your argument should move smoothly through paragraphs that are held together by a clear thesis sentence. But if a transitional tag will help, by all means use one.

Provide a Satisfying Conclusion

Almost every example of human communication has a beginning, a middle, and an end. Even a simple phone call begins with "hello" and ends with "goodbye." If one of those elements is missing, we are uncomfortable and we usually aren't sure what to do. If a phone call ends abruptly, we might feel we had been hung up on or that the line had been disconnected.

The same is true in writing an essay. You do not want your reader to feel that you have hung up without saying goodbye, which is the purpose of a conclusion. It lets your readers know that the essay is complete, that there are no missing pages, that you have said what you intended to say. How you say goodbye will depend on your thesis statement, your organization, your details, and even the length of your argument. If, for example, you have written a short piece—say, an editorial for your campus newspaper—there may be no reason to repeat what you have said in your thesis statement or your central premises. After all, most readers can remember the claim and the topic ideas in a short piece, so repeating them may look like an attempt to take up space. If, on the other hand, you write a more lengthy or more complicated argument, you might find it necessary to summarize your main ideas. Whatever you do, don't attach a cookie-cutter ending to everything you write. Each essay or argument that you write is unique; try writing conclusions that fit the essay.

Try one of the following ways to conclude your argument:

Return to the opening. Your readers might find your essay more satisfying if it comes full circle to its opening. Suppose you began with a quotation or a story; you might find a way to return to the quotation, providing a new interpretation or reminding your reader of its aptness, or to return to the story, telling the reader what happened next or simply referring to some of the details.

Make a prediction. Tell your readers that things might get worse or better or that new problems might arise. Be careful not to make an unfair appeal to your readers' emotions. They may feel that you have taken a cheap shot to end your argument.

Ask a question. Let your readers know that your argument raises some questions that must be answered.

Call for action. Very often, a good argument will leave readers wondering what they can do. Encourage your readers, if appropriate, to take action in support of your claim: spread the word, avoid certain behaviors, write letters, join a campaign, and so forth. Be careful not to preach at your readers.

End with a story different from the one you started with. If returning to your original opening is not an option, a new story may help close your argument. If you do opt to tell a story, be sure it is a true one. Making something up—pretending in the argument for a traffic light that a child's life was saved because of the presence of a traffic light, for instance—will only anger readers who know or suspect that the story is untrue.

Emphasize the importance of your claim. This strategy works very well if you feel your readers might not see the significance of your argument. For example, in the paper about 7:00 A.M. classes, your readers might say that with all the important issues on campus, this one doesn't deserve the attention you have lavished upon it. The conclusion might provide an opportunity to say that it does indeed.

Whatever method you choose to conclude your essay, keep in mind that your purpose is to end the essay, to say goodbye. Try to do so in a manner that is pleasing and satisfying to the readers and that fits your purpose and your point.

EXERCISE 13.6

Write an argument. Although the exercises throughout this chapter have been designed to help you create a group paper, your professor may prefer that you write your argument individually.

If you are to work as a group, keep in mind that collaborating on the writing is somewhat more difficult than working as a group to gather and organize ideas. There are several ways to collaborate on a paper: One member can write the entire draft and hand it to the next group member for revisions, who hands it to the third. Or group members could sit in a circle and, like a "three-headed" writer, draft the argument. Or each member could take a certain section or a number of paragraphs. Although any method will work, the last works best for longer papers such as business reports. For a short paper, the first or the second works well. The first method (one draft writer at a time) is a good option if your group will be writing more than one argument during the semester, since each member can have his or her turn at the first draft. If your professor has no prefer-ence, your group will have to choose which method to employ as your group writes the first draft of your argument.

After the First Draft

Once you have organized and defended your argument, you will have a draft of your essay. Most writers like to set their work aside for a short time before they begin revising or editing. Doing so helps those writers "get distance" from their own words, which, as you probably know, seem too familiar if you read them too soon after writing them. It is easy to miss errors if our minds are filling in what we meant instead of what actually appears on the page.

When you return to your first draft, you must be willing to see it as a rough sketch of what your final draft will look like. Few writers are entirely happy with the first words that flow from their pens or appear on the screen. Can you imagine what life would be like if in conversations with one another we had no opportunity to correct what we said or take back a comment or clarify our meaning? Take advantage of the opportunity to correct and clarify your first draft, and take as many drafts as you need to get the argument as you want it.

Read What You Have Written and Revise

After you have written a draft of your essay and given your brain time to cool, return to your essay and read it again with a critical eye. Don't look only for clumsy expressions, grammatical problems, meaningless or repetitive sen-tences, and the like. Look, too, for the large issues and evaluate your argument from the point of view of someone who disagrees with you. Be honest with yourself; question your evidence. Ask yourself if you are simply repeating what you have heard or what you assume to be true. Check your logic. Put your es-say through the same rigorous test you have put other arguments through. Re-vise your draft to correct any problems.

Consider What You Have Not Written and Revise

Most important, consider what you *have not* said. Very often, we are so com-mitted to our viewpoints that we fail to examine the ideas and assumptions upon which those views are based. When you look critically at your essay, try to disagree with what you have written by finding a way to reject each of the premises you have offered as support. It may sound like you're being awfully rough on yourself, but it will help reveal areas where connections are left un-explored or where unexamined assumptions are guiding your thinking. You don't have to abandon what you have written; you may simply have to defend it better. Suppose the topic were salaries and someone had suggested that salaries in the United States should be capped at, say, a quarter-million dollars. You are asked for your argument on the issue, and you write: "Capping salaries is not a good idea, since it would reduce competition." You might write a brilliant paragraph showing that capping salaries would indeed reduce competition. You might provide historical examples and the testimony of experts to back you up. But you need to ask, "So what?" So what if competition is reduced? What's so great about competition anyway? It may be great, but you need to show that it is. Your reader may not have the same values that you have. In a case such as this, it is best not to leave anything to chance. If you discover that you have taken too much for granted or that you need to better defend your assertions, revise your essay.

Show Your Work

Show your draft to someone—a friend, a family member, a professor, a tutor in the writing lab—someone who will do you the favor of critically reviewing your essay. Don't let a friend tell you what you want to hear: "It's great. Hand it in." Ask if anything is confusing or undeveloped. Ask your reader to show you where the argument may be weak or unconvincing. Ask if the organization is clear and effective, if the opening paragraph is interesting, if the conclusion is satisfying. Never hesitate to get advice from a reader. It is not a sign of weakness or insecurity but of strength and intelligence to ask for advice on a draft. Not even a professional writer considers a piece finished until it has been seen by someone or several people who can offer advice for improving the writing.

Edit Your Work

When you have revised your argument several times and are happy with the content and organization, look your sentences over very carefully one last time for grammatical mistakes, misused or missing punctuation, misspellings, and typographical errors. And, again, there is no shame in seeking help if you are unsure about things such as comma usage and sentence fragments. Finally, try reading your paper out loud to hear how it sounds. Doing so can sometimes help reveal awkward phrases or repetitive sentence structures.

Hand It In

Someone once said that good writing is never finished, it's just published or, in this case, handed in. You can probably rest assured that your reader—your professor—is the intelligent, impartial, sensitive reader that you have been advised to write for and that your argument will be evaluated on its strength, its form and content, its support, and so forth. If you have done your work well, you will at least get a fair hearing.

Evans   1

Samantha Evans

Professor Gaughran

Humanities 101: Critical Thinking

December 5, 2000

No Public Prayer in Public Schools

Interesting opening.

Not long after the Columbine massacre in the spring of 1999, a Gallup poll showed what could be considered a very understandable reaction to the killings: more than two-thirds of Americans favor returning organized prayer to our public schools (Gillespie). Undoubtedly, daily prayer is important in the lives of

Offers a balanced view: doesn't try to argue in either/or terms; shows good sense of audience.

many Americans, and we are all entitled to offer private, silent prayers whenever and wherever we wish and even to shout our prayers in our backyards or on street corners. And some prayer must be permitted even in public schools; no one would deny Muslim students, for example, the right to gather to pray at prescribed times during the school day. But such prayers should be conducted in areas removed from the student body, not publicly in classrooms or assemblies where non-Muslim students are gathered. As tragic as the Columbine killings were, public

Defines "prayer" in a specific context.

prayer on public school grounds, whether organized by school officials or by groups within the student body, must be

Thesis provides some idea of how paper will proceed.

prohibited. While prayer is permitted in exclusively religious schools, private schools or colleges, organized public prayer

This essay is published with the kind permission of the author.

Evans   2

in public schools not only violates the First Amendment, it discourages students from expressing minority views for fear of appearing to go against the majority. Furthermore, allowing prayers in school interferes with parents' rights to raise their children as they see fit.

    First, prayer in public schools violates the First Amendment: "Congress shall make no law respecting an establishment of religion, or prohibiting the free exercise thereof, or abridging the freedom of speech, or of the press; or the right of the people peaceably to assemble, and to petition the government for a redress of grievances." The rights guaranteed by the First Amendment of the Constitution are familiar to most Americans, and the amendment's underlying principle—personal freedom— plays a part in our daily lives: we may, without government interference, choose our spouse, job, place of residence, college, and so on. That same freedom also applies to religion, a concept that is explicitly protected by two constitutional provisions, namely the establishment and free exercise clauses. Briefly, the establishment clause, in the most basic sense, prohibits the government (interpreted by the Supreme Court to mean both national and state governments) from promoting or assisting a specific religion or from interfering in one. The second provision—the free exercise clause—allows an individual to practice whatever religion he or she chooses. We take advantage of that simple freedom when we worship at a church or synagogue, or when we choose not to worship at all.

First premise: Public school prayer violates First Amendment.

Quotes First Amendment, since some readers might be unfamiliar with the exact language.

Uses illustrations to explain "personal freedoms."

Divides the First Amendment statement on religious freedom into two parts, establishment clause and free exercise clause, and defines each.

Evans   3

Shows how school prayer violates the establishment clause.

Supports claim with analogy.

Provides illlustrations.

School-sponsored prayer violates the establishment clause, since a public school is funded by tax money and acts as an agent of the state. Just as the government couldn't lead us in a prayer before our driver's test at the Department of Motor Vehicles, it cannot conduct prayer in its schools. As decided in a 1963 case questioning a school's required reading of ten Bible passages per day and in a 2000 case involving the constitutionality of displaying the motto "In God We Trust" in Colorado classrooms, schools cannot perpetuate established religions associated with the Bible and God (Epstein 201-2; Janofsky A9). This fact holds true regardless of how many people believe in and practice that religion. Even if the school did not require but merely supervised organized prayer on school grounds, the school would be in violation of the establishment clause since it would appear to promote or assist in religion.

Shows how school prayer violates the free exercise clause.

Considers opposing point of view: shouldn't free exercise clause permit us to freely exercise our religious beliefs?

If a school did require its students to pray, it would also, obviously, violate the second provision, the free exercise clause, which allows us to choose *not* to worship if that's what we desire. But, some might ask, doesn't the free exercise also give us the right to freely express our religious views? In other words, shouldn't the students themselves be free to assemble to pray in the cafeteria, in the school yard or parking lot, or in the locker room, for example? This very position was recently taken by a school district in Sante Fe, Texas, where a student was chosen by her classmates, and therefore not a school official, to recite "an invocation and/or message" over the loud speaker during

Evans   4

home football games. The school was obviously aware that this practice was occurring and claimed that it was allowable considering the students' right to free exercise (Richey). Unfortunately, the argument is flawed in two areas. Primarily, the activity of prayer itself continues to occur on school grounds, and regardless of whether or not a school official chose the speaker, simply allowing prayer on school property in this context could be interpreted as promoting the religion advocated by the student representative. Put more plainly, the school is not remaining neutral on issues of religion.

Secondly, such an argument overlooks the tension inherent in the establishment and free exercise provisions, a tension so strong that it may seem to be contradiction: On the one hand, if the government *permits* us to pray on public property, it promotes a religion; if the government *prohibits* prayer, it is denying our freedom to exercise our religious beliefs. Since tension unquestionably exists, one clause must take precedence over the other in certain public locations such as schools. In a public school setting, the precedence of the establishment clause preserves the school's neutrality. Simultaneously, such a choice still allows for and encourages the free exercise of religion to occur elsewhere, namely in the privacy of one's home (or anywhere else not linked to a public school). Those who argue that the free exercise clause should prevail sometimes resort to emotional appeals, as does Armstrong William in "Supreme Court Quivers Over Prayer Possibility." Mr. William suggests, in

---

Responds to opponent's argument: first, prayer is still taking place on school grounds in violation of establishment clause.

Further response to opponent's argument: two clauses create a tension that can be resolved only by giving precedence to the establishment clause, not to the free exercise clause.

Considers one opposing argument—that if one clause should take precedence, it should be the free exercise clause.

the wake of recent Supreme Court decisions regarding school prayer, that the Supreme Court will eventually abolish Christmas and similar religious holidays. By overstating the case and playing on the fear of the public, he makes it seem as if all religious values are being questioned and that we are on the slippery slope toward a completely secular society. What the Court correctly questioned, however, was a school's *position* in perpetuating religious values. Upholding the establishment clause ensures that schools do not promote a single religion while allowing personal religious practices to continue without restriction.

What if a school's officials, however, are unaware of and therefore unable to stop attempts to pray collectively and publicly on school grounds? Couldn't we simply ignore the small prayer groups formed, sometimes spontaneously, by students who pray aloud in hallways and during assemblies? Couldn't we somehow get around the First Amendment and let students who want to pray gather with one another the way some NFL players do on the field after a game? After all, what harm is done? Actually, the potential exists for much harm. All of us have felt in grade school and high school (and yes, even in college) pressure to conform to the wishes of the group around us. It's often better to laugh at a friend's unfunny joke simply to be accepted by that friend. The same can and does hold true for young adults who practice a religion other than that of their classmates. If public prayer is allowed, we are creating an extremely tense and stressful situation for students who might fear that their choice

Responds to the opposing argument.

Introduces second premise with questions

and with an analogy.

Second premise: One effect of school prayer: creates stressful situation for some students.

Evans   6

of a "different" religion could divide them from classmates and friends, resulting, possibly, in their being ostracized or ridiculed. And their fear is warranted. Recently, in a school located in Maryland, one young man, refusing to participate in a spontaneous prayer begun by audience members at commencement, left the auditorium as a way of expressing his disapproval of the intended religious message. Security guards refused to allow the student back into the proceedings, and school officials subsequently barred him from a school party occurring on the same evening (Chavez). In the Sante Fe, Texas, case, Debbie Mason, a mother of four children attending a public school, testified that the school's promotion of one religion (through prayer) pitted students of conflicting faiths against one another, "If a child was Jewish in this community, the child was made fun of by other students who were Christians" (Alford 19). Or, as a final example of what can happen when an individual refuses to participate in a majority prayer, consider the case of Greg Thomas. A former teacher in Hamilton High School, Thomas suddenly lost the support of his once friendly neighbors after complaining about the predominance of Christian teachings in the schools. Fellow teachers, previous supporters of the community art program, stopped bringing their students to plays produced by Thomas, leading eventually to the cutting of the program and loss of Thomas' job. The consensus seemed to be that the community feared Thomas' attempts at turning the Christian school into "the Jewish league" (Reeves). Without a

Premise supported through illustrations.

doubt, if adults are willing to treat fellow adults with such disdain over a difference of religion, it sends the message to students of minority faiths to keep quiet. We should not be placing children, or even young adults, in a situation where they must choose between their faith and their friends. Students are learning that choosing the former may result in ridicule, while choosing the latter is a denial of oneself. Simply keeping public, collective prayer out of school eliminates any such dilemma.

Third premise: School prayer interferes with a parents' right to instruct children on religious matters.

A final reason to reject school prayer is to prevent influencing individuals whose religious beliefs have not been completely forged. Schools that permit or ignore even spontaneous prayer are in effect robbing parents of the right to instruct their children on religious matters if their children are hearing beliefs in school contrary to those being taught at home.

Considers opposing view that morality must be injected into schools.

Some proponents of school prayer argue that morality must be injected into our classrooms. In the case involving the use of "In God We Trust," advocates for prayer feared a replay of the tragic events at Columbine, contending that such a phrase might help "reinforce the precepts of moral rectitude" throughout our schools (Janofsky). Although no one denies the hideous nature of the events at Columbine, it is conceivable that some parents do not define "morality" on the basis of any established religious teachings and may wish to inculcate moral values through a process that does not involve religion. Religion must remain a private family issue. This is not a question of shared responsibility among parents, community and schools. Realistically, that type of

Responds to opposing argument: parents will not all agree on how morality should be taught.

Evans   8

cooperation is beneficial when used to encourage student involvement in school sports teams, clubs or community programs. We can identify a unified goal for this type of cooperation, such as helping children make friends. On the contrary, it is nearly impossible to find one religious absolute that would cover all students in a school. And not only do we hold beliefs different from those held in another denomination, but even within our own faith what we accept and do not accept may vary widely among members of the same church or synagogue. Therefore, worrying about what should be and should not be included when designing a prayer is an overwhelmingly difficult task. The task is much easier when religion is not addressed in public schools at all, but remains a subject dealt with at home.

For many of us, prayer is a vital part of our lives; it can help us cope with and understand our earthly existence. No doubt a bit more religion in our lives could help curb our violent tendencies. But prayer does not belong in schools. Schools should teach subjects that are beneficial to all students, while refraining from getting involved in subjects certain to increase tension between classmates and within individual students. Surely much could be done in our schools to decrease the overwhelming tension that already exists between factions or to provide a more secure and safe environment. But while we might pray at home for providential guidance for ourselves, our teachers and our classmates, praying together in school can only cause more harm than good.

Development through contrasts: some shared goals, such as helping students make friends, can be achieved, but we do not all share the same religious beliefs.

Satisfying conclusion: shows sensitivity to audience and

Comes back to issues addressed in opening paragraph.

Works Cited

Alford, Deann. "Pregame Prayer Barred." *Christianity Today* 7
    Aug. 2000: 19–20.

Chavez, Linda. "Most Americans Want to Return to a
    Tradition of Public Prayer." *Salt Lake City Enterprise* 7
    June 1999: 24.

Epstein, Lee, and Thomas G. Walker. *Constitutional Law for a
    Changing America: Rights, Liberties, and Justice.* 3rd ed.
    Washington, D.C.: Congressional Quarterly Inc., 1998.

Gillespie, Mark. "Most Americans Support Prayer in Public
    Schools." Poll Releases July 9, 1999. The Gallup
    Organization.
        <http://www.gallup.com/poll/releases/pr990709.asp>

Janofsky, Michael. "Colorado Asks: Is 'In God We Trust' a
    Religious Statement?" *New York Times* 3 July 2000, natl.
    ed.: A9.

Reeves, Jay. "Alabama Man Crusades Against School Prayer."
    Community College Week 10 July 2000: 32.

Richey, Warren. "Can Students Mix Prayer and Football?"
    Christian Science Monitor 29 March 2000: 1.

William, Armstrong. "Supreme Court Quivers Over Prayer
    Possibility." *New York Amsterdam News* 29 June 2000: 8.

Summary

1. An argument is not a fight. Although your objective might be to win, your success in an argument should be measured by how well you defend your claim and how fair, accurate, and honest you are in presenting your case. Whether in the end your opponent agrees or disagrees with you, you should strive to put forward the most rational and even-handed presentation you can muster.

2. Before writing an argument, know yourself, your audience, and your topic. Present yourself as a humane and generous person. Don't try to write an argument on an issue you know nothing about even though you might have strong opinions concerning it. Know your topic well, even if you have to conduct research. Speak to your audience; don't lecture, antagonize, or bully them. Expect your readers to be fair but skeptical. Try to foresee your readers' reactions and objections.

3. To get started, focus your topic so that you can cover the issue in the number of pages assigned. Brainstorm for ideas and organize your thoughts.

4. In writing the argument, provide a single statement of your central claim and organize your material in a manner that will allow your readers to easily recognize your premises. Try organizing your argument around one of the standard developmental patterns for writing essays (narration, description, illustration, definition, comparison/contrast, cause-effect, classification), one of the more familiar organization schemes for presenting an argument (deductive, problem-solution, evaluation), or a combination of several patterns. Give your argument a conclusion that your readers will find satisfying.

5. Defend your central claim with factual evidence, expert opinion, examples, and, when appropriate, analogies. Don't hesitate to research your topic to provide the best support possible.

6. After you have written your argument, read what you have written. Be certain that you have defended your premises and any assumptions upon which your argument is based. Before you write your final, edited draft, seek the advice of your professor, a tutor, or a peer who might alert you to any shortcomings in the argument you may have failed to notice.

CHAPTER 14

THINKING CRITICALLY ABOUT THE MEDIA

In the previous two chapters we looked at how you might apply your critical thinking skills to the evaluation of sources you find in a library or on the Internet and at how you might use your skills and sources in writing an argument. In actively seeking facts and opinions to support your claims, you need to do the difficult, demanding, but ultimately rewarding work of scrutinizing the sources you intend to rely upon in your argument. The lesson, although sometimes difficult to apply, is not hard to remember; after all, you've heard it since childhood: "Don't believe everything you read." Reading carefully and skeptically—with respect for truth, clarity, and fairness, and disdain for lies, manipulation, contradiction and illogic—will keep you alert to fallacies, slanted language, fraudulent authorities and specious arguments.

In this chapter we look at other, more common sources of information, ones that we encounter every day whether we are actively seeking them or not. Think about how much information from an almost overwhelming number of sources you may have absorbed, even unconsciously, just since you awoke this morning—information from the radio, television, newspapers, magazines, billboards, road signs, posters, fliers, textbooks, brochures, lectures, phone calls, faxes, CDs—you can probably think of others. We may avoid some of these sources—reading newspapers and novels is not as popular an activity for some as watching television or chatting in cyberspace—but a substantial amount of information assails our ears and eyes on any given day.

Because we are daily pelted with messages and because of the supposed ease of finding information about almost anything we need, our time in history has often been referred to as "the information age." But the onslaught of information can be so overpowering that many people, even while they often profess to distrust the media, can easily slip into the habit of absorbing whatever is thrown at them. The daily barrage of information, though it should invite the most rigorous application of our critical thinking skills, frequently dulls our senses and teases us out of skepticism. Perhaps we have become so accustomed to "relaxing" in front of the television or with a magazine that we allow our intellectual filters to shut down. Whereas actively conducting research requires that we possess the skills of a detective—digging for evidence, interrogating sources, examining the issue from every angle, following leads, avoiding hasty conclusions, and, if we are lucky and smart, solving the case—watching television, listening to the radio, and reading magazines seem to encourage a kind of mental complacency. Although we may occasionally heed the admonition not to believe everything we read and see, too often we let a great deal of misinformation slip under our critical radar. This chapter will help you develop methods for applying your critical thinking skills to the evaluation of information you hear and read in your daily life.

THE MASS MEDIA

Much of what you hear and read comes to you through what is called the *mass media*. Some people mistakenly believe that the word "mass" in this context refers to the size of the organization that delivers news and entertainment, and, certainly, mass-media organizations such as ABC and The New York Times Company are quite large. But the mass media are defined not so much by the size of the organizations as by the size of the audience they reach through devices such as televisions, radios, computers, cameras, printing presses, and copy machines. These two elements—a large audience and a mechanical means of reaching that audience—are essential to the definition of mass media. A conversation with a friend obviously does not qualify as an example of mass media, but neither does shouting from a rooftop to a crowd gathered in the street. One of the additional defining characteristics of the mass media is that the audience being addressed usually cannot reply immediately to the communicator, who is delivering a message through a device that separates him or her from the audience. Although some media organizations provide means for immediate "feedback"—radio call-in shows, for example—the mass media usually allow only for one-way communication. In fact, one could argue that even radio talk shows are one-way communication, since calls to a show are "screened"—approved, in other words—by the producers of the show.

The mass media, then, include all electronic communication intended to inform, entertain, or persuade *large* audiences and includes news broadcasts, sitcoms, talk shows, soap operas, music videos, movies, magazines, newspapers, radio shows, record albums (does anyone remember them?), CDs, posters, fliers, advertisements of every sort wherever they appear, comic books, novels, and textbooks. The term "media" is also used to indicate the producers of, and contributors to, media creations; thus, we refer to journalists, news anchors, camera operators, performers, and so forth as "the media."

The media in America face an enormous challenge in their effort to reach a very large and diverse audience. In some cases, the prospective audience is narrowed by the content of the particular production. *The Sporting News, Field and Stream, Popular Science, Cosmopolitan, Harper's,* and many other specialized publications are aimed at audiences whose interests or needs distinguish them from other groups. Other publications and productions, such as the *New York Times,* the *Washington Post,* the *Wall Street Journal, All Things Considered* (on National Public Radio), and *The Week in Review* (on the Public Broadcasting System [PBS]), are aimed at educated audiences interested in more extensive coverage and analysis of national and international events. Another branch of the media narrows its audience through editorial policies that openly declare a political point of view. Often referred to as journals of opinion, partisan publications such as *The Nation, Commentary, The New Republic,* and *National Review* occasionally report the news but more frequently comment on current events from one side of the political spectrum or the other. A reader has a slightly easier task of evaluating materials from these sources, since the editorial policies are stated forthrightly.[1]

But the majority of media productions in the United States profess to maintain an objective political stance and are aimed at audiences whose diversity makes it difficult to assume any common ground, political or otherwise. Local and national daily papers and radio programs; the local and national nightly news on ABC, NBC, and CBS; programming on CNN, MSNBC, and FoxNews, and the popular newsmagazines (*Time, Newsweek, U.S. News and World Report*) all reach audiences whose political viewpoints run the spectrum from the most liberal to the most conservative. Although these productions may target particular groups of people defined by age and literacy, they all reach a larger audience than specialized publications. The editors of *Field and Stream* can safely assume that their magazine is being read primarily by hunting and fishing enthusiasts. The magazine *Mother Jones* is aimed at progressives, or liberals, who are interested in its investigative reporting and coverage regarding labor, political and environmental issues. But the managing editor of *World News Tonight,* the editor of your local paper, and the writers for *Time* magazine must assume that their watchers and readers have widely varied interests and viewpoints. A perceived or stated bias on the part of the network, newspaper, or magazine would speak to one segment of the audience and alienate others.

Clearly, the media constitute a large and complex institution. Because a thorough discussion of critical thinking and the media would be impossible in a single chapter, we will limit ourselves to a discussion of two related institutions that critical thinkers encounter every day—news and advertising, and we will examine how they appear in newspapers and magazines and on television and radio.

THE NEWS MEDIA

To begin our analysis of the news media, let's take a closer look at the word "media." "Media" is the plural form of "medium," a word derived from the Latin *medius,* from which we get many words—"mediate," "medieval," "mediocre," "meridian," and others—with a common meaning: they all refer to something *in the middle*. A mediator tries to resolve conflicts by working with both sides, helping them communicate and perhaps find a middle ground; the Medieval period of art and literature bridged the ancient world and the Renaissance. Similarly, the media—especially the news media—act as middle-agents, mediators, a bridge between us and the world of events occurring all around us. Since we cannot be in Iraq or South Africa or Mexico this afternoon to see for ourselves the events taking place there, the media will bring those events, in some shape or form, to us.

But the news media do not and cannot deliver those real events in a transparent fashion as if we were merely looking through a window on the world. Instead, the media "mediate" reality, passing the day's events, the data of real life, through a lens or filter that interprets and sometimes distorts reality. It's not hard to see how this happens. If you were to act as a mediator for two friends having a quarrel, you would carry messages back and forth, but you would most likely inject your opinion, occasionally (perhaps inadvertently) misconstrue one person's intentions or report information incorrectly, exclude minor details and select what you think are the most important points, forget some details, and so forth. Even if you attempted to deliver messages precisely and accurately, the tone and volume of your voice, your expressions and gestures, your stance and posture, even the clothes you wear might aid or alter the message or the way it is perceived. Your friends, standing on either side with you in the middle, would have to remain conscious of your mediating role and decide whether you are a reliable source. They may have to decide at some point whether you as mediator have something to lose or gain in reuniting them or in keeping them apart. Your friends would have to admit that neither knows for sure what the other feels or thinks; they know only what you present or impart. One friend may begin to take advantage of you, using your weaknesses as a mediator to his advantage. And, finally, your influence might be so profound that when your friends finally do get together, they might not see each other as each truly is, but in the way you have prepared them to see.

Similarly, when we watch the nightly news, we cannot say for certain that we *know* what happened in the world today; we only know what a complex web of journalists, writers, editors, camera operators, technicians, engineers, news anchors, and so forth have shown us and told us about the world's events. The network might have something to gain by its portrayal of events, might have distorted reality, might have focused on the wrong details or excluded important ones, might have allowed itself to be exploited by government or business sources of information. Our understanding of and response to the events depicted will be influenced by the way they are presented—the electronic or print equivalent of facial expressions, posture, and clothing.

As a mediator, the news media act as a sort of sieve through which the world's events are sifted and prepared for delivery to the homes of a massive audience. When we talk about the media, we are talking not about the real world beyond our sight and hearing, but about that sieve and what comes through it—the messages we've received about the world and how the delivery of those message might influence the way we perceive reality and the way we think. If we are told again and again, in overt and subtle ways, in images and words, in newspapers and on television, that a people are dangerous and violent, do we eventually begin to perceive them that way? Immediately following the Oklahoma City bombing, some Americans were so convinced that "Arab terrorists" were involved that they refused to fly on planes with passengers who appeared to be from the Middle East. The assumption of Arab involvement was incorrect, of course, but where did it come from? In part from the media. A *Wall Street Journal* article on the bombing began with the sentence, "A "Beirut-style car bombing ripped the face of a nine-story federal building. . . ." Several paragraphs in the article examined the "possible motivation of Islamic extremists." The *Washington Post* reported that "hundreds of leads were being investigated," but the paper highlighted one in particular: ". . . a number of law enforcement sources and private terrorism experts said that the bomb apparently used bore the basic characteristics of devices that Muslim extremists have detonated in such places as Beirut, Lebanon and Buenos Aires." The article carried a sidebar with a list of "Terrorists Acts Against U.S. Targets" that included only attacks committed by militant Arab groups.[2] It's not hard to argue that the media, standing between us and the vast, complicated world, greatly influence the way we view that world.

The Importance of Context

As critically thinking consumers of messages sifted from the world's events, we must first remember that those messages have been sifted, removed from their much larger contexts. Context refers to the environment within which events take place, the conditions and circumstances surrounding an event in the way rings of water encircle a pebble dropped in a lake. In mediating between your friends, your messages are understood because you and they have a shared context, a shared history; they know what caused the quarrel. In our communication with one another we often assume a context. We phone someone and leave a voice message that will make perfect sense: "I'll meet you at our favorite table after your last class." But without context, messages often have very little meaning to us. It's like coming home to find a message on the answering machine left by a caller who dialed the wrong number.

Imagine, then, the challenge faced by the producers of television, radio, newspapers, and magazines face every day when they attempt to deliver messages to anywhere from a few hundred to several million people of varying intelligence, education, critical thinking skills, interests, concerns, and so on, who can't immediately respond to the message, who can't ask for clarification or details, and who may have no context for messages about politics, the arts, higher education, crime, terrorism, foreign relations, and so forth. To be sure, messages are not divorced completely from their contexts; we know who the president is, where Oklahoma is located, that guns and bombs kill, that fires destroy. So some context can be assumed. But, rather than spend the enormous amount of time and effort required to provide the context necessary for a mass audience to fully understand a message, the popular media focus almost exclusively on the message itself, with little regard for what the message may mean. We are left with a great deal of information—a crime was committed, a house burned down, a politician was elected, a hurricane hit, a war broke out, interest rates rose, a plane crashed, a president lied, a bomb exploded—and very little meaning other than what we might ourselves attach to the message given our prejudices, experiences, and opinions. We often put down the paper or turn off the television with no greater insight, background, or knowledge than what we had before we read or watched the day's news. And, in fact, because the media tend to highlight the most sensational, unusual, or spectacular events—the crashes, fires, accidents, murders—we more often than not walk away with information that is not only useless to us but detrimental as well in that it encourages us to believe that crashes, fires, accidents, and murders are more common than they are and that they represent what is truly important, ignoring other significant and perhaps more meaningful occurrences.

The "Meaning" of the News

Perhaps we should pause briefly here to ask what sort of "meaning" we have in mind when we talk about the *meaning* of the news. Information, as we receive it through the media, can affect us in a variety of ways: it might teach us something new about our world, help correct a misconception or an assumption, alert us to the presence of danger or misfortune, inspire us to look deeper into an issue, or awaken our empathy and compassion. Sometimes, among the thousands of messages delivered to us by the media, we will find one that moves us or affects our lives in some way. From the news we might draw our own conclusions about the condition of our world or the state of human affairs.

But of the many messages we receive daily we might find ourselves asking, "What does that mean?" or "What does that mean to me?" One measure of a news item's meaning might be its usefulness to us. We might ask ourselves, "Now that I have been informed of this event, what will I do with the information?" Although some news is *immediately* useful—we might be cautioned to avoid roads under construction or to prepare for higher gasoline prices—all news does not have to be useful in this sense; if immediate usefulness were the sole measure of the value of news, we would have only endless gardening and home-improvement tips, consumer alerts, weather warnings, and the like.

In *Breaking the News,* James Fallows offers some idea of what is meant by the "usefulness" of news:

> . . . [F]or journalism to matter it must be useful in one particular way. It must give people the sense that life is not just a sequence of random occurrences. That is how a cat or a horse sees the world. For a cat, everything happens by surprise

and then ends without consequence. Useful information helps people under-stand what can be changed and what must be endured.[3]

In other words, the news should help us to gain some measure of control over our lives and the events occurring all around us. The news should provide what we need to make informed, intelligent decisions that result in reasonable and effective actions. If we all lived alone in isolated cottages in inaccessible places, it wouldn't really matter what news we received. We could sit like human recording devices, simply, pointlessly gathering data. But as members of larger communities, we need information to help guide our conversations, decisions, and actions. In *Amusing Ourselves to Death,* a book that demonstrates how television has undone our capacity to think, Neil Postman proposes a simple question to help us get a sense of what is meant by useless information:

> How often does it occur that the information provided you on morning radio or television, or in the morning newspaper, causes you to alter your plans for the day, or to take some action you would not otherwise have taken, or provides you insight into some problem you are required to solve?[4]

As Postman goes on to suggest, some reports might alter our behavior; perhaps we'll carry an umbrella or sell some stock. And on occasion the news media have provided the kinds of information necessary for informed decisions and significant action: some writers, for example, have argued that the Vietnam War was shortened because the news media helped mobilize protesters by providing information that contradicted government propaganda. But the way we *generally* receive information—in brief, flashy bursts, with more graphic distractions than meaningful analysis—provides us little means for furthering our understanding of the world and precious few tools for controlling or contributing to our environment. Although there is no harm in picking up a few loose facts to contribute to our store of information about the world, most mass media news outlets provide only tidbits of information that are useful primarily for answering questions in trivia games. It is this excessive overflow of insignificant information that makes the majority of what we see and hear useless.

The press owes to society a truthful, comprehensive and intelligent account of the day's events in a context that gives them meaning.

—Freedom of the Press Commission, 1947

EXERCISE 14.1

Form groups of three and, for the next class, get a copy of *USA Today,* another paper with national distribution (the *New York Times,* the *Washington Post,* the *Wall Street Journal,* etc.), and a local paper. Each member of the group can be responsible for one paper; be sure to decide in advance and to get papers issued on the same day.

Working as a group in the next class, look through the papers until you find a story that is covered by all three. Read the longest of the articles first, then the second longest, then the shortest. As a group, compare the coverage, paying close attention to the following questions:

- Which paper covers the story in greatest depth? List some specific differences in the details that are included and excluded. Be careful not to assume that the longest piece is the most developed, since it may simply be repetitive.
- Do any of the papers attempt to discuss the event in a broader context—looking, for example, at historical episodes that may have led to the current event, discussing the impact or possible consequences of the event, comparing the event with similar occurrences, or discussing it in terms of larger political, social, or economic issues? You don't have to know a great deal about these broader issues; just ascertain which paper attempts to set the events in a larger context.
- Looking at the difference in how the three papers cover the same issue, try to determine how readers might react to each paper. If one paper has excluded some important contextual information, what is the effect on the reader? What kinds of questions might an interested reader have?
- Compare the headlines for similar stories. What does each headline emphasize? How might the headline affect the reader's conception of the story?

When you have finished discussing these questions in your group, report your findings to the whole class.

How Lack of Context Affects Meaning

Because of space limitations and because the audience is so large and diverse, most popular media are forced to exclude any broad discussion of contexts that would give information more meaning or make it more useful to us. Important, even vital stories are pared down to bite-sized morsels of information. One example with which many readers will be familiar is the "sound bite." The broadcast media often snip very small segments of a speaker's comments from a longer, more complex discourse. Although the media may try to clip the most important passages for broadcast, ones that, for example, summarize a political candidate's position on an issue, the practice of using sound bites extracts a comment from its context, which means that a listener has no way of knowing *precisely* what may have been intended by a comment or how to interpret the comment. Knowing the media's penchant for using sound bites, political advisors and speech writers often attempt to stay a step ahead of the media by including succinct, snappy lines that will make the nightly news as "sound bites." Some of these lines, such as George Bush's "Read my lips; no new taxes," have become very well known. Although politicians can use the sound-bite phenomenon to their advantage, the practice does little to help viewers and readers understand intentions and meanings, since the surrounding introductions, explanations, qualifiers, and so forth are missing. In fact, in the worst examples of the practice, a speaker is "quoted out of context" and the audience is given a false impression of the speaker's intentions.

The practice of using sound bites illustrates what amounts to a minor problem given the larger, more consequential effect of stripping information from its context. In many cases, the media, rather than offering a thorough examination of an issue in all its complexity, actually distort meaning in its presentation of the news. In place of complexity, which would require an audience's active, intelligent participation, the media usually employ attention-grabbing techniques that do little to increase our knowledge of a topic. Although some media productions, most notably national newspapers such as the *New York Times* and the *Washington Post,* do attempt to provide extended coverage and analysis, most news outlets provide little, if any, insight into events and issues. Ironically, some network news organizations label segments of the news "In-Depth" or "A Closer Look," even though these segments are only a minute or two longer than other segments of the news. The titles do little more than call attention to the lack of depth and close analysis.[5]

Yet another illustration of how the lack of context can make information meaningless can be found in the clipped stories that take up much space and time in the media. In an effort to pack as many stories as possible into a broadcast or a newspaper, managers and editors may devote a few moments of time or a few inches of newsprint to the selected national and international events in a segment usually titled something like "The World in a Minute," "Around the Nation," or "Nationline." Newsmagazines are especially fond of presenting pages full of abbreviated news, statistics, quotes, snapshots, and so forth. These brief segments and scraps of information are usually so far removed from their contexts as to be not only useless but sometimes dangerously misleading as well. In a typical broadcast fragment, an announcer might declare that a foreign government official has stepped down and that a celebrity has filed a protection-from-abuse order, giving the impression that these events are of equal importance and leaving us with no idea why the foreign leader resigned or what will happen next. A brief segment on health issues, such as the introduction of new medications or the latest research findings on nutrition, can be especially hazardous to audiences who fail to realize that the whole story is far more complicated than the segment suggests. Even more useless and potentially detrimental are popular reports of scientific findings, which are often misrepresented by science writers working under deadlines and with limited scientific knowledge. Without sufficient training in the practice of interpreting results and measuring the value of evidence, science writers, unlike scientists who write, often overstate the significance of scientific news, predicting, for example, that cures for deadly diseases are close at hand.

Even with the slightly more extended coverage and analysis found in such shows as *Nightline, 60 Minutes, 20/20,* and *Dateline,* there will inevitably remain in every story cultural, political, and social implications that the media fail to examine. Very few news organizations can afford to make the effort to help us understand isolated events by examining them in larger social or political contexts. To put the matter in personal terms, imagine a decision you made in your life that took a great deal of thought (choosing to live with one parent or the other, breaking up with a girlfriend, quitting a job, selecting a college); then imagine that you have two minutes or approximately three hundred words to tell your entire story to the world so that listeners or readers fully understand your motives, feelings, attitudes, regrets, and so on. Would five minutes be enough? Ten?

But let's suppose you had all of thirty minutes to tell your story, and, to make the task still more challenging, suppose you were only one of several people with a story to tell and your audience could get up and walk out on you at any point in your tale. You might first find yourself inventing more ways to hold your audience's attention than ways to persuade them of your innocence or convince them of your regret. In a similar manner, the news media are motivated not by the desire to educate an audience or to provide the tools necessary to make good decisions or take some measure of control over our lives, but by the need to get and hold the attention of the largest possible audience.

EXERCISE 14.2

Find and compare two articles about the same subject. Choose one article from a newspaper and the other from a news magazine. Read the newspaper article first and then the one from the newsmagazine. List the aspects of the magazine story not covered in the newspaper story, and answer this question: How is your understanding of the subject changed by the inclusion of additional information in the magazine?

GETTING US TO PAY ATTENTION: WHAT REALLY DRIVES THE MEDIA

So why do the news media go to all this trouble to attract and hold the attention of a large audience? After all, if the purpose is to deliver news into our homes, what does it matter how many of us are reading or watching? The mainstream news media do not exist solely to deliver the news, however, just as sitcoms and dramas are not intended only to entertain us. Although the news media certainly hope to inform us of daily events, they are impeded and constrained by the need to achieve an additional objective: to promote and sell commercial products and services to a large audience. The sitcoms and newscasts, radio talk shows and newspaper headlines are intended first to grab our attention so that we will stay tuned for the commercials or read the ads.

This revelation might not startle those of us who have grown accustomed to full-page newspaper ads, annoying radio jingles, and the constant interruption of television commercials. But surely the news is exempt from such commercialism; surely the news operates on a higher plane. Unfortunately, no.

When distant and unfamiliar and complex things are communicated to great masses of people, the truth suffers a considerable and often radical distortion. The complex is made over into the simple, the hypothetical into the dogmatic, and the relative into the absolute.

—Walter Lippmann

"Are you a businessman or a newsman?"

—Lowell Bergman (Al Pacino) in *The Insider*

Whereas we might hope in a perfect world to tune in to a half-hour of uninterrupted news every night or buy a paper that devoted all of its space to detailed reporting and analysis, the news media could not survive without advertisements, since it is not the consumers but the sponsors who pay for the production of the news. Take one large network as an example. Although many viewers receive CBS from their local cable provider, CBS is a free, "commercial" network. Anyone with a television set and an antenna can receive CBS provided the viewer lives close enough to a transmitter. Radio may be a better example: no one gets a radio bill each month. And the fifty cents or so you pay for your daily paper makes hardly a dent in the costs of producing it.

How can these media afford to provide services at little or no charge to consumers? By selling advertising space. A sponsor, say Ford Motor Company, buys ad space on CBS, which uses the money to produce the news. If viewers stay tuned to the news and the ad is successful, Ford will sell cars and buy more ad space on CBS. Ford and other corporations keep a close eye on CBS's nightly news "ratings" to see how many people are watching the broadcasts. If the ratings are too low, meaning that a relatively smaller number of people are watching the news on CBS, Ford might go to another network, one with higher ratings and a greater share of the news-watching audience. Without sponsorship to pay the bills, the mainstream media would simply collapse.

Some exceptions to commercial media should be noted. In the case of *public* television and radio (Public Broadcasting Service, National Public Radio, Public Radio International), survival depends on contributions from private corporations, contributing members, and government grants. Church-affiliated radio and television stations survive with contributions from listeners and viewers and, of course, with church sponsorship. And the United States government, funded by tax money, produces many informative documents. But for almost everyone else in the media, survival depends on advertising revenue. This, obviously, presents a problem, a clash of values represented on the one hand by an audience's need for information and on the other by the media's need to survive. Put bluntly, the mass media in America are businesses, powerfully motivated by the need to sustain themselves and, in the case of privately owned corporations, to make a profit. Certainly, making money is no crime, and because most of us like to be informed, the mass media should have no trouble garnering audiences large enough to sustain the individual companies that supply the information. But it's not that simple.

Simply presenting information—often complicated, detailed, and dense—won't usually do the trick in holding our attention and coaxing us back to the same newspaper or television network again and again. Let's be brutally honest with ourselves here: many Americans do not enjoy reading long and complicated articles about issues unconnected with their everyday lives or watching detailed and serious analysis of those issues. And, to be fair, a large number of American adults (estimates go as high as 50 percent) cannot read complicated material or follow intricate and demanding analysis. Because

The Nielsen Ratings

Nielsen Media Research collects data on the television viewing habits of Americans and provides "ratings" to indicate which TV shows were the most popular during a given week. A single *ratings* point represents 1 percent of the number of households with television sets (currently about 100 million). *Share* is the percentage of television sets that are turned on and tuned to the specific program.

The following tables indicate the popularity of *Who Wants to Be a Millionaire,* a game show airing three times a week on ABC, usually at 8:00 or 9:00 p.m. As the second table demonstrates, when the game show was aired on Sunday, April 30, at 7:00, opposite CBS's perennial favorite *60 Minutes,* the game show knocked the news show out of the top ten.

April 17 to April 23, 2000

Rank	Program	Network	Time	Rating	Share	Homes
1	Who Wants to Be a Millionaire? (Tues.)	ABC	8:00pm	17.0	29.0	17,093,000
2	Who Wants to Be a Millionaire? (Thurs.)	ABC	9:00pm	16.8	27.0	16,907,000
3	Who Wants to Be a Millionaire? (Sun.)	ABC	9:00pm	16.7	27.0	16,848,000
4	The Practice	ABC	10:00pm	11.7	20.0	11,780,000
5	Everybody Loves Raymond	CBS	9:00pm	11.3	17.0	11,363,000
6	NYPD Blue	ABC	10:00pm	10.4	18.0	10,465,000
7	60 Minutes	CBS	7:00pm	10.3	21.0	10,351,000
8	E.R.	NBC	10:00pm	10.1	17.0	10,199,000
9	20/20—Downtown	ABC	10:00pm	10.0	17.0	10,043,000
10	Becker	CBS	9:30pm	9.9	15.0	9,999,000

April 24 to April 30, 2000

Rank	Program	Network	Time	Rating	Share	Homes
1	E.R.	NBC	10:00pm	19.6	32.0	19,759,000
2	Who Wants to Be a Millionaire? (Tues.)	ABC	8:00pm	17.0	28.0	17,172,000
3	Who Wants to Be a Millionaire? (Thurs.)	ABC	9:00pm	16.0	24.0	16,098,000
4	Friends	NBC	8:00pm	14.7	25.0	14,794,000
5	Frasier	NBC	9:00pm	14.4	22.0	14,565,000
6	Frasier 9:30	NBC	9:30pm	13.0	20.0	13,150,000
6	Who Wants to Be a Millionaire? (Sun.)	ABC	7:00pm	13.0	25.0	13,056,000
8	Just Shoot Me	NBC	8:30pm	12.9	21.0	12,960,000
9	Law and Order	NBC	10:00pm	12.8	21.0	12,947,000
10	Touched by an Angel	CBS	8:00pm	11.8	19.0	11,851,000

Source: UltimateTV.com, April 28, 2000, and May 8, 2000; available from http://www.ultimatetv.com/news/nielsen/.

the media know this (and may, in fact, be partly responsible for it), they surround the advertisements with stories and reports that will not tax our intelligence and that will instead attract and keep the interest of a large, often bored, impatient, easily distracted, and busy audience. The competition for our attention and loyalty is so stiff among news organizations that bizarre and sometimes disastrous consequences often result from attempts to keep us tuned in.

The need to be first in calling the 2000 presidential election, for example, resulted in a long evening of embarrassment for the major news networks and may have sent the message to voters in western states that voting was a waste of their time.

There are many contenders for our attention (the Internet, video games, movies, other shows, family obligations, work, relationships); the remote control allows us to silence a news reporter in midsentence; there is a growing lack of interest in reading the printed word. The mass media in America, therefore, must deliver information in a way that will keep us tuned in and reading, keep us buying automobiles, laxatives, allergy medicines, or whatever else is being sold on the nightly news or in the paper.

EXERCISE 14.3

Compare the ads in a local newspaper, a national newsmagazine such as *Time* or *Newsweek,* and a more upscale news commentary magazine such as *The New Republic* or *National Review.* How do the ads reflect differences in the readership of the newspaper and magazines you have selected? Consider such characteristics as the education, interests, hobbies, economic class, political views, and social status of the intended readers.

KEEPING OUR INTEREST: THE NEWS AS ENTERTAINMENT

Operating on the premise that our interest is held best by what we find entertaining, the media direct almost all their efforts, even those involved in the production of news, toward keeping us entertained by making the delivery of information more fun, enjoyable, amusing, and pleasant, not so easy to do when the news involves earthquakes and plane crashes. But as you will see, the news media in the United States have made entertainment, not information, their primary concern.

We should admit quickly that for most of us, this is perfectly all right. After all, who among us doesn't like to be entertained? In fact, it is probably safe to say that the desire for entertainment—pleasure, amusement, diversion—is universal. Many people, of course, enjoy intellectual pursuits and are entertained by working out complex ideas, but many of us find that complicated information is more palatable when it has been made enjoyable to consume. The book you are reading is one example. It has been our purpose throughout to provide information useful in your effort to become a better thinker, but how successful would we be if you found the text dull and boring? So, information couched in entertaining language or structured in an amusing manner is perfectly acceptable. As long as the information has not been compromised, no harm is done.

But in their effort to hold our attention, the mass media often *do* compromise information in that they sacrifice complexity, context, and meaning for captivating and entertaining techniques. The goal is to keep us in front of the set or holding on to the newspaper so that we will absorb (even subconsciously) the messages of the advertisers and buy the products that keep the money coming in so that the media operations will survive.

How the Media Entertain Us

We all know just how hard critical thinking can be. Were it simple and easy, everyone would be doing it, and there would be no need for textbooks and courses. Critical thinking requires self-knowledge, concentration, mental discipline, respect for others, awareness of fallacious reasoning, sensitivity to language, and above all, a willingness to look carefully at arguments and to base evaluations on standards and criteria. Now, of course, the reason we have told you all this is not that you are undisciplined, disrespectful, and intellectually lazy, but that we know (from experience and study) that for most of us thinking *uncritically*—jumping to conclusions, generalizing, reducing complexities to either/or choices, and so forth—is easier and often more fun than thinking critically. In fact, consider how many jokes are based on violations of critical thinking traits—on generalities, ambiguities, imprecision, oversimplification, weak analogies, questionable cause arguments, and so forth. Of course, to get the joke, you often have to be a critical thinker or you won't see the humor in the violation of critical thinking standards. Nonetheless, we are often more entertained by noncritical reasoning—by generalities, emotional appeals, exaggerations, simple conflicts, and so forth—than by critical reasoning.

The news media take advantage of our unwillingness to think too rigorously and deliver the news in a noncontextual, entertaining manner that has the added result of tricking us out of critical analysis. In some respects, the news media do precisely the opposite of what the authors of this textbook have been encouraging you to do. In place of information that can help sustain and nourish our thinking and help us make decisions, we get what F. Scott Fitzgerald called, in *This Side of Paradise,* "predigested food"—the "politics, prejudices, and philosophy" appetizingly served up by the media for our consumption. Rather than provide a thorough look at the world's events, the media often carefully select events, exaggerate them or play them down, and present them without helpful analysis. The result is an entertaining array of facts and opinions intended to satisfy our less critical faculties. In the sections that follow, we shall look at some of the ways in which the media dole out what amounts to a sort of intellectual candy—fun to eat, but ultimately unsatisfying and unhealthy.

Cinema, radio, television, magazines are a school of inattention: people look without seeing, listen in without hearing.
—Robert Bresson

Selecting Events   In a world of six billion people, enough events are taking place at this very moment that recording even a small fraction of them would take thousands of hours and millions of pages. But to find out what happened during the time you have been reading your critical thinking textbook, you can tune in this evening to one of the three main television networks and watch, subtracting commercials, about twenty minutes of world news, or buy tomorrow's paper and "read all about it" in a few dozen pages. The entire world in twenty minutes? Twenty pages?

Obviously, not everything makes the papers or the news broadcast. In selecting some events and excluding others, the media determine what is and is not important for us to know, and because thoroughly examining an event in all its complexities, causes, and consequences is virtually impossible given time and space limitations, the media select from each newsworthy occurrence a relatively small sliver of the event itself, ignoring much of the greater context that might help make the event more meaningful to us. Some selectivity is inescapable. A reporter working under a deadline and allocated only a few inches of space or a few minutes of time in which to file a report inevitably selects what he or she believes to be essential or interesting moments, comments, or facts. But where a reporter decides to set his or her focus can reveal much about the reporter's attentiveness, worldview, attitudes, political opinions, and social philosophy. In some cases, a journalist's deliberate or unwitting failure to "see" or recognize certain key facts can call the accuracy of the report into question. How can we be sure that we have been told everything? And how can we be sure, without all the relevant information, that we aren't being manipulated by carefully chosen facts to "see" the event in the way the reporter wants us to? Think back to your own story for a moment. If you had only a few moments to tell your story, you would most likely decide what effect you wanted to produce in your audience—approval or sympathy, for example—and then cautiously select some details and ignore others in an effort to create the desired effect and avoid negative responses. The effect, of course, can be far different from the one at which your readers or listeners might have arrived with *all* the facts in their possession. Like a funhouse mirror, a reporter's selectivity distorts reality so that the original event and our perception of the event diverge greatly.

News editors and managers must be selective when deciding which of the thousands of stories that are collected every day will make the papers or the nightly news. Traditionally, editors and managers have insisted that "newsworthiness" is determined solely on two criteria: a story must be true, and it must serve the "public interest," meaning that it must somehow benefit the audience. Although the great majority of mass-media news outlets do not lie to their audiences, news organizations often select stories with questionable benefit to the public. In fact, most stories are chosen not because they *serve* the public interest but because they reflect the entertainment preferences of the majority of viewers or readers.

What Makes the News   With daily events too plentiful and complicated for the space available, what makes the cut? Judging from what is selected, we would have to conclude that newsworthy events are those which a reader or viewer will find entertaining; that is, exciting, titillating, shocking, disturbing, frightening, unusual, heartwarming, or easy to comprehend and identify with—"all sex, scandal, brutal crime, sports, children with incurable diseases, and lost puppies," as Diana Christensen describes the nightly news in *Network*. In an effort to hold the attention of a large and diverse audience, the news media generally appeal to the lowest common interests among us—sex, gossip, scandal, violence, death, crime—and to our common emotions—fear for our safety, joy over rescues, anger at injustice, sympathy for victims. The news media's view of their audiences is hinted at in the recent increase in stories intended to alert us to all the potential dangers in our homes, on the road, in the air, at work, on the athletic field, and so forth. Are we really in such grave danger, or is it simply hard to turn off the television when, "coming up next," we'll be told just how our mattresses might be killing us in our sleep?

And, of course, if there is video or a photo of some disturbing or violent event, it is almost guaranteed to make the news. Many local news stations air videotape of such events as parachute failures and police chases even though neither event may be of significance to a large audience. Without a context, the medium itself becomes context: the importance of the event is determined merely by its being "caught on tape." In fact, for the broadcast media, an event's newsworthiness is often determined not by its true importance but by its visual impact. In a particularly gruesome example, a major network affiliate in the area where this book is being written recently aired video of a man drowning. A state trooper in a distant state, the man had gone into a raging river to save someone and had become trapped between rocks. The video showed his desperate, futile attempts to free himself. According to the news anchor, "no additional information" was available. His name, his age, his history, his relationship, if any, to the local area, the reasons for showing his awful death—none of those points was ever made. The video was selected for broadcast apparently because it was attention-grabbing and available for broadcast.

To hold our attention, much of the news is presented with all the drama and excitement of literature, complete with suspense, intriguing characters, surprise endings, and, especially, conflict between opposing parties. Because court trials contain all those elements, the media seldom miss a chance to provide extensive coverage of criminal cases, but other favorites in the media include battles between neighbors, political candidates and parties, school boards and teachers, and the government and constituents. In fact, most current coverage of politics in America concerns political campaigns, wars between "mudslinging" advertisers, investigations of special prosecutors, accusations of misconduct and corruption, and responses to those allegations. Often, the first time we hear about high-ranking political figures such as senators and representatives is when the press covers a bitter campaign or an investigation of wrongdoing. The fixation on conflict has spilled over into the coverage itself as reporters and analysts (often called, sarcastically, "pundits") take sides and shout one another down or one-up one another on political talk shows such as *Meet the Press, This Week, Crossfire,* and *The McLaughlin Group.* Lost in all this focus on conflict and controversy are the important political issues that affect our lives. And because we are apparently drawn to battles, quarrels, and confrontations, the media often play up and extend conflicts that might have otherwise amounted to no more than minor, short-lived disagreements.

What Doesn't Make the News   What doesn't make the newspapers and the nightly broadcast usually includes stories too complicated for quick and painless consumption and stories too critical of American corporations, powerful nonprofit organizations, the government, and the news media themselves. Each year for the past quarter-century, Project Censored, a media-watch organization at Sonoma State University, has endeavored, according to its Web site,

> to explore and publicize the extent of censorship in our society by locating stories about significant issues of which the public should be aware, but is not, for one reason or another. The essential issue raised by the project is the failure of the mass media to provide the people with all the information they need to make informed decisions concerning their own lives and in the voting booth. (www.projectcensored.org/about.htm)

Among the topics largely ignored by the mass media in 1999 were the collaboration between multinational corporations and governments suspected of "significant human rights violations," the custom among pharmaceutical companies to devote their resources to the development of profit-making drugs rather than much-needed cures for deadly diseases, the apparent misdirection of revenue within the "increasingly wealthy" American Cancer Society, and the Department of Defense's contract with an American "sweatshop" manufacturer of uniforms. All these stories appeared somewhere in the media, but primarily in journals of opinion (*The Nation, Mother Jones*) and not in the mainstream press. Some might accuse the news media of having an "agenda" in excluding certain topics, and because news organizations are increasingly under the control of corporate parent companies (NBC is owned by General Electric, ABC by Disney, *Time* magazine by AOL/Time Warner, and so on), news organizations may, indeed, be reluctant or forbidden to investigate their owners and subsidiaries. So, the accusation that the news media have an agenda has some grounding. But in many instances complicated and discouraging stories about the Defense Department or the American Cancer Society are omitted merely to make room for stories presumably more interesting to a mass audience. Whatever the reason, it is clear from a study of the mainstream press that some topics get very little coverage.

Of course, some media sources are more guilty than others of pandering to their audiences, and, conversely, some publications take great pains to publish more than just the scurrilous and salacious, to publish, in the motto of the *New York Times,* "all the news that's fit to print." But even the *Times* has to make choices, and although the bar might be set higher for determining what's fit to print in national papers, all media, even the most venerable, must decide what to select and what to exclude. In fact, news does not really happen; events are not news until they are selected and labeled "news" by the media. The effect of all this cannot be overstated. Because we tend to talk around the dinner table or at work or in the classroom about "the day's news," what is selected becomes part of the social dialogue; what doesn't make the news, obviously, draws little attention from us. The news media, as the saying goes, "set the agenda," determining what is important enough to warrant our concern and perhaps our involvement. Unfortunately, when time and space that might be better spent unraveling complicated issues of race relations, public education, labor, poverty, pollution, and so forth are sacrificed to stories of sex scandals and plane crashes, the public receives little education in issues that really matter in our lives.

> *The most important service rendered by the press and the magazines is that of educating people to approach printed matter with distrust.*
> —Samuel Butler

EXERCISE 14.4

I. List all of the stories covered in one edition of your local nightly news and on one of the major networks. How many of those stories center on a conflict? What are the two sides that are apparently pitted against each another? Does the news seem to be creating a battle where one does not exist, exaggerating a battle that does exist but that could be easily resolved, or justly calling attention to a serious conflict? Are broader, more important issues being ignored in favor of the conflict, or is the controversy a serious one that you feel should be examined? What use will you make of what you learned about the conflict?

II. Visit any Web site that features news headlines—yahoo.com (http://dailynews.yahoo.com/h/ts/), cnn.com, msnbc.com, iwon.com. Look carefully at the headlines to determine how many of them focus on a conflict of one sort or another in an apparent effort to entice us into clicking on the headline to read further.

III. Watch the local and national news broadcasts for one evening in your town and make a list of the stories they carry. You can ignore the sports and the weather. Do the same for one edition of a local paper, concentrating on the news sections and ignoring sports. When your list is complete, answer the following: How many stories are apparently intended to appeal to our emotions and our sympathies? Which stories seem to have been intended to grab our attention by appealing to our curiosity or love of scandal? Which seem to have been selected for their entertainment value? How many stories seem intended to make us fearful for our safety or grateful for our security?

IV. If you are reading this chapter during an election year, choose two or three days' worth of broadcast or print news concerning political candidates. How many of the reports center on campaign strategies, including how one candidate responds to another's attacks and insinuations? How many reports and commentaries focus on the candidate's style, such as whether he or she is relaxed or stiff, as opposed to the candidate's positions on certain issues? How many reports focus instead on the candidate's stance on key issues?

V. Most people have been close to at least one story covered in the local media. Perhaps you were interviewed for your comments on an event, or an event that you were part of was covered in the press. Give the details of a story you were close to. How accurately did the media report the story? What did they leave out? Emphasize? Minimize? Distort? Were you quoted accurately?

EXERCISE 14.5

For each of the following names, indicate, first, whether you *recognize* the name, then whether you can *identify* the person.

Robert Reich	Linda Tripp	Richard Riley
Madeline Albright	Kenneth Starr	Janet Reno
Monica Lewinsky	William Cohen	Donna Shalala
Vince Foster	Kathleen Willey	Bruce Babbit

Now find out who each of these people was (clue: they were all involved in the life of President Bill Clinton). Why do you think that some names are more familiar to you than others? Why do you think it is so hard to *identify* some of the people on the list even though you may have heard their names?

EXERCISE 14.6

This exercise requires a partner and a stopwatch (or a watch with a second hand). Pair off with someone in your class and designate yourselves Person A and Person B. Now spend twenty minutes talking to each another. Tell each other about your hometowns, your families, your high schools, your greatest accomplishments, your proudest moments, your major, your plans, your living situation, your sport teams, and so forth. Take notes as you listen to each another, but don't merely transcribe each other's comments. Your objective here is to see what you can find out about each other.

After your conversation, each of you must write an introduction of the other that you can read aloud to the class in only *ten* seconds at a normal, natural pace. Although our speaking patterns differ, you should be able to read between twenty-five and forty words aloud in ten seconds. Your job is to tell the class something about your partner in the allotted time. After everyone in the class has written a ten-second introduction, everyone takes a turn reading to the class. So that no one exceeds the limit, have someone with a stopwatch keep time.

After you have read your ten-second presentation, write an additional ten seconds' worth of material. And then another. You should now have three ten-second segments. Your instructor may or may not choose to have you read these additions.

When the exercise is complete, consider the following questions. Be prepared to discuss these in class.

1. In your first ten-second spot, what facts did you select and which did you omit? When you chose details for the first ten seconds, you were probably trying to capture the essence of the stories or the person you listened to. Explain how you selected the details that found their way into your first report.

2. What frustrations, if any, did you feel at trying to select ten seconds' worth of material? Did you at any point get the feeling that you were pulling facts out of context and that your listeners in the class would fail to understand what you were trying to get at?

3. Look carefully at your selections. Does what you chose to include say anything about you? Are you more impressed with education, accomplishments in sports, work history, personal achievements, family background, where a person lives or comes from, his or her current status (sophomore English major), plans (wants to be a doctor)? Your selections are not wrong; no one can say you should have chosen differently. But what you selected *may* reveal something about your values.

4. When you chose details for the first ten seconds, were you trying to achieve a particular effect in the students who would be listening to your words? Did you want to evoke their awe, wonder, amazement, sympathy, curiosity about your partner?

5. How concerned were you about the impression you would make as a writer, reader, or presenter? Perhaps you treated the assignment lightly, writing a few sentences to evoke laughter or entertain your listeners. Were you concerned at all about how you would come across? Did you want to give the class an impression about yourself?

6. Now look at your twenty- and thirty-second lists. How are they different from the first list? Is there a pattern to your selections? Did you, for example, start with what you thought was most important and add details of decreasing importance? Did you add any direct quotes from your partner?

7. When *your* story was being told in ten seconds, how did you feel about the events that were chosen? Do you think the narrator caught the essential elements of your life? Were you surprised at what was selected?

8. Write a paragraph in which you reflect on this exercise. What you have done here is play the role of a news writer or reporter. Of course, in the "real world" you would have a little more time to collect your facts, but, interestingly, many "stories" on television and radio broadcasts take to no more than ten to thirty seconds. What has this exercise shown you about the nature of news-gathering?

Emphasizing Stories and Parts of Stories   Along with selecting events or parts of events that will appeal to us, the media employ other techniques for attracting our attention and challenging our critical thinking skills—namely, making events seem more or less important than they are. The print media use a variety of techniques. A newspaper can highlight a story by placing it on the front page or diminish a story's worth by burying it deep inside, where it is likely to be overlooked. Editors of traditional papers (nontabloid style) must decide what front-page stories to prominently display "above the fold" to attract the attention of potential readers as they pass the newsstand or coin-operated dispensers. The paper can further heighten the sense of importance by including a dramatic photo, placing the event in the top headline, using large font sizes, or giving more space to a story. Details can be arranged to slant a story in one direction or the other: the paragraph telling you that an arrested suspect has an ironclad alibi might appear so late in a story that you'll quit reading before you get to it, thereby emphasizing the crime over the suspect's apparent innocence.[6] Mass-media magazines can elevate a story to grand status by featuring the event on the cover. This isn't to say that a story covered in this manner by newspapers and magazines isn't significant, but we have become so accustomed to seeing screaming headlines on page one that whatever we see there takes on a aura of great importance simply by virtue of its location and the attention given the story by media editors. Is it really an important story? Does it mean anything to us? Is it there just to attract our attention? To keep us buying?

Similarly, television and radio news editors can determine the worth of a story in several ways. Stories deemed most important will "lead" the broadcast or receive extended coverage, whereas less important stories are quickly covered later in the broadcast. Extensive, wall-to-wall broadcast coverage is rare and predictable: plane crashes, dead celebrities, military actions, and grand-scale violence will almost always set off round-the-clock reporting complete, when carried by the networks, with an attention-grabbing tagline: "Crisis in the Heartland," "Death of a Princess," "War in the Gulf." This kind of end-less attention is reserved for the "big event," such as the 1999 crash of John F. Kennedy, Jr.'s plane, which the major networks and CNN covered from the first word of the plane's disappearance through the search for and burial of the bodies of Kennedy, his wife, and her sister.

In these extensive-coverage episodes (the war in Serbia, the Gulf War, the Oklahoma City bombing, the standoff at Waco, the O. J. Simpson trial, the crash of TWA Flight 800, the death of Princess Diana, the murder of Jon-Benet Ramsey, the Columbine massacre, the Elián Gonzalez case, the recount of ballots in Florida), additional effort is given to providing context as analysts and commentators examine the event from a variety of angles and fill air time and news space with some exploration of causes and implications, but the result is usually the same: we are left with far more questions than answers. In some cases, the exaggerated coverage distorts the truth. The saturation cover-age of the Columbine shootings, for example, although powerful and moving in many respects, might have left us with the impression that young people are hyperviolent or that only single, isolated cases of extreme violence against youth are worth investigating. News organizations could, but usually don't, devote their extensive resources to exploring persistent trends, perennial issues, or the root causes and possible solutions of common, everyday problems such as violence against young people. We seldom hear about certain topics until they become "newsworthy" events, when they are sprung on us as isolated, shocking occurrences. When war breaks out in what we regard as a "remote" part of the world, we are finally informed about the conflict even though tensions may have been present for many decades. Likewise, what was once presented as vital and urgent will disappear from the spotlight when the topic has worn thin. We are told of widespread starvation in Ethiopia, but after the story has run its course it disappears from the headlines, leaving us to wonder if the situation has been rectified or if large-scale starvation has simply become boring. The ethnic Albanians who fled Kosovo were at one time the hottest topic in America. Where are they now? Whatever happened to the warlords in Somalia, the victims of Hurricane Mitch in Nicaragua, the drug cartels in Colombia, the people of Kuwait?

Ironically, the media often exhaust issues that mean nothing to us in the long run. We receive nightly updates on the success of a corporation's new advertising campaign or the popularity or failure of a television game show. The broadcast news "magazines," such as *20/20* and *Dateline,* will take a long, dramatic, sensationalized look at a single rescue, crime, or police investigation and tell us all there is to know about these inconsequential or trifling matters. One reason for the media's reluctance to investigate and report on trends and enduring issues and to concentrate instead on big events and trivial subjects is that long-term investigations cost money, whereas sending a camera crew and reporters to the scene of an accident or the front lawn of the White House takes far fewer resources and less work. But, perhaps more important, the media are merely giving us what we apparently want, and the big stories have it all—conflict, mystery, death, violence. The big and trivial stories allow the media to feed a great many mouths cheaply.

> *The greatest felony in the news business today is to be behind or miss a big story. So speed and quantity substitute for thoroughness and quality, for accuracy and context. The pressure to compete, the fear somebody else will make the splash first, creates a frenzied environment in which a blizzard of information is presented and serious questions may not be raised.*
>
> —Carl Bernstein

Commenting—or Not—on the News   Earlier in this textbook, we proposed the notion that total objectivity—the ability to perceive or describe an event or a situation without being influenced by personal attitudes, emotions, beliefs, and so forth—is almost impossible. We may be able to report a simple event without bias ("The cat is on the kitchen table again"), but *how* we report even that simple event—in this case, the tone of our voice—can reveal whether we are amazed, amused, or angered at the cat's disregard of authority. Obviously, more complicated events are even more difficult to report without allowing our point of view to intrude: we ignore certain facts and focus on others, choose language that evokes emotional or prejudicial responses in our audiences, reveal our attitudes through tone and organization, and so forth.

When it comes to objectivity, the news media appear to have responded in two completely different ways. On the one hand, many journalists and editors continue to strive for objective detachment, total neutrality, a "just the facts" approach to news reporting. Others appear to have rejected objectivity altogether, surrendering to the notion that all truth depends on point of view, openly offering opinion and commentary on the news. Both responses have led to some serious problems.

Attempting Objectivity   In the first—maintaining an apparently objective approach—the media fall into the trap of simply delivering information that has been gathered. The result is an outpouring of information, a chaos of facts and data that a journalist has collected without sorting out what is reliable, useful, and meaningful. Often, the media will publish unedited, unverified press releases that public relations directors routinely send to newspapers or provide uncritical coverage of staged events such as award ceremonies and press conferences. One famous example comes from the 1990 Gulf War. Reporters stationed at the Pentagon acted more as intermediaries, some might say "agents," of the military, dutifully reporting whatever information the military presented and asking few questions that challenged official proclamations. Military accounts of the accuracy of "smart bombs" and the success of Patriot missiles were channeled through reporters into American homes with little investigation of the truth of the military's claims. It should be noted that several news organizations *did* question the United States' involvement in the Gulf War, but only after the war had ended did several non-mass-media publications begin asking for evidence of the military's success rate. In situations such as this, reporters are often accused of helpfully delivering the official "spin," the interpretation that public relations officials and press secretaries have put on events. Rather than learning whether the Pentagon's report is accurate, we receive only the Pentagon's report. Not surprisingly, the media learned nothing from the experience, and during the war in Kosovo again obligingly channeled to the American people the Defense Department's press briefings on smart bombs and precision missiles.

The danger in this kind of "objectivity" is apparent. We are left knowing only what someone has said, but not the truth of what was said, and news becomes indistinguishable from rumor. After the explosion of TWA Flight 800, the media diligently reported every theory on what could have caused the crash, including the claim that the plane had been downed by a wayward missile fired from a U.S. Navy ship. Rather than investigating the rumor, finding it baseless, and dismissing it, news outlets across the country, most likely fearful of missing out on a big story, reported the theory immediately after it was raised. Of course, for entertainment value, the theory was priceless. In this case, as in all others involving "sources" of information, readers would be better served by a reporter's willingness to test the veracity of the source and not just repeat information. Unfortunately, many journalists today are, in the most limited sense of the word, "reporters," merely reporting what they have been told by sources. Although journalists may be reluctant to give their opinions on an issue, they wrongfully assume that objectivity can be achieved without a *thorough* report that includes all points of view and known facts. A reporter honestly striving for a detached and neutral perspective would have to be aware of the lenses through which he or she filters the world's events and do everything possible to see things clearly and in their entirety. The best journalist, in other words, would be a good critical thinker.

Perceived Bias: Is There a Liberal Press?   Although most mainstream journalists would insist that political partisanship does not infect their view of events and that their coverage of the news is neutral and balanced, some media critics contend that the news in the United States shows a pronounced liberal slant. A 1996 survey of 1,037 journalists conducted by the American Society of Newspaper Editors might appear to support this contention. The survey revealed that a large majority of journalists place themselves left of center on the political spectrum, as the following table shows.[7]

Political Orientation	Percent of Respondents	Percent of Respondents to 1988 Survey
Democrat or liberal	36	34
Republican or conservative	8	11
Lean to Democrat/liberal	25	28
Lean to Republican/ conservative	7	11
Independent	24	17

Of course, the fact that an individual journalist may be liberal (or conservative, for that matter) does not mean that his or her news coverage reflects personal attitudes. The survey shows only the reported political orientation of journalists, not the effect of their political views on their coverage of the news. In fact, it is closer to the truth to suggest that even though the political orientation of many journalists seems clear, and though editorial writers often take a stand on political issues, it is not likely that a mainstream newspaper, network, or magazine has a pronounced and consistent political bias, since doing so would alienate too many potential audience members. An analysis of the overall coverage by a mainstream news organization will show that, although an individual reporter may take a liberal or conservative slant on an issue, the great majority of articles are going to fit into a narrow band of ideology that hovers around the center of the political spectrum, where most Americans locate themselves. It is especially difficult to argue convincingly that any *single* mainstream news organization is demonstrably liberal while another is conservative.

In fact, the products of the mainstream press are often interchangeable. An article in *Time* could easily appear in *Newsweek* (in fact, the covers are often similar), and the nightly news on CBS, ABC, and NBC are hardly distinguishable from one another. Local newscasts and newspapers may lean toward one side of the political spectrum depending on the voter registration in a particular area, and many newspapers adhere to the tradition of endorsing a political candidate during campaigns, a practice recalling the fact that many newspapers in America were founded by political parties. And some newspapers—the *Washington Times,* for one—*do* have an advertised political slant. But the goal of reaching a large and diverse audience is more easily achieved in avoiding controversy and in appearing to strike a political balance in the reporting of news. The news sells better when the media dodge stories involving hallowed subjects (corporate sponsors) and stories deemed boring or unpopular (welfare, pollution), and avoid swimming against the current of prevailing public opinion. It is much safer and more lucrative to simply float safely on the surface.

Nonetheless, the media will often give the impression of favoring or opposing, depending on your own political point of view, one political perspective over another. Conservatives charge that the media are soft on Democrats and sympathetic to liberal causes such as gay rights, environmental protection, entitlement programs, and gender equality. Liberals claim that corporate ownership and sponsorship of the mainstream press preclude covering issues and events embarrassing to big business or examining issues from the perspective of the poor and disenfranchised. Several organizations are committed to watching for bias in the media whether from the right or the left. Groups like FAIR (Fairness and Accuracy in Reporting) and NewsWatch root out inaccuracies and incidents of perceived bias in the mainstream press. FAIR provides an additional service to media watchers by alerting readers to the lack of context in some national newspaper articles and flagging articles that are especially good in providing context. The Web address for FAIR is www.fair.org; for NewsWatch it is www.newswatch.org.

True Bias: The Personal Touch   Whatever bias exists in reporting—and it does exist—results not so much from journalists' political partisanship as from the common practice of personalizing the news in an effort to appeal to a large audience. A growing number of journalists now report the news in a highly subjective, often sentimental, overly dramatized, or exaggerated manner, routinely dressing up the news to feed into readers' prejudices, expectations, and emotions. Rather than working to find the most precise way to describe an event, to find language that best fits a situation, some journalists struggle to describe events in a manner that emphasizes the "human" perspective, a look at the events through the writer's eyes. So rather than a straightforward description of events,

> Daniel Morris, a Carbondale borough police officer, was shot and wounded last night by an unidentified man.

Thoughtfully written analysis is out. . . . Do powder-puff, not probing, interviews. Stay away from controversial subjects. Kiss ass, move with the mass, and for heaven's and the ratings' sake don't make anybody mad. . . . Make nice, not news.

—Dan Rather

The corporate grip on opinion in the United States is one of the wonders of the Western World. No First World country has ever managed to eliminate so entirely from its media all objectivity—much less dissent.

—Gore Vidal

we get, instead,

> Borough police officer Daniel Morris came dressed for the occasion.
>
> A routine traffic stop early Thursday morning nearly cost the 22-year-old police officer his life when an unidentified gunman allegedly shot him.
>
> Luckily, Morris was wearing a bulletproof vest.[8]

Although there is surely nothing wrong with noting Officer Morris's good fortune, the language and style in which the event is described draws more attention to the writer than to the event itself. Such breezy writing is clearly intended to appeal to the audience's softer side and to create a bond that the majority of readers will enjoy. The same phenomenon appears in television and radio news broadcasts where even the most mundane stories can be overly sensationalized to ensure our rapt attention or cast in weepy tones to warm our hearts. News readers often engage in what is called "happy talk," the overly chummy delivery of news that makes the anchor seem neighborly and trustworthy. Phrases like "Wait till you hear this," and "You won't believe this" make the newscaster appear to be a friend who knows us and would never mislead us. These and similar tactics give the impression that the reporter is on our side, an advocate for our best interests, looking out for our safety, our children, our taxes. Now who wouldn't want to tune into such a friend every night?

Perhaps sentimentality and chumminess can be overlooked in a medium that survives on keeping the audience content and entertained. But reporters can and do sometimes slant stories in a manner that *may* reveal their opinion of the topic, letting us know through language, tone, organization, and the selection of details how the individual reporter feels about the fact that the cat is on the kitchen table again. As you may recall from Chapter 4, writers can use vague terms ("sources close to the president"), euphemisms ("Mr. Jennings left school early in his academic career to pursue a job in the food industry"), and emotionally charged words ("the GOP's campaign tactics") to influence how readers and listeners will respond to an event. They can ignore, twist, or exaggerate facts It is no real challenge for a good writer to manipulate a reader into liking or disliking a person, supporting or condemning an action or a decision, endorsing or rejecting a cause or a policy, and so forth. Critical thinkers need to be especially sensitive to this slanting of the news, since some writers are so adept at blending opinion and fact that it is hard to distinguish the two. But critical thinkers also need to be careful not to jump to conclusions about a journalist's attitude. It may be impossible to say for certain that a writer believes one way or another about a topic, since what appears to be advocacy for a position may simply be an effort to indulge an audience's prejudices. The best a consumer of news can do is to assume that the news cannot be reported in a fully objective manner, to remain aware of the difference between fact and opinion as they appear in the news, to distinguish between verifiable historical events and *how* those events are depicted in language, and to root out all efforts to manipulate readers and viewers.

EXERCISE 14.7

The following excerpts contain opening paragraphs from several newspapers' accounts of an event that took place on April 22, 2000. As you read the various accounts, look for appeals to the reader's emotions, attempts to heighten the drama, possible exaggerations, or other attempts on the writer's part to connect with the reader. Look for any signs of sensationalism or sentimentality. Look at how each writer organizes information: What does the writer begin with? What facts are given early in the article? Try to determine whether you could infer from the excerpt the writer's position on the issue; in other words, could you argue that the writer approves or disapproves of the actions taken by the government? Try to find places where the writer has used unnecessary exaggeration or biased language. Finally, when you are finished reading, see if you can write, using only what you find in the excerpts, a fact-based, unemotional, unexaggerated first paragraph for a news story about the event.

1. Armed United States immigration agents smashed their way into the Little Havana home of Elián Gonzalez's Miami relatives before dawn today, took the sobbing 6-year-old boy from a bedroom closet and flew him to a reunion with his father outside Washington.

   As demonstrators wept in rage and coughed from pepper spray and tear gas, the agents wrapped the child in a blanket and carried him to an airport to fly him to Washington. The action touched off a fury in the streets outside the Miami home, where Cuban exiles have kept a vigil since November.

   "What's happening? What's happening?" Elián said in Spanish as he was taken away. "Help me. Help me."

   The agents, wearing shirts with the words "INS FEDERAL AGENT" in bold yellow letters, ended a bitter standoff between Miami's exile community and a federal government that stopped fruitless negotiations with the child's defiant great-uncle and a community that saw Elián as a symbol of freedom and a precious victory, now perhaps lost, over President Fidel Castro of Cuba. (Rick Bragg, "Cuban Boy Seized by U.S. Agents and Reunited with His Father," *New York Times,* April 23, 2000, early edition, p. A-1)

2. Eight helmeted, SWAT-equipped federal agents broke down the front door of the Miami home of Elián Gonzalez's relatives shortly before dawn yesterday and removed the boy, avoiding serious injury but sparking a day of sporadic violence and demonstrations in Little Havana. Four hours later, Elián's Cuban father walked alone onto a government jet at Andrews Air Force Base and emerged cradling his 6-year-old son.

   Miami's Cuban American community erupted in outrage in the wake of the surprise raid by more than 130 Immigration and Naturalization Service agents, who arrived in a convoy of white vans about 5:10 a.m., fanned out around the house and used pepper spray to push back demonstrators gathered outside.

   The agents corralled the frightened family inside at gunpoint. Elián was found in a bedroom, halfway inside a small closet, in the arms of one of the

Florida fishermen who had rescued him from the Atlantic Ocean on Thanksgiving Day.

A female agent bundled the boy into a blanket and rushed him out the door and into a van that quickly backed away from the home. (Karen DeYoung, "Raid Reunites Elián and Father," *Washington Post*, April 23, 2000, p. A-1)

3. Elián Gonzalez was reunited with his father Saturday after a SWAT team of federal agents, armed with semiautomatic weapons and firing pepper spray, rushed the home of the Cuban boy's Miami relatives and seized the child near a back bedroom closet.

Crying "Help me! Help me!" in both English and Spanish, the frightened 6-year-old was hurried from Miami's Little Havana neighborhood in a predawn raid, taken by helicopter to a waiting government jet and flown to Andrews Air Force Base in suburban Washington, where he was turned over to the long-waiting arms of his father, Juan Miguel Gonzalez.

The reunion was warm and emotional, said the father's attorney, Gregory B. Craig. It followed five months of anxiety and extremely harsh feelings that have consumed the case of the little refugee, whose mother drowned as he was set adrift on an inner tube in the Florida Straits.

"There was a huge relief on Juan Miguel's face and a huge smile," Craig said after watching the initial embrace of father and son. "I saw absolutely no evidence of any kind of trauma or any kind of fear or any kind of uncertainty" on Elián's part. (Richard A. Serrano and Mike Clary, "Elián, Dad Reunited After Raid," *Los Angeles Times*, April 23, 2000, p. A1)

4. Heavily armed federal agents stormed a modest bungalow in Miami's Little Havana yesterday, seizing 6-year-old Elián Gonzalez and flying him to suburban Washington for a reunion with his father nearly five months after the boy was plucked from the ocean trying to reach the United States.

President Clinton called the pre-dawn raid "the right thing to do."

Eight U.S. Immigration and Naturalization Service officers and Border Patrol agents entered the house of the Cuban boy's great-uncle about 5:15 a.m. on the orders of Attorney General Janet Reno.

One agent shoved the barrel of an automatic rifle toward Elián and snatched him from the arms of a fisherman who had rescued the boy as he clung to an inner tube Thanksgiving Day.

A female INS agent spoke in Spanish to the terrified, crying boy as she ran with him in her arms to an unmarked van. She told him: "This may seem very scary right now, but it will soon be better. We are taking you to see your papa."

The federal agents took the little shipwreck survivor to Watson Island near Miami, where they put him aboard a helicopter that flew him to Homestead Air Force Base south of Miami. He was examined by a doctor and then put on a U.S. Marshals plane for the flight to Andrews Air Force Base in Maryland. (Jerry Seper, "U.S. Agents Seize Elián, Fly Him to Father Here," *Washington Times*, April 23, 2000, p. C-1)

5. It took five months for the custody battle over Elián Gonzalez to build to a tense stand-off. It took federal agents less than three minutes to end it.

In a cleanly executed predawn raid that caught Elián's Miami relatives off guard, armed and helmeted U.S. Border Patrol officers pushed aside a handful of demonstrators to batter in the door of the Little Havana home. At gunpoint, they took the boy from the grip of his Thanksgiving Day rescuer, fisherman Donato Dalrymple.

"We are taking you to see your papa," a Spanish-speaking female agent, Betty Mills, told the terrified boy as she carried him out of the house to a government van.

Before most of Miami awoke Saturday to what had occurred, Elián had been reunited with his father, Juan Miguel Gonzalez, at Andrews Air Force Base outside Washington D.C. (Manny Garcia, Carolyn Salazar, and Andres Viglucci, "Taking Elián," Wilkes-Barre *Times Leader,* April 23, 2000, pp. A1–2) (*Note:* The *Times Leader* is a Knight-Ridder newspaper.)

6. Armed with automatic weapons and firing occasional rounds of tear gas, federal agents seized Elián Gonzalez from the home of his Miami relatives before dawn Saturday.

About 30 agents arrived at the home in white vans shortly after 5 a.m. and used rams on the chain-link fence and on the front door. A short time later, a woman brought Elián out of the home and put him in a van that drove away.

Some of the approximately 100 protesters gathered at the home climbed over barricades to try to stop the agents. The agents, wearing Immigration and Naturalization Service shirts, shouted, "Everybody move out of the way. Everybody get out of the way."

They fired tear gas in front of the home and behind barricades, before departing with the boy.

"The world is watching!" yelled Delfin Gonzalez, the brother of the little boy's caretaker and great-uncle, Lazaro Gonzalez.

"They were animals," said Jess Garcia, a bystander. "They gassed women and children to take a defenseless child out of here. We were assaulted with no provocation." (Carolyn Salazar and Manny Garcia, "Elián Seized. Crying Boy Carried Off Amid Guns, Tear Gas," *The Miami Herald,* April 23, 2000, p. A1)

7. "Estan Aqui!" "They're here! They're here!" someone cried out. It was just after dawn on Saturday. The Miami relatives of Elián González and various of their advisers and hangers-on were awake, or half awake, in the cluttered living room of the small bungalow in Little Havana. Some were sitting around a speakerphone, in negotiations with the Justice Department. Or so they thought, before two federal agents in black body armor jumped the back fence, and eight more burst through the front, firing stinging pepper spray and shouting, "Get down! Get down! Give us the boy!" Elián himself was lying awake on the couch with his great-uncle Lázaro. Donato Dalrymple, the fisherman who first plucked the Miracle Boy out of an inner tube off the Florida coast on Thanksgiving Day, swept Elián into his arms and ran into a bedroom, where he stood in a closet as the boy cowered. An AP photographer snapped the photo of a black-helmeted, begoggled *federale*

menacing the fisherman and his terrified charge with an automatic weapon (Evan Thomas and Martha Brant, "Raid and Reunion for Elián," *Newsweek,* May 1, 2000, p. 22)

8. Elián was having trouble sleeping. He kept climbing out of his little race-car bed and going into the living room, where his great-uncle Lázaro lay on the white leather couch. The boy had been watching his relatives fight over him all this time; he had seen the news reports. It had been another long day. He snuggled next to Lázaro, who stroked the boy's hair. "I'm afraid. Are they coming for me?" Elián asked again and again. Lázaro tried to comfort him, explaining in a calm voice that everything would be O.K. "*Relax,*" Lázaro said in Spanish. "Relax, Eliancito."

Donato Dalrymple was dozing on another couch nearby, still dressed in his jeans and polo shirt. One of the fishermen who rescued Elián on Thanksgiving Day, the former missionary had practically moved into the González house these past few days, convinced that he had a calling to protect this kid, no matter what. When he heard the pounding and the screaming, he thought it was a dream. (Nancy Gibbs and Michael Duffy, "The Taking of Elián," *Time,* May 1, 2000, p. 24)

EXERCISE 14.8[9]

The following is the chronology of Daria Jones, a fictitious person. Suppose you were going to write about her for your local paper. Write one short biography (about one hundred words) to make your readers like her and a second short biography to make your readers dislike her. Select and omit details as you wish, but don't make anything up. Try not to reveal your opinion overtly. Use language that will evoke the response you are looking for. Remember: Don't falsify any of the information.

- She was born in October of 1966.
- Her father worked as a printer for a newspaper; her mother was a nurse.
- She was one of five children.
- She attended a Catholic grade school, where she played basketball and earned A's in 65 percent of her classes and B+'s in the other 35 percent.
- She attended a preparatory high school, where she played basketball for a team that never lost a game in the four years she was there.
- When she was sixteen, her ten-year-old brother died suddenly of a misdiagnosed illness.
- Her GPA in high school was 3.05. She finished 109th in a class of 220.
- She attended Barre College, a Division III school, and played in the national title game in basketball in her freshman year. The team lost.
- She transferred to a Division I school, Maine State University, on a full athletic scholarship, but a knee injury in the first season ended her career. She continued on the scholarship and graduated from the school.

- She switched majors from accounting to communications and earned a GPA of 2.99 over three years.
- In her senior year, she had an internship at a recognized public relations firm in New York City and met many of the day's most famous athletes, including Muhammad Ali, Mike Schmidt, Michael Jordan, and Martina Navratilova.
- Her job for the PR firm was to drive the athletes from the airport to the company's headquarters.
- After college, she worked in a day-care center for a year, then as a fitness trainer for children, then again at a day-care center, then as an office assistant at the paper where her father worked. She earned less than $8,000 a year in each position.
- In 1988, she married an executive in an advertising firm.
- In 1988, she returned to school for a degree in elementary education and started a teaching career.
- She divorced in 1993.
- After several years of teaching, she received two master's degrees and published several articles on teaching methods.
- She remarried in 1996.
- She received her first teaching job in 1997 and has taught in three different school districts since then.
- She has no children.

Unsubstantiated Opinions   Although most slanting in the mainstream results from efforts to write in a personal, reader-friendly way, serious breaches of neutrality do sometimes occur, and journalists have on occasion blatantly offered their opinions, often with disastrous consequences. One example comes from the 1996 Summer Olympics in Atlanta, Georgia. On the evening of July 27, Richard Jewell, a security guard working at an outdoor concert site, noticed a suspicious-looking green knapsack, alerted the police, and helped to move people away from the area moments before a bomb in the knapsack exploded, killing one person and injuring more than one hundred people. Three days later, the *Atlanta Constitution* newspaper published a story under the headline "FBI Suspects 'Hero' Guard May Have Planted Bomb," setting off a media circus that included interviews with psychologists who assured reporters and the public that Jewell fit the profile of a lone bomber and that his actions were consistent with those of a guilty man. Well-respected journalists and news reporters, including NBC's Tom Brokaw, began talking less and less about Jewell's "alleged" involvement and focused instead on evidence that proved him guilty. Jewell's trial in the press ended three months later when he was cleared of all suspicion by the FBI. The media cannot be faulted for accurately reporting that the FBI was investigating Jewell, but the media failed to examine the "evidence" against Jewell from a truly objective, all-inclusive viewpoint.[10]

Even though the Jewell case alerted many news consumers to the power of journalists, who can slant a story on the scantest evidence and easily mislead an audience, the trend over the past few decades has been to elevate reporters and other media members to celebrity status as insightful and thoughtful speakers whose opinions on current events are apparently of great value. Lecture fees for the top anchors at the major networks range from $5,000 to $35,000 per speech, and journalists are routinely invited by lobbying groups to speak at corporate events.[11] Although it seems odd, given how often people claim to distrust and even to despise the media, newscasters' names commonly appear on lists of the most trusted people in America. This is easily explained by the tactics news reporters use to ensure that we continue to trust them. For example, after a live broadcast from the field, television reporters will often be asked apparently spontaneous questions by the anchor in the studio. A reporter's quick and perceptive response might suggest that he or she knows a great deal about the issue, but very often these exchanges are set up in advance; the reporter knows exactly what's coming. The same sort of behind-the-curtain scripting allows political commentators on Sunday morning talk shows to seem exceptionally well versed in politics, thus giving viewers the impression that the commentator's opinions can be trusted. Whereas we once asked our news reporters to gather and report the facts, we now routinely ask them for their opinions and treat them as if they are players in the political arena. In some cases the results can be comical. Sam Donaldson insisted one week after the discovery of President Clinton's affair with a White House intern that the president would be out of office within a week.

Arguably, one result of the willingness of some in the media to abandon any notions of objectivity has been an explosion of opinion in the press. Traditionally, claims and arguments could be located in the editorial and letters-to-the-editor sections of newspapers and journals. These sections were (and still are) clearly labeled—"editorial," "commentary," "opinion," "letters"—to differentiate them from the more objective, fact-based reports. More and more, however, the media are filled with opinion, much of it unsupported and prejudicial. Reporters routinely speculate about causes of events and support their conjecture with the opinion of "experts" who may have no familiarity with the topic immediately at issue, and too often the experts being consulted are merely other reporters and journalists happy to voice their opinion on the subject. Radio talk-show hosts fill hours with nothing but personal attacks and unsubstantiated claims, mainly in an effort to keep both fans *and* detractors tuned in to the show (sponsors don't care if the listeners love or hate the host). Listeners are invited to call radio shows and television "talkback" lines and air their perspectives on complicated issues. Some newspapers have taken the almost ludicrous step of publishing anonymous phone calls to the paper. Surely we are all "entitled to an opinion," but the proliferation of published opinions that are too often undefended makes even more important our need to stay alert and think critically when reading and watching media productions. An opinion, whether from a news anchor, a reporter, a writer or a reader, is only as valuable as its support.

We have focused in this chapter on only some of the methods that news producers use to entertain us in an effort to keep and hold our attention and to influence our reactions. There are, of course, many other techniques, such as using music during newsmagazine shows to heighten dramatic effects, editing film to juxtapose events that may not have occurred near one another in real time, using sharp camera angles to distort a subject's size, cropping photos to eliminate context, doctoring photos to suggest relationships or to achieve desired effects, and on and on. All these techniques work toward keeping us interested, even if truth might be sacrificed in the effort. Because the "facts" in a news story are often subordinated to efforts to entertain an audience, today's consumer of news needs a high degree of what is called "media literacy."

EXERCISE 14.9

One of the best sources for an examination of the news media is your own college newspaper. Pick up a copy of your campus paper and examine it for the qualities we have discussed in the preceding sections. Look especially for how events are selected for inclusion in the paper, the emphasis that is placed on some stories, the appearance of objectivity (are sources quoted without analysis and comment?), and evidence of slanting on the part of individual writers.

MEDIA LITERACY

It is easy and fun to trash the media, to blame them for everything from the moral degradation of children to violence in the schools to the dumbing down of higher education. The movie industry, part of the mass media, ironically, has reveled in pointing out the shallowness, laziness, deception, manipulation, and even cowardice of television news broadcasts in such movies as *Network, Broadcast News, Wag the Dog,* and *The Insider.* And television occasionally pokes fun at its own news industry in such shows as *Saturday Night Live* and *The Daily Show.* Flaws notwithstanding, the media have contributed greatly to our understanding and acceptance of other cultures, alerted us to the pain and suffering endured by victims of natural and human-created disasters, shown us the surface of the moon and the faces of refugees, celebrated the accomplishments of our neighbors, warned us about fraud and consumer rip-offs, fought for the release of the unjustly imprisoned, uncovered political malfeasance, and in some cases taken bold steps in challenging our assumptions and provincial attitudes. In short, the news media have done much good, and our lives would be diminished without them.

But although we admit that the media are not the villains they are sometimes portrayed to be, we can also admit that their need to survive has forced the media to provide a service more entertaining than informative. And they have done so very successfully. Without getting into the irresolvable argument over whether the media are responding to a need in their readers, listeners, and viewers or whether the media have created the need they now fill, let's deal only with the fact that the media have successfully blurred the line between news, entertainment, and advertisement and that audiences for the most part seem to have played along. In other words, the media have met their objectives to sustain themselves and to prosper.

Today the task is more daunting than ever for a critical thinker faced with media that have substituted entertainment for context. The relationship between news, entertainment, and advertising has become so sophisticated and seamless that it is difficult to tell them apart. A growing percentage of airtime in nightly news broadcasts is dedicated to promoting upcoming stories and other news shows. Gossip shows about the lives of celebrities and the making of movies, shows such as *Entertainment Tonight,* which are intended primarily to promote the entertainment industry, are presented in the format of a news broadcast.[12] News organizations routinely "reenact" events using actors and stage sets, which only helps to blur the distinction between what is real and what is not. Advertisers have been very creative recently in further blurring the line. Many products, for example, are now advertised through "infomercials," usually thirty-minute-long commercials that often take the form of documentaries, talk shows, or news broadcasts. We may be fooled momentarily into thinking that the expert or eyewitness commentary in support of beauty products, exercise equipment, and hair-replacement procedures is unscripted and objective.

Other examples are plentiful. In early 2000, ABC News sent the actor Leonardo DiCaprio to interview the president of the United States. When the *Orlando Sentinel* newspaper is delivered to tourists' hotel doors, the paper sometimes carries a false front page that advertises local attractions such as Disney World. A tourist seeing the paper for the first time might be surprised to read the headline "Drama Unfolds at Disney" before realizing that the "news" is bogus. Many radio stations across the country carry a syndicated show called "News and Comment," by noted radio newsman Paul Harvey. A listener to the show is hard pressed to tell where the news, comment, and advertisements begin and end, since opinions are blended into factual reports and advertisements are read in the same tone as the news, complete with quotes from sources. For example, an advertisement for a diet supplement will sound precisely like a report on recent scientific discoveries regarding health and nutrition. Likewise, advertisements in newspapers often appear in the style and format of news articles. Finally, on the major network morning shows, a news segment on a rapidly spreading flu virus might be followed immediately— perhaps coincidentally, perhaps not—by an advertisement for an over-the-counter flu remedy. Critical thinkers struggling to separate fact and opinion in today's media, when the producers of news and the manufacturers of products are often controlled by the same parent company, have their work cut out for them.

There is little hope that the media will change anytime soon. Despite campaigns by parents' groups, political organizations, and media watchdogs, despite the portrayal in Hollywood movies, despite a growing distrust among audiences, despite the fact that we know the tricks, the news media will continue to carefully study their audiences and provide them with entertainment, and we will dutifully oblige by watching and reading. Critical thinkers can, of course, take countermeasures to ensure that they are not among the audience members so easily entertained, that they are unwilling to settle for blurred or scant information, and that entertainment will not silence their critical faculties.

To counter the mind-numbing effects of news media devoted primarily to entertaining us, critical thinkers can demonstrate a high degree of what is called media literacy by asking the following questions when they encounter a news item, whether on television or the radio, in the papers or newsmagazines. Many of the questions call upon critical thinking skills that we have discussed throughout this book.

1. What message is being sent? What specific, factual information is being delivered? If I were to write down the information I am hearing or reading, what would I record? What more would I know now than I knew before the report? Am I willing to regard the information as accurate? Or should I investigate other sources to be certain that the source has the facts straight?

2. Can I separate the information from how the information is delivered? How much of a reporter's involvement can I detect in the information? Does the reporter, news anchor, or writer subtly or blatantly offer opinion and speculation? Does the report appear to be slanted in any direction? Is the reporter's language emotionally charged, euphemistic, vague, or ambiguous?

3. What is the larger context from which the information has been selected? What do I need to know about what happened before this event took place? What questions do I have about the history leading up to this event? What more would I need to know about this event and its history before I could make any use of this information?

4. What can I do with what I have heard, read, or seen? Is the information I've just received giving me nothing more than a cat's-eye view of the world, or can I use it to change my plans, take some action, or solve a problem? Or is the information essentially useless, nothing more than trivia? Is the information meaningful and important?

5. What methods did the media use to attract my attention to this piece of information and to hold my interest? In the selection of the story and the elements of the story, what appeals were made to the

audience's interest in conflict, violence, and tragedy? What appeals were made to the audience's emotions?

6. Who appears to be best served by the way in which the story is told? Is there a clear tie-in with a manufacturer, corporation, or service provider?

ADVERTISEMENTS AND THE MEDIA

As we have seen, the media have a great influence on our beliefs and values. As television, newspaper, radio, billboards, junk mail, and now the Internet insert themselves into every aspect of our lives, so advertising, using those media, is a pervasive, powerful force shaping attitudes and behavior in today's world. The typical person sees 250 commercial messages daily and more than two million of them by the time he or she is twenty-five years old.[13] It is very difficult, if not impossible, to avoid exposure to advertising. Studying advertising and the strategies used by advertisers helps us to become more critical, insightful, and selective consumers, even under the barrage of advertising appeals we experience. When it comes to commercial advertisements, for the most part, skepticism is a virtue.

Definition and Functions of an Advertisement

Advertising is an extremely diverse phenomenon. It is as varied in its purposes as it is in its use of different media and techniques. As a consequence, it is important to distinguish among the various types. The most common forms of advertising include public service advertising on behalf of various institutions, programs, and causes; commercials for products and services; and, a variety of increasing importance today, political advertising in the interests of parties and candidates. Advertising can be as simple as a poster in a school classroom, or it can be very complex, entailing sophisticated research and multimedia campaigns that span the globe. In general terms, an *advertisement* is simply a public notice meant to convey information and invite patronage or some other response.

An analysis of this definition reveals that advertisements have two basic functions: *to inform* and *to motivate*. Sometimes these two functions support each other, but often they do not. A good ad—for example, a public service advertisement for a flu vaccination—can both inform and motivate. A good ad, whether a commercial or a public service ad, meets the following criteria: it is truthful; it is informative; it is motivational; and it appeals to but does not insult one's intelligence. If it can be humorous as well, that's a plus.

A bad ad, on the other hand, may motivate but not correctly inform. Conflicts between informing and motivating occur in many commercial advertisements. The reason for this is fairly obvious: providing the consumer with *complete* information about the best product at the lowest possible price

> *The superior man understands what is right; the inferior man understands what will sell.*
>
> —Confucius

may conflict with motivating the consumer to buy the product from the manufacturer or retailer who sponsors the ad. That manufacturer or retailer may not have the best product at the lowest possible price.

Some advertisements seek to motivate without providing any information at all. Either ads offer reasons for buying a product or they do not. Slogans and jingles such as "Sony, the One and Only," "You deserve a break today at McDonald's," "Always Coca Cola," and "Nike. Just Do It" are examples of ads that seek to sell on the basis of "brand recognition" alone. No product claims are made; only seductive phrases or catchy jingles are used.

Some advertisements make a mockery of the function of informing by making false or misleading claims. Listerine mouthwash was long advertised as preventing colds and sore throats or lessening their severity. The Federal Trade Commission (FTC) required the manufacturer to drop the advertisement and to do "corrective advertisements" to inform consumers that using Listerine does not, in fact, prevent colds and sore throats or lessen their severity.[14]

Advertisements directed at children can be harmful. For example, advertisements aired on television during after-school and Saturday-morning cartoon shows typically pitch a variety of dolls, guns, and other toys as well as sugared cereals. Some shows are really just program-long commercials for toys based on the show's characters. Critics contend that children are simply not capable of evaluating the worth of advertised claims. Television commercials for children's toys are now required to end with the toy being shown in actual size against a neutral background. This is obligatory because production techniques such as low camera angles and close-ups can make these toys seem larger or better than they actually are. Ads aimed at children have a great impact. The average child sees more than 20,000 television commercials a year as well as countless ads in magazines and other sources, including school materials.

Do ads create or mirror society's values? That may be an unanswerable question, but it is still an important one to consider. The view that ads simply mirror the culture is overly simplistic. No doubt, advertising, like the media it uses, does act like a mirror to some degree. But as a multi-billion-dollar commercial enterprise, advertising does more than passively reflect the attitudes and values of its culture—it contributes to their creation. It does this by selecting certain values and attitudes and ignoring others. Subtly, and not so subtly, ads suggest that consumers should possess wealth, status, success, and power; that it is important to "belong"; that consumers need the good opinions of others, popularity, security, and cleanliness; and so forth. What ads largely ignore are the values of being one's own person and thinking for oneself; of cooperation rather than competitiveness; of thriftiness and efficiency; of caring for the environment, being aware of its fragility and the limits of our natural resources.

Currently, the United States is experiencing a craze of sport utility vehicles (SUVs). Are ads creating or simply reflecting that craze? Sport utility vehicles yield high profits, and, as a result, most car manufacturers offer one. It also appears that many SUV owners want to control the drivers around them. Manufacturers respond by designing their SUVs with seats mounted high to help drivers feel like lords of all they survey, and the ads reinforce the feeling that those drivers are powerful defenders of the good life. Finally, SUVs are very fuel-inefficient, environmentally unfriendly, dangerous to normal-size cars on the road, and expensive, typically costing about $40,000. At that price, owning one is clearly a status symbol. Given these circumstances, can anyone hold that the desire to own an SUV is simply a reflection of cultural values and not at all of the ads that push them?

This selectivity gives the lie to the notion that advertising does no more than simply reflect or echo its culture. Television, which has been the dominant medium for the last fifty years, best illustrates the point. Given the enormous financial resources that TV programs require, corporate advertisers such as Procter & Gamble, General Motors, and RJR Nabisco largely determine what we see and how we see it. Television is much more than a mere medium. It is also an industry and an institution that has as great an influence on people's lives as the institutions of family and government. George Gerbner, former dean of the University of Pennsylvania's Annenberg School of Communications, calls television the contemporary mythmaker, much in the way that the church was in the Middle Ages. A myth, as Gerbner uses the term, refers to the stories that teach, explain, and justify the practices and institutions of a given society to the people in that society. Myths deal with what is most important to us—things as fundamental as life's meaning, love, death, and sex—and have a profound influence on the way we see the world and ourselves. They are found in television's dramas, sitcoms, and sports programs—and in its advertisements.[15]

Moreover, corporate advertisers do not want just any audience. They seek the largest possible audience that is receptive to the advertiser's message. This is why, rather than simply reflecting culture and its values as a mirror does, advertisements tend to distort our conception of culture and its values. They do this by targeting or selecting certain groups of people according to their age, race, gender, or economic status to more effectively deliver their message. Every year billions of dollars are spent on advertising in the mass media. The largest part of this expenditure goes to commercial advertisements on television, which have the highest per-minute production costs of anything in the media. Given this financial investment and commitment, it is only natural that advertisements seek the largest audience with the most expendable income. With this emphasis, advertisers inevitably will present a warped view of society's real interests and needs.

> *You can tell the ideals of a nation by its advertisements.*
> —Norman Douglas

> *Advertising may be described as the science of arresting the human intelligence long enough to get money from it*
> —Stephen Leacock

EXERCISE 14.10

I. Get a copy of a local daily paper, a national paper, and a national newsmagazine, and bring each to class. Rather than look at the articles, focus on the advertisements. You can ignore the "supplements" that often come with the paper. Count the number of ads in the first section of each newspaper or an entire newsmagazine, and compare these with the number of news articles. Before you do this take a guess at what percentage you might expect it to be. Look at the sizes of ads and their content. Take note of the ads that appear in particular sections, such as Sports or Business. Can you conclude anything about what kind of audience the ads are directed toward? Are there any obvious or subtle connections between any of the advertisements and the stories in the paper? Do any of the stories have the quality of an ad—announcing the opening of a new store, for example? Or are there any ads that have the quality of a news story—making claims about a new weight-reducing pill, for example? Are the ads clearly labeled as advertisements or distinguished from the news in other ways, such as being enclosed in a border?

II. Divide the three major television networks—ABC, CBS, and NBC—among your group members, watch the nightly news on your assigned network, and do the same with the evening news that you did with the print media. Take careful notes of how many ads appear, when they appear, and what they are for. If possible, use a watch to estimate how much of the half-hour is taken up with ads. What audience is indicated in the ads? Is there any connection between ads and news? Also, within the news itself, take note of the promotions for upcoming news shows and tie-ins with Internet sites and other broadcast stations. Finally, note the "teasers" that are intended to keep your finger off the remote control—phrases such as "When we return . . ." and "Coming up later in our broadcast . . .". What sorts of appeals do these self-advertisements make?

Defenses of Advertising

Defenders of advertising claim that it provides many benefits. In addition to employing a large workforce of talented writers and producers, it informs consumers about available products and services. Many ads promote the public interest by informing consumers about health and safety issues and about new treatments for medical problems. Volvos, for example, were among the first to provide side-door air bags, a definite safety advantage.

Defenders of advertising also argue that by giving the media the financial backing they require, advertisements allow "free" non-government-regulated programming, thus permitting greater freedom of expression. The survival of many media outlets, such as television and radio stations, depends on the revenues from advertisements. Finally, proponents of advertising claim that advertising stimulates competition and fuels our mass-consumption economy, raising the standard of living for everyone by making possible what economists call the "the economy of large-scale production." Mass production reduces the cost of manufacturing a product, thus making it less expensive to buy; but mass production requires mass consumption, and mass consumption of a product cannot occur unless consumers know that the product exists. So, advertising is required if we are to reap the benefits of large-scale production.

Criticisms of Advertising

Despite these benefits, a number of criticisms have been leveled at advertising. First, some argue, advertising is intrusive. It interferes with almost everything we do (reading, driving, viewing TV, watching a ball game, lying on the beach) in order to deliver a message and therefore constitutes an invasion of privacy. Second, critics say, advertising demeans and corrupts culture, making citizens materialistic, preoccupied with things and with possessing more and more. Of course, there is nothing wrong with improving one's standard of living, but by encouraging consumers to measure their worth solely by what they *have* rather than by who they *are,* advertising contributes to a breakdown in interpersonal relationships, such as family and community. Critics argue that this push to acquire what commercials label "the good life" is done at the expense of the environment, the economy, and civilization itself. Third, and particularly relevant to critical thinking, critics argue that advertising is a manipulative, deceptive process that reinforces sexist and other stereotypes and treats people as a mere "means to an end."

That last criticism of advertising, that it manipulates and deceives us with sophisticated psychological ploys and other strategies, is one we are the least likely to believe. We don't like to think of ourselves as mere pawns of advertising geniuses, buying products we neither want nor need. Young people, including college students, usually claim advertising does not influence them. They claim that they buy what they want and need. They reject the notion that advertisements influence what they buy. The ad makers know better. Sales figures and market studies reveal that a well-designed ad campaign can greatly increase a product's impact. The next time you are in your university bookstore, notice how many credit-card ads are placed in your bag along with the books or other items you purchased.

Most Americans see advertising as peripheral to their lives. They consider advertisements as messages and images that they can easily tune in and out. Advertisers want us to believe this is true: they want to influence us not through blatant, overt messages but through more subtle messages and the value atmosphere they create. For example, you see the female Calvin Klein models on television looking great and having fun, and without making it explicit to yourself, you conclude, "If I get a pair of jeans like theirs, I'll attract men and have fun, too!" Beer ads typically have a good many sexual ploys, and soft-drink ads offer the promise of adventure. If you buy the right the beer or soda, the ads suggest, you will also get approval from your family and friends. Covertly the ads argue, "You bought the best-selling beer in the country for your party. You must be cool!" or "You bought the cheap no-name brand. You must be a nerd!"

Why do we find it so difficult to realize how profoundly advertising influences us? Max Sutherland, author of *Advertising and the Mind of the Consumer,* tells us that it is because we ask the wrong questions, make the wrong assumptions, and look for major effects rather than minor effects.[16] The major effects of most ads fall well short of persuasion. To appreciate the power of advertising, one has to measure and understand the minor effects, which are not obvious but are more characteristic of how advertisements achieve their goals. No one notices the effects of the calories one takes in from that second helping of food at dinner or that second bottle of beer. Determining how much weight you put on in twenty-four hours is like evaluating the effect of being exposed to a single commercial. In both cases, the changes are too small for one to notice. But even the small effects of advertising can influence which brands we choose—-especially when all other factors are equal and when one brand is much the same as another.

The majority of the things we buy—toothpaste, shampoo, or soft drinks, for example—are what Sutherland calls "low-involvement buying." These are purchases we give little thought to. High-involvement items are high-cost possessions, such as homes and cars. When people are spending a good deal of their hard-earned money to buy a TV, a car, or a home, they do not take the decision lightly. Before buying such items, they talk with friends, read *Consumer Reports,* and generally get as much information as they can about the item. At this level of cost, too, there usually are significant differences between one brand and another. Low-involvement buying, on the other hand, because it involves low-cost items, is no big deal. We have more important things to do, and we are not going to agonize over which brand to buy every time we need a box of facial tissue. This is the way low-involvement buying works. It is a "balance-beam" situation in which each brand weighs the same. With one brand on each side, the beam is balanced. However, it takes only a feather added to one side of the balance to tip it in favor of the brand on that side. The brands consumers have to pick from are often very similar. Which one will the buying balance tip toward?

When we look for advertising effects, as Sutherland notes, "we are looking for feathers rather than heavy weights."[17] In these low-involvement product categories, the brands are very similar and sometimes almost identical. These are called parity products. No matter how similar these products are, however, each advertiser must create an important perceived difference for his or her products—the USP (unique selling proposition). Cola is cola, for example, but when you're drinking a Coke, "it adds life!" Underwear is underwear, but if an ad shows Harrison Ford wearing Fruit of the Loom then it's more than just underwear, it's Harrison Ford's brand of underwear. In these situations, it often doesn't matter to consumers which one they buy. And, it is in these low-involvement categories that the effects of advertising can be greatest and yet hardest to think clearly about.

EXERCISE 14.11

Group discussion: For a week or more before you answer the following questions, consider how many times during the week you have thought about the things you really need as opposed to the things you think you would like to have. Where did these needs and desires come from? From an ad or something that a friend had? Do you see your fellow students walking around campus talking into cell phones? Are these phones really necessary or just a status symbol? Does our culture put too much emphasis on material things? Are ads primarily responsible for persuading us that we cannot be happy without the latest fad clothing, record album, or vehicle?

If you owned an advertising agency, would you produce ads for cigarettes directed at young people or ads for toys based on cartoon shows directed at children? The producers of such products have the right to freedom of speech, but do you think that the legal regulation of such ads constitutes indefensible censorship? Defend your answer to your classmates.

Strategies Used in Advertisements

Humor   Most ads attempt to persuade us primarily by engaging our emotions and emotional needs rather than by appealing to reason. The use of humor can be very effective in grabbing our attention. Who doesn't enjoy a good laugh? Ads that use humor can be very effective in closing down our critical defenses. An advertisement for Visa debit cards, for example, pitches them as being better than cash. The ad shows actor Jason Alexander (George Costanza of *Seinfeld*) at a movie theater without enough cash for tickets for both himself and his girlfriend. Unflustered, Alexander's character says to his girlfriend as they part, "I'll call you." In the next scene we see him with a bag of popcorn sitting in the theater alone. The pleasure he seems to be taking in eating his popcorn and preparing to enjoy the movie makes him forget any guilt he may have had for his date's missing the movie. The advertisement is effective simply because it is so humorous, and hence so memorable.

Catchy Slogans and Jingles   Although the strategies used in advertisements are often very subtle and difficult to categorize, most ads use some variety of the fallacies we have already studied. An example of a strategy difficult to categorize is the endlessly repeated slogans and jingles we see and hear. We might label these "the repetitive slogan" ploy. Over time, through the process of repetition, such slogans as "Nobody beats Midas. Nobody"; "It's Miller Time"; and "Tastes great, Less filling" can, by small increments, produce major perceived differences between brands. But we are rarely aware that this process is taking place.

EXERCISE 14.12

1. See how well you can match a jingle or a slogan from column A with a product, or a company from column B. Like most of us, you will probably do well on this quiz. What does that tell you about the effectiveness of advertisements?

	Column A		Column B

Column A	Column B
⬜ ___ 1. They're great!	a. Hallmark cards
___ 2. When it rains, it pours.	b. Bounty paper towels
___ 3. Good to the last drop.	c. Virginia Slims cigarettes
⬜ ___ 4. Just do it!	d. Oscar Meyer bologna
___ 5. When you care enough to send the very best.	e. Prudential Insurance
___ 6. We can't hide the pride.	f. Kellogg's Sugar Frosted Flakes
⬜ ___ 7. Come to where the flavor is.	g. Allstate Insurance
___ 8. They keep going and going and going.	h. Chevrolet trucks
___ 9. We try harder.	i. McDonald's
⬜ ___ 10. My bologna has a first name.	j. Maxwell House coffee
___ 11. Get a piece of the rock.	k. Marlboro cigarettes
___ 12. You've come a long way, baby.	l. Avis rental cars
⬜ ___ 13. The quicker picker-upper.	m. Nike
___ 14. You're in good hands.	n. Morton salt
___ 15. Like a rock.	o. Energizer batteries
⬜ ___ 16. Finger-lickin' good.	p. Timex watches
___ 17. Reach out and touch someone.	q. Kentucky Fried Chicken
___ 18. Takes a lickin' but keeps on tickin'.	r. United Negro College Fund
⬜ ___ 19. M'm M'm Good.	s. Lay's potato chips
___ 20. I love what you do for me.	t. U.S. Army
___ 21. How do you spell relief?	u. BMW
⬜ ___ 22. We bring good things to life.	v. Debeers
___ 23. Don't leave home without it.	w. Texaco
___ 24. The ultimate driving machine.	x. Campbell's soup
⬜ ___ 25. You can trust your car to the man who wears the star.	y. Toyota
___ 26. A diamond is forever.	z. The Marines
___ 27. Betcha can't eat just one.	aa. American Express
⬜ ___ 28. A mind is a terrible thing to waste.	bb. Rolaids
___ 29. Be all that you can be.	cc. General Electric
___ 30. We are looking for a few good men.	dd. AT&T

Fears of Rejection and Hopes for Acceptance and Approval   Other advertisements appeal to our fears and our desire for acceptance and approval. Most of us strive for what psychologists call cognitive balance.[18] Simply put, we are most comfortable when all our beliefs, actions, attitudes, and relationships are harmoniously balanced. Advertisers attempt to upset this balance, this symmetry, by making you worry that you are not as attractive as you may believe: an ad might suggest that you have dandruff or bad breath. This loss of balance will, of course, be restored by the use of the advertised hair treatment or breath mint. Ads for Michelin tires attempt to upset your sense of balance, your happy perception of yourself as a responsible parent, by showing you a baby floating safely in one of its tires. Tires are more than a mere part of your car; they protect your child. The suggestion is that if you buy the wrong tires, you don't care about your family's safety. The correct choice of tires—Michelin's, of course—will restore your balance and relieve your guilt by providing the needed protection.

There are plenty of ads that work on the reader's or viewer's fears and emotions. If you are a young man, you probably fear losing your hair, and, of course, there's an advertisement for a product that's guaranteed to get your hair growing again. If you are a young woman, you may fear that your bosom is too big or too small. Again, of course, there's an ad for a bra that will solve your problem and give you the look you are after. Worries about having body odor or bad breath, being overweight or underweight, having teeth that aren't white or straight enough can all upset your cognitive balance, your self-confidence. You can be certain there is an ad that will promise to allay your fears and restore that confidence. Sometimes, these products really do live up to their claims and allay your fears. In many cases, however, the results are disappointing and you are off searching for another product that will restore that lost hair or that lost self-esteem.

Promise, large promise, is the soul of advertising.
—Samuel Johnson

Emotive Words   As we have already seen, language is often imprecise, vague, or ambiguous. Advertisers use this imprecision for their own purposes. They carefully choose their words so that the very language they use will work independently without needing to give any evidence for the advertisers' claims. Often, use of the correct word can create an enticing mood and attitude. Think of what is implied, for example, by "joystick," a control handle used with some computer games, or a computer game itself called *PlayStation2*. When you go fishing, you do not just want bait, an ad proclaims, you want "Power Bait." "Power" is a positive and dynamic emotive word, useful in selling many things. On the other hand, think of the unfortunate connotations of a restaurant named for a family called "Hare," "Foote," or "Mudd"!

Advertisers favor words that help create a positive, emotional feeling about a product. Among these are "pleasure," "fresh," "clean," and "natural." Smoking Camel cigarettes, says the ad, gives you "Pleasure to burn." An ad for Newport cigarettes claims they are "Alive with pleasure." An ad for Winston cigarettes claims "It's only natural." (Is there such a thing as an artificial tobacco?) Finally, Kool cigarettes aren't just Kool, they're Kool Natural Lights. That's because, as the copy in the advertisement reads, "they are a blend of tobaccos and natural menthol with other natural flavors for a smooth, fresh taste." To drive the point home, this one ad uses the word "natural" three times.

Weasel Words   Weasel words are words or phrases used to water down or qualify a claim so that the claim ends up saying much less than it seems to at first glance. A weasel word allows an advertisement to give a product the *appearance* that it is the best one or that it will actually cure or eliminate your problem, when, in fact, it is not or will not. The designation "weasel word" is appropriately taken from the egg-eating habits of weasels. Weasels suck out the inside of an egg, giving the appearance to the casual observer that the egg is still whole. Claims couched in weasel language either practically evaporate on closer examination or claim much less than they initially appeared to be asserting.

Commonly used weasel words include "helps" (probably the most-used one), "virtual" or "virtually," "can be," "fights," "up to," and "looks like." This ad appears on the back of the Weis Premium Orange Juice container: "Low fat diets rich in fruits and vegetables containing Vitamin A, Vitamin C, and fiber may reduce the risk of some types of cancer. Florida Orange Juice is an excellent source of Vitamin C." An ad for a popular dishwashing detergent claims that it "leaves dishes *virtually* spotless"; you can be sure that the advertisers are presuming you will just think that their detergent will leave your dishes "spotless" rather than "virtually spotless." When a sign in a storefront says, "Everything is discounted up to 75 percent," you can bet that only a few items (some things no one wants) will be discounted 75 percent and that the majority of things on sale will be far less than 75 percent off.

Fine-Print Disclaimers   How many times have you seen an ad in newspaper in big, bold letters claiming, "Sale. 50% off," at one of your favorite stores, only to notice at the bottom of the page, in very small, easy-to-overlook type that the price cut is only on certain marked items? These are called *fine-print disclaimers*. You will often walk into a department store and face a large sign with foot-high letters saying, "25% OFF Everything.*" Only when you get up close will you notice the little sneaky asterisk and the fine print down at the bottom of the sign saying, "*except for TVs, VCRs, and major appliances."

Puffery   "Prices so hot the fire department comes by to hose off the store every half hour." That's a Radio Shack ad and a good example of what is called *puffery* in advertising.

One of the greatest problems for the FTC (Federal Trade Commission) is finding the line between false or deceptive advertising and puffery—that little lie or exaggeration that skirts the literal truth but does so in a way that does not deceive most audiences and is often entertaining. One can reasonably presume that the viewing or reading public does not take many commercials literally. Most of us know that, although hair dyes will hide the gray, they are

Fictitious Fine-Print Disclaimer from Humorist Writer Dave Barry

Warning: Use of this product may cause nausea, insomnia, euphoria, déjà vu, menopause, tax audits, demonic possession, lung flukes, eyeball worms, decapitation, and mudslides. We would not even dare to sell this product if we did not have a huge, carnivorous legal department that could squash you in court like a baby mouse under a sledgehammer. We frankly can't believe that you were so stupid as to purchase this product. Your only hope is to set this product down very gently, back slowly away from it, then turn and sprint for your home, never to return.

not going to make us look as great as the models in their commercials. On the other hand, what about these: a beer that advertises "The best beer in America," an appliance dealer who claims that "Nobody sells for less," or a car dealer who claims, "We will not knowingly be undersold"? Such puffery is very common. An ad for newly minted quarters touts "The Historic Opportunity of the Millennium . . . The 1999 America's Commemorative Quarters Program!" A final example: When does a Big Mac ever look the way it does on TV? Is this deception or acceptable puffery?

The Promise of Sex   There is hardly a brand of soap, car, cigarette, beer, or jeans that has not used the promise of sex, or better sex, in its ads. An ad for Marlboro cigarettes shows two cowboys resting their horses beside a beautiful stream. The ad's copy reads: "Come to where the flavor is. Come to Marlboro Country." Next to their horses, beneath an arching tree, the men have paused from their cattle-herding chores for a well-deserved cigarette break. In front of them a wood fire burns. This is a very subtle ad. It seems to suggest that smoking Marlboro and riding horses in the open country is the manly thing to do. And such men, of course, must attract the opposite sex. What woman could resist?

Is there a connection between shampooing your hair and sexual pleasure and excitement? Ads for Herbal Essence shampoo would you like to believe there is. The commercial shows a woman stepping into her shower about to wash her hair. She is using Herbal Essence shampoo. As she lathers up with the shampoo, she cries loudly, "Yes, yes, yes," and then there's an "ooh" and an "ah." It clearly suggests that using this shampoo will send you into a state of orgasmic sexual pleasure and excitement.

An ad for Virginia Slims pictures a woman with beautiful eyes and hair, wearing beautiful earrings, saying, "I made a promise to bring romance back into my life, to kiss negativity good-bye and love the dawning of each new day," followed by the words, "Virginia Slims: Find your Voice." Does having tobacco-breath really help your love life? Another magazine advertisement shows a smiling, beautiful, young woman with a copy that reads: "Amber

O'Brien, 25, is having the time of her life. Recently, she decided it was time to have breast augmentation." The suggestion being made by this advertisement is obvious. If you want a happy sex life, you should have your breasts augmented as well. It's clear: Sex or the promise of sex sells.

Other Advertising Ploys

Enviable Situations   Take a closer look at the next new-car commercial you see. The ones on television almost always show a car on a quiet rained-soaked country road. *There's no traffic.* There's never any traffic in car commercials, even when they film these ads in the middle of downtown in major cities. All you see is a traffic-free street or a wide-open highway with no other cars in sight. The camera zooms in on the driver behind the wheel, the music picks up, and the car takes off, purring smoothly as it gracefully zips out of sight down the road into a beautiful sunset. Who would not like to be in a beautiful new car on some deserted highway in Arizona or a mountain road in the Colorado Rockies?

Cigarette advertisements targeted at women, such as those for Virginia Slims, typically show a young, attractive, very slim woman at a table in a fashionable restaurant with a handsome young man staring into her eyes, or the same woman walking along a beautiful, sunlit beach, again with a handsome young man at her side. The message is clear: If you want to be in similar surroundings, looking slim and attractive and pursued by a lover, smoke Virginia Slims.

Enviable People   We all tend to identify with people we admire for their celebrity status, accomplishments, wealth, intelligence, or athletic abilities. Advertisers play on this tendency by featuring celebrities or the people we admire or identify with. Maybe you will never play ball as well as Michael Jordan, but you can feel a little more like him if you wear the same brand of basketball shoes he does. Such ads don't just sell a product, they also sell a lifestyle that people identify with. Such ads don't even attempt to give reasons for purchasing the product; it is enough in the consumer's mind that some celebrity uses or endorses the shoes, clothes, perfume, beer, cars, or automotive oil. The "Got milk?" ads do no more than show a famous celebrity with a milk-mustache. Apparently, that's enough to get consumers to think about adding more milk to their diets. This is an example of an ad that effectively combines humor and celebrity status to sell a product.

Such ads are similar to "target ads," or ads aimed at segments of the population most likely and able to buy a particular product. Target ads are frequently aimed at children, teenagers, young women, and certain ethnic minorities. Such ads frequently raise ethical as well as critical thinking issues.

Although they are no longer in use, "Joe Camel" ads were heavily criticized for the use of this cool-camel figure. Critics argued that it enticed young children to smoke. The popularity of Camel cigarettes skyrocketed during the tenure of the Joe Camel campaign. Surprisingly, many people begin smoking as early as eight years old. Virginia Slims cigarettes have been criticized because they are aimed primarily at young women who aspire to be as skinny as the models they see. Sadly, some young women, in an attempt to imitate the skinny ideal embodied in so many commercials, develop eating disorders such as anorexia nervosa or bulimia.

Compliments   Many ads seek to butter up consumers or play on their image of themselves as being better than the average person is. Virginia Slims says, "You've come a long way, baby." Hallmark claims, "When you care enough to send the very best." Piaget watches have "Exceptional character." Saks Fifth Avenue claims its clothes are "Defining style."

Many people believe that if a product is the most expensive in its class, then it must be the best. Many advertisements play on this belief, including ads for Mont Blanc pens, Rolex wristwatches, and BMWs. Their ads assure their consumers that they are buying the very best product and one that is known to be the very best. A young newlywed wants to impress her mother-in-law, who is coming to her house for Thanksgiving for the first time. If she risks buying a cheaper brand of turkey, the turkey may be too dry, and the hapless bride is sure to be seen as a failure in her mother-in-law's eyes. The ad for Butterball, well known to be more expensive than most frozen turkeys, assures her that her Thanksgiving turkey will be moist and sure to impress.

Political Ads

Political advertising, truthfully and honestly made, can make a valuable contribution to democracy. As we discussed earlier, political freedom requires knowledge. Unfortunately, the high costs of political ads can limit political competition to wealthy candidates or require that office seekers compromise their integrity and independence on special interests for campaign funds.

The same psychological strategies used to sell a product can also be used to "sell" a candidate. Images and text can be designed to appeal primarily to the emotions rather than to reason. The familiar tactics used to market a product—emotive language, weasel words, puffery, and the like—can be used as the basis for a political campaign. Political ads can appeal to bias, hostility, fear, or prejudice, rather than to a reasoned sense of justice and the common good.

"Negative" political ads misrepresent or distort a candidate's policies and record. Televised political advertising can invite the visual-image stereotype and the gut-level response to replace a reasoned response to a policy question. Powerful visual images coupled with evocative music can invite strong emotional reactions to what is seen and heard.

One of the most blatant examples of this occurred in the 1964 presidential campaign between incumbent President Lyndon Johnson and his opponent, Barry Goldwater. During Goldwater's acceptance speech as the Republican candidate for president, he uttered the famous line, "Extremism in

There are some politicians who, if their constituents were cannibals, would promise them missionaries for dinner.

—H. L. Mencken

the defense of liberty is no vice." Johnson's campaign managers used this statement against Goldwater in an infamous ad, known as the "Daisy" ad. In the
ad, a little girl pulls petals from a daisy matching a background countdown, 5,
4, 3, 2, 1, that ends with a nuclear blast that fills the screen with a mushroom
cloud. Although he never had much of a chance of beating President Johnson,
this ad effectively destroyed Goldwater's candidacy.

EXERCISE 14.13

I. Read the advertisements in current newspapers and magazines and find five
that give no reasons for buying their product but are based on mere emotional
appeals, slogans, or jingles. Check the criteria given in this chapter for a good ad
and then find five ads that do what ads are supposed to do as they are supposed
to do it.

II. Choose an ad from a current magazine or newspaper, then analyze it in the
following manner:
- If it is a promise ad, describe the audience to which it appears to be
  addressed.
- Tell what promise is it making.
- Identify the strategy the ad uses to reach its audience.
- Determine if the ad uses a fallacious appeal and explain what it is.

III. Below are examples of advertisements taken from various sources. Evaluate
each for its informational and motivational aspects; then explain which, if any, of
the various ploys and strategies we examined in this chapter are being used.
Some may be legitimate and not based upon a fallacious appeal.
1. "The best things in life are basic." (Ad for Basic brand cigarettes)
2. "On Mother's Day give her your best! Our oversized pale pink cotton t-
   shirt that says, 'Mom's the best,' with our signature rose embroidered on the
   sleeve." (Lord and Taylor ad)
3. "This is your last chance. Drive home in one of these 2000's or one of our
   carefully selected pre-owned vehicles today for less than you ever imagined.
   Hurry, this savings event ends this weekend!" (Car ad)
4. "You're thinking, 'I need a bank that offers me more.' We are thinking,
   'How about a certificate for two airline tickets?'" (Bank ad)
5. "New Charmin's so good, it brought Mr. Whipple out of retirement."
6. "This will change the way you clean. Forever. New Mr. Clean Antibacter-
   ial Wipe-ups."
7. "For moms who have a lot of love, but not a lot of time." (Ad for Quaker
   Oatmeal)
8. "Like a rock." (Ad for Chevrolet Suburban truck)
9. "Excedrin Migraine is now the #1 doctor-recommended brand* for the relief of migraine pain." (Note the following "*nonprescription" at the bottom of the page.)

10. "Totally liquid way to make color stay! Liquid-y smooth. Liquid-y sexy! And Kiss Off? No Way!" (Ad for Revlon lipstick)

11. "Let me give you the secrets of fearless conversation! I promise you the ability to walk into a room full of strangers—and talk to <u>anyone</u> with total confidence, authority and flair." (Ad for Verbal Advantage)

12. "Damn the tuxedos, full speed ahead. Lincoln Navigator. American Luxury." (Ad for Lincoln's sport utility vehicle)

13. "Urban Assault Luxury Vehicle. Lincoln Navigator. American Luxury." (Ad for Lincoln's sport utility vehicle)

14. "I wanted a light, not his life story. No Additives. No Bull." [At the bottom of the page the following appears: "No additives in our cigarette does NOT mean a safer cigarette."] (Ad for Winston cigarettes)

15. "You won't find a better service provider, British Airways, The world's favorite airline."

16. "Love is blind but not senseless. Scope. Feel the tingle. Nothing kills more bad breath germs."

17. "Real men. Real allure. The new men's fragrance from Chanel." (Ad for Allure Homme)

18. "Virtually impervious to dust, dirt and water, not to mention the shifting winds of fashion." (Ad for Rolex watches)

19. "For those who like to fly in the face of convention." (Ad for Jaguar)

20. "5 million dollar handmade, oriental rug Tent Sale. A sale so big we have to hold it outdoors in the parking lot! An assortment so spectacular we've set up a 10,000 sq. ft. tent to hold it all." (Macy's ad)

21. "Try our delicious homemade rice pudding!" (Sign in KFC restaurant)

22. "If you don't need ACT! to manage your business relationships, you probably don't have many relationships to manage." (Ad for business software product)

23. "The best olive oil in the world comes from Spain. Just ask the Italians." (Ad for Alvaros Extra Virgin Olive Oil, a product of Spain)

24. "The views are spectacular and our prices are unbelievable." (Ad for home-site properties)

25. "Hollywood's new diet phenomenon. Lose up to 10 lbs this weekend! The Hollywood 'Miracle' diet features delicious, all-natural juices that help you lose weight while you cleanse, detoxify and rejuvenate your body." (Ad for Hollywood 48-Hour Miracle Diet)

Summary

1. We are assailed daily by messages from the media. Although some media sources target specific audiences, the mass media deliver their messages to a large and diverse audience with varying interests, education, political viewpoints, and so forth.

2. To assign meaning to a message, we need to know something about the context of the message—the background of the information, the intentions or perceived intentions of the speaker, the wider implications and circumstances that surround a message. Without context, messages can be meaningless and useless. Unfortunately, the news media extract information from the wider context, leaving us with some facts but little knowledge.

3. For context, which would require thorough, extensive investigation and demand much of the audience, the media substitute appeals to our noncritical natures and common emotions, selecting stories of crime, scandal, violence, and whatever else will disturb, frighten, or shock audiences. Heartwarming stories about animals and children are common as well, as are stories of rescues and warnings about hidden dangers. Stories critical of corporations and the media do not usually appear in the mainstream press. In general, stories are selected for their entertainment value.

4. The media employ a number of techniques to exaggerate the importance of some stories and to play others down. Often these techniques result in a distortion of reality, especially since extensive coverage is reserved for big events that are uncommon or for trivial matters. Persistent issues and trends receive relatively little coverage.

5. Although "objectivity" is difficult to attain, some members of the news media attempt to be objective by reporting news without commentary or analysis. This approach to the news often leads to problems when the media pass along information that is not credible or that has not been verified. Although some critics contend that the news media are biased toward a political viewpoint, most media organizations, preferring not to alienate current or potential customers, choose not to stir up controversy with pronounced political viewpoints. Individual writers, on the other hand, often appear to slant a story toward personal biases, although what seems to be personal opinion is often just an effort to appear chummy or to appeal to readers' prejudices. Finally, some news personnel have on occasion blatantly offered their opinions on issues. In fact, audiences now, unfortunately, look more and more to news reporters for their opinions and insights.

6. The media-literate critical thinker is aware of the techniques used in the news media to entertain an audience in the effort to keep them reading and watching. A media-literate consumer of news knows that stories have been stripped of their contexts and can separate fact from opinion in news stories.

7. The point of studying advertising ploys and strategies is to become a more critical, insightful, and selective consumer.

8. Advertising permeates our environment. Using a host of ploys that appeal both to our physiological needs—food, drink, sleep, etc.—and to our psychological needs—affiliation, affection, acceptance, self-esteem, status, etc.—advertisers invest vast amounts of money to break through our rational defenses to sell their products. They employ researchers and psychologists to maximize the impact of their ads on consumers.

9. Some of the more common strategies of advertisements include mindless slogans and jingles, psychological appeals, promises of being accepted and approved, the promise of sex or improved sex, the association of products with people we admire and identify with, and snob appeal. Advertisers use emotive language, weasel words, fine-print disclaimers, and puffery in many ads. Political ads use many of these same strategies.

CHAPTER 15

SCIENCE AND PSEUDOSCIENCE

Science is the most powerful intellectual tool ever discovered. It has transformed the way we live, work, travel, and communicate. It has given us computers, telephones, televisions, VCRs, CD players, refrigerators, and a thousand other conveniences of modern life. It has improved health care, raised living standards, and significantly increased average life expectancy worldwide. Most significant, science has added enormously to the sum of human knowledge and has, after ages of more or less blind groping, finally provided human beings with a proven, reliable method for answering age-old questions about ourselves and the awe-inspiring physical universe in which we live.

Despite the profound impact science has on our daily lives, studies show that a large percentage of Americans are "scientifically illiterate."[1] Evidence of this can be seen in scientific literacy surveys (see box, "What Americans Believe . . ."), in the dismal performance of American high school students on international math and science tests,[2] and in the recent upsurge in interest in "New Age" or occult phenomena such as ESP, astrology, reincarnation, ghosts, psychic prediction, levitation, psychic surgery, the Bermuda Triangle, the lost continent of Atlantis, the prophecies of Nostradamus, healing crystals, pyramid power, out-of-body experiences, and trance channeling.

In this chapter we offer a brief introduction to science and scientific reasoning, discuss the limitations of science, explain how to distinguish real science from pseudoscience, and explore in detail two examples of pseudoscientific or allegedly paranormal phenomena: astrology and near-death experiences.

THE BASIC PATTERN OF SCIENTIFIC REASONING

Science is a method of inquiry that seeks to describe, explain, and predict occurrences in the physical or natural world by means of careful observation and experiment.[3] Although there is no single "scientific method" all scientists use,

What Americans Believe about Science and the Paranormal

The term **paranormal** refers to mysterious, unusual, or supernatural phenomena that supposedly transcend the limits of existing science and are due to hidden or occult causes.[4] Here is a sampling of things Americans believe about science and the paranormal:

18 percent of adult Americans believe that the sun revolves around the earth, rather than vice versa.[5]

More than 50 percent of adult Americans don't know that the earth takes a year to orbit the sun.[6]

63 percent of adult Americans don't know that the last dinosaur died before the first human arose.

57 percent of adult Americans don't know that electrons are smaller than atoms.[7]

47 percent of adult Americans believe that God created human beings at one time within the last 10,000 years pretty much in their present form.[8]

93 percent of adult Americans believe in some form of paranormal phenomena.[9]

48 percent of adult Americans believe in ESP.

25 percent of adult Americans believe in astrology.[10]

28 percent of adult Americans believe in communication with the dead.[11]

most scientific reasoning does follow a certain general pattern. That pattern can be summarized as follows:

The Basic Pattern of Scientific Reasoning

1. Identifying the problem
2. Gathering relevant data
3. Formulating hypotheses to explain the data
4. Testing the hypotheses by observation or experiment

Identifying the Problem   Try to remember the last time you thought really hard about something. We'd be willing to bet there was some *problem* you were trying to solve: Should I change my major? Quit my dead-end job? Move into my own apartment? Talk to my friend about his drinking problem? Tell my boyfriend about my planned sex-change operation? In fact, as John Dewey and other philosophers have pointed out, most of the serious thinking we do is problem-solving thinking.

Science, by its very nature, is a kind of problem-solving activity. It always begins with a question or puzzle that researchers believe can be answered by means of observation or experiment: Do oral contraceptives cause breast cancer? Does drinking red wine lower the risk of heart attack? Did the universe begin with a big bang? What are the fundamental building blocks of matter? Were dinosaurs wiped out by the impact of a large asteroid? How do honeybees communicate? What genes determine eye color? Did life once exist on Mars? What causes those amazing bubbles to percolate up from the bottom of a glass of beer? Science seeks to answer such puzzles by means of careful observation and rigorous testing.

Gathering Relevant Data   The ultimate test of a scientific theory or hypothesis is whether it fits the observable facts. No matter how popular, comforting, or long accepted a scientific idea may be, it must be rejected if it fails to agree with the clear evidence of our senses.

Sometimes it is possible to confirm or refute a scientific hypothesis by means of a single decisive observation or experiment. That was the case, for example, when Galileo, according to a famous but possibly apocryphal story, refuted Aristotle's claim that heavy objects fall faster than light objects by dropping two iron balls of different weights from the Leaning Tower of Pisa and noting that the two balls struck the ground at the same instant. In most cases, however, a scientific hypothesis can be effectively confirmed or refuted only by collecting a great deal of observational evidence. To find out, for example, whether coffee drinking contributes to coronary heart disease, scientists would need to collect information on the coffee-drinking habits and other health-related characteristics of literally thousands of people over a period of many years. The patient, methodical collection of facts is what consumes most of the time and energy of most working scientists.

Formulating Hypotheses   Contrary to a popular misconception, scientists don't just go around collecting facts blindly or indiscriminately. All scientific investigation is guided by certain presuppositions that influence the kinds of observations and experiments scientists think are worth making. Among these presuppositions are a class of tentative or "working" assumptions scientists call **hypotheses.** Let's consider a few examples.

Suppose you are a doctor investigating an outbreak of serious stomach-flu-like symptoms onboard a commercial jet airliner. Five passengers, all from the same family and all seated in the first-class cabin, became sick during a long overseas flight. Your job is to find out why. How would you begin?

Clearly, you wouldn't begin just by collecting facts at random: noting the color of the sick passengers' socks, the number of coins in their pockets, their favorite sports teams, the kinds of toothpaste they prefer, and so on. Based on your knowledge of how things normally work in the world, you would assume that those facts aren't pertinent to your investigation. Instead, you would start by looking for *relevant* facts, guided by a kind of working hypothesis such as the following:

H_1: The passengers became sick because of the food they ate on the plane.

Suppose you do some quick checking, however, and discover that two of the five sick passengers were fasting and ate nothing on the plane. Naturally, you would then set aside your initial hypothesis and formulate another, such as the following:

> *The great tragedy of Science—the slaying of a beautiful hypothesis by an ugly fact.*
> —Thomas Henry Huxley

H_2: The passengers became sick because they all came down with the stomach flu.

You then might then call for some medical tests, which, let's suppose, confirm that the passengers did indeed come down with a severe case of viral gastroenteritis, more commonly known as stomach flu.

As this example makes clear, there is a complex interplay between observations and hypotheses in science. Hypotheses inevitably *guide* observations, since scientists wouldn't have a clue where to begin their investigations without at least some initial assumptions about what sorts of data are worth collecting. Observations, in turn, are used to *test* hypotheses—to modify, confirm, or refute them in the light of empirical evidence and experimentation. It is this complex interplay between careful observation and rigorous testing that is the touchstone of modern science.

> *Science is nothing but trained and organized common sense, differing from the latter only as a veteran may differ from a raw recruit.*
>
> —Thomas Henry Huxley

Testing the Hypotheses   Scientific hypotheses are tested by *considering their implications* and then *testing those implications* by means of observation or experiment. Consider, again, the problem of the sick airline passengers.

Recall that we were able to quickly rule out our initial hypothesis—that the passengers became sick because of the food they ate on the plane—simply by noting that two of the passengers who became sick did not eat on the plane. In effect, we reasoned like this:

1. If the passengers became sick because of the food they ate on the plane, then all the passengers who became sick must have eaten on the plane.

2. But it is not the case that all the passengers who became sick ate on the plane.

3. So, it is not the case that the passengers became sick because of the food they ate on the plane.

Let *H* stand for the hypothesis that the five passengers became sick because of the food they ate on the plane. Let *I* stand for the implication of *H*, that all the five passengers did, in fact, eat on the plane. The pattern of our reasoning is thus:

1. If *H*, then *I*.
2. Not *I*.
3. So, not *H*.

As you will recall from Chapter 3, this is a deductively valid pattern of reasoning called *modus tollens*. *Modus tollens* arguments are widely used in scientific reasoning as a way of *disconfirming,* or falsifying, scientific hypotheses.

A different pattern of scientific reasoning is often used to *confirm* scientific hypotheses. Consider the reasoning we used to verify our second hypothesis—the stomach flu hypothesis—in our example above:

1. If the five passengers became sick because they came down with the stomach flu, then medical tests should confirm that diagnosis.

2. Medical tests do confirm that diagnosis.

3. So, the five passengers did become sick because they came down with the stomach flu.

Here the pattern of reasoning is

1. If *H,* then *I.*

2. *I.*

3. So, *H.*

This is a pattern of reasoning called *affirming the consequent.* As we saw in Chapter 3, arguments of this pattern are *not* deductively valid. For example:

1. If JFK died in a bungee-jumping accident, then JFK is dead.

2. JFK is dead.

3. So, JFK did die in a bungee-jumping accident.

In this argument, the premises are both true and the conclusion is clearly false. Thus, arguments of this pattern are not deductively valid.

Does this mean that scientific reasoning is inherently flawed? No. Arguments of this pattern can provide *persuasive evidence* for a conclusion, even though they are not deductively valid. For example:

If it rained, then the streets are wet.

The streets are wet.

Therefore, it rained.

Clearly, this argument does not *prove* that it rained. It might be the case that the streets are wet because some pranksters from the local volunteer fire department hosed them down during the night. But given the fact that rain and wet streets are regularly associated in our experience, the fact that the streets are wet does provide strong *presumptive* evidence that it rained. By a similar process of reasoning, scientists are often able to provide strong (but not logically conclusive) evidence for a hypothesis by a process of (1) deducing specific implications from the hypothesis (i.e., asking what *would be true* if the hypothesis were true); (2) testing those implications by observation or experiment; and (3) finding that those implications consistently turn out to be true across a variety of demanding test conditions.

Because of the inherent theoretical and practical difficulties in confirming scientific hypotheses, scientific conclusions can never be 100 percent certain. No matter how much evidence we amass for a scientific "law" of the form "All A's are B's," it is always possible that tomorrow we will discover an A that is *not* a B. No matter how carefully we make our observations or conduct our experiments, it is always possible that some hidden cause or overlooked variable will bias our conclusions. For those reasons, scientific conclusions are always tentative and open to revision.

Does this mean that everything is up for grabs in science? By no means. Many scientific conclusions *can* be affirmed with a high degree of confidence.

One way in which scientists are able to achieve such confident conclusions is by conducting controlled studies.

A *controlled study,* as we noted briefly in Chapter 11, is a rigorous, carefully structured study in which scientists use a baseline comparison, or control group, to answer questions of the form "Does A cause B?" Suppose you want to discover, for example, whether vitamin C prevents colds. Here is the most reliable way to find out:

1. You randomly select a large number of people from the whole population.
2. You randomly divide them into two groups: an *experimental group* and a *control group.*
3. You treat the two groups exactly alike, except that you give the experimental group a specified dosage of vitamin C and you give the control group a *placebo*—that is, a sugar pill or some other known inactive substance.
4. You conduct the study *double-blind.* That is, you make sure that neither the scientists nor the subjects know which of the subjects is getting the vitamin C and which is getting the placebo.
5. You check to see if there is a *statistically significant difference* in the frequency with which the two groups get colds. If the experimental group gets significantly fewer colds than the control group, then it is reasonable to conclude that vitamin C does help prevent colds.[12]

Each of these five steps is generally necessary to establish the effectiveness of a treatment beyond a reasonable doubt.

Randomly selecting a *large* number of subjects from the population as a whole is necessary to ensure that you have a sample that is representative of the population as a whole.

Using a *control group* is necessary to determine that it is the substance being tested, and not some other factor, that explains any apparent causal effects.

Using a *placebo* is necessary because studies have shown that many people will experience improvement in their condition even if they are given a sugar pill or some other treatment that is known to be worthless. The only way to control for this "placebo effect" is to give one group the real stuff (the substance being tested) and another group a placebo, without telling either group which they are receiving.

Making the study *double-blind* is necessary to make sure, first, that the *scientists* don't bias the results by consciously or unconsciously treating one group differently from the other, and second, that the *subjects* don't bias the results by knowing which group is receiving the real stuff and which isn't.

Last, checking to see if there is a *statistically significant difference* in the frequencies of the measured effect is necessary to ensure that any observed differences are not simply due to chance.

The type of controlled study just described is called a *randomized experimental study,* since it involves deliberate "interventions," or tests, on groups that have been randomly selected. Sometimes, for ethical or other reasons, it is not possible to conduct studies of this kind. For example, suppose you wanted to find out if low-level lead poisoning causes hearing loss in young children. Clearly, it would unethical to deliberately expose children to potentially harmful levels of lead. Nevertheless, there are two types of controlled tests you could use to try to answer your question scientifically. Specifically, you could perform either a nonrandomized prospective study or a nonrandomized retrospective study.

In a *nonrandomized prospective study,* you begin with a group of people that has *already been exposed* to a suspected causal agent (in our example, low levels of lead poisoning). This group (or a representative sample) serves as your experimental group. You then find a group of people that has not been exposed to the suspected causal agent but matches the first group in all other relevant respects. (For the study to be reliable, great care must be taken to ensure that the two groups really are alike in all relevant respects.) This second group serves as your control group. You then track the two groups over time. If the experimental group exhibits the suspected effect at significantly higher rates than the control group, this provides evidence for the suspected cause-and-effect relationship.

In a *nonrandomized retrospective study,* you start with a group of people that *already exhibits a certain effect.* You then find a control group that is as similar as possible to the first group except that its members do *not* exhibit the observed effect. You then work backward to try to determine the cause of the observed effect. In our lead-poisoning example, for instance, if a researcher were to find that children with hearing loss suffer from low-level lead poisoning at significantly higher rates than children in the control group, this would provide evidence that such poisoning does cause hearing loss in children.

We are constantly bombarded by claims about "miracle" or "alternative" cures. Does shark cartilage cure cancer? Do magnets ease back pain? Does zinc cure colds? Do copper bracelets alleviate motion sickness? To answer these questions, you might try one or more of the following ever-popular techniques:

Popular Methods for Assessing "Miracle" or "Alternative" Cures

The method of personal experience:	"I tried it, and it worked."
The method of anecdotal evidence:	"Someone else tried it, and it worked."
The method of paid testimonials:	"A famous actor or sports hero was paid to say it works."
The method of ancient practice:	"An ancient practice or folklore says it works." [13]

He who proves things by experience increases his knowledge; he who believes blindly increases his errors.

—Chinese proverb

However, each of these methods has been proven time and again to be unreliable. Sick people often feel better for all sorts of reasons that have nothing to do with any treatments they may be receiving. So, the only way to know be-

Critical Thinking Lapse

Shortly before his death, science writer Carl Sagan published an article in *Parade* magazine, in which he bemoaned the fact that American high school students perform poorly on international math and science tests. A tenth-grade teacher in Minnesota handed out copies of the article to her class and asked what they thought. Here's what some of the students wrote in response (all quotes are verbatim):

· Not a Americans are stupid We just rank lower in school big deal.
· Maybe that's good that we are not as smart as the other countries. So then we can just import all of their products and then we don't have to spend all of our money on the parts for the goods.
· And if other countries are doing better, what does it matter, their most likely going to come over the U.S. anyway?
· Not one kid in this school likes science. I really didn't understand the point of the article. I thought it was very boreing. I'm just not into anything like that.
· I think your facts were inconclusive and the evidence very flimsy. All in all, you raised a good point.[14]

yond a reasonable doubt that an alleged "cure" is effective is through careful, controlled scientific testing.

EXERCISE 15.1

In small groups, design reliable scientific studies to test the following hypotheses. Be prepared to share your study designs with the class as a whole.

1. Magnets can ease chronic back pain.
2. Sleeping with a night-light can cause near-sightedness in young children.
3. Drinking two or three cups of green tea a day reduces the risk of heart attack.
4. Teen pregnancy-prevention programs that emphasize abstinence are less effective than programs that emphasize both abstinence and safe-sex education.
5. The chemical defoliant Agent Orange caused birth defects in the children of American soldiers who served in Vietnam.

THE LIMITATIONS OF SCIENCE

Science is the most reliable method we have for discovering empirically verifiable truths about the physical universe. However, there are many important questions science cannot answer. Among these are fundamental questions of *meaning* and *value*.

Questions of Meaning   Science deals with empirically observable facts. But many of life's most important questions deal not with empirically observable facts but with the meaning or significance of those facts. Thus, for example, science cannot answer fundamental questions such as these:

- Does the universe have a purpose?
- Does life have a purpose?
- Does my life have a purpose?
- What things in life are truly meaningful and important?
- Does my suffering have meaning?
- Does anything I do have enduring meaning or significance?

Although science can provide evidence relevant to these questions, these are not scientific questions, because they are not questions of objective, empirically verifiable fact.[15]

Questions of Value   Questions of value, or *normative questions,* are questions about what is good or bad, right or wrong, better or worse, beautiful or ugly, desirable or undesirable. Here are some examples of questions of value:

- Is abortion always wrong?
- Is capital punishment justifiable?
- Should gay marriage be legal?
- Is it ever right to lie?
- Should human cloning be permitted?
- What is a just society?
- Is freedom more important than equality?

These are important questions we can argue about well or badly, reasonably or unreasonably. But they are not scientific questions, because they cannot be settled by any conceivable empirical observation or experiment.

Some people claim that science can, in fact, answer questions of meaning and value. Specifically, they claim that modern science shows us that the universe has *no* meaning or purpose and that values are only subjective. Often, they defend this claim with some version of the following argument:

1. Either beliefs are mere subjective opinions or they are facts.
2. All facts are scientific facts.
3. Beliefs about meanings or values are not scientific facts.
4. Therefore, beliefs about meanings or values are mere subjective opinions.

This argument can be challenged in several ways. Here let's focus just on (2), the claim that

All facts are scientific facts.

A little reflection shows that this claim cannot possibly be true. The statement "All facts are scientific facts" is not itself a scientific fact. It cannot be validated by any scientific observation or procedure. Consequently, the statement is *self-refuting*—that is, false even in its own terms. The statement cannot be true, because it undermines itself.

Statements such as "All facts are scientific facts" or "Science is the only reliable guide to truth" are not, in fact, scientific claims but expressions of an uncritical form of science-worship called *scientism*. **Scientism** is the view that science is the only reliable way of knowing.[16]

Scientism must be carefully distinguished from science. Whereas science is cautious and empirical, scientism is arrogant and dogmatic. For example, defenders of scientism often claim that science has shown that all the following beliefs are false or unwarranted:

- God exists.
- There is life after death.
- The universe has a purpose.
- Religious experience is sometimes a valid way of knowing.
- Some things are objectively right or wrong.

These claims may be true or false, warranted or unwarranted. Our point is simply that they are philosophical or religious claims, not scientific ones. No amount of scientific evidence will ever prove that the universe has no purpose. You will never hear a scientist exclaim, "Aha! The litmus paper turned blue. I *told* you there are no objective moral values!" Science limits itself to what can be observed, measured, and tested. It doesn't pretend to answer fundamental questions of meaning or value.

Wisdom lies in understanding our limitations.

—Carl Sagan

How to Distinguish Science from Pseudoscience

Pseudoscience is false science—that is, unscientific thinking masquerading as scientific thinking. It is thinking that appears to be scientific but is, in fact, faithless to science's basic values and methods.[17] Because pseudoscientific thinking often looks and sounds like real science, it can be hard for nonscientists to tell them apart. Luckily, there are certain marks of pseudoscience that any educated person can use to distinguish it from true science,[18] including the following:

Six Marks of Pseudoscience
1. It makes claims that are not testable.
2. It makes claims that are inconsistent with well-established scientific truths.
3. It explains away or ignores falsifying data.
4. It uses vague language.

5. It is not progressive.
6. It often involves no serious effort to conduct research.

Scientists, of course, aren't perfect. Consequently, even genuine science will sometimes display one or two of these marks (though rarely in a serious or systematic way). But if an allegedly "scientific" discipline displays several of these marks (or even one in a particularly blatant way), that is a strong indication that it is pseudoscience rather than science.

Absence of Testability   Science seeks to answer questions about the natural world, not through myth, intuition, or guesswork, but through careful observation and experiment. Thus, by the very nature of the scientific enterprise, all genuinely scientific claims must be testable.

A scientific claim is *testable* when we can make observations that would show the claim to be true or false. In thinking about this criterion, we must avoid two common mistakes.

First, scientific claims need not be *directly* testable. Obviously, we can never go back in time to obtain direct observational evidence that birds evolved from dinosaurs. However, there is a great deal of *indirect* evidence that supports this hypothesis, including DNA evidence, structural similarities ("homologies") between birds and certain species of dinosaurs, and transitional fossil forms. The fact that scientists can argue for or against this hypothesis by appealing to such indirect evidence is enough to make the hypothesis a genuinely scientific one.

Second, scientific claims need not be *immediately* testable. For example, when Einstein proposed in 1916 that clocks run faster in space than they do on Earth, it wasn't possible to test this hypothesis experimentally with the technology available at the time. It wasn't until many decades later that the invention of jet aircraft and high-precision atomic clocks allowed scientists to test Einstein's hypothesis and prove that it was true.[19]

Although scientific claims need not be directly or immediately testable, they must at least be *testable in principle*. That is, there must be at least some observations we can realistically imagine making that would show the claim to be true or false. If we can't conceive of any observations that would count for or against the claim, then it is not a claim about empirically observable reality, and hence not a claim that can be studied scientifically.

Here are some examples of claims that are *not* scientifically testable:

There are invisible, completely undetectable gremlins that live deep in the interior of the earth.

An exact duplicate of you exists in a parallel universe that is completely inaccessible to us.

All reality is spiritual; matter is only an illusion.

The earth was once visited by superintelligent aliens who left no trace of their visit.

Every time a bell rings, an angel gets its wings.

Each of these claims may, for all we know, be true. But they are not scientific claims because there is no possible observation or experiment that would tell us whether they are true or false.[20]

To be scientific, a claim must be testable in two senses: it must be verifiable in principle and falsifiable in principle. A claim is *verifiable in principle* when we can imagine some possible observation that would provide good reason to believe that the claim is true. A claim is *falsifiable in principle* when we can imagine some possible observation that would provide good reason to believe that the claim is false.

Pseudoscientists commonly make claims that violate the second of these two conditions. That is, they often make claims that are not falsifiable even in principle.

A good example of this comes from the field of ESP research. ESP (extrasensory perception) is the alleged ability to sense or perceive things without the aid of the five senses. Believers in ESP often point to experiments that seem to provide evidence for claims of the form

> X has genuine powers of ESP.

Unfortunately, every time scientists have sought to repeat such experiments under tightly controlled conditions, no evidence of ESP abilities has been found. To explain this failure, believers in ESP often offer the following two excuses:

- ESP works sometimes but not others.
- ESP doesn't work when skeptics are present.[21]

These excuses may sound plausible—until you notice the kind of "heads-I-win, tails-you-lose" logic behind them. For those who offer such excuses, there can be evidence *for* ESP but not evidence *against* it. By resorting to such rationalizations, believers in ESP render their claim unfalsifiable, and hence unscientific.

Catch-22 cop-outs like this are commonplace in pseudoscience. For example, when researchers in the 1970s failed to confirm poorly controlled experiments suggesting that plants were sensitive and aware, die-hard believers in plant consciousness retorted that this was because the skeptical researchers weren't emotionally "in tune" with the plants.[22] Similarly, when scientists in the 1960s failed to find evidence supporting James V. McConnell's startling claim that cannibalistic flatworms acquired their fellow worms' knowledge, McConnell's colleague Allan Jacobson defended McConnell's work by charging that the scientists lacked feelings for the worms.[23]

> *Fallibility is the hallmark of science.*
> —Philip Kitcher

> *The human species has a perverse streak that runs deep in its nature. It is the capacity for being deceived, the tendency to allow wishes, desires, fantasies, hopes or fears to color the imagination or influence judgment or beliefs.*
> —Paul Kurtz

EXERCISE 15.2

Determine whether the following items are scientifically testable. If so, how? If not, why not?

1. Joey swims well because he was a dolphin in a previous life.
2. Everyone has a guardian angel.

3. Razor blades stay sharp when placed inside a pyramid.
4. Disobeying the law is always morally wrong.
5. The entire universe sprang into existence from nothing five minutes ago, exactly as it then was, apparent fossils in the ground, wrinkles on people's faces, and other signs of age all instantly formed and thoroughly deceptive.[24]
6. The Loch Ness monster exists.
7. Human beings are the most intelligent species in the universe.
8. "The chief purpose of life, for anyone of us, is to increase according to our capacity our knowledge of God by all the means we have, and to be moved by it to praise and thanks" (J. R. R. Tolkien).[25]
9. *Tarot card reader:* You have unresolved issues in your love life.
10. The last surviving dinosaur was a Triceratops.
11. All human actions and choices are fundamentally selfish.
12. Some diseases can be cured by prayer.

Inconsistency with Well-Established Scientific Truths   Science is cumulative and progressive. It constantly changes and grows. Sometimes these changes involve big "paradigm shifts"—whole new ways of looking at the world or a particular area of science, such as that which occurred in the seventeenth century when scientists abandoned the traditional Earth-centered view of the universe. Even in these big revolutions, however, science advances not by throwing out well-established scientific truths but by extending those truths into new domains. Science progresses by building on existing knowledge, not by starting from scratch.

By contrast, in pseudoscience one often encounters claims that conflict with well-confirmed scientific conclusions. Young-earth creationism is a case in point.

Young-earth creationists are religious conservatives who believe, as a literal reading of Genesis would have it, that the universe is only 6,000–10,000 years old, that the theory of evolution is false, and that the fossil record and the major geological features of the earth can be explained by the Great Flood described in Genesis 6:5–8:22.

Young-earth creationism conflicts with many well-established scientific findings. In fact, as Isaac Asimov notes with only slight exaggeration, young-earth creationism cannot be accepted "without discarding all of modern biology, biochemistry, geology, astronomy—in short, without discarding all of science."[26] Consider just a few of the problems faced by those who insist on a literal reading of the Genesis account of Noah's ark and the Great Flood:

- How could a 600-year-old man have constructed a wooden boat larger than any supertanker? How many years would this have taken? How much wood would this have required?

- There are well over a million species of animals alive today. Millions of other animal species are now extinct. According to Genesis, Noah took into the ark seven pairs of all "clean" animals, seven pairs of all birds, and two pairs of all "unclean" animals (Gen. 7:2–5). How could all these living and now-extinct animals have fit on the ark? How could Noah, his wife, three sons, and their wives have gathered and stored enough food and water for all these animals? (Did Noah, for example, travel to Australia to gather the fresh eucalyptus leaves that koalas need to survive? If so, how did he keep them fresh on the journey home?) How could all these creatures have gotten to the ark from the far-flung portions of the globe? How could saltwater marine species have survived in a freshwater environment? How could plants and trees have survived underwater for nearly a year? What did the animals eat when they got off the ark? How did they travel to their current habitats? Why did marsupials, but no placental mammals, manage to get to Australia?

- Young-earth creationists claim that floodwaters covered the entire earth to a depth of three miles. Scientists have calculated that this would require 3.4 times more water than exists in all the earth's oceans.[27] Where did all of this water come from? Where did it all go?

- Earth's continents are covered with sedimentary deposits to an average depth of one mile. In some places, these deposits consist of millions of distinct, alternating layers of light and dark sediment. Geological observations indicate that such deposits take millions of years to form. How could these millions of alternating layers have been laid down in a single flood that lasted less than a year?[28]

- Earth's fossil record shows a remarkably consistent pattern: more primitive plant and animal species in the lower geological strata, more advanced species in the higher. Young-earth creationists seek to explain the fossil record by invoking three principles of "flood geology": (1) lower-dwelling creatures (e.g., marine invertebrates) would be deposited before higher-dwelling creatures (e.g., amphibians and reptiles), (2) less buoyant creatures would be deposited before more buoyant creatures, and (3) less mobile creatures (e.g., tortoises and snails) would be deposited before more mobile creatures (e.g., humans and horses), since the latter would be able to flee to the hilltops before being overwhelmed by the flood.[29]

   This explanation, however, conflicts starkly with both the fossil record and common sense. Marine invertebrates are found at all levels of the fossil record. Flowering plants and trees are never found with more primitive plants and trees. Modern fish are never found at the same levels as ancient extinct fish. Whales and dolphins are always found at higher levels than extinct marine reptiles. And many highly mobile creatures, such as carnivorous dinosaurs and flying reptiles, are always found at lower levels than modern mammals and birds.

In short, young-earth creationism conflicts at many points with extremely well confirmed scientific findings. This demonstrates clearly that it is pseudoscience rather than science.

Explaining Away or Ignoring Falsifying Evidence   Science is self-correcting. It advances by continually seeking to *disprove* its own hypotheses and then learning from its own mistakes. For this reason, scientists don't fear or ignore falsifying evidence; they welcome it as essential to scientific progress. This attitude is reflected in the following story told by the Oxford biologist Richard Dawkins:

> One of the formative experiences of my Oxford undergraduate years occurred when a visiting lecturer from America presented evidence that conclusively disproved the pet theory of a deeply respected elder statesman of our zoology department, the theory that we had all been brought up on. At the end of the lecture, the old man rose, strode to the front of the hall, shook the American warmly by the hand and declared, in ringing emotional tones, "My dear fellow, I wish to thank you. I have been wrong these fifteen years." We clapped our hands red. Is any other profession so generous towards its admitted mistakes?[30]

By contrast, pseudoscientists often ignore or seek to explain away evidence that conflicts with their favored theories. A good example of this involves the famed Israeli entertainer Uri Geller.

Geller, a nightclub magician, became something of a psychic celebrity in the 1970s. Audiences and even respected scientists were astounded at his apparent ability to read minds, peer inside sealed envelopes, and bend keys and spoons with the power of his mind alone. In fact, Geller was a complete fraud, who used parlor tricks and sleight-of-hand to perform his "psychic" feats. He was finally exposed when hidden cameras caught him blatantly cheating. When proof of Geller's guilt was shown to his fans, some sought to explain this by claiming that Geller resorted to cheating only when his psychic powers failed![31]

Or consider another form of psychic humbug that created a stir in the 1970s: "psychic surgery." Psychic surgeons are people who claim to be able to remove diseased tissue or dangerous tumors from a patient's body without conventional surgery. Psychologist Terence Hines describes how the procedure supposedly works:

> As the psychic surgeon performs "surgery," his hand is seen to disappear into the patient's belly and a pool of blood appears. After groping around, apparently inside the body cavity, the psychic surgeon dramatically pulls his hand "out" of the body, clutching what is said to be the tumor or diseased tissue that was causing the patient's problem. The offending tissue is promptly tossed in a handy nearby fire to be purified. When the patient's belly is wiped clean of the blood, no incision is found.[32]

In fact, the procedure is performed through simple sleight-of-hand, with fake blood and animal tissue typically concealed in a false plastic thumb. When

The hallmark of science is not the question "Do I wish to believe this?" but the question "What is the evidence?"

—Douglas J. Futuyma

Those who lose an argument win if, in the discipline or tradition with which they identify, better arguments prevail.

—Holmes Rolston III

laboratory tests showed that the "tumors" were actually chicken livers or other animal remains, some hard-core believers in the procedure remained unconvinced. How amazing, they said, that these miracle workers can not only perform operations without making an incision but can also transform deadly tumors into harmless animal tissue![33]

Rationalizations of this sort are completely opposed to the spirit of science. Science learns from its mistakes or failures; it does not ignore them or sweep them under the rug.

Use of Vague Language   To be scientific, a claim must be testable, and to be testable it must be expressed in clear, specific language. A prediction like "A big change will occur in your life next year" is not a scientific prediction, because it is so vague that almost anything could be counted as confirming it.

Pseudoscientists often use language that is too vague to be testable. Consider "psychic readers," for example. Psychic readers claim to be able to know all sorts of things about people through mysterious "psychic" abilities. Although there is no credible scientific evidence that such abilities are real, psychics employ a variety of ploys to convince people that they are. One of these ploys involves the skillful use of vague or general language.

To be successful, a psychic reader must be able to convince complete strangers that he knows all about their problems and experiences. To accomplish this, psychics use a technique called "cold reading."

Cold reading is a sophisticated set of skills used by palm readers, psychics, tarot card readers, and other professional "readers" for gathering surprisingly accurate information about persons the reader has never met before. The method works largely through a combination of close observation, knowledge of human commonalities, flattering "feel-good" statements, the use of vague, general language, and the natural human tendency to remember hits and forget misses. Here let's focus on psychic readers' use of vague or general language.

A psychic reading usually begins with a "stock spiel"—a set of general statements that apply to practically everybody. Here is a stock spiel that has been shown to be particularly effective with college students:

> Some of your aspirations tend to be pretty unrealistic. At times you are extroverted, affable, sociable, while at other times you are introverted, wary and reserved. You have found it unwise to be too frank in revealing yourself to others. You pride yourself on being an independent thinker and do not accept others' opinions without satisfactory proof. You prefer a certain amount of change and variety, and become dissatisfied when hemmed in by restrictions and limitations. At times you have serious doubts as to whether you have made the right decision or done the right thing. Disciplined and controlled on the outside, you tend to be worrisome and insecure on the inside. . . .
>
> While you have some personality weaknesses, you are generally able to compensate for them. You have a great deal of unused capacity which you have not turned to your advantage. You have a tendency to be critical of yourself. You have a strong need for other people to like you and for them to admire you.[34]

> *A man should never be ashamed to own he has been in the wrong, which is but saying, in other words, that he is wiser today than he was yesterday.*
>
> —Jonathan Swift

Studies have shown that when people are presented with general personality descriptions like this, they are often amazed at their accuracy. Psychologists call this the "Barnum effect," after the nineteenth-century showman P. T. Barnum, who once famously declared, "There's a sucker born every minute."

Psychic readers also use vague, general language in a manipulative technique called *fishing for details*. This is a method in which readers use a combination of vague, exploratory language and close observation of verbal and visual clues to subtly elicit detailed information from a subject. Two types of vague expressions are especially crucial to this technique: multiple-out expressions and try-ons.

Multiple-out expressions are statements or questions that are so vague that they can easily be interpreted, often after the fact, as fitting many different outcomes.[35] For example, a reader might say, "Someone close to you is having problems in his or her love life." Her surprised client might respond, "That's amazing! How did you know my friend Marta is getting a divorce?" Of course, the reader didn't know anything about Marta or her divorce, but the expressions "close to you" and "having problems in his or her love life" are so broad and elastic that almost anyone can think of at least one person (and on reflection, probably several) that fits these descriptions.

Try-ons are subtle statements designed to prompt a reaction, but carefully phrased so that they are easily interpreted as hits but not easily interpreted as misses.[36] For example, a reader might say, "I'm getting a feeling you may have some serious financial concerns you're dealing with." If the client does have "serious financial concerns" (note the vague language), this will naturally be counted as a hit. On the other hand, if the client does not have serious financial concerns, this may not be counted as a miss. After all, the reader hasn't positively stated that the client *does* have serious financial worries—only that that he's *getting a feeling* that the client *may* have such worries.

A skilled cold reader can learn an amazing amount of information about a client simply by making a few vague statements and then watching closely how the client reacts. Extremely subtle visual clues—downcast eyes, a slight nod of the head, an almost imperceptible flushing of the cheeks—can tell an experienced cold reader whether she's on the right track or not. Such abilities can seem uncanny, but in reality there is nothing mysterious or "paranormal" about them. In fact, now that you know the secrets of cold reading, you, too, can amaze your friends with your "psychic" abilities.

Lack of Progressiveness   Science is progressive. It continually advances and grows. Pseudoscience, by contrast, is often intellectually static. It gets stuck at a certain point and stops changing and progressing.

A good example of this is the flat-earth hypothesis supported by the International Flat Earth Research Society. (Yes, there really is such a society.) Flat-Earthers believe that the earth is shaped like a pancake, with the North Pole at the center and an enormous wall of ice at the perimeter. It is this wall of ice, presumably, that prevents ships and planes from falling off the edge of the world or flying off into space.

Many centuries ago, belief in a flat earth was perfectly reasonable. After all, the earth *looks* flat, even from a high mountaintop. Moreover, it doesn't feel like we're whirling around at a thousand miles per hour, as scientists tell us we are. And if the earth is spinning at a thousand miles per hour, why is it that when we shoot an arrow straight up in the air, it lands at our feet instead of many miles away?

These may have been more or less reasonable grounds for belief in a flat earth at one time. But, of course, not any longer. To paraphrase Richard Dawkins: It is absolutely safe to say that if you meet someone who claims not to believe that the earth is round, that person is ignorant, stupid, or insane (or joking, which we would hope is the case).

Failure to Conduct Research   Science is a body of well-confirmed facts. More important, science is a *method,* a set of proven techniques for advancing the frontiers of human understanding. As we have seen, science by its very nature is constantly asking questions, seeking solutions, collecting data, trying out hypotheses, and searching for new insights and deeper understanding. Thus, systematic, disciplined inquiry—in short, *research*—lies at the heart of the scientific enterprise.

Pseudosciences, on the other hand, often fail to engage in any serious program of research. Consider the "water cure," an alternative medical treatment touted by Dr. Fereydoon Batmanghelidj, author of the 1992 book *Your Body's Many Cries for Water.*[37]

The idea behind the water cure is simple. The root cause of most illnesses is lack of water in the body—chronic dehydration. To maintain proper hydration, people should drink eight or ten glasses of water a day, consume salt liberally, and avoid caffeine and alcohol. Among the many diseases Dr. Batmanghelidj claims can be prevented or cured by this simple natural remedy are asthma, arthritis, back pain, cancer, depression, erectile dysfunction, high blood pressure, migraines, muscular dystrophy, and multiple sclerosis.

What proof does Dr. Batmanghelidj have that drinking large amounts of water can actually prevent and cure all of these various diseases? The evidence he presents is almost purely anecdotal. Both Dr. Batmanghelidj's book and his Web site are full of testimonials by people saying, "I tried it and it worked!"

We have seen, however, that anecdotal evidence of this sort is highly unreliable. Every useless quack remedy and snake-oil treatment since the dawn of civilization has been supported by anecdotal evidence. The only way to be sure that a treatment is effective is to test it scientifically under rigorous, controlled conditions.

Bob Butts, a prominent supporter of Dr. Batmanghelidj, has argued that it is pointless to test the water cure scientifically. "The need for testing makes about as much sense as someone suggesting that we do research to see if daylight exists," Butts claims. It is just common sense, he argues, that "the body's cure for drought is water."[38]

It may be common sense that chronic dehydration can be harmful to one's health, but it is not common sense to suppose that dehydration is the root cause of most diseases. This is, in fact, quite implausible in the light of modern medical knowledge. The causes of most diseases are now well understood, and there is no reason to suspect that chronic dehydration is a significant causal factor in most diseases. The water cure may indeed have the amazing health benefits Dr. Batmanghelidj claims, but the only way to *know* whether it does is to subject it to rigorous scientific testing.

In summary, science can be contrasted with pseudoscience in the following ways:

Science	*Pseudoscience*
Makes claims that can be rigorously tested through observation or experiment.	Makes claims that cannot be tested, even in principle.
Makes claims that are consistent with well-established scientific findings.	Makes claims that conflict with well-established scientific findings.
Actively seeks out falsifying data and confronts it openly and honestly.	Ignores or explains away falsifying data.
Uses language that is clear and specific.	Uses language that is vague and imprecise.
Constantly changes and progresses.	Often fails to change or progress.
Engages in serious ongoing research.	Usually makes no serious effort to conduct research.

EXERCISE 15.3

Use what you have learned in this chapter and in previous chapters to evaluate the thinking in the following passages. Identify any marks of pseudoscientific thinking you find.

1. I know herbal medicines work for me. Last night, I had a splitting headache after work. I drank a cup of herbal tea, and before I knew it the headache was gone.

2. I'm convinced Nostradamus, the sixteenth-century astrologer and physician, could foresee the future. Consider this prophecy, for example:

   At night they will think they have seen the sun,
   When they see the half pig man:

> Noise, screams, battles seen fought in the skies:
> The brute beast will be heard to speak.

Clearly, this is a prophecy of the bombing of Baghdad at the outset of the Gulf War. The sun is the light of exploding bombs, the half pig man is a Stealth bomber pilot wearing goggles and an oxygen mask, and the beast that speaks refers to the use of the radio.[39]

3. This paper has been sent to you for Good Luck! The original copy is in New England. It has been around the world nine times. The Luck has been sent to you. You will receive Good Luck in four days. This is no joke.

   You will receive it in the mail. Send copies to the people you think need Good Luck. Do not send cash, as fate has no price. Do not keep this letter. It must leave your hands with 96 hours. . . . Since the copy must make the tour of the world, you must make twenty copies and send them to your friends and associates. After a few days you will get a surprise. This is true even if you are not superstitious.

   Note the following: Constantine Dess received the chain in 1953. He asked his secretary to make twenty copies and send them out. A few days later he won the lottery for two million dollars. Andy Duddit, an office employee, received the letter and he forgot it had to leave his hands in 96 hours. He lost his job. Later, after finding the letter again, he mailed out twenty copies. A few days later he got a better job. Mr. Fairchild received the letter and not believing it, threw it away. Nine days later he died.

   Please send no money. Please do not ignore it! It works. . . . Good Luck is coming your way! (Chain letter)

4. I see where the guy that took the famous 1934 photograph of the Loch Ness monster has confessed the picture was a fake. But I don't believe him. How do we know the guy isn't saying that just to get his name in the newspapers again?

5. Sure, psychics disagree all the time, but so do scientists. One month they tell us coffee is bad for us, the next month they tell us it's not. So science isn't any more reliable than what you call "pseudoscience."

6. I believe in ESP. A few years ago, I woke up in the middle of the night in a cold sweat. I had this terrible feeling my sister was in trouble. I phoned her immediately, and her husband told me she had been in a serious car accident and was in the hospital. Surely that couldn't have been a mere coincidence.

7. *Graphologist* (handwriting expert): I can tell from your firm, flowing script that you like feeling happy, but don't like feeling lonely, depressed, or anxious. In fact, the more miserable you are, the more you dislike it.[40]

8. *Stefan:* Nothing bad ever happens to a person unless he or she deserves it.
   Lucy: O yeah? What about babies that die from AIDS? What have they done to deserve that?
   Stefan: Obviously, they did something bad in a previous life.

9. *Seventeeth-century Cardinal* (explaining why he refuses to look into Galileo's telescope): I have no reason to look in your telescope; I know what I shall see. Aristotle has said there are no moons around planets other than our own, and I trust the authority of Aristotle more than I trust that newfangled instrument of yours.

10. If astrology were valid, twins would presumably have similar fates, since the stars and planets were all in the same positions at the time of their births. Yet plainly there are cases in which one twin dies in childhood and the other lives to a ripe old age. Astrologer Robert Parry offers the following response to this obvious objection: "Twins may not always share the same characteristics, of course, but their lives do generally develop at a similar pace. The differences when they occur are subtle ones, which is exactly what astrology would expect. Even in your example, where one twin dies while the other lives, clearly the same event, namely death, has entered both lives at the same time. One twin dies, while the other is touched radically by the sorrow and tragedy of the death of the other. Surely this is an argument for, rather than against astrology."[41]

11. *Earl:* Aliens abduct millions of people every year. They take them up to their spaceships and conduct all kinds of weird genetic and reproductive experiments on them.
    Zoe: Why don't these alien spacecraft ever show up on our radar?
    Earl: They have cloaking devices. Their technology is vastly superior to ours.
    Zoe: How come these aliens never set off burglar alarms or appear on home surveillance cameras? Why don't husbands or wives ever wake up and notice their spouses are missing?
    Earl: I told you, they're much too advanced ever to be detected by us. They probably just beam people up to their spaceships and put android lookalikes in their places.

12. God always answers prayers. But sometimes He gives us what is good for us, not what we ask for.

13. Of course dowsing works. I've seen my grandfather do it several times. Every time his well on his farm runs dry, he takes a forked stick and walks out into his pasture. When the stick dips toward to the ground, he knows just where to dig. Works every time.

14. Many so-called "scientific" studies have cast doubt on magnet therapy—a form of alternative treatment that claims that magnets can relieve pain and a host of other bodily ills. But why should we trust these studies? Doctors, scientists, and pharmaceutical companies stand to lose billions if this simple, natural remedy were shown to be effective.

15. Whenever harmonious music is being played in the presence of your crystal or amethyst, the mood and thoughts of the composer become deeply embedded within the very heart of the crystal and if you "listen" to the crystal afterward with your inner ear, you will often be able to pick up the esoteric meaning of the music itself. (From a healing crystals Web site)

Two Case Studies in Pseudoscience and the Paranormal

Let's now consider two extended examples of pseudoscientific thinking: astrology and paranormal explanations of near-death experiences.

Astrology

Can the stars and the planets affect people's personality and destiny? For thousands of years, believers in the ancient divinatory art of astrology have claimed that they can. Even in our own advanced scientific age, belief in astrology remains surprisingly strong. Polls show that about 25 percent of adult Americans believe that astrology works.[42] More than 1,200 U.S. newspapers have a daily column on astrology. There are ten times more astrologers in the United States than there are astronomers.[43] And more money is spent each year in the United States on astrology than is spent on all astronomical research combined (excluding NASA).

You can make a better living in the world as a soothsayer than as a truthsayer.

—George Lichtenberg

Belief in astrology is very ancient. It began more than 4,000 years ago in Mesopotamia (modern-day Iraq and Syria), and then spread throughout the ancient world. The form in which astrology exists today in the Western world is based largely on the work of Ptolemy, a Greek astronomer and astrologer who lived in Alexandria in the second century A.D.

Astrologers claim that human personality, behavior, and destiny are all strongly influenced by the position of the sun, moon, planets, and stars at the time of one's birth. Here, in a nutshell, is how astrology supposedly works:

Each year the sun appears to travel a certain path around the earth. This path is called the *ecliptic.* Astrologers take a 16-degree-wide belt of sky centering on the ecliptic and divide it into twelve equal 30-degree parts. These are the familiar *signs of the zodiac:* Aquarius, Pisces, Libra, Capricorn, and so forth. These signs are so named because they correspond roughly with the star-groupings, or constellations, that bear the same names. A person's "sun sign" is the sign of the zodiac the sun appeared to be in on the day of his or her birth. Thus, for example, anyone born between December 23 and January 19 is a Capricorn because the sun appears to be in the same part of the sky as the constellation Capricorn during that period.[44]

Sun signs are the basis for "pop astrology," the kind of astrology you find in newspaper horoscopes and popular astrology Web sites. Professional astrologers tend to be highly skeptical of these one-size-fits-all daily horoscopes. For really serious astrology, they insist, you need to take into account not only a person's sun sign but also the precise time and place of his or her birth, the positions of the planets, and a host of other factors.

Despite its antiquity and widespread acceptance, astrology has absolutely no scientific basis. Let's look at six reasons why this is so:[45]

1. Astrologers fail to identify a plausible physical force or mechanism that could explain astrology's alleged influences.
2. Astrologers fail to provide a convincing response to the problem of precession.
3. Astrologers fail to deal adequately with the discovery of three new planets and other recent astronomical discoveries.
4. Astrologers often use vague, untestable language.

5. Astrologers fail to offer a convincing response to the problems of time twins and mass disasters.
6. Scientific tests do not support astrology's claims.

Astrologers Fail to Identify a Plausible Physical Force or Mechanism
Astrologers claim that extremely remote celestial objects have powerful effects on human personality, destiny, and behavior. But how, exactly? What forces or mechanisms could possibly explain such remarkable effects?

For the ancients, the answer was simple: magic. The stars and planets were believed to be divine and were often associated with particular mythological beings. The planet Venus, for example, was named after the Roman goddess of love and beauty. Accordingly, it was believed that anyone born under the influence of the planet Venus must be romantic, sensitive, emotional, and artistic. Similarly, anyone born under the influence of the planet Mars was thought to be aggressive and courageous, since Mars was the Roman god of war.

We, of course, no longer believe in these mythical associations. So what mechanisms or forces could possibly explain astrology's alleged influences?

Astrologers have proposed five possible explanations:

• Gravity
• Tidal forces
• Electromagnetic forces
• Magnetic fields
• Emitted particles

Unfortunately, none of these mechanisms is an even remotely plausible candidate. Gravity, tidal forces, and electromagnetic forces are all far too weak to have any significant effect on human behavior over the vast distances of space. In fact, many ordinary objects around you exert far stronger forces on you than remote planets and stars. For example, the book you are now holding exerts about *one billion times* as much tidal force on you as does the planet Mars.[46] And magnetic fields and emitted particles are even less plausible mechanisms, since not all astrologically significant celestial objects have magnetic fields (Venus and the moon do not, for example), and none of the planets in our solar system emits any particles.[47]

Of course, it is possible that there is some mysterious, not-yet-discovered force that could explain astrology's alleged influences on human life. But as astronomer George Abell points out, this force would have to be one with very strange properties:

[I]t would have to emanate from some but not all celestial bodies, have to affect some but not all things on earth, and its strength could not depend on the distances, masses, or other characteristics of those [celestial bodies] giving rise to it. In other words it would lack the universality, order, and harmony found for every other force and natural law ever discovered that applies in the real universe.[48]

Although the existence of such a force cannot be completely ruled out, it seems very unlikely given what we know about the fundamental laws and forces of nature.

The Problem of Precession   Scientists have long known that, owing to the gravitational pull of the sun and the moon, the earth slowly "wobbles" in its orbit, much like a spinning top or gyroscope. As a consequence, the apparent positions of the stars relative to the sun slowly change over time. This is a phenomenon astronomers call *precession*. This shift in the apparent positions of the stars is extremely slow—only about 1 degree every 71 years—but in the two thousand years since the signs of the zodiac became fixed, the change has been significant. The position of the sun relative to the constellations has now shifted almost a whole astrological sign to the east. So, for example, if your horoscope says you are an Aries, it is very likely that the sun was actually in the constellation of Pisces on the day of your birth. Professional astrologers are well aware of this fact but are divided over the best way to deal with it. Most astrologers simply shrug off the problem, claiming that "constellations are simply not that important."[49] This response, however, is inconsistent with the vital role constellations have always played in astrological theory, and it leaves it utterly mysterious how an arbitrary division of signs can fundamentally affect human character and destiny. Other astrologers claim that the constellations "remember" the influences they had two thousand years ago! However, they fail to explain why the constellations don't remember the influences they had in even earlier epochs.[50]

Astrology Is Not Progressive   We have seen that pseudoscience, unlike real science, is often static; it fails to change in the light of advancing knowledge. Let's consider two examples of astrology's stagnant character: its inability to deal convincingly with the discovery of three new planets and other recently discovered celestial objects, and its failure to take into account the arbitrary nature of constellations.

For thousands of years, astrologers consistently taught that there are only seven celestial bodies in the solar system other than Earth: the sun, the moon, Mercury, Venus, Mars, Saturn, and Jupiter. In recent centuries, however, astronomers have discovered three new planets (Uranus in 1781, Neptune in 1846, and Pluto in 1930), as well as a multitude of new moons and many large asteroids and comets. These recent discoveries pose two major problems for astrology.

First, if astrology were true, why weren't astrologers able to deduce the existence of Uranus, Neptune, and Pluto long before scientists discovered them? If, as astrologers now claim, these planets have effects on human life, then astrologers' predictions must have been systematically in error for the past two thousand years.[51] Why during these centuries wasn't there even a single astrologer who noticed these errors and predicted the eventual discovery of unknown planets to account for them?[52]

Second, why is it that only stars, planets, the sun, and our own moon have any astrological influences? Since the time of Galileo (1564–1642), scientists have discovered more than fifty additional moons in our solar system. Two of these moons (Ganymede and Titan) are larger than the planets Pluto and Mercury. In addition, many thousands of asteroids have been discovered. Some of these asteroids are larger than all but a few of the moons in our solar system. (One asteroid has even been found to have its own satellite.) Why does remote Pluto, for example, have astrological influences when closer and, in a few instances, more massive moons and asteroids do not?[53]

Another problem for astrology is its failure to deal convincingly with our modern scientific understanding of constellations. Ancient astrologers believed that the constellations really were fixed, neutrally observable "pictures in the sky." We now know that this is totally false. Other cultures see quite different pictures from those we see; the appearance of the constellations changes over time (1 million years ago the Big Dipper looked like a spear to our ancestors on the African savanna); and stars that appear to us to be close together in space may in fact be millions of light-years apart from one another.

Why is this a problem for astrology? Because the personality characteristics astrologers associate with particular sun signs presuppose that the constellations are real rather than merely perceiver-relative human constructions. Consider the following list, which shows the constellations of the zodiac, their namesakes, and selected sun-sign personality characteristics:

Constellation and Symbol	Namesake	Selected Characteristics
Aries	ram	headstrong, impulsive, quick-tempered
Taurus	bull	plodding, patient, stubborn
Gemini	twins	vacillating, split personality
Cancer	crab	clinging, protective exterior shell
Leo	lion	proud, forceful, born leader
Virgo	virgin	reticent, modest
Libra	scales	just, harmonious, balanced
Scorpius	scorpion	secretive, troublesome, aggressive
Sagittarius	archer	active, aims for target
Capricornus	goat	tenacious
Aquarius	water carrier	humanitarian, serving mankind
Pisces	fish	attracted to sea and alcohol[54]

Notice the kind of thinking implicit in these associations: "The constellation Taurus sort of looks like a bull. Bulls are stubborn and plodding. Therefore,

Tauruses must be stubborn and plodding." This makes clear at a glance the kind of magical thinking that has always been the true basis of astrology.

Astrology Uses Vague, Untestable Language   One of the clearest signs that astrology is a pseudoscience is its frequent use of vague, untestable language. Here, for example, is the November 6, 2000, daily horoscope for Taurus people offered on the Excite.com astrology Web site:

> *Taurus* (April 20–May 20): Your plans with friends could go awry. If you're stubborn enough to keep going, you may still achieve your goals. The longer you hang on, the more likely you are to achieve your goals.

This passage contains two deceptive uses of language. First, it uses the weasel words "could" and "may." *Weasel words,* as you will recall, are words used to water down a claim so that it ends up saying much less than it may appear to say. In saying only that "your plans with friends *could* go awry" and that "you *may* achieve your goals," the writer is making claims that are so vague and highly qualified that almost nothing could be counted as disproving them. Second, the passage uses general Barnum-type language that can readily be interpreted as applying to almost anyone. (Isn't it virtually true by definition that the longer you keep going the more likely you are to achieve your goals?) By using vague and deceptive language like this, a skillful horoscope writer can fool millions into believing that he or she can really foresee the future.

Of course, astrologers do sometimes make statements that are specific enough to be checked. For example, according to the astrology.com Web site, the principal writer of this chapter, as an Aquarian, should have the following preferences in music:

> **Music:** The Water Bearer's favorite goal is to change the world. You've already worn out several copies of the *Hair* soundtrack, as you like to listen to music based on an era where everyone was trying to make the world a better and more unified place. From the Grateful Dead to the Allman Brothers, you are now likely to be an avid fan of Phish—or any party band for that matter. Aquarians are social and appreciate a good sing-along classic.[55]

As a matter of fact, my tastes run more to classical and folk music—though I confess I do sometimes find myself humming some of the racier lyrics from *Hair.*

—————
EXERCISE 15.4
—————

I. Visit the astrology.com Web site at http://www.astrology.com (or a similar Web site) and check out the supposed preferences for food, music, sports, and television for people with your sun sign. Then check out the alleged preferences for your parents. Do you find any difference in the accuracy of the profiles? If so, what might explain the difference?

Science is what we have learned about how not to fool ourselves.
—Richard Feynman

The astrologers have an easy game when they warn us, as they do, of great and imminent changes and revolutions; their prophecies are present and palpable; no need to go to the stars for that.
—Montaigne

Astrology rests on a proven principle, namely that if you know the exact positions where the moon and the various planets were when a person was born, you can get this person to give you money.
—Dave Barry

II. Can people accurately pick out their own daily horoscopes? Here is a simple way to find out. The day before your next class meeting, a student volunteer will copy down the twelve daily horoscopes from a major daily newspaper or an astrology Web site. The horoscopes should be typed or pasted randomly on a single page, numbered 1–12, with all references to specific zodiac signs removed. Here's an example of how the page might look:

> **Please write your zodiac sign here:** _____
> **Circle the number that best describes the type of day you had yesterday.**
> (1) Love is a whirlwind. This is a day when you'll explain, announce and persuade. On the job, realize that you have more to offer.
> (2) A lucky meeting produces revenue. There are monetary limits on fun, but this should only be an incentive to the creative imagination.
> (3) A dashing, desirous urgency manifests itself in marvelous romantic gestures. Ignore one who tries to compete with you. . . .[56]

[And so on, for all twelve horoscopes.]
Make enough copies for each student in the class, then administer the test and tabulate the results.

The Problems of Time Twins and Mass Disasters   Most astrologers claim that a person's destiny is strongly influenced by the position of the stars and the planets at the moment of that person's birth. Since ancient times, critics have noted two obvious objections to such a claim. First, if astrology were true, shouldn't *time twins* (i.e., biologically unrelated persons born at exactly the same time and place) have very similar destinies?[57] Second, how can astrologers explain *mass disasters*—tragic events such as earthquakes or hurricanes in which hundreds or thousands of people may die at the same time? Are we to believe, for example, that everyone who drowned aboard the *Titanic* had the same foreboding horoscope?

Astrologers commonly respond to the time-twins objection by claiming that there are many well-documented cases in which time twins have been found to have led remarkably similar lives.[58] One often-cited example involves actor Rudolph Valentino. When Valentino died, the movie industry launched a nationwide search for a double. One of the most convincing candidates turned out to have been born in the same area and on the same day as Valentino.[59]

However, isolated examples like this don't prove anything. One would expect to find a certain number of "amazing parallels" like this purely by chance. The relevant question is whether time twins exhibit similarities in personality, destiny, career choice, and so forth *that cannot be explained by mere chance*. Studies of time twins have found no evidence that this is the case.[60]

Astrologers often attempt to explain mass disasters by claiming that whole *nations* have horoscopes just as individuals do, and that sometimes the horoscopes of nations override those of individuals.[61] This response is unconvincing for several reasons. First, many mass disasters (e.g., some hurricanes, earthquakes, and plane crashes) involve people from many different nations.

Second, there are many relevant differences between nations and individuals. For example, nations, unlike individuals, often have fluid borders and no clear "date of birth." Third, there is no agreement among astrologers about how to determine when a nation's horoscope will override those of individuals. Finally, numerous studies have found no evidence that astrologers can accurately predict major national events.[62]

Scientific Tests Do Not Support Astrology's Claims   In science, the bottom-line question is always: Does it work? Dozens of scientific studies of astrology have been conducted over the past few decades. The clear verdict of these studies is that astrology does *not* work. Let's look at a few representative studies.

Many astrologers claim there is a correlation between sun sign and physical appearance. According to astrologer Sandra Shulman, for example, those born under the sign of Aries tend to be roundheaded and snub-nosed, with reddish or light brown hair.[63] To test such claims, R. B. Culver and P. A. Ianna surveyed hundreds of college students. They studied more than thirty physical characteristics, including height, weight, hair color, skin complexion, and head size. Not a single physical feature they examined had any correlation with sun sign.[64]

Most astrologers also claim that some sun signs make for compatible personal relationships and others do not. If that were true, reasoned psychologist Bernard I. Silverman, then pairs with compatible sun signs should show higher rates of marriage and lower rates of divorce than pairs with incompatible sun signs. However, when Silverman looked at the birth dates of 2,978 Michigan couples who were getting married and 478 couples who were getting divorced, he found no correlation between sun sign and rates of marriage or divorce.[65]

Another claim commonly made by astrologers is that a person's sun sign strongly influences his or her choice of a career. Many astrologers claim, for example, that Leos tend to become politicians. To test such claims, John D. McGervey looked at the birth dates of 16,634 scientists and 6,475 politicians. He found no correlation between sun sign and either of these two career choices.[66] Studies of some sixty other careers and occupations have likewise found no correlation between astrological sign and choice of profession.[67]

In addition, most astrologers also claim that personality is strongly influenced by sun signs. Psychologist W. Grant Dahlstrom and his associates tested this claim by administering the Minnesota Multiphasic Personality Inventory (MMPI) to 2,600 adults. They found no significant correlations between sun sign and any of the many personality traits measured by the MMPI.[68]

It might be objected that statistical studies of this kind are not fair tests of astrology, since sun signs alone are not enough for an accurate astrological reading. However, virtually all astrologers admit that sun signs have at least some influence on personality, career choice, and so on. If that were true, then some systematic statistical correlations should be discoverable.

In fact, several scientific studies have been done that involved complete astrological birth charts, not just subjects' sun signs. One of the best known of these studies was conducted by San Diego State University physicist Shawn Carlson.

Carlson gave thirty of the world's most prominent astrologers the complete natal horoscopes of 116 subjects. He then asked the astrologers to match these horoscopes against three California Personality Inventory (CPI) psychological profiles. One profile was the subject's actual psychological profile; the other two were chosen at random. The result: the astrologers did no better than chance.[69]

A few scientific studies have found evidence that *weakly* supports certain claims of astrology. For example, Michael Gauquelin, a respected French researcher, published a study in 1955 that indicated a statistically significant correlation between certain positions of the planet Mars and the births of sports champions. More recent studies, however, have generally failed to replicate Gauquelin's findings, and serious questions have been raised about the reliability of his data.[70]

In short, scientific tests do *not* support astrology's claims. For these and other reasons we have noted, astrology must be regarded as a pseudoscience.

> My business is to teach my aspirations to conform themselves to fact, not to try to make facts harmonize with my aspirations.
>
> —Thomas Henry Huxley

EXERCISE 15.5

I. Discuss the following questions in small groups. Be prepared to share the highlights of your discussions with the class as a whole.

1. Do you agree that astrology is a pseudoscience? Why or why not?
2. If astrology has no scientific basis, why do so many people believe in it? What accounts for its persistent appeal?

II. In small groups, design a scientific study to test the hypothesis that time twins tend to have similar personalities and destinies.

Near-Death Experiences

What happens to us when we die? Do we simply cease to exist, our brief flicker of consciousness extinguished forever? Or is there an afterlife, another realm or dimension in which our lives, and the lives of those we love, will in some way continue? Belief in some form of life after death has been common in virtually all cultures and ages. In general, these beliefs have been based purely on religious faith or philosophical arguments. However, many people now claim there is convincing *scientific* evidence for life after death. The most compelling evidence of this kind comes from near-death experiences (NDEs).

The current interest in near-death experiences began with the publication, in 1975, of Raymond Moody's best-selling book *Life After Life*.[71] In it he documented the experiences of more than a hundred people who had been declared "clinically dead" or had come close to death and had then been revived. Many of these people reported strikingly similar experiences. Based on their reports, Moody composed the following now-famous "composite" account of a typical near-death experience (NDE):

> A man is dying and, as he reaches the point of greatest physical distress, he hears himself pronounced dead by his doctor. He begins to hear an uncomfortable noise, a loud ringing or buzzing, and at the same time feels himself moving very rapidly through a long dark tunnel. After this, he suddenly finds himself outside of his own physical body, but still in the immediate physical environment, and he sees his own body from a distance, as though he is a spectator. He watches the resuscitation attempt from this unusual vantage point and is in a state of emotional upheaval.
>
> After a while, he collects himself and becomes more accustomed to his odd condition. He notices that he still has a "body," but one of a very different nature and with very different powers from the physical body he has left behind. Soon other things begin to happen. Others come to meet and to help him. He glimpses the spirits of relatives and friends who have already died, and a loving, warm spirit of a kind he has never encountered before—a being of light—appears before him. This being asks him a question, nonverbally, to make him evaluate his life and helps him along by showing him a panoramic, instantaneous playback of the major events of his life. At some point he finds himself approaching some sort of barrier or border, apparently representing the limit between earthly life and the next life. Yet, he finds that he must go back to earth, that the time for his death has not yet come. At this point he resists, for by now he is taken up with his experiences in the afterlife and does not want to return. He is overwhelmed by intense feelings of joy, love and peace. Despite his attitude, though, he somehow reunites with his physical body and lives.
>
> Later he tries to tell others, but he has trouble doing so. In the first place, he can find no human words adequate to describe these unearthly episodes. He also finds that others scoff, so he stops telling other people. Still, the experience affects his life profoundly, especially his views about death and its relationship to life.[72]

Since Moody's book appeared, an enormous amount of research has been done on NDEs. For the most part, this research has supported Moody's findings. Studies have found that NDEs are relatively common (about 40 percent of people who survive cardiac arrest report them);[73] that they are fundamentally similar in people of all ages, backgrounds, and cultures; and that they have often have many of the characteristic features Moody describes. Based on the research to date, we can identify the following core features of NDEs:

1. Feelings of peace and serenity
2. The buzzing or ringing noise
3. Separation from the body
4. The dark tunnel

5. Meeting others
6. The Being of Light
7. The life review
8. The barrier or border
9. Reluctance to come back

Studies have shown that those elements tend to occur in that order, and that the first few features occur much more often than the others.[74]

Susan Blackmore, Reader in Psychology at the University of the West of England, Bristol, has been researching paranormal phenomena for over twenty years and is widely considered one of the world's leading experts on NDEs. In her 1993 book, *Dying to Live: Near-Death Experiences,* Blackmore argues that there are two main alternative explanations for NDEs: the "afterlife hypothesis" and the "dying brain hypothesis." According to the afterlife hypothesis, NDEs really are what they appear to be: paranormal glimpses of a postmortem spiritual world. According to the dying brain hypothesis, NDEs are creations of the dying brain: hallucinations, fantasies, and mental constructs that will ultimately stop when the brain's activity stops. Let's consider which of these two hypotheses is better supported by the available evidence.

Arguments for the Afterlife Hypothesis   Blackmore considers four arguments for the afterlife hypothesis. She calls these the consistency argument, the reality argument, the paranormal argument, and the transformational argument. Let's look at each in turn.

The Consistency Argument   NDEs are remarkably consistent in broad detail. The core features of NDEs appear to be very similar in people of all ages and religious and cultural backgrounds. The best explanation for this amazing uniformity, it is claimed, is that NDEs really are glimpses of a spiritual world.

This argument is unconvincing for two reasons. First, NDEs are by no means always the same. Some people have terrifying, hell-like experiences.[75] Only a small percentage of NDEers report seeing a light, meeting others, or experiencing a panoramic life review.[76] Some NDEers report having a grayish, transparent "astral" body, and others do not.[77] Children often report being met by living playmates (or even animals) rather than by deceased relatives or a Being of Light.[78] And people of different religious backgrounds often report meeting religious figures or receiving messages that are unique to their own religious traditions.[79]

Second, even if NDEs are often consistent in basic detail, that doesn't mean the experiences are genuinely paranormal. As Blackmore argues, it might mean only that we have similar brains that react in similar ways to the physical and psychological stresses of dying.

The Reality Argument   Unlike vivid dreams or hallucinations, NDEs often feel totally real and compelling. The best explanation for this, it is claimed, is that they are genuine experiences of a paranormal reality.

There are two major problems with this argument. First, something's seeming real doesn't mean that it is. It is common, in fact, for people to experience vivid visual or auditory hallucinations that they mistakenly believe to be real. (There is good reason to think many alien abduction stories fall into this category.[80]) Second, NDEs often include features that can't possibly be real. Studies have shown, for example, that a significant number of people allegedly encountered on "the other side" in NDEs are in fact still living.[81] This makes clear how problematic it is to infer that NDEs must be real because they feel real.

The Paranormal Argument   Many NDEs ostensibly involve paranormal phenomena (e.g., out-of-body experiences and ESP) that cannot be explained by science. Some unconscious or "clinically dead" NDEers, for example, have described in detail the hospital procedures used to resuscitate them from cardiac arrest. They describe specific visual or auditory experiences (e.g., how their bodies looked from above) that apparently could not have been obtained through ordinary means. This is proof, it is claimed, that these experiences are real.

Arguments of this sort can never be refuted completely, because of the inherent difficulties in "proving a negative." No one could possibly prove, for example, that *no* alleged UFO or Bigfoot sightings are genuine. No matter how successful skeptics are in producing ordinary explanations for apparently extraordinary phenomena, there will always be a residuum of cases that cannot readily be explained. However, as Blackmore argues, there are good reasons to doubt that any NDE experiences are truly paranormal or supernatural.

Being declared "clinically dead" does not mean that a person is totally unconscious. Studies have shown that people who appear to be completely unconscious or even dead sometimes have a great deal of sensory information about what is happening around them. For this reason, hospital personnel are trained not to discuss a dying or anesthetized patient's illness or possible demise as though he or she were known to be completely unconscious.[82]

Moreover, memory and imagination also seem to play a key role in many typical NDEs. As Blackmore notes, when our normal sources of information about the world are cut off, as often happens when we are dying, the brain tries to construct a coherent model of reality by using the only sources of information still available to it, namely, memory and imagination. But memories, as psychologist Ronald Siegel points out, are often reconstructed from a fictitious bird's-eye point of view. Try to recall, for example, the last time you walked on a beach. If you are like most people, you will see yourself from above. According to Blackmore, this feature of our memories helps explain out-of-body experiences that often occur in NDEs.[83]

It is also noteworthy that there appear to be no well-confirmed cases in which a person who has been blind from birth has experienced an accurate visual perception as part of a NDE.[84] This is further evidence that NDEs take place within the body, rather than outside it.

In short, as Blackmore argues at length, there appear to be no clear-cut, well-documented cases in which a NDEer could *not* have obtained information by some ordinary means.[85] Critical thinking, as we have seen, requires that extraordinary claims be accepted only if they are supported by extraordinary evidence. Consequently, the paranormal argument does not give us good reason to accept the afterlife hypothesis.

The Transformational Argument   NDEs change lives. People who experience NDEs often become more hopeful, generous, spiritual, and joyful. Their attitudes toward life and death are often permanently altered. This is evidence, it is claimed, that these experiences are real.

> *How easily . . . do our dreams turn out to be wishful dreaming, our images illusions, our revelations imaginations!*
>
> —Hans Küng

This argument also faces two major problems. First, as Theodore Schick, Jr., and Lewis Vaughn point out, the fact that one has been transformed by an experience does not prove its reality.[86] Think of the life-changing insights one can gain by reading a great novel or play, for example. Similarly, dreams, drug-induced hallucinations, and false alien abduction experiences can also produce momentous life changes.

Second, simply coming close to death can affect one's priorities deeply. Those who experience a close brush with death often come away with a renewed sense of life's preciousness and fragility. That alone can prompt many people to rethink their fundamental attitudes toward life and death.[87]

In sum, none of the four main arguments for the afterlife hypothesis provides good reason to accept it. Let us turn, then, to consider the major alternative explanation of NDEs: the dying brain hypothesis.

Arguments for the Dying Brain Hypothesis   The dying brain hypothesis asserts that NDEs are fantasies, hallucinations, and distorted perceptions of the dying brain. There are several leading versions of the dying brain hypothesis. Let's consider three: the birth memory hypothesis, the cerebral anoxia hypothesis, and the neurochemistry hypothesis.

The Birth Memory Hypothesis   According to the birth memory hypothesis, NDEs are vivid recollections of the birth experience. In this interpretation, the traumatic experience of dying triggers long-forgotten memories of moving down the birth canal (the dark tunnel), emerging into the dazzling radiance of the hospital delivery room (moving into the light), and being welcomed by heroic, dimly perceived beings of light (the birth attendants and one's parents).[88]

This is an intriguing hypothesis, but it confronts many problems. First, studies of infant cognition show that newborns' brains are probably too undeveloped to preserve any memories of the birth experience. Second, the birth canal is an extremely tight fit for babies and probably wouldn't feel at all like moving through a tunnel. Third, birth is almost certainly an intensely stressful experience for babies, not the calm, blissful experience NDEers report. Finally, and most tellingly, studies have shown that people who were born by

Cesarean section (and hence never moved through the birth canal) are just as likely to have NDEs as people who were not.[89]

The Cerebral Anoxia Hypothesis   When we die, we stop breathing and our brains are deprived of oxygen. Studies have shown that cerebral anoxia (lack of oxygen to the brain) can produce experiences very similar to NDEs, including loud ringing or buzzing noises, feelings of calm and well-being, experiences of floating above the body, and bright lights. Anoxia can also cause sensations of moving down a dark tunnel. When the brain is deprived of oxygen, nerve cells in the visual cortex can begin to fire randomly. This, in turn, causes "stripes" in the visual field that the brain may interpret as moving down a tunnel. Because cerebral anoxia can cause many of the same experiences commonly reported in NDEs, some researchers have suggested that NDEs simply _are_ hallucinations caused by oxygen deprivation to the brain.[90]

Most NDE researchers acknowledge that cerebral anoxia plays some role in producing at least some NDEs. But there are many reasons why anoxia is unlikely to be the complete explanation. First, anoxia often causes effects that are not typically found in NDEs (e.g., tiredness and confusion). Moreover, hallucinations caused by anoxia rarely involve features such as the panoramic life review or a meeting others. Further, hallucinations due to oxygen deprivation are almost always recognized as being mere hallucinations and rarely produce permanent, life-transforming changes. Finally, blood-gas tests suggest that NDEs _may_ occur in persons who are not suffering from anoxia.[91]

The Neurochemistry Hypothesis   According to the neurochemistry hypothesis, NDEs are vivid hallucinations resulting from a combination of biochemical and psychological causes. Like Blackmore, we shall argue that the neurochemistry hypothesis offers the best explanation of NDEs.[92]

In support of the neurochemistry hypothesis, Blackmore notes that NDE-type experiences occur frequently in persons who are not, in fact, close to dying. We have seen that many NDE-like effects can be caused by oxygen deprivation. NDE-type experiences can also be obtained by sensory deprivation or, more commonly, by drugs, such as hashish, LSD, opium, or dissociative anesthetics such as ketamine. Sometimes such drugs produce NDE-type features in isolation; for example, sensations of moving down a dark tunnel are common drug-induced hallucinations. Occasionally, an apparently _complete_ NDE, one having all the elements of an NDE-type experience, can occur under the influence of various drugs.[93]

Blackmore argues that NDEs are hallucinations caused mainly by neurochemical events in the dying brain. She suggests there are two principal neurochemical causes: endorphins and cerebral anoxia.

Endorphins are natural morphinelike substances produced by the brain in response to pain, injury, or certain other kinds of stress. The "runner's high" often reported by long-distance runners is caused by endorphins, for example. When people are dying, their brains and spinal cords may be bathed in these natural painkillers. This explains why so many NDEers report feelings of peace, serenity, and well-being, Blackmore argues.[94]

We have also seen that cerebral anoxia can produce many of the same effects as NDEs, including loud ringing or buzzing noises, sensations of floating, out-of-body experiences, tunnel experiences, and bright lights. According to Blackmore, all these features commonly associated with NDEs are plausibly explained by anoxia.

However, as Blackmore acknowledges, this fails to explain a number of other features commonly reported in NDEs. In particular, it doesn't explain experiences of meeting others, the loving Being of Light, and the panoramic life review. How can these be accounted for on Blackmore's neurochemistry hypothesis?

The life review, Blackmore believes, has a straightforward psychological explanation. Rapid, even seemingly "instantaneous" life reviews ("My whole life flashed before my eyes!") are common in people who believe, rightly or wrongly, that they are close to death. Blackmore also suggests that there may be a neurochemical basis for at least some near-death life reviews. Studies have shown that endorphins and anoxia can cause nerve cells to fire randomly in certain parts of the brain that store memories, producing rapid and extremely vivid flashbacks.[95]

Finally, how can we explain experiences of meeting departed relatives and the loving Being of Light? As real as these may seem, they are simply comforting hallucinations, says Blackmore—consoling fantasies created by the dying brain as it faces the fear and uncertainty of its own imminent extinction.

The neurochemistry hypothesis has two major advantages over the afterlife hypothesis, Blackmore notes. First, it is theoretically simpler. It posits no mysterious immaterial souls or "other realms." Instead, it explains all the core elements of NDEs in terms of relatively well understood physiological and psychological causes. Second, it explains features of NDEs that are not satisfactorily explained by the afterlife hypothesis—such as why many NDEs include encounters with still-living persons and why people of different religious backgrounds often encounter religious figures and receive messages that are distinctive to their own cultural or religious traditions. For these reasons, we agree with Blackmore that the neurochemistry hypothesis offers the best available interpretation of NDEs.

It is important to note, however, that the neurochemistry hypothesis does not imply that NDEs lack religious or spiritual significance. Science, as we have seen, addresses questions of empirical fact, not questions of value or meaning. Thus, that NDEs can be understood scientifically does not mean that they lack religious meaning or significance. To the eyes of faith, happenings in nature and in history can possess a "depth" or spiritual significance that no purely scientific examination can reveal or exclude. NDEs can be seen as biological, scientifically explainable phenomena, but they can also be seen as providential, revelatory events pointing to a transcendent spiritual reality. To discuss this question here, however, would take us into philosophical and theological issues far beyond the scope of this textbook.

Exercise 15.6

I. Discuss the following questions in small groups. Be prepared to share the highlights of your discussion with the class as a whole.

   a. We argue that none of the four main arguments for the afterlife hypothesis is convincing. Do you agree? Why or why not?

   b. We argue that the neurochemistry hypothesis is the best available explanation of NDEs. Do you agree? Why or why not?

II. Is Blackmore right that there are no clear-cut, well-documented cases in which a NDRer could *not* have obtained certain information through ordinary sensory and cognitive means? Do some research on this issue and report your findings to the class.

III. In small groups, research and present to the class one of the following topics. Is the phenomenon an example of pseudoscience? Why or why not?

alien abductions	creation science	palmistry
ancient astronauts	dowsing	precognition
Atlantis	healing crystals	pyramid power
Bermuda Triangle	homeopathy	reflexology
Bible code	Loch Ness monster	reincarnation
Bigfoot	magnet therapy	Roswell crash
channeling	moon madness	therapeutic touch
clairvoyance	Nostradamus	UFOs

IV. Write a short argumentative paper (the precise length will be determined by your instructor) on one of the topics listed in the preceding exercise. Consult Chapters 12 and 13 for guidelines on writing argumentative papers.

Summary

1. *Science* is a method of inquiry that seeks to describe, explain, and predict occurrences in the physical or natural world by means of careful observation and experiment. Science is the most powerful intellectual tool ever discovered, and it profoundly influences almost every aspect of our daily lives. Yet surveys show that a large percentage of Americans know distressingly little about science or its methods and values.

2. Although there is no single "scientific method" all scientists use, most scientific reasoning does follow a basic pattern. That pattern consists of four steps:

- Identifying the problem
- Gathering relevant data
- Formulating hypotheses to explain the data
- Testing the hypotheses by observation or experiment

3. Science is the most reliable method we have for discovering empirically verifiable truths about the physical or natural world. But there are many important questions science cannot answer. Among these are questions of meaning and questions of value.

4. *Pseudoscience* is false science—that is, unscientific thinking masquerading as scientific thinking. We looked at six common marks of pseudoscience:

- It makes claims that are not testable.
- It makes claims that are inconsistent with well-established scientific truths.
- It explains away or ignores falsifying data.
- It uses vague language.
- It is not progressive.
- It often involves no serious effort to conduct research.

5. We looked in detail at two examples of pseudoscientific thinking: astrology and paranormal explanations of near-death experiences. We argued that astrology is a pseudoscience for the following reasons:

- Astrologers fail to identify a plausible mechanism or force that could explain astrology's alleged influences.
- Astrologers fail to provide a convincing response to the problem of precession.
- Astrologers fail to deal adequately with the discovery of three new planets and other recent astronomical discoveries.
- Astrologers often use vague, untestable language.
- Astrologers fail to offer a convincing response to the problems of time twins and mass disasters.
- Scientific tests do not support astrology's claims.

6. The term *near-death experiences* (NDEs) refers to a cluster of striking paranormal or spiritual experiences commonly reported by people who have come very close to death or have been resuscitated after being pronounced clinically dead. According to researcher Susan Blackmore, there are two main alternative explanations of NDEs: the afterlife hypothesis and the dying brain hypothesis. According to the *afterlife hypothesis,* NDEs are what they appear to be: paranormal glimpses of a postmortem spiritual world. According to the *dying brain hypothesis,* NDEs are hallucinations, fantasies, or distorted perceptions of the dying brain.

7. There are four major arguments for the afterlife hypothesis:

   - *The consistency argument:* NDEs are often remarkably similar in people of many different backgrounds and ages. The best explanation of this similarity is that the experiences are real rather than mere hallucinations.

   - *The reality argument:* NDEs feel so real—so vivid and compelling—that they cannot be mere fantasies or hallucinations.

   - *The paranormal argument:* Many NDEs involve paranormal experiences—such as accurately perceiving what is going on in other rooms in a hospital while one's unconscious body is being resuscitated—that cannot be explained scientifically. The only reasonable explanation of such experiences is that the soul can leave the body during NDEs.

   - *The transformational argument:* People who have experienced NDEs are often permanently and positively changed by their experiences. The best explanation of these personal transformations is that NDEs are real.

   For a variety of reasons, we argued that none of these arguments provides good reason to accept the afterlife hypothesis.

8. There are three leading versions of the dying brain hypothesis: the birth memory hypothesis, the cerebral anoxia hypothesis, and the neurochemistry hypothesis. According to the *birth memory hypothesis,* NDEs are vivid recollections of the birth experience. According to the *cerebral anoxia hypothesis,* NDEs are hallucinations caused by cerebral anoxia (lack of oxygen to the brain). According to the *neurochemistry hypothesis,* NDEs are hallucinatory wishful-thinking experiences that result from both neurochemical and psychological causes. We argued, on a variety of grounds, that the neurochemistry hypothesis offers the best explanation of NDEs.

Notes

Chapter 1

1. Our discussion of critical thinking standards is indebted to Richard Paul, *Critical Thinking: What Every Person Needs to Survive in a Rapidly Changing World* (Rohnert Park, CA: Center for Critical Thinking and Moral Critique, 1990), pp. 51–52.
2. Martin Heidegger, *Being and Time,* trans. John Macquarrie and Edward Robinson (San Francisco: HarperSanFrancisco, 1962), pp. 376–77. Originally published in 1927.
3. William Strunk, Jr., and E. B. White, *The Elements of Style,* 3rd ed. (New York: Macmillan, 1979), p. 79.
4. William H. Herndon, quoted in David Hackett Fischer, *Historians' Fallacies: Toward a Logic of Historical Thought* (New York: Harper & Row, 1970), p. 291.
5. Harold Kushner, *When All You've Ever Wanted Isn't Enough: The Search for a Life That Matters* (New York: Pocket Books, 1986), p. 15.
6. Bertrand Russell, *Unpopular Essays* (New York: Simon & Schuster, 1950), pp. 75–76.
7. Used by permission of Kenneth R. Merrill. This is an abridged and slightly adapted version of Merrill's unpublished "Advice for Writers." An unabridged version may be obtained by writing to Prof. Kenneth R. Merrill, Department of Philosophy, University of Oklahoma, Norman, OK 73019.
8. Erma Bombeck, *All I Know about Animal Behavior I Learned in Loehmann's Dressing Room* (New York: HarperPaperbacks, 1995), p. 66.
9. Cited in Thomas Gilovich, *How We Know What Isn't So: The Fallibility of Human Reason in Everyday Life* (New York: Free Press, 1991), p. 77. The same survey found that only 2 percent of respondents rated themselves below average in their leadership ability.
10. Adapted from J. E. Russo and P. J. H. Schoemaker, *Decision Traps: Ten Barriers to Brilliant Decision Making and How to Overcome Them* (New York: Simon & Schuster, 1989), p. 71.
11. Answers: 1. 39 years; 2. 4,187 miles; 3. 12.68% (1997); 4. 39 books; 5. 2,160 miles; 6. 390,000 lbs.; 7. 33,871,678 (2000); 8. 1756; 9. 5,959 miles; 10. 36,198 feet.

12. Quoted in Paul, *Critical Thinking,* pp. 91–92.
13. See Stanley Milgram, *Obedience to Authority: An Experimental View* (New York: Harper & Row, 1974).
14. Joel Rudinow and Vincent E. Barry, *Invitation to Critical Thinking,* 4th ed. (Ft. Worth: Harcourt College Publishers, 1999), p. 20.
15. *Weekly World News,* March 11, 2000.
16. This list of critical thinking dispositions is largely drawn from three sources: Vincent Ryan Ruggiero, *Beyond Feelings: A Guide to Critical Thinking,* 5th ed. (Mountain View, CA: Mayfield, 1998), pp. 13–14; John Chaffee, *The Thinker's Way* (Boston: Little, Brown, 1998), pp. 34–37; and Paul, *Critical Thinking,* p. 54.

Chapter 2

1. More precisely, a statement (or proposition) is the truth claim asserted by a sentence or part of a sentence that is capable of standing alone as a declarative sentence. Thus, the French sentence "Le ciel est bleu" and the English sentence "The sky is blue" have the same meaning and, hence, express the same statement, even though they are different sentences in different languages. For purposes of this text, the distinction between sentences and statements will largely be ignored.
2. *Washington Post,* December 26, 1999, p. B3.
3. This list is adapted from Sherry Diestler, *Becoming a Critical Thinker: A User-Friendly Manual,* 2nd ed. (Upper Saddle River, NJ: Prentice Hall, 1998), pp. 8, 10.
4. "Truck Driver Takes to Skies in Lawn Chair," *New York Times,* July 3, 1982; "Lawn-Chair Pilot Faces $4,000 in Fines," *New York Times,* December 19, 1982.
5. Jonathan Kozol, *Amazing Grace: The Lives of Children and the Conscience of a Nation* (New York: HarperPerennial, 1995), p. 21.
6. Stephen Nathanson, *Should We Consent to Be Governed? A Short Introduction to Political Philosophy* (Belmont, CA: Wadsworth, 1992), p. 70.
7. Harold Kushner, *When All You've Ever Wanted Isn't Enough: The Search for a Life That Matters* (New York: Pocket Books, 1986), p. 156.

8. Note that conditional statements need not explicitly contain the words "if" and "then." For instance, the statements "In the event of rain, the picnic will be canceled" and "Should it rain, the picnic will be canceled" are both conditional statements.

9. Adapted from an example in Wilson Follett, *Modern American Usage* (New York: Hill & Wang, 1966), p. 93.

10. Nadine Strossen, "Regulating Racist Speech on Campus: A Modest Proposal?" *1990 Duke Law Journal* (June 1990), p. 489.

11. *Portland Oregonian,* August 23, 1999.

CHAPTER 3

1. These exercises are loosely adapted from similar exercises in Kathleen Dean Moore, *Reasoning and Writing* (New York: Macmillan, 1993), p. 103.

2. Adapted from John Hoagland, *Critical Thinking,* 2nd ed. (Newport News, VA: Vale Press, 1995), p. 68.

3. Irving M. Copi and Carl Cohen, *Introduction to Logic,* 10th ed. (Upper Saddle River, NJ: Prentice-Hall, 1998), p. 80 (slightly adapted).

4. Ibid., p. 80 (slightly adapted).

5. A particular statement, as we use the term, is a statement that refers to a specific person, place, or thing. For example, "Tom Cruise is an actor" is a particular statement. A general statement is a statement that refers to all or most members of a particular class—for example, "All dogs are mammals" or "Most Democrats are liberals."

6. There are cases in which an arguer mistakenly believes that his premises provide only probable support for the truth of his conclusion when, in fact, they provide logically conclusive support. Such cases are rare, however, and for purposes of this text they will be ignored.

7. The traditional name for this argument pattern is "affirming the consequent." For more on arguments of this pattern, see pages 64–65.

8. Bill Bryson, *A Walk in the Woods: Rediscovering America on the Appalachian Trail* (New York: Broadway Books, 1999), p. 91 (slightly paraphrased).

9. In this section and the following we are indebted to Patrick J. Hurley, *A Concise Introduction to Logic,* 7th ed. (Belmont, CA: Wadsworth Publishing Co., 2000), pp. 35–39.

10. Some critical thinking texts define "hypothetical syllogism" more narrowly as an argument that has the following form: "If A then B; If B then C; therefore, If A then C." We prefer to call arguments of this pattern "pure hypothetical syllogisms" or "chain arguments."

11. Latin for "denying mode" or "the way of denying."

12. A more precise definition will be provided in Chapter 9.

13. Notice the pattern of this argument: Either A is true or B is true. But A isn't true; therefore, B is true. Arguments of this pattern are known as "disjunctive syllogisms." Disjunctive syllogisms are one variety of argument by elimination.

14. Thus, not all arguments that refer to numbers or quantities are arguments based on mathematics. For example, statistical arguments, as we see shortly, are usually best treated as inductive.

15. Dave Barry, *Dave Barry Turns 50* (New York: Crown Publishers, 1998), p. 176.

16. Robert Fulghum, *It Was on Fire When I Lay Down on It* (New York: Ivy Books, 1989), p. 3.

17. This example is borrowed from David A. Conway and Ronald Munson, *The Elements of Reasoning,* 2nd ed. (Belmont, CA: Wadsworth, 1997), p. 40.

18. This is a stock example that exists in many versions. This version is borrowed from Hurley, *A Concise Introduction to Logic,* p. 153.

19. Daniel Butler, Alan Ray, Leland Gregory, *America's Dumbest Criminals* (Nashville, TN: Rutledge Hill Press, 1995), pp. 147–48 (slightly adapted).

20. In later chapters we shall present some more formal tests of validity.

21. Whether all valid arguments have a valid argument form is a disputed question in logic. For purposes of this text, we shall assume that they do.

22. This means that on exams, students should never have premises or conclusions in their counterexamples that say things like "My boyfriend lives in Ohio" or "My brother likes spinach." In most cases, your instructor will have no way of knowing whether such statements are true or false.

CHAPTER 4

1. Adapted from an example in Andrea Lunsford and Robert Connors, *The St. Martin's Handbook,* 2nd ed. (New York: St. Martin's Press, 1992), p. 288.

2. S. Morris Engel, *With Good Reason: An Introduction to Informal Fallacies,* 5th ed. (New York: St. Martin's Press, 1994), p. 119.

3. Ibid., p. 121.

4. Richard L. Epstein, *Workbook for Critical Thinking* (Belmont, CA: Wadsworth, 1999), p. 19.

5. Quoted in Clifton Fadiman, ed., *The Little, Brown Book of Anecdotes* (Boston: Little, Brown, 1985), p. 504.

6. Quoted in Sherry Diestler, *Becoming a Critical Thinker: A User-Friendly Manual,* 2nd ed. (Upper Saddle River, NJ: Prentice Hall, 1998), p. 282.

7. Quoted in *Wilkes-Barre Times Leader,* May 15, 1999.

8. Fadiman, *The Little, Brown Book of Anecdotes,* p. 140.

9. Ibid., p. 171.

10. Quoted in Anders Henriksson, "The Ultimate Rewrite: A Plague of Boobs," *The Wilson Quarterly* (Fall 1983), p. 5.

11. John J. Kohut and Roland Sweet, *Dumb, Dumber, Dumbest: True News of the World's Least Competent People* (New York: Penguin-Plume, 1996), pp. 83–84.

12. Leon Jaroff, "The Magic Is Back," *Time,* October 10, 1988, p. 20.

13. Steve Goldstein, "Soviets Bask in Success of First Shuttle," *Philadelphia Inquirer,* November 16, 1988, p. A-3.

14. William Lutz, "The New Doublespeak," *Newsweek,* August 12, 1996, p. 57.

15. Kohut and Sweet, *Dumb, Dumber, Dumbest,* p. 240.

CHAPTER 5

1. It follows from this definition that an argument is not fallacious simply because it contains false premises. Some logicians prefer to define "fallacy" more broadly as "any faulty or defective argument." Given the eclectic mix of argumentative errors and deceptive tactics traditionally classified as fallacies, neither definition is completely adequate. We prefer our narrower definition because it fits more closely with traditional usage.

2. Many critical thinking texts distinguish between "formal" and "informal" fallacies. The distinction is roughly this: formal fallacies are fallacious arguments that involve *explicit* use of an invalid argument form, whereas informal fallacies are fallacious arguments that do not. According to this definition, most of the arguments we discuss in this chapter and the next are informal fallacies. In this text, we avoid the distinction between formal and informal fallacies because (a) students find it confusing and (b) in practice the distinction often breaks down. For more on the traditional distinction between formal and informal fallacies, see Patrick J. Hurley, *A Concise Introduction to Logic,* 7th ed. (Belmont, CA: Wadsworth, 2000), pp. 118–20.

3. These helpful distinctions are borrowed from Trudy Govier, *A Practical Study of Argument,* 5th ed. (Belmont, CA: Wadsworth, 2001), pp. 172–73.

4. An argument's premises provide "probable reasons" for a conclusion if the premises, if true, make the conclusion likely.

5. Scott Adams, *The Dilbert Principle* (New York: Harper Business, 1996), p. 9.

6. The traditional name of this fallacy is "*ad hominem* abusive." (*Ad hominem* is a Latin phrase meaning "against the person.")

7. Quoted in Clifton Fadiman, ed., *The Little, Brown Book of Anecdotes* (Boston: Little, Brown, 1985), p. 357.

8. The traditional name for this fallacy is "*ad hominem* circumstantial." Some critical thinking texts define the fallacy slightly more broadly than we do.

9. The traditional name for this fallacy is "*tu quoque*" (pronounced *too-kwo-kway*), which is Latin for "you too." The fallacy is often treated as a variety of the personal attack fallacy.

10. Quoted in the *Wilkes-Barre Times Leader,* January 27, 2000.

11. Often called "appeal to fear" or "scare tactics." The traditional Latin name for this fallacy is "*argumentum ad baculum*" (literally, "argument to the stick").

12. As this example makes clear, the fallacy of appeal to force need not involve a threat of *physical* force. Any kind of threat can be involved, and the threat may be veiled.

13. Scare tactics can, however, provide good *non*evidential reasons for action. If a mad gunman says to you, "Say that the Pythagorean Theorem is false or I'll fill you full of lead," the right thing to do under the circumstances is to *say* that the theorem is false. But, of course, the gunman's threat provides no relevant evidence that the theorem is, in fact, false.

14. The traditional name for this fallacy is "*argumentum ad misericordiam*" (Latin for "argument to mercy").

15. Quoted in Elanor and Reginald Jebb, *Belloc, The Man* (Westminster, MD: The Newman Press, 1957), p. 19.

16. Adapted from Alan Brinton, "Pathos and the 'Appeal to Emotion': An Aristotelian Analysis," *History of Philosophy Quarterly* 5 (1989), p. 211.

17. See the definition of "red herring" and the supporting passage cited from the third edition of Nicholas Cox's *The Gentleman's Recreation* (1686) in *The Compact Edition of the Oxford English Dictionary* (New York : Oxford University Press, 1971).

18. This example is adapted from Hurley, *A Concise Introduction to Logic,* p. 164.

19. Thomas V. Morris, *Making Sense of It All: Pascal and the Meaning of Life* (Grand Rapids, MI: William B. Eerdmans Publishing Co., 1992), p. 38.

CHAPTER 6

1. Alvin Plantinga, *Warrant and Proper Function* (New York: Oxford University Press, 1993), p. 77.

2. Notice that this is consistent with what we said in Chapter 5 about the fallacy of attacking the motive. Attacking the motive is the fallacy of criticizing a person's motivation for offering a particular argument or claim, *rather than examining the worth of the argument or claim itself.* In these examples, questioning the testifier's motives is necessary to evaluate the worth of the argument.

3. *Weekly World News,* October 10, 1999.

4. Quoted in Dr. Laurence J. Peter, *Peter's Quotations* (New York: Morrow, 1977), p. 296.

5. *USA Today News,* July 22, 2000; available online at http://www.usatoday.com/news/nweird.htm.

6. Other names for this fallacy include "false dilemma," "false dichotomy," "the either-or fallacy," and the "black-and-white fallacy." Our discussion of this fallacy is indebted to Patrick Hurley, *A Concise Introduction to Logic,* 7th ed. (Belmont, CA: Wadsworth, 2000), pp. 161–62.

7. Notice that the only thing wrong with these arguments is that they have a false premise: they falsely claim that there are only two relevant alternatives when, in fact, there are more than two. Strictly speaking, therefore, the fallacy of false alternatives, like the fallacy of begging the question, is not a fallacy. We shall follow convention, however, in treating them as fallacies.

8. *Weekly World News,* June 3, 1999.

9. Dave Barry, *Dave Barry's Guide to Life* (New York: Wing Books, 1987), p. 67.

10. House of Commons Debates of Canada, June 10, 1982. Quoted in Douglas N. Walton, *Begging the Question* (New York: Greenwood Press, 1991), p. 239.

11. For a fuller discussion of the *post hoc* fallacy and other forms of the questionable cause fallacy, see pages 334–40.

12. This example is adapted from Hurley, *A Concise Introduction to Logic,* p. 153.

13. This example is adapted from a similar example in C. Stephen Layman, *The Power of Logic* (Mountain View, CA: Mayfield, 1999), p. 180.

14. According to a 1996 poll, only 39 percent of American scientists believe in a personal God, compared with over 90 percent of the general population. See Edward J. Larson and Larry Witham, "Scientists Are Still Keeping the Faith," *Nature* 386 (1997), pp. 435–36.

15. The argument does commit a fallacy. Specifically, it commits the fallacy of hasty conclusion. The *fallacy of hasty conclusion* occurs when an arguer jumps to a conclusion without adequate evidence. Most of the fallacies we discuss in this chapter are subvarieties of the fallacy of hasty conclusion.

16. This threefold analysis is adapted from Ralph H. Johnson and J. Anthony Blair, *Logical Self-Defense,* U.S. ed. (New York: McGraw-Hill, 1994), p. 183.

17. From a newspaper call-in column, *Wilkes-Barre Times Leader,* January 23, 2000.

18. For a fuller discussion of reasoning by analogy, see pages 323–33.

19. Adapted from an oft-quoted saying of Yogi Berra. See Clifton Fadiman, ed., *The Little, Brown Book of Anecdotes* (Boston: Little, Brown, 1985), p. 61.
20. *USA Today News,* January 12, 2000; available online at http://www.usatoday.com/news/nweird.htm.
21. This example is adapted from an anecdote told by Bertrand Russell in his book *Human Knowledge: Its Scope and Limits* (New York: Simon & Schuster, 1948), p. 180.
22. This example was inspired by a remark made by Ronald Reagan.
23. Quoted in Marc Ramirez, "Powter Power," *Wilkes-Barre Times Leader,* June 19, 1999.
24. Quoted in David Halberstam, *The Fifties* (New York: Fawcett Columbine, 1993), p. 10.
25. Quoted in Stephen E. Ambrose, *Citizen Soldiers* (New York: Simon & Schuster, 1997), p. 105 (slightly adapted).
26. Quoted in Al Franken, *Rush Limbaugh Is a Big Fat Idiot and Other Observations* (New York: Island Books, 1996), p. 292.
27. Our thanks to Brooke Moore and Richard Parker for helpful suggestions on this exercise.

Chapter 7

1. More precisely still, a premise is *linked* just in case (1) the amount of support it provides for the conclusion would be affected (i.e., either weakened or strengthened) by the omission of some other premise in the argument, or (2) its omission from the argument would affect the amount of support provided by some other premise in the argument. Similarly, a premise is *independent* when neither of these two conditions obtains. For purposes of this introductory text, these technical refinements can be safely ignored.
2. Thomas Lickona, *Educating for Character: How Our Schools Can Teach Respect and Responsibility* (New York: Bantam, 1991), p. 77.
3. Our discussion in this section is indebted to C. Stephen Layman, *The Power of Logic* (Mountain View, CA: Mayfield, 1999), pp. 73–74.
4. This example is adapted from an argument discussed (but not endorsed) by C. S. Lewis in his book *God in the Dock: Essays on Theology and Ethics* (Grand Rapids, MI: William B. Eerdmans Publishing Co., 1970), p. 105.
5. This argument is stated but not endorsed by Morris.
6. This argument is a restatement of an argument originally presented by the seventeenth-century French philosopher René Descartes.
7. *Washington Post,* December 26, 1999.
8. This argument is stated but not endorsed by Pierce and VanDeveer.
9. We owe this example to the Plain English Homepage; available at http://www.plainenglish.couk/examples.html.
10. Thanks to our colleague Len Gorney for passing along this (slightly adapted) example to us.
11. This example is borrowed from William Strunk, Jr., and E. B. White, *The Elements of Style,* 3rd ed. (New York: Macmillan, 1979), p. 25.
12. David Hume, *Dialogues concerning Natural Religion,* ed. Norman Kemp Smith (Indianapolis: Bobbs-Merrill Educational Publishing, 1947), p. 143.
13. See pages 41–42 for a discussion of the principle of charity.
14. "No Sex in Show Me State?" *Wilkes-Barre Times Leader,* November 6, 1994.

15. Our formulation of these rules is indebted to Robert Paul Churchill, *Logic: An Introduction,* 2nd ed. (New York: St. Martin's Press, 1990), pp. 61–63; and David A. Conway and Ronald Munson, *The Elements of Reasoning,* 2nd ed. (Belmont, CA: Wadsworth, 1997), pp. 9–10.
16. This example is borrowed from Thomas V. Morris, *Making Sense of It All: Pascal and the Meaning of Life* (Grand Rapids, MI: William B. Eerdmans Publishing Co., 1992), p. 55.
17. Charles E. Sheedy, *The Christian Virtues,* 2nd ed. (Notre Dame, IN: University of Notre Dame Press, 1951), p. 15.
18. Tom Morris, *Philosophy for Dummies* (Foster City, CA: IDG Books Worldwide, 1999), p. 218. (The argument is stated but not endorsed by Morris.)
19. Notice that in listing the reasons that support the conclusion, we list only those premises that *directly* support the conclusion, not all the premises that appear in the argument. Premises that provide only *indirect* support for the conclusion—that is, premises that have already been cited once in the argument in support of some subconclusion—should not be cited a second time in justification of the main conclusion. Citing only premises that directly support conclusions helps us see more clearly the logical structure of the argument.
20. The *Baton Rouge Advocate,* April 4, 1998. Our thanks to Professor Barbara Forrest for this example and the accompanying standardization.
21. Bob Butts, Letter to the Editor, *Wilkes-Barre Times Leader,* September 16, 1998.
22. Notice how we keep referring to "one reader's" attempt to summarize a particular argument? This is because there is almost never a single uniquely correct way to summarize a long and complex argument. This doesn't mean that "anything goes," that one summary is as good as any other. But it does mean that we should be open to the idea that another person's rather different summary may be just as "correct" as our own.

Chapter 8

1. Some of these examples are borrowed from Tom Morris, *Philosophy for Dummies* (Forest City, CA: IDG Books Worldwide, 1999), pp. 92–94.
2. One exception should be noted here. In some arguments, the premises may still provide good reasons for the conclusion even though the argument contains a premise that is false. This occurs when the false premise is *superfluous*—that is, not needed to prove or establish the conclusion. Having noted this complication, we shall ignore it in what follows.
3. If an argument is inconsistent, then at least one of its claims must be false. Strictly speaking, therefore, consistency is included in the standard of accuracy and is not a separate standard in its own right. However, inconsistency is such an important and pervasive form of inaccuracy that it is useful for our purposes to treat it as a separate standard.
4. It should be noted that these guidelines are not intended to be complete. Many specific guidelines for evaluating arguments are presented throughout the text.
5. Our discussion of this principle is indebted to Brooke Noel Moore and Richard Parker, *Critical Thinking,* 5th ed. (Mountain View, CA: Mayfield, 1998), pp. 71–79.
6. Ibid., p. 84.

7. For a helpful general discussion, see Theodore Schick, Jr., and Lewis Vaughn, *How to Think about Weird Things: Critical Thinking for a New Age,* 2nd ed., 1999), chap. 3.

8. Answer: 11. (Many people overlook the *f*'s in the word "of.") This exercise is borrowed from Scott Plous, *The Psychology of Judgment and Decision Making* (New York: McGraw-Hill, 1993), p. 16.

9. This exercise is inspired by one in John Chaffee, *The Thinker's Way* (Boston: Little, Brown, 1998), p. 64.

10. "Gun Safety Training"; available online at http://www.darwinawards.com.

11. This exercise is adapted from Moore and Parker, *Critical Thinking,* p. 74.

12. *Weekly World News,* June 25, 1999.

13. *Weekly World News,* September 3, 1999.

14. "I'm a Man, I Can Handle It"; available online at http://www.darwin awards.com/darwin/index_darwin1997.html.

CHAPTER 9

1. The method is named after its inventor, the English logician John Venn (1834–1923).

2. These numbers aren't normally included in Venn diagrams. They are added here temporarily to make it easier to refer to the relevant areas.

3. In math, shading an area generally means that the area is *not* empty. In logic, shading has just the opposite meaning.

4. "The 1999 Darwin Award Wannabes"; available online at http//www.tiac.net/users/cri/darwin99a.html.

5. Many logic and critical thinking texts adopt the convention that ambiguous generalizations like these should always be translated as "all." Although this convention certainly simplifies matters for students, it is more important, we think, to respect the principle that speakers' intentions be interpreted plausibly and charitably.

6. Our discussion of stylistic variants of standard categorical forms is indebted to C. Stephen Layman, *The Power of Logic* (Mountain View, CA: Mayfield, 1999), pp. 129–31.

7. Strictly speaking, quantifying expressions such as "many," "most," and "nearly all" aren't really stylistic variants of "some," since they convey more specific quantitative information than "some" does. For example, "Nearly all Canadians are friendly" clearly says something much stronger than "Some (i.e., at least one) Canadian is friendly." With rare exceptions, however, these verbal differences are irrelevant for purposes of categorical logic. Thus, so long as due care is exercised, quantifying expressions such as "many," "most," and "nearly all" can be safely translated as "some."

8. William H. Halverson, *A Concise Logic* (New York: Random House, 1984), p. 83.

9. "The 1999 Darwin Award Wannabes"; available online at http://www.tiac.net/users/cri/darwin99a.html.

CHAPTER 10

1. In this chapter we will not consider arguments with more than three variables, since such arguments become impractical to analyze by means of truth tables. The number of columns needed is determined exponentially. With two variables we need four columns, two squared. With three variables we need eight columns, two cubed. With four variables we would need sixteen columns, two to the fourth power. This quickly becomes work that is more suitable for a computer than a human being.

2. A horseshoe, $\supset$, is also an acceptable symbol for this operation.

3. Counterfactual conditionals, such as "If Caesar had fought in the Revolutionary War, he would have used firearms," are another matter altogether. Consideration of counterfactuals would take us beyond the aims and scope of this chapter.

CHAPTER 11

1. In Chapter 3 we discussed six patterns, but here our discussion will focus on four.

2. For a thorough explanation of how this figure is calculated, see A. Agresti and B. Finley, *Statistical Methods for the Social Sciences,* 2nd ed. (San Francisco: Dellen Publishing Company, 1986), p. 103.

3. These are the figures used and made available by the Gallup poll. See Charles W. Roll and Albert H. Cantril, *Polls: Their Use and Misuse in Politics* (New York: Basic Books, 1972), p. 72.

4. Statistics can also be used to make inductive generalizations, especially when they argue to a conclusion about most members of a class. Some, but not all, statistical arguments are also inductive generalizations. And clearly, not all inductive generalizations are statistical arguments.

5. It is also possible to have negative arguments from analogy. For example, x and y are not similar in ways a, b, and c. So they are probably not similar in d, either.

6. This example is adapted from Jostein Gaarder's *Sophie's World: A Novel about the History of Philosophy* (New York: Berkley Books, 1994), p. 328.

CHAPTER 12

1. Jorge Luis Borges, "The Library of Babel," in *Labyrinths* (New York: Penguin, 1970), pp. 81–82.

2. Gary Ink, "Book Title Output and Average Prices: 1996 Final and 1997 Preliminary Figures," *The Bowker Annual Library and Book Trade Almanac,* 43rd ed. (New Providence, NJ: R. R. Bowker, 1998), p. 521.

3. "Leading U.S. Daily Newspapers" and "U.S. Commercial Radio Stations, by Format, 1992–98," *The World Almanac and Book of Facts,* 1999 (Mahwah, NJ: World Almanac Books, 1999), pp. 185, 186.

4. John J. Kohut and Roland Sweet, *Dumb, Dumber, Dumbest: True News of the World's Least Competent People* (New York: Penguin-Plume, 1996), pp. 80–81.

5. Sigmund Freud, "Femininity," in *New Introductory Lectures on Psychoanalysis* (New York: Norton, 1965).

6. "The Gun Under Fire," *Time,* June 12, 1969, p. 13.

7. *Answers to the Most Asked Questions about Cigarettes* (Washington, DC: The Tobacco Institute, n.d.).

8. Kohut and Sweet, *Dumb, Dumber, Dumbest,* p. 152.

9. In 1981, a *Washington Post* Pulitzer Prize–winning article about an eight-year-old heroin addict had been fabricated.

10. Although the terms are often used interchangeably, a "journal" is a periodical limited to a particular subject (medicine, politics, literature, sociology, etc.) and aimed at an audience familiar with the subject. A "magazine" includes articles on various subjects and is aimed at a more general readership.

11. William Carlos Williams, "The Virtue of History," in *In the American Grain* (New York: New Directions, 1925, 1956), p. 201.
12. "Of Studies," in *Essays or Counsels Civil and Moral* (1625).
13. *The Affluent Society* (Boston: Houghton-Riverside, 1958), p. 21.

CHAPTER 13

1. John J. Kohut and Roland Sweet, *Dumb, Dumber, Dumbest: True News of the World's Least Competent People* (New York: Penguin-Plume, 1996), p. 51.
2. Op. cit., pp. 54, 107, 233.

CHAPTER 14

1. For recommendations on evaluating information in journals of opinion, see Chapter 12.
2. Laura E. Keeton, Mark Pawlosky, and Robert Tomsho, "Terrorism Hits Home: U.S. Building Bombed; Dead Include Children," *Wall Street Journal,* April 20, 1995, pp. A1, A6; Pierre Thomas and Ann Devroy, "Clinton Condemns 'Evil Cowards' for Blast," *Washington Post,* April 20, 1995, pp. A1, A24. Interestingly, the online version of the *Wall Street Journal* article carries a revised version of the original opening sentence.
3. New York: Vintage Books, 1997, pp. 139–140.
4. New York: Viking Penguin, 1985, p. 68.
5. The Internet has allowed major newspapers such as the *New York Times* to provide extended, more contextualized coverage. An article can be linked to archived articles, commentaries, editorials, cartoons, and letters regarding the topic of the current story. A reader interested in an event or issue can study the topic in greater detail. Although covered from the point of view of only one newspaper, the topic is at least more fully analyzed than is usually possible.
6. Because stories sent to local papers by wire service (AP, Reuters, United Press International) are trimmed from the bottom to fit available space, the endings of national and international stories are often missing in local papers, which helps explain why some articles seem to end abruptly.
7. Paul S. Voakes, "The Newspaper Journalists of the '90's: Who They Are . . . and What They Think about the Major Issues Facing Their Profession." American Society of Newspaper Editors, 1997; accessed May 11, 2000. http://www.asne.org/kiosk/reports/97reports/journalists90s/coverpage.html.
8. John Decker. "Carbondale Cop Shot, Vest Stopped Bullet," *Wilkes-Barre Times Leader,* April 21, 2000, p. A1.
9. Inspired by an exercise in Stephen S. Carey, *The Uses and Abuses of Argument: Critical Thinking and Fallacious Reasoning* (Mountain View, CA: Mayfield, 2000), p. 167.
10. For his "conviction" in the press, Jewell was paid undisclosed amounts in out-of-court settlements with the *Atlantic Constitution* and NBC News.
11. Arthur E. Rowse, *Drive-By Journalism: The Assault on Your Need to Know* (Monroe, ME: Common Courage Press, 2000), p. 215.
12. Since Neal Postman first alerted viewers to this phenomenon, "infotainment" shows like *Entertainment Tonight* have proliferated. Shows that inform us in entertaining ways about current events, shows like *Inside Edition, Extra, Access Hollywood,* and *RealTV* effectively erase the line between news and entertainment.

13. Stanley J. Baran, *Introduction to Mass Communication* (Mountain View, CA: Mayfield Publishing Company, 1999), p. 278.
14. FTC, In the matter of Warner-Lambert, Federal Trade Commission Decisions 86, July 1, 1975 to December 31, 1975 (Washington, D.C.: Government Printing Office), p. 1399.
15. George Gerbner, "The Stories We Tell," *Media Development* (April 1996), pp. 13–17.
16. Max Sutherland (St Leonards, Australia: Allen & Unwin Pty Ltd, 1993), pp. 6–12.
17. Ibid, p. 6.
18. Philip Patterson and Lee Wilkins, *Media Ethics: Issues and Cases* (New York: McGraw-Hill, 1998), p. 61.

CHAPTER 15

1. Carl Sagan, *The Demon-Haunted World: Science as a Candle in the Dark* (New York: Random House, 1995), p. 6.
2. For example, in a 1998 international test, American high school students finished eighteenth out of twenty-one nations in math and science literacy, and the test didn't even include any of the traditionally high-performing Asian countries. James Freeman, "To Improve Schools, Forget Computers," *USA Today Online,* September 10, 1999; available online at http://www.usatoday.com/news/comment/columnists/freeman/ncjf38.htm.
3. Sometimes, "science" is defined more broadly to include nonempirical disciplines such as logic and mathematics. When we speak of "science," we mean *empirical* science in the sense defined.
4. This definition is adapted from Paul Kurtz, "Believing the Unbelievable: The Scientific Response—A Foreword," in *Science and the Paranormal: Probing the Existence of the Supernatural,* ed. George O. Abell and Barry Singer (New York: Scribner's, 1981), pp. vii–viii.
5. Poll cited in *Parade,* December 26, 1999, p. 7.
6. National Science Foundation poll, reported in the *Wilkes-Barre Times Leader,* May 23, 1996.
7. This and the preceding statistic are cited in Sagan, *The Demon-Haunted World,* p. 324.
8. Poll cited in *The Gallup Poll Monthly,* August 1999, p. 35.
9. 1990 Gallup poll cited in *Paranormal Phenomena: Opposing Viewpoints,* ed. Terry O'Neill (San Diego, CA: Greenhaven Press, 1991), p. 13.
10. This and the preceding statistic are cited in a poll published in the *Gallup Poll Monthly,* September 1996, p. 23.
11. 1994 Gallup poll cited in Stuart A. Vyse, *Believing in Magic: The Psychology of Superstition* (New York: Oxford University Press, 1997), p. 17.
12. In fact, controlled studies have found no evidence that vitamin C prevents or cures colds.
13. Our discussion of these methods is indebted to Theodore Schick, Jr., and Lewis Vaughn, *How to Think about Weird Things: Critical Thinking for a New Age,* 2nd ed. (Mountain View, CA: Mayfield, 1999), p. 196.
14. Sagan, *The Demon-Haunted World,* pp. 339–40.
15. When we speak of "questions of meaning or purpose," we have in mind primarily questions of "existential" or cosmic meaning or purpose. We don't mean to deny that there are some kinds of "meanings" and "purposes" that science is competent to deal with.

16. This is one standard sense of "scientism." See, for example, John F. Haught, *Science and Religion: From Conflict to Conversation* (Mahwah, NJ: Paulist Press, 1995), p. 16. In a weaker sense, scientism is the view that the methods of the natural sciences should be applied in every field of human knowing. Robert Todd Carroll, "Scientism"; available online at http://skeptic.com/scientism/html.

17. This definition is indebted to Sagan, *The Demon-Haunted World,* p. 13.

18. Our discussion in this section is indebted to William D. Gray, *Thinking Critically about New Age Ideas* (Belmont, CA: Wadsworth, 1991), Chapter 5.

19. Nigel Calder, *Einstein's Universe* (Harmondsworth, England: Penguin Books, 1980), pp. 72–83.

20. Of course, any of these statements might reasonably be believed on the basis of religious revelation, provided there is ample proof that the revelation is genuine. When we speak of "possible observations or experiments," we have in mind observations or experiments that don't rely upon supernatural agencies or rest on mere appeals to authority.

21. For representative statements of these excuses, see Robert H. Ashby, *The Guidebook for the Study of Psychical Research* (London: Rider and Company, 1972), excerpt reprinted in O'Neill, *Paranormal Phenomena,* p. 132; D. Scott Rogo, "The Making of Psi Failure," *Fate* (April 1986), pp. 76–80. For a helpful critical discussion, see Ray Hyman, *The Elusive Quarry: A Scientific Appraisal of Psychical Research* (Buffalo, NY: Prometheus Books, 1989), pp. 210–15.

22. See Arthur W. Galston and Clifford L. Slayman, "The Not-So-Secret Life of Plants," *American Scientist* 67 (May 1979), pp. 337–44.

23. Barry Singer, "Double Standards," in Abell and Singer, *Science and the Paranormal,* p. 144.

24. This is Bertrand Russell's famous "five minute hypothesis." This formulation of the argument is borrowed from Tom Morris, *Philosophy for Dummies* (Foster City, CA: IDG Books Worldwide, 1999), p. 62.

25. Humphrey Carpenter, ed., *The Letters of J. R. R. Tolkien* (Boston: Houghton Mifflin, 1981), p. 400.

26. Isaac Asimov and Duane Gish, "The Genesis War," *Science Digest,* October 1981, pp. 82–87.

27. Lee Tiffin, *Creationism's Upside-Down Pyramid: How Science Refutes Fundamentalism* (Buffalo, NY: Prometheus Books, 1994), p. 28.

28. Robert J. Schadewald, "Six 'Flood' Arguments Creationists Can't Answer," in *Evolution versus Creationism: The Public Education Controversy,* ed. J. Peter Zetterberg (Phoenix: Oryx Press, 1983), p. 450.

29. See, for example, Henry M. Morris, ed., *Scientific Creationism* (San Diego, CA: Creation-Life Publishers, 1974), pp. 118–19.

30. Richard Dawkins, *Unweaving the Rainbow: Science, Delusion and the Appetite for Wonder* (Boston: Houghton Mifflin, 1998), p. 31.

31. Terence Hines, *Pseudoscience and the Paranormal* (Buffalo, NY: Prometheus Books, 1988), p. 93. See generally James Randi, *The Truth about Uri Geller* (Buffalo, NY: Prometheus Books, 1975).

32. Hines, *Pseudoscience and the Paranormal,* pp. 245–46.

33. James Randi, "Science and the Chimera," in Abell and Singer, *Science and the Paranormal,* p. 214.

34. C. R. Snyder and R. J. Shenkel, "The P. T. Barnum Effect," *Psychology Today* 8 (March 1975), pp. 52–54.

35. Hines, *Pseudoscience and the Paranormal,* p. 34.

36. Robert Novella, "Cold Reading"; available online at http://www.factsource.com/cut/coldreading.html. This article originally appeared in *The Connecticut Skeptic* 2, No. 2 (Spring 1997), p. 3.

37. Fereydoon Batmanghelidj, *Your Body's Many Cries for Water,* 2nd ed. (Falls River, VA: Global Health Solutions, 1997). For more on Dr. Batmanghelidj and the water cure, click on the Global Health Solutions Web site at http://www.watercure.com.

38. Bob Butts, Letter to the Editor, *Wilkes-Barre Times Leader,* September 3, 1997. Butts, owner of an auto-parts store in Moosic, Pennsylvania, has spent over $300,000 of his own money in recent years touting the water cure. For more on Butts and his crusade, see Michael Rubinkam, "The Water Man," online at http://www.abcnews.go.com/sections/living/DailyNews/water000619.html.

39. This example is inspired by an example in Gray, *Thinking Critically about New Age Ideas,* p. 110.

40. This example is adapted from an example in David A. Levy, *Tools of Critical Thinking: Metathoughts for Psychology* (Boston: Allyn & Bacon, 1997), p. 53.

41. Robert Parry, *In Defense of Astrology: Astrology's Answers to Its Critics* (St. Paul, MN: Llewellyn Publications, 1991), p. 88.

42. *Gallup Poll Monthly,* September 1996, p. 23. A 1984 Gallup poll found that 55 percent of American teenagers believe in astrology. Paul Kurtz and Andrew Franknoi, "Scientific Tests of Astrology Do Not Support Its Claims," reprinted in *The Outer Edge: Classic Investigations of the Paranormal,* ed. Joe Nickell, Barry Karr, and Tom Genoni (Amherst, NY: Committee for the Scientific Investigation of Claims of the Paranormal, 1996), p. 36.

43. Carl Sagan, *Cosmos* (New York: Random House, 1980), p. 48.

44. An important qualification to this statement will be noted below.

45. Our discussion in this section is indebted to Hines, *Pseudoscience and the Paranormal,* pp. 141–56.

46. George O. Abell, "Astrology," in Abell and Singer, *Science and the Paranormal,* p. 87.

47. Hines, *Pseudoscience and the Paranormal,* p. 147. It can also be asked why these forces have no effect on human behavior until the precise moment of birth. After all, most of these forces also operate in the womb.

48. Abell, "Astrology," p. 88.

49. Parry, *In Defense of Astrology,* p. 113.

50. Abell, "Astrology," p. 86.

51. Many astrologers are reluctant to concede that the discovery of the three new planets proves that astrologers' predictions have been systematically in error for the past two thousand years. Noted astrologer Linda Goodman, for example, argues that ancient astrologers' claims weren't mistaken, because planets *have* no astrological influences until they are discovered! Cited in Hines, *Pseudoscience and the Paranormal,* p. 146.

52. It is also instructive to note how astrologers sought to determine what astrological influences the newly discovered planets possessed. They did this not by empirical investigation but by resort to Greek and Roman mythology. For ex-

ample, Pluto (Hades) was the Greek god of the underworld. From this it was inferred that the planet Pluto must influence matters connected with death. See Ronny Martens and Tim Trachet, *Making Sense of Astrology* (Buffalo, NY: Prometheus Books, 1998), pp. 100–101.

53. Some astrologers do claim that asteroids (at least the larger ones) do have astrological influences. The claimed influences, however, are invariably based on myth, not empirical observation. See, for example, "Astrology on the Web," available online at http://www.astrologycom.cm/aster.html.

54. Paul Kurtz, *The Transcendental Temptation: A Critique of Religion and the Paranormal* (Buffalo, NY: Prometheus Books, 1986); excerpt reprinted in O'Neill, *Paranormal Phenomena,* pp. 154–55.

55. "Aquarius: Your Preferences"; available online at http://www.astrology.com/prefs_aquarius.htm.

56. These horoscopes are taken from astrologer Joyce Jillson's syndicated column, *Wilkes-Barre Times Leader,* November 24, 2000.

57. As St. Augustine pointed out, essentially the same problem arises with biological twins. However, time twins present an even greater challenge for astrologers, since with time twins quibbles cannot be raised about their being born even a few minutes apart.

58. See, for example, Parry, *In Defense of Astrology,* p. 100.

59. Ibid.

60. See, for example, Christopher C. French, Antony Leadbetter, and Geoffrey Dean, "The Anatomy of Time Twins: A Re-Analysis," *The Journal of Scientific Exploration,* 11, No. 2, (1997), p. 147.

61. See, for example, Parry, *In Defense of Astrology,* pp. 106–7.

62. R. B. Culver and P. A. Ianna, *The Gemini Syndrome: A Scientific Evaluation of Astrology* (Buffalo, NY: Prometheus Books, 1984), pp. 169–70; R. N. Hunter and J. S. Derr, "Prediction Monitoring and Evaluation Program: A Progress Report," *Earthquake Information Bulletin,* 10, No. 3 (1978), pp. 93–96.

63. Sandra Shulman, *The Encyclopedia of Astrology* (New York: Hamlyn Publishing Group, Ltd., 1976), p. 168; cited in Culver and Ianna, *The Gemini Syndrome,* p. 125.

64. Culver and Ianna, *The Gemini Syndrome,* pp. 125–27.

65. Bernard Silverman, "Studies of Astrology," *Journal of Psychology* 77 (1971), pp. 141–49; cited in Culver and Ianna, *The Gemini Syndrome,* p. 131.

66. John D. McGervey, "A Statistical Test of Sun-Sign Astrology," in *Paranormal Borderlands of Science,* ed. Frazier (Amherst, NY: Prometheus Books, 1981), pp. 235–40.

67. Culver and Ianna, *The Gemini Syndrome,* pp. 127–29.

68. W. Grant Dahlstrom et al., "MMPI Findings on Astrological and Other Folklore Concepts of Personality," *Psychological Reports* 78 (1996), pp. 1059–70.

69. Shawn Carlson, "A Double-Blind Test of Astrology," *Nature* 318 (December 5, 1985), pp. 419–25. A follow-up study, addressing astrologers' objections to the design of Carlson's study, was conducted a few years later by J. H. McGrew and R. M. McFall. See J. H. McGrew and R. M. McFall, "A Scientific Inquiry into the Validity of Astrology," *Journal of Scientific Exploration* 4 (1990), pp. 75–83. This study also failed to support astrology's claims.

70. See, for example, Claude Benski et al., *The Mars Effect: A French Test of Over 1,000 Sports Champions* (Buffalo, NY:

Prometheus Books, 1996); P. Kurtz, J. W. Nienhuys, and R. Sandhu, "Is the 'Mars Effect' Genuine?" *Journal of Scientific Exploration* 11 (1997), pp. 19–39.

71. Raymond A. Moody, *Life after Life* (New York: Bantam Books, 1975).

72. Ibid., pp. 21–23.

73. Susan Blackmore, *Dying to Live: Near-Death Experiences* (Buffalo, NY: Prometheus Books, 1993), p. 33.

74. Ibid., pp. 25–26.

75. Ibid., pp. 98–102.

76. Ibid., pp. 25–27.

77. Ibid., p. 181.

78. Ibid., p. 126.

79. Ibid., p. 17.

80. Sagan, *The Demon-Haunted World,* pp. 101–11, 180–88. Studies show that 10 to 25 percent of ordinary people have experienced vivid auditory or visual hallucinations at least once in their lives. Ibid., p. 104. Interestingly, some researchers have found that NDEers are significantly more likely to experience paranormal "visions" (other than the NDE itself) than are nonNDEers. See Michael Sabom, *Light and Death* (Grand Rapids, MI: Zondervan, 1998), pp. 151–57.

81. Susan Blackmore, "Near-Death Experiences: In or Out of the Body?" in Nickell, Carr, and Genoni, *The Outer Edge,* p. 88.

82. Blackmore, *Dying to Live,* pp. 120–25. Even patients who are completely flatlined—no detectable activity in the cerebral cortex *or* the brain stem—have later reported having had conscious experiences during that time. See Sabom, *Light and Death,* pp. 37–51, for one remarkable account.

83. This paragraph draws freely on Schick and Vaughn, *How to Think about Weird Things,* p. 278.

84. Blackmore, *Dying to Live,* pp. 128–33.

85. See generally ibid., pp. 113–35.

86. Schick and Vaughn, *How to Think about Weird Things,* pp. 271–72.

87. Studies show, however, that life-transforming attitudinal changes are significantly more frequent in patients that have had a NDE than they are in patients who narrowly escaped death but did not have a NDE. See Sabom, *Light and Death,* pp. 96–97.

88. See, for example, Sagan, *Broca's Brain,* p. 304.

89. Blackmore, *Dying to Live,* pp. 79–80.

90. See, for example, Hines, *Pseudoscience and the Paranormal,* pp. 69–70.

91. Blackmore, *Dying to Live,* pp. 49–61. As Blackmore points out (p. 52), however, these blood-gas tests cannot be taken as conclusive, since blood samples taken from peripheral areas are not reliable indicators of the amount of blood present in the brain.

92. The term "neurochemistry hypothesis" is ours, not Blackmore's. She calls her view simply the "dying brain hypothesis." As we note, however, there are several versions of the dying brain hypothesis, and it is important to distinguish among them.

93. Blackmore, *Dying to Live,* p. 42.

94. Ibid., pp. 106–10. As we shall see, Blackmore also speculates that endorphins, by activating parts of the brain where memories are stored, may help explain the panoramic life reviews often associated with NDEs. Ibid., pp. 210–14.

95. Ibid., pp. 183–225.

Answers to Selected Exercises

Chapter 2

Exercise 2.1

1. Statement.
4. Nonstatement; request or suggestion.
7. Statement. (Sentences that report personal feelings can be true or false. After all, someone who says, "I love you," might be lying.)
10. Statement.
13. Statement. (You might be lying.)
16. Statement. (You might be lying.)
19. Nonstatement; exhortation. (This could be a statement in certain contexts.)
22. Nonstatement; petition or request.
25. Statement or nonstatement, depending on the context. If it's an ought imperative, it's a statement. If it's a command, it's not.

Exercise 2.2

I.

1. *Premise:* Pain is a state of consciousness, a mental event.
   Conclusion: It can never be directly observed.
4. *Premise:* A man's own fundamental thoughts are the only ones that he can fully and wholly understand.
   Conclusion: If a man's thoughts are to have truth and life in them, they must after all be his own fundamental thoughts.
7. *Premise 1:* Without symbols, no intellectual advance is possible.
   Premise 2: With symbols, there is no limit set to intellectual development except inherent stupidity.
   Conclusion: The invention or discovery of symbols is doubtless by far the single greatest event in the history of man.
10. *Premise:* The extent of a man's or a people's liberty to live as they desire must be weighed against the claims of many other values, of which equality, or justice, or happiness, or security, or public order are perhaps the most obvious examples.
    Conclusion: The extent of a man's or a people's liberty cannot be unlimited.
13. *Premise:* The more stupid a member of Parliament is, the more stupid his constituents were to elect him.
    Conclusion: Democracy has at least one merit, namely, that a member of Parliament cannot be stupider than his constituents.
16. *Premise:* Everyone recalls the famous incident at Sybil Seretsky's when her goldfish sang "I Got Rhythm"— a favorite tune of her deceased nephew.
    Conclusion: There is no doubt that certain events recorded at seances are genuine.
19. *Premise 1:* In great contests each party claims to act in accordance with the will of God.
    Premise 2: God cannot be for and against the same thing at the same time.
    Conclusion: Both parties in great contests may be, and one must be, wrong.
22. *Premise:* Philosophy is nothing else but the study of wisdom and truth.
    Conclusion: It may with reason be expected that those who have spent most time and pains in philosophy should enjoy a greater calm and serenity of mind, and greater clearness and evidence of knowledge, and be less disturbed with doubts and difficulties than other men.
25. *Premise 1:* When the universe has crushed him, man knows that he is dying.

Answers to Selected Exercises   **551**

Premise 2: Of its victory the universe knows nothing.

Conclusion: When the universe has crushed him, man will still be nobler than that which kills him.

EXERCISE 2.2

II.

1. *Premise:* If you put a pen in the breast pocket of your pajamas and roll over in the middle of the night, you kill yourself.

   Conclusion: You don't need a breast pocket on your pajamas.

4. *Premise:* If we engage the authority of Scripture in disputes about the natural world, in opposition to reason, then time, which brings all things to light, may discover that to be false, which we had made scripture assert.

   Conclusion: 'Tis a dangerous thing to engage the authority of Scripture in disputes about the natural world, in opposition to reason.

7. *Premise 1:* Philosophy is dangerous whenever it is taken seriously.

   Premise 2: So is life.

   Premise 3: Safety is not an option.

   Conclusion: Our choices are not between risk and security, but between a life lived consciously, fully, humanly in the most complete sense and a life that just happens.

10. *Premise 1:* You have to exist in order for your neighbor to present you with an argument that you do not really exist.

    Premise 2 (subconclusion): If your neighbor presents you with an apparently flawless scientific case that you do not really exist, there are mistakes in the argument.

    Conclusion: If your neighbor presents you with an apparently flawless scientific case that you do not really exist, don't get too rattled even if you cannot find any obvious mistakes in the case.

13. *Premise 1:* Virtually everyone and every group claim they know what constitutes right versus wrong action.

    Premise 2: Virtually all of these moralities differ from all others to a greater and lesser extent.

    Conclusion: Reason alone tells us these moralities cannot all be correct.

16. *Premise 1:* People who believe that they are responsible for what they do will also demand the conditions of responsible choice.

    Premise 2: They will insist that they not be denied information that is relevant to their choice.

    Premise 3: They will want the opportunity to discuss and debate with others.

    Conclusion: Free speech and free press are essential components of a society that regards human beings as responsible moral agents.

19. *Premise 1:* It is because of ethics (moral reasoning) that we have law in the first place.

    Premise 2: We continue to need ethics to refine and perfect our legal system.

    Premise 3: We need ethics in order to discuss the practical implications of our religious beliefs with others who do not share that belief.

    Premise 4: In situations when the reasonableness of a particular article of belief is at issue, we need ethics to help us reach a sound decision.

    Conclusion: It is foolish to argue that we don't need ethics because we have law and religious belief.

EXERCISE 2.4

I.

1. Nonargument; explanation.
4. Nonargument; conditional statement.
7. Argument.
10. Nonargument; illustration.
13. Nonargument; report of argument. (The writer is reporting, not endorsing, Gladstone's argument.)
16. Argument.
19. Nonargument; unsupported statement of belief or opinion. (Notice that the word "because" does not function as a premise indicator in either sentence of this passage.)
22. Argument.
25. Nonargument; unsupported statement of belief or opinion.
28. Nonargument; illustration.
31. Nonargument; conditional statement. (The claim is of the form: If you believe A, then you must also believe B.)
34. Nonargument; explanation of why so many people have become vegetarians.
37. Nonargument; explanation of why she never throws away a key.
40. Argument.

EXERCISE 2.4

II.

1. Explanation.
4. Argument.
7. Explanation.
10. Explanation.
13. Explanation.
16. Explanation.
19. Explanation.
22. Argument.
25. Explanation.

CHAPTER 3

EXERCISE 3.1

I.
Problem 1: Moriarty.

EXERCISE 3.1

II.
Problem 1: Mike: Grape juice.
Amy: Pepsi.
Brian: Diet Coke.
Lisa: Iced tea.
Bill: 7-Up.

EXERCISE 3.2

1. Deductive (argument based on mathematics; also, the conclusion follows necessarily from the premises).
4. Deductive (argument by elimination).
7. Inductive. (Given that signs can be wrong, the conclusion follows only probably from the premises.)
10. Inductive (argument from authority; also a prediction; also, "probably" is an induction indicator word).
13. Inductive. (The principle of charity dictates that the argument be regarded as inductive, since the conclusion follows at best probably from the premises.)
16. Inductive. (Argument from authority; also, the conclusion does not follow necessarily from the premises.)
19. Inductive. (The principle of charity dictates that the argument be regarded as inductive, since the conclusion does not follow necessarily from the premises.)
22. Deductive (argument by elimination; also, the conclusion follows necessarily from the premises.)
25. Deductive (argument based on mathematics; also, conclusion follows necessarily from the premises; also, "it necessarily follows" is a deduction indicator phrase).
28. Inductive (argument from analogy; also, the conclusion does not follow necessarily from the premises).
31. Deductive. (Conclusion follows necessarily from the premises.)
34. Inductive (causal argument; also, the conclusion follows only probably from the premises).

EXERCISE 3.3

1. Beta.
4. Delta is not an alpha.
7. If Delta is an alpha, then Delta is a theta.
10. Some alphas are thetas. (Or: Some thetas are alphas.)

EXERCISE 3.4

I.
1. Valid.
4. Invalid (denying the antecedent).
7. Invalid.
10. Invalid.

EXERCISE 3.4

II.
1. Sound.
4. Unsound (invalid argument: affirming the consequent).
7. Unsound (invalid argument: denying the antecedent).
10. Unsound (false premise).

EXERCISE 3.4

III.
1. Cogent.
4. Uncogent. (The argument compares cities that are different in relevant respects. Gun violence is a much less serious problem in Montreal than it is in Detroit, Miami, or Houston, in part because there are far fewer guns in Canada.)
7. Cogent.
10. Uncogent. (The conclusion does not follow probably from the premises.)

EXERCISE 3.4

IV.
1. Deductive, valid.
4. Inductive, weak.
7. Inductive, strong.
10. Inductive, weak.
13. Inductive, weak.
16. Inductive, weak.
19. Inductive, strong.
22. Deductive, valid.
25. Deductive, invalid.

EXERCISE 3.5

1. 1. All A's are B's.   1. All dogs are animals.   (T)
   2. All C's are B's.   2. All cats are animals.   (T)
   3. So, all A's are C's. 3. So, all dogs are cats. (F)

4. 1. If O is an A,
      then O is a B.   Valid (*modus tollens*).
   2. O is not a B.
   3. So, O is not an A.

7. 1. No A's are B's.   1. No ants are birds.   (T)
    2. Some A's are   2. Some ants are
       not C's.   not crows.   (T)
    3. So, some C's are   3. So, some crows are
       not B's.   not birds.   (F)

10. 1. All A's are B's.   1. All dogs are animals.   (T)
    2. Some A's are C's.   2. Some dogs are collies.   (T)
    3. So, some C's are   3. So, some collies are
       not B's.   not animals.   (F)

CHAPTER 4

EXERCISE 4.2

1. Ambiguous. The headline could be read to mean that tires with metal studs have been prohibited or that a breeding animal (or a sexually active man) has become exhausted.

4. Ambiguous. Should the security officer have experience as a shoplifter or as someone who has enforced laws against shoplifting?

7. Ambiguous because of unclear pronoun reference. Which nephew is getting the watch, and which is getting the car? Or are the nephews supposed to share the items?

10. Ambiguous. "With relish" could refer to the condiment made of chopped pickles, or it could describe the enjoyment with which the cheesecake was eaten.

13. Vague. The meaning of "the loving thing" is fuzzy.

16. Ambiguous. Without parentheses it is impossible to know how to proceed in solving this equation. Is it $(3 + 5) \times 3 = 24$? Or is it $3 + (5 \times 3) = 18$?

19. Ambiguous. Is "left" a verb or a noun? The same could be asked of "waffles." In one reading of the headline, the British Labor party has changed its mind regarding England's defense of the Falkland Islands. In another reading, the British have deposited a popular breakfast food on the islands.

22. Vague and overgeneral. The words "small," "brown," and "dog" have fuzzy meanings. (How small? What shade of brown? What kind of dog?) And the phrase "small brown dog" is not specific enough to distinguish the lost dog from many other dogs. "Generous reward" is also vague, since there are many borderline cases. A million dollars is clearly generous; a nickel is not. But what about one hundred dollars?

25. Ambiguous. Does the statement suggest that we *give* our loved ones herpes or *inform* them that we have the disease?

28. Vague. Just what counts as a "religion" or "the free exercise thereof" is not clear. Arguably, however, the language in such a broad legal statement is appropriate and necessary.

EXERCISE 4.5

I.

4. Possible choices: *begged, pleaded, requested, implored, insisted, demanded. Begged, pleaded,* and *implored* suggest that the speaker is dependent on the listener or that she is desperate. *Demanded* shows that she has more power over the listener, making "please" in the sentence merely courteous or perhaps sarcastic.

7. Possible choices: *gripped, grabbed, clutched, seized, squeezed. Gripped* connotes aggression or dominance; *clutched* might suggest fear or protection.

10. Possible choices: *cold, hard-hearted, apathetic, callous, insensitive, unsympathetic.* These words are all close in meaning, but *callous* might imply a roughness developed after many disappointments, and *apathetic* suggests indifference and a lack of concern.

13. Possible choices: *accepted, okayed, endorsed, praised, admired, celebrated.* These words all have different meanings, but they share the notion of approval. However, some of the words (*praised, celebrated*) suggest something far more positive than others (*accepted, okayed*).

EXERCISE 4.5

II.

1. In many contexts, "dreamer" would elicit a negative reaction. More positive words include "optimistic," "goal-oriented," and "visionary." "Hopeful" might be more neutral. What about "idealistic"?

4. "Dresses well" sounds neutral enough, although it could generate positive responses toward the person described. To say that "he's so into his looks," however, would probably generate a negative response to the person, as would "fashion plate," "clothes horse," or the dated expressions "fop" and "dandy" (ask your grandparents).

7. "Old treasures" sounds much more valuable and precious than "junk" or "garbage." Neutral words might be the ubiquitous "stuff," "things," or "items." Other words that generate positive reactions include "collectibles" and "antiques."

10. We might be impressed by a student who "stood up for" himself, but what about a student who "had an excuse," "offered an alibi," or "talked back"? Those descriptions would most likely elicit a negative response. More neutral descriptors include "explained" or even "defended."

13. "Assertive" is a neutral word, although some readers or listeners might respond negatively. "Aggressive" would elicit negative reactions, as would "pushy." How about "forceful" or "firm"? How would you respond to the sentence "The new employee was firm with her boss?"

16. "Scheme" is negative; a tax "plan" or "program" is more neutral, perhaps even positive. "Tax initiatives"

softens everything. (More on this when we get to euphemisms.)

19. "Tactics" is negative. "Actions" would be neutral; "efforts" sounds positive.

EXERCISE 4.5

III.

1. Emotive words and phrases in the advertisement include *charming, cozy* (code for small?), *older neighborhood, lower-level recreation room* (basement?), *modern, tender loving care* (needs lots of work?). All these words are used to create a warm and receptive attitude in the prospective buyer.

4. Emotive words and phrases include *admitted bisexual, oddball, dumped, four-time loser at the altar, spousal abuse, walked away, on-the-mouth kisses, spawned, incest, nuptials.* Some of these words (*oddball, dumped, loser*) are clearly intended to reveal the writer's negative attitude and to encourage the reader to feel the same. Other words, though emotive, might be appropriate and accurate—*bisexual, spousal abuse*—though both are vague.

7. Emotive words include *laziest, slapdash, crummy, cornball, feeble, contemptible, gross, ingratiating, smarm, perfunctory, of course, maudlin, lame.* Apparently this reviewer didn't like *Big Daddy*. We'll leave it up to you to say whether the emotive language is accurate or not.

CHAPTER 5

EXERCISE 5.1

1. Positively relevant.
4. Irrelevant.
7. Negatively relevant.
10. Positively relevant. (Although the premises don't provide evidence for God's existence, they do provide prudential, or self-interested, reasons for *belief* in God. Whether these prudential reasons are properly convincing is, of course, another question.)
13. The first premise is negatively relevant, and the second premise is positively relevant.

EXERCISE 5.2

1. Bandwagon argument.
4. Straw man.
7. Begging the question.
10. Two wrongs make a right.
13. Equivocation.
16. No fallacy.
19. No fallacy.

22. Straw man.
25. Red herring.
28. Attacking the motive.
31. Bandwagon argument.
34. Bandwagon argument.
37. Red herring.
40. No fallacy.

CHAPTER 6

EXERCISE 6.1

I.

1. Inappropriate appeal to authority.
4. Inappropriate appeal to authority.
7. Hasty generalization.
10. Inappropriate appeal to authority.
13. Weak analogy.
16. Inappropriate appeal to authority.
19. No fallacy.
22. Hasty generalization.
25. Inappropriate appeal to authority.
28. Inconsistency.
31. No fallacy. (No argument is given.)
34. Weak analogy.
37. Hasty generalization.
40. Slippery slope.

EXERCISE 6.1

II.

1. Loaded question.
4. False alternatives (assuming that an argument is being given).
7. Personal attack.
10. Weak analogy.
13. Red herring; possible personal attack.
16. Questionable cause.
19. Questionable cause.
22. Begging the question.
25. Personal attack; also weak analogy.
28. Questionable cause.
31. Look who's talking; also personal attack.
34. Hasty generalization.
37. False alternatives.
40. Questionable cause.

CHAPTER 7

EXERCISE 7.1

1. ① All humans are mortal. ② Socrates is a human. Therefore, ③ Socrates is mortal.

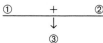

4. ① Affirmative action in higher education is morally justifiable, because ② it compensates for past discrimination, ③ provides valuable role models for women and minorities, and ④ promotes multicultural understanding.

7. Several states have abolished the insanity defense against criminal responsibility. ① This may be popular with voters, but it is morally indefensible. ② Insanity removes moral responsibility, and ③ it is wrong to punish someone who is not morally responsible for his crime. Moreover, ④ it is pointless to punish the insane, because ⑤ punishment has no deterrent effect on a person who cannot appreciate the wrongfulness or criminality of his or her actions.

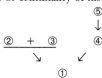

10. ① If today is Saturday, then tomorrow is Sunday. ② If tomorrow is Sunday, then we'll be having pasta for dinner. ③ If we'll be having pasta for dinner, then I should pick up some red wine today, since ④ in this state wine can be purchased only at liquor stores, and ⑤ the liquor stores are closed on Sundays. ⑥ Today is Saturday. Therefore, ⑦ I should pick up some red wine today.

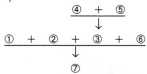

13. ① Most drugs should be legalized. Since ② drugs such as heroin and cocaine are literally worth more than their weight in gold, ③ it's foolish to think we can ever prevent drugs from being smuggled into this country. Moreover, ④ the drug war is enormously expensive to fight. ⑤ According to a recent FBI report, local, state, and federal governments spent over $20 billion last year enforcing our nation's drug laws. In addition, ⑥ it distracts police from the task of fighting more serious crimes, ⑦ clogs our courts and

⑧ leads to grossly overcrowded prisons. Finally, ⑨ just as in the days of Prohibition, making drugs illegal funnels huge profits into the hands of a dangerous criminal underground.

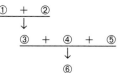

16. Brute beasts, not having understanding and therefore not being persons, cannot have rights. [Elaborated version: ① Brute beasts have no understanding. Therefore, ② they are not persons. Therefore, ③ they cannot have rights.]

19. ① All humans have equal positive value. ② There is no morally relevant difference between humans and some animals (such as mammals). Therefore, ③ some animals have equal positive worth with humans. ④ Moral rights derive from the possession of value. Since ⑤ humans have rights (to life, not to be harmed, and so forth), ⑥ animals have those same rights.

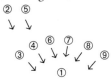

22. ① Planetary exploration has many virtues. ② It permits us to refine insights derived from such Earth-bound sciences as meteorology, climatology, geology, and biology, to broaden their powers and improve their practical applications here on Earth. ③ It provides cautionary tales on the alternative fates of worlds. ④ It is an aperture to future high technologies important for life here on Earth. ⑤ It provides an outlet for the traditional human zest for exploration and discovery, our passion to find out, which has been to a very large degree responsible for our success as a species. And ⑥ it permits us, for the first time in history, to approach with rigor, with a significant chance of finding out the true answers, questions on the origins and destinies of worlds, the beginnings and ends of life, and the possibilities of other beings who live in the skies—questions as basic to the human enterprise as thinking is, as natural as breathing.

25. ① Here is a gentleman of a medical type, but with the air of a military man. ② Clearly an army doctor, then. ③ He has just come from the tropics, for ④ his face is dark, and ⑤ that is not the natural tint of his skin, as ⑥ his wrists are fair. ⑦ He has undergone hardship and sickness, as ⑧ his haggard face says clearly. ⑨ His left arm has been injured. ⑩ He holds it in a stiff and unnatural manner. Where in the tropics could an English doctor have seen much hardship and get his arm wounded? ⑪ Clearly in Afghanistan.

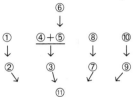

EXERCISE 7.2

1. Most Californians are friendly.
4. Having a lot of money is not the secret to true happiness.
7. People often make light of hardships or sorrows that they themselves have never experienced.
10. Since human reason is so weak and uncertain, some people should simply be told what their moral duties are. Otherwise, they will make bad choices that may cause serious harm.

EXERCISE 7.3

I.
1. Missing premise: All Mazda Miatas are convertibles.
4. Missing premise: This is not a Honda.
7. Missing premise (subconclusion): This is a Toyota.
10. Missing premise: Some Fords are Rangers.

EXERCISE 7.3

II.
1. Missing premise: Most people from Singapore speak English.
4. Missing premise: Abortion is the intentional killing of an innocent human person.
7. Missing premise: Anyone who graduated from Princeton must be smart. Missing premise: Anyone who is smart should be able to solve this logic problem in the time allotted.
10. Missing premise: Anything that comes to an end is meaningless.
13. Missing premise: All facts are scientific facts.

EXERCISE 7.4

Essay 1: Why Teachers Shouldn't Assign Homework
1. Teachers already have enough time during the school day to instruct children.
2. There are too many children that come home with either no adult there or no adult with the ability to help them with their homework.
3. This places many children at a disadvantage compared to other children who have their parents there to help them with their homework.
4. [Teachers should not give assignments that place some children at a disadvantage compared to others.]
5. Children, like adults, should have the luxury of being able to come home after a long day and have the rest of the day to themselves.
6. Therefore, teachers should assign no homework whatsoever. (from 1–5)

Essay 4: Nation Isn't Ready for Same-Sex Marriages
1. Despite all the turmoil that swirls around marriage, most people continue to see it as a legal and/or religious bond between a man and a woman.
2. Government should not legalize same-sex marriages until a substantial portion of Americans is ready to do so.
3. A recent Gallup Poll indicates Americans oppose same-sex marriages by 68 to 27 percent.
4. Marriage is a beleaguered institution that still lends much-needed stability to individuals and the community.
5. A proposal to redefine marriage to include homosexuals would offend millions of Americans and would never be approved by Congress.
6. A battle over gay marriage might further weaken the troubled institution of marriage and threaten hard-won gay rights in housing, employment and other areas.
7. Therefore, in this election year the gay community would be wise to follow President Clinton's lead and not demand the legalization of same-sex marriages. (from 1–6)

CHAPTER 9

EXERCISE 9.1

1.

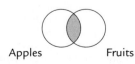

4.

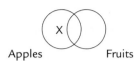

Apples   Fruits

7.

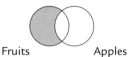

Fruits   Apples

10.

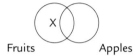

Fruits   Apples

EXERCISE 9.2

1. All persons who may use the Jacuzzi are hotel guests.
4. All ladybugs are insects.
7. All persons permitted in the faculty locker room are faculty members.
10. All dogs allowed in the store are Seeing Eye dogs.

EXERCISE 9.3

I.
1. All maples are trees.
4. All insects are animals.
7. No cheaters are persons who prosper.
10. All cars are vehicles.
13. Some sheep are not white sheep.
16. Some polar bears are animals that live in Canada.
19. All free persons are educated persons.
22. No questions that have answers are questions that are worth asking.
25. All lives that are worth living are examined lives.
28. All persons who are any good are persons who are different from anybody else.

EXERCISE 9.4

I.
1. Some bankers are vegetarians.
   No anarchists are bankers.
   So, some anarchists are not vegetarians.

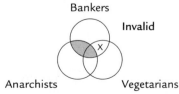

4. No barracuda are pets.
   No sharks are barracuda.
   So, no sharks are pets.

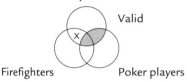

7. No poker players are early risers.
   Some firefighters are early risers.
   So, some firefighters are not poker players.

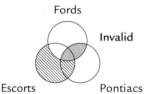

10. No Fords are Pontiacs.
    All Escorts are Fords.
    So, some Escorts are not Pontiacs.

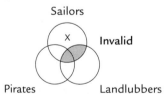

13. No landlubbers are sailors.
    Some sailors are not pirates.
    So, some pirates are not landlubbers.

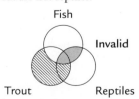

16. No fish are reptiles.
    All trout are fish.
    So, some trout are not reptiles.

19. Some butchers are not bakers.
No butchers are candlestick makers.
Therefore, some candlestick makers are not bakers.

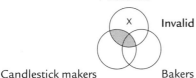

EXERCISE 9.4

II.
1. No Nobel Prize winners are rock stars.
Some astrophysicists are Nobel Prize winners.
Therefore, some astrophysicists are not rock stars.

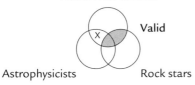

4. All liberals are big spenders.
All persons identical to Senator Crumley are big spenders.
So, all persons identical to Senator Crumley are liberals.

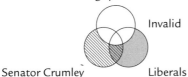

7. Some lawyers are not golfers.
All lawyers are persons who have attended law school.
So, some persons who have attended law school are not golfers.

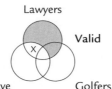

10. All political scientists are social scientists.
Some political scientists are persons who favor campaign finance reform.
So, some persons who favor campaign finance reform are social scientists.

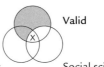

13. All tax evaders are lawbreakers.
No lawbreakers are model citizens.
So, no model citizens are tax evaders.

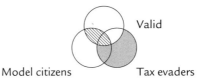

16. No harmless acts are immoral acts.
Some lies are not harmless acts.
So, some lies are not immoral acts.

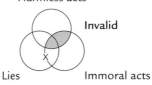

19. All persons who eat pizza every night are persons at risk for heart disease.
Some persons who are at risk for heart disease are cab drivers.
So, some cab drivers are persons who eat pizza every night.

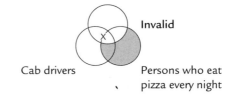

CHAPTER 10

EXERCISE 10.1

I.
1. p
4. $p \& q$
7. $p \& q$
10. $p \& q$

II.
1. T
4. T
7. F
10. F

III.
1. T
4. T
7. F
10. T

EXERCISE 10.2

I.
1.

p^*	q^*	$p \& q$ C
T	T	T
T	F	F
F	T	F
F	F	F

Valid.

4.

r^*	s C
T	T
T	F
F	T
F	F

Invalid.

II.
1.

p
q
$\therefore p \& q$

p^*	q^*	$p \& q$ C
T	T	T
T	F	F
F	T	F
F	F	F

Valid.

EXERCISE 10.3

I.
1. F
4. F
7. F
10. T

III.
1. $p \& \sim q$
4. $\sim p \& q$
7. $p \& \sim q$
10. $\sim (p \& q)$

IV.
1.

p	q^*	$\sim p^*$	$\sim p \& q$ C
T	T	F	F
T	F	F	F
F	T	T	T
F	F	T	F

Valid.

4.

p	q	$p \& q$	$\sim (p \& q)^*$	p^*	$\sim q$ C
T	T	T	F	T	F
T	F	F	T	T	T
F	T	F	T	F	F
F	F	F	T	F	T

Valid.

V.
1.

$\sim p \& \sim q$
$\therefore \sim (p \& q)$

p	q	$\sim p$	$\sim q$	$p \& q$	$\sim p \& \sim q^*$	$\sim (p \& q)$ C
T	T	F	F	T	F	F
T	F	F	T	F	F	T
F	T	T	F	F	F	T
F	F	T	T	F	T	T

Valid.

4.

$\sim (p \& q)$
p
$\therefore \sim q$

p	q	$p \& q$	$\sim (p \& q)^*$	p^*	$\sim q$ C
T	T	T	F	T	F
T	F	F	T	T	T
F	T	F	T	F	F
F	F	F	T	F	T

Valid.

EXERCISE 10.4

I.
1. T
4. F
7. F
10. T

III.

1. (c & d) & ~k
4. (t & b) & ~w

IV.

1.

p & q
~ (q & r)
∴ ~r

	p	q	r	q & r	p & q*	~(q & r)*	~r C
1.	T	T	T	T	T	F	F
2.	T	T	F	F	T	T	T
3.	T	F	T	F	F	T	F
4.	T	F	F	F	F	T	T
5.	F	T	T	T	F	F	F
6.	F	T	F	F	F	T	T
7.	F	F	T	F	F	T	F
8.	F	F	F	F	F	T	T

Valid.

4.

b & ~t
~(m & b)
∴ ~m & ~t

	b	m	t	~m	~t	m & b	b & ~t*	~(m & b)*	~m & ~t C
1.	T	T	T	F	F	T	F	F	F
2.	T	T	F	F	T	T	T	F	F
3.	T	F	T	T	F	F	F	T	F
4.	T	F	F	T	T	F	T	T	T
5.	F	T	T	F	F	F	F	T	F
6.	F	T	F	F	T	F	F	T	F
7.	F	F	T	T	F	F	F	T	F
8.	F	F	F	T	T	F	F	T	T

Valid.

V.

1.

f & t
~s
∴ ~(f & s)

	f	t	s	f & s	f & t*	~s*	~(f & s)C
1.	T	T	T	T	T	F	F
2.	T	T	F	F	T	T	T
3.	T	F	T	T	F	F	F
4.	T	F	F	F	F	T	T
5.	F	T	T	F	F	F	T
6.	F	T	F	F	F	T	T
7.	F	F	T	F	F	F	T
8.	F	F	F	F	F	T	T

Valid.

4.

s & ~e
~(e & t)
∴ s & t

	s	e	t	~e	e&t	s&~e*	~(e & t)*	s & t C
1.	T	T	T	F	T	F	F	T
2.	T	T	F	F	F	F	T	F
3.	T	F	T	T	F	T	T	T
4.	T	F	F	T	F	T	T	F
5.	F	T	T	F	T	F	F	F
6.	F	T	F	F	F	F	T	F
7.	F	F	T	T	F	F	T	F
8.	F	F	F	T	F	F	T	F

Invalid.

EXERCISE 10.5

I.

1. T
4. T
7. T
10. F

III.

1. d v r
4. w v d
7. p v f
10. ~(t v a) & w

IV.

1.

p	q	p v q*	~p*	q C
T	T	T	F	T
T	F	T	F	F
F	T	T	T	T
F	F	F	T	F

Valid.

4.

	t	a	w	~t	t & a	~(t & a)*	a v w*	~t & a C
1.	T	T	T	F	T	F	T	F
2.	T	T	F	F	T	F	T	F
3.	T	F	T	F	F	T	T	F
4.	T	F	F	F	F	T	F	F
5.	F	T	T	T	F	T	T	T
6.	F	T	F	T	F	T	T	T
7.	F	F	T	T	F	T	T	F
8.	F	F	F	T	F	T	F	F

Invalid.

V.

1.

$d \lor r$

$\sim r$

$\therefore d$

d	r	d v r*	~r*	d C
T	T	T	F	T
T	F	T	T	T
F	T	T	F	F
F	F	F	T	F

Valid.

4.

$s \lor a$

$\sim(s \,\&\, a)$

a

$\therefore s$

s	a	s & a	s v a*	~(s & a)*	a*	s C
T	T	T	T	F	T	T
T	F	F	T	T	F	T
F	T	F	T	T	T	F
F	F	F	F	T	F	F

Invalid.

EXERCISE 10.6

I.

1. F
4. T
7. F
10. T

III.

1. $b \to e$
4. $h \to f$
7. $\sim c \to \sim e$
10. $(s \to g) \to (\sim s \to p)$

IV.

1.

p	q	p → q*	~p*	~q C
1. T	T	T	F	F
2. T	F	F	F	T
3. F	T	T	T	F
4. F	F	T	T	T

Invalid.

4.

p	q	r	~p	~q	p → q*	~q v r*	~p & r
1. T	T	T	F	F	T	T	F
2. T	T	F	F	F	T	F	F
3. T	F	T	F	T	F	T	F
4. T	F	F	F	T	F	T	F
5. F	T	T	T	F	T	T	T
6. F	T	F	T	F	T	F	F
7. F	F	T	T	T	T	T	T
8. F	F	F	T	T	T	T	F

Invalid.

V.

1. $b \to e$

$\sim e$

$\therefore b$

b	e	b → e*	~e*	~b C
1. T	T	T	F	F
2. T	F	F	T	F
3. F	T	T	F	T
4. F	F	T	T	T

Valid.

4.

$g \to s$

$\therefore \sim g \to \sim s$

g	s	~g	~s	g → s*	~g → ~s C
1. T	T	F	F	T	T
2. T	F	F	T	F	T
3. F	T	T	F	T	F
4. F	F	T	T	T	T

Invalid.

CHAPTER 11

EXERCISE 11.1

1. Strong.
4. Strong.
7. Strong.
10. Weak.

EXERCISE 11.2

I.

1. Strong. Is the sample large enough? Yes. Is the sample representative? Yes.
4. Weak. Is the sample large enough? Yes. Is the sample representative? No.

EXERCISE 11.2

II.
1. Is the sample large enough? No, there are just three cities. Is the sample representative? No, not necessarily; for example, at least two of the cities have problems with illegal immigration that may add to the crime problem.
4. Is the sample large enough? Possibly, depending on the size of the faculty. Is the sample representative? No, they are all from one department. Other departments may grant tenure to far fewer applicants.

EXERCISE 11.4

I.
1. (c) Strong and reliable.
4. (c) Strong and reliable.
7. (c) Strong and reliable.
10. (c) Strong and reliable.

EXERCISE 11.6

1. 2: The skills involved are very different.
4. 5: There are big differences between a small family budget and a large city budget.
7. 7: The argument does not claim very much, and considering Jordan's athletic ability, love for the game, and practice, it isn't unreasonable to claim that he could learn to play fairly well.
10. 3: The conclusion is too strong in claiming that he must be "just like" the character. There are a couple of important similarities but not enough to fully support the conclusion.

EXERCISE 11.8

I.
1. Strong.
4. Weak.

EXERCISE 11.8

II.
1. a. Strengthen.
   b. Strengthen.
   c. Weaken.
   d. Strengthen.
4. a. Strengthen.
   b. Weaken.
   c. Weaken.
   d. Strengthen.

EXERCISE 11.10

I.
1. Bad evidence.
4. Good evidence.
7. Good evidence.
10. Good evidence.

EXERCISE 11.10

II.
1. What else did he eat? Did anyone else become sick from eating it?
4. The percentage of women with breast implants who have connective tissue disease; the percentage of women in the general public who have connective tissue disease; the percentage of women with silicon breast implants who have connective tissue disease; the percentage of women with saline breast implants who have connective tissue disease.
7. Why do students choose to sit in the front row?
10. How do we define a "healthy heart"? Just red wine, or other alcoholic beverages?

EXERCISE 11.11

1. Relative frequency.
4. Epistemic.
7. Relative frequency.
10. A priori.

EXERCISE 11.12

I.
1. Negative.
4. Negative.

CHAPTER 12

EXERCISE 12.2

II.
1. Facts: Cal Thomas worked for NBC News in the late 1960s. Robert Kitner was at one time president of NBC, as was Sylvester Weaver, who went by the name of "Pat." Matters of fact: Stories were selected on the basis of the audience they would attract. (This could be verified with interviews, for example, or with corporate correspondence.) Whether or not "ratings for news started to matter, as they did for entertainment" could be verified in similar ways, though some words, such as "mattered," would need to be clarified. The decline in the ratings could easily be documented. But what about the claim that "the respect most people once had for the journalism

profession" also declined? Could that be documented through surveys or opinion polls? Could such a statement be shown to be factual?

4. There are many facts in this item: Harvard is the oldest institution of higher learning in America; thirty-three Nobel Prize winners graduated from Harvard; Bill Gates developed the programming language BASIC; Radcliff was founded in 1879 and started admitting men in 1973; Martin Luther King, Jr., received a doctorate in theology from Boston University, and so forth. Some statements, however, are not immediately verifiable. For example, it would be very difficult to document the claim that MIT is "generally acknowledged to be the nation's top school for science and engineering." The imprecise language—"generally acknowledged"—makes the statement more opinion than fact. Qualifying the statement might bring it closer to a matter of fact: "MIT is regarded among college presidents as the nation's best school for engineering." At least, such a claim could be verified.

Exercise 12.3

1. Rush Limbaugh is a radio-talk-show host and author who espouses a conservative point of view. His claim that condoms fail "around" 17 percent of the time should be cautiously considered and verified with more reliable sources. One key to Limbaugh's bias is his characterization of liberals in the first sentence of the quoted item. (Could he be charged here with a straw man fallacy?)

4. The billboards proclaiming these "facts" are sponsored by someone who is attempting to reduce the level of immigration into the United States. The figures on the billboards may or may not be correct, but anyone hoping to use them in an argument would do well to corroborate the information with other sources. (A careful reader will notice the slippery language in less-than-reliable information. In the first billboard, how little is "very little"? In the second, "arrive" is a vague word with several possible meanings, including "visit.")

7. It may well be true that 67 percent of listeners "would prefer that the races be separated," but that doesn't prove that "67 percent of people" prefer the same. Are the callers to a radio talk show a representative sample of "people" everywhere? Hardly.

10. The *Washington Times* reporter has relied on comments from several organizations—Landmark Legal Foundation, the Southeastern Legal Foundation, and Judicial Watch—to support its claim that that American Bar Association "was widely criticized" for hosting President Clinton. All three organizations have a pronounced conservative political bias and would be expected to support the claim. For information about each, visit their Web sites:

http://www.southeasternlegal.org/; http://www.landmarklegal.org/; http://www.judicialwatch.org.

13. As a student at Harvard and editor of one of the student newspapers, Mr. Douthat is most likely very bright and perceptive. Still, his comments represent only one person's view of higher education, and his observations may be limited to what he sees at his own school. It would be unwise to use Mr. Douthat's comments as support for an argument about college life and work in general. The writer's point of view and attitude are very clear in the passage, and the fact that it was published in *The American Spectator* hints at the author's bias and intended audience. A description of *The American Spectator* can be found earlier in this chapter.

Exercise 12.4

1. Answers will vary. Here is one possibility: In her book, *Starting Out Suburban: A Frosh Year Survival Guide,* Linda Polland Puner suggests that most freshmen find it difficult to be away from home for the first time. They miss some of the comforts, such as good meals and privacy. Some are lucky enough, particularly if their family lives nearby, to get home within the first month of school, but others must wait until Thanksgiving or even Christmas. Even just a semester away from home can seem very long and the distances can seem longer than they really are. (121)

4. Answers will vary. Here is one possibility: In her article "A Test for Assessing Phonemic Awareness in Young Children," Hallie Kay Yopp claims that researchers have found that phonemic awareness, or the ability to sound out words, is perhaps the most important requirement for good reading skills. This ability appears to be a more important indicator of reading success than IQ scores and vocabulary and listening comprehension tests. Having a proper assessment tool in place, therefore, can help direct the teacher to awareness of potential problems and to the use of available exercises that will enable the student to acquire stronger spelling and reading skills (28).

Exercise 12.5

1. Because rules are precise and must be followed to the letter, it would be best to quote the rule or the relevant part of the rule exactly as it appears in the book. In claiming that a player should have lost a tournament, someone might write, "In hitting the ball twice, Samprassi clearly violated Rule 20d, which prohibits the player from 'deliberately touch[ing] it [the ball] with his racket more than once' in a given point." The writer would need, of course, to prove that the action was "deliberate."

4. The passage could be paraphrased or summarized with some phrases quoted if necessary. The following sentence might appear in a student's paper: "Athletes who push themselves to the limit often incur injuries, but the medical community is now considering whether athletes who push too hard might be susceptible to 'a host of chronic diseases, even cancer'" (Tabor).

EXERCISE 12.6

1. Fact available in wide variety of sources: does not need to be documented.

4. Although many people might be able to list from memory the five best-selling albums of all time, this fact should be documented. One clue that this information needs to be cited is the inclusion of a date, "as of August 1999." The fact may have changed since then, so it would be wise to say where the information came from.

7. No need to document this fact; it is widely known and available.

10. This one is tricky. For scholars of Dickens's life and work, this is a commonly known fact: Dickens's childhood experiences are indeed reflected in several of his novels. Therefore, in preparing an argument for a literature class, you would most likely find this information in several sources and would not have to cite it. However, you would not be incorrect in giving a source if you chose to do so. In your paper you might write, "According to Charles Dickens's friend and biographer, John Forster, the novelist's childhood experiences, including his father's imprisonment for debt and Dickens's subsequent work in a shoe-polish factory, influenced his work as a novelist." (You would also need, of course, to supply the appropriate reference information.)

13. This is still being debated, so it would be best to tell your reader what source you are using.

16. This fact should be documented.

19. This is common knowledge or information that could be located in wide variety of sources. Remember that even if information is news to you, it might not need to be documented.

22. These are historical facts in wide circulation.

25. This fact is so shocking that the source should be acknowledged.

CHAPTER 14

EXERCISE 14.12

1. f
4. m
7. k

10. d
13. b
16. q
19. x
22. cc
25. w
28. r

EXERCISE 14.13

III.

1. "The best things in life are basic." (Ad for Basic brand cigarettes)

   This advertisement gives no information about the product. It is a clever but ironic play on words aimed at price-conscious cigarette-consuming buyers and seeks to compliment them for knowing how to get the pleasure they seek but at a sensible, lower price.

4. "You're thinking, 'I need a bank that offers me more.' We're thinking, 'How about a certificate for two airline tickets?'" (Bank ad)

   This advertisement gives no information about the bank's services or fees but cleverly gives the impression of being able to read the consumer's mind and his or her desire to get the most for his or her money. It is a promise ad telling consumers it will give them more than competing banks, but it fails to disclose the fees involved.

7. "For moms who have a lot of love, but not a lot of time." (Ad for Quaker Oatmeal)

   This is an emotionally effective ad but one that gives no information about the product. It is addressed to working moms who probably feel a little guilty for not having enough time for their kids: it compliments them for having enough love to give their kids a hot breakfast.

10. "Totally liquid way to make color stay! Liquid-y smooth. Liquid-y sexy! And Kiss Off? No Way!" (Ad for Revlon lipstick)

    This ad does give some information about the product: it is smooth and it won't kiss off. It is a catchy promise ad, promising sex.

13. "Urban Assault Luxury Vehicle. Lincoln Navigator. American Luxury." (Ad for Lincoln's sport utility vehicle)

    This advertisement gives no information about the product but is a promise ad, aimed at men who want the power, dominance, and luxury to match their conception of themselves as successful, macho, aggressive, SUV drivers.

16. "Love is blind but not senseless. Scope. Feel the tingle. Nothing kills more bad breath germs."

Another compliment ad aimed at the consumer who is moved by the promise of love and sex.

19. "For those who like to fly in the face of convention." (Ad for Jaguar)

This advertisement gives the consumer no information about the product; instead it makes a snob appeal to those consumers who conceive of themselves as independent thinkers.

22. "If you don't need ACT! to manage your business relationships, you probably don't have many relationships to manage." (Ad for business software product)

This advertisement offers no information about the product but implies that the consumer who does not use their product has a business that is somehow inadequate.

25. "Hollywood's new diet phenomenon. Lose up to 10 lbs this weekend! The Hollywood 'Miracle' diet features delicious, all-natural juices that help you lose weight while you cleanse, detoxify and rejuvenate your body." (Ad for Hollywood 48-Hour Miracle Diet)

This is basically a promise advertisement. It uses the weasel words "up to" and "help" as well as "all-natural" to give the impression that it is a safe and effective weight-loss program. Calling it a "new diet phenomenon" also employs hyperbole.

CHAPTER 15

EXERCISE 15.2

1. Not testable (not realistically verifiable or falsifiable, though scientific evidence no doubt bears on the issue).

4. Not testable (value statement).

7. Not testable. (We can imagine evidence that would falsify the claim—superintelligent extraterrestrials might visit the earth, for example—but the claim is not realistically verifiable, since we have no way to search the immensity of space.)

10. Testable. (We can imagine finding fossilized remains that would verify or falsify the claim.)

EXERCISE 15.3

1. Pseudoscientific thinking. The arguer relies on an appeal to personal experience ("I tried it and it worked"). The herbal tea might have worked because of the placebo effect. Alternatively, the headache might have gone away by itself.

4. Pseudoscientific thinking. The arguer is explaining away falsifying evidence.

7. Pseudoscientific thinking. The graphologist is relying upon general, Barnum-type language that applies to practically everybody.

10. Pseudoscientific thinking. Parry is explaining away falsifying data.

13. Pseudoscientific thinking. It is not surprising that dowsing sometimes works, since underground water is abundant. However, the only way to know whether dowsing consistently works is to test it under controlled conditions.

15. Pseudoscientific thinking. Claims about the "esoteric meaning[s]" of music are not scientifically testable.

CREDITS

7 Reprinted by permission of Kenneth R. Merrill. **14** Adapted from *Decision Traps* by J. Edward Russo and Paul J. H. Shoemaker. Copyright 1989 by J. Edward Russo and Paul J. H. Shoemaker. Used by permission of Doubleday, a division of Random House, Inc. **54** Adapted from John Hoaglund, *Critical Thinking*, Third Edition, Newport News, VA: Vale Press, 1999, p. 65. Reprinted with permission from the publisher; from *Introduction to Logic*, Tenth Edition by Irving M. Copi and Carl Cohen. Copyright © 1998 Prentice-Hall, Inc. Reprinted by permission of Prentice-Hall, Inc., Upper Saddle River, NJ. **87** "Dwayne" adapted from Daniel R. Butler, Alan Ray and Leland Gregory, *America's Dumbest Criminals,* Nashville, TN: Rutledge Hill Press, 1995, pp. 147–148. With permission from the publisher. **113, 136** From *Dumb, Dumber, Dumbest* by John J. Kohut and Roland Sweet. Copyright © 1996 by John J. Kohut and Roland Sweet. Used by permission of Plume, a division of Penguin Putnam Inc. **133** Reprinted by arrangement with The Heirs to the Estate of Martin Luther King, Jr., c/o Writers House, Inc., as agent for the proprietors. Copyright © 1963 Martin Luther King, Jr., renewed 1991 by Coretta Scott King. **210** "EBR's Students Need Your Vote" editorial, *The Baton Rouge Advocate,* April 4, 1998. Reprinted with permission from the publisher. **211** "SAT Scores," Letter to the Editor, *Wilkes-Barre Times Leader,* September 16, 1998. Reprinted with permission from Robert Butts. **215** "Don't Rush to Adopt Mail Voting System," editorial, *The Baton Rouge Advocate,* February 8, 1996. **216** From Paul B. Kelter et al., *Chemistry: A World of Choices,* McGraw-Hill, 1999. Reprinted with permission from The McGraw-Hill Companies; "Nation Isn't Ready for Same-Sex Marriages," editorial, *The Seattle Times,* May 21, 1996. Copyright © 1996 Seattle Times Company. Reprinted with permission from the editorial pages of May 21, 1996. **217** Carmen F. Ambrosino, "Legalizing Drugs Spawns Many Problems, Solves None," *Wilkes-Barre Times Leader,* February 17, 1997. Reprinted with permission from the publisher. **218** From *Dave Barry Is Not Taking This Sitting Down* by Dave Barry. Copyright © 2000 by Dave Barry. Used by permission of Crown Books, a division of Random House. **230** Letter to the Editor of *Wilkes-Barre Times Leader,* June 10, 1996. Reprinted with permission from Stan Daniels, "A Slap on the Wrist to Crusaders Against Spank-

ing," editorial, *Wilkes-Barre Times Leader,* May 25, 1996. Reprinted with permission from the publisher. **231** From Leonard Pitts, Jr., "Don't Use God's Law to Beat Up on Gays," *Wilkes-Barre Times Leader,* June 8, 1997. **232** Editorial, *USA Today,* December 17, 1993. Copyright © 1993 USA Today. Reprinted with permission. **233** Kurt Wiesenfeld, "Making the Grade," *Newsweek,* June 17, 1996, p. 16. Copyright © 1996 Newsweek, Inc. All rights reserved. **234** Editorial, "End the Death Penalty; Use Life Without Parole," *USA Today,* April 8, 1994. Copyright © 1994 USA Today. Reprinted with permission. **235** Thomas Sowell, "Improve Way We Educate Teachers and Kids' Education Will Improve," *Wilkes-Barre Times Leader,* February 28, 1998. Reprinted with permission from Creators Syndicate. **238** Jack Pytleski, "Defending My Right to Claim My 'Steak' in the Animal Kingdom," *Wilkes-Barre Times Leader,* July 10, 1997. Reprinted with permission from the author. **366, 375** From *Dumb, Dumber, Dumbest* by John J. Kohut and Roland Sweet. Copyright © 1996 by John J. Kohut and Roland Sweet. Used by permission of Plume, a division of Penguin Putnam Inc. **376** Descriptions of *The American Spectator* and *The Nation,* from *Magazines for Libraries,* Tenth Edition, pp. 1046, 1048. Reprinted with permission from R. R. Bowker Company. **389** Anna Quindlen, "Raised on Rock and Roll," *The New York Times,* February 25, 1997. Copyright © 1997 by the New York Times Co. Reprinted by permission. **416** Letter to the Editor, *Wilkes-Barre Times Leader,* August 1998. Reprinted with permission from George R. Race. **433, 437** From *Dumb, Dumber, Dumbest* by John J. Kohut and Roland Sweet. Copyright © 1996 by John J. Kohut and Roland Sweet. Used by permission of Plume, a division of Penguin Putnam Inc. **437** From *Amusing Ourselves to Death* by Neil Postman. Copyright 1985 by Neil Postman. Used by permission of Viking Penguin, a division of Penguin Putnam Inc. **463** Used with permission from Nielsen Media Research. **475** From "The Newspaper Journalists of the 90's." Used with permission from the American Society of Newspaper Editors. **497** From Dave Barry, *Dave Barry Turns 50,* New York: Crown Publishers, 1998, p. 14. **528** From Paul Kurtz, *The Transcendental Temptation,* Prometheus Books. Copyright © 1986 Prometheus Books. Reprinted by permission of the publisher.

GLOSSARY/INDEX